D0514740

THE PRESIDENTIAL ELECTION OF 2016

Hillary Clinton (Democrat) margin of victory

Total electoral votes: 232

less than 5%   5–10%   more than 10%

Donald Trump (Republican) margin of victory

Total electoral votes: 306

less than 5%   5–10%   more than 10%

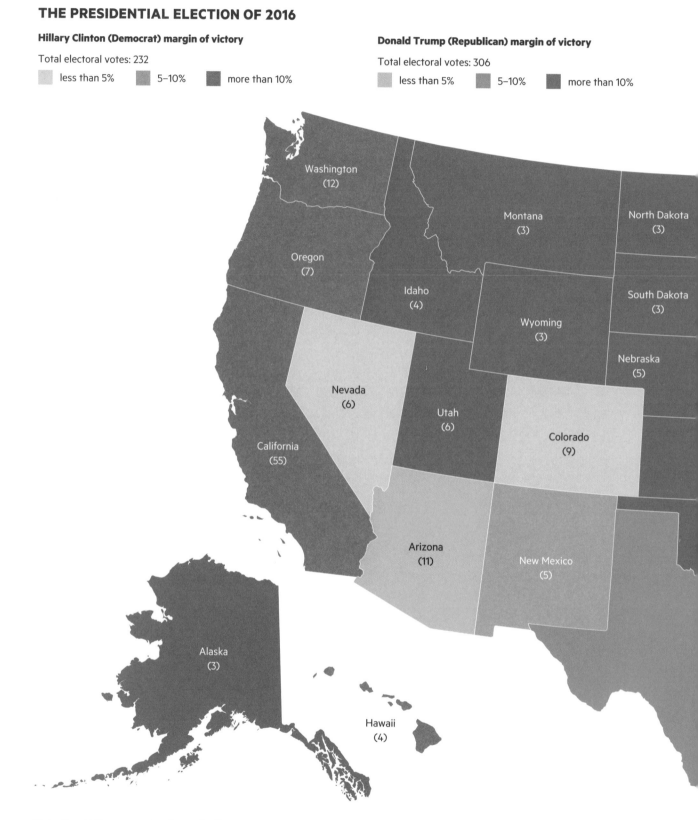

Washington
(12)

Montana
(3)

North Dakota
(3)

Oregon
(7)

Idaho
(4)

South Dakota
(3)

Wyoming
(3)

Nebraska
(5)

Nevada
(6)

Utah
(6)

Colorado
(9)

California
(55)

Arizona
(11)

New Mexico
(5)

Alaska
(3)

Hawaii
(4)

Note: Donald Trump won the electoral college with 304 votes to Hillary Clinton's 227.
Seven electors voted for someone other than their party's candidate.

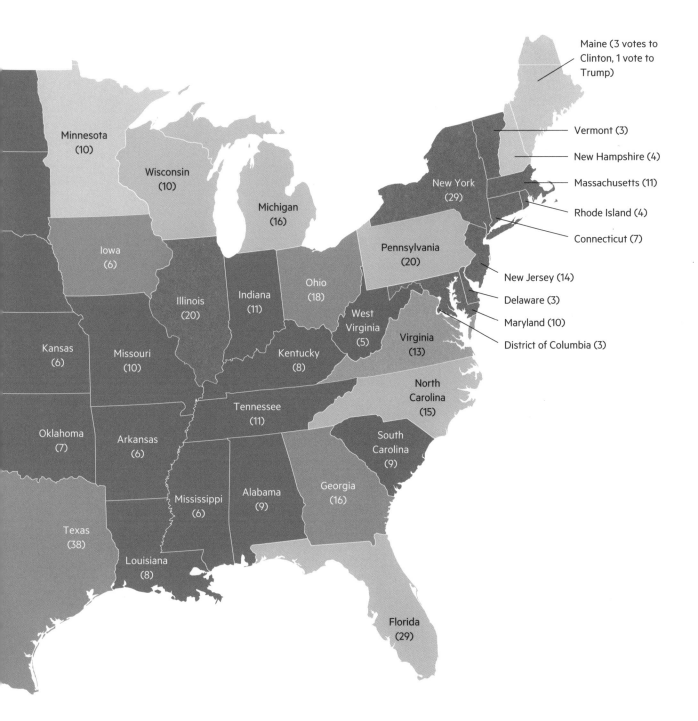

Maine (3 votes to Clinton, 1 vote to Trump)

Vermont (3)

New Hampshire (4)

Massachusetts (11)

Rhode Island (4)

Connecticut (7)

New Jersey (14)

Delaware (3)

Maryland (10)

District of Columbia (3)

Minnesota (10)

Wisconsin (10)

Michigan (16)

Iowa (6)

New York (29)

Pennsylvania (20)

Ohio (18)

Indiana (11)

Illinois (20)

West Virginia (5)

Virginia (13)

Kansas (6)

Missouri (10)

Kentucky (8)

Tennessee (11)

North Carolina (15)

South Carolina (9)

Oklahoma (7)

Arkansas (6)

Mississippi (6)

Alabama (9)

Georgia (16)

Texas (38)

Louisiana (8)

Florida (29)

American Politics Today

Fifth Essentials Edition

Fifth Essentials Edition

American Politics Today

William T. Bianco
Indiana University, Bloomington

David T. Canon
University of Wisconsin, Madison

W. W. NORTON & COMPANY · NEW YORK · LONDON

W. W. Norton & Company has been independent since its founding in 1923, when William Warder Norton and Mary D. Herter Norton first published lectures delivered at the People's Institute, the adult education division of New York City's Cooper Union. The firm soon expanded its program beyond the Institute, publishing books by celebrated academics from America and abroad. By midcentury, the two major pillars of Norton's publishing program—trade books and college texts—were firmly established. In the 1950s, the Norton family transferred control of the company to its employees, and today—with a staff of four hundred and a comparable number of trade, college, and professional titles published each year—W. W. Norton & Company stands as the largest and oldest publishing house owned wholly by its employees.

Copyright © 2017, 2015, 2013, 2011, 2009 by W. W. Norton & Company, Inc.

All rights reserved.

Editor: Peter Lesser
Project Editor: Linda Feldman
Assistant Editor: Samantha Held
Managing Editor, College: Marian Johnson
Managing Editor, College Digital Media: Kim Yi
Production Manager: Ashley Horna
Media Editor: Spencer Richardson-Jones
Associate Media Editor: Michael Jaoui
Media Project Editor: Marcus Van Harpen
Media Editorial Assistant: Ariel Eaton
Digital Production: Mateus Teixeira
Marketing Manager, Political Science: Erin Brown
Design Director: Jillian Burr
Text Designer: Open, N.Y.
Photo Editor: Catherine Abelman
Photo Researcher: Donna Ranieri
Permissions Manager: Megan Schindel
Permissions Clearer: Elizabeth Trammell
Composition: Cenveo® Publisher Services
Manufacturing: LSC Communications-Kendallville

Permission to use copyrighted material is included on p. A45.

The Library of Congress has catalogued the full edition as follows:

Names: Bianco, William T., 1960- author. | Canon, David T., author.
Title: American politics today / William T. Bianco, Indiana University,
    Bloomington, David T. Canon, University of Wisconsin, Madison.
Description: New York : W.W. Norton & Company, [2017] | Includes
    bibliographical references and index.
Identifiers: LCCN 2016049890 | ISBN 9780393283594 (hardcover)
Subjects: LCSH: United States—Politics and government.
Classification: LCC JK275 .B53 2017 | DDC 320.473—dc23 LC record available at
https://lccn.loc.gov/2016049890

This edition:
ISBN 978-0-393-28361-7

W. W. Norton & Company, Inc., 500 Fifth Avenue, New York, NY 10110
wwnorton.com
W. W. Norton & Company Ltd., 15 Carlisle Street, London W1D 3BS

4 5 6 7 8 9 0

For our families,
Regina, Anna, and Catherine,
Sarah, Neal, Katherine, and Sophia,
who encouraged, empathized, and
helped, with patience,
grace, and love.

About the Authors

William T. Bianco

is professor of political science at Indiana University, Bloomington. His research focuses on congressional institutions, representation, and international cooperation in crewed spaceflight. He received his undergraduate degree from SUNY Stony Brook and his MA and Ph.D. from the University of Rochester. He is the author of *Trust: Representatives and Constituents*; American Politics: Strategy and Choice; and numerous articles on American politics. His research and graduate students have received funding from the National Science Foundation and the national Council for Eurasian and Eastern European Research. He has also served as a consultant to congressional candidates and party campaign committees, as well as to the U.S. Department of Energy, the U.S. Department of Health and Human Services, and other state and local government agencies. He was also a Fulbright Senior Scholar in Moscow, Russia, during 2011-12.

David T. Canon

is professor of political science at the University of Wisconsin, Madison. His teaching and research interests focus on American political institutions, especially Congress, and racial representation. He is the author of *Actors, Athletes, and Astronauts: Political Amateurs in the U.S. Congress*; *Race, Redistricting, and Representation: The Unintended Consequences of Black Majority Districts* (winner of the Richard F. Fenno Prize); *The Dysfunctional Congress?* (with Kenneth Mayer); and various articles and book chapters. He served as the Congress editor of *Legislative Studies Quarterly*. He is an AP consultant and has taught in the University of Wisconsin Summer AP Institute for U.S. Government & Politics since 1997. Professor Canon is the recipient of a University of Wisconsin Chancellor's Distinguished Teaching Award.

Contents in Brief

Contents

3. Federalism   56

4. Civil Liberties   88

5. Civil Rights   122

Part II: Politics

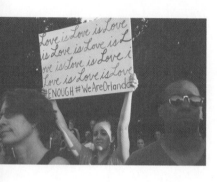

6. Public Opinion and the Media   160

7. Political Parties   190

8. Elections 216

9. Interest Groups 250

Part III: Institutions

10. Congress   276

11. The Presidency   312

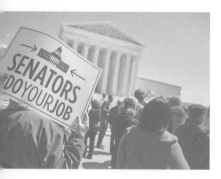

13. The Courts 370

Part IV: Policy

14. Economic and Social Policy 402

Preface

This book is based on three simple premises: politics is conflictual, political process matters, and politics is everywhere. It reflects our belief that politics is explainable, that political outcomes can be understood in terms of decisions made by individuals—and that the average college undergraduate can make sense of the political world in these terms. It focuses on contemporary American politics, the events and outcomes that our students have lived through and know something about. The result, we believe, is a book that provides an accessible but rigorous account of the American political system.

American Politics Today is also the product of our dissatisfaction with existing texts. Thirty years ago we were assistant professors together at the same university, assigned to teach the introductory class in alternate semesters. Though our graduate training was quite different, we found that we shared a deep disappointment with available texts. Their wholesale focus on grand normative concepts such as civic responsibility or their use of advanced analytic themes left students with little idea of how American politics really works, how events in Washington, D.C., affect their everyday lives, and how to piece together all the facts about American politics into a coherent explanation of why things happen as they do. These texts did not engender excitement, fascination, or even passing interest. What they did was put students to sleep.

As with previous editions, the overarching goal of the Fifth Edition is to move beyond simply describing what happens in American politics to explaining behavior and outcomes. In part we wish to counter the widespread belief among students that politics is too complicated, too chaotic, or too secretive to make sense of. More than that, we want to empower our students, to demonstrate that everyday American politics is relevant to their lives. This emphasis is also a response to the typical complaint about American government textbooks—that they are full of facts but devoid of useful information, and that after students finish reading, they are no better able to answer "why" questions than they were before they cracked the book.

In this edition, we maintain our focus on conflict and compromise in American politics—identifying what Americans agree and disagree about and assessing how conflict shapes American politics, from campaign platforms to policy outcomes. Though this emphasis seems especially timely given the 2016 elections and the prospect of continued deadlock in Washington, our aim is to go beyond these events to identify a fundamental constant in American politics: the reality that much of politics is driven by disagreements over the scope and form of government policy, and that compromise is an essential component of virtually all significant changes in government policy. Indeed, it is impossible to imagine politics without conflict. Conflict was embedded in the American political system by the Founders, who set up a system of checks and balances to make sure that no single group could dominate. The Constitution's division of power guarantees that enacting and implementing laws will involve conflict and compromise. Furthermore, the Constitution itself was constructed as one long series of compromises. Accordingly, despite the general dislike people have for conflict, our students must recognize that conflict and compromise lie at the heart of politics.

Throughout the text, we emphasize common sense, showing students that politics inside the Beltway is often strikingly similar to the students' own everyday interactions. For example, what sustains policy compromises made by members of Congress?

The fact that the members typically have long careers, that they interact frequently with each other, and that they only deal with colleagues who have kept their word in the past. These strategies are not unique to the political world. Rather, they embody rules of thumb that most people follow (or are at least aware of) in their everyday interactions. In short, we try to help students understand American politics by emphasizing how it is not all that different from the world they know.

This focus on common sense is coupled with many references to the political science literature. We believe that contemporary research has something to say about prediction and explanation of events that students care about—and that these insights can be taught without turning students into game theorists or statisticians. Our text presents the essential insights of contemporary research, motivated by real-world political phenomena and explained using text or simple diagrams. This approach gives students a set of tools for understanding politics, provides an introduction to the political science literature, and matches up well with students' common-sense intuitions about everyday life. Moreover, by showing that academic scholarship is not a blind alley or irrelevant, this approach helps to bridge the gap between an instructor's teaching and his or her research.

The Fifth Edition builds on these strengths. We've continued to streamline and improve the presentation of text and graphics, and added a new section, "What Do the Numbers Say," that guides students through interpreting quantitative information. Our focus on explanation is hammered home throughout the chapters with new "Why Should I Care" call-outs. New or revised chapter openers use contemporary stories and examples (from student loans to the threats posed by ISIS) to highlight the conflict and compromise theme. We refer to these openers throughout the chapters to illustrate and extend our discussion. The "Take a Stand" sections now explicitly argue both sides of policy questions. Finally, we have added new pull quotes and other sidebar material to enhance the liveliness of the text.

The text continues to be ruthlessly contemporary, but also places recent events in context. Although we do not ignore American history, our stress is on contemporary politics—on the debates, actions, and outcomes that most college students are aware of. Focusing on recent events emphasizes the utility of the concepts and insights that we develop in the text. It also goes a long way toward establishing the relevance of the intro class. The new edition discusses the acceptance of same-sex marriage, the debate over immigration reform, and debates over income inequality—all issues that Americans care about. We have also devoted considerable space to describing the 2016 presidential race, working to show how the contest between Hillary Clinton and Donald Trump fits into a broader theory of how candidates campaign and how voters decide.

Finally, our book offers an individual-level perspective on America's government. The essential message is that politics—elections, legislative proceedings, regulatory choices, and everything else we see—is a product of the decisions made by real flesh-and-blood people. This approach grounds our discussion of politics in the real world. Many texts focus on abstractions such as "the eternal debate," "the great questions," or "the pulse of democracy." We believe that these constructs don't explain where the debate, the questions, or even democracy come from. Nor do they help students understand what's going on in Washington, D.C., and elsewhere, as it's not obvious that the participants themselves care much about these sorts of abstractions—quite the opposite, in fact.

We replace these constructs with a focus on real people and actual choices. The primary goal is to make sense of American politics by understanding why politicians, bureaucrats, judges, and citizens act as they do. That is, we are grounding our description of American politics at the most fundamental level—an individual facing a decision. How, for example, does a voter choose among candidates? Stated that way, it is reasonably easy to talk about where the choice came from, how the individual might evaluate different options, and why one choice might look better than the others. Voters' decisions may be understood by examining the different feasible strategies they employ (issue voting, retrospective evaluations, stereotyping, etc.) and by asking why some voters use one strategy while others use a different one.

By focusing on individuals and choices, we can place students in the shoes of the decision makers, and in so doing, give them insight into why people act as they do. We can discuss, for example, why a House member might favor enacting wasteful pork-barrel spending, even though a proposal full of such projects will make his constituents economically worse off—and why constituents might reward such behavior, even if they suspect the truth. By taking this approach, we are not trying to let legislators off the hook. Rather, we believe that any real understanding of the political process must begin with a sense of the decisions the participants make and why they make them. Focusing on individuals also segues naturally into a discussion of consequences, allowing us to move from examining decisions to describing and evaluating outcomes. In this way, we can show students how large-scale outcomes in politics, such as inefficient programs, don't happen by accident or because of malfeasance. Rather, they are the predictable results of choices made by individuals (here, politicians and voters).

The policy chapters in the Full and Essentials Editions also represent a distinctive feature of this book. The discussion of policy at the end of an intro class often fits awkwardly with the material covered earlier. It is supposed to be a culmination of the semester-long discussion of institutions, politicians, and political behavior, but instead it often becomes an afterthought that gets discarded when time runs out in the last few weeks of class. Our policy chapters explicitly draw on previous chapters' discussions of the actors that shape policy: the president, Congress, the courts, interest groups, and parties. By doing so, these chapters show how all the pieces of the puzzle fit together.

Finally, this book reflects our experience as practicing scholars and teachers, as well as interactions with more than fifteen thousand students in introductory classes at several universities. Rather than thinking of the intro class as a service obligation, we believe it offers a unique opportunity for faculty to develop a broader sense of American politics and American political science, while at the same time giving students the tools they need to behave as knowledgeable citizens or enthusiastic political science majors. We hope that it works for you as well as it does for us.

Features of the Text and Media Package

The book's "three key ideas"
are fully integrated throughout the text.

- **Politics Is Conflictual** and conflict and compromise are a normal, healthy part of politics. The questions debated in elections and the policy options considered by people in government are generally marked by disagreement at all levels. Making policy typically involves important issues on which people disagree, sometimes strongly; so compromise, bargaining, and tough choices about trade-offs are often necessary.

- **Political Process Matters** because it is the mechanism we have established to resolve conflicts and achieve compromise. Governmental actions result from conscious choices made by voters, elected officials, and bureaucrats. The media often cover political issues in the same way they do sporting events, and though this makes for entertaining news, it also leads citizens to overlook the institutions, rules, and procedures that have a decisive influence on American life. Politics really is not just a game.

- **Politics Is Everywhere** in that the results of the political process affect all aspects of Americans' everyday lives. Politics governs what people can and cannot do, their quality of life, and how they think about events, other people, and situations.

New and revised "How It Works" chapter openers
feature hot-button political issues and pose the kinds of questions students might ask. For example, "When is discrimination legal and when is it not?" (Civil Liberties) and "How do interest groups work? Do lobbying victories always go to the side with the most money?" (Interest Groups).

Organization around chapter goals
stresses learning objectives and mastery of core material.

- **Chapter Goals** appear at the beginning of the chapter and then recur at the start of the relevant sections throughout the chapter to create a more active reading experience that emphasizes important learning objectives.

- **Extensive end-of-chapter review sections organized around the Chapter Goals** include section summaries, practice quiz questions, key terms, and suggested reading lists. Students have everything they need to master the material in each section of the chapter.

Special features for critical thinking
reinforce the three key ideas while introducing other important ways to think about American politics.

- **"How It Works" graphics,** newly redesigned for greater clarity, highlight key political processes and structures and build graphical literacy. The "How It Works in Practice" section of these graphics show how the processes presented play out in a real-world political event.

- **NEW "What Do the Numbers Say?" features** develop quantitative reasoning skills by teaching students to read and interpret data on important political issues and current events.

- **NEW "Why Should I Care?" sections** draw explicit connections between the chapter material and students' lives.
- **NEW "Did you know?" features and pull quotes** give students tidbits of information that may induce questions, anger, and may even inspire students to get involved.
- **Revised "Take a Stand" features** address contemporary issues in a pro/con format and invite students to consider how they would argue their own position on the topic. Each feature concludes with two critical-thinking questions.
- **"Nuts & Bolts" features provide students with concise explanations of key concepts,** like the difference between civil liberties and civil rights, different kinds of gerrymanders, and brief summaries of campaign finance rules. These features provide an easy way for quick study and review.

Tools for a dynamic classroom

- **InQuizitive, Norton's formative, adaptive assessment tool,** accompanies the Fifth Edition of *American Politics Today* and reinforces reading comprehension with a focus on the foundations of government and major political science concepts. Guiding feedback helps students understand why their answers were right or wrong and steers them back to the text. Student knowledge is strengthened through questions that compel analysis of the systems of government, animated and static infographics, and images, charts, and graphs from this text. With InQuizitive, students have the opportunity to achieve the maximum score in a low-risk environment.

  To learn more about InQuizitive, visit http://books.wwnorton.com/books/inquizitive/overview/.

- **Norton Coursepacks are free and open with no access codes,** allowing you to easily bring Norton's high-quality digital content into your existing learning management system. The content is fully editable and is yours to keep forever. The Norton Coursepack for *American Politics Today,* Fifth Edition, contains the following activities and quizzes:
    - **How to Read Charts and Graphs tutorial** that provides students with extra practice and guidance interpreting common representations of data that they will encounter in this textbook and in the world,
    - **Pre- and post-test chapter quizzes** that assess student knowledge of core concepts,
    - **Video exercises** that engage students and help them retain and apply information through significant events,
    - **"How It Works" and "How It Works In Practice" animated graphics** that guide students through understanding political processes and institutions,
    - **Updated simulations** that show students how concepts work in the real world,
    - **"By the Numbers" activities** that give students more practice with quantitative skills and more familiarity with how political scientists know what they know, and
    - **"Take a Stand" exercises** that present students with multiple sides of contemporary debates and ask them to consider and refine their own views based on what they've learned.
- **Test bank** contains more than 1,800 questions tagged to chapter-learning objectives and keyed to Bloom's taxonomy.
- **Instructor's manual** includes chapter outlines, class activities, and discussion questions.
- **Instructor PowerPoints** contains fully customizable lecture slides with clicker questions and "How It Works" and "How It Works in Practice" animated PowerPoint slides for optimal classroom presentation.

Acknowledgments

This edition of *American Politics Today* is again dedicated to our families. Our wives, Regina and Sarah, have continued to accommodate our deadlines and schedules and have again served as our most accurate critics and sources of insight and inspiration. Our children have again been forced to contend with politics and textbook writing as a perennial topic of conversation in their visits home, and have responded with critiques and ideas of their own, which appear throughout the text.

Our colleagues at Indiana University and the University of Wisconsin (and before that, Duke University for both of us) provided many opportunities to talk about American politics and teaching this course.

Bill thanks his colleagues at Indiana University and elsewhere, including Christine Barbour, John Brehm, Ted Carmines, Chris DeSante, Mike Ensley, Bernard Fraga, Russ Hansen, Matthew Hayes, Yanna Krupnikov, Lin Ostrom, Regina Smyth, Will Winecoff, and Jerry Wright, for sharp insights and encouragement at crucial moments. He is also grateful to many teaching assistants who have helped him organize and teach the intro class at three universities. Finally, he thanks the students at the Higher School of Economics in Moscow, Russia, where he taught the introductory class as a Fulbright Scholar in 2012.

David gives special thanks to Ken Mayer, whose daily "reality checks" and consistently thoughtful professional and personal advice are greatly appreciated. Barry Burden, Ben Marquez, Don Moynihan, Ryan Owens, Ellie Powell, Howard Schweber, Byron Shafer, Alex Tahk, Dave Weimer, Kathy Cramer, Susan Yackee, and all the great people at Wisconsin have provided a wonderful community within which to teach and research American politics. John Coleman, who has moved on to become a dean at the University of Minnesota, also deserves special thanks as a former member of the intro American team and good friend and colleague. David would also like to thank the students at the University of Debrecen in Hungary, where he taught American politics as a Fulbright Scholar in 2003–2004, and the Eberhard Karls University of Tübingen, Germany, where he taught as a Fulbright Scholar in 2011–2012. The Hungarian students' unique perspective on democracy, civil liberties, and the role of government required David to think about American politics in a different way. The German students' views on the role of political parties, campaigns, and the social welfare state also provided a strong contrast to the views of his American students.

Both of us are grateful to the political science faculty at Duke University, who, in addition to giving us our first academic jobs, worked to construct a hospitable and invigorating place to research and to teach. In particular, Rom Coles, Ruth Grant, John Aldrich, Tom Spragens, Taylor Cole, and David Barber were model teachers, colleagues, and scholars. We both learned to teach by watching them, and we are better instructors and scholars for it.

We are indebted to the outstanding people at W. W. Norton who have been our full partners through all five editions. Peter Lesser's relentless combination of wit, insight, and expertise is evident throughout the book. Sam Held kept us all on the same page, and was a graceful editor and deadline-enforcer. Steve Dunn was responsible for getting the process started and providing good counsel from beginning to end. Roby Harrington has been a source of constant encouragement and feedback. Linda Feldman has been a superb project editor, bringing to the project her talent for clarity of words and visuals. Cat Abelman put together an excellent photo program. Megan Jackson cleared reprint permissions for the figures and tables. Ashley Horna handled production with efficiency and good humor. Jillian Burr and Open design studio created a beautiful design for the book's interior and cover. Spencer Richardson-Jones and Michael Jaoui's clear vision for the ever-more-complex and rich digital media package has been a major help. We also would like to thank Aaron Javsicas and Ann Shin for their outstanding work on earlier editions. The entire crew at Norton has been incredibly professional and supportive in ways we never knew when we started writing this book. Signing with them fifteen years ago was an eyes-shut home run.

We are also indebted to the many reviewers who have commented on the text.

First Edition Reviewers

Dave Adler, *Idaho State University*

Rick Almeida, *Francis Marion University*

Jim Bailey, *Arkansas State University, Mountain Home*

Todd Belt, *University of Hawaii, Hilo*

Scott Buchanan, *Columbus State University*

Randy Burnside, *Southern Illinois University, Carbondale*

Carolyn Cocca, *SUNY College at Old Westbury*

Tom Dolan, *Columbus State University*

Dave Dulio, *Oakland University*

Matt Eshbaugh-Soha, *University of North Texas*

Kevin Esterling, *University of California, Riverside*

Peter Francia, *East Carolina University*

Scott Frisch, *California State University, Channel Islands*

Sarah Fulton, *Texas A&M University*

Keith Gaddie, *University of Oklahoma*

Joe Giammo, *University of Arkansas, Little Rock*

Kate Greene, *University of Southern Mississippi*

Steven Greene, *North Carolina State University*

Phil Habel, *Southern Illinois University, Carbondale*

Charles Hartwig, *Arkansas State University, Jonesboro*

Ted Jelen, *University of Nevada, Las Vegas*

Jennifer Jensen, *Binghamton University, SUNY*

Terri Johnson, *University of Wisconsin, Green Bay*

Luke Keele, *Ohio State University*

Linda Keith, *University of Texas, Dallas*

Chris Kelley, *Miami University*

Jason Kirksey, *Oklahoma State University*

Jeffrey Kraus, *Wagner College*

Chris Kukk, *Western Connecticut State University*

Mel Kulbicki, *York College*

Joel Lieske, *Cleveland State University*

Steve Light, *University of North Dakota*

Baodong (Paul) Liu, *University of Utah*

Ken Long, *Saint Joseph College, Connecticut*

Michael Lynch, *University of Kansas*

Cherie Maestas, *Florida State University*

Tom Marshall, *University of Texas, Arlington*

Scott McClurg, *Southern Illinois University, Carbondale*

Jonathan Morris, *East Carolina University*

Jason Mycoff, *University of Delaware*

Sean Nicholson-Crotty, *University of Missouri, Columbia*

Timothy Nokken, *Texas Tech University*

Sandra O'Brien, *Florida Gulf Coast University*

John Orman, *Fairfield University*

L. Marvin Overby, *University of Missouri, Columbia*

Catherine Paden, *Simmons College*

Dan Ponder, *Drury University*

Paul Posner, *George Mason University*

David Redlawsk, *University of Iowa*

Russell Renka, *Southeast Missouri State University*

Travis Ridout, *Washington State University*

Andy Rudalevige, *Dickinson College*

Denise Scheberle, *University of Wisconsin, Green Bay*

Tom Schmeling, *Rhode Island College*

Pat Sellers, *Davidson College*

Dan Smith, *Northwest Missouri State University*

Dale Story, *University of Texas, Arlington*

John Vile, *Middle Tennessee State University*

Mike Wagner, *University of Nebraska*

Dave Wigg, *St. Louis Community College*

Maggie Zetts, *Purdue University*

Second Edition Reviewers

Danny Adkison, *Oklahoma State University*
Hunter Bacot, *Elon College*
Tim Barnett, *Jacksonville State University*
Robert Bruhl, *University of Illinois, Chicago*
Daniel Butler, *Yale University*
Jennifer Byrne, *James Madison University*
Jason Casellas, *University of Texas, Austin*
Jeffrey Christiansen, *Seminole State College*
Richard Conley, *University of Florida*
Michael Crespin, *University of Georgia*
Brian DiSarro, *California State University, Sacramento*
Ryan Emenaker, *College of the Redwoods*
John Evans, *California State University, Northridge*
John Fliter, *Kansas State University*
Jimmy Gleason, *Purdue University*
Dana Glencross, *Oklahoma City Community College*
Jeannie Grussendorf, *Georgia State University*
Phil Habel, *Southern Illinois University, Carbondale*
Lori Han, *Chapman University*
Katy Harriger, *Wake Forest University*
Richard Himelfarb, *Hofstra University*
Doug Imig, *University of Memphis*
Daniel Klinghard, *College of the Holy Cross*
Eddie Meaders, *University of North Texas*

Kristy Michaud, *California State University, Northridge*
Kris Miler, *University of Illinois, Urbana-Champaign*
Melinda Mueller, *Eastern Illinois University*
Michael Mundt, *Oakton Community College*
Emily Neff-Sharum, *University of North Carolina, Pembroke*
David Nice, *Washington State University*
Tim Nokken, *Texas Tech University*
Stephen Nuño, *Northern Arizona University*
Richard Powell, *University of Maine, Orono*
Travis Ridout, *Washington State University*
Sara Rinfret, *University of Wisconsin, Green Bay*
Martin Saiz, *California State University, Northridge*
Gabriel Ramon Sanchez, *University of New Mexico*
Charles Shipan, *University of Michigan*
Dan Smith, *Northwest Missouri State University*
Rachel Sondheimer, *United States Military Academy*
Chris Soper, *Pepperdine University*
Walt Stone, *University of California, Davis*
Greg Streich, *University of Central Missouri*
Charles Walcott, *Virginia Tech*
Rick Waterman, *University of Kentucky*
Edward Weber, *Washington State University*
Jack Wright, *Ohio State University*

Third Edition Reviewers

Steve Anthony, *Georgia State University*
Marcos Arandia, *North Lake College*
Richard Barberio, *SUNY College at Oneonta*
Jody Baumgartner, *East Carolina University*
Brian Berry, *University of Texas, Dallas*
David Birch, *Lone Star College, Tomball*
Eileen Burgin, *University of Vermont*
Randolph Burnside, *Southern Illinois University, Carbondale*
Kim Casey, *Northwest Missouri State University*
Christopher Chapp, *University of Wisconsin, Whitewater*
Daniel Coffey, *University of Akron*
William Corbett, *University of Texas at El Paso*
Jonathan Day, *Western Illinois University*
Rebecca Deen, *University of Texas, Arlington*
Brian DiSarro, *California State University, Sacramento*
Nelson Dometrius, *Texas Tech University*

Stan Dupree, *College of the Desert*
David Edwards, *University of Texas, Austin*
Ryan Emenaker, *College of the Redwoods*
John Evans, *University of Wisconsin, Eau Claire*
Brandon Franke, *Blinn College, Bryan*
Rodd Freitag, *University of Wisconsin, Eau Claire*
Donna Godwin, *Trinity Valley Community College*
Craig Goodman, *Texas Tech University*
Amy Gossett, *Lincoln University*
Tobin Grant, *Southern Illinois University*
Stephanie Hallock, *Harford Community College*
Alexander Hogan, *Lone Star College, CyFair*
Marvin King, *University of Mississippi*
Timothy LaPira, *James Madison University*
Mary Linder, *Grayson University*
Christine Lipsmeyer, *Texas A&M University*
Michael Lyons, *Utah State University*
Jill Marshall, *University of Texas, Arlington*

Thomas Masterson, *Butte College*
Daniel Matisoff, *Georgia Institute of Technology*
Jason McDaniel, *San Francisco State University*
Mark McKenzie, *Texas Tech University*
Leonard McNeil, *Contra Costa College*
Melissa Merry, *University of Louisville*
Ann Mezzell, *Lincoln University*
Eric Miller, *Blinn College, Bryan*
Jonathan Morris, *East Carolina University*
Leah Murray, *Weber State University*
Farzeen Nasri, *Ventura College*
Brian Newman, *Pepperdine University*
David Nice, *Washington State University*
Stephen Nichols, *California State University, San Marcos*

Tim Nokken, *Texas Tech University*
Barbara Norrander, *University of Arizona*
Andrew Reeves, *Boston University*
Michelle Rodriguez, *San Diego Mesa College*
Dan Smith, *Northwest Missouri State University*
Christopher Soper, *Pepperdine University*
Jim Startin, *University of Texas, San Antonio*
Jeffrey Stonecash, *Syracuse University*
Linda Trautman, *Ohio University*
Kevin Unter, *University of Louisiana, Monroe*
Michelle Wade, *Northwest Missouri State University*
Michael Wagner, *University of Nebraska, Lincoln*
Adam Warber, *Clemson University*
Wayne Wolf, *South Suburban College*

Fourth Edition Reviewers

Rickert Althaus, *Southeast Missouri State University*
Eric K. Austin, *Montana State University*
Evelyn Ballard, *Houston Community College Southeast*
Jim Battista, *University at Buffalo, SUNY*
Kenneth C. Blanchard Jr., *Northern State University*
Heidi Brockmann, *United States Military Academy*
Adriana Buliga-Stoian, *Mount Mercy University*
Abbe Allen DeBolt, *Sandhills Community College*
John C. Evans, *University of Wisconsin, Eau Claire*
Babette Faehmel, *Schenectady County Community College*
Daniel Fuerstman, *State College of Florida*
Stephanie Hallock, *Harford Community College*
John Hitt, *North Lake College*
Debra Jenke, *Angelina College*
Ronald A. Kuykendall, *Trident Technical College*
Paul Lewis, *Arizona State University*
Mary Linder, *Grayson College*
Michael Lyons, *Utah State University*

Wendy Martinek, *Binghamton University, SUNY*
Melissa Merry, *University of Louisville*
Javan "J. D." Mesnard, *Mesa Community College*
Monique Mironesco, *University of Hawai'i, West O'ahu*
Tim Nokken, *Texas Tech University*
David Parker, *Montana State University*
Sylvia Peregrino, *El Paso Community College*
Blayne Primozich, *El Paso Community College*
Bryan Rasmussen, *Collin College*
Suzanne M. Robbins, *George Mason University*
Susan Roomberg, *University of Texas at San Antonio*
Michael Shamgochian, *Worcester State University*
Geoffrey Shine, *Wharton County Junior College*
Rachel Milstein Sondheimer, *United States Military Academy*
Gregory Streich, *University of Central Missouri*
Jeremy Teigen, *Ramapo College*
Dave Wells, *Arizona State University*

Fifth Edition Reviewers

Leslie Baker, *Mississippi State University*
Evelyn Ballard, *Houston Community College*
Jim Battista, *University at Buffalo, SUNY*
Nathaniel A. Birkhead, *Kansas State University*
William Blake, *Indiana University, IUPUI*

Kenneth C. Blanchard Jr., *Northern State University*
Michael P. Bobic, *Glenville State College*
Ben Christ, *Harrisburg Area Community College*
Rosalyn Crain, *Houston Community College, Northwest College*

Brian Cravens, *Blinn College–Schulenburg*

Stephanie R. Davis, *University of South Carolina*

Christi Dayley, *Weatherford College*

Justin B. Dyer, *University of Missouri*

Jonathan P. Euchner, *Missouri Western State University*

John W. Eyster, *University of Wisconsin, Whitewater*

Eddie Feng, *Weatherford College*

John P. Flanagan, *Weatherford College*

Peter L. Francia, *East Carolina University*

Daniel Fuerstman, *State College of Florida*

Willie Hamilton, *Mt. San Jacinto College*

David Huseman, *Butler County Community College*

Debra Jenke, *Angelina College*

Catherine Johnson, *Weatherford College*

Joshua Kaplan, *University of Notre Dame*

Tim LaPira, *James Madison University*

Alan Lehmann, *Blinn College*

Morris Levy, *University of Southern California*

Michael S. Lynch, *University of Georgia*

Rob Mellen Jr., *Mississippi State University*

Timothy Nokken, *Texas Tech University*

Anthony O'Regan, *Los Angeles Valley College*

Hyung Lae Park, *El Paso Community College*

Donna Rhea, *Houston Community College*

Joseph Romance, *Fort Hays State University*

Sam Scinta, *Viterbo University*

Michael Shamgochian, *Worcester State University*

Lenore VanderZee, *SUNY Canton*

Abram J. Trosky, *United States Coast Guard Academy*

Ronald W. Vardy, *Wharton County Community College; University of Houston*

Gordan Vurusic, *Grand Rapids Community College*

Jeremy Walling, *Southeast Missouri State University*

It is a humbling experience to have so many smart people involved in the process of writing and revising this book. Their reviews were often critical, but always insightful, and you the reader are the beneficiaries of their efforts. In many cases, the improvements in this edition are the direct result of their suggestions. They have our profound thanks.

William T. Bianco
David T. Canon
November 2016

American Politics Today

Fifth Essentials Edition

"

In a democracy, oftentimes other people win.

— C. J. Cregg, *The West Wing*

1

Understanding American Politics

How does politics work and why does politics matter?

You have just lived through one of the most interesting presidential elections in American history. For the first time, a major party nominated a woman as their candidate. Even so, the election was won by a newcomer to politics, Republican Donald Trump, who won his party's nomination despite having a deeply problematic past, no political experience, and a campaign style that emphasized insult, innuendo, and attack. The campaign was one of the nastiest ever, exemplified by Trump's repeated threats to jail Clinton if he became president, and his claim that a conspiracy of elites, media companies, and banks were working to rig the election and ensure his defeat. Yet Trump was able to win by rallying voters who wanted change and opposed immigration reform, and by raising questions about Clinton's use of a private e-mail server while secretary of state and vowing to change the "culture of corruption."

For most of you, this is the first presidential election you have paid much attention to, and it would be no surprise if you asked whether American politics always worked this way. Are presidential contests always drawn-out, controversial, and conflictual? Do they typically feature candidates as widely disliked as Clinton and Trump? Do candidates often attack their opponents in intensely personal terms, such as Trump's referring to Clinton as "Crooked Hillary," alleging that she lacked the stamina and the judgment to be president, criticizing her appearance, or claiming she used drugs to enhance her debate performance? How often do significant numbers of party leaders abandon their nominees?

The easy answer is no: the 2016 presidential election is not typical. Trump's focus on general themes such as "make America great again" rather than specific policy proposals, his rejection of well-accepted campaign tactics, his charges of a rigged electoral process, claims of sexual assault against him, the dissention within Republican ranks—all of these things are highly unusual. Even so, political science does a good job of explaining what happened in 2016. Trump's nomination reflected the relatively extreme policy preferences held by the

★
___

CHAPTER
GOALS

Describe the basic functions of government.
pages 4–8

Define *politics* and identify three key ideas that help explain politics.
pages 8–14

Identify major sources of conflict in American politics.
pages 15–19

Explain how the American values of democracy, liberty, and equality work to resolve political conflict.
pages 20–23

📷

The 2016 presidential campaign and the surprising election of Republican Donald Trump highlighted the conflicts deeply embedded in American political life. Issues surrounding race, ethnicity, gender, geography, education, income level, and sexual orientation all seemed to further divide an already polarized country. Now the questions emerge: How will Trump govern? Will the divisions in American politics only become deeper, or will President Trump fulfill his election-night pledge to represent all Americans and work to unite the country?

average Republican primary voter and an anti-Washington mood. The closeness of the general election reflects the role of party identification and economic conditions in vote decisions. And the omnipresent conflict seen in 2016 was not only due to candidates or their campaign strategies—rather, it reflects sharp, sincere underlying differences between the parties (and their supporters) over what the federal government should and shouldn't be doing.

In fact, the outcome of the 2016 elections illustrates how digging below the surface of political events can help to explain why things happen in American politics—the conflicts and the political process that deals with them. But is conflict natural in American politics? Is this how politics really works? And why does politics matter in our lives?

★

DESCRIBE THE BASIC FUNCTIONS OF GOVERNMENT

Making sense of American government and politics

The premise of this book is simple: *American politics makes sense.* What happens in elections, in Washington, D.C., and everywhere else—even the 2016 election—has a logical and often simple explanation; we just have to know how to look for it. By the end of the book, we hope you get really good at analyzing the politics you see everywhere—in the news and in your own life.

This claim may seem unrealistic or even naive. On the surface, American politics often makes no sense. Polls show strong support for extreme, unconstitutional, or downright silly proposals. Candidates put more time into insulting their opponents than making credible campaign promises. Members of Congress seem more interested in beating their political opponents than getting something done. Elections look random or even chaotic. And many policy questions, from reforming immigration to deciding what to do about climate change, seem hopelessly intractable.

Many people, we believe, have given up on American politics because they don't understand the political process, feel helpless to influence election outcomes or policy making, and believe that politics is irrelevant to their lives. Many people disliked both

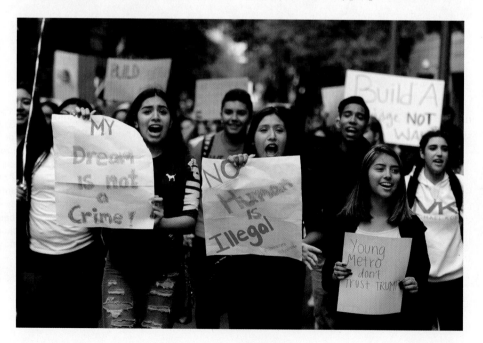

Conflicts within the government—say, over immigration policy—often reflect real divisions among American citizens about what government should do about certain issues. Groups on all sides of controversial issues pressure the government to enact their preferred policies.

of the candidates running in 2016, and saw this as more evidence that American politics do not work well. Since you are taking a class on American politics, we hope you have not given up on politics entirely. It is *not* our goal to turn you into a political junkie or a policy expert. You don't need to be completely immersed in politics to make sense of it, but we hope that after finishing this book you will have a basic understanding of the political process and why it matters.

One goal of this book is to help you take an active role in the political process. A functioning democracy allows citizens to defer complicated policy decisions to their elected leaders, but it also requires citizens to monitor what politicians do and to hold them accountable at the voting booth. This book will help you accomplish this important duty by providing the analytical skills you need to make sense of politics, even when it initially appears to make no sense at all.

We are not going to spend much time talking about how American politics should be. Rather, our focus will be on explaining American politics as it is. Here are some other questions we will examine:

- Why don't people vote? Why *do* people vote? How do they decide who to vote for?
- Why do so many people mistrust politicians and the political system?
- Why can't Congress get things done? Why can they get anything done?
- Why is the Supreme Court so political?
- Can presidents do whatever they want? Why can't they do more?
- Is the media biased?

We will answer these questions and many others by applying three key ideas about the nature of politics: politics is conflictual, political process matters, and politics is everywhere. But first, we begin with an even more basic question: Why do we have a government?

Why do we have a government?

As we prepare to address this question, let's agree on a definition: **government** is the system for implementing decisions made through the political process. All countries have some form of government, which in general serves two broad purposes: to provide order and to promote the general welfare.

government
The system for implementing decisions made through the political process.

To Provide Order At a basic level, the answer to the question "Why do we have a government?" seems obvious: without government there would be chaos. As the seventeenth-century British philosopher Thomas Hobbes said, life in the "state of nature" (that is, without government) would be "solitary, poor, nasty, brutish, and short."[1] Without government there would be no laws—people could do whatever they wanted. Even if people tried to develop informal rules, there would be no way to guarantee enforcement of those rules. Accordingly, one of the most important rules of government is policing—making sure that people obey the law and protecting citizens from threats coming from outside the nation.

The Founders of the United States noted this crucial role in the Constitution's preamble: two of the central goals of government are to "provide for the common defense" and to "insure domestic Tranquility." The former refers to military protection against foreign invasion and the defense of our nation's common security interests. The latter refers to law enforcement within the nation, which today includes the National Guard, Federal Bureau of Investigation (FBI), Department of Homeland Security, state and local police, and the courts. So at a minimal level, government is necessary to provide security.

However, there's more to it than that. The Founders cited the desire to "establish Justice ... and secure the Blessings of Liberty to ourselves and our Posterity." But do we need government to do these things? It may be obvious that the police power of the nation is required to prevent anarchy, but can't people have justice and liberty without government? In a perfect world, maybe, but the Founders had a more realistic view of human nature. As James Madison, one of the founding fathers (and the fourth president of the United States), said, "But what is government itself, but the greatest of all reflections on human nature? If men were angels, no government would be necessary. If angels were to govern men, neither external nor internal controls on government would be necessary."[2] Furthermore, Madison continued, people have a variety of interests that have "divided mankind into parties, inflamed them with mutual animosity, and rendered them much more disposed to vex and oppress each other than to co-operate for their common good."[3] That is, without government we would quickly be headed toward Hobbes's nasty and brutish state of nature because of differences in opinion about what society should look like. Having a government means that people cannot act unilaterally against each other, but it also creates a new problem: people will try to use the government and its powers to impose their views on the rest of society.

Madison's view of human nature might sound pessimistic, but it was also realistic. He assumed that people were self-interested: we want what is best for ourselves and for our families, and to satisfy those interests we tend to form groups with like-minded people. Madison saw these groups, which he called **factions**, as being opposed to the public good, and his greatest fear was of tyranny by a faction imposing its will on the rest of the nation. For example, if one group took power and established an official state religion, that faction would be tyrannizing people who practiced a different religion. This type of oppression is precisely why many of the early American colonists fled Europe in the first place.

So government is necessary to avoid the anarchy of the state of nature and the right kind of government is needed to avoid oppression by whoever controls the policy-making process. As we will discuss in Chapters 2 and 3, America's government seeks to control the effects of factions by dividing government power in three main ways. First, the **separation of powers** divides the government into three branches—judicial, executive, and legislative—and assigns distinct duties to each branch. Second, the system of **checks and balances** gives each branch some power over the other two. (For example, the president can veto legislation passed by Congress; Congress can impeach the president; and the Supreme Court has the power to interpret laws written by Congress to determine whether they are constitutional.) Third, **federalism** divides power yet again by allotting different responsibilities to local, state, and national governments. With power divided in this fashion, Madison reasoned, no single faction could dominate the government.

To Promote the General Welfare The preamble to the Constitution also states that the federal government exists to "promote the general Welfare." This means tackling the hard problems that Americans cannot solve on their own, such as taking care of the poor, the sick, or the aged, and dealing with global issues like climate change, terrorist threats, and poverty in other countries. However, government intervention is not inevitable—people can decide that these problems aren't worth solving. But if people *do* want to address these large problems, government action is necessary because **public goods** such as these are not efficiently provided by the free market, either because of **collective action problems** or for other reasons.

It is easy for two people or even a small group to tackle a common problem without the help of government, but 1,000 people (to say nothing of the more than 320 million in the United States today) would have a very difficult time. They would suffer from the

factions
Groups of like-minded people who try to influence the government. American government is set up to avoid domination by any one of these groups.

separation of powers
The division of government power across the judicial, executive, and legislative branches.

checks and balances
A system in which each branch of government has some power over the others.

federalism
The division of power across the local, state, and national levels of government.

public goods
Services or actions (such as protecting the environment) that, once provided to one person, become available to everyone. Government is typically needed to provide public goods because they will be under-provided by the free market.

collective action problems
Situations in which the members of a group would benefit by working together to produce some outcome, but each individual is better off refusing to cooperate and reaping benefits from those who do the work.

free rider problem—that is, because it is in everyone's own interest to let someone else do the work, the danger is that no one will contribute, even though everyone wants the outcome that collective contributions would create. A government representing more than 320 million people can provide public goods, such as protecting the environment or defending the nation, that all those people acting on their own would be unable to provide, so people elect leaders and pay taxes to provide those public goods.

Collective action problems are common in modern society. Education is a great example. You benefit personally from your college education in terms of the knowledge and experience you gain and perhaps from the higher salary you will earn because of your college degree. However, society also benefits from your education. Your employer will benefit from your knowledge and skills, as will people you interact with. If education were provided solely by the free market, those who could afford schooling would be educated, but the rest would not, leaving a large segment of society with little or no education and therefore unemployable. So, public education, like many important services, benefits all levels of society and must be provided by the government for the general welfare.

Now that we understand *why* we have a government, the next question is: *What* does the government do to "insure domestic Tranquility" and "promote the general Welfare"? Many visible components of the government promote these goals, from the police and armed services to the Internal Revenue Service, Federal Reserve, Postal Service, Social Security Administration, National Aeronautics and Space Administration, Department of Education, and Food and Drug Administration. In fact, it is hard to find an aspect of everyday life that does not involve the government in some way, either as a provider of public goods, such as national defense, interstate highways, and national parks, as a protector of civil liberties, as an enforcer of laws and property rights, or as a regulator of individual or corporate behavior.

Two important government functions described in the Constitution are to "provide for the common defense" and "insure domestic Tranquility." The military and local police are two of the most commonly used forces the government maintains to fulfill those roles.

free rider problem
The incentive to benefit from others' work without making a contribution, which leads individuals in a collective action situation to refuse to work together.

Forms of government

While all governments must provide order and promote the general welfare, there are different types of governments. Greek political philosopher Aristotle, writing in the fourth century BC, developed a classification scheme for governments that is still useful. Aristotle distinguished three pure types of government based on the number of rulers versus the number of people ruled: monarchy (rule by one), aristocracy (rule by the few), and polity (rule by the many—such as the general population).

DID YOU KNOW?

64%

of the world's population lives in countries considered to be free or partly free. All countries considered not free are in Asia or Africa.
Source: Freedom House

Additional distinctions can be made within Aristotle's third type—constitutional republican governments—based on how they allocate power among the executive, legislative, and judicial branches. Presidential systems such as we have in the United States tend to follow a separation of power among the three branches, while parliamentary systems such as the one in the United Kingdom elect the chief executive from the legislature, so there is much closer coordination between those two branches.

We can further refine Aristotle's third type by considering the relationships among different levels of the government. In a federal system such as the United States, power is shared among the local, state, and national levels of government. In a unitary system (such as the United Kingdom), all power is held at the national level. A confederation (like Switzerland) is a less common form of government in which states retain their sovereignty and autonomy but form a loose association at the national level.

★

DEFINE *POLITICS* AND IDENTIFY THREE KEY IDEAS THAT HELP EXPLAIN POLITICS

politics
The process that determines what government does.

What is politics?

We define **politics** as the process that determines what government does. You may consider politics the same thing as government, but we view politics as being much broader; it includes ways of behaving and making decisions that are common in everyday life. Many aspects of our discussion of politics will probably sound familiar because your life involves politics on a regular basis. This may sound a little abstract, but it should become clear in light of the three key ideas of this book (see the How It Works graphic in this chapter).

First, *politics is conflictual*. The questions debated in election campaigns and in Washington and the options considered by policy makers generally involve disagreement at all levels. The federal government does not spend much time resolving issues that everyone agrees should be decided in a particular way. Rather, making government policy involves issues on which people disagree, sometimes strongly, which makes compromise difficult—and this is a normal, healthy part of politics. Although compromise may be difficult, it is often necessary to produce an outcome that can be enacted and implemented.

Second, *political process matters*. Governmental actions don't happen by accident—they result from conscious choices made by elected officials and bureaucrats. Politics, as the process that determines what governments do, puts certain individuals into positions of power and makes the rules that structure their choices. The media often cover political campaigns the way they would report on a boxing match or the Super Bowl, focusing on the competition, rivalries, and entertaining stories, which can lead people to overlook the institutions, rules, and procedures that have a decisive influence on politics. Indeed, the political process is the mechanism for resolving conflict. The most obvious example of the political process at work is elections, which democracies use to resolve a fundamental conflict in society: deciding who should lead the country.

Third, *politics is everywhere*. Decisions about what government should do or who should be in charge are integral to society, and they influence the everyday lives of all Americans. Politics helps to determine what people can and cannot do, their quality of life, and how they think about events, people, and situations. Moreover, people's political thought and behavior are driven by the same types of calculations and decision-making rules that shape beliefs and actions in other parts of life. For example,

Three Key Ideas for Understanding Politics

Politics Is Conflictual

Conflict and compromise are natural parts of politics. Political conflict over issues like the national debt, abortion, and health care **reflects disagreements among the American people** and often requires compromises within government.

Vote aquí

Political Process Matters

How political conflicts are resolved is important. Elections determine who represents citizens in government. **Rules and procedures determine who has power** in Congress and other branches of government.

Politics Is Everywhere

What happens in government affects our lives in countless ways. Policies related to jobs and the economy, food safety and nutrition, student loans, and many other areas shape **our everyday lives**. We see political information in the news and encounter political situations in many areas of our lives.

? Critical Thinking

1. **One implication of the idea that politics is conflictual is that politicians** may not want to negotiate compromises on important policy questions. Why do you think politicians sometimes refuse to compromise rather than work together to get things done?

2. **Think back to the discussion** of the 2016 election at the beginning of this chapter. Even though this election was not typical, in what ways does it illustrate the three key ideas described here?

deciding which presidential candidate to vote for is similar to deciding which college to attend. For candidates, you might consider issue positions, character, and leadership ability, while for college you would weigh which school fits your academic goals, how much tuition you can afford, and where different schools are located. In both cases you are making a decision that will satisfy the criteria most important to you.

Politics is conflictual

Political scientists have long recognized the central role of conflict in politics. In fact, one prominent theory in the mid-twentieth century saw conflict between interest groups as explaining most outcomes in American politics. The political scientist E. E. Schattschneider argued that the scope of political conflict—that is, how many people are involved in the fight—determines who wins in politics. Others have argued that some conflict is helpful for small groups: if nobody challenges a widely shared but flawed view, people may convince themselves that the obvious flaws are not a problem. Bureaucratic politics, congressional politics, elections, and even Supreme Court decision making have all been studied through the lens of political conflict.[4]

Despite the consensus that conflict in politics is inevitable, most people do not like conflict, either in their personal lives or in politics. You probably have heard people say that the three topics one should not discuss in polite company are money, religion, and politics. Indeed, since the 1950s political scientists have found strong evidence that people avoid discussing politics in order to maintain social harmony.[5]

Many people apply their disdain for conflict to politicians as well. "Why is there so much partisan bickering?" our students frequently ask. "Why can't they just get along?" Many such comments were voiced during recent negotiations over budgets,

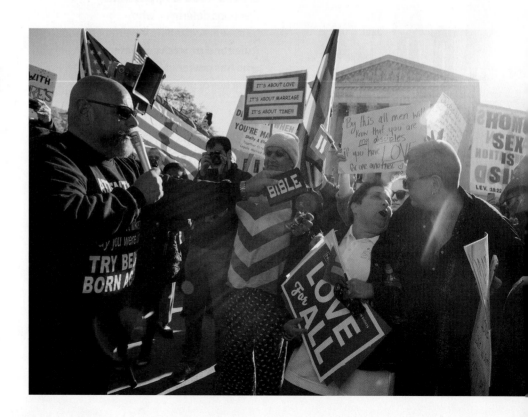

Conflict is inherent in American politics, a fact that has been driven home by the ongoing national debate over health care reform. Here, supporters and opponents of same-sex marriage argue in front of the Supreme Court building in Washington on the day the Court heard arguments in *Obergefell v. Hodges,* the 2015 case that legalized same-sex marriage throughout the nation. #Obergefell #SCOTUS surveillance, and foreign policy, and during many other legislative fights in recent years.

This dislike of conflict, and of politics more generally, produces a desire for what political scientists John R. Hibbing and Elizabeth Theiss-Morse call "stealth democracy"—that is, nondemocratic practices such as running government like a business or taking action without political debate. In essence, this idea reflects the hope that everything would be better if we could just take the politics out of politics. Hibbing and Theiss-Morse argue that, to combat this belief, we need to do a better job of educating people about conflict and policy differences and that the failure to do so "is encouraging students to conclude that real democracy is unnecessary and stealth democracy will do just fine."[6] Conflict cannot be avoided in politics; ignoring fundamental disagreements will not make conflict go away.

The argument over abortion is a good example. Abortion rights have been a perennial topic of debate since a 1973 Supreme Court decision held that state laws banning abortion were unconstitutional. Surveys about abortion rights show that public opinion spans a wide range of policy options, with little agreement about which policy is best. (In Chapter 6, we will examine the political implications of this kind of broad disagreement.) Such conflicts reflect intense differences of opinion that are rooted in self-interest, ideology, and personal beliefs. Moreover, in such situations, no matter what Congress does, many people will be unhappy with the result. You might expect that politicians will ultimately find a way to compromise that satisfies everyone, but this is not always true. In many cases, no single policy choice satisfies even a slight majority of elected officials or citizens.

The idea that conflict is nearly always a part of politics should be no surprise. Situations in which everyone (or almost everyone) agrees about what government should be doing are easy to resolve: either a popular new policy is enacted or an unpopular issue is avoided, and the debate moves off the political agenda. Although issues where there is consensus resolve quickly and disappear, conflictual issues remain on the agenda as the winners try to extend their gains and the losers work to roll back policies. Thus, one reason that abortion rights is a perennial issue in campaigns and congressional debates is that there is no national consensus on when to allow abortions, no indication that the issue is becoming less important to citizens or elected officials, and no sign of a compromise policy that would attract widespread support.

An important consequence of the inevitable conflicts in American politics is that compromise and bargaining are essential to getting things done. Politicians who bargain with opponents are not necessarily abandoning their principles; striking a deal may be the only way to make some of the policy changes they want. Moreover, agreement sometimes exists even in the midst of controversy. For example, surveys that measure attitudes about abortion find widespread support for measures such as prohibiting government funding for abortions, requiring parental notification when a minor has an abortion, or requiring doctors who perform the procedure to present their patients with information on alternatives such as adoption.

Another consequence of conflict is that it is almost impossible to get exactly what you want from the political process. Even when a significant percentage of the population is united behind common goals—such as supporters of Barack Obama after the 2012 election, who favored immigration reform and additional control on handguns, or Republicans, who wanted to shrink government and repeal Obamacare—these individuals almost always find that they need to accept something short of their ideal to attract enough support to implement policy change. Republicans, for example, had to accept that Obamacare was here to stay, at least for the moment. The need for compromise does not mean that change is impossible, only that what is achievable often falls short of individuals' demands.

When everyone (or almost everyone) agrees about a policy or problem, the issue is generally dealt with quickly and without much conflict. In a rare example of compromise and cooperation, Republican and Democratic members of Congress along with students, teachers, and administrators applaud as President Obama signs the Every Student Succeeds Act in December 2015, which reduced the federal government's authority over state education standards. #EveryStudentSucceeds

As long as the reason of man continues fallible, and he is at liberty to exercise it, different opinions will be formed.

— James Madison

Political process matters

The political process is often described like a sporting event, with a focus on strategies and ultimately on "winning." In fact, the *National Journal* magazine regularly published a segment titled "The Play of the Day" on its online site. This focus overlooks an important point: politics is the process that determines what government does, none of which is inevitable. Public policy—everything from defending the nation to spending on Medicare—is up for grabs. And the political process determines these government actions. It is not just a game.

Elections are an excellent example of the importance of the political process. Elections allow voters to give fellow citizens the power to enact laws, write budgets, and appoint senior bureaucrats and federal judges. It matters who gets elected. After the 2008 election, when Democrats strengthened their control of Congress and captured the presidency, they enacted a massive economic stimulus package and new policies for alternative energy, global warming, education, health care, regulation of the mortgage and financial sectors, and the plan for fighting the wars in Iraq and Afghanistan. Clearly, political process matters: if the 2008 election had gone the other way, policies in all these important areas would have been significantly different. The same is true for the 2016 election, given the candidates' sharp disagreements on trade, gun rights, immigration, and other issues. Again, elections matter.

Yet politics is more than elections. As you will see, many members of the federal bureaucracy have influence over what government does by virtue of their roles in developing and implementing government policies. The same is true for federal judges, who review government actions to see if they are consistent with the Constitution and other federal laws. These individuals' decisions are part of the political process, even though they are not elected to their positions.

Ordinary citizens are also part of politics. They can vote; donate time or money to interest groups, party organizations, or individual candidates; or demand action from these groups or individuals. Such actions can influence government policy, either by determining who holds the power to change policy directly or by signaling to policy makers which options have public support.

The political process mattered in the 2016 presidential election, from determining who the candidates were, to affecting which states received the most attention from the campaigns. Here, Hillary Clinton is shown debating Donald Trump.

Another important element of politics is the web of rules and procedures that determines who has the power to make choices about government policy. These rules range from the requirement that the president must be born a U.S. citizen, to the rules that structure debates and voting in the House and the Senate, to the procedures for approving new federal regulations. Seemingly innocuous rules can have an enormous impact on what can or does happen, which means that choices about these rules are actually choices about outcomes. The ability to determine political rules empowers the people who make these choices.

Politics is everywhere

Even though most Americans have little interest in politics, most of us encounter it every day. When you read the newspaper, watch television, go online, or listen to the radio you'll almost surely encounter a political story. When you are walking down the street, you may see billboards, bumper stickers, or T-shirts advertising a candidate, a political party, an interest group, or an issue position. Someone may ask you to sign a petition. You may walk past a homeless person and wonder whether a winning candidate followed through on her promise to help. You may glance at a headline about violence in the Middle East and wonder if America should be "putting boots on the ground" (sending in troops).

Many people have an interest in putting politics in front of us on a daily basis. Interest groups, political parties, and candidates work to raise public awareness of the political process and to shape what people know and want. Moreover, the news media offer extensive coverage of elections and governing and how government policies affect ordinary Americans. Through efforts like these, politics really is everywhere.

Politics is also a fundamental part of how Americans think about themselves. Virtually all of us can name our party identification (Democrat, Republican, or independent)[7] and can place our views on a continuum between liberal and conservative.[8]

Politics is everywhere in another important way, too: actions by the federal government touch virtually every aspect of your life. Figure 1.1 shows a time line for a typical college student on a typical day. As you can see, from the moment this student wakes up until the end of the day his or her actions are influenced by federal programs, spending, and regulations. As you will see in later chapters, it's not surprising that the federal government touches your everyday life in so many ways. The federal government is extraordinarily large regardless of whether you measure spending (nearly $4 trillion a year), number of employees (over two million if you include contract workers and postal service employees), or new regulations (over 80,000 pages per year).[9]

> **I'll let you write the substance, you let me write the procedure, and I'll screw you every time.**
>
> **—John Dingell**

The idea that "politics is everywhere" means that government actions touch virtually all aspects of our lives, from requiring drone owners to register with the Federal Aviation Administration to mandating equal funding for men's and women's sports in high schools and colleges. Moreover, everyday life often helps us to make sense of politics and politicians, such as Republican presidential candidate Ted Cruz's claim that *Star Trek*'s Captain Picard was a Democrat while Captain Kirk was a Republican. #FAADrones #TitleIX #StarTrek

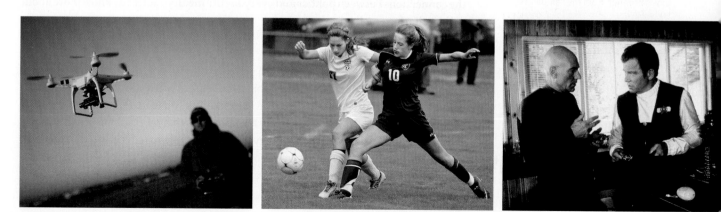

FIGURE 1.1

Government in a Student's Daily Life

On a typical day, the government plays a critical role in a student's daily life through federal programs, regulation, and spending. In addition to what is listed here, in what other aspects of your life does government play a part?

Time	Activity
7:30	Wake up in dorm funded by federal program.
8:00	Eat cereal regulated by Food and Drug Administration.
8:15	Get dressed in clothing subject to import tariffs and regulations.
8:30	Read weather reports that use data from the National Weather Service.
9:00	Check e-mail using Internet developed with federal funding.
10:00	Drive to school in car whose design is shaped by federal regulations.
10:30	Drive past post office, military recruitment office, and environmental cleanup site.
11:00	Attend lecture by professor whose research receives federal funding.
4:00	Ride home from school on federally subsidized mass transit.
7:30	Pay bursar bill using federally funded student loan.
8:00	Call friend on cellular network regulated by the Federal Communications Commission.
10:00	Watch TV program on station that has federal license.

”

Just because you do not take an interest in politics does not mean that politics will not take an interest in you.

—Pericles

Moreover, the idea that politics is everywhere has a deeper meaning: people's political behavior is similar to their behavior in the rest of their lives. For example, collective action problems occur when you live with roommates and need to keep common areas neat and clean. Everyone has an interest in a clean area, but each person is inclined to let someone else do the work. The same principles help us to understand campus protests of tuition hikes, alcohol bans, or changes in graduation requirements in terms of which kinds of issues and circumstances foster cooperation. In each case, individual free riders acting in their own self-interest may undermine the outcome that most people prefer.

Similarly, convincing like-minded individuals to contribute to a political group's lobbying efforts is no easy task. Each would-be contributor of time or money also has the opportunity to be a free rider who refuses to participate yet reaps the benefits of others' participation. Because of these difficulties, some groups of people with common goals remain unorganized. College students are a good example: many want more student aid and lower interest rates on government-subsidized student loans, but they fail to organize politically toward those ends.

This similarity, between behavior in political situations and in the rest of life is no surprise; everything that happens in politics is the result of individuals' choices. And the connections between politics and everyday life mean you already know more about politics than you realize.

"Why Should I Care?"

The three key ideas should be the first thing you think of when you are trying to make sense of a political situation. Focusing on conflict helps you to understand what is at stake. Focusing on rules helps to explain the strategies that participants use to achieve their goals. And the idea that politics is everywhere is there to remind you that conflicts over government policy are not something that happen to other people—for better or worse, the outcome of political conflicts can touch virtually all aspects of our lives.

Sources of conflict in American politics

Conflict must be addressed in order to find compromise and enact policy. Sometimes, however, disagreements resist resolution because of inherent differences among people and their opinions about government and politics.

Economic Interests

People's economic interests today vary widely, and they constitute a source of conflict in politics. In contrast, relative economic equality was a defining characteristic of our nation's early history—at least among white men, since small landowners, businessmen, craftsmen, and their families constituted a large majority of the nation's population. Compared with our European counterparts, the United States has been relatively free from class-based politics. Over time, our nation has become more stratified by class, to the point that the United States has one of the highest levels of income inequality among developed nations. Nonetheless, a commitment to the **free market** (an economic system based on competition among businesses without government interference) and to *economic individualism* (the autonomy of individuals to manage their own financial decisions without government interference) remains central to our national identity.

free market
An economic system based on competition among businesses without government interference.

Today there are important differences among American citizens, interest groups, and political parties in terms of their economic interests and favored economic policies. Democratic politicians and activists tend to favor more **redistributive tax policies** and social spending on programs for the poor. Democrats are also more inclined to regulate industry to protect the environment and ensure worker and product safety, but they tend to favor fewer restrictions on the personal behavior of individuals. Republicans favor lower taxes and less spending on social policies. They are also more supportive than Democrats of the free market and less inclined to interfere with business interests, although many Republicans favor regulation of individual behaviors, such as abortion and same-sex marriage.

redistributive tax policies
Politics, generally favored by Democratic politicians, that use taxation to attempt to create social equality (for example, higher taxation of the rich to provide programs for the poor).

Cultural values

Another source of conflict in American politics is differing cultural values. For example, political analysts often focus attention on the **culture wars** in the United States between "red-state" Americans, who tend to have strong religious beliefs, and "blue-state" Americans, who tend to be more secular. (The color coding of the states comes from the election-night maps on television that show the states carried by Republican candidates in red and those won by Democrats in blue—but see the What Do the Numbers Say? feature for a more nuanced take on this.)

culture wars
Political conflict in the United States between "red-state" Americans, who tend to have strong religious beliefs, and "blue-state" Americans, who tend to be more secular.

Although the precise makeup and impact of "values voters" is still debated, there is no doubt that many Americans disagree on cultural and moral issues. These include the broad category of "family values" (such as whether and how to regulate pornography, gambling, and media obscenity and violence); whether to supplement the teaching of evolution in public schools with intelligent design and creationism; same-sex

Purple America: The 2016 Presidential Election

The media create maps of the country on election night with red states where Republicans win and blue states where Democrats win (see the very first pages of this book). But what do we see if we look beyond the state level to the county level? And what if we look not just at who won and who lost, but which party was stronger relative to the other? This is what this map, created by Robert Vanderbei at Princeton University, shows. The simple view of two Americas—Republican versus Democrat, red versus blue—starts to look a lot more purple.

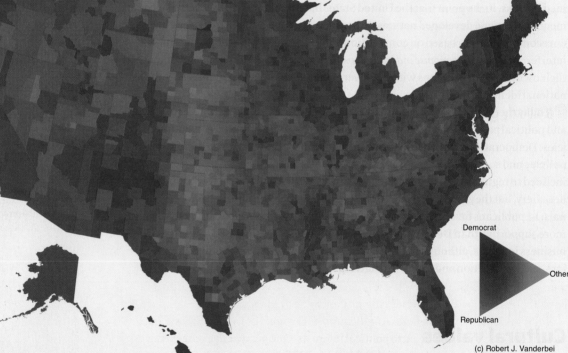

Democrat

Other

Republican

(c) Robert J. Vanderbei

Think about it

- Which sections of the country were the strongest for Clinton and which were strongest for Trump?
- Which areas are the most mixed (light purple)?
- How do you think the color of the map will shift over the next 20 years as the nation becomes more racially and ethnically diverse?

Source: Provided by Robert J. Vanderbei, Princeton University, "2016 Presidential Election, Purple America," www.princeton.edu/~rvdb/JAVA/election 2016 (accessed 11/14/16).

The debate over income inequality in America and what should be done about it (raising the minimum wage, for example) was one of the important issues that divided Republicans and Democrats and their supporters in the 2016 elections. #WageAction #FightFor15

marriage; abortion; school prayer; the War on Drugs; gun control; school vouchers; immigration policy, including allowing political refugees to enter the country; the federal Common Core curriculum for K–12 schools; and religious displays in public places. These are all hot-button issues that interest groups and activists on all sides attempt to keep at the top of the policy agenda.

Racial, gender, and ethnic differences

Many political differences are correlated with racial, gender, and ethnic differences. For example, over the last generation about 90 percent of African Americans have been strong supporters of Democratic candidates. Other racial groups have been less cohesive in their voting, with their support for a particular party ranging from 55 to 70 percent. Whites tend to vote Republican; Latinos tend to vote Democratic, with the exception of Cuban Americans, who tend to vote Republican; Asian Americans tend to support Democrats with about 70 percent of the vote. A gender gap in national politics is also evident, with women being somewhat more likely to vote for Democrats and men for Republicans.[10] Because these tendencies are not fixed, however, the political implications of racial, gender, and ethnic differences can change over time.

One of the enduring debates in American politics concerns whether ethnic and racial differences *should* be tied to political interests. One perspective reflects the melting pot image of America, which holds that as different racial and ethnic groups come to this country they should mostly leave their native languages and customs behind.

However, there are varied alternatives to the melting pot view. These range from racial separatists such as the Nation of Islam, whose members see white-dominated society as oppressive and discriminatory, to multiculturalists, who argue that there is strength in diversity and embrace a "tossed salad" version of assimilation (that is, each ingredient remains distinct but contributes to the overall quality of the salad).[11]

This debate over culture is one reason why recent discussions about immigration law have been so conflictual—the two sides start from very different premises about the value of diversity. But regardless of how this debate is resolved, our multiracial makeup is clear, as Table 1.1 shows. In fact, trends in population growth suggest that by

Civil and voting rights contributed to the realignment of the South in the second half of the twentieth century, as more whites began supporting the Republican Party and the Democratic Party came to be seen as the champion of minority rights. Here, blacks and whites in Alabama wait in line together to vote at a city hall after enactment of the 1965 Voting Rights Act.

DID YOU KNOW?

One year after graduation, college-educated women working full time earn on average

7%

less than their male peers, even after controlling for differences in major, training, parenthood, hours worked, and other factors.

Source: American Association of University Women

ideology
A cohesive set of ideas and beliefs used to organize and evaluate the political world.

conservative
One side of the ideological spectrum defined by support for lower taxes, a free market, and a more-limited government; generally associated with Republicans.

liberal
One side of the ideological spectrum defined by support for stronger government programs and more market regulation; generally associated with Democrats.

2042 whites will no longer constitute a majority of the U.S. population. The extent to which this diversity continues to be a source of political conflict depends on the broader role of race in our society. As long as there are racial differences in employment, education, health, housing, and crime and as long as racial discrimination is present in our society, race will continue to be a source of political conflict.

Many of the same observations apply to gender and politics. The women's movement is usually viewed as beginning in 1848 at the first Women's Rights Convention at Seneca Falls, New York. The fight for women's suffrage and legal rights dominated the movement through the late nineteenth and early twentieth centuries. Beginning in the 1960s and 1970s, feminism and the women's liberation movement highlighted a broad range of issues: workplace issues such as maternity leave, equal pay, and sexual harassment; reproductive rights and abortion; domestic violence; and sexual violence. Progress has been made on many fronts, including at the most basic level of electing women to political office. While Clinton failed to win the 2016 presidential election, the new Congress has more than 80 female House members and more than 20 female senators. Even so, these percentages are far lower than in the general population, confirming that gender equality remains an important source of political conflict.

Ideology

Another source of differences in interests is **ideology**: a cohesive set of ideas and beliefs that allows an individual to organize and evaluate the political world. Ideology may seem most obviously related to political interests through political parties, since Republicans tend to be **conservative** and Democrats tend to be **liberal**. While this is true in a relative sense (most Republicans are more conservative than most Democrats), few Americans consider their own views ideologically extreme.[12]

Ideology shapes specific beliefs. Conservatives promote traditional social practices and favor lower taxes, a free market, and more-limited government, whereas liberals support social tolerance, stronger government programs, and more market regulation.

TABLE 1.1

The Racial Composition of the United States

Only about 62 percent of Americans describe themselves as white. Moreover, the proportion of Hispanics and Latinos in the population is about 18 percent and rising, although this category contains many distinct subgroups. What changes would you expect in American politics and federal policy if the actual population in 2060 matches the projections?

| | % of population | |
	2015	2060
White	61.7	43.6
Hispanic or Latino	17.7	28.6
Black or African American	12.4	13.0
Asian	5.3	9.1
American Indian and Alaska Native	0.7	0.6
Native Hawaiian and Other Pacific Islander	0.2	0.2
Two or More Races	2.1	4.9

Source: Census data aggregated by author. Raw data available at www.census.gov/projections (accessed 6/21/16).

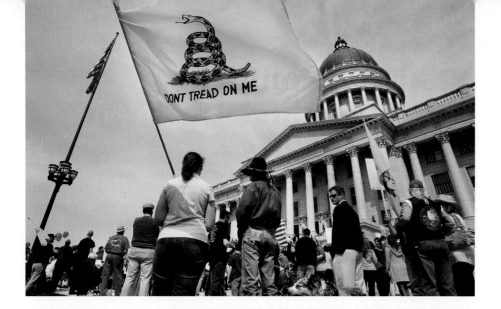

Libertarians, including those in the Tea Party, believe in very limited government. These Tea Party activists at the Utah state capitol in Salt Lake City hold a flag with the libertarian motto "Don't Tread on Me" while protesting against high taxes and government programs. #TeaParty #Libertarian #LibertyForAll

However, the picture gets cloudy if we look more closely. **Libertarians**, for example, prefer very limited government—that is, they believe that the government should provide for the national defense and should only have a few other narrowly defined responsibilities. Because they are at the extreme end of the ideological continuum on this issue, libertarians are generally conservative in areas such as social welfare policy, environmental policy, and government funding for education and generally liberal on issues involving personal liberty such as free speech, abortion, and the legalization of drugs. For libertarians, the consistent ideological theme is limiting the role of government in our lives.

Personal ideologies are not always consistent. Someone can be both a fiscal conservative (favoring balanced budgets) and a social liberal (favoring the pro-choice position on abortion and marital rights for gay men and lesbians), or a liberal on foreign policy issues (supporting humanitarian aid and opposing military intervention overseas) and a conservative on moral issues (being pro-life on abortion and opposing stem-cell research). Ideology is a significant source of conflict in politics, and it does not always operate in a straightforward manner. In Chapter 6, we explore whether America is becoming more ideological and polarized, deepening our conflicts and making compromise more difficult.

Even so, there are clear areas of agreement in American politics, even on issues that once divided us. For example, while there is still considerable disagreement over same-sex marriage, public opinion has clearly shifted toward making such unions legal. Along the same lines, two generations ago Americans were divided on the legality of mixed-race marriage, while today very few people would object. Thus, even though conflict is a constant in American politics, it is wrong to say that we are divided into two groups, red and blue, that oppose each other on all issues of significance.

libertarians
Those who prefer very limited government and therefore tend to be conservative on issues such as welfare policy, environmental policy, and public support for education but liberal on issues of personal liberty such as free speech, abortion, and the legalization of drugs.

DID YOU KNOW?

38%
of millennials call themselves conservative on economic issues, while 33 percent call themselves liberal.
Source: *USA Today*/Rock the Vote Poll

"Why Should I Care?"

The first step in understanding politics is to determine who wants what. Who is involved in this conflict? What do they, or their side, want? In modern American politics, citizens' demands are often connected to their economic interests, values, race, gender, ethnicity, and ideology. As a result, an individual's group affiliations often tell us a lot about what they want from candidates and the government, and why they want it.

Resolving conflict: democracy and American political values

When we say that rules shape how conflicts are worked out in American politics, most of the time we are referring to formal (written-down) constraints that describe how the actions taken by each participant shape the ultimate outcome. For example, most American House and Senate elections are decided using plurality voting (whichever candidate gets the most votes wins), while a few states require winners to receive a majority (50% + 1) of votes cast. However, some of the most important rules are not written down—these constitute America's political culture, or a collective idea of how a government and society should operate, including democracy, equality, and liberty.[13]

Democracy

democracy
Government by the people. In most contexts, this means representative democracy in which the people elect leaders to enact policies. Democracies must have fair elections with at least two options.

The idea of democracy means that policy disagreements are ultimately resolved through politics—through decisions made by citizens, such as their votes in elections. In the simplest terms, "democracy" means government by the people. As put into practice, this typically means representative democracy rather than direct democracy—that is, the people elect representatives who decide policies and pass laws, rather than determining those things directly. There are some examples of direct democracy in the United States, such as the New England town meeting[14] and the referendum process, in which people in a state directly determine policy. But for the most part, Americans elect politicians to represent us, from school board and city council members at the local level, to state legislators and governors at the state level, to U.S. House members, senators, and the president at the national level.

Democracy is not the only way to resolve conflict, nor do all societies have as strong a belief in democracy as in America. One mechanism used by authoritarian governments is to suppress conflict though violence and limiting freedom. Some governments, such as those of China and Russia, control political outcomes while allowing relatively free markets. The Iranian government is a theocracy, where religious figures have a veto over the government's policy choices. Part of the reason why these governments have remained in place over time is that their citizens have less of a preference for democracy—they favor, for example, a strong leader who can implement policy change without needing elected officials or the people to consent.

Liberty

Democracy means resolving conflict through voting and elections rather than through violence or coercion. When the second president of the United States, John Adams, turned over power to his bitter rival, Thomas Jefferson, after losing a hotly contested election in 1800, it demonstrated that democratic government by the people had real meaning. Democracy depends on the consent of the governed: if the views of the people change, then the government must eventually be responsive to those views or the people will choose new leaders. It also means that citizens must accept election results as authoritative—you have to obey the laws passed by a new Congress, even if you voted for the other party's candidates.

Democracy also means that resolving conflict requires compromise. In a dictatorship, totalitarian state, or monarchy, no compromise is required. The government simply chooses its preferred policies and implements them. Any dissent is either ignored or quashed. Representative democracies must be more open to dissent, or they lose legitimacy. Given the broad range of interests outlined in the previous section, no single group can get its way all of the time. Having a functioning democracy means compromising on issues that we may care deeply about.

The American ethos is to embrace conflict as a natural consequence of the differences between people and to create a system that gives people the political freedom to express views based on those differences. To the Founders, **liberty** was the central principle for their new government: they believed that people must have the freedom to express their political views. The Bill of Rights of the Constitution, discussed in Chapter 4, outlines the nature of those liberties: the freedom of speech, press, assembly, and religion, as well as many legal and due process rights protecting individuals from government control. James Madison recognized this essential trade-off between liberty and conflict. He argued that suppressing conflict by limiting freedom was "worse than the disease" (worse than conflict). Therefore, any political system with political freedom will have conflict.

liberty
Political freedom, such as the freedom of speech, press, assembly, and religion. These and other legal and due process rights protecting individuals from government control are outlined in the Bill of Rights of the U.S. Constitution.

Equality

Another principle of democracy is **equality**. Even though the Declaration of Independence boldly declared "all Men are created equal," this did not mean that all people were entitled to the same income or even the same social status. Instead, the most widely embraced notion of equality is the equality of opportunity—that is, everyone should have the same chance to realize his or her potential. Political equality also means that people are treated the same in the political system. Everyone has one vote in an election, and everyone is equal in the eyes of the law—that is, we are all subject to the same rules that limit how we can lobby, contribute, work for a candidate, or express our opinions. In practice, political equality has not always existed in America. In our early history, only white men could vote and in many states those men needed to be property owners in order to vote. Slowly, political equality expanded as property requirements were dropped; black men (in 1870, but restrictions persisted into the 1960s), women (in 1919), and 18- to 20-year-olds (in 1971) got the right to vote (for more on the expansion of the right to vote, see Chapter 5). Today, although wealthy people clearly can have their voices heard more easily than poor people (through campaign contributions or independent expenditures on political ads), the notion of political equality is central to our democracy.

equality
In the context of American politics, "equality" means equality before the law, political equality (one person, one vote), and equality of opportunity (the equal chance for everyone to realize their potential), but not material equality (equal income or wealth).

Like democracy, political equality also contributes to resolving conflict. First, if people know that they will be treated equally by the political system they are more likely to respect the system. Indeed, one of the triggers for revolutions around the world is reaction against rigged elections or policies that benefit only the supporters of winning candidates. Political equality also gives us cues about how to get involved in politics. Most fundamentally, it suggests that the way to change policy is to elect candidates who share your views, rather than appealing to a friend or relative who works in the government or offering a bribe to a bureaucrat.

While America's political culture has many other aspects, the concepts of democracy, liberty, and equality are central to understanding how American politics works.

Agreement on these principles helps to lessen conflicts and limits their scope. For example, when Republican legislators lost the battle to prevent Obamacare from being enacted they didn't have to worry that Democrats would throw them in jail for opposing the program or force them to pay for health care for everyone else. (Indeed, this equality norm is one reason why Trump's threat to jail Clinton was so controversial.) Rather, the benefits of Obamacare are given to everyone regardless of who they voted for. Moreover, Republicans have a clear path to ending Obamacare: attract enough supporters to win the presidency and enough seats in Congress to repeal the program. Americans have been more willing to grant one another political equality and to take political defeats in stride because there is more agreement on the basic boundaries of political debate. Again, this consensus does not imply there is no conflict—quite the contrary. However, conflict is easier to resolve if it is over a narrower range of options.

Not surprisingly, many aspects of America's political culture will come up throughout this book. You also might want to look out for them when you are watching the news or reading about national politics. When Hillary Clinton talked about the need to provide subsidized college tuition for all Americans, she was emphasizing equality, and when President Trump argues that minimizing government involvement and allowing people more choice would lead to a better system he is emphasizing liberty. Moreover, as this example suggests, part of the conflict in American politics is over which aspect of political culture should carry the day. The fact that issues such as education were central in recent elections is a reminder of the importance of elections in a democracy, and our belief that elections are one venue where conflicts are debated and resolved.

In democracies like the United States, voting is one of the most visible ways citizens use the political process to express their opinions and resolve conflict.

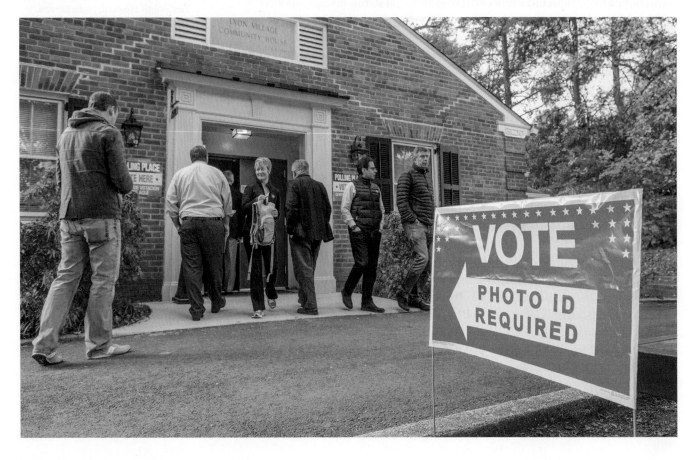

To truly understand American politics, you must understand America's core values: democracy, liberty, and equality. These values set broad limits on how political conflicts will be resolved. Democracy implies that the people are the ultimate authority over political outcomes. Equality means that everyone has an equal share of decision-making power. And liberty implies that people are able to express whatever demands they want and to choose among a wide range of strategies in trying to shape the outcomes of political decisions. Despite conflicts over their interpretations, most Americans believe in these core values, and reminding ourselves of this can help us work toward resolving political conflicts.

Conclusion

By understanding that politics is conflictual, that it is rooted in process, and that it is everywhere, you will see that modern American political life makes more sense than you might have thought. As you read this book, we hope you will learn important "nuts and bolts" of the American political process as well as some political history. In general, however, your reading in this book will focus on contemporary questions, debates, and examples to illustrate broader points about our nation's political system. After all, American politics in its current form is the politics that will have the greatest impact on your life. To return to the case of the 2016 election, regardless of how you feel about the campaign or the outcome, you need to know how things work in order to understand why your preferred candidate won or lost—and to determine what actions you might take to help your cause.

Although you will no doubt disagree with some aspects of American politics and other parts may even make you angry, our goal in this book is to provide you with the tools to understand *why* government operates as it does. We are not arguing that the federal government is perfect or that imperfect responses to policy problems are inevitable. Rather, we believe that any attempt to explain these outcomes, or to devise ways to prevent similar problems, requires an understanding of why they happened in the first place. After reading this book, you will have a better sense of how American politics really works, and why it matters.

STUDY GUIDE

Making sense of American government and politics

Describe the basic functions of government. (Pages 4–8)

Summary

Forms of government can be characterized by the number of people who hold power (many versus few) and the number of levels over which power is distributed (national versus state versus local). Government exists primarily to provide order, although it must do so while avoiding oppression by the rulers. Government also needs to provide public goods because they will be underprovided by the free market.

Key terms

government (p. 5)

factions (p. 6)

separation of powers (p. 6)

checks and balances (p. 6)

federalism (p. 6)

public goods (p. 6)

collective action problems (p. 6)

free rider problem (p. 7)

Practice Quiz Questions

1. **What did Aristotle call "a government ruled by the many"?**
   a. monarchy
   b. aristocracy
   c. polity
   d. unitary system
   e. democracy

2. **Which term describes giving each branch of government power over the other two?**
   a. separation of powers
   b. checks and balances
   c. federalism
   d. plutocracy
   e. unitary system

3. **Which term describes the inability to get individuals to cooperate to achieve a common goal?**
   a. positive externality
   b. the Samaritan's dilemma
   c. collective action problem
   d. principal-agent problem
   e. public goods

What is politics?

Define *politics* and identify three key ideas that help explain politics. (Pages 8–14)

Summary

Conflict in politics cannot be avoided: the American people disagree on nearly every issue on which politicians make policy decisions. Compromise and bargaining are essential to enacting policy, but this means that it is almost impossible to get exactly what you want from the political process. Policy outcomes are also influenced by the policy process itself—different procedures of making policy can lead to different outcomes. Whether it is on the news or influencing most aspects of your life, politics is all around us.

Key term

politics (p. 8)

Practice Quiz Questions

4. **What is the main reason why politicians have a hard time resolving the issue of abortion?**
   a. Politicians don't listen to the people.
   b. The parties are divided on what abortion policy should look like.
   c. Politicians don't know what their constituents' views are.
   d. The country is closely divided on what abortion policy should look like.
   e. Abortion is a relatively new issue.

5. **Which concept describes the idea that actions by the government touch most aspects of your life?**
   a. Politics is understandable.
   b. Politics is conflictual.
   c. Political process matters.
   d. Politics is everywhere.
   e. People have different interests.

6. **Rules, such as those regulating debate in the Senate, or limiting who can vote in elections, serve as evidence that _____.**
   a. politics is understandable
   b. politics is conflictual
   c. political process matters
   d. politics is everywhere
   e. people have different interests

Sources of conflict in American politics

Identify major sources of conflict in American politics. (Pages 15–19)

Summary

Although Americans generally agree on a free market system, there is considerable conflict over how much the government should support tax policies that redistribute wealth. Conflict also arises on cultural grounds, pitting religious "red-state" Americans against the more secular "blue-state" Americans. There is also disagreement on the extent to which racial, gender, and ethnic diversity should be celebrated or minimized.

Key terms

free market (p. 15)   conservative (p. 18)
redistributive tax policies (p. 15)   liberal (p. 18)
culture wars (p. 15)   libertarians (p. 19)
ideology (p. 18)

Practice Quiz Questions

7. **Democrats tend to favor _____ tax policies and are _____ inclined to regulate industry.**

   a. redistributive; more
   b. conservative; more
   c. redistributive; less
   d. conservative; less
   e. regressive; less

8. **Which issue is commonly associated with the culture wars?**

   a. the national debt
   b. environmental regulation
   c. affirmative action
   d. the tax code
   e. same-sex marriage

9. **An individual who opposes government social welfare policy and supports the legalization of drugs is most likely a _____.**

   a. libertarian
   b. socialist
   c. Democrat
   d. Republican
   e. centrist

Resolving conflict: democracy and American political values

Explain how the American values of democracy, liberty, and equality work to resolve political conflict. (Pages 20–23)

Summary

Democracy, liberty, and equality are American political values that are essential for understanding how conflict is resolved. Representative democracies resolve conflict through elections rather than through violence. Although liberty ensures that people will have the freedom to express differing views, democracy is the best system for resolving those conflicts. Political equality ensures that everyone is treated the same before the law and that all votes are equal, and the equality of opportunity means that every person has an equal chance to realize his or her potential.

Key terms

democracy (p. 20)   equality (p. 21)
liberty (p. 21)

Practice Quiz Questions

10. **Which type of equality is *not* typically agreed upon in American politics?**

    a. equality of opportunity
    b. equality before the law
    c. political equality
    d. one person, one vote
    e. material equality (such as equal income)

11. **What did James Madison argue was "worse than the disease"?**

    a. giving too much power to state legislatures
    b. allowing people to have too much freedom, which would lead to chaos
    c. giving up liberty to get rid of conflict
    d. allowing politicians to exercise their judgment rather than listen to the people
    e. taking cod liver oil to treat various ailments

Suggested Reading

Dahl, Robert. *A Preface to Democratic Theory*, expanded ed. Chicago: University of Chicago Press, 2013.

Fiorina, Morris P., with Samuel J. Abrams and Jeremy C. Pope. *Culture War? The Myth of a Polarized America*, 3rd ed. New York: Pearson, Longman, 2010.

Gelman, Andrew, David Park, Boris Shor, Joseph Bafumi, and Jeronimo Cortina. *Red State, Blue State, Rich State, Poor State: Why Americans Vote the Way They Do*. Princeton, NJ: Princeton University Press, 2008.

Putnam, Robert D. *Bowling Alone: The Collapse and Revival of American Community*. New York: Simon and Schuster, 2000.

Schattschneider, E. E. *The Semisovereign People: A Realist's View of Democracy in America*. New York: Holt, Rinehart, and Winston, 1960.

2

The Constitution and the Founding

What are the rules of the political game?

Recently, the Constitution itself has become the focus of political debate and conflict. Starting in the 2010 midterm elections and continuing through the last three elections, a popular movement known as the Tea Party has supported candidates who endorse a return to the Constitution's founding principles. While the range of views within the Tea Party movement is vast, its supporters generally see the expansion of federal power—which began with Theodore Roosevelt, exploded during the New Deal of the 1930s and Great Society of the 1960s, and continues today with President Barack Obama's health care reform—as constitutional overreach. Many Tea Partiers see Social Security, Medicare, and the Federal Reserve as unconstitutional because they are not expressly permitted by the Constitution. Jim DeMint, head of the conservative Heritage Foundation and a leading Tea Partier, recently wrote, "If President Obama's motto is 'Yes, we can,' the Constitution's is 'No, you can't.' ... Although the Constitution does give some defined powers to the federal government, it is overwhelmingly a document of limits, and those limits must be respected."[1]

The Tea Party's efforts to establish constitutional limits on government activity have met resistance from those who challenge the Tea Party's take on the Constitution and the Founding. These critics argue that rather than serving as a document that created a limited national government and protected state power, the Constitution was intended to create a strong national government while limiting state power.[2] Differences of opinion about the Constitution have been part of American politics since the debates between Federalists and Antifederalists over its ratification. Unfortunately, the Constitution itself provides few definitive answers because its language was intentionally general so that it would stand the test of time. Consequently, in every major political debate in our nation's history both sides have claimed to ground their views in the Constitution. Proslavery and antislavery factions during the pre–Civil War period, New

★

CHAPTER GOALS

Describe the historical circumstances that led to the Constitutional Convention of 1787.
pages 28–33

Analyze the major issues debated by the framers of the Constitution.
pages 34–40

Contrast the arguments of the Federalists with those of the Antifederalists.
pages 40–42

Outline the major provisions of the Constitution.
pages 42–47

Explore how the meaning of the Constitution has evolved.
pages 47–51

Supporters of the Tea Party movement think the federal government has overstepped the powers granted to it by the Constitution. Here, Tea Party activists protest against big government. Throughout American history, debates over the meaning of the Constitution have persisted. #TeaParty

Deal supporters and opponents during the Great Depression, and civil rights activists and segregationists all claimed to have the Constitution on their side. Today's vigorous debate about the proper scope of the national government's powers on issues such as health care, immigration, and economic policy is only the most recent chapter in this perpetual conflict. This debate is likely to shift sharply in the direction of less national power now that Republicans have unified control of government.

One reason that Tea Partiers revere the document is the stability it provides to our political system. The Constitution provides the basis for resolving conflict through elections and representative government rather than by taking up arms. Losers of one round of elections know that they have an opportunity to compete in the next election and that their voices can be heard in another part of the government. The peaceful transitions of power and stability in our political system may be attributed to the hallmark characteristics of U.S. constitutional government: the separation of power across the levels of government (national, state, and local) and within government (legislative, executive, and judicial), as well as the checks and balances of power across the institutions of government.

The separation of powers in government does not mean that the Constitution *resolves* our political conflicts. The Founders recognized that self-interest and conflict are inherent parts of human nature and cannot be eliminated, so they attempted to control conflict by dispersing power across different parts of government. Thus, parts of the political system are always competing with one another in pursuit of various interests. For example, Republicans in Congress may want to cut spending to balance the budget, while a Democratic president may want a mix of spending cuts and tax increases. This conflictual process is often criticized as "gridlock" and "partisan bickering." But that is the system our Founders created. Think about it this way: dictatorships do not have political conflict because dissenters are imprisoned or murdered; in contrast, we *do* have political conflict because under our constitutional government there is free and open competition among different interests and ideas. Why is conflict inherent in our political system? And what does the Constitution say about how we deal with that conflict?

★

DESCRIBE THE HISTORICAL CIRCUMSTANCES THAT LED TO THE CONSTITUTIONAL CONVENTION OF 1787

The historical context of the Constitution

The Constitution was created through conflict and compromise, and understanding the historical context can help clarify *why* the framers made the specific choices they did.

The first event that led many American colonists to question the fairness of British rule and shaped their ideas about self-governance was the Stamp Act of 1765, which imposed a tax on many publications and legal documents in the colonies. The British Parliament enacted the tax to help pay for the French and Indian War (1754–1763), claiming the tax was fair because the American colonists were benefiting from the protection of British troops. Many colonists saw this as unfair "taxation without representation" because they had no say in the legislation's passage (because they had no representation in the British Parliament). A series of escalating events, including the Tea Act (1773) and the Boston Tea Party later that year, in which colonists dumped tea from the British East India Company into the harbor rather than pay the new tax on tea, moved the colonies closer to the inevitable break with Great Britain. Attempts at a political solution failed, so the Continental Congress declared independence from Britain on July 4, 1776.[3]

The Founders wanted to create a constitution that was general enough to stand the test of time. Their approach succeeded, and the U.S. Constitution is the oldest written constitution still in use today. However, by leaving some passages open to interpretation they also set the stage for conflict over the meaning of the Constitution. This painting depicts the signing of the document at the Constitutional Convention of 1787.

The Articles of Confederation: the first attempt at government

Throughout the Revolutionary and early post-Revolutionary era, the future of the American colonies was very much in doubt. While many Americans were eager to sever ties with the oppressive British government and establish a new nation that rejected the trappings of royalty, there was still a large contingent of Tories (supporters of the British monarchy) and probably an even larger group of Americans who wished the conflict would just go away. This context of uncertainty and conflict made the Founders' task of creating a lasting republic extremely difficult.

The first attempt to structure an American government, the **Articles of Confederation**, swung too far in the direction of decentralized and **limited government**. The Articles were written in the summer of 1776 during the Second Continental Congress, which also authorized and approved the Declaration of Independence. The Articles were submitted to all 13 states in 1777 for approval, but they did not take effect until the last state ratified them in 1781. However, in the absence of any alternative, the Articles of Confederation served as the basis for organizing the government during the Revolutionary War (see Figure 2.1).

In their zeal to reject monarchy, the authors of the Articles did not even include a president or any other executive leader. Instead, they assigned all national power to a Congress in which each state had a single vote. Members of Congress were elected by state legislatures rather than directly by the people. There was no judicial branch. All legal matters were left to the states, with the exception of disputes among the states, which would be resolved by special panels of judges appointed on an as-needed basis by Congress. In their eagerness to limit the power of government, the authors of the Articles gave each state veto power over any changes to the Articles and required approval from nine of the thirteen states on any legislation.

More important, the states maintained autonomy and did not sacrifice any significant power to the national government; thus, government power was decentralized

Articles of Confederation
Sent to the states for ratification in 1777, these were the first attempt at a new American government. It was later decided that the Articles restricted national government too much, and they were replaced by the Constitution.

limited government
A political system in which the powers of the government are restricted to prevent tyranny by protecting property and individual rights.

Constitutional Time Line

The sequence of important events leading to independence and the writing and ratification of the Constitution.

September
First Continental Congress

May
Second Continental Congress

January
First publication of Thomas Paine's *Common Sense*

July
Congress adopts the Declaration of Independence

November 15
Articles of Confederation adopted by Congress, sent to the states for ratification

February 6
Treaty of Alliance with France

October 19
Cornwallis surrenders the British army at Yorktown

March 1
Articles of Confederation are ratified by the requisite number of states

1774   1775   1776   1777   1778   1779   1780   1781

1775–1783 Revolutionary War

in the states, rather than centralized in the national government. For example, the national government and the states could both make treaties and coin money. Congress also lacked any real authority over the states. For example, Congress could suggest the amount of money each state owed to support the Revolutionary army but could not enforce payment. After the Revolutionary War ended with the British surrender in 1781, the same weaknesses continued to plague Congress. For example, even though the new government owed millions of dollars to foreign governments and domestic creditors, it had no way to make the states pay their share. And if a foreign government negotiated a trade agreement with Congress, any state government could veto or amend the agreement, which meant that the foreign government might have to negotiate separate agreements with Congress and each state legislature. Even trade among states was complicated and inefficient.

In the face of such issues, a small group of leaders decided that something had to be done. A group from Virginia urged state legislatures to send delegates to a convention on interstate commerce in Annapolis, Maryland, in September 1786. Only five sent delegates. However, Alexander Hamilton and James Madison salvaged the effort by getting those delegates to agree to convene again in Philadelphia the following May. They also proposed that the next convention examine the defects of the current government and "devise such further provisions as shall appear to them necessary to render the Constitution of the Federal Government adequate to the exigencies of the Union."[4]

The issues that motivated the Annapolis Convention gained new urgency as subsequent events unfolded. In the years after the war, economic chaos led to a depression and many farmers lost their land because they could not pay their debts or state taxes. Frustration mounted, and early in 1787 a former captain in the Revolutionary army, Daniel Shays, led a force of 1,000 farmers in an attempt to take over the Massachusetts state government arsenal in Springfield. Their goal was to force the state courts to stop

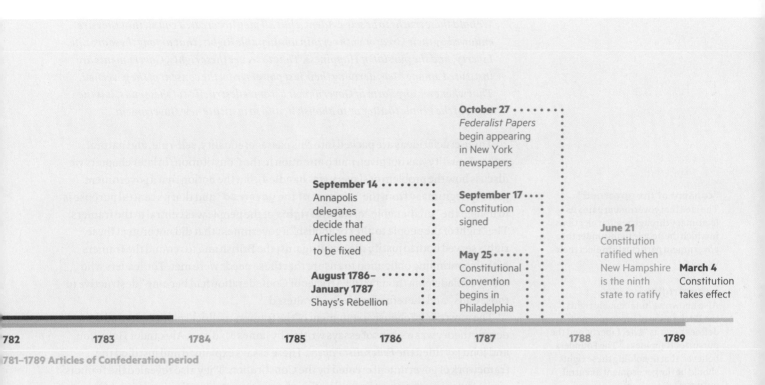

October 27
Federalist Papers begin appearing in New York newspapers

September 14
Annapolis delegates decide that Articles need to be fixed

September 17
Constitution signed

June 21
Constitution ratified when New Hampshire is the ninth state to ratify

August 1786– January 1787
Shays's Rebellion

May 25
Constitutional Convention begins in Philadelphia

March 4
Constitution takes effect

1782 1783 1784 1785 1786 1787 1788 1789

1781–1789 Articles of Confederation period

prosecuting debtors and taking their land, but the rebels were repelled by a state militia. Similar protests on a smaller scale happened in Pennsylvania and Virginia. Some state legislatures gave in to the debtors' demands, causing national leaders to fear that **Shays's Rebellion** had exposed fundamental discontent with the new government. The very future of the fledgling nation was at risk.

Political theories of the framers

Although the leaders who gathered in Philadelphia in the summer of 1787 to write the Constitution were chastened by the failure of the Articles of Confederation, they still supported many of the principles that motivated the Revolution. There was broad consensus on (1) rejection of **monarchy**, (2) popular control of government through a republican democracy, and (3) limitations on government power that would protect individual rights and personal property (that is, protect against tyranny).

First among these principles was rejection of monarchy in favor of a form of government based on self-rule. **Republicanism** as understood by the framers is a government in which elected leaders represent the views of the people. Thomas Paine, an influential political writer of the Revolutionary era, wrote a pamphlet titled *Common Sense* in 1776 that was a widely read[5] indictment of monarchy and an endorsement of the principles that fueled the Revolution and underpinned the framers' thinking. Paine wrote that monarchy was the "most bare-faced falsity ever imposed on mankind" and that the common interests of the community should be served by elected representatives.

The Founders' views of republicanism, together with liberal principles of liberty and individual rights, shaped their vision of the proper form of government. The Declaration of Independence expresses these core principles:

Shays's Rebellion
An uprising of about 4,000 men in Massachusetts in 1786 and 1787 to protest oppressive laws and gain payment of war debts. The unrest prompted calls for a new Constitution.

monarchy
A form of government in which power is held by a single person, or monarch, who comes to power through inheritance rather than election.

republicanism
As understood by James Madison and the framers, the belief that a form of government in which the interests of the people are represented through elected leaders is the best form of government. Our form of government is known as a republican democracy.

We hold these truths to be self-evident, that all men are created equal, that they are endowed by their Creator with certain unalienable Rights, that among these are Life, Liberty, and the pursuit of Happiness. That to secure these rights, Governments are instituted among Men, deriving their just powers from the consent of the governed. That whenever any Form of Government becomes destructive of these ends, it is the Right of the People to alter or to abolish it, and to institute new Government.

Three crucial ideas are packed into this passage: equality, self-rule, and natural rights. Equality was not given much attention in the Constitution (in later chapters we discuss how the problem of slavery was handled), but the notion that a government gains its legitimacy from the **"consent of the governed"** and that its central purpose is to uphold the "unalienable" or **natural rights** of the people was central to the framers. The "right of the people to alter or abolish" a government that did not protect these rights served both to justify the revolt against the British and to remind the framers of their continuing obligation to ensure that those needs were met. The leaders who met in Philadelphia thought the Articles of Confederation had become "destructive to those ends" and therefore needed to be altered.

The most comprehensive statement of the framers' political philosophy and democratic theory was a series of essays written by James Madison, Alexander Hamilton, and John Jay titled the *Federalist Papers*. These essays explained and justified the framework of government created by the Constitution. They also revealed the framers' view of human nature and its implications for democracy. The framers' view of human nature as basically being driven by self-interest led to Madison's assessment that "[i]n framing a government which is to be administered by men over men, the great difficulty lies in this: you must first enable the government to control the governed; and in the next place oblige it to control itself." This analysis (from *Federalist 51*) is often considered the clearest articulation of the need for republican government and a system of separated powers.

In *Federalist 10*, Madison described the central problem for government as the need to control factions. He argued that governments cannot control the causes of factions, because differences of opinion—based on the fallibility of reason; differences in wealth, property, and native abilities; and attachments to different leaders—are part of human nature. The only way to eliminate factions would be to either remove liberty or try to make everyone the same. The first remedy Madison called "worse than the disease," and the second he found "as impracticable as the first would be unwise." Because people are driven by self-interest, which sometimes conflicts with the common good, government must, however, try to control the effects of factions. This was the task facing the framers at the Constitutional Convention.

Economic interests

Political ideas were central to the framers' thinking at the Constitutional Convention, but economic interests were equally important.

First, while there were certainly class differences among Americans in the late eighteenth century, they were insignificant compared with those in Europe. America did not have the history of feudalism that had created tremendous inequality in Europe between landowners and propertyless serfs who worked the land. In contrast, most Americans owned small farms or worked as middle-class artisans and craftsmen. Thus, while political equality did not figure prominently in the Constitution, citizens'

"consent of the governed"
The idea that government gains its legitimacy through regular elections in which the people living under that government participate to elect their leaders.

natural rights
Also known as "unalienable rights," the Declaration of Independence defines them as "Life, Liberty, and the pursuit of Happiness." The Founders believed that upholding these rights should be the government's central purpose.

The economic context of the American Founding had an important impact on the framing of the Constitution. Most Americans worked on small farms or as artisans or business owners, which meant that economic power was broadly distributed. This woodcut shows New York City around the time the Constitution was written, viewed from upper Manhattan.

relative economic equality did indeed influence the context of debates at the Constitutional Convention.

Second, despite Americans' general economic equality, there were significant regional differences. The South was largely agricultural, with cotton and tobacco plantations that depended on slave labor. The South favored free trade because of its export-based economy (bolstered by westward expansion) and the slave trade. The middle Atlantic and northern states, however, had smaller farms and a broad economic base of manufacturing, fishing, and trade. These states favored government-managed trade and commercial development.

Despite these differences, the diverse population favored a stronger national government and reform of the Articles of Confederation (see Nuts & Bolts 2.1). Creditors wanted a government that could pay off its debts to them, southern farmers wanted free trade that could only be efficiently promoted by a central government, and manufacturers and traders wanted a single national currency and uniform interstate commerce regulations. However, there was a deep division between those who supported empowering the national government and those who still favored strong state governments and a weak national government. These two groups became known as the **Federalists** and the **Antifederalists**. The stage was set for a productive but contentious convention.

Federalists
Those at the Constitutional Convention who favored a strong national government and a system of separated powers.

Antifederalists
Those at the Constitutional Convention who favored strong state governments and feared that a strong national government would be a threat to individual rights.

Comparing the Articles of Confederation and the Constitution

Issue	Articles of Confederation	Constitution
Legislature	Unicameral Congress	Bicameral Congress divided into the House of Representatives and the Senate
Members of Congress	Between two and seven per state (the number was determined by each state)	Two senators per state; representatives apportioned according to population of each state
Voting in Congress	One vote per state	One vote per representative or senator
Selection of members	Appointed by state legislatures	Representatives elected by popular vote; senators appointed by state legislatures
Chief executive	None (there was an Executive Council within Congress, but it had limited executive power)	President
National judiciary	No general federal courts	Supreme Court; Congress authorized to establish national judiciary
Amendments to the document	When approved by all states	When approved by two-thirds of each house of Congress and three-fourths of the states
Power to coin money	Federal government and the states	Federal government only
Taxes	Apportioned by Congress, collected by the states	Apportioned and collected by Congress
Ratification	Unanimous consent required	Consent of nine states required

DID YOU KNOW?

The average age of the delegates to the Constitutional Convention was

42

Four of the delegates were in their 20s, and 14 were in their 30s.
Source: teachingamericanhistory.org

James Madison argued that it is beneficial to put the interests of one group in competition with the interests of other groups, so that no one group can dominate government. He hoped to achieve this through the separation of powers across different branches of the national government and across the national, state, and local levels.

The politics of compromise at the Constitutional Convention

Although the delegates to the Constitutional Convention generally agreed that the Articles of Confederation needed to be changed, there were many tensions over the issues that required political compromise (see Nuts & Bolts 2.2). Among them were the following:

- majority rule versus minority rights
- small states versus large states
- legislative power versus executive power (and how to elect the executive)
- national power versus state and local power
- slave states versus nonslave states

These complex and competing interests meant that the delegates had to focus on pragmatic, achievable solutions rather than on proposals that represented particular groups' ideals but could not gain majority support. The most important initial decision they made was to give up on the original plan to revise the Articles of Confederation; instead they decided to start from scratch with a new blueprint for government.

Majority rule versus minority rights

A central problem for any representative democracy is protecting minority rights within a system ruled by the majority. The framers did not think of this issue in terms of racial and ethnic minorities (as we might today), but in terms of regional and economic minorities. How could the framers be sure that small landowners and poorer people would not impose onerous taxes on the wealthier minority? How could they guarantee that dominant agricultural interests would not impose punitive tariffs on manufacturing while allowing the free export of farmed commodities? The answers to these questions can be found in Madison's writings on the problem of factions.

Madison defined a "faction" as a group motivated by selfish interests against the common good. If these interests prevailed, he felt, it could produce the very kind of tyranny that the Americans had fought to escape during the Revolutionary War. Madison's solution to this problem provided justification for the American form of government. To control majority tyranny, he argued, factions must be set against one another to counter one another's ambitions and prevent the tyranny of any single majority faction. This would be accomplished through the "double protection" of the separation of powers within the national government in the form of checks and balances, and also through the further division of power across the levels of state and local governments.

Madison also argued that additional protection against majority tyranny would come from the "size principle." That is, the new nation would be a large and diverse republic in which majority interests would be less likely to organize and therefore less able to dominate. This insight provides the basis for

Major Compromises at the Constitutional Convention

Conflict	Position of the Large States	Position of the Small States	Compromise
Apportionment in Congress	By population	State equality	Great Compromise created the Senate and House
Method of election to Congress	By the people	By the states	House elected by the people; Senate elected by the state legislatures
Electing the executive (president)	By Congress	By the states	By the Electoral College
Who decides federal–state conflicts?	Some federal authority	State courts	State courts to decide*
	Position of the Slave States	**Position of the Nonslave States**	**Compromise**
Control over commerce	By the states	By Congress	By Congress, but with 20-year exemption for the importation of slaves
Counting slaves toward apportionment	Counted 1:1 like citizens	Not counted	Three-Fifths Compromise
	Position of the Federalists	**Position of the Antifederalists**	**Compromise**
Protection for individual rights†	Secured by state constitutions; national Bill of Rights not needed	National Bill of Rights needed	Bill of Rights passed by the 1st Congress; ratified by all states as of December 1791

*This was changed by the Judiciary Act of 1789, which provided for appeals from state to federal courts.
†This issue was raised but not resolved until after the convention.

modern **pluralism**, a political theory that makes the same argument about the cross-cutting interests of groups today.

The precise contours of Madison's solution still had to be hammered out at the Constitutional Convention, but the general principle pleased both the Antifederalists and the Federalists. State governments would maintain some autonomy, but the national government would become stronger than it had been under the Articles. The issue was how to strike an appropriate balance: none of the framers favored a pure populist majoritarian democracy, and few wanted to protect minority rights to the extent that the Articles had.

pluralism
The idea that having a variety of parties and interests within a government will strengthen the system, ensuring that no group possesses total control.

Small states versus large states

The question of the appropriate balance came to a head in a debate between small- and large-population states over representation in the national legislature. Under the

Virginia Plan
A plan proposed by the larger states during the Constitutional Convention that based representation in the national legislature on population. The plan also included a variety of other proposals to strengthen the national government.

New Jersey Plan
In response to the Virginia Plan, smaller states at the Constitutional Convention proposed that each state should receive equal representation in the national legislature, regardless of size.

Great Compromise
A compromise between the large and small states, proposed by Connecticut, in which Congress would have two houses: a Senate with two legislators per state and a House of Representatives in which each state's representation would be based on population (also known as the Connecticut Compromise).

Articles, every state had a single vote, but this did not seem fair to large states. They were pushing for representation based on population. This proposal, along with other proposals to strengthen the national government, constituted the **Virginia Plan**. The small states countered with the **New Jersey Plan**, which proposed maintaining equal representation for every state. Rhode Island, the smallest state, was so concerned about small-state power that it boycotted the convention. Tensions were running high; this issue appeared to have all the elements of a deal breaker, and there seemed to be no way to break the impasse.

Just as it appeared that the convention might grind to a halt before it really got started, Connecticut proposed what became known as the **Great Compromise**, or Connecticut Compromise. The plan suggested establishing a Congress with two houses: a Senate would have two senators from each state, and in the House of Representatives each state's number of representatives would be based on its population. Interestingly, Connecticut's population was ranked seventh of the 13 states (see What Do the Numbers Say?). It was in a perfect position to offer a compromise because it did not have strong vested interests in the plans offered by either the small states or the large states.

Legislative power versus executive power

An equally difficult challenge was how to divide power at the national level. Here the central issues revolved around the executive—the president. How much power should the president have relative to the legislative branch? (The courts also figured here, but they were less central to the discussions.) And how would the president be elected?

Limiting Presidential Power The delegates knew what they did not want: the king of England and his colonial governors were viewed as tramplers of liberty. Many delegates rejected outright the idea of a single executive because they believed it was impossible to have an executive who would not be oppressive. The delegates finally agreed on the single executive because the president would have the most "energy, dispatch, and responsibility for the office," but they constrained the president's power through the system of checks and balances. One significant power they granted to the executive was the veto. It could be overridden by Congress, but only with the support of two-thirds of both chambers. This requirement gave the president a significant role in the legislative process.

The arguments for a strong executive relied heavily on the work of the English philosopher John Locke. Locke recognized the general superiority of a government of laws created by legislatures, but he also saw the need for an executive with more flexible leadership powers, or what he called "prerogative powers." Legislatures are unable, Locke wrote, "to foresee, and so by laws to provide for all accidents and necessities." They also are, by virtue of their size and unwieldiness, too slow to alter and adapt the law in times of crisis, when the executive could step in to pursue policies in the public's interest.

Although there was support for this view, the Antifederalists were concerned that if such powers were viewed as open-ended, they could give rise to the type of oppressive leader the framers were trying to avoid. Madison attempted to reassure the opponents of executive power, arguing that any prerogative powers would have to be clearly enumerated in the Constitution. In fact, the Constitution explicitly provides only one extraordinary executive power: the right to grant reprieves and pardons, which means that the president can forgive any crimes against the federal government.

Connecticut's Pivotal Place at the Constitutional Convention

Though there were many disagreements over the details of America's new constitution, one of the most intense focused on how states would be represented in Congress, either allocating representatives equally or based on population. After other plans were considered and rejected, the Connecticut Compromise won out. But why Connecticut? What do the numbers say?

State Populations at the Time of the Constitutional Convention

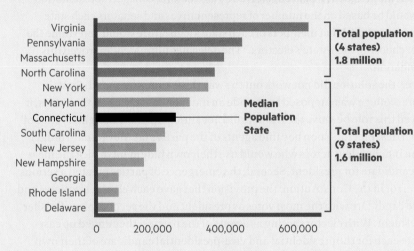

Virginia
Pennsylvania
Massachusetts
North Carolina
New York
Maryland
Connecticut
South Carolina
New Jersey
New Hampshire
Georgia
Rhode Island
Delaware

Total population (4 states) 1.8 million

Median Population State

Total population (9 states) 1.6 million

0   200,000   400,000   600,000

Votes at the Constitutional Convention

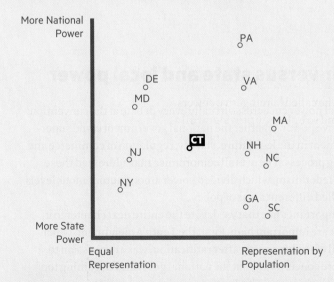

More National Power

PA
DE
MD
VA
MA
CT
NJ
NHNC
NY
GA SC

More State Power

Equal Representation   Representation by Population

Source: Keith L. Doughterty and Jac C. Heckelman, "A Pivotal Voter from a Pivotal State: Roger Sherman at the Constitutional Convention," *American Political Science Review* 100:2 (May 2006): 298.

At first glance, the Connecticut Compromise seems to make perfect sense: as the seventh of 13 states in terms of population, Connecticut was positioned to offer a compromise that would appeal to both large and small states. But it actually was much more complicated. First, Rhode Island did not attend the convention, so there was no true median state (with only 12 states at the convention, no one stood alone at the center). Second, given that each state had one vote at the convention, the smallest states could have easily outvoted the biggest ones and insisted on equal representation for each state.

Why didn't the smaller states impose their view? Two of the smaller states, Georgia and South Carolina, focused on their future growth, so they supported representation based on population, the Virginia Plan. But when other smaller states balked at their loss of power, the Connecticut Compromise was able to win the support of North Carolina (and Massachusetts's delegates were divided), so the compromise passed 5-4-1.

Despite this more complex picture, an analysis of all 569 votes at the Constitutional Convention clearly shows that Connecticut occupied a pivotal place at the convention. Connecticut was in the middle in terms of desire for representation based on population and in terms of desire for more state power. Connecticut's right in the center of this graph—no wonder they could broker a compromise!

Think about it

1. Looking at the graph "Votes at the Constitutional Convention," why do you think Connecticut was well positioned to find a compromise?

2. How do these graphs help us understand why the Virginia and New Jersey plans were in conflict and ultimately rejected?

Selecting the President The second contentious issue concerning the executive was the method of selecting a president. The way the president was to be elected incorporated the issues of majority rule and minority rights, state versus national power, and the nature of executive power itself. Would the president be elected by the nation as a whole, by the states, or by coalitions within Congress? If the state-level governments played a central role, would this mean that the president could not speak for national interests? If Congress elected the president, could the executive still provide a check on the legislative branch?

Most Americans do not realize (1) that our presidential system is unique and (2) that we came close to having a parliamentary system, which is the form of government that exists in most other established democracies. In a **parliamentary system**, the executive branch depends on the support of the legislative branch. The Virginia Plan proposed that Congress elect the president, just as Parliament elects the British prime minister. However, facing lingering concerns that the president would be too beholden to Congress, a committee of framers subsequently made the following recommendations: (1) that the president would be selected by an electoral college, representation in which would be based on the number of representatives and senators each state has in Congress, and (2) that members of each state's legislature would determine the method for choosing their state's electors.[6] The delegates ultimately approved this recommendation.

However, the solution did not work out the way the framers intended. First, if the electoral college was supposed to provide an independent check on the voters, it never played this role because the framers did not anticipate the quick emergence of political parties. Electors soon became agents of the parties (as they remain today) rather than independent actors who would use their own judgment to pick the most qualified candidate for president. Second, the emergence of parties created a serious technical error in the Constitution: the provision that gave each elector two votes and elected the candidate with the most votes as president and the second-place finisher as vice president. With electors acting as agents of the parties, they ended up casting one vote each for the presidential and vice-presidential candidate of their own party. This created a tie in the 1800 presidential election when Thomas Jefferson and Aaron Burr each received 73 electoral votes. The problem was fixed by the Twelfth Amendment, which required that electors cast separate votes for president and vice president.

National power versus state and local power

Tensions over the balance of power cut across virtually every debate at the convention: presidential versus legislative power, whether the national government could supersede state laws, apportionment in the legislature, slavery, regulation of commerce and taxation, and the amending process. The overall compromise that addressed these tensions was the system of federalism, which divided power among autonomous levels of government that controlled different areas of policy.

Federalism is such an important topic that we devote the entire next chapter to it, but two brief points about it are important here. First, the Tenth Amendment, which was added as part of the Bill of Rights shortly after ratification, was a concession to the Antifederalists who were concerned about the national government gaining too much power in the new political system. The Tenth Amendment says: "The powers not delegated to the United States by the Constitution, nor prohibited by it to the States,

---

parliamentary system
A system of government in which legislative and executive power are closely joined. The legislature (parliament) selects the chief executive (prime minister), who forms the cabinet from members of the parliament.

"

Yo.

The people are asking to hear my voice . . .

For the country is facing a difficult choice.

. . . And if you were to ask me who I'd promote . . .

Jefferson has my vote.

—*Hamilton,* the musical

are reserved to the States respectively, or to the people." This definition of **reserved powers** was viewed as setting outer limits on the reach of national power.

Second, the **national supremacy clause** of the Constitution (Article VI) says that any national law is the supreme law of the land and takes precedence over any state law that conflicts with it. This is especially important in areas where the national and state governments have overlapping responsibilities for policy. (The relationship between the national government and the states is discussed in Chapter 3.)

Slave states versus nonslave states

Slavery was another nearly insurmountable issue for the delegates. Southern states would not agree to any provisions limiting slavery. Although the nonslave states opposed the practice, they were not willing to scuttle the entire Constitution by taking a principled stand. Even after these basic divisions had been recognized, many unresolved issues remained. Could the importation of slaves be restricted in the future? How would northern states deal with runaway slaves? Most important in terms of the politics of the issue, how would the slave population be counted for the purpose of slave states' representation in Congress?

In reaching compromises on these questions, the delegates went through similar negotiations over how slaves would be counted for purposes of states' congressional representation. The states had been through this debate once before, when they addressed the issue of taxation under the Articles of Confederation. At that point, slave states had argued that slaves should not be counted because they did not receive the same benefits as citizens and were not the same burden to the government. Nonslave states had countered that slaves should be counted in the same way as citizens when determining a state's fair share of the tax burden. They had reached a compromise by agreeing that each slave would count as three-fifths of a person for purposes of taxation. Now the arguments over the issue of representation were even more contentious at the Constitutional Convention. Here the positions were reversed, with slave states arguing that slaves should be counted like everyone else for the purposes of determining the number of House representatives for each state. Ultimately, both sides managed to agree on the **Three-Fifths Compromise**.

The other two issues involved the importation of slaves and how to deal with runaway slaves. In terms of the latter issue, northern states either would be obligated to return runaway slaves to their southern owners or would not. Because there was no middle ground, the opposing sides looked for other issues on which to trade votes. The nonslave states wanted more national government control over commerce and trade than under the Articles, a change that the slave states opposed. So a vote trade developed as a way to compromise the competing regional interests of slavery and regulation of commerce. Northern states agreed to return runaway slaves (the Fugitive Slave Clause), and southern states agreed to allow Congress to regulate commerce and tax imports with a majority vote (rather than the supermajority required under the Articles).

The importation of slaves was included as part of this solution. Northern states wanted to allow future Congresses to ban the importation of slaves; southern states wanted to allow the importation of slaves to continue indefinitely, arguing that slavery was essential to produce their labor-intensive crops. After much negotiation, the final language prevented a constitutional amendment from banning the slave trade until 1808.[7]

reserved powers
As defined in the Tenth Amendment, powers that are not given to the national government by the Constitution, or not prohibited to the states, are reserved by the states or the people.

national supremacy clause
Part of Article VI, Section 2, of the Constitution stating that the Constitution and the laws and treaties of the United States are the "supreme Law of the Land," meaning national laws take precedence over state laws if the two conflict.

DID YOU KNOW?

At only about

8,700

words, the U.S. Constitution is much shorter than the average state constitution (39,604 words).
Source: PARCA, Tableau Public

Three-Fifths Compromise
The states' decision during the Constitutional Convention to count each slave as three-fifths of a person in a state's population for the purposes of determining the number of House members and the distribution of taxes.

A slave auction in Virginia. Slavery proved problematic at the Constitutional Convention: Would there be limits on the importation of slaves? How would runaway slaves be dealt with by nonslave states? And how would slaves be counted for the purposes of congressional representation?

From a modern perspective, it is difficult to understand how the framers could have taken such a purely political approach to the moral issue of slavery. Many of the delegates believed slavery was immoral, yet they were willing to negotiate in order to gain the southern states' support of the Constitution. Some southern delegates were apologetic about slavery, even as they argued for protecting their own interests. Numerous constitutional scholars view the convention's treatment of slavery as its central failure. In fairness to the delegates, the issue of slavery could not be settled, since the goal was to create a document that all states would support. However, the delegates' inability to resolve this issue meant that it would simmer below the surface for the next 70 years, finally boiling over into the bloodiest of all American wars, the Civil War.

The convention ended on a relatively harmonious note with Benjamin Franklin moving for adoption. His motion was worded ambiguously to allow those who still had reservations to sign the Constitution anyway: "Done in Convention by the unanimous consent of the States present the 17th of September . . . In Witness whereof we have hereunto subscribed our names." His clever wording meant that the signers were only bearing witness to the approval by the states and therefore could still, in good faith, oppose substantial parts of the document. Franklin's motion passed with 10 ayes, no nays, and one delegation divided. All but three of the remaining delegates signed.

★

CONTRAST THE ARGUMENTS OF THE FEDERALISTS WITH THOSE OF THE ANTIFEDERALISTS

Ratification

Article VII of the Constitution, which described the process for ratifying the document, was also designed to maximize its chance of success. Only nine states were needed to ratify, rather than the unanimity rule that had applied to changing the Articles of Confederation. Equally important, ratification votes would be taken in state conventions set up specifically for that purpose, bypassing the state legislatures, which would be more likely to resist some of the Constitution's state–federal power-sharing arrangements.

The near-unanimous approval at the Constitutional Convention's end masked the very strong opposition that remained. Subsequently, the ratifying conventions in each state subjected the Constitution to intense scrutiny, as attendees examined every sentence for possible objections. A national debate raged over the next nine months.

"

A lady asked Dr. [Benjamin] Franklin, "Well Doctor what have we got a republic or a monarchy?" "A republic," replied the Doctor, "if you can keep it."

—James McHenry, *The Records of the Federal Convention of 1787*

The Antifederalists' concerns

The Antifederalists were most worried about the role of the president, the transfer of power from the states to the national government, and the lack of specific guarantees of civil liberties. In short, they feared that the national government would become tyrannical. State power and the ability to regulate commerce were also central concerns. States such as New York would lose substantial revenue if they could no longer charge tariffs on goods that came into their ports. Other states were concerned that they would pay a disproportionate share of national taxes.

Union and Confederate troops clash in close combat in the Battle of Cold Harbor, Virginia, in June 1864. The inability of the framers to resolve the issue of slavery allowed tensions over the issue to grow throughout the early nineteenth century, culminating in the Civil War.

The Antifederalists' foremost objection was to the lack of protections for civil liberties in the new political system. During the last week of the convention, Elbridge Gerry and George Mason offered a resolution "to prepare a Bill of Rights." However, the resolution was unanimously defeated by the state delegations. Some believed that the national government posed no threat to liberties such as freedom of the press because it did not have the power to restrict them in the first place. Others thought that because it would be impossible to enumerate all rights, it was better to list none at all. Federalists such as Roger Sherman argued that state constitutions, most of which protected freedom of speech, freedom of the press, right to a trial by jury, and other civil liberties, would be sufficient to protect liberty. However, many Antifederalists still wanted assurances that the *national* government would not trample their rights.

The Federalists' strategies

The Federalists counterattacked on several fronts. First, they published a series of articles that came to be known as the *Federalist Papers*. Although originally published in New York newspapers, these articles were widely read throughout the nation. The *Federalist Papers* were one-sided arguments aimed at changing public opinion. The authors downplayed potentially unpopular aspects of the new system, such as the power of the president, while emphasizing points they knew would appeal to the opposition. Despite their biased arguments, the *Federalist Papers* are considered the best comprehensive discussion of the political theory underlying the Constitution and the framers' interpretations of many of its key provisions.

Second, the Federalists agreed that the new Congress's first order of business would be to add a **Bill of Rights** to the Constitution to protect individual rights and liberties. This promise was essential for securing the support of New York, Massachusetts, and Virginia. The crucial ninth state, New Hampshire, ratified the Constitution on June 21, 1788, but New York and Virginia were still dragging their heels, and their support was viewed as necessary for the legitimacy of the United States, even if it technically was

Alexander Hamilton authored a majority of the *Federalist Papers* and was a strong advocate for ratification of the Constitution.

Bill of Rights
The first 10 amendments to the Constitution; they protect individual rights and liberties.

not needed. By the end of the summer, both Virginia and New York finally voted for ratification. Rhode Island and North Carolina refused to ratify until Congress made good on its promise of a Bill of Rights. The 1st Congress submitted 12 amendments to the states, and 10 were ratified by all the states as of December 15, 1791. We will take a close look at the Bill of Rights in Chapter 4.

"Why Should I Care?"

Politicians today have a very difficult time compromising on issues like gun control, abortion rights, and even the proper levels of taxation and spending. At the Constitutional Convention, the framers had to struggle with fundamental issues such as executive power and state versus national power as well as incredibly divisive issues like slavery. The framers were facing uncertainty about the very survival of their new nation and the nearly impossible task of creating a new framework that would allow our nation to not only survive but also flourish. Yet the framers were able to arrive at workable compromises on all of these issues. Without compromise, our nation would not exist. When you hear a politician today say, "I am going to stick to my principles; I am not going to compromise," reflect on the fact that governing is not possible without compromise. "Compromise" is not a dirty word; it is an essential feature of politics.

★

OUTLINE THE MAJOR PROVISIONS OF THE CONSTITUTION

The Constitution: a framework for government

The Constitution certainly has its flaws (some of which have been corrected through amendments), but the document's longevity is testimony to the framers' foresight in crafting a flexible framework for government. Perhaps its most important feature is the system of separation of powers and checks and balances that prevent majority tyranny while maintaining sufficient flexibility for decisive leadership during times of crisis. The system of checks and balances means that each branch of national government has certain exclusive powers, some shared powers, and the ability to check the other two branches (see How It Works: Checks and Balances).

> "
> **The Constitution is the guide which I never will abandon.**
>
> —George Washington

Exclusive powers

The framers viewed Congress as the "first branch" of government and granted it significant exclusive powers. Congress was given the power to raise revenue for the federal government through taxes and borrowing, regulate interstate and foreign commerce, coin money, establish post offices and roads, grant patents and copyrights, create the system of federal courts, declare war, "raise and support armies," make rules for the military, and create and maintain a navy. Most important is the so-called power of the purse—control over taxation and spending.

Congress's exclusive powers take on additional significance through the **necessary and proper clause**, also known as the elastic clause. It gives Congress the flexibility to "make all Laws which shall be necessary and proper for carrying into Execution the

necessary and proper clause Part of Article I, Section 8, of the Constitution that grants Congress the power to pass all laws related to its expressed powers; also known as the elastic clause.

foregoing Powers, and all other Powers vested by this Constitution in the Government of the United States, or in any Department or Officer thereof." In other words, Congress could pass laws related to any of its exclusive powers. For example, while the Constitution did not explicitly mention Congress's right to compel people to serve in the military, its power to enact a draft was clearly given by the necessary and proper clause, in conjunction with its power to "raise and support armies."

The exclusive powers of Congress are more numerous and specific than the limited powers granted to the president. As commander in chief of the armed forces, the president has the power to receive ambassadors and foreign ministers and to issue pardons. The president's most important powers are contained in the executive powers clause, which says: "The executive power shall be vested in a President of the United States of America," and in the directive to ensure "that the laws are faithfully executed."

The courts did not receive as much attention in the Constitution as either Congress or the president. The most important positive powers that the framers gave the Supreme Court were lifetime tenure for justices in good behavior and relative independence from the other two branches. The critical negative power of judicial review, the ability to strike down the laws and actions of other branches, will be discussed later.

Shared powers

Along with dividing the exclusive powers among the branches of government, checks and balances designate some shared powers. These are areas where no branch has exclusive control. For example, the president has the power to negotiate treaties and make appointments to the federal courts and other government offices, but these executive actions are to be undertaken with the "advice and consent" of the Senate, which means they were intended to be shared powers. In the twentieth century, these particular powers became executive centered, with the Senate providing almost no advice to the president and routinely giving its consent. However, the Senate still can assert its shared power, as shown by the Senate's relatively recent blocking of several of President George W. Bush's and President Obama's lower-court nominees and Obama's nomination of Merrick Garland to the Supreme Court in 2016.

The war powers, which include decisions about when and how to use military force, were also intended to be shared but have become executive-dominated powers. After serious disagreements, the ultimate compromise that the framers reached shows checks and balances at work, with the president serving as commander in chief of the armed forces, while Congress has the power to declare war and to appropriate the funds to conduct a war. Since very early in the nation's history, the president has taken a lead role in the war powers. Presidents have authorized the use of American troops on hundreds of occasions, but Congress has declared war only five times. Of these, Congress debated the merits of entering only one war, the War of 1812. The other "declarations" recognized a state of war that already existed. If a president is intent on going to war, Congress must go along or get out of the way.

However, since the Vietnam War Congress has tried to redress the imbalance in the war powers in other ways. In 1970, during the Vietnam War, Congress passed a resolution that prevented any funds from supporting ground troops in Laos or Cambodia (nations that bordered Vietnam). In 2013, Congress was strongly opposed to a military strike against Syria in response to its use of chemical weapons against its own people.

The president and the Senate share the appointment power to many federal offices: the president makes the nominations, and the Senate provides its "advice and consent." The nomination of Merrick Garland (pictured here at left) to the Supreme Court was stopped by Republican Senate leaders who decided to allow the next president to fill the vacancy on the Court.

Checks and Balances

In the Constitution, if one branch tries to assert too much power, the other branches have certain key powers that allow them to fight back and restore the balance. (In addition to the powers noted in the diagram, Congress can impeach the president and remove him or her from office.)

The president nominates judges.

The president can veto congressional legislation.

The Senate confirms the president's judicial nominations. Congress can impeach and remove judges from office.

Executive

Legislative

Judicial

The Senate approves presidential nominations, and Congress can pass laws over the president's veto.

The Court interprets the laws passed by Congress.

The Court interprets actions by the executive branch.

Checks and Balances in the War on Terror

Since shortly after the attacks of September 11, 2001, the president, acting on his power as commander in chief, authorized the Guantánamo Bay detention center in Cuba to be used as a place to detain, interrogate, and try prisoners related to the War on Terror. There have been allegations of human rights violations, including torture. The controversies and policies surrounding Guantánamo show how checks and balances work in practice.

So...

First prisoners are taken to Guantánamo on January 11, 2002.

He said...

President George W. Bush asserts that Guantánamo is **outside the legal jurisdiction** of the United States and that the prisoners held there do not have protections guaranteed to prisoners of war under the Geneva Convention.

But then...

The Supreme Court disagrees in *Hamdan v. Rumsfeld* on June 29, 2006, ruling that the detainees were entitled to basic legal rights and that the Geneva Convention did apply.

It's still a problem.

The detention center is increasingly controversial as Amnesty International, a human rights organization, calls it **"the gulag of our time,"** and in 2006, the United Nations urges the United States to close the facility.

New idea.

Two days after taking office, President Obama **signs an order to close the center** by the end of the year and to suspend all Guantánamo military commission hearings for 120 days.

Nope.

A week later, a military court judge **overturns the order** to suspend hearings at Guantánamo.

Sounds like a plan.

President Obama **wants to move Guantánamo prisoners** to a federal prison in Illinois.

Plan blocked.

A few months later, **Congress votes to block funds** needed for the transfer or release of prisoners held at the facility.

Sigh.

Going into the last year of President Obama's presidency, **more than 100 prisoners remain,** some of whom have been detained for 14 years without a trial.

❓ Critical Thinking

1. **Why do you think it has been so difficult to close the detention center in Guantánamo?** Is it because of the issue of terrorism and national security? Or is it because of our system of checks and balances? Why?

2. **Do you think our system of checks and balances creates** too much gridlock, or is it an essential check on potential tyranny?

A showdown with President Obama was averted when Syria agreed to allow weapons inspectors to destroy their chemical weapon stockpile. These examples show that while the president continues to dominate the war powers, Congress can assert its power when it has the will—just as it can by advising the president in treaty negotiations or by withholding approval of the president's nominees for appointed positions.

Negative or checking powers

The last part of the system of checks and balances is the negative power that the branches have over one another. These powers are especially important because they ensure that no single branch dominates the national government.

Congressional Checks Congress has two important negative checks on the other two branches: impeachment and the power of the purse. **Impeachment** is where the president, vice president, or other "officers of the United States" (including federal judges) can be removed for abuses of power—specifically, "Treason, Bribery, or other high Crimes or Misdemeanors."

Through the **power of the purse**, Congress can punish executive agencies by freezing or cutting their funding or by holding hearings on, investigations of, or audits of their operations to make sure money is being spent properly. Congress can also freeze judges' salaries to show displeasure with court decisions, and it has the power to limit the issues that federal courts can consider. Even today, the system of checks and balances is not fixed in stone but evolves according to the changing political climate.

Presidential Checks The framers placed important checks on congressional power as well, and the president's most important check on Congress is the veto. Again there was very little agreement on this topic. The Antifederalists argued that it was "a political error of the greatest magnitude, to allow the executive power a negative, or in fact any kind of control over the proceedings of the legislature." But the Federalists worried that Congress would slowly strip away presidential powers and leave the president too weak. Ultimately, the Federalist view won the day. However, the veto has developed into a major policy-making tool for the president, which is probably broader than the check against "depredations" envisioned by the framers. The Constitution also gives the president a formal check on the courts through the power to appoint judges.

Judicial Review The Constitution did not provide the Supreme Court with any formal checks on the other two branches. Instead, the Court itself (in the landmark decision of *Marbury v. Madison* in 1803) established the practice of **judicial review**—the ability of the Supreme Court to strike down a law or an executive branch action as unconstitutional. While judicial review is not explicitly mentioned in the Constitution, supporters of the practice point to the supremacy clause, which states that the "Constitution, and the Laws of the United States which shall be made in Pursuance thereof . . . shall be the supreme Law of the Land."

As Chief Justice John Marshall argued in *Marbury v. Madison*, in order to enforce the Constitution as the supreme law of the land the Court must determine which laws are "in pursuance thereof." Critics of judicial review argue that the Constitution is supreme because it gains its legitimacy from the people, and therefore elected officials—Congress and the president—should be the primary

impeachment
A negative or checking power over the other branches that allows Congress to remove the president, the vice president, or other "officers of the United States" (including federal judges) for abuses of power.

power of the purse
The constitutional power of Congress to raise and spend money. Congress can use this as a negative or checking power over the other branches by freezing or cutting their funding.

judicial review
The Supreme Court's power to strike down a law or an executive branch action that it finds unconstitutional.

Congress alone has "the power of the purse" to fund government programs. Although President Obama ordered the "troop surge" in Afghanistan, Congress had to continue appropriating money to pay for the war.

interpreters of the Constitution rather than the courts. This dispute may never fully be resolved, but Marshall's bold assertion of judicial review made the Supreme Court an equal partner in the system of separate powers and checks and balances.

"Why Should I Care?"

If you remember anything from your elementary civics class it is probably some foggy memory of the system of checks and balances and separation of powers. But why is this so important? This institutional framework provides the basis for our government and explains the nature of political conflict and outcomes. When the government shuts down because of a dispute over spending or the Senate blocks the president's court nominees, this is because the president and Congress have different roles but can check each other's powers. Understanding checks and balances and separation of powers helps us be realistic about what government can do and shows us that all parts of the government are critical but not dominant in making policy and enforcing laws.

Is the Constitution a "living" document?

★

EXPLORE HOW THE MEANING OF THE CONSTITUTION HAS EVOLVED

How has the Constitution remained relevant after more than 200 years? Why does this framework of government still work? How can the framers' values still be meaningful to us? There are several reasons that the Constitution continues to be a "living" document that evolves with the changing values and norms of the nation (see the Take a Stand feature).

Changing the Constitution

The most obvious way that the Constitution keeps up with the times is by allowing for changes to its language. The framers broadly supported the idea behind Article V, which lays out the formal process for amending the Constitution: the people must control their own political system, which includes the ability to change it through a regular, nonviolent process.

Proposal and Ratification While there was strong consensus on including in the Constitution a set of provisions for amending it, there was no agreement on how this should be done. The Virginia Plan envisioned a relatively easy process of changing the Constitution "whensoever it shall seem necessary" by means of ratification by the people, while the New Jersey Plan proposed a central role for state governments. Madison suggested the plan that was eventually adopted, which accommodated both those who wanted a stronger national government and those who favored the states. Article V describes the two steps necessary to change the Constitution: proposal and ratification. Congress may *propose* an amendment that has the approval of two-thirds of the members in both houses, or an amendment may be proposed by a national convention that has been called by two-thirds of the states' legislatures. In either case, the amendment

The people made the Constitution, and the people can unmake it. It is the creature of their will, and lives only by their will.

—Justice John Marshall

A Living Constitution?

Should the Constitution be viewed as a flexible framework or a document that has fixed meaning? The public is evenly split on this issue, with 49 percent saying that constitutional interpretation should be based on "what it means in current time" (the living Constitution) and 46 percent on "what it originally meant" (originalism). However, there is a deep partisan divide on this issue, with 70 percent of Democrats taking the living constitution approach and 69 percent of Republicans supporting originalism.[a]

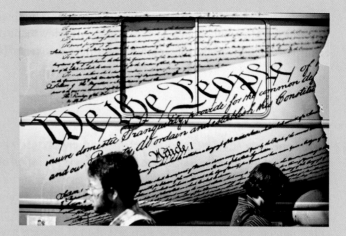

📷 There is a vigorous debate among justices of the Supreme Court as to whether the Constitution is a living document or should be interpreted more strictly according to the original intent of the framers.

The meaning of the Constitution doesn't change.

Justice Clarence Thomas is perhaps the strongest advocate of the originalist view. He wrote: "Let me put it this way; there are really only two ways to interpret the Constitution—try to discern as best we can what the framers intended or make it up."[b] Former chief justice William Rehnquist, although generally adhering to the originalist view, took a more nuanced approach. He favorably cites a 1920 Supreme Court opinion by Oliver Wendell Holmes: "When we are dealing with words that also are a constituent act, like the Constitution of the United States, we must realize that they have called into life a being the development of which could not have been foreseen completely by the most gifted of its begetters."[c] John Marshall in *McCulloch v. Maryland* also endorses this view, saying the Constitution was "intended to endure for ages to come, and consequently to be adapted to the various crises of human affairs." Rehnquist says that "scarcely anyone would disagree" with the idea that the Constitution was written broadly enough to allow principles such as the prohibition against illegal searches and seizures to apply to technologies, such as the telephone or the Internet, that could not have been envisioned by the framers.[d]

However, according to this view, the *meaning* of the Constitution cannot change with the times. Rehnquist writes that "mere change in public opinion since the adoption of the Constitution, unaccompanied by a constitutional amendment, should not change the meaning of the Constitution. A merely temporary majoritarian groundswell should not abrogate some individual liberty truly protected by the Constitution."[e] Therefore, recent rulings restricting the death penalty (which is clearly endorsed by the Constitution), expanding gay rights, or allowing a child to testify remotely against her sexual abuser rather than having to confront him directly in court (as guaranteed by the Sixth Amendment) would all be inconsistent with the originalist view. This view would also hold that anything other than relying on the meaning of the words of the Constitution allows justices to "legislate from the bench," which is undemocratic given that the judges are not elected.

The meaning of the Constitution changes with the times.

Proponents of a living constitution argue for a more flexible view. Justice Thurgood Marshall advocated a living constitution, noting that the framers "could not have imagined, nor would they have accepted, that the document they were drafting would one day be construed by a Supreme Court to which had been appointed a woman and the descendent of an African slave."[f] If the meaning of the Constitution is fixed, then the Court would have to uphold a state law allowing the death penalty for horse stealing, which was common during the Founding era. Executing horse thieves, or, more realistically, children and the mentally impaired (which was allowed in many states until 2005), is unacceptable in a modern society, even if it would be allowed by a strict reading of the Constitution.

Answering the question about how justices should interpret the Constitution ultimately depends on one's broader views of the proper role of the Court within a representative democracy. Should justices be constrained by the original meaning of the Constitution, or should that meaning evolve over time? Take a stand.

take a stand

1. If you were on the Supreme Court, would you adopt an originalist or a living constitution approach? Justify your position.

2. Based on the originalist view, should a state be allowed to execute whomever it wants to, including minors (or horse thieves)? Based on the living constitution approach, should limits be placed on justices to prevent them from "legislating from the bench"?

must be *ratified* by three-fourths of the states' legislatures or state conventions (see Nuts & Bolts 2.3). A national convention has never been used to propose an amendment, and every amendment except for the Twenty-First, which repealed Prohibition, has been ratified by state legislatures rather than state conventions.

A Range of Amendments Amendments have ranged from fairly narrow, technical corrections of errors in the original document (Eleventh and Twelfth Amendments) to important topics such as abolishing slavery (Thirteenth), mandating equal protection of the laws for all citizens (Fourteenth), providing for the popular election of senators (Seventeenth), giving blacks and then women the right to vote (Fifteenth and Nineteenth), and allowing a national income tax (Sixteenth). Potential constitutional amendments have addressed many other issues, with more than 10,000 proposed; of those, 33 were sent to the states and 27 have made it through the amending process (the first 10 came at once in the Bill of Rights). Table 2.1 shows several amendments that were introduced but not ratified.

Flexibility and interpretation

The Constitution also remains relevant because it allows for some flexibility in how it is interpreted. First, some parts of the Constitution are simply ignored today because they have no meaning in a modern context. For example, Article I, Section 4, says that "Congress shall assemble at least once in every Year," but the modern Congress is in session throughout the year (with various recesses). Nobody pays attention to this passage anymore because it simply does not matter.

Ambiguity The Constitution's inherent ambiguity is a characteristic that has kept the document relevant. Key passages were written in very general language, which has enabled the Constitution to evolve along with changing norms, values, and political contexts. This ambiguity was a political necessity: not only were the framers aware that the document would need to survive for generations, but in many instances the language that they chose was simply the only wording that all the framers could agree on.

Proposal	Ratification	Frequency of use
Congress proposes amendment by at least a two-thirds vote	By at least **three-fourths of the state legislatures**	All but once
	By at least **three-fourths of state conventions** called for the purpose of ratifying the amendment	Once
Amendment is proposed by a national convention that is called by at least two-thirds of the state legislatures	By at least **three-fourths of the state legislatures**	Never
	By at least **three-fourths of state conventions** called for the purpose of ratifying the amendment	Never

NUTS & BOLTS 2.3

Amending the Constitution

This flowchart shows how amendments to the Constitution can be proposed and ratified and the frequency with which each method has been used. Interestingly, the president is not a part of the formal process of amending the Constitution.

TABLE
2.1

Amendments Introduced in Congress That Did Not Pass

Many proposed constitutional amendments have almost no chance of passing. Indeed, most of those listed here did not even make it to the floor of the House or Senate for a vote. Why do you think a member of Congress would propose an amendment that he or she knew would fail?

114th Congress (2015–2016)	Require that the rights extended by the Constitution be granted only to natural persons (not corporations). Repeal the Sixteenth Amendment (income tax).
113th Congress (2013–2014)	No treaty, executive order, or agreement with another nation can diminish the rights of U.S. citizens. All laws that apply to U.S. citizens must apply equally to U.S. senators and representatives.
112th Congress (2011–2012)	Impose 12-year term limits for the House and Senate. Amend the First Amendment to allow limitations on federal campaign contributions and expenditures. Protect the right of parents to raise and educate their children without interference from government. Require that the federal budget be balanced.

Sources: The U.S. Constitution Online: Some Proposed Amendments, www.usconstitution.net (accessed 3/22/12); http://thomas.loc.gov (accessed 2/21/16).

enumerated powers
Powers explicitly granted to Congress, the president, or the Supreme Court in the first three articles of the Constitution. Examples include Congress's power to "raise and support Armies" and the president's power as commander in chief.

implied powers
Powers supported by the Constitution that are not expressly stated in it.

For instance, the necessary and proper clause gives Congress the power to enact laws that are related to its **enumerated powers**, or those that are explicitly granted. But what does "necessary and proper" mean? Congress, for the most part, gets to answer that question.

Implied Powers Furthermore, there have been significant changes in the way that the Constitution structures the policy-making process, even though the pertinent text of the Constitution has not changed.[8] This point is best understood by examining the concept of **implied powers**—that is, powers not explicitly stated in the Constitution but that can be inferred from an enumerated power. The Supreme Court often defines the boundaries of implied powers, but Congress, the president, and the public can also play key roles.

To take a recent example of Congress's interpretation of implied powers, the president's appointment powers have evolved as the Senate has become much more aggressive in providing "advice and consent" on presidential nominations to the federal courts. As we explore in Chapter 13, in the past 20 years the Senate has blocked court appointments at a significantly higher rate than it did in the first half of the twentieth century. The relevant language in the Constitution is the same, yet the Senate's understanding of its role in this important process has changed. President Obama's use of executive powers to go around Congress when they declined to act also demonstrates the ambiguous nature of constitutional powers. Obama's action on EPA rules concerning carbon emissions and immigration policy were viewed as either appropriate and necessary executive action or "constitutional overreach."

Changing Social Norms Public opinion and social norms also influence the prevailing interpretation of the Constitution, as is evident in the evolving meanings of capital punishment (the death penalty) and freedom of speech. When the Constitution was written, capital punishment was broadly accepted, even for horse thieves. Therefore, the prohibition in the Eighth Amendment against "cruel and unusual punishments"

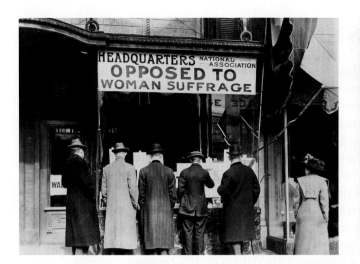

certainly did not mean to the framers that the death penalty was unconstitutional. However, in 1972 the Supreme Court struck down capital punishment as unconstitutional because it was being applied arbitrarily.[9] Subsequently, after procedural changes were made, the Court once again upheld the practice. However, the Court has since decided that capital punishment for a mentally impaired person and minors constituted cruel and unusual punishment—a decision that reflects modern sensibilities but not the framers' thinking.[10] Similarly, the text of the First Amendment protections for freedom of speech has never changed, but the Supreme Court has been willing to uphold significant limitations on free speech, especially in wartime. When external threats are less severe, the Court has been more tolerant of controversial speech.

The line between a new interpretation of the Constitution and constitutional change is difficult to define. Clearly, not every new direction taken by the Court or new interpretation of the constitutional roles of the president or Congress is comparable to a constitutional amendment. In one respect, a constitutional amendment is much more permanent than a new interpretation. For example, the Supreme Court could not unilaterally decide that 18- to 20-year-olds, women, and African Americans no longer have the right to vote. Constitutional amendments expanded the right to vote to include these groups, and only further amendments could either expand or restrict the right to vote. However, gradual changes in constitutional interpretation are probably just as important as the amending process in explaining the Constitution's ability to keep pace with the times.

Amending the Constitution is difficult and can be controversial. Some amendments that are widely accepted today, like the Nineteenth Amendment giving women the right to vote, were intensely debated prior to their ratification.

> 99

They keep talking about drafting a constitution for Iraq. Why don't we just give them ours? It was written by a lot of really smart guys. It's worked for over 200 years, and hell, we're not using it anymore.

—Jay Leno

One of the most remarkable things about the Constitution is its longevity. While there are intense debates about whether a "living Constitution" is a good thing, there is no doubt its ability to change with the times, whether because of its amending process, multiple interpreters, or ambiguity, has helped make it the oldest constitution in the world. People may joke that the Constitution isn't relevant anymore, but it shapes the boundaries for all of today's policy debates and institutional struggles.

"Why Should I Care?"

Conclusion

The debate between Tea Party supporters and opponents outlined in this chapter's introduction illustrates many of the chapter's themes: the conflictual nature of politics established by the Constitution, multiple interpreters, and ambiguous language. The separation of powers and the system of checks and balances in our political system divide power to protect against majority tyranny. To Tea Party supporters, we have strayed too far from the limited government roots of the Founding. Tea Party opponents claim that the Constitution centralized power in the national government, while moving away from the state-centered Articles of Confederation. Which side is right? The rather unsatisfying answer is that both are correct. The Founders *did* create a system of limited government that was intended to protect individual liberty from government tyranny, but at the same time the Founders wanted a strong and effective government that could overcome the limitations of state-centered government.

Congress, the president, and the Supreme Court all must interpret the Constitution in the normal course of playing their institutional roles. The general and ambiguous language of the Constitution means that both supporters and opponents of the Tea Party can stake a claim to having views that are informed by the Constitution. When a Tea Party advocate claims that the Federal Reserve is unconstitutional because it is not specifically mentioned in the document, the other side can point out that under that logic the air force is unconstitutional as well (the Constitution mentions Congress's power to support the army and navy but obviously not the air force). Furthermore, Tea Party opponents would say, the commerce clause and the necessary and proper clause give Congress all the power it needs.

The Constitution's flexibility and general language mean that there will never be definitive answers to the conflict over its meaning, but they ensure that these debates will be enduring and meaningful.

The Eighth Amendment's ban on "cruel and unusual punishments" is generally viewed as excluding capital punishment, but the execution of juveniles and the mentally impaired has been found unconstitutional. This picture shows the electric chair in the Southern Ohio Correctional Facility in Lucasville, Ohio.

STUDY GUIDE

The historical context of the Constitution

Describe the historical circumstances that led to the Constitutional Convention of 1787. (Pages 28–33)

Summary

The U.S. Constitution was shaped by historical events preceding its creation, particularly the period of British rule over the colonies, the Revolutionary War, and the states' experience under the Articles of Confederation. Under British rule, the colonies were relatively independent of one another, and the framers sought to create a strong nation while still maintaining the autonomy of the states in the system. The framers based the Constitution on three key principles: the rejection of a monarchy, popular control of the government, and a limited government that protected against tyranny.

Key terms

Articles of Confederation (p. 29)
limited government (p. 29)
Shays's Rebellion (p. 31)
monarchy (p. 31)
republicanism (p. 31)

"consent of the governed" (p. 32)
natural rights (p. 32)
Federalists (p. 33)
Antifederalists (p. 33)

Practice Quiz Questions

1. **How were members of Congress selected under the Articles of Confederation?**
   a. by the state governor
   b. by the state legislature
   c. by the state supreme court
   d. by popular election
   e. by random lot

2. **What power did the president have under the Articles of Confederation?**
   a. power to raise an army
   b. power to veto congressional legislation
   c. power to negotiate foreign agreements
   d. power to nominate federal judges
   e. There was no president under the Articles of Confederation.

3. **At the American Founding, what is the best way to describe the economic inequality among classes and the economic diversity among regions?**
   a. high inequality / high diversity
   b. high inequality / low diversity
   c. low inequality / high diversity
   d. low inequality / low diversity

The politics of compromise at the Constitutional Convention

Analyze the major issues debated by the framers of the Constitution. (Pages 34–40)

Summary

While the framers of the Constitution agreed that the Articles of Confederation needed to be changed, there was little consensus otherwise. The Federalists and Antifederalists clashed on several issues, though the most important were (1) balancing majority rule with minority rights, (2) allocating power between large and small states, (3) allocating power between the legislature and executive, (4) allocating power between the national government and the states, and (5) determining how to handle slavery.

Key terms

pluralism (p. 35)
Virginia Plan (p. 36)
New Jersey Plan (p. 36)
Great Compromise (p. 36)

parliamentary system (p. 38)
reserved powers (p. 39)
national supremacy clause (p. 39)
Three-Fifths Compromise (p. 39)

Practice Quiz Questions

4. **Madison argued that the best way to prevent the tyranny of factions was to _____.**
   a. outlaw political parties
   b. establish a strong national government
   c. have various groups compete against one another in the government
   d. establish strong local governments
   e. try to ensure that all people were equal

5. **The Great Compromise provided solutions to which issue?**
   a. balancing majority rule with minority rights
   b. allocating power between big and small states
   c. allocating power between the legislature and executive
   d. allocating power between national and state governments
   e. determining how to handle slavery

6. **How are executives chosen in most other established democracies?**
   a. by popular election
   b. by the Electoral College
   c. through selection by the judiciary
   d. through selection by the legislature
   e. by the United Nations

7. **The outcome of the Three-Fifths Compromise was that each slave counted for three-fifths of a person for the purposes of _____ and _____.**
   a. voting; taxation
   b. congressional representation; taxation
   c. voting; congressional representation
   d. taxation; congressional appropriations
   e. congressional representation; agricultural subsidies

Ratification

Contrast the arguments of the Federalists with those of the Antifederalists. (Pages 40–42)

Summary

After the Constitution was written and approved at the Constitutional Convention, it still needed to be ratified by nine states. The Constitution was primarily criticized by the Antifederalists, which gave way to a lengthy public debate over the merits of the proposed framework. Ultimately, the framers had to include the Bill of Rights, which was tailored to protect the rights of states and individuals from the national government, in order to win over the necessary support in the states.

Key term
Bill of Rights (p. 41)

Practice Quiz Questions

8. **What group was concerned about the Constitution's provisions for the strength of the president and the lack of specific guarantees of civil liberties?**
   a. Tories
   b. Unionists
   c. Federalists
   d. Antifederalists
   e. Free Soilers

9. **A series of arguments originally published in New York newspapers supported the Constitution and outlined the political theory behind it. What are these assembled works called?**
   a. *Pickwick Papers*
   b. *Federalist Papers*
   c. *Antifederalist Papers*
   d. *Common Sense*
   e. *The Second Treatise of Government*

The Constitution: a framework for government

Outline the major provisions of the Constitution. (Pages 42–47)

Summary

The defining feature of the Constitution is its separation of powers while still maintaining flexibility for leadership in times of crisis. The system of checks and balances gives each branch of the federal government some explicit powers, some shared powers, and some ability to limit the power of the other two branches of government.

Key terms
necessary and proper clause (p. 42) **power of the purse** (p. 46)
impeachment (p. 46) **judicial review** (p. 46)

Practice Quiz Questions

10. **The "necessary and proper" clause gives flexibility to which part of government?**
    a. the president
    b. the Supreme Court
    c. the bureaucracy
    d. the Congress
    e. interest groups

11. **Which branch has the fewest explicit powers?**
    a. the president
    b. the Supreme Court
    c. the bureaucracy
    d. the Congress

12. **Which of the following negative powers does the president enjoy?**
    a. the power to veto legislation
    b. the power to freeze judicial salaries
    c. the power to review the constitutionality of a law
    d. the power to impeach federal justices
    e. the power to dissolve Congress and call new elections

Is the Constitution a "living" document?

Explore how the meaning of the Constitution has evolved. (Pages 47–52)

Summary

The Constitution is more than 200 years old, yet it still provides a blueprint for modern governance. It has maintained its relevance because of its ambiguity on several key passages, its ability to be amended rather than entirely rewritten, and the designation of multiple interpreters of the Constitution.

Key terms

enumerated powers (p. 50)   implied powers (p. 50)

Practice Quiz Questions

13. **Which route for *proposing* a constitutional amendment has been used for all successful amendments to date?**
    a. approval by two-thirds of the members of Congress
    b. approval by a national convention
    c. approval by two-thirds of the state legislatures
    d. approval by the Supreme Court
    e. approval by the president

14. **After an amendment is successfully proposed, what step must occur in order for it to become part of the Constitution?**
    a. signature by the president
    b. approval by a popular vote
    c. ratification by three-fourths of the states
    d. nullification by all 50 state legislatures
    e. a national referendum vote

15. **Which part of government often defines the boundaries of implied powers?**
    a. the president
    b. the Supreme Court
    c. the bureaucracy
    d. the Congress
    e. the people

Suggested Reading

Allen, Danielle. *Our Declaration: A Reading of the Declaration of Independence in Defense of Equality.* New York: W.W. Norton, 2014.

Currie, David P. *The Constitution of the United States: A Primer for the People*, 2nd ed. Chicago: University of Chicago Press, 2000.

Dahl, Robert A. *How Democratic Is the American Constitution?* New Haven, CT: Yale University Press, 2001.

Davis, Sue. *Corwin and Peltason's Understanding the Constitution*, 17th ed. Boston: Wadsworth, 2008.

Hamilton, Alexander, James Madison, and John Jay. *The Federalist Papers.* 1788. Reprint, 2nd ed., edited by Roy P. Fairfield. Baltimore, MD: Johns Hopkins University Press, 1981.

Ketcham, Ralph. *The Anti-Federalist Papers and the Constitutional Convention Debates.* New York: Signet Classics, 2003.

Rossiter, Clinton. *1787: The Grand Convention.* New York: Macmillan, 1966.

Sunstein, Cass R. *Designing Democracy: What Constitutions Do.* New York: Oxford University Press, 2001.

Wood, Gordon S. *The Creation of the American Republic.* New York: W. W. Norton, 1969.

3

Federalism

States or the federal government: Who's got the power?

Following passage of the 2010 Affordable Care Act (ACA), sometimes called Obamacare,[1] 26 states sued the national government over the new law. Intended to provide health care coverage to more than 30 million Americans who were uninsured, the law seemed to these states to be an unconstitutional overreach of federal power: "the individual mandate exceeds Congress's enumerated powers, the Medicaid expansions are unconstitutionally coercive, and the employer mandates impermissibly interfere with state sovereignty."[2] This is the federalism trifecta, hitting on all three major themes concerning the balance of power among levels of government: (1) Congress's power to enact broad national legislation under the Constitution's commerce clause, (2) Congress's power to compel states to act through "coercive federalism," and (3) states' sovereign powers under the Tenth and Eleventh Amendments.

The Supreme Court largely upheld the ACA in 2012, but there was one important point of agreement with the states: the Court ruled that the expansion of Medicaid, which would provide health care for an additional 17 million low-income Americans, was unconstitutionally coercive in requiring states to expand Medicaid or lose all their federal funding for the existing Medicaid program. States could still choose to accept the federal funding to expand Medicaid, but they would not lose their other Medicaid funding if they opted out of the expansion. However, the battle between the national governments and the states did not end with the Court's ruling. Nineteen states decided not to accept the federal incentives to expand Medicaid, leaving 4.3 million poor Americans without health insurance.[3] Thirty-four states opted to not run the health insurance exchanges, requiring the federal government to do it for them (entirely, or at least in part). A few states have actively tried to obstruct implementation of the law by forbidding state employees to do anything to help that is not specifically required by the law.[4]

Some of these disputes continued to work their way up to the Supreme Court. In 2015, the Court ruled that federal subsidies to purchase insurance applied to all 50 states, despite language in the law that said subsidies would only apply in an "exchange established by the State." If the Court had followed a narrow interpretation of the legislative language, 6.4 million Americans would have lost their

CHAPTER GOALS

Define *federalism* and explain its significance.
pages 58–60

Explain what the Constitution says about federalism.
pages 60–63

Trace the major shifts in state and federal government power over time.
pages 63–70

Describe the major trends and debates in federalism today.
pages 71–84

📷

Should the government require all Americans to have health insurance? While individual Americans disagreed about this question, the states and the federal government also disagreed about the states' role in implementing the ACA.

insurance and likely created a "death spiral" for the ACA. In the majority opinion Chief Justice John Roberts wrote: "Congress passed the ACA to improve health insurance markets, not to destroy them." By deferring to Congress's broad legislative intent, the Supreme Court gave a huge victory to supporters of national power over state power. However, now that Republicans have unified control of national government, they will likely try to "repeal and replace" Obamacare, which will probably include returning more power to the states.

The conflict over the ACA is a great example of the tensions over how power is distributed between the states and the national government. What are the responsibilities of the states and what is the domain of the national government? What happens when levels of government disagree on a policy? Can the national government simply force the states to do something? Is this how federalism works?

★

DEFINE *FEDERALISM* **AND EXPLAIN ITS SIGNIFICANCE**

federalism
The division of power across the local, state, and national governments.

sovereign power
The supreme power of an independent state to regulate its internal affairs without foreign interference.

What is federalism and why does it matter?

Federalism is a form of government that divides sovereign power across at least two political units. Dividing **sovereign power** means that each unit of government (in the U.S. context, the national and state governments) has some degree of authority and autonomy. As discussed in Chapter 2, this division of power across levels of government is central to the system of separated powers in the United States. The concept of dividing power across levels of government seems simple, but as we will see later in this chapter, the political battles over *how* that power is divided have been intense.

In practical terms, federalism is about intergovernmental relations: how the different levels of government interact and how power is divided. But even that may seem a little abstract. Why does federalism matter? On a broad range of issues, the level of government that dictates policy can make a real difference. The conflict over health care reform is an obvious example, but other policies include whether the national government can prevent states from allowing marijuana use for medical and recreational purposes, from allowing "aid in dying" (or what opponents to the practice label "assisted suicides"), from discriminating against their employees based on age or disability, or from fighting national immigration laws. These questions involve defining the disputed boundaries between what the states and national government are allowed to do. Much of U.S. history has been rooted in this struggle to define American federalism.

📷

The relationship between the national government and the states also involves cooperation. After unprecedented flash flooding devastated South Carolina in October 2015, FEMA partnered with state officials to provide relief at outposts like this one. @FEMA

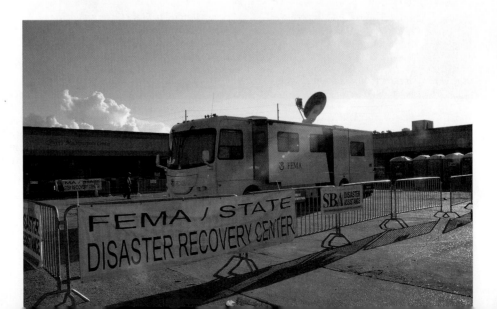

Levels of government and their degrees of autonomy

A distinguishing feature of federalism is that each level of government has some degree of autonomy from the other levels—that is, each level can carry out some policies without interference from the others. In the United States, this means that the national and state governments have distinct powers and responsibilities. The national government, for example, is responsible for national defense and foreign policy. State and local governments have primary responsibility for conducting elections and promoting public safety, or **police powers**. In other areas, such as transportation, the different levels of government have **concurrent powers**—that is, they share responsbilities (see Nuts & Bolts 3.1). The national government also has additional responsibilities through implied powers that are inferred from the powers explicitly granted in the Constitution (see the later discussion in this chapter). Local governments—cities, towns, school districts, and counties—are not autonomous units of government. State governments create them and control the types of activities they can engage in by specifying in the state

police powers
The power to enforce laws and provide for public safety.

concurrent powers
Responsibilities for particular policy areas, such as transportation, that are shared by federal, state, and local governments.

National and State Responsibilities

NUTS
& BOLTS
3.1

National Government Powers	State Government Powers	Concurrent Powers
Print money	Issue licenses	Collect taxes
Regulate interstate commerce and international trade	Regulate intrastate (within the state) businesses	Build roads
Make treaties and conduct foreign policy	Conduct elections	Borrow money
Declare war	Establish local governments	Establish courts
Provide an army and navy	Ratify amendments to the Constitution	Make and enforce laws
Establish post offices	Promote public health and safety	Charter banks and corporations
Make laws necessary and proper to carry out these powers	May exert powers the Constitution does not delegate to the national government or does not prohibit the states from using	Spend money for the general welfare; take private property for public purposes, with just compensation

Powers Denied to the National Government	Powers Denied to State Governments
May not violate the Bill of Rights	May not enter into treaties with other countries
May not impose export taxes among states	May not print money
May not use money from the Treasury without an appropriation from Congress	May not tax imports or exports
May not change state boundaries	May not interfere with contracts
	May not suspend a person's rights without due process

Source: GPO Access: Guide to the U.S. Government, http://bensguide.gpo.gov/3-5/government/federalism.html (accessed 12/5/11).

charter either what they *can* do or only what they *cannot* do (that is, they are allowed to do anything not prohibited in the charter). Despite this lack of autonomy, local governments play an important role in providing public education, police and fire departments, and land use policies. They also raise money through property taxes, user fees, and in some cases local sales taxes. But overall, because of their lack of autonomy, local governments do not directly share power within our federal system with the state and national governments.

A comparative perspective

It is useful to compare U.S. federalism with forms of government in other countries. In some countries, power is centralized within the national government. This system is known as a **unitary government**. Unitary governments are the most common in the modern world (about 80 percent); examples include the United Kingdom, Israel, Italy, France, Japan, and Sweden. In these countries, the states or subunit governments are not autonomous; they cannot carry out policies if the national government opposes them. At the opposite end of the spectrum is a **confederal government**, in which the states have most of the power and often can veto the actions of the central government. This was the first type of government in the United States under the Articles of Confederation. Because there are many problems associated with having such a weak national government (see Chapter 2), few successful modern examples exist. The Commonwealth of Independent States (CIS), which formed in 1991 after the breakup of the Soviet Union, was initially successful as a confederal structure, but rifts among the member states today are making it largely ineffective.[5]

Although true confederations are rare, **intergovernmental organizations** have proliferated in recent decades. More than 1,200 multilateral organizations have been created by member nations seeking to coordinate their policies on, for example, economic activity, security, or environmental protection. The United Nations (UN), the International Monetary Fund (IMF), and the North Atlantic Treaty Organization (NATO) are important examples. The European Union (EU) is an intergovernmental organization that began as a loose confederation, but it is becoming more federalist in its decision-making process and structure.

unitary government
A system in which the national, centralized government holds ultimate authority. It is the most common form of government in the world.

confederal government
A form of government in which states hold power over a limited national government.

intergovernmental organizations
Organizations that seek to coordinate policy across member nations.

★

EXPLAIN WHAT THE CONSTITUTION SAYS ABOUT FEDERALISM

Balancing national and state power in the Constitution

Although our nation's Founders wanted a national government that was stronger than it had been under the Articles of Confederation, they also wanted to preserve states' autonomy. These goals are reflected in different parts of the Constitution, which provides ample evidence for advocates of both state-centered and nation-centered federalism. The nation-centered position appears in the document's preamble, which begins: "We the People of the United States," compared with the Articles of Confederation, which began: "We the undersigned delegates of the States." The Constitution's phrasing emphasizes the nation as a whole over the separate states. The competing perspectives of nation- and state-centered federalism is a lens through which we can understand the evolving conceptions of federalism and current conflict over intergovernmental power.

A strong national government

Other aspects of the Constitution also support the nation-centered perspective. These reflect the Founders' desire for a strong national government to provide national security and a healthy, efficient economy.

In terms of national security, Congress was granted the power to raise and support armies, declare war, and "suppress Insurrections and repel Invasion," while the president, as commander in chief of the armed forces, would oversee the conduct of war. Congress's power to regulate interstate commerce promoted economic efficiency and centralized an important economic power at the national level, and many restrictions on state power had similar effects. States were *prohibited* from entering into "any Treaty, Alliance, or Confederation" or keeping troops or "Ships of War" during peacetime. They also could not coin money or impose duties on imports or exports (see Article I, Section 10). These provisions ensured that states would not interfere with the smooth operation of interstate commerce or create problems for national defense. Imagine, for example, that Oklahoma had the power to tax oil produced in other states or that California decided to create its own army. This would create inefficiencies and potential danger for the rest of the country.

The necessary and proper clause (Article I, Section 8) was another broad grant of power to the national government: it gave Congress the power "[t]o make all Laws which shall be necessary and proper for carrying into Execution the foregoing Powers." Similarly, the national supremacy clause (Article VI) says that the Constitution and all laws and treaties that are made under the Constitution shall be the "supreme Law of the Land" and that "the Judges in every State shall be bound thereby, any Thing in the Constitution or Laws of any State to the Contrary notwithstanding." This is perhaps the clearest statement of the nation-centered focus of the Constitution. If any state law or state constitution conflicts with national law or the Constitution, the national perspective wins. Thus, the laws passed by states to limit implementation of the ACA had no effect after the Supreme Court upheld the central parts of the national law. The only way to change the law would be at the national level.

DID YOU KNOW?

7

of the thirteen states printed large quantities of their own currency under the Articles of Confederation.
Source: U.S. Information Agency

State powers and limits on national power

Despite the Founders' nation-centered bias, many parts of the Constitution also address state powers and limits on national power. Article II gives the states the power to choose electors for the electoral college, and Article V grants the states a central role in the process of amending the Constitution. Three-fourths of the states must ratify any constitutional amendment (through either conventions or the state legislatures, as specified by Congress), but the states can also bypass Congress in proposing amendments if two-thirds of the states call for a convention. This route to amending the Constitution has never been used, but the Founders clearly wanted to provide an additional check on national power.

Article I of the Constitution enumerates many powers for Congress, but the list of state powers is much shorter. One could interpret this as more evidence for the nation-centered perspective, but at the time of the Founding the default position was to keep most power at the state level. Therefore, the federal powers that were exceptions to this rule had to be clearly specified, while state governments received authority over all other matters. The Tenth Amendment supports this view, saying: "The powers not delegated to the United States by the Constitution, nor prohibited by it to the states, are reserved to the states respectively, or to the people."

The Eleventh Amendment, the first one passed after the Bill of Rights, was another important affirmation of state sovereignty. Antifederalists were concerned that the part of Article III that gave the Supreme Court authority over cases involving a "State and Citizens of another State" would undermine state sovereignty by giving the Court too much power over state laws. Federalists assured them this would not happen, but the Supreme Court ruled in *Chisholm v. Georgia* (1793) that citizens of one state could sue the government of another state. The majority opinion ridiculed the "haughty notions of state independence, state sovereignty, and state supremacy." The states struck back by adopting the Eleventh Amendment, which made such lawsuits unconstitutional. While the Supreme Court lost this skirmish over state power, it continued to serve as the umpire in disputes between the national and state governments.

Clauses that favor both perspectives

Article IV of the Constitution has elements that favor both the state-centered and the nation-centered perspectives. For example, its **full faith and credit clause** specifies that states must respect one another's laws, granting citizens the "Full Faith and Credit" of their home state's laws if they go to another state. At the same time, though, the article's **privileges and immunities clause** says that citizens of each state are "entitled to all Privileges and Immunities" of citizens in the other states, which means that states must treat visitors from other states the same as their own residents. This part of the Constitution favors a nation-centered perspective because it was intended to promote free travel and economic activity among the states.

There are many examples of the full faith and credit clause at work today. If you have a New York driver's license and are traveling to California, you do not need to stop at every state line to get a new license; each state will honor your New York license. Similarly, a legal marriage in one state must be honored by another state, a provision that has fueled the ongoing controversy over same-sex marriage. In 1996, after Hawaiian courts gave homosexual marriages most of the same legal rights as heterosexual marriages, many states passed laws saying they would not have to honor those marriages. Congress passed the Defense of Marriage Act (DOMA) in 1996, which said that states would not have to recognize same-sex marriages. But in 2013 the Supreme Court struck

full faith and credit clause
Part of Article IV of the Constitution requiring that each state's laws be honored by the other states. For example, a legal marriage in one state must be recognized across state lines.

privileges and immunities clause
Part of Article IV of the Constitution requiring that states must treat nonstate residents within their borders as they would treat their own residents. This was meant to promote commerce and travel between states.

Jim Obergefell, the plaintiff in the *Obergefell v. Hodges* Supreme Court case that legalized same-sex marriage nationwide, is backed by supporters of the ruling on the steps of the Texas capitol during a rally on June 29, 2015, in Austin. This ruling shows the power of the supremacy clause, as it struck down laws in 14 states. #LoveWins #Obergefell down the part of this law that denied federal benefits to same-sex couples[6] and then in 2015 the Court ruled that a marriage is a fundamental right that cannot be denied by the states (see Chapter 5 for a discussion of these important cases).[7]

We can also cite examples of the privileges and immunities clause at work in a modern context. For example, states may not deny welfare benefits to new residents or deny police protection to visitors even though they do not pay state taxes.[8] However, states are allowed to make some distinctions between residents and nonresidents. For example, states do not have to permit nonresidents to vote in state elections and public colleges and universities may charge out-of-state residents higher tuition than in-state residents. Therefore, the privileges and immunities clause cuts both ways on the question of the balance of power: it allows the states to determine and uphold these laws autonomously, but it also emphasizes that national citizenship is more important than state citizenship.

"Why Should I Care?"

Why is it important to understand the Constitution's role in federalism? The Constitution sets the boundaries for the battles over state and federal power. For example, no state can decide to print its own currency, and the U.S. government cannot take over the public schools. But within those broad boundaries, the balance between national and state power at any given point in history is a political decision, the product of choices made by elected leaders and the courts. The struggle over the implementation of the ACA was a perfect example: the national government passed the law, the Supreme Court upheld most of it and struck down part of it, and the states implemented the law with varying levels of cooperation and resistance. This meant that you would be able to stay on your parents' health insurance until you are 26 (part of the national law that was upheld), but once you had to buy your own insurance, the process of getting signed up would vary depending on which state you live in.

★

TRACE THE MAJOR SHIFTS IN STATE AND FEDERAL GOVERNMENT POWER OVER TIME

The evolving concept of federalism

The nature of federalism has changed as the relative positions of the national and state governments have evolved. In the first century of our nation's history, the national government played a relatively limited role and the boundaries between the levels of government were distinct. As the national government took on more power in the twentieth century, intergovernmental relations became more cooperative and the boundaries less distinct. Even within this more cooperative framework, federalism remains a source of conflict within our political system, as the levels of government share lawmaking authority (as the health care example that opened this chapter illustrates).

The early years

As the United States gained its footing, clashes between the advocates of state-centered and nation-centered federalism evolved into a partisan struggle. The Federalists—the party of George Washington, John Adams, and Alexander Hamilton—controlled the new government for its first 12 years and favored strong national power. Their opponents, the Democratic-Republicans (led by Thomas Jefferson and James Madison), favored state power.

Establishing National Supremacy The first confrontation came when the Federalists established a national bank in 1791, over Jefferson's objections. This controversy did not come to a head until Congress chartered the second national bank in 1816. At that time, the state of Maryland, which was controlled by the Democratic-Republicans, tried to tax the National Bank's Baltimore branch out of existence, but the head cashier of the bank refused to pay the tax and the case eventually ended up at the Supreme Court. The Court had to decide whether Congress had the power to create the bank and, if it did, whether Maryland had the right to tax the bank.

In the landmark decision *McCulloch v. Maryland* (1819), the Court ruled in favor of the national government on both counts. In deciding whether Congress could create the bank, the Court held that even though the word "bank" does not appear in the Constitution, Congress's power to create one is implied through its relevant enumerated powers—such as the power to coin money, levy taxes, and borrow money. The Court also ruled that Maryland did not have the right to tax the bank because of the Constitution's national supremacy clause. Both the concept of implied powers and the validation of national supremacy were critical for establishing the centrality of the national government.

A few years later, the Supreme Court decided another case that cemented Congress's power to act based on the commerce clause. In *Gibbons v. Ogden* (1824), the Supreme Court held that Congress has broad power to regulate interstate commerce and struck down a New York law that had granted a monopoly to a private company operating steamboats on the Hudson River between New York and New Jersey. By granting this monopoly, the ruling stated, New York was interfering with interstate commerce.

Pressing for States' Rights Despite such Court rulings in favor of national government, the following decades saw a push for broader **states' rights**, as when the southern states challenged federalism on issues such as civil liberties (in response to a law passed in 1798 that made it illegal to criticize the government), tariffs, and slavery. John Calhoun, a South Carolina senator, used the term "nullification" to refer to a state's right to ignore a law passed by Congress if the state believed the law was unconstitutional (for example, Calhoun urged South Carolina to ignore a tariff law passed by Congress in 1832). The states' rights perspective was at the center of the dispute between

states' rights
The idea that states are entitled to a certain amount of self-government, free of federal government intervention. This became a central issue in the period leading up to the Civil War.

In the early 1800s, the Supreme Court confirmed the national government's right to regulate commerce between the states. The state of New York granted a monopoly to a ferry company serving ports in New York and New Jersey, but this was found to interfere with interstate commerce and was therefore subject to federal intervention.

southern and northern states over slavery, which ultimately led to the secession of the Confederate states and, subsequently, the Civil War. The stakes were enormous in the battles over federalism: about 528,000 people died in that bloodiest of American wars.[9] As Abraham Lincoln forcefully argued, concepts such as nullification and states' rights, when taken to their logical extremes, were too divisive to be allowed to stand. If states were allowed to ignore national laws, the basis of the United States would fall apart.

Dual federalism

The ideas of states' rights and nullification did not produce the Civil War by themselves. They had some help from the Supreme Court's infamous *Dred Scott* decision. In this section, we will discuss the significance of that case as well as the broader system of dual federalism, which defined intergovernmental relations for nearly the first 150 years of our nation's history.

For nearly three decades during the mid-1800s, the Supreme Court was able to limit the reach of the national government through Chief Justice Roger Taney's vision of federalism, which is known as dual federalism (see Table 3.1). Under **dual federalism**, the national and state governments were viewed as distinct, with little overlap in their activities or the services they provided. In this view, the national government's activities are confined to powers strictly enumerated in the Constitution, despite the necessary and proper clause and the implied powers endorsed in *McCulloch v. Maryland*.

dual federalism
The form of federalism favored by Chief Justice Roger Taney in which national and state governments are seen as distinct entities providing separate services. This model limits the power of the national government.

Early Landmark Supreme Court Decisions on Federalism

TABLE 3.1

Case	Holding and Significance for States' Rights	Direction of the Decision
Chisholm v. Georgia (1793)	Held that citizens of one state could sue another state; led to the Eleventh Amendment, which prohibited such lawsuits.	Less state power
McCulloch v. Maryland (1819)	Upheld the national government's right to create a bank and reaffirmed the idea of "national supremacy."	Less state power
Gibbons v. Ogden (1824)	Held that Congress, rather than the states, has broad power to regulate interstate commerce.	Less state power
Barron v. Baltimore (1833)	Endorsed a notion of "dual federalism" in which the rights of a U.S. citizen under the Bill of Rights did not apply to that same person under state law.	More state power
Dred Scott v. Sandford (1857)	Sided with southern states' view that slaves were property and ruled that the Missouri Compromise violated the Fifth Amendment, because making slavery illegal in some states deprived slave owners of property. Contributed to the start of the Civil War.	More state power
National Labor Relations Board v. Jones and Laughlin Steel Corporation (1937)	Upheld the National Labor Relations Act of 1935 as consistent with Congress's commerce clause powers, reversing the Court's more narrow interpretation of that clause.	Less state power

Dred Scott and Civil War The state-centered views of the Taney Court also produced a tragic decision, *Dred Scott v. Sandford* (1857). Dred Scott was a slave who had lived for many years with his owner in the free Wisconsin Territory but was living in Missouri, a slave state, when his master died. Scott petitioned for his freedom under the Missouri Compromise, which said that slavery was illegal in any free state. The Taney Court's decision held that slaves were not citizens but private property and that therefore the Missouri Compromise violated the Fifth Amendment because it deprived people (slave owners) of property without the due process of law. This unfortunate decision contributed to the Civil War, which started four years later, because it indicated that there could not be a political solution to the problem of slavery.

Ultimately the Civil War ended the dispute over slavery, but it did not resolve basic questions about the balance of power between the national and state systems. Right after the Civil War, the Constitution was amended to ensure that the Union's views on states' rights were the law of the land. The Civil War amendments banned slavery (the Thirteenth), prohibited states from denying citizens due process or equal protection of the laws (Fourteenth), and gave newly freed male slaves the right to vote (Fifteenth). The Fourteenth Amendment was the most important in terms of federalism because it served as the constitutional basis for many of the civil rights laws passed by Congress during Reconstruction. The Civil War fundamentally changed the way Americans thought about the relationship between the national government and the states: before the war people said "the United States *are* . . ." but after the war they said "the United States *is* . . . ," highlighting the feeling that the United States was a unified nation, not merely a loose collection of states.

The Supreme Court and Limited National Government The assertion of power by Congress during Reconstruction was short-lived, as the Supreme Court soon stepped in again to limit the power of the national government. In 1873, the Court reinforced the notion of dual federalism, ruling that the Fourteenth Amendment did not change the balance of power between the national and state governments despite its clear language aimed at state action. Moreover, the Court ruled that the Fourteenth Amendment right to due process and equal treatment under the law only applied to individuals' rights as citizens of the United States, not to their state citizenship.[10] By extension, freedom of speech, freedom of the press, and the other liberties protected in the Bill of Rights applied only to laws passed by Congress, not to state laws. This distinction between state and national citizenship sounds odd today, partly because the Fourteenth Amendment has long been viewed as the basis for ensuring that states do not violate basic rights.

In 1883, the Court overturned the 1875 Civil Rights Act, which had guaranteed equal treatment in public accommodations. The Court argued that the Fourteenth Amendment did not give Congress the power to regulate private conduct, such as whether a white restaurant owner had to serve a black customer, but only the conduct of state governments.[11] This narrow view of the Fourteenth Amendment left the national government powerless to prevent southern states from implementing state and local laws that led to complete segregation of blacks and whites in the South (called Jim Crow laws) and the denial of many basic rights to blacks after northern troops left the South at the end of Reconstruction.

The other area in which the Supreme Court limited the reach of the national government concerned Congress's authority to regulate the economy through its commerce clause powers. In several cases in the late nineteenth and early twentieth centuries, the Supreme Court endorsed a view of laissez-faire—French for "leave alone"—capitalism aimed at protecting business from regulation by the national government. To this end, the Court defined clear boundaries between *inter*state and *intra*state commerce, ruling that Congress could not regulate any economic activity that occurred *within* a state (intrastate).

On similar grounds, the Court also struck down attempts by Congress to regulate child labor.[12] In some instances, the Court's laissez-faire perspective even led the justices to strike down state laws, as in one case that ruled unconstitutional a New York law limiting the working hours of bakers to no more than 60 hours a week or 10 hours a day.[13] Therefore, the limits that the Court placed on Congress during this antiregulation phase did not necessarily tip the balance to the state governments. Rather, big business was the clear winner over both national and state governments.

Cooperative federalism

In the early years of the twentieth century and through the 1930s, a new era of American federalism emerged. The first step was taking the election of U.S. senators away from state legislatures and providing for their direct election in the Seventeenth Amendment. This change was prompted by the Progressives' desire to shift power away from corrupt state legislatures.[14] Now the national government became much more involved in activities that were formerly reserved for the states, such as education, transportation, civil rights, agriculture, social welfare, and management–labor relations. Starting in 1937 with the landmark ruling *National Labor Relations Board v. Jones and Laughlin Steel Corporation*, the Supreme Court gave Congress far more latitude in shaping economic and social policy for the nation.[15]

After the Supreme Court struck down the 1875 Civil Rights Act, southern states were free to impose Jim Crow laws. These state and local laws led to complete racial segregation, even for public drinking fountains.

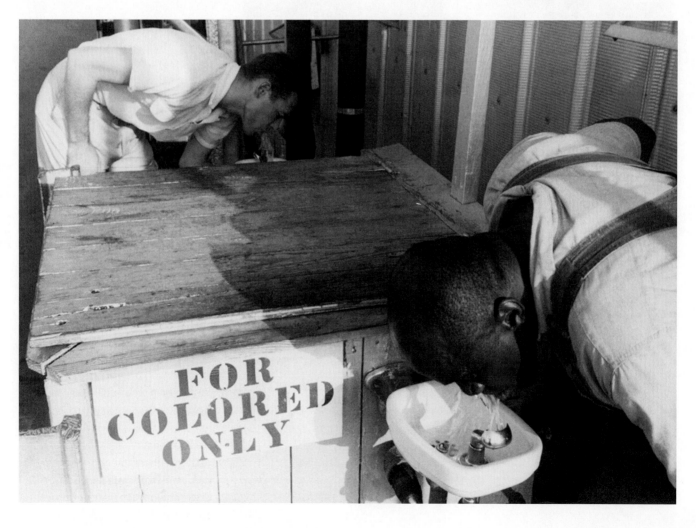

Versions of Federalism

Version 1:
Layer Cake Federalism

1789–1937
No interactions between the levels of government.

Version 2:
Marble Cake Federalism

1937–today
Interactions between the levels of government are common.

National

State

Local

Version 3:
Picket Fence Federalism

1960s–today
Horizontal boards represent different levels of government, and the pickets are policy areas within which coordination happens across those levels.

National

State

Local

Agriculture Environment Highways Housing Education Medical Care Tax Policy

Version 4:
Coercive Federalism

1970s–today
National government uses regulations, mandates, and conditions to pressure states to fall into line with national policy goals.

National

Regulations
National government provides new policy goals.

State   Local

Incentives
National government pressures or incentivizes state and local governments to act according to new goals.

Federalism and Environmental Policy

This is who carries out environmental policy in...

The National Government:
Environmental Protection Agency (EPA), Department of the Interior, Department of Energy

The State Government:
State Department of Natural Resources, State Park Service, State Environmental Protection Agencies

The Local Government:
City park system, city and county oversight boards for land use policy and zoning

Environmental policy shows contemporary federalism in action. As you can see on the right, all levels of government combine to effect environmental policy (exemplifying picket fence federalism). Also, the national government provides both rules and incentives for state and local governments to change their environmental policies (exemplifying coercive federalism).

Congress passed new acts.

Over the last few decades, Congress has passed the **Coastal Zone Management Act**, the **Clean Water Act**, the **Endangered Species Act**, and the **Clean Air Act**.

What does that mean?

These have all provided states and localities with **federal regulations and mandates.**

Stricter rules.

In 2015, the EPA set **new tougher standards** for ozone and proposed stricter limits on greenhouse gases.

Also...

The federal government **provides many incentives** designed to preserve the environment.

Cool bonus.

These include **tax credits** for electric cars, biodiesel and hydrogen fuel cells, and home improvements that increase energy efficiency.

Good deal.

In 2015, the EPA introduced a Clean Energy Incentive Program to promote expansion of renewable energy and energy efficiency. **States receive emission credits** for the clean energy they produce.

Critical Thinking

1. **Which do you think is a more effective tool** to change environmental policy—the "stick" of regulation or the "carrot" of incentives? Why?

2. **Should the government provide tax credits and other incentives** for things like electric cars and alternative energy, or leave such things up to the free market?

In short:

The federal government **imposes new rules** on **state** and **local governments** and **provides incentives** to follow these new rules and goals. Goals such as: **increased energy efficiency and independence**

cooperative federalism
A form of federalism in which national and state governments work together to provide services efficiently. This form emerged in the late 1930s, representing a profound shift toward less concrete boundaries of responsibility in national–state relations.

picket fence federalism
A more refined and realistic form of cooperative federalism in which policy makers within a particular policy area work together across the levels of government.

Franklin Delano Roosevelt's New Deal shifted more power than ever to the national government. Through major new programs to address the Great Depression, such as the Works Progress Administration construction projects pictured here, the federal government expanded its reach into areas that had been primarily the responsibility of state and local governments.

Shifting National–State Relations The type of federalism that emerged in the Progressive Era of the early twentieth century and blossomed in the late 1930s is called **cooperative federalism**, or "marble cake" federalism, as opposed to the "layer cake" model of dual federalism.[16] As the image of a marble cake suggests, the boundaries of state and national responsibilities are not as well defined under cooperative federalism as under dual federalism. With the increasing industrialization and urbanization of the late 1930s and 1940s, more complex problems arose that could not be solved at one level of government. The Great Depression made it painfully clear that states did not have the resources necessary to address major economic crises. Cooperative federalism adopted a more practical focus on intergovernmental relations and how to efficiently provide services. State and local governments maintained some influence as the implementers of national programs, but the national government played an enhanced role as the initiator of key policies.

"Cooperative federalism" accurately describes this important shift in national–state relations in the first half of the twentieth century, but it does not capture the complexity of modern federalism. The marble cake metaphor falls short in one important way: the lines of authority and patterns of cooperation are not as messy as implied by the swirly flow of chocolate through white cake. Instead, the 1960s metaphor of **picket fence federalism** is a better description of cooperative federalism in action. As the How It Works graphic shows, each picket of the fence represents a different policy area and the horizontal boards that hold the pickets together represent the different levels of government. This is a much more orderly image than the marble cake, and it has important implications about how policy is made across levels of government.

The most important point to be drawn from this analogy is that activity within the cooperative federal system occurs *within* pickets of the fence—that is, within policy areas. Policy makers within a given policy area will have more in common with others in that area (even if they are at different levels of government) than they do with people who work in different areas (even if they are at the same level of government). For example, someone working in a state's Department of Natural Resources will have more contact with people working in local park programs and the national Department of the Interior than with people who also work at the state level but who focus on, say, transportation policy. Overall, this version of federalism provides good opportunities for coordination and the sharing of expertise within policy areas.

"Why Should I Care?"

Why is it important to understand the history of federalism? You might think that the Civil War ended the debates over nation-centered versus state-centered federalism (in favor of the national government), but disputes today over immigration, health care, welfare, and education policy all revolve around the balance of power between the levels of government. State legislatures that talk about ignoring the ACA today are invoking the same arguments used by advocates of states' rights in the 1830s and 1840s concerning tariffs and slavery.

Federalism today

Federalism today is a complex mix of all the elements our nation's political system has experienced in the past. Our current system is predominantly characterized by cooperative federalism, but it has retained strong elements of national supremacy, dual federalism, and states' rights. Therefore, rather than categorizing types of federalism into neat time periods, the following discussion characterizes the dominant tendency within each period, keeping in mind that competing versions of federalism have always been just below the surface (see Nuts & Bolts 3.2). In the past 20 years, the competing versions are so evident that this period could be considered the "era of balanced federalism."[17]

Cooperative federalism lives on: fiscal federalism

The cooperative relationship between the national and state governments is rooted in the system of transfer payments, or grants from the national government to lower levels of government. This is called **fiscal federalism**. However, just because money flows from Washington does not mean that cooperation by the recipients follows. Depending on how the money is transferred, the national government can either help the local and state governments to achieve their own goals or use its centralized fiscal power to impose its will.

★
DESCRIBE THE MAJOR TRENDS AND DEBATES IN FEDERALISM TODAY

fiscal federalism
A form of federalism in which federal funds are allocated to the lower levels of government through transfer payments or grants.

The Evolution of Federalism

NUTS & BOLTS 3.2

Type of Federalism	Period	Characteristics
Dual federalism (layer cake)	1789–1937	The national and state governments were viewed as very distinct with little overlap in their activities or the services they provided. Within this period, federalism could have been state centered or nation centered, but relations between levels of government were limited.
Cooperative federalism (marble cake)	1937–present	This indicates greater cooperation and collaboration between the levels of government.
Fiscal federalism	1937–present	This system of transfer payments or grants from the national government to lower-level governments involves varying degrees of national control over how the money is spent: categorical grants give the national government a great deal of control whereas block grants involve less national control.
Picket fence federalism	1961–present	This version of cooperative federalism emphasizes that policy makers within a given policy area have more in common with others in their area at different levels of government than with people at the same level of government who work on different issues.
New Federalism	1969–present	New Federalism attempts to shift power to the states by consolidating categorical grants into block grants and giving the states authority over programs such as welfare.
Coercive federalism	1970s–present	This involves federal preemptions of state and local authority and unfunded mandates on state and local governments to force the states to change their policies to match national goals or policies established by Congress.

categorical grants
Federal aid to state or local governments that is provided for a specific purpose, such as a mass-transit program within the transportation budget or a school lunch program within the education budget.

block grants
Federal aid provided to a state government to be spent within a certain policy area, but the state can decide how to spend the money within that area.

Grants in Aid Today most federal aid to the states comes in one of two forms. **Categorical grants** are for specific purposes—they have strings attached, and therefore we discuss them in the section on coercive federalism later. **Block grants** are financial aid to states for use within a specific policy area, but within that area the states have discretion on how to spend the money. For example, Community Development Block Grants were started in 1974 to help state and local governments revitalize their communities; such grants may support ongoing programs or help with large capital expenditures, such as building a waste treatment plant or a highway. Since the 1970s, grants to the states as a proportion of the size of the national economy (gross domestic product, or GDP) have been relatively constant, while the rate of state and local spending has inched up (see What Do the Numbers Say?).

New Federalism

New Federalism, the idea of giving states more control over programs, was introduced in a limited form by President Richard Nixon in the early 1970s and was revived during Ronald Reagan's presidency in the 1980s. In his inaugural address, Reagan emphasized, "All of us need to be reminded that the federal government did not create the states. The states created the federal government." This classic statement of the states' rights position is similar to the Antifederalists' position at the Constitutional Convention.

Reagan's goal of returning more power to the states involved consolidating 77 categorical grants into nine general block grants that gave local politicians more control over how money was spent. This change reflected the belief that because state and local politicians were closer to the people, they would know better how to spend the money. However, the increase in state control came with a 25 percent cut in the amount of federal money granted to the states.

The next phase of New Federalism came when Republicans won control of Congress in 1994. Working with President Bill Clinton, a moderate Democrat, Republicans passed several pieces of significant legislation that shifted power toward the states. For example, in 1996 the Personal Responsibility and Work Opportunity Act reformed welfare by creating a block grant to the states, Temporary Assistance to Needy Families (TANF), to replace the largest nationally administered welfare program. Another piece of legislation, the Unfunded Mandate Reform Act of 1995, made it more difficult for Congress to impose **unfunded mandates** on the states.

The shift from categorical grants to block grants has not substantially affected the balance of power between the national and state governments. In fact, the amount of money going to the states through block grants has been surpassed by categorical grants since 1982. We will explore the reason for this later: Congress prefers categorical grants because they give Congress more control over how the money is spent.

unfunded mandates
Federal laws that require the states to do certain things but do not provide state governments with funding to implement these policies.

"

The operations of the federal government will be most extensive and important in times of war and danger; those of the State governments, in times of peace and security.

—**James Madison,** *Federalist 45*

The rise of coercive federalism

Despite the overall shift toward cooperative federalism, strong overtones of national government supremacy remain. Three important characteristics of American politics in the past 60 years have reinforced the role of the national government: (1) reliance on the national government in times of crisis and war; (2) the "rights revolution" of the 1950s and 1960s, as well as the Great Society programs of the 1960s; and (3) the rise of coercive federalism.

Federal and State/Local Government Spending

Advocates for smaller government often make the argument that spending in Washington is out of control and that state and local governments should have more power. What do the numbers say? What are the trends in state and local spending as a share of the total economy compared to federal spending?

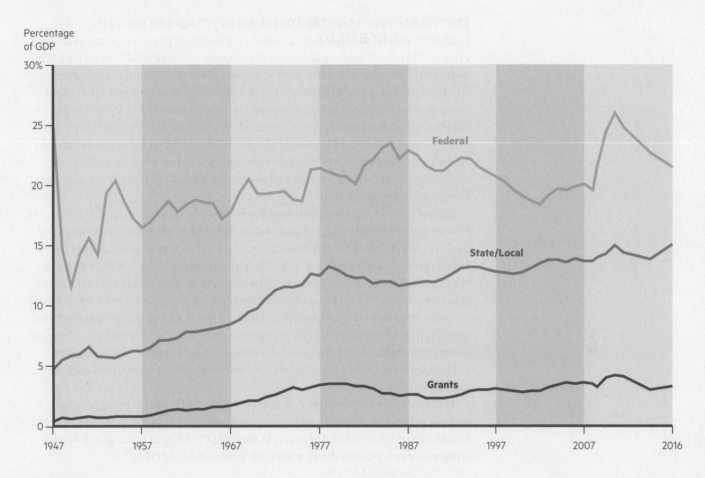

Percentage of GDP

Think about it

- How much is the federal government helping the states in terms of grants? Has this greatly increased? What does this say about the debates between nation-centered and state-centered federalism?
- Should the national government provide more grants to state and local governments to help even out inequalities and address national problems, or leave decisions about funding up to the states?
- What determines the appropriate level of government for spending on a given policy?

Source: 2012 Statistical Abstract of the United States, Table 4.31, and the Bureau of Economic Analysis, "Government Current Receipts and Expenditures" (accessed 5/31/16).

Crisis and War Even in the 1800s, during the period of dual federalism and strong state power, the national government's decisive actions were needed during the Civil War to hold the nation together. More recently, following the September 11, 2001, terrorist attacks, most Americans expected the national government to improve national security and retaliate for the attacks. Even Republicans, who normally oppose increasing the size of government, largely supported President George W. Bush's proposal to create a cabinet-level Department of Homeland Security and the USA PATRIOT Act. Policy responses to the other major crises that occurred during the twentieth century (the Great Depression's New Deal policies and the massive mobilization for World War II), as well as the response to the banking meltdown of 2008–2009, also dramatically shifted the balance of power toward Washington.

The "Rights Revolution" and Great Society Programs During the mid-twentieth century, the "rights revolution" created by the Supreme Court, as well as President Lyndon Johnson's Great Society programs, contributed to more national control over state policies. Landmark Court decisions thrust the national government into policy areas that had typically been reserved to the states. In the school desegregation and busing cases of the 1950s and 1960s, for example, the Court upheld the national goal of promoting racial equality and fighting discrimination over the earlier norm of local control of school districts.[18] The rights revolution also applied to police powers, another area of traditional state control, including protection against self-incrimination and preventing illegally obtained evidence from being used in a criminal trial.[19]

These Court actions were paralleled by a burst of legislation that tackled civil rights, education, the environment, medical care for the poor, and housing. These so-called Great Society policies gave the national government much more leverage over policy areas previously controlled by state and local governments. For example, under the 1965 Voting Rights Act federal marshals were sent to the South to ensure that African Americans were allowed to vote. Another part of this act required some state and local governments to submit changes in their electoral practices, including the boundaries of voting districts, to the Justice Department to make sure they did not have a discriminatory impact. But in 2013 the Court effectively overturned this part of the law by striking down the formula that determined which state and local governments were covered by the act.[20]

In the 1960s, the national government also expanded its reach through a large increase in categorical grants, which the states sorely needed even though the monies came with strings attached. For example, the 1964 Civil Rights Act required nondiscrimination as a condition for receiving any kind of federal grants.

Other Shifts toward National Supremacy Categorical grants aimed at a broad national goal have also reinforced national supremacy in recent decades—for example, requiring a state drinking age of 21 before granting federal highway funds. This policy direction from Washington is part of a trend known as **coercive federalism**. The practice involves the use of federal regulations, mandates, or conditions to force or entice the states to change their policies to match national goals or policies established by Congress. The Clean Air and Clean Water Acts, the Americans with Disabilities Act (ADA) (which promotes handicapped access to public buildings and commercial facilities), and the Motor Voter Act (which requires states to provide voter registration services at motor vehicle departments) are all laws that forced states to change their policies. The laws most objectionable to the states are unfunded mandates, which require states to do certain things but carry no federal money to pay for them.

coercive federalism
A form of federalism in which the federal government pressures the states to change their policies by using regulations, mandates, and conditions (often involving threats to withdraw federal funding).

Along with these mandates, federal preemption is another method of coercive federalism. Derived from the Constitution's national supremacy clause, **federal preemptions** involve the imposition of national priorities on the states. Many preemptions also include unfunded mandates, making the state and local governments pick up the tab for policies that the national government wants them to implement. The presidency of George W. Bush provided strong evidence of this shift toward national power. Beyond the centralization of power associated with fighting terrorism, Bush pushed the national government into more areas that previously had been dominated by the states—including significant mandates and preemptions in education testing, sales tax collection, emergency management, infrastructure, and election administration.[21]

President Obama continued the shift toward national power with one of the most active domestic policy agendas since the New Deal of the 1930s. A $787 billion economic stimulus package of tax cuts and spending designed to address the financial collapse of 2008–2009, a $938 billion health care reform law, cap-and-trade legislation, efforts to prop up and stimulate the battered housing industry, strengthened regulations of finance and banking, and an expanded jobs program all were on the agenda in Obama's first term. His objectives for the second term were more modest given the persistence of budget deficits and split-party control of government. But Obama still pushed for comprehensive immigration reform, action on climate change, and job creation. When Congress wouldn't work with the president, he increasingly relied on executive orders to implement a more limited agenda (for example, on immigration and climate change). This was not popular with Republicans in Congress, who saw it as presidential overreach. Health care reform has been especially controversial with state governments, many of which see the law as an unwarranted expansion of federal power (recall this chapter's opening discussion). This view was supported by the Supreme Court's ruling that states could not be coerced by the federal government into expanding their Medicaid coverage. This Court decision means that there are limits on the scope of coercive federalism. While the overall impact of national health care reform is to centralize more power at the national level, states remain very important in this period of "balanced federalism," as the next section demonstrates.

The States Fight Back Most Americans support the national policies that have been imposed on the states: racial equality, clean air and water, a fair legal process, safer highways, and equal access to the voting booth. At the same time, there has always been strong support for state and local governments. In most national surveys, Americans typically say that they trust state and local government more than the national government. Indeed, the shift in public opinion toward favoring national power after the terrorist attacks of September 11 was temporary, and it appears that state and local governments quickly reasserted their position as the more trusted level of government. For example, a Gallup poll taken in late 2015 showed that 70 percent of Americans trust their local government "a great deal or a fair amount" to "handle local problems," compared with 58 percent who trust their state governments to handle state problems and 38 percent who trust the national government to handle domestic problems.[22]

States appear to be reversing their traditional role of resisting change and protecting the status quo. Lately, for example, they have taken the lead on environmental policy. Many policies to address climate change—including the development of renewable energy sources, carbon emissions limits, and carbon cap-and-trade programs—have been advocated at the state level.[23] States have also taken a lead role on health care

federal preemptions
Impositions of national priorities on the states through national legislation that is based on the Constitution's supremacy clause.

With the No Child Left Behind Act, the Bush administration increased the national government's power over education. This law was replaced by the Every Student Succeeds Act in 2015, which provides more flexibility to states to meet the needs of their students. #NCLB #edreform

competitive federalism
A form of federalism in which states compete to attract businesses and jobs through the policies they adopt.

99

Crucial to understanding federalism in modern day America is the concept of mobility, or "the ability to vote with your feet." If you don't support the death penalty and citizens packing a pistol—don't come to Texas. If you don't like medicinal marijuana and gay marriage, don't move to California.

—**Rick Perry,** former Texas governor

policy, immigration, same-sex marriage, and stem-cell research. However, this willingness to fight back in recent years has not always been for progressive causes. Indeed, with the Republican gains in the 2010 midterm elections and the influence of the Tea Party movement, many states have been attempting to curb national power and protect their more conservative policies in a broad range of areas, including land use, gun control, immigration, and health care. For example, Kansas and Montana passed laws holding that federal gun laws do not apply to guns that are manufactured in their states (and making it a felony to try to enforce those laws).[24]

Many of these state laws will not stand up in federal court. Indeed, the Montana gun law has already been struck down. But the laws are clearly a reflection of state frustration with assertions of federal power.

States have one important advantage over the national government when it comes to experimenting with new policies: their numbers. There are 50 states potentially trying a mix of different policies—another reason that advocates of state-centered federalism see the states as the proper repository of government power. In this view, such a mix of policies produces **competitive federalism**—competition among states to provide the best policies to attract businesses, create jobs, and maintain a healthy social fabric.[25] Supporters point out that competitive federalism is also a check on tyranny because people will "vote with their feet"—that is, move to a different state—if they do not like a given state's policies. One advocate of this view argues that it "disciplines government and forces the states to compete for the citizens' business, talents, and assets," which makes government act more like a free market.

But competitive federalism can also create a "race to the bottom" as states compete in a negative way. For example, when states compete for businesses and jobs they may do so by eliminating more environmental or occupational regulations than would be desirable. Likewise, a priority to keep taxes low may lead to cuts in benefits to those who can least afford it, such as welfare or Medicaid recipients.[26] Thus, while competitive federalism provides citizens with a broad range of choices about the type of government they prefer, it also can be a source of political conflict over the national direction of policy.

Fighting for states' rights: the role of the modern Supreme Court

Just as the Supreme Court played a central role in defining the boundaries of dual federalism in the nineteenth and early twentieth centuries and in introducing a more nation-centered cooperative federalism in the late 1930s, today's Court is once again reshaping federalism. But this time, the move is decidedly in the direction of state power.

The Tenth Amendment The Tenth Amendment ensures that all powers not delegated to the national government are reserved to the states or to the people. Interestingly, the amendment has had little significance except during the early 1930s and in the recent era.

Forty years ago, a leading text on the Constitution said that the Tenth Amendment "does not alter the distribution of power between the national and state governments. It adds nothing to the Constitution."[27] To understand why, consider the following example. State and local governments have always controlled their own public schools. Thus, public education is a power reserved to the states under the Tenth Amendment. However, a state law concerning public education is void if it conflicts with the Constitution or with a national law based on an enumerated power. For example, a state could not compel an 18-year-old to attend school if the student had been drafted to serve in the army. Under the Tenth Amendment, the constitutionally enumerated national power to "raise and support armies" would trump the reserved state power to support public education. This view supporting the primacy of national government power was validated as recently as 1985, when the Supreme Court ruled that Congress had the power to impose a national minimum wage law on state governments, even if this was an area of traditional state power.[28]

But times change. With the appointment of three conservative justices in the 1980s who favored a stronger role for the states, the Court started to limit Congress's reach. One technique has been to require that Congress provide an unambiguous statement of its intent to overrule state authority when issuing legislation that does so.

The Fourteenth Amendment The Fourteenth Amendment was intended to give the national government control over the potentially discriminatory laws of southern states after the Civil War. Section 1 guarantees that no state shall make or enforce any law depriving any person of "life, liberty, or property, without due process of law" or denying any person the "equal protection of the laws." Section 5 empowers Congress "to enforce" those guarantees by "appropriate legislation."

The Supreme Court narrowly interpreted the Fourteenth Amendment in the late nineteenth century, severely limiting Congress's ability to affect state policy. However, throughout most of the twentieth century the Court interpreted Section 5 to give Congress broad discretion to pass legislation to remedy bad state laws. For example, discriminatory application of literacy tests prevented millions of African Americans from voting in the South before Congress passed the Voting Rights Act in 1965. As part of the federalism revolution of the 1990s, the Court started to chip away at Congress's Fourteenth Amendment powers.

An important case in 1997 established a new standard to justify **remedial legislation**—national legislation that fixes discriminatory state law—under Section 5, saying: "There must be a congruence and proportionality between the injury to be prevented or remedied and the means adopted to that end."[29] In one application of the new standard, the Court struck down the portion of the ADA that applied to the

> 99
>
> **State sovereignty is not just an end in itself: "Rather, federalism secures to citizens the liberties that derive from the diffusion of sovereign power."**
>
> **—Justice Anthony Kennedy**

remedial legislation
National laws that address discriminatory state laws. Authority for such legislation comes from Section 5 of the Fourteenth Amendment.

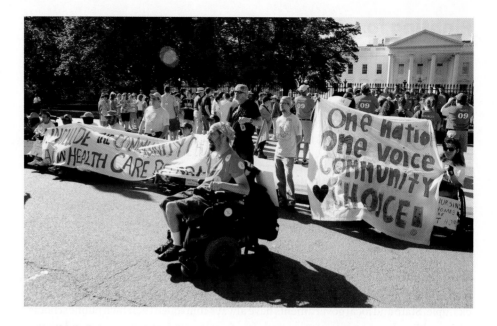

The Americans with Disabilities Act of 1990 requires that public accommodations and commercial facilities be accessible, but recent Supreme Court rulings have held that the law does not apply to most state and local government buildings. Here, activists for the disabled community are shown in front of the White House lobbying for stronger legislation. #ADA #EEOC #BecauseOfTheADA

states, saying that "[s]tates are not required . . . to make special accommodations for the disabled."[30]

In 2013 the Court demonstrated that it would stick up for states' rights even when the issue concerned race. In striking down an important part of the Voting Rights Act, the Court established a new principle of "equal sovereignty" in saying that Congress had placed an unfair burden on the states (see Table 3.2).[31] The key point here is that laws passed by Congress cannot violate a state's sovereignty in a broad range of cases.

The Commerce Clause Another category of cases leading to more state power concerns the commerce clause of the Constitution. A significant recent Court case that limited Congress's commerce powers involved the Gun-Free School Zones Act of 1990, which made it a federal offense to have a gun within 1,000 feet of a school. Congress assumed that it had the power to pass this legislation, given the Court's previously expansive interpretation of the commerce clause, even though it concerned a traditional area of state power. Although it was a stretch to claim that carrying a gun in or around a school was related to interstate commerce, Congress could have demonstrated the point by showing that (1) most guns are made in one state and sold in another (thus commercially crossing state lines); (2) crime affects the economy and commerce; and (3) the quality of education, which is also crucial to the economy, is harmed if students and teachers are worrying about guns in their schools. However, members of Congress did not present this evidence because they did not think it was necessary.

Alfonso Lopez, a high school senior, was arrested for carrying a concealed handgun with five bullets in it. Lopez moved to dismiss the charges, arguing that the law was unconstitutional because carrying a gun in a school could not be regulated as "interstate commerce." The Court agreed in *United States v. Lopez*.[32] If Congress wanted to encroach on the states' turf in the future, the Court indicated, Congress would have to demonstrate that the law in question was a legitimate exercise of the commerce clause powers.

As a result, the next time Congress passed legislation that affected law enforcement at the state level, it documented the impact on interstate commerce. The Violence

TABLE
3.2

Recent Important Supreme Court Decisions on Federalism

Case	Holding and Significance for States' Rights	Direction of the Decision
Gregory v. Ashcroft (1991)	The Missouri constitution's requirement that state judges retire by age 70 did not violate the Age Discrimination in Employment Act.	More state power
United States v. Lopez (1995)	Carrying a gun in a school did not fall within "interstate commerce"; thus, Congress could not prohibit the possession of guns on school property.	More state power
Seminole Tribe v. Florida (1996)	The Court used the Eleventh Amendment to strengthen states' sovereign immunity, ruling that Congress could not compel a state to negotiate with Native American tribes about gaming and casinos.	More state power
City of Boerne v. Flores (1997)	The Court struck down the Religious Freedom Restoration Act as an overly broad attempt to curtail the state-sponsored harassment of religion, saying that national legislation aimed at remedying states' discrimination must be "congruent and proportional" to the harm.	More state power
United States v. Morrison (2000)	The Court struck down part of the Violence Against Women Act, saying that Congress did not have the power under the commerce clause to provide a national remedy for gender-based crimes.	More state power
Alabama v. Garrett (2001)	The Court struck down the portion of the ADA that applied to the states, saying that state governments are not required to make special accommodations for the disabled.	More state power
Nevada Department of Human Resources v. Hibbs (2003)	The Court upheld Congress's power to apply the 1993 Family Leave Act to state employees as "appropriate legislation" under Section 5 of the Fourteenth Amendment.	Less state power
United States v. Bond (2011)	The Court upheld an individual's right to challenge the constitutionality of a federal law under the Tenth Amendment.	More state power
National Federation of Independent Business v. Sebelius (2012)	The Court upheld most provisions of the ACA but struck down the expansion of Medicaid as an unconstitutional use of coercive federalism (states could voluntarily take the additional funding to cover the expansion, but they would not lose existing funds if they opted out).	Mixed
United States v. Windsor (2013)	The Court held that Section 3 of DOMA was unconstitutional because it denied federal benefits to same-sex couples who were legally married under state law.	More state power
Shelby County v. Holder (2013)	The Court struck down Section 4 of the Voting Rights Act on the grounds that it violated the "equal sovereignty" of the states.	More state power

Against Women Act was passed in 1994 after weeks of testimony and evidence showing the links between violence against women and commerce. Nevertheless, the Supreme Court subsequently ruled that Congress did not have the power under the commerce clause to make a national law that gave victims of gender-motivated violence the right to sue their attackers in federal court (however, the Court struck down only that part of the law; the program funding remained unaffected).[33]

The Lopez decision struck down the 1990 Gun-Free School Zones Act, ruling that Congress did not have the power to forbid people to carry guns near schools. After the shooting of 12 students and one teacher at Columbine High School in Jefferson County, Colorado, on April 20, 1999, there were renewed calls nationwide for strengthening gun control laws.

> [A] state may, if its citizens choose, serve as a laboratory; and try novel social and economic experiments without risk to the rest of the country.
>
> —Justice Louis Brandeis, 1932

The significance of such rulings is enormous. Not only has the Court set new limits on Congress's ability to address national problems (the "congruence and proportionality" test), but it has also clearly stated that the Court alone will determine which rights warrant protection by Congress. However, the Court does not consistently rule against Congress; it often rules against the states because of broader constitutional principles or general public consensus behind a specific issue. For example, the Court has struck down state laws limiting gay rights as a violation of the equal protection clause of the Fourteenth Amendment[34] and has upheld Congress's power to regulate marijuana over states that had attempted to allow its medical use.[35] And while the Court rejected the commerce clause as the constitutional justification for national health care reform, it did uphold the ACA based on Congress's taxing power.[36]

Based on these and other cases, some would argue that the shift in power toward the states has been relatively marginal. Furthermore, the national government still has the upper hand in the balance of power and can readily blunt the impact of a Court decision: First, Congress can pass new laws to clarify its legislative intent and can overturn any cases that involve statutory interpretation. Second, Congress can use its financial power to impose its will on the states. So, for example, Congress could pass a law stating that before a state could receive money from the federal government related to the relevant law it would have to agree to abide by the ADA or the Age Discrimination in Employment Act. Thus, while the Supreme Court has limited Congress's power under the commerce clause, Congress still may induce states to act according to its policy goals. However, as noted earlier, there are new limits on budgetary coercion. In the health care reform case, the Court ruled that the threat to withhold Medicaid funds was a "gun to the head" of states,[37] meaning states did not have a real choice. This was the first time the Court limited Congress's coercive budgetary power over the states, and the boundaries of the new limits will have to be decided in future cases.

Assessing federalism today

From protecting individual liberty to allowing states to be "laboratories of democracy" in policy innovation, there is much to recommend federalism as a cornerstone of our political system. However, there are disadvantages as well, such as inefficiency in the policy process and inequality in policy outcomes. How does federalism in the United States fare from a twenty-first-century perspective?

Ideological Complexities Historically, issues concerning federalism have seemed to break down along traditional liberal and conservative lines. Liberals generally favor strong national power to fight discrimination, and they push for progressive national policies on issues such as protecting the environment, providing national health care, and supporting the poor. Conservatives, in contrast, tend to favor limited intrusion from the national government and allowing the states to decide their own mix of social welfare and regulatory policies.

However, in recent years the tables have turned, and in many cases liberals today are arguing for states' rights while conservatives are advocating the virtues of uniform national laws. On a broad range of new issues, such as medical use of marijuana, gay rights, cloning, and aid in dying, state governments are passing socially liberal legislation.[38] And the Court's earlier, state-centered rulings give it little precedent for striking down these laws. The Court's current conservative majority will have to either continue applying its state-centered federalism and uphold these liberal state laws or strike them down on ideological grounds, which would undermine the Court's credibility (see the Take a Stand feature).

Advantages of a Strong Role for the States The advantages of a strong role for the states can be summarized in four main points: states can be laboratories of democracy, state and local government is closer to the people, states provide more access to the political system, and states provide an important check on national power.

The first point refers to the role that states play as the source of policy diversity and innovation. If many states are trying to solve problems creatively, they can complement the efforts of the national government. Likewise, successful policies first adopted at the state level often percolate up to the national level. Welfare reform, health care, and environmental policy are key areas in which states have innovated.

Second, government that is closer to the people encourages participation in the political process and is responsive to their needs. Local politicians know better what their constituents want than further-removed national politicians do. On the one hand, if voters want higher taxes to pay for more public benefits, such as public parks and better schools, they can enact these changes at the state and local levels. On the other hand, if they prefer lower taxes and fewer services, local politicians can be responsive to those desires. There is strong evidence that "statehouse democracy" is at work: more liberal states enact more liberal policies and conservative states have more conservative policies. State policy is also responsive to state public opinion across different policy areas.[39] In addition, local government provides a broad range of opportunities for direct involvement in politics, from working on local political campaigns to attending school board or city council meetings. When citizens are able to directly affect policies, they are more likely to get involved in the political process.

Third, our federalist system provides more potential paths to address problems. For example, the court system allows citizens to pursue complaints under

DID YOU KNOW?

Owing to a state program signed by then-governor Mitt Romney, and similar to Obamacare, only

3%

of people in Massachusetts don't have health insurance. Nineteen percent of Texans do not have health insurance—the highest percentage in the nation.
Source: Census.gov

In the debate over health care reform and the Affordable Care Act, supporters of nationalized health care argued the federal government could do a better job than the patchwork of state policies to ensure that all Americans receive sufficient care. #ACA #Obamacare

HEALTH CARE FOR AMERICA NOW!

www.healthcareforamericanow.org

TAKE A STAND

Medical Marijuana and Aid in Dying

Should Congress be able to tell a state that it cannot allow the use of medical marijuana? Can the U.S. attorney general interpret a congressional law as prohibition of aid in dying? The debate over the balance of state and national power has grown increasingly complicated in the past several years. The courts have played a larger but inconsistent role, and issues of states' rights have increasingly cut across normal ideological and partisan divisions. Since the mid-1990s, the Supreme Court has played a central role in the shift of power to the states, but two cases involving medical marijuana (*Gonzales v. Raich*, 2005) and aid in dying—or assisted suicide, as it was called at the time of the decision (*Gonzales v. Oregon*, 2006)—show how the typical debate between national and state power can change when a moral dimension is introduced.

In both cases, state voters supported liberal policies. In 1996, California voters passed the Compassionate Use Act, by 56 to 44 percent. This law allowed seriously ill Californians, typically AIDS and cancer patients, to use marijuana as part of their medical treatment with the permission of a doctor. Oregon voters approved the Death with Dignity Act twice, the second time by a margin of 60 to 40 percent. This law allows physicians to prescribe a lethal drug dose for terminally ill patients who wish to end their lives. Both of these states' laws were challenged in federal court in classic confrontations between the states' rights and national power perspectives. Surprisingly, the Supreme Court ruled against medical marijuana and in favor of assisted suicide. (This summary oversimplifies the legal arguments, but these were the bottom-line outcomes.) If you were on the Court, how would you have ruled?

The states should decide these issues.

Unlike many of the cases discussed in this chapter, the states' rights position in these cases represented the liberal perspective, rather than the conservative position typically associated with state-centered federalism. Social liberals tended to support both the medical marijuana law and the assisted suicide law. However, if you examine these cases in terms of the question of federal versus state power, the traditional liberal and conservative perspectives are reversed: conservatives tend to favor state power, but that would put them on the socially liberal side of these issues. That is, if you support this side of the issue, you would be a states' rights conservative and a social liberal.

Congress should be able to tell the states what to do.

If you endorse this side of the debate, that Congress should have the power to regulate medical marijuana and assisted

Federal drug enforcement agents raid a medical marijuana club.

suicide, you would be taking the socially conservative and national-power liberal position. In sorting out which side you take, you should consider which is more important to you—taking a consistent position on state versus national power or just figuring out which specific policy you support, regardless of whether the national or state government gets to call the shots.

As it turns out, the Court wasn't consistent on the question of federalism: in the medical marijuana case, the Court upheld Congress's power to regulate the medical use of marijuana under the Controlled Substances Act. But in the assisted suicide case, the Court said that under that same congressional law the U.S. attorney general did not have the power to limit the drugs that doctors in Oregon could prescribe for aid in dying.

Despite the Court's endorsement of Congress's power to regulate medical marijuana, the actual situation is more complex because of the evolving federal position on enforcing the law. Initially, the Obama administration said it would not enforce the federal law in states that had legalized or decriminalized medical marijuana. But then the Drug Enforcement Administration (DEA) shifted course, cracking down on large medical marijuana dispensaries, saying that the drug had become widely available for recreational use, not just medical use. Congress responded in 2014 by passing a law denying funds to the DEA to crack down on dispensaries.[a] However, the DEA continues to enforce federal law in the eight states that have legalized all uses of marijuana. The struggle between the national and state governments is likely to continue on this issue in the foreseeable future.

take a stand

1. As a matter of policy, should doctors be able to prescribe marijuana to alleviate pain? Should they be able to prescribe lethal drugs to terminally ill patients?

2. Do you tend to support a state-centered or nation-centered perspective on federalism? Now revisit your answers to question 1. Are your positions more consistent with your views on federalism or with your policy concerns?

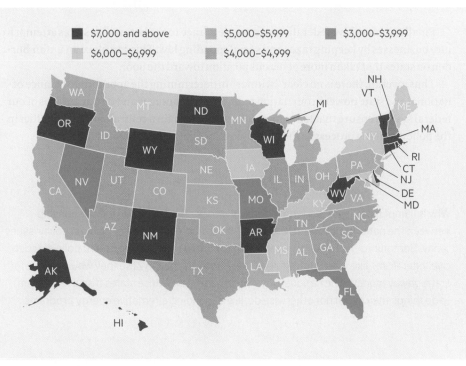

FIGURE 3.1

State Spending per Person

Spending per person varies dramatically by state. What are some of the advantages and disadvantages of living in a low-spending state or in a high-spending state? What type of state would you rather live in? Why?

Source: State and Local Government Finance Data Query System, http://slfdqs. taxpolicycenter.org (accessed 10/17/16).

Legend: $7,000 and above · $6,000–$6,999 · $5,000–$5,999 · $4,000–$4,999 · $3,000–$3,999

either state or federal law. Likewise, cooperative federalism can draw on the strengths of different levels of government to solve problems.

Finally, federalism provides a check on national tyranny. Competitive federalism ensures that Americans have a broad range of social policies, levels of taxation and regulation, and public services to choose from (see Figure 3.1). When people "vote with their feet" by deciding whether to move and where to live, they encourage healthy competition among states that would be impossible under a unitary government.

Disadvantages of Too Much State Power A balanced assessment of state and national power must acknowledge that there are problems with a federalist system that gives too much power to the states. The disadvantages include unequal distribution of resources across the states, unequal protection for civil rights, and competitive federalism that produces a "race to the bottom."

One problem of giving too much responsibility to the states is the huge variation in the distribution of resources. Without federal funding, poor states simply cannot provide an adequate level of benefits because they have the greatest needs but the lowest incomes—a situation that leads to significant disparities in important areas such as public education. The resource problem becomes more acute in dealing with national-level problems that are intractable at the local or state level. For example, pollution spills across state lines and the deteriorating public infrastructure, like the highway system, crosses state boundaries. Solving such problems individually would vastly outstrip the resources of state and local governments.[40]

The second problem, unequal civil rights protection, is evident in various federalism cases that have passed before the Supreme Court. These clearly show that states are not uniformly willing to protect the civil liberties and civil rights of their citizens. This was critically important during the 1950s and 1960s when the national government forced southern states to end segregation and passed laws outlawing discrimination in housing, employment, transportation, and voting. The Supreme Court recently stepped in to provide equal rights to marry, but states vary a great deal in terms of antidiscrimination laws based on sexual orientation. Without national laws, there will continue to be large differences in the levels of protection against discrimination based on age, disability, and sexual orientation.

Finally, competitive federalism can create a "race to the bottom" as states attempt to lure businesses by keeping taxes and social spending low. This can place an unfair burden on states that take a more generous position toward the poor.

Thus, overall, there is no clear "winner" in determining the appropriate balance of national and state power in our nation today. The advantages and disadvantages of our federal system ensure that federalism will always remain a central source of conflict in the policy-making process as the various levels of government fight it out.

"Why Should I Care?"

Why is it important to understand federalism today? The nature of the relationship between the national government and the states has a huge impact on most policy issues today. Sometimes the national government can force states to implement policies (coercive federalism), like when states raised their drinking ages to 21 so they wouldn't lose federal highway money. The national government may also entice states (fiscal federalism) to do things they might not otherwise do, like expanding alternative energy programs.

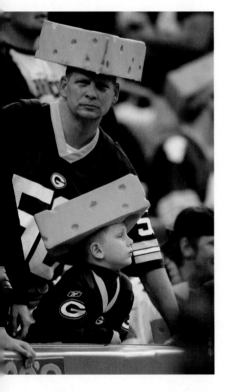

One of the strengths of federalism is that it allows regional diversity to flourish. Green Bay Packers fans proudly wear their cheesehead hats at Lambeau Field, showing that what passes for normal behavior in one part of the country would be viewed differently in other areas. #PackersNation

Conclusion

Alexis de Tocqueville, a French observer of American politics in the early nineteenth century, noted the tendency of democratic governments to centralize. This is especially true during wartime or times of crisis, as in the aftermath of the September 11 attacks, but it is also true during normal political times.

The health care reform example at the beginning of this chapter also illustrates the incentive to govern from Washington instead of the states. Passing a single piece of legislation was a much more efficient way to provide health insurance for more than 30 million Americans than attempting to get each state to pass similar legislation. This scenario occurs again and again across many issues and creates a powerful centralizing force. Within that pattern of centralization, however, there have been lengthy periods when states' rights held sway over the national government. And even when laws are passed at the national level, states often play a vital role in their implementation, as with Obamacare.

This evolving balance of power between the national government and the states obscures a broader reality of federalism: we are citizens of several levels of government simultaneously. One leading scholar of American federalism says that the basic question of federalism involves choices about how many communities we will be.[42] If you asked most people in our nation about their primary geopolitical community, they would probably not say "I am a Montanan" or "I am an Arizonan"; most would likely say "I am an American." Yet we have strong attachments to our local communities and state identities. Most Texans would not be caught dead wearing a Styrofoam cheesehead, but thousands of football fans in Green Bay, Wisconsin, regularly don the funny-looking things to watch their beloved Packers. We are members of multiple communities, a fact that has had an indelible impact on our political system.

STUDY GUIDE

What is federalism and why does it matter?

Define *federalism* and explain its significance. (Pages 58–60)

Summary

A federal system simultaneously allocates power to both the state and federal governments, while a confederal system gives power only to the states, and a unitary government gives power only to the federal government.

Key terms

federalism (p. 58)
sovereign power (p. 58)
police powers (p. 59)
concurrent powers (p. 59)
unitary government (p. 60)
confederal government (p. 60)
intergovernmental organizations (p. 60)

Practice Quiz Questions

1. **What system of government did the Articles of Confederation establish?**
   a. unitary
   b. federal
   c. confederal
   d. monarchy
   e. dictatorship

2. **Which is an example of a concurrent power?**
   a. printing money
   b. building roads
   c. conducting elections
   d. declaring war
   e. establishing post offices

Balancing national and state power in the Constitution

Explain what the Constitution says about federalism. (Pages 60–63)

Summary

The framers of the Constitution wanted a federal government that was stronger than under the Articles of Confederation, but they also wanted to preserve the autonomy of the states. While the state governments have considerable power in our system, the Founders ultimately favored the federal government in the Constitution, so that the federal government's powers superseded those of the states in the event of a conflict.

Key terms

full faith and credit clause (p. 62)
privileges and immunities clause (p. 62)

Practice Quiz Questions

3. **States' rights are protected in which constitutional provisions?**
   a. the Ninth Amendment
   b. the Tenth Amendment
   c. Article I of the Constitution
   d. Article III of the Constitution
   e. the First Amendment

4. **Which of the following would be best explained by the Tenth Amendment?**
   a. Congress increasing the minimum wage to $10 an hour
   b. the California state legislature declaring it was going to create its own navy
   c. state and local control over education policy
   d. the Supreme Court's recent decisions in same-sex marriage cases
   e. the Environmental Protection Agency passing a new regulation on carbon emissions that applies to all 50 states

The evolving concept of federalism

Trace the major shifts in state and federal government power over time. (Pages 63–71)

Summary

The relationship between the state and federal governments has changed dramatically over time. Whereas the federal and state governments traditionally operated with little interaction under the era of dual federalism, the trend over the past 80 years has been one of increasing federal interaction with state governments to address particular policy areas.

Key terms

states' rights (p. 64)
dual federalism (p. 65)
cooperative federalism (p. 70)
picket fence federalism (p. 70)

5. **Which analogy best describes the federalism arrangement today?**
   a. layer cake federalism
   b. marble cake federalism
   c. picket fence federalism
   d. gumbo federalism
   e. dual federalism

6. **Which case bolstered the federal government's power over the states?**
   a. *United States v. Lopez*
   b. *McCulloch v. Maryland*
   c. *Dred Scott v. Sandford*
   d. *Mapp v. Ohio*
   e. *Shelby County v. Holder*

7. **When did the federal government begin cooperating with the states on policy goals?**
   a. 1890s
   b. 1930s
   c. 1950s
   d. 1970s
   e. 1990s

Federalism today

Describe the major trends and debates in federalism today. (Pages 71–83)

Summary

Today's federal structure offers a complex mix of all previous components of federalism: some elements of national supremacy combine with states' rights for a varied federal landscape. While the federal and state governments still exercise cooperative federalism to achieve joint policy goals, the federal government has utilized coercive federalism to impose federal priorities on the states without offering compensation. However, in several recent cases the Supreme Court has ruled in favor of the states, limiting federal power.

Key terms

fiscal federalism (p. 71)
categorical grants (p. 72)
block grants (p. 72)
unfunded mandates (p. 72)

coercive federalism (p. 74)
federal preemptions (p. 75)
competitive federalism (p. 76)
remedial legislation (p. 77)

8. **Which form of revenue sharing is given to the states by the federal government with explicit conditions on how it is to be allocated?**
   a. block grant
   b. categorical grant
   c. general revenue sharing
   d. federal mandates
   e. tax refund

9. **Ronald Reagan's efforts to increase states' rights led to an increase in _____.**
   a. block grants
   b. categorical grants
   c. federal taxes
   d. federal mandates
   e. state taxes

10. **The imposition of national priorities on the states through congressional legislation and imposition of the national supremacy clause is called _____.**
    a. cooperative federalism
    b. dual federalism
    c. competitive federalism
    d. federal preemption
    e. remedial legislation

11. **A state would usually challenge the constitutionality of a federal law under which of the following amendments?**
    a. Eighth Amendment
    b. Tenth Amendment
    c. Thirteenth Amendment
    d. Fourteenth Amendment
    e. First Amendment

12. **The Court has recently overturned a number of congressional laws rooted in the _____.**
    a. national supremacy clause
    b. reserve clause
    c. establishment clause
    d. commerce clause
    e. free exercise clause

Suggested Reading

Banks, Christopher P., and John C. Blakeman. *The U.S. Supreme Court and New Federalism: From the Rehnquist to the Roberts Court*. Lanhan, MD: Rowman & Littlefield, 2012.

Beer, Samuel. *To Make a Nation: The Rediscovery of American Federalism*. Cambridge, MA: Harvard University Press, 1993.

Conlan, Timothy. *From New Federalism to Devolution: Twenty-Five Years of Intergovernmental Reform*. Washington, DC: Brookings Institution, 1998.

Derthick, Martha. *Keeping the Compound Republic: Essays on American Federalism*. Washington, DC: Brookings Institution, 2001.

Elkins, Stanley, and Eric McKitrick. *The Age of Federalism: The Early American Republic, 1788-1800*. New York: Oxford University Press, 1993.

Grodzins, Martin. *The American System: A New View of Government in the United States*. Chicago: Rand McNally, 1966.

LaCroix, Alison L. *The Ideological Origins of American Federalism*. Cambridge, MA: Harvard University Press, 2010.

Manna, Paul. *School's In: Federalism and the National Education Agenda*. Washington, DC: Georgetown University Press, 2006.

McDonald, Forrest. *States' Rights and the Union: Imperium in Imperio, 1776-1876*. Lawrence: University Press of Kansas, 2000.

Nagel, Robert F. *The Implosion of American Federalism*. New York: Oxford University Press, 2001.

Peterson, Paul E. *The Price of Federalism*. Washington, DC: Brookings Institution, 1995.

Posner, Paul L. *The Politics of Unfunded Mandates: Whither Federalism?* Washington, DC: Georgetown University Press, 1998.

Scheberle, Denise. *Federalism and Environmental Policy: Trust and the Politics of Implementation*, 2nd ed. Washington, DC: Georgetown University Press, 2004.

4

Civil Liberties

It's a free country ... right?

The constitutional protections for religious freedom are clear and strong: "Congress shall make no law respecting an establishment of religion, or prohibiting the free exercise thereof." But what happens when one person's religious beliefs collide with another person's constitutional right? Shortly after the Supreme Court upheld the constitutionality of same-sex marriage for all Americans, a county clerk in Rowan County, Kentucky, Kim Davis, refused to provide marriage licenses to same-sex couples because of her religious beliefs. Davis described herself as a "soldier for Christ" and said, "I am confident that God is in control of all of this!"

The issue came to a head when a district court judge, David Bunning, appointed to the bench by President George W. Bush, sentenced Davis to jail for five days, saying that public officials are not allowed to pick which laws and court orders they obey: "We expect at the end of the day for the court's orders to be complied with. That's how things work here in America."[1] After she got out of jail, Davis continued to refuse to put her name on the marriage licenses but did issue them. Late in 2015, the newly elected governor, Matt Bevin, issued an executive order saying the county clerks did not have to put their names on the licenses. Governor Bevin issued his order "to ensure that the sincerely held religious beliefs of all Kentuckians are honored."[2] However, same-sex couples were able to be married.

In general, religious beliefs do not provide legal grounds for discrimination. For example, a religious belief that women should not work outside the home would not provide the basis for refusing to hire a woman. The same applies to discrimination based on race, ethnicity, or sexual orientation. However, the Supreme Court recently ruled that a "closely held" private corporation could not be forced to provide contraception to women under the Affordable Care Act (ACA) if there was a "less restrictive" means available to have the insurance provide it. This was the first time that a corporation, Hobby Lobby, was given First Amendment protections based on the religious beliefs of the owners of the corporation. Family Research Council president Tony Perkins said, "The Supreme Court has delivered one of the most significant victories for religious freedom in our generation."[3] The American Civil Liberties Union had a very different view, saying: "This is a deeply

Should freedom of religious expression be
protected even when acting on those views
means discriminating against someone
else? In general, discrimination based on
religious views is not allowed, but Rowan
County Clerk of Courts Kim Davis served
time in jail for contempt of court after
refusing a court order to issue marriage
licenses to same-sex couples.

Civil Liberties　**89**

troubling decision. For the first time, the highest court in the country has said that business owners can use their religious beliefs to deny their employees a benefit that they are guaranteed by law."[4] This is fundamentally a clash of whose rights are at stake—the owners of the corporation with their specific religious beliefs or the employees who want their health insurance to pay for contraception.

Is this how civil liberties work? Unfortunately, yes, it is messy and complicated figuring out what our liberties and freedoms actually mean. Even central freedoms such as the freedom of speech, the press, and religious practices are subject to limitations if there are threats to national security or public safety or if these freedoms conflict with another fundamental right (such as the right to marry). Simply put, civil liberties are not absolute. How should political actors draw the lines between protected behavior and actions that may be regulated? People say that America is a free country, but are there limits to those freedoms?

★

DEFINE *CIVIL LIBERTIES* AND EXPLAIN HOW THE BILL OF RIGHTS CAME TO APPLY TO THE STATES

civil liberties
Basic political freedoms that protect citizens from governmental abuses of power.

Defining civil liberties

The terms "civil rights" and "civil liberties" are often used interchangeably, but there are some important differences (see Nuts & Bolts 4.1). To oversimplify a bit, **civil liberties** are about freedom and civil rights are about equality. (For more on this distinction, see Chapter 5.)

Civil liberties are deeply rooted in our key idea that politics is conflictual and that it involves trade-offs. When the Supreme Court rules on civil liberties cases, it must balance an individual's freedom with the government's interests and the public good. For example, in the war on terrorism the government must balance civil liberties with national security. Many Americans have been concerned that government surveillance invades people's privacy and that the treatment of suspected terrorists violates due process rights.[5] At the same time, most Americans would probably agree that in some instances these measures might be warranted. For example, if a nuclear device were set to detonate in Manhattan in three hours few would insist on protecting the civil liberties of someone who knew where the bomb was hidden. Once we recognize that our freedoms are not absolute, it becomes a question of how they are balanced against other interests, such as national security, public safety, and public health.

⬡

NUTS & BOLTS 4.1

Distinguishing Civil Liberties from Civil Rights

Civil Liberties	Civil Rights
Basic freedoms and liberties	Protection from discrimination
Rooted in the Bill of Rights and the "due process" protection of the Fourteenth Amendment	Rooted in laws and the "equal protection" clause of the Fourteenth Amendment
Primarily restrict what the government can do to you ("*Congress* shall make no law . . . abridging the freedom of speech")	Protect you from discrimination both by the government and by individuals

Along with balancing competing interests, court rulings must also draw the lines to define the limits of permissible conduct by the government or by an individual in the context of a specific civil liberty. For example, despite the First Amendment's protection of freedom of speech, it is obvious that some speech absolutely cannot be permitted. The classic example is falsely yelling "fire!" in a crowded theater. Therefore, the courts must interpret the law to draw the line between protected speech and impermissible speech. The same challenge applies to other civil liberties such as the establishment of religion, freedom of the press, freedom from illegal searches, or other due process rights (see How It Works: The First Amendment).

Courts define the boundaries of civil liberties, but the other branches of government and the public often get involved as well. The earliest debates during the American Founding illustrate the broad public involvement concerning the basic questions of how our civil liberties would be defined: Should government be limited by an explicit statement of individual liberties? Would these limitations apply to the state governments or just the national government? How should these freedoms evolve as our society changes? As we will see in this section, interpretations of these constitutional protections have changed over time.

How can conflicts be resolved between civil liberties and other legitimate interests, such as public safety and public health? Sometimes freedom is forced to give way. Courts have upheld bans on the religious practice of snake handling and laws requiring the Amish to display reflective triangles when driving slow-moving buggies on public roads, despite religious objections to doing so.

Origins of the Bill of Rights

Originally, the Constitution provided very limited protection of civil liberties: a guarantee of habeas corpus rights (a protection against illegal incarceration) and a prohibition of bills of attainder (legislation punishing someone for a crime without the benefit of a trial) and ex post facto laws (laws that retroactively change the legal consequences of some behavior). There were a few attempts to include a broader statement of civil liberties, including one proposed by George Mason and Elbridge Gerry five days before the Constitutional Convention adjourned, but their motion to appoint a committee to draft a bill of rights was rejected. Charles Pinckney and Gerry also tried to add a provision protecting the freedom of the press, but that too was rejected.[6]

Mason and Gerry opposed ratification of the Constitution partly because it did not include a bill of rights, and many Antifederalists echoed this view. Some states ratified the Constitution but urged Congress to draft specific protections for individuals' and states' rights from federal action. (They believed that protection of civil liberties from

How it works: in theory

The First Amendment

The First Amendment states:
"Congress shall make no law respecting an establishment of religion, or prohibiting the free exercise thereof; or abridging the freedom of speech, or of the press; or the right of the people peaceably to assemble, and to petition the government for a redress of grievances."

Freedom of Expression

Freedom of Religion

Freedom of Assembly

Freedom to Petition the Government

Freedom of the Press

Freedom of Speech

Establishment
The government cannot establish an official state religion or favor one religion over others.

Free Exercise
The government cannot prevent people from practicing their religion.

@user
!!!!!!
Less protected forms of speech

Political speech and symbolic speech

Balancing Interests and Drawing Lines: Government and Religion

While the different branches of the First Amendment on the opposite page are an accurate representation of the various aspects of our religious and expressive freedoms, in practice, the implementation of these civil liberties is more complicated.

Free Exercise:

When she refused...

When county clerk Kim Davis **refused to issue marriage licenses to same-sex couples,**

They said no.

the court ruled that her religious convictions **did not allow her to discriminate.**

Here's why.

In cases like these, **courts must balance religious freedom against other state interests,** such as freedom from discrimination.

Critical Thinking

1. **Balancing interests can be tricky. Consider these two scenarios** in which competing interests are in play: Company policy restricts employees from wearing political T-shirts or buttons at work. A pharmacist denies birth control pills to a customer for religious reasons. Which (if either) do you think should be allowed? Why did you select the one(s) you did?

2. **Drawing lines for a given civil liberty** can also be difficult. What if Kim Davis, instead of refusing to issue marriage licenses to same-sex couples, wore a necklace with a large crucifix at work? Should that be allowed? Or, consider a different scenario: Should Congress be able to start its sessions with a prayer? Reference the First Amendment and its interpretations in your answer.

Establishment Clause:

Banned.

Since 1962 the Supreme Court has **banned school prayer as a violation of the establishment clause.**

What about...?

But does the separation of church and state also apply to town board members who **start their meetings with a prayer?** In 2014, the Court decided by a 5–4 vote that it did not.

It's tough.

The establishment clause often asks courts to **draw lines between what type of religious conduct is allowed** and what would be considered an "excessive entanglement" between church and state.

In some cases,

the free exercise and establishment clauses are in tension with one another. For example, while the establishment clause prohibits school-sponsored prayer, the free exercise clause guarantees that any student can pray at any time in school on their own, **as long as they are not bothering others.**

The Bill of Rights: A Statement of Our Civil Liberties

First Amendment	Freedom of religion, speech, press, and assembly; the separation of church and state; and the right to petition the government.
Second Amendment	Right to bear arms.
Third Amendment	Protection against the forced quartering of troops in one's home.
Fourth Amendment	Protection from unreasonable searches and seizures; requirement of "probable cause" for search warrants.
Fifth Amendment	Protection from forced self-incrimination or double jeopardy (being tried twice for the same crime); no person can be deprived of life, liberty, or property without due process of law; private property cannot be taken for public use without just compensation; and no person can be tried for a serious crime without the indictment of a grand jury.
Sixth Amendment	Right of the accused to a speedy and public trial by an impartial jury, to an attorney, to confront witnesses, to a compulsory process for obtaining witnesses in his or her favor, and to counsel in all felony cases.
Seventh Amendment	Right to a trial by jury in civil cases involving common law.
Eighth Amendment	Protection from excessive bail, excessive fines, and cruel and unusual punishment.
Ninth Amendment	The enumeration of specific rights in the Constitution shall not be construed to deny other rights retained by the people. This has been interpreted to include a general right to privacy and other fundamental rights.
Tenth Amendment	Powers not delegated by the Constitution to the national government, nor prohibited by it to the states, are reserved to the states or to the people.

state actions should reside in state constitutions.) In other states, the Antifederalists who lost the ratification battle continued making their case to the public and Congress.

Madison and other supporters of the Constitution agreed that the 1st Congress would take up the issue, despite their reservations that a Bill of Rights could lead the people into falsely believing that it was an exhaustive list of all their rights. State conventions submitted 124 amendments for consideration. That list was whittled down to 17 by the House and then to 12 by the Senate. This even dozen was approved by the House and sent to the states, which in 1791 ratified the 10 amendments that became the Bill of Rights (see Nuts & Bolts 4.2).[7] Despite the document's profound significance, one point limited its reach: it applied only to the national government, not to the states. This decision proved consequential because the national government was quite weak for the first half of our nation's history. Given that the states exercised at least as much power over people's lives as the national government, it would have been more important for the Bill of Rights to limit the states rather than the federal government, but this did not occur.

The Supreme Court used the Bill of Rights only once before 1866 to invalidate a federal action—in the infamous *Dred Scott* case that contributed to the Civil War (see Chapter 3).

Civil War amendments
The Thirteenth, Fourteenth, and Fifteenth Amendments to the Constitution, which abolished slavery and granted civil liberties and voting rights to freed slaves after the Civil War.

Selective incorporation and the Fourteenth Amendment

The significance of the Bill of Rights increased somewhat with ratification of the Fourteenth Amendment in 1868. It was one of the three **Civil War amendments** that attempted to guarantee the newly freed slaves equal rights as citizens of the United States. (The other two Civil War amendments were the Thirteenth, which abolished slavery, and the Fifteenth, which gave male former slaves the right to vote.) Northern politicians were concerned that southerners would deny basic rights to the former slaves, so the sweeping language of the Fourteenth Amendment was adopted. Section 1 of the Fourteenth Amendment says:

> *All persons born or naturalized in the United States, and subject to the jurisdiction thereof, are citizens of the United States and of the State wherein they reside. No State shall make or enforce any law which shall abridge the privileges or immunities of citizens of the United States; nor shall any State deprive any person of life, liberty, or property, without due process of law; nor deny to any person within its jurisdiction the equal protection of the laws.*

This language sought to ensure that states would not deny newly freed slaves the full protection of the law.[8] The **due process clause**, which forbids any state from denying "life, liberty, or property, without due process of law," led to an especially important expansion of civil liberties because the Supreme Court had previously interpreted a similar clause in the Fifth Amendment to apply only to the federal government.

Despite the clear language of the amendment saying that "no State shall make or enforce any law," in its first opportunity to interpret the Fourteenth Amendment in 1873 the Court continued to rule in favor of protecting states from national government actions only, embracing the "dual citizenship" idea set forth in *Barron v. Baltimore*.[9] Over the next 50 years, a few justices tried mightily to interpret the Fourteenth Amendment to protect civil liberties against state government action, culminating in the 1925 case *Gitlow v. New York*.[10] Here the Court said for the first time that the Fourteenth Amendment incorporated one of the amendments in the Bill of Rights and applied it to the states. The case involved Benjamin Gitlow, a radical socialist convicted under New York's Criminal Anarchy Act of 1902 for advocating the overthrow of the government. The Court upheld his conviction, arguing that his writings were the "language of direct incitement," but it also warned state governments that there were limits on such suppression of speech.

Over the ensuing decades, most civil liberties covered in the Bill of Rights were applied to the states on a right-by-right, case-by-case basis through the Fourteenth Amendment. However, this process of **selective incorporation** was not smooth and incremental. Rather, it progressed in surges with flurries of activity in the 1930s and the 1960s (see Table 4.1). As a result, the Bill of Rights has evolved from the nineteenth century's limitations that affected only national government action to a robust set of widespread protections for freedom and liberty today.

due process clause
Part of the Fourteenth Amendment that forbids states from denying "life, liberty, or property" to any person without due process of law. (A nearly identical clause in the Fifth Amendment applies only to the national government.)

selective incorporation
The process through which the civil liberties granted in the Bill of Rights were applied to the states on a case-by-case basis through the Fourteenth Amendment.

"Why Should I Care?"

Today the Bill of Rights is one of the most revered and important parts of the Constitution. But it didn't start out that way. Initially, the Bill of Rights only applied to the national government, not the states. But through the Fourteenth Amendment and the process of selective incorporation, the Supreme Court has gradually applied the Bill of Rights to the states. While all levels of government must respect our civil liberties today, there are many unresolved areas in terms of balancing interests and drawing lines. Do religious beliefs allow a county clerk to deny a marriage license to a same-sex couple? How do we balance our freedom of speech or freedom from illegal searches with the need for national security? These are central questions in today's politics.

TABLE 4.1

Selective Incorporation

The process of applying the Bill of Rights to the states progressed in two stages. The first, coming in the 1920s and 1930s, applied the First Amendment to the states; the second came a few decades later and involved criminal defendants' rights.

Amendment	Issue	Case
First Amendment	Freedom of speech	*Gitlow v. New York* (1925)
	Freedom of the press	*Near v. Minnesota* (1931)
	Freedom of assembly	*De Jonge v. Oregon* (1937)
	Right to petition the government	*Hague v. CIO* (1939)
	Free exercise of religion	*Hamilton v. Regents of the University of California* (1934); *Cantwell v. Connecticut* (1940)
	Separation of church and state	*Everson v. Board of Education of Ewing Township* (1947)
Second Amendment	Right to bear arms	*McDonald v. Chicago* (2010)
Fourth Amendment	Protection from unreasonable search and seizure	*Wolf v. Colorado* (1949); *Mapp v. Ohio* (1961)*
Fifth Amendment	Protection from forced self-incrimination	*Malloy v. Hogan* (1964)
	Protection from double jeopardy	*Benton v. Maryland* (1969)
Sixth Amendment	Right to a public trial	*In re Oliver* 333 U.S. 257 (1948)
	Right to a fair trial and an attorney in death-penalty cases	*Powell v. Alabama* (1932)
	Right to an attorney in all felony cases	*Gideon v. Wainwright* (1963)
	Right to an attorney in cases involving jail time	*Argersinger v. Hamlin* (1972)
	Right to a jury trial in a criminal case	*Duncan v. Louisiana* (1968)
	Right to cross-examine a witness	*Pointer v. Texas* (1965)
	Right to compel the testimony of witnesses who are vital for the defendant's case	*Washington v. Texas* (1967)
Eighth Amendment	Protection from cruel and unusual punishment	*Robinson v. California* (1962)[†]
	Protection from excessive bail	*Schilb v. Kuebel* (1971)[‡]
Ninth Amendment	Right to privacy and other nonenumerated, fundamental rights	*Griswold v. Connecticut* (1965)[§]

Not Incorporated

Third Amendment	Prohibition against the quartering of troops in private homes	
Fifth Amendment	Right to indictment by a grand jury	
Seventh Amendment	Right to a jury trial in a civil case	
Eighth Amendment	Prohibition against excessive fines	

Wolf v. Colorado applied the Fourth Amendment to the states (which meant that states could not engage in unreasonable searches and seizures); *Mapp v. Ohio* applied the exclusionary rule to the states (which excludes the use in a trial of illegally obtained evidence).

[†]Some sources list *Louisiana ex rel. Francis v. Resweber* (1947) as the first case that incorporated the Eighth Amendment. While the decision mentioned the Fifth and Eighth Amendments in the context of the due process clause of the Fourteenth Amendment, this argument was not included in the majority opinion that upheld as constitutional the bizarre double electrocution of prisoner Willie Francis (the electric chair malfunctioned on the first attempt but was successful on the second attempt; see Abraham and Perry, *Freedom and the Court*, pp. 71–72).

[‡]Justice Blackmun "assumed" in this case that "the Eighth Amendment's proscription of excessive bail [applies] to the states through the Fourteenth Amendment," but later decisions did not seem to share this view. However, Justices Stevens and O'Connor agreed with Blackmun's view in *Browning-Ferris v. Kelco Disposal* (1989). Some sources argue that the excessive bail clause of the Eighth Amendment is unincorporated.

[§]Justice Goldberg argued for explicit incorporation of the Ninth Amendment in a concurring opinion joined by Justices Warren and Brennan. The opinion of the Court referred more generally to a privacy right rooted in five amendments, including the Ninth, but did not explicitly argue for incorporation.

Freedom of religion

The First Amendment has two parts that deal with religion: the **establishment clause**, which has been interpreted to mean that Congress cannot sponsor or endorse any particular religion, and the **free exercise clause**, which has been interpreted to mean that Congress cannot interfere in the practice of religion unless there are important secular reasons for doing so. Essentially, the former says that Congress should not *help* religion and the latter that it should not *hurt* religion. The establishment clause is primarily concerned with drawing lines. For example, does a prayer at a public high school football game or a Nativity scene on government property constitute state sponsorship of religion? The free exercise clause has more to do with balancing interests, such as balancing public safety concerns against snake handling in religious services and the use of Amish buggies on public highways.

The combination of the establishment and free exercise clauses results in a general policy of noninterference and government neutrality toward religion. As Thomas Jefferson said in 1802, the First Amendment provides a "wall of eternal separation between church and state." This language continues to be cited in Court cases[11] in which religion and politics intersect. Since both areas carry great moral weight and emotional charge, the boundaries of religious expression remain difficult to draw, as the case of Kim Davis and same-sex marriage demonstrated.

The establishment clause and separation of church and state

Determining the boundaries between church and state—the central issue of the establishment clause—is very difficult. We know that the Founders did not want an official state religion or for the government to favor one religion over another, but beyond that it's hard to say. Jefferson's "wall of eternal separation" has been cited in Court decisions that prohibit state aid for religious activities, but lately the Court has been displaying a more "accommodationist" perspective that sometimes allows religious activity in public institutions.

School Prayer The issue of prohibition of prayer in public schools exploded onto the political scene in 1962 when the Court ruled in *Engel v. Vitale* that a prayer written by the New York Board of State Regents and read every day in the state's public schools violated the separation of church and state.[12] Banning the prayer caused a public outcry protesting the perceived attack on religion.

Over the next 50 years, Congress repeatedly tried, unsuccessfully, to amend the Constitution to allow school prayer. Meanwhile, the Court continued to take a hard line on school-sponsored prayer. In 1985, the Court struck down the practice of observing a one-minute moment of silence for "meditation or voluntary prayer" in the Alabama public schools.[13] More recently, the Court said that benedictions or prayers at public school graduations and a school policy that allowed an elected student representative to lead a prayer at a high school football game also violated the establishment clause. The former established a strong "coercion test" that prohibited prayers that may appear to be voluntary (students are not required to attend their high school graduation) but in effect are compulsory.[14] Yet the Court has upheld the practice of opening every session of Congress with a prayer, has let stand without comment a lower-court ruling that allowed a prayer that was planned and led by students (rather than being school policy)

establishment clause
Part of the First Amendment that states "Congress shall make no law respecting an establishment of religion," which has been interpreted to mean that Congress cannot sponsor or favor any religion.

free exercise clause
Part of the First Amendment that states that Congress cannot prohibit or interfere with the practice of religion.

> ❞
>
> **The number, the industry, and the morality of the Priesthood, & the devotion of the people have been manifestly increased by the total separation of the Church from the State.**
>
> **—James Madison**

at a high school graduation, and in 2014 upheld prayers by voluntary chaplains for town board meetings in Greece, New York.[15] The latter case was especially significant because the town meetings included residents, unlike the previously approved legislative prayers that were intended for the elected leaders.[16]

Aid to Religious Organizations The Court has had an even more difficult time determining principles to govern aid to religious organizations, either directly, through tax dollars, or indirectly, through the use of public space. One early attempt was known as the **Lemon test**, after one of the parties in a 1971 case involving government support for religious schools (*Lemon v. Kurtzman*). Here the justices ruled that a practice violated the establishment clause if it (1) did not have a "secular legislative purpose," (2) either advanced or inhibited religion, or (3) fostered "an excessive government entanglement with religion."[17] The third part of the test was later found open to interpretation by lower courts and therefore led to conflicting rulings.

The Court started to move away from the Lemon test in a 1984 case involving a city-owned crèche that was displayed in a park owned by a nonprofit corporation. The Court allowed the Nativity display, saying: "The Constitution does not require complete separation of church and state; it affirmatively mandates accommodation, not merely tolerance, of all religions, and forbids hostility toward any."[18] This "endorsement test" simply says that government action is unconstitutional if a "reasonable observer" would think that the action either endorses or disapproves of religion. Later rulings upheld similar religious displays, especially if they conformed to what observers have labeled the "three plastic animals rule"—if the baby Jesus is surrounded by Rudolph the red-nosed reindeer and other secular symbols, the overall display is considered sufficiently nonreligious to pass constitutional muster.[19]

The Court has also applied the accommodationist perspective to funding for religious schools by looking more favorably on providing tax dollars to students' families to subsidize tuition costs rather than funding parochial schools directly. In 2011, the Court expanded taxpayer support for religious education when it upheld an Arizona law that provides state tax credits for contributions to organizations that provide tuition for religious schools.[20] The Court has also ruled that it is acceptable to use federal funds to buy computers and other educational equipment to be used in public and private schools for "secular, neutral, and nonideological programs"[21] and tax dollars for a sign language interpreter for a deaf student who attended a parochial school.[22]

The free exercise clause

While the freedom of belief is absolute, freedom of religious conduct cannot be unrestricted. That is, you can believe whatever you want without government interference, but if you *act* on those beliefs the government may regulate your behavior. And while the government has restricted religious conduct in dozens of cases, the freedom of religion has been among the most consistently protected civil liberties.

Hundreds of cases have come before the Court in the area of the free exercise of religion. Here are some examples of the questions they addressed[23]: May Amish parents be forced to send their children to schools beyond the eighth grade? (no); Is animal sacrifice as part of a religious ceremony protected by the First Amendment? (generally yes); May Mormons have multiple wives? (no); May the Amish be compelled to follow traffic laws and put license plates on their buggies? (yes); May people be forced to work on Friday night and Saturday if those are their days of worship? (no); May religious dress

Lemon test
The Supreme Court uses this test, established in *Lemon v. Kurtzman*, to determine whether a practice violates the First Amendment's establishment clause.

Can a cross be displayed on federal land? The Supreme Court has ruled that religious displays on government property must be part of larger, secular displays. This cross on federal land in the Mojave Desert was covered up after it became controversial. Now it looks like a sign.

Demonstrators rally outside of the U.S. Supreme Court during oral arguments in the 2014 Hobby Lobby case. The court ruled that a for-profit corporation may exclude contraceptives from their employees' health insurance, which is otherwise entitled by federal law, based on the religious objections of the corporation's owners. #TeamLife

be regulated? (generally no, but in some contexts, such as the military, yes). Keep in mind that this list is not exhaustive.

One case had broad implications that defined the general basis for government restrictions of religious expression. The Court ruled that the state of Oregon had not violated the free exercise clause in denying unemployment benefits to the plaintiffs in the case who were fired for using peyote as part of a religious ceremony. The broader significance of the ruling came with the Court's announcement of a new interpretation of the free exercise clause: the government does not need a "compelling interest" in regulating a particular behavior to justify a law that limits a religious practice.[24] In other words, after this decision it would be easier for the government to limit the exercise of religion because the Court would no longer require a "compelling" reason for the restrictions but rather demonstration that the legislation was a "neutral law of general applicability."

Congress responded by passing the Religious Freedom Restoration Act (RFRA) in 1993, reinstating the need to demonstrate a "compelling state interest" before limiting religious freedoms. After several cases and congressional actions, the Court made it clear that it would have the final word in deciding when a compelling interest is required in order to limit religious practice.[25] The Court relied on this standard in the controversial 2014 case discussed in the chapter opener involving the family-owned Hobby Lobby stores.[26]

Would you, or do you, send your children to religious schools? Should the government pay for it? If you attend a public college or university, should it be allowed to organize a prayer before a football or basketball game? These questions, and more, are at the heart of the controversies around religious freedoms—one of the most deeply personal freedoms debated today.

"Why Should I Care?"

Freedom of speech, assembly, and the press

As noted earlier, defining the scope of our civil liberties depends on balancing interests and drawing lines. This is especially true of the First Amendment's freedom of speech, which can best be envisioned on a continuum from most to least protected types of speech based on the Supreme Court cases that have tested their limits.

Generally protected expression

Any time you attend a religious service or a political rally, post a Tweet, write a blog post or letter to the editor, or express a political idea, you are being protected by the First Amendment. However, the nature of this protection is continually evolving due to political forces and shifting constitutional interpretations. Only recently have the courts developed a complex continuum ranging from strongly protected political speech to less-protected speech.

Standards for Protection The basis for the continuum of protected speech is rooted in the content of the speech. Typically, the Court does not allow content-based regulation of speech (unless it falls into one of the categories of exceptions we discuss later). For example, in 1972 the Court struck down a local ordinance that banned picketing outside of schools except for labor picketing.[27] This ordinance was deemed to be content-based regulation because it favored one form of speech (from labor unions) over others. Such regulation is subject to the **strict scrutiny** standard of judicial review, which means the regulation must be narrowly tailored (that is, the least restrictive means) to serve a compelling state interest. In most cases, this means that the speech will be protected and the regulation struck down. If a regulation is "content neutral" and does not favor any given viewpoint, then it is subject to the less demanding **intermediate scrutiny** standard. This means that the government must demonstrate only a substantial interest, the interest must be unrelated to the content of the speech, and there must be alternative opportunities for communication.[28]

strict scrutiny
The highest level of scrutiny the courts can use when determining whether a law is constitutional. To meet this standard, the law or policy must be shown to serve a "compelling state interest" or goal, it must be narrowly tailored to achieve that goal, and it must be the least restrictive means of achieving that goal.

intermediate scrutiny
The middle level of scrutiny the courts can use when determining whether a law is constitutional. To meet this standard, the law or policy must be "content neutral," must further an important government interest in a way that is "substantially related" to that interest, and must use means that are a close fit to the government's goal and not substantially broader than is necessary to accomplish that goal.

Political Speech Freedom of speech got off to a rocky start when Congress passed the Alien and Sedition Acts in 1798. The controversial Sedition Act made it a crime to "write, print, utter or publish . . . any false, scandalous and malicious writing or writings against the government of the United States." Supporters of the acts claimed they were necessary to strengthen the national government in response to the French Revolution, but in reality they were an attempt by the governing Federalist Party to neutralize the opposition—the Democratic-Republican Party. The outcry against the laws helped propel Thomas Jefferson to the presidency in 1800. Jefferson pardoned those who had been convicted under the law (mostly newspaper editors), Congress repealed one of the acts in 1802, and the others were allowed to expire before the Supreme Court had a chance to rule them unconstitutional.

In the twentieth century, World War I prompted the harshest crackdowns on free speech since the Sedition Act of 1798. The most important case from this period involved the general secretary of the Socialist Party, Charles Schenck, who opposed U.S. involvement in the war. He had printed a leaflet urging young men to resist the draft. Schenck was arrested, and he appealed all the way to the Supreme Court, arguing that the First Amendment permitted him to protest the war and urge others to resist the draft. But the Court sustained his conviction, noting that free speech is not an absolute right:

> *The most stringent protection of free speech would not protect a man in falsely shouting fire in a theatre and causing a panic. . . . The question in every case is whether the words used are used in such circumstances and are of such a nature as to create a clear and present danger that they will bring about the substantive evils that Congress has a right to prevent.*[29]

This **clear and present danger test** meant that the government could suppress any speech it thought was dangerous—in this instance, preventing the government from fighting the war. However, critics of the decision argue that Schenck's actions were not dangerous for the country and should have been allowed.[30]

Over the next several decades, the Court struggled to draw the line between dangerous speech and words that were simply unpopular. Then, in 1969, the Court established a strong protection for free speech that still holds today. This case involved a Ku Klux Klan leader who made a threatening speech at a cross-burning rally that was subsequently shown on television. Twelve hooded figures were shown, many with weapons. The speech said that "revengence [*sic*]" might be taken if "our president, our Congress, our Supreme Court continues to suppress the white, Caucasian race." It continued, "We are marching on Congress July the Fourth, four hundred thousand strong." The Klan leader was convicted under an Ohio law banning "sabotage, violence, or unlawful methods of terrorism as a means of accomplishing industrial or political reform," but the Court unanimously reversed his conviction, arguing that threatening speech could not be suppressed just because it sounded dangerous. Specifically, the **direct incitement test** holds that speech is protected "except where such advocacy is directed to inciting or producing imminent lawless action and is likely to incite or produce such action."[31] Under this new standard, *Schenck* and many other previous sedition convictions would have been overturned.

Perhaps the strongest example of protecting unpopular speech comes from the case of the Westboro Baptist Church (WBC). Since 2005, members of the WBC have protested at hundreds of funerals of members of the armed services who were killed in Iraq and Afghanistan. However, these are not typical antiwar protests. Instead, the protesters claim that the troops' deaths were God's punishment for "the homosexual lifestyle of soul-damning, nation-destroying filth." The church and its members have drawn strong reactions and counterprotests for their confrontational approach at the military funerals, including their use of signs that say "God Hates Fags," "Thank God for Dead Soldiers," "God Killed Your Sons," and "God Hates America." Critics, including many veterans groups and attorneys general from 48 states, argue that the protests should not be considered protected speech under the First Amendment. The Veterans of Foreign Wars issued a statement saying: "In a time of profound grief and emotional vulnerability, these personal attacks are an affront of the most egregious kind." However, in 2011 the Supreme Court ruled 8–1 that the WBC's protests were protected speech.[32]

Symbolic Speech The use of signs, symbols, or other unspoken acts or methods to communicate in a political manner—**symbolic speech**—enjoys many of the same protections as regular speech. For example, during the Vietnam War the Court protected the right of a protester to wear an American flag patch sewn on the seat of his pants,[33] a high school student's right to wear an armband to protest the war,[34] and an individual's right to tape a peace symbol on the flag and fly it upside down outside an apartment window.[35]

A 1989 case provided the strongest protection for symbolic speech yet, overturning a flag desecration law in Texas on the grounds that symbolic political speech is protected

clear and present danger test
Established in *Schenck v. United States*, this test allows the government to restrict certain types of speech deemed dangerous.

direct incitement test
Established in *Brandenburg v. Ohio*, this test protects threatening speech under the First Amendment unless that speech aims to and is likely to cause imminent "lawless action."

"

Restriction of free thought and free speech is the most dangerous of all subversions. It is the one un-American act that could most easily defeat us.

—Supreme Court Justice William O. Douglas, 1952

symbolic speech
Nonverbal expression, such as the use of signs or symbols. It benefits from many of the same constitutional protections as verbal speech.

💡

DID YOU KNOW?

75%

of black Americans and 25 percent of white Americans view the Confederate battle flag primarily as a symbol of racism.
Source: ORC International

by the First Amendment.[36] In response to this unpopular decision, Congress passed the Flag Protection Act of 1989, which the Court also struck down as an unconstitutional infringement on political expression.[37] Congress then attempted six times to pass a constitutional amendment to overturn the Court decision, but each time the measure failed in the Senate.

Money as Speech Spending money in political campaigns may also be protected by the First Amendment, since it provides the means for more conventional types of political speech. Here the question is whether the government can control campaign contributions and spending for a broader public purpose such as controlling corruption, or whether such laws violate the First Amendment rights of candidates or their supporters. You probably have heard the old saying "Money talks," which implies that money is speech. Given the importance of advertising in modern campaigns, limitations on raising and spending money could limit the ability of candidates and groups to reach voters with their message. The Court has walked a tightrope on this one, balancing the public interest in honest and ethical elections and the First Amendment rights of candidates and their advocates. The Court has upheld individual candidates' right to spend their own money in federal elections, but presidential candidates give up that right if they accept federal campaign funds (taxpayers' money) in a presidential election. Also, candidates in federal elections are subject to limits on the types and size of contributions they can receive, and they must report all contributions and spending to the Federal Election Commission.[38]

The Bipartisan Campaign Reform Act, which went into effect for the 2004 elections, included a "Millionaires' Amendment" that lifted restrictions on campaign contributions for candidates whose opponent spent more than $350,000 of his or her own money in the election. This attempt to level the campaign finance playing field was struck down by the Supreme Court in 2008 as a violation of wealthy candidates' First Amendment rights.[39] In 2010, the Court also extended First Amendment rights to corporations and labor unions that want to spend money on campaign ads.[40] In 2014, the Court struck down aggregate limits placed on individual contributions.[41] However, the Court upheld a ban on unlimited "soft money" contributions because they have the most potential for corruption.[42]

📷

The American flag is a popular target for protesters: it has been spat upon, shredded, turned into underwear, and burned. Here, protesters burn a U.S. flag as they march through downtown Washington, D.C., following the Ferguson, Missouri, grand jury's decision not to indict Officer Darren Wilson for the shooting death of Michael Brown. #BlackLivesMatter #Ferguson

Hate Speech Free speech has been a hot topic on many college campuses in the context of hate speech. Do people have a right to say things that are offensive or abusive, especially in terms of race, gender, and sexual orientation? By the mid-1990s, more than 350 public colleges and universities said no by regulating some forms of hate speech.[43] One example was a speech code adopted at the University of Michigan that prohibited "any behavior, verbal or physical, that stigmatizes or victimizes an individual on the basis of race, ethnicity, religion, sex, sexual orientation, creed, national origin, ancestry, age, marital status, handicap, or Vietnam veteran status" and "creates an intimidating, hostile, or demeaning environment for educational pursuits, employment or participation in University-sponsored extra-curricular activities."[44] Many of these speech codes were struck down in federal court, but late in 2015 the issue resurfaced on many college campuses. At Yale University, controversy erupted over the response of a residential college faculty administrator, Erika Christakis, to an e-mail students received cautioning them not to wear Halloween costumes that could be racially or culturally insensitive. Christakis wrote that universities no longer allowed students to be "a little bit inappropriate or provocative or, yes, offensive."[45] She resigned a few weeks later saying, " . . . the current climate at Yale is not, in my view, conducive to the civil dialogue and open inquiry required to solve our urgent societal problems."[46] The president at the University of Missouri also resigned after students, including the football team, said that he was racially insensitive and not open to their demands for a more inclusive and supportive environment on campus. President Obama weighed in on this issue largely on the free speech side, saying college students shouldn't be "coddled and protected from different points of view."[47]

Another significant issue combines the topics of symbolic speech and hate speech. For example, can a person who burned a cross on a black family's lawn be convicted under a city ordinance that prohibits conduct "arous[ing] anger, alarm, or resentment in others on the basis of race, color, creed, religion, or gender"? Or is the ordinance an unconstitutional limit on First Amendment rights? In this case, the Court said the cross burner could be punished for arson, terrorism, trespassing, or other violations of the law, but he could not be convicted under that particular city ordinance because it was overly broad and vague.[48] However, the Court has since upheld more carefully worded bans of cross burning.[49]

Internet hate speech has become increasingly controversial in recent years. Cyberbullying precipitated several suicides, and then in 2013 Facebook cracked down on offensive content that glorified violence against women, such as pages with headlines like "Violently Raping Your Friend Just for Laughs."[50] Facebook's "community standards" have a more restrictive definition of hate speech than is allowed by the direct incitement test. While Facebook makes a distinction between humor and serious speech, they "do not permit individuals or groups to attack others based on their race, ethnicity, national origin, religion, sex, gender, sexual orientation, disability or medical condition."[51] This led law professor Jeffrey Rosen to conclude "today, lawyers at Google, YouTube, Facebook, and Twitter have more power over who can speak and who can be heard than any president, judge, or monarch."[52] This may sound like hyperbole, but he is right: corporations are not restricted by the First Amendment (which, after all, says "*Congress* shall make no law . . ."). So if Facebook and other social media want to restrict hate speech, they can. While free speech advocates are concerned about restrictions on Internet hate speech, civil rights groups such as the Anti-Defamation League, the Leadership Conference on Civil Rights, and the National Organization of Women all support the move. Early in 2014, Congress got in on the act when 13 House Democrats proposed a bill that would mandate a study of how the Internet, cell phones, television, and radio are used to advocate and encourage violent acts and the commission of crimes of hate.[53]

hate speech
Expression that is offensive or abusive, particularly in terms of race, gender, or sexual orientation. It is currently protected under the First Amendment.

Freedom of Assembly The Supreme Court has consistently protected the right to assemble peaceably. Perhaps the most famous assembly case involved a neo-Nazi group that wanted to march in a suburb of Chicago whose population of 70,000 was nearly 60 percent Jewish. (And of those, many were Holocaust survivors.) The village passed ordinances that banned the group from marching, arguing that residents would be so upset by the Nazi marchers that they might become violent. But the lower courts did not accept this argument, ruling that if "the audience is so offended by the ideas being expressed that it becomes disorderly and attempts to silence the speaker, it is the duty of the police to attempt to protect the speaker, not to silence his speech."[54] Otherwise, the right to assemble would be restricted by a "heckler's veto."

Are laws banning hate speech constitutional? Sometimes yes, but the threshold is relatively high. These Ku Klux Klan members are free to hold rallies, preach racism and xenophobia, and burn crosses, as long as they do not directly incite violence or display an "intent to intimidate."

While broad protection is provided for peaceable assemblies, governments may regulate the time, manner, and place of expression as long as these regulations do not favor certain groups or messages over others. For example, anti-abortion protesters were not allowed to picket a doctor's home in Brookfield, Wisconsin. The Court ruled that the ordinance banning all residential picketing was content neutral and that there was a government interest in preserving the "sanctity of the home, the one retreat to which men and women can repair to escape from the tribulations of their daily pursuits."[55] "Time, manner, and place" restrictions also may be invoked for practical reasons. For example, if the Ku Klux Klan planned to hold a march around a football stadium on the day of a game, the local city council could deny them a permit and suggest they choose another day that would be more convenient. The legal standard for these regulations is that they are "reasonable." For example, in 2014 the Court ruled that a Massachusetts state law creating a 35-foot buffer zone around entrances to abortion clinics violated the First Amendment. While the buffer zone was content neutral, it was unreasonable because it was more restrictive than necessary to allow access to the clinics. While the "reasonableness" standard is vague, it allows the courts to balance the right to assemble against other practical considerations.

Freedom of the Press The task of balancing interests is central to many First Amendment cases involving the freedom of the press. The general issue here is **prior restraint**, the government's right to prevent the media from publishing (or, later, broadcasting) something of social or political significance. Prior restraint has never been

prior restraint
A limit on freedom of the press that allows the government to prohibit the media from publishing certain materials.

clearly defined by the Supreme Court, but several landmark cases have set a very high bar for applying it. One suit, brought in 1971 and known as the Pentagon Papers case, involved disclosure of parts of a top-secret report on internal planning for the Vietnam War. Ultimately, the Court decided that the government could not prevent publication of the Pentagon Papers, but at least five justices supported the view that under some circumstances the government could use prior restraint—though they could not agree on the standard.[56]

Recently, prior restraint has gained new significance in the war on terrorism. The media, especially the *New York Times*, skirmished with the Bush administration over publishing stories on classified programs, including taking suspected terrorists to foreign countries and torturing them, domestic surveillance, and the Terrorist Finance Tracking Program, which monitors all large financial transactions in the international banking system. The sensational leaking of more than 91,000 reports concerning the war in Afghanistan by WikiLeaks ratcheted up the stakes. Some members of Congress labeled the leaks "treason" and called for prosecution. However, supporters of an unrestrained press point to the Pentagon Papers case as precedent for the role of journalists in holding the government accountable. They argue that the conduct of war and programs such as warrantless wiretapping of U.S. citizens may violate international or domestic law and that the public has the right to know about them. None of these issues has yet to appear in a suit before the Supreme Court.

The forms of expression discussed in this section—speech, assembly, and press—all have strong protection from the First Amendment. The strongest protections are for content-based expression. However, there are exceptions, such as speech that directly incites an imminent danger. If the regulation is content neutral and does not favor one viewpoint over another, then it is easier to uphold. But even then, the government must have a substantial reason for limiting expression.

Less-protected speech and publications

Some forms of speech do not warrant the same level of protection as political speech because they do not contribute to public debate or express ideas that have important social value. Governments may more easily regulate four categories of such speech: fighting words, slander and libel, commercial speech, and obscenity.

Fighting Words Governments may regulate **fighting words**, "which by their very utterance inflict injury or tend to incite an immediate breach of the peace."[57] Such laws must be narrowly written; it is not acceptable to ban all foul language, and the prohibited speech must target a single person rather than a group. Moreover, the question of whether certain words provoke a backlash depends on the reaction of the targeted person. Inflammatory words directed at a pacifist would not be fighting words because he or she would turn the other cheek, whereas the same words yelled at a hothead *would* be fighting words because that individual would likely respond with violence. The Court has further clarified the test, based on "what persons of common intelligence would understand to be words likely to cause an average addressee to fight."[58]

Slander and Libel A more extensive line of cases prohibiting speech concerns **slander**, spoken false statements that damage someone's reputation, and **libel**, written statements that do the same thing. However, it is difficult to draw the line between permissible speech and slander or libel. The current legal standard distinguishes between speech about a public figure, such as a politician or celebrity, and speech about a regular person. It is much more difficult for public figures to prove libel because they must

Bradley Manning (center), whose job in the U.S. military gave him access to classified information, downloaded thousands of classified videos, diplomatic cables, reports, and other information and gave them to the website WikiLeaks.

> The freedom of the press is one of the greatest bulwarks of liberty, and can never be restrained but by despotic governments.
>
> —George Mason

fighting words
Forms of expression that "by their very utterance" can incite violence. These can be regulated by the government but are often difficult to define.

slander
Spoken false statements that damage a person's reputation. They can be regulated by the government but are often difficult to distinguish from permissible speech.

libel
Written false statements that damage a person's reputation. They can be regulated by the government but are often difficult to distinguish from permissible speech.

demonstrate that the defamatory statement was made with "actual malice" and "with knowledge that it was false or with reckless disregard of whether it was false or not."[59]

One of the most famous libel cases occurred when Reverend Jerry Falwell, a well-known televangelist and political activist, sued *Hustler* magazine for libel and emotional distress after the magazine published a parody of a liquor advertisement depicting him in a "drunken incestuous rendezvous with his mother in an outhouse" (this quote is from the Supreme Court case).[60] The Court ruled against Falwell, saying that public figures and public officials have to put up with such things and compared the parody to outrageous political cartoons, which have always been protected by the First Amendment.

Commercial Speech Commercial speech, which mostly refers to advertising, has evolved from having almost no protection under the First Amendment to enjoying quite strong protection by the 1970s. In a 1976 case, the Court struck down a law against advertising prescription drug prices and one prohibiting placing newspaper racks on city streets to distribute commercial publications such as real estate guides.[61] Another key decision in 1980 established a test that is still central today: the government may regulate commercial speech if it concerns an illegal activity, if the advertisement is misleading, or if regulating speech directly advances a substantial government interest and the regulation is not excessive. In practice, this test means that commercial speech can be regulated but that the government has to have a very good reason to do it.[62] Even public health concerns have not been allowed to override commercial speech rights. For example, the Court struck down a Massachusetts regulation that limited the content of advertisements aimed at children (the ban on R. J. Reynolds's Joe Camel character is the classic example) in a manner that was more restrictive than federal law.[63]

Obscenity One area in which the press has never experienced complete freedom involves the publication of pornography and material considered obscene. The difficulty arises in deciding where to draw the line. Nearly everyone would agree that child pornography should not be published[64] and that pornography should not be available to minors. However, beyond these points there is little consensus. For example, some people are offended by nude paintings in art museums, while others enjoy watching hard-core X-rated movies.

commercial speech
Public expression with the aim of making a profit. It has received greater protection under the First Amendment in recent years but remains less protected than political speech.

📷

Joe Camel peddles his wares on a New York City billboard. Commercial speech, as a general category, is not as strongly protected by the First Amendment as political speech, but advertising can be limited by the government only in specific circumstances.

Defining obscenity has proven difficult for the courts. In an often-quoted moment of frustration, Justice Potter Stewart wrote that he could not define obscenity, but "I know it when I see it."[65] The Supreme Court took a stab at it in 1973 in a case that gave rise to the **Miller test**, which is still applied today.[66] The test has three standards that must all be met in order for material to be banned as obscene: if it appeals to prurient interests; if it is "patently offensive"; and if the work as a whole lacks serious literary, artistic, political, or scientific value. The Court also clarified that *local* community standards are to apply rather than a single national standard.

Congress and the president also get in on the act of controlling obscenity. Recent efforts have focused on the Internet as a pornography medium. Congress passed the Communications Decency Act in 1996, which criminalized the use of any computer network to display "indecent" material, unless the provider could offer an effective way of screening out potential users under age 18. The Court struck down the law in 1997 because it was vague and because it is technically impossible to limit access to websites based on age. This ruling gives the Internet the same free speech protection as print.[67] But in 1998 Congress enacted the Child Online Protection Act, which prohibited commercial websites from distributing material that is "harmful to minors," using the Miller test to specify what this means. The law bounced around in federal courts for six years before the Supreme Court ultimately struck it down.[68]

Miller test
Established in *Miller v. California*, this three-part test is used by the Supreme Court to determine whether speech meets the criteria for obscenity. If so, it can be restricted by the government.

"Why Should I Care?"

Even if you are not a journalist, don't engage in political protest, or contribute to political campaigns, the freedom of speech, the press, and assembly still shapes the world around you. The "marketplace of ideas" ensures that policies are debated and a range of voices can be heard. Our political leaders are held accountable by the free exchange of ideas and a strong independent media that can criticize their actions. Also, other areas of your everyday life that you may not consider to be "speech," such as video games, are protected by the First Amendment.

The right to bear arms

★
EXPLORE WHY THE SECOND AMENDMENT'S MEANING ON GUN RIGHTS IS OFTEN DEBATED

Between 1791 and 2007, the Court issued only four rulings directly pertaining to the Second Amendment and the right to bear arms. The federal courts had always interpreted the Second Amendment's awkward phrasing—"A well regulated Militia, being necessary to the security of a free State, the right of the people to keep and bear Arms, shall not be infringed"—as a right to bear arms within the context of serving in a militia, rather than an individual right to own a gun.

Interest groups such as the National Rifle Association have long asserted that the Second Amendment guarantees an individual the right to bear arms. Critics of this view emphasize the first clause of the amendment and point to the frequent mentions of state militias in congressional debates at the time the Bill of Rights was adopted. They argue that the Second Amendment was adopted to reassure Antifederalist advocates of states' rights that state militias, not a national standing army, would provide national security. In this view, the national armed forces and the National Guard have made the Second Amendment obsolete.

DID YOU KNOW?

33,304

people were killed by guns in the United States in 2014 (the most recent year with complete data). About 60 percent of these deaths were from suicides.

Source: U.S. Centers for Disease Control

While the Constitution guarantees the individual right to bear arms (as shown by the woman taking target practice), the shootings at Umpqua Community College in Roseburg, Oregon, shocked the nation. In response, college students organized a demonstration on Capitol Hill urging Congress to vote on gun reform. #SecondAmendment #GunControl #GunSense

Before the Court's recent entry into this debate, Congress and state and local lawmakers had largely defined gun ownership and carrying rights, creating significant variation among the states. (Wyoming and Montana have virtually no restrictions on gun ownership, for example, whereas California and Connecticut have many.) However, following an assassination attempt on President Ronald Reagan in 1981 a push for stronger gun control laws intensified. In 1993, Congress passed the Brady bill, which mandates a background check and a five-day waiting period for any handgun purchase.

But not all gun tragedies lead to more gun control. In 2014 and 2015 there were 610 mass shootings, defined as incidents in which at least four people were killed or injured, not counting the shooter. By the FBI's definition—at least three people killed—there were 86 mass shootings in those two years, including those at San Bernardino, California, Charleston, South Carolina, and Roseburg, Oregon. In the deadliest mass shooting by a single gunman, 49 people were killed and 53 injured in June 2016 at an Orlando, Florida, nightclub. While in the past three years 41 states passed new "smart gun" laws, 19 states strengthened laws concerning mental health and gun ownership, and 5 passed laws restricting ownership of assault weapons, there were 12 states that expanded the places in which guns may be carried.[69]

In 2008, a landmark Supreme Court ruling recognized for the first time an individual right to bear arms for self-defense and hunting.[70] The decision struck down the District of Columbia's ban on handguns, while noting that state and local governments could enforce ownership restrictions, such as preventing felons or the mentally impaired from buying guns. The Court did not apply the Second Amendment to the states in this decision but did so two years later in striking down a gun control ordinance in Chicago, while reaffirming the ownership restrictions noted in the Washington, D.C., case.[71]

Given the strong public support for gun ownership (there are about 300 million privately owned guns in the United States) and the Supreme Court's endorsement of an individual right to bear arms, stronger gun control at the national level is highly unlikely (especially given the unsuccessful pushes after the shootings at Sandy Hook Elementary School in 2012 and Orlando, Florida, in 2016). Early in 2016 President Obama issued an executive order requiring all gun sales to be through federally licensed dealers who would conduct background checks.[72] In addition to this limited executive action, extensive litigation will be necessary to define the acceptable boundaries of gun control and to identify which state and local restrictions will be allowed to stand.

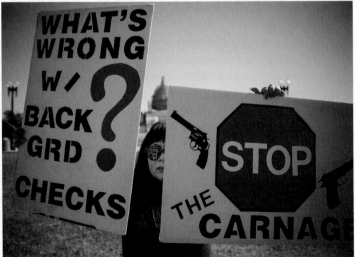

Law, order, and the rights of criminal defendants

Every advanced democracy protects the rights of people who have been accused of a crime. In the United States, the **due process rights** of the Fourth, Fifth, Sixth, and Eighth Amendments include the right to a fair trial, the right to consult a lawyer, freedom from self-incrimination, the right to know what crime you are accused of, the right to confront the accuser in court, and freedom from unreasonable police searches. Difficulties in applying these abstract principles to concrete situations indicate how hard it is to define due process, especially in a way that protects civil liberties without jeopardizing order.

The difference between abstract principles of due process and their specific application also raises difficult political questions. Most people endorse the principle of "due process of law" and general ideas such as requiring that police legally obtain any evidence used in court. However, when the Court applies these principles to protect the rights of criminal defendants there is a public outcry that too many suspects are going free on "legal technicalities" (such as having to inform a suspect of his or her right to talk to an attorney before being questioned by the police).

due process rights
The idea that laws and legal proceedings must be fair. The Constitution guarantees that the government cannot take away a person's "life, liberty, or property, without due process of law." Other specific due process rights are found in the Fourth, Fifth, Sixth, and Eighth Amendments, such as protection from self-incrimination and freedom from illegal searches.

The Fourth Amendment: unreasonable searches and seizures

The Fourth Amendment says: "The right of the people to be secure in their persons, houses, papers, and effects, against unreasonable searches and seizures, shall not be violated." Over the years, the Court has provided strong protections against searches within a person's physical space, typically defined as his or her home. With the introduction of new technology—telephones and wiretapping, then more sophisticated listening and searching devices—the Court has had to confront a broad array of complicated questions. It has attempted to achieve a balance between security and privacy by requiring court approval for search warrants, while carving out limited exceptions to this general rule (see the Take a Stand feature).

Searches and Warrants Under most circumstances, a law-enforcement official seeking a search warrant must provide the court with "personal knowledge" of a "probable cause" of specific criminal activity and outline the evidence that is the target of the search. Broad "fishing expeditions" for evidence are not allowed.

Police searches inherently involve a clash between public safety and the private freedom from government intrusions. These issues came to the fore with passage of the USA PATRIOT Act of 2001 after the terrorist attacks of September 11. Several of the most controversial parts of the act strengthen police surveillance powers; make it easier to conduct "sneak and peek" searches (the police enter a home with a warrant, look for evidence, and do not tell the suspect of their search until months later); broaden Internet surveillance; increase the government's access to library, banking, and medical records; and permit roving wiretaps for suspected terrorists.

Most police searches without warrants occur because suspects consent to being searched; officers are not required to tell a suspect that he or she may say no or request a warrant. Other cases in which the Court allows a warrantless search include conducting a search that happens at the time of a legal arrest and "is confined to the immediate vicinity of the arrest"; collecting evidence that was not included in the search warrant but is out in plain view; searching the passenger area and passengers of a car if the

Drug-Sniffing Dogs: An Illegal Search?

In 2013, the Supreme Court was presented with the case of Joelis Jardines, whom police suspected of growing marijuana inside his Miami home based on an anonymous tip. Police went to the home with a trained drug-detection dog. On the front porch, the dog gave a positive signal indicating the presence of drugs. The police returned with a search warrant, found a marijuana-growing operation, and arrested Jardines. However, the Florida Supreme Court threw out the evidence, arguing it was an illegal search. The case then made its way to the Supreme Court, which was faced with this question: Should drug-sniffing dogs be allowed outside a home without a warrant? More broadly, in the context of rapidly changing technology, what is the public's "reasonable expectation" for privacy? Take a stand.

A drug-sniffing dog is no more invasive than the surveillance technologies we encounter every day.
The Court has ruled that police do not need a search warrant to have drug-sniffing dogs search luggage at an airport or a car that has been stopped for a traffic violation unrelated to drugs. Lower courts have also ruled that sniffs are not considered searches in a hotel hallway, at a school locker, outside a passenger train's sleeper compartments, or outside an apartment door. Is a sniff outside someone's home any more invasive?

It might not seem that way, especially when you consider the reach of new surveillance methods that are on the horizon. Other technologies that are becoming more common or will be used soon include RFIDs (radio frequency identifications), which are the size of a grain of rice and transmit information wirelessly through radio waves; facial recognition software and iris scanners; "smart dust devices"—tiny wireless micromechanical sensors—that can detect light and movement; and drones, which have primarily been used for military purposes but also have vast potential for tracking suspects in any situation.

Warrantless surveillance of somebody's home crosses a line.
Lower courts have been split on whether drug-sniffing dogs may be used outside a home without a warrant, due, in part, to a Supreme Court precedent giving homes stronger Fourth Amendment protection than cars, lockers, or other areas. For example, in 2001 the Court ruled that police needed a warrant to use a thermal-imaging device outside a home when trying

to detect marijuana that was believed to be growing under heat lamps inside.

The U.S. Supreme Court ultimately agreed in the Jardines case, saying that there is a general expectation that anyone may come onto a front porch as long as the uninvited person simply knocks and then leaves if there is no answer. The majority opinion wryly noted: "Complying with the terms of that traditional invitation does not require fine-grained legal knowledge; it is generally managed without incident by the Nation's Girl Scouts and trick-or-treaters." But, they continued, "introducing a trained police dog to explore the area around the home in hopes of discovering incriminating evidence is something else. There is no customary invitation to do *that*."[a]

📷 Federal agents use a drug-sniffing dog to inspect a car.

New and future technologies continue to complicate the question of just what is "reasonable." Justice Alito raised this question in oral arguments in a Supreme Court case involving a GPS tracking device. He said, "Technology is changing people's expectations of privacy. . . . Maybe 10 years from now 90 percent of the population will be using social networking sites and they will have on average 500 friends and they will have allowed their friends to monitor their location 24 hours a day, 365 days a year, through the use of their cell phones. Then—what would the expectation of privacy be then?"[b]

take a stand

1. If you had to decide the case of the drug-sniffing dog, how would you have ruled? Do you think that homes should have stronger privacy expectations than cars or school lockers? Even when it concerns illegal drugs?

2. How would you answer Justice Alito's question about the expectation of privacy in an era of rapidly changing technology? When should law-enforcement officials have to get a warrant to monitor our behavior?

driver has been stopped for a traffic offense; and searching school lockers with probable cause.[73] The Supreme Court recently upheld strip searches after an arrest and before the suspect is put in jail even when there is no suspicion of illegal substances. Dissenting justices argued that "the humiliation of a visual strip-search" after being "arrested for driving with a noisy muffler, failing to use a turn signal and riding a bicycle without an audible bell" should not be allowed under the Fourth Amendment.[74]

In 2013, the Court ruled that a DNA swab of an arrested suspect is simply for identification and therefore is no more intrusive than a photograph or fingerprint. The late Justice Scalia, a strong defender of privacy rights, argued in his dissent that DNA evidence could be used to identify the arrestee as a suspect in an unrelated crime and therefore the standard of individualized suspicion should hold before the swab can be taken.

The Court has generally made it easier for law-enforcement officials to conduct searches without warrants, but two important decisions in the other direction were a 2014 case that required a warrant to search cell phones of people who are arrested[75] and a 2012 case that required a warrant to place a GPS tracking device on a vehicle. In the latter case, the FBI suspected Antoine Jones of selling cocaine, so they placed a tracking device on his vehicle without a warrant, monitored his movements for four weeks, and then used the evidence to convict him. Jones was sentenced to life in prison. While the Court required a warrant in this specific case, the basis for the majority's decision was fairly narrow: the placement of the device was a "physical trespass," and the lengthy monitoring of his movement constituted an illegal search.[76] Remote tracking without physical trespass or shorter-term monitoring with a GPS device without a warrant may be acceptable to the Court. Additional cases will be required to sort this out.

If the police illegally obtain evidence, the need to balance security and privacy becomes concrete. Either the evidence is excluded from a criminal trial to protect privacy rights or it is allowed in order to support conviction of the suspect.

The Exclusionary Rule In 1961, the Fourth Amendment was incorporated (applied to the states through the Fourteenth Amendment) in a case that established the **exclusionary rule** for all courts.[77] Previously, the rule, which states that illegally obtained evidence cannot be used in a criminal trial, had applied only at the national level. The landmark case involved police breaking into a woman's residence without a warrant to look for a suspect thought to be hiding there. The officers did not find the suspect, but they did find illegal pornographic material. Although the woman was convicted of possessing it, the Court ultimately threw out the conviction.

Subsequent Courts started weakening the exclusionary rule. For example, the Court established a "good faith exception" to the exclusionary rule, allowing evidence to be used as long as the officer believed that he or she had conducted a legal search. In the specific case, the officer had a warrant with the wrong address.[78] The bottom line is that the exclusionary rule remains in effect, but lately it has become easier for prosecutors to use evidence obtained under questionable circumstances.

Drug Testing Another area of Fourth Amendment law concerns drug testing. The clause granting people the right "to be secure in their persons" certainly seems to cover drug testing. However, the courts have long recognized the right of private companies to test their employees for illegal drugs, and testing for performance-enhancing drugs is increasingly common in professional sports.

What about drug testing by the state? The Court has upheld random drug testing for high school athletes and mandatory drug testing for any junior high or high school students involved in extracurricular activities.[79] Federal employees became subject to drug testing in 1986, with all employees required to refrain from using illegal drugs as a condition of federal employment and with each agency required to implement drug testing for sensitive positions. Two years later, the Drug-Free Workplace Act applied

exclusionary rule
The principle that illegally or unconstitutionally acquired evidence cannot be used in a criminal trial.

Can the police search your home without a warrant? After Dollree Mapp was arrested for possession of pornographic material, the case made its way to the Supreme Court and the search was ruled unconstitutional. This case established the exclusionary rule for evidence that is obtained without a warrant.

the same rule to all executive agencies, the uniformed services, and any service providers under contract with the federal government. Despite these prohibitions, drug testing of federal employees is actually limited to people who hold security clearances, carry firearms, or work in public safety or national security. Some employees receive random tests; others are tested only when they apply for a job, are involved in a workplace accident, or show signs of drug use.

The Court has upheld drug testing of public employees, with one exception. It struck down a Georgia law that would have required all candidates for state office to pass a drug test within 30 days of announcing a run for office, because candidates are not public employees.[80] Rather than appealing to the courts, former senator Ernest Hollings of South Carolina had a different approach to avoid drug testing. When his opponent, Representative Tommy Hartnett, challenged him to take a drug test, the senator shot back, "I'll take a drug test if you take an IQ test."

The Post–September 11 Politics of Domestic Surveillance The debate over the trade-off between civil liberties and security intensified in 2005, when a White House-approved domestic surveillance program was revealed. Since the September 11, 2001, attacks, the National Security Agency (NSA) had been monitoring the phone calls of many U.S. citizens who have had contact with suspected terrorists overseas. These calls were intercepted without the approval of the Foreign Intelligence Surveillance Court (FISA), which Congress created in 1978 for approving the interception of calls. A few months later in 2005, another NSA program aimed at creating a database of every phone call made within the borders of the United States was revealed. Phone companies AT&T, Verizon, and BellSouth reportedly had turned over records of millions of customers' phone calls to the government.[81] In 2013, classified information revealed by Edward Snowden showed that the NSA monitored the phone calls of German chancellor Angela Merkel and other leaders of allied countries. Outrage over these practices prompted President Obama to outline important changes to how information would be gathered and stored. Critics warn that phone surveillance may be just the tip of the domestic surveillance iceberg because the government might be monitoring travel, credit card, and banking records more widely than we think.[82]

As you can imagine, the debate over domestic surveillance has generated intense disagreement. The idea that politics is everywhere may seem threatening if you are concerned about protecting your civil liberties, or it may seem reassuring if you are more concerned about national security. Either way, this issue will remain significant in your daily life for the foreseeable future.

The Fifth Amendment

The familiar phrase "I plead the Fifth" has been part of our criminal justice system since the Bill of Rights was ratified, ensuring that a suspect cannot be compelled to provide court testimony that would cause him or her to be prosecuted for a crime. However, what about outside a court of law? If a police officer coerces a confession out of a suspect, is that self-incrimination?

Coercive police interrogations were allowed until a landmark case in 1966. Ernesto Miranda had been convicted in an Arizona court of kidnapping and rape, on the basis of a confession extracted after two hours of questioning in which he was not read his rights. The Court overturned the conviction, saying that police interrogation "is inherently intimidating" and in these circumstances "no statement obtained from the defendant can truly be the product of his free choice."[83] To ensure that a confession is

DEFENDANT | **LOCATION**

SPECIFIC WARNING REGARDING INTERROGATIONS

1. YOU HAVE THE RIGHT TO REMAIN SILENT.

2. ANYTHING YOU SAY CAN AND WILL BE USED AGAINST YOU IN A COURT OF LAW.

3. YOU HAVE THE RIGHT TO TALK TO A LAWYER AND HAVE HIM PRESENT WITH YOU WHILE YOU ARE BEING QUESTIONED.

4. IF YOU CANNOT AFFORD TO HIRE A LAWYER ONE WILL BE APPOINTED TO REPRESENT YOU BEFORE ANY QUESTIONING, IF YOU WISH ONE.

SIGNATURE OF DEFENDANT | **DATE**

WITNESS | **TIME**

☐ REFUSED SIGNATURE   SAN FRANCISCO POLICE DEPARTMENT   PR.9.1.4

This is a typical example of the Miranda warning card that police officers carry with them and read to every suspect after an arrest.

truly a free choice, the Court established **Miranda rights**. If police do not read a suspect these rights, nothing the suspect says can be used in court.

Over time, the Court has carved out exceptions to the Miranda rights requirement because the public has viewed the practice as "coddling criminals" and letting too many people go free on legal technicalities. However, in 2000 the Court rejected Congress's attempt to overturn *Miranda* by designating all voluntary confessions as legally admissible evidence. The Court ruled that it, not Congress, has the power to determine constitutional protections for criminal defendants. The justices also affirmed their intent to protect the *Miranda* rule, saying: "*Miranda* has become embedded in routine police practice to the point where the warnings have become part of our national culture."[84]

Another Fifth Amendment right for defendants is protection against being tried more than once for a particular crime. This **double jeopardy** prohibition was extended to the states in 1969.[85] However, prosecutors can exploit two loopholes in this civil liberty: (1) a suspect may be tried in federal court and state court for the same crime, and (2) if a suspect is found innocent of one set of *criminal* charges brought by the state he or she may still be found guilty of the same or similar offenses based on *civil* charges brought by a private individual.

The final part of the Fifth Amendment is at the heart of a legal debate over property rights. The clause says "nor shall private property be taken for public use, without just compensation." For most of American history, this civil liberty has been noncontroversial. When the government needs private property for a public use such as a highway or a park, it may enforce "physical takings" by making a property owner sell at a fair market value in a practice known as eminent domain. But lately a controversial interpretation of the "takings" clause has attempted to expand just compensation for "regulatory takings" as well. For example, if the Endangered Species Act protects an animal whose habitat is on your land, you would not be able to develop that property and thus its market value would probably drop. Therefore, the argument goes, because of this law the government has "taken" some of your land's value by protecting the species, so the government should compensate you.

One key case ruled that if a regulation "deprives a property owner of all beneficial use of his property" the owner must receive compensation.[86] The issue became especially controversial around a case involving a development project in New London, Connecticut. A working-class neighborhood was sold to a private developer to build

Miranda rights
The list of civil liberties described in the Fifth Amendment that must be read to a suspect before anything the suspect says can be used in a trial.

double jeopardy
Being tried twice for the same crime. This is prevented by the Fifth Amendment.

a waterfront hotel, office space, and higher-end housing, but a homeowner sued the city to stop the development. The Court supported the local government, saying that "promoting economic development is a traditional and long accepted function of government," so a "plausible public use" is satisfied.[87] In reaction to this decision, 42 states passed legislation or constitutional amendments restricting the use of eminent domain for economic development.[88]

The Sixth Amendment: the right to legal counsel and a jury trial

The right to an attorney is a key civil liberty, because the legal system is too complicated for a layperson to navigate. However, at one time poor people accused of a felony had to defend themselves in court if they could not afford a lawyer (except in death-penalty cases, for which the state would provide a lawyer).[89] This changed in 1963 with *Gideon v. Wainwright*, when the Court overturned the conviction of a man who had been accused of breaking into a pool hall to steal beer, wine, and money. Unable to afford an attorney, Clarence Gideon defended himself—quite well, in fact—but the (false) testimony of the actual guilty party brought Gideon a conviction. Ultimately, the Court overturned it, saying: "In our adversary system of criminal justice, any person hauled into court who is too poor to hire a lawyer cannot be assured a fair trial unless counsel is provided for him."[90]

The right to an attorney has been strengthened over time, through both legislation and subsequent Court rulings. One year after *Gideon*, Congress passed the Criminal Justice Act, which provided better legal representation for criminal defendants in federal court; soon 23 states had taken similar action. The Court has defined a general right to *effective* counsel (although the bar is set low in defining "effective") and recently mandated that defense attorneys must conduct any reasonable investigation into possible lines of defense when presenting evidence that could help the defendant.[91]

The Sixth Amendment also protects the right to a speedy and public trial by an impartial jury in criminal cases. The Court affirmed the right to a speedy trial in 1967,[92] and today under the Federal Speedy Trial Act a trial must begin within 70 days of the defendant's arrest or first appearance in court. In addition, a defendant may not waive the right to a speedy trial.[93] The most important disputes over the "impartial jury" issue concern jury selection and peremptory challenges, in which lawyers may eliminate certain people from the jury pool without providing any reason. Race and gender may not be the basis for a peremptory challenge.[94]

The Eighth Amendment: cruel and unusual punishment

The Founders would be surprised by the intense debates over whether the Eighth Amendment prohibition against "cruel and unusual punishments" applies to the death penalty. Clearly, the death penalty was accepted in their time (even stealing a horse was a capital offense!), and the language of the Constitution reflects that. Both the Fifth and Fourteenth Amendments say that a person may not be deprived of "life, liberty, or property, without due process of law," which implies that someone *could* be deprived of life as long as the state follows due process. In the United States, 31 states still allow capital punishment. However, seven states have abolished the death penalty since 2007 (and four more states have moratoriums on the death penalty imposed by their governors, but Nebraska reinstated the death penalty by state referendum in 2016), and dozens of other countries have done the same in recent years. There were only 28 executions in the

The fight against terrorism has raised controversial questions about due process rights. After the United States killed Anwar al-Awlaki—an Al Qaeda leader living in Yemen, and a U.S. citizen—critics argued that his due process rights, such as the right to a fair trial, had been violated.

United States in 2015, which is the second-lowest number since 1991 and well below the peak of 99 in 1999.[95] A botched execution in Oklahoma in 2014, in which Clayton Lockett writhed and gasped for nearly 30 minutes when one of the lines filled with the lethal drugs failed, led to renewed calls for abolishing the death penalty.[96]

After being silent on this issue for nearly two centuries, in 1972 the Supreme Court ruled that the death penalty was unconstitutional because the process of applying it was inconsistent. Thereafter, Congress and 35 states rushed to make their laws compliant with the Court decision. The typical fix was to make explicit which crimes were punishable by death and to make capital sentencing a two-step process: first the determination of guilt or innocence and then a sentencing phase after a guilty finding. Four years later, the Court allowed states to bring back the death penalty.[97]

While never again challenging the death penalty, the Court has been chipping away at its edges for two decades. The Court has struck down state laws mandating the death penalty in murder cases and another law requiring it for rape. It has also prohibited the execution of insane prisoners and abolished the death penalty for the "mentally retarded," for juveniles, and for child rapists.[98]

Privacy rights

You may be surprised to learn that the word "privacy" does not actually appear in the Constitution. **Privacy rights** were developed in a 1965 case that questioned the constitutionality of an 1879 Connecticut law against using birth control. Estelle Griswold, the director of Planned Parenthood in Connecticut, was arrested after opening a clinic that dispensed contraceptives. She was fined $100 and appealed her conviction all the way to the Supreme Court, which overturned it.

In a fractured decision, the Court agreed that the law was outdated, but the justices agreed on little else. Even those who based their opinions on an implied constitutional right to privacy cited various constitutional roots: the First Amendment right of association, the Third's protection against the quartering of troops, the Fourth's prohibition against unreasonable searches and seizures, the Fifth's protection against self-incrimination, and the Ninth's statement "The enumeration in the Constitution, of certain rights, shall not be construed to deny or disparage others retained by the people."[99] *Griswold* was significant for establishing the constitutional basis for a right to privacy, but the dissenters worried where this right would lead. Justice Black warned that privacy "is a broad, abstract and ambiguous concept" that could be shrunken or expanded in subsequent decisions as judges determine what is constitutional on the basis of their own appraisal of what laws are unwise or unnecessary.[100]

Abortion rights

Eight years after *Griswold*, the landmark ruling in *Roe v. Wade* struck down laws in 46 states that limited abortion. Twelve of those states allowed abortions for pregnancies due to rape or incest, to protect the life of the mother, and in cases of severe fetal handicap. The much-criticized trimester analysis in the *Roe* ruling said that states could not limit abortions in the first trimester; in the second trimester, states could regulate abortions in the interests of the health of the mother; and in the third trimester, states could forbid all abortions except those necessary to protect the health or life of the mother.[101]

Subsequent decisions have upheld *Roe* but endorsed various state restrictions on abortion, such as requiring parental consent, a waiting period, or counseling sessions

DID YOU KNOW?

337

people have been exonerated post-conviction in the United States based on DNA evidence, out of 1,700 total exonerations. Twenty of those served time on death row and 16 more had been convicted of capital offenses.
Source: The Innocence Project

★

EXPLAIN WHY THE RIGHTS ASSOCIATED WITH PRIVACY ARE OFTEN CONTROVERSIAL

privacy rights
Liberties protected by several amendments in the Bill of Rights that shield certain personal aspects of citizens' lives from governmental interference, such as the Fourth Amendment's protection against unreasonable searches and seizures.

aimed at convincing the woman not to have an abortion (see the What Do the Numbers Say? feature for more on restrictions currently in effect). Most significant, the trimester analysis of *Roe* has been replaced by a focus on fetal viability. When the fetus would be viable (generally at 22 or 23 weeks), states can ban abortions "except where it is necessary, in appropriate medical judgment, for the preservation of the life or health of the mother."[102] Laws passed in 2013 by Arkansas and North Dakota limiting abortions as soon as a fetal heartbeat can be detected (as early as 6 weeks) were struck down by federal courts, but laws in nine states now ban abortions at 20 weeks, in apparent contradiction with *Roe v. Wade*.

Since *Roe*, most political action concerning abortion has taken place in the courts, but that could all change if the Supreme Court overturns this decision. Overturning *Roe* would shift the politics of abortion back to state legislatures and make it an even more highly contested political issue. One effort to force a challenge to *Roe* was a "personhood amendment" to the Mississippi constitution that defined life as beginning at conception. However, the amendment was soundly defeated in a statewide vote in 2011.[103] The pace of state restrictions on abortions accelerated from 2011 to 2013, with more than 200 limitations on abortion services. In 2013, 22 states enacted 70 new restrictions, including a requirement that abortion doctors have admitting privileges at local hospitals—which would close up one-third of abortion clinics in affected states.[104] In 2016, the Supreme Court struck down the latter as an "undue burden" on the right to an abortion.[105]

Gay rights

Gay rights have typically been seen more as a civil right (that is, freedom from discrimination) than a civil liberty, so these issues will be discussed in the next chapter. However, a recent Court ruling established very broad privacy rights for sexual behavior. The case involved two Houston men who were prosecuted for same-sex sodomy after police entered one of the men's apartments—upon receiving a false tip about an armed man in an apartment complex—and found the two having sex. Under Texas law, sodomy was illegal for homosexuals but not for heterosexuals. In a landmark ruling, the Court said that the liberty guaranteed by the Fourteenth Amendment's due process clause allows homosexuals to have sexual relations. "Freedom presumes an autonomy of self that includes freedom of thought, belief, expression, and certain intimate conduct."[106]

Tyron Garner and John Geddes Lawrence after the Supreme Court decision in *Lawrence v. Texas* in 2003 established broad privacy rights for sexual behavior (including homosexual behavior).

Parental Consent Laws for Abortions for Minors

- No parental notification or consent laws
- One or both parents must consent
- One or both parents must be informed
- Both parental consent and notification required
- Parental consent or notification laws blocked

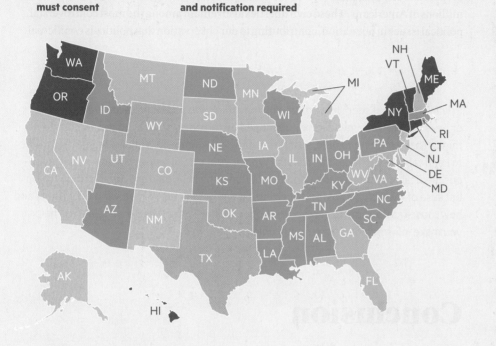

Abortion Rights Today

The Court's 1973 decision in *Roe v. Wade* made abortion legal throughout the United States. How do abortion rights look today? What do the numbers say?

Source: Guttmacher Institute, *State Policies in Brief,* "An Overview of Abortion Laws," October 1, 2016, www.guttmacher.org (accessed 10/17/16).

Pre-Abortion Mandatory Waiting Period Laws

- No mandatory waiting period
- Waiting period of less than 24 hours
- Waiting period of 24 hours or more
- Waiting period law blocked

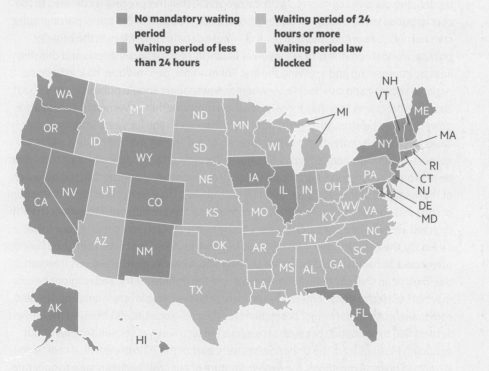

Think about it

1. Which states have the most restrictive policies concerning access to abortions?
2. How do you think waiting periods and parental notification affect the number of abortions in a state? What about the number of abortions nationwide?

Five members of the majority signed on to the broad "due process" reasoning of the decision, while Justice O'Connor wrote a concurring opinion in which she agreed that the Texas law was unconstitutional but on narrower grounds. With the broader due process logic, 13 state laws that banned sodomy were struck down.

While privacy rights may not be as firmly grounded in the Constitution as the freedom of speech or religion, this evolving area of the law has provided important protections for millions of Americans. These civil liberties also remain among the most controversial political issues in our nation, contributing to our observation that politics is conflictual.

"Why Should I Care?"

Privacy might not seem important. You may think you'll never be accused of a crime or have your privacy invaded or questioned by the government. Indeed, many people think, "I have nothing to hide, so it is fine if the NSA monitors e-mail and Internet traffic to keep tabs on suspected terrorists." What if your e-mail revealed that you had a serious medical or mental health condition? What if the NSA paid special attention to you because of tweets you posted criticizing a government policy? Knowing your rights and how those rights apply to everyone—both criminals and innocent people—will help you make informed decisions about which policies to support.

Conclusion

Every day you are likely affected by your civil liberties, whether speaking in a public place, attending church, participating in a political demonstration, writing or reading an article in your school newspaper, or being free from illegal police searches in your home. Because civil liberties are defined as those things the government *cannot* do to us, defining our civil liberties is a political process. Often this process is confined to the courts; but on many issues—including free speech, freedom of the press, pornography, criminal rights, abortion, and gun control—these debates take place in the broader political world where the process involves balancing competing interests and drawing lines by interpreting and applying the law. For example, debates over how to balance national security and civil liberties—whether newspapers should publish stories about classified programs that may threaten civil liberties; whether government surveillance powers should be strengthened to fight terrorism—will rage for years to come. Other cases, such as the protests at military funerals or protecting the due process rights of suspected criminals and terrorists, illustrate how difficult and politically unpopular it can be to protect our freedoms and liberty. Nearly everyone would agree that the behavior of the members of the WBC is completely outrageous. However, protecting the freedom of speech is easy if you agree with it. It becomes much more difficult if the speech is filth directed at the families of fallen soldiers or the rights of Nazis marching in your town.

Finally, the chapter opener on religious freedom revealed that even cherished liberties often must be balanced against other policy goals. A county clerk's religious freedom does not mean she may deny a same-sex couple the right to marry, and religious beliefs may not be used to deny someone health care (however, employers in small family-held companies may have stronger protections for their religious beliefs). Many of the earliest settlers fled to our nation because of religious persecution, yet serious debates about excluding Muslims from the United States were part of the 2016 presidential campaign. As with all political questions, the evolving nature of our civil liberties is sure to generate more political conflict. But that process affirms the essence of our political system.

STUDY GUIDE

Defining civil liberties

Define *civil liberties* and explain how the Bill of Rights came to apply to the states. (Pages 90–96)

Summary

The Bill of Rights—the first 10 amendments to the Constitution—lists individual protections from the federal government. For the majority of the nineteenth century, these individual freedoms were guaranteed only from the *federal* government and did not extend to protections from *state* governments. With the ratification of the Fourteenth Amendment and the process of selective incorporation, federal freedoms have been gradually extended to the state level.

Key terms
civil liberties (p. 90)　　　　due process clause (p. 95)
Civil War amendments (p. 94)　　selective incorporation (p. 95)

Practice Quiz Questions

1. **The Bill of Rights originally protected individuals from which level of government?**
   a. all levels of American government
   b. state governments
   c. local governments
   d. federal government
   e. the bureaucracy

2. **Which amendment has been used as the basis for selective incorporation?**
   a. the Eighth Amendment
   b. the Fourteenth Amendment
   c. the Tenth Amendment
   d. the Nineteenth Amendment
   e. the Fifth Amendment

Freedom of religion

Describe the First Amendment rights related to freedom of religion. (Pages 97–99)

Summary

Religious freedoms are defined by two clauses in the First Amendment: the establishment clause and the free exercise clause. Together, they do not allow the government to do anything to benefit any particular religion, nor is the government allowed to do anything to hinder religious practice. As is often the case, the Court has struggled to define exactly what constitutes "excessive government entanglement" in religion.

Key terms
establishment clause (p. 97)　　Lemon test (p. 98)
free exercise clause (p. 97)

Practice Quiz Questions

3. **The establishment clause is invoked under which of the following circumstances?**
   a. allowing "conscientious objectors" to avoid the military draft
   b. outlawing polygamy
   c. prohibiting prayer in public schools
   d. allowing the Amish to keep children home from school after the eighth grade
   e. banning the handling of snakes in church services

4. **Which test does the Supreme Court use to establish whether there has been "excessive government entanglement with religion"?**
   a. Lemon test
   b. Kreutz test
   c. Miller test
   d. Meyer test
   e. Brandenburg test

Freedom of speech, assembly, and the press

Describe the major First Amendment rights related to freedom of speech. (Pages 100–107)

Summary

The Court's attempt to balance individual freedoms and public good is reflected in the scope of protections guaranteed by the First Amendment. The Court generally prioritizes protecting individual rights to political speech, hate speech, symbolic speech, the freedom to assemble, and the freedom of the press unless under extreme circumstances (such as speech that directly incites violence). By contrast, the Court regularly places a lower priority on, and affords less protection to, fighting words, slander, libel, and commercial speech.

Key terms

strict scrutiny (p. 100)

intermediate scrutiny (p. 100)

clear and present danger test (p. 101)

direct incitement test (p. 101)

symbolic speech (p. 101)

hate speech (p. 103)

prior restraint (p. 104)

fighting words (p. 105)

slander (p. 105)

libel (p. 105)

commercial speech (p. 106)

Miller test (p. 107)

Practice Quiz Questions

5. **Which test does the Court use to determine if speech is considered dangerous and should not be legally protected?**

   a. Lemon test

   b. clear and present danger test

   c. Miller test

   d. direct incitement test

   e. balancing test

6. **Flag burning is an example of _____ that is currently _____ under the First Amendment.**

   a. symbolic speech; protected

   b. symbolic speech; not protected

   c. hate speech; protected

   d. hate speech; not protected

   e. offensive slander; not protected

7. **Prior restraint involves limits on what form of expression?**

   a. freedom of assembly

   b. freedom of association

   c. freedom of speech

   d. freedom of the press

   e. freedom of religion

The right to bear arms

Explore why the Second Amendment's meaning on gun rights is often debated. (Pages 107–108)

Summary

The Supreme Court has done little to define exactly what freedoms are established in the Second Amendment, largely preferring to allow the national, state, and local governments to make their own laws. The majority of public sentiment appears in favor of continued gun ownership, and limitations on Second Amendment rights appear unlikely.

Practice Quiz Question

8. **What is the best summary of the current position of the Supreme Court on the Second Amendment?**

   a. The Court has upheld most gun control laws, both at the state and national level, arguing that there is no individual right to own guns.

   b. The Court has upheld most gun control laws at the state level but struck down federal gun control laws, arguing that the Second Amendment only applies to Congress.

   c. The Court has struck down some state and national limitations on gun ownership, arguing that the Second Amendment protects an individual right to bear arms.

   d. The Court has struck down *all* state and national limitations on gun ownership, arguing that the Second Amendment protects an individual right to bear arms.

   e. The Court has refused to take a general position on the individual right to bear arms.

Law, order, and the rights of criminal defendants

Describe the protections provided for people accused of a crime. (Pages 109–115)

Summary

The Fourth, Fifth, Sixth, and Eighth Amendments provide protections to individuals accused of a crime, known as due process rights. Interpreting these general due process rights in specific cases is difficult, however, because specific standards of fairness and justice are very hard to define.

Key terms

due process rights (p. 109)

exclusionary rule (p. 111)

Miranda rights (p. 113)

double jeopardy (p. 113)

Practice Quiz Questions

9. **Protections from unreasonable searches and seizures are guaranteed by which constitutional amendment?**

   a. the Third Amendment

   b. the Fourth Amendment

   c. the Fifth Amendment

   d. the Seventh Amendment

   e. the Eighth Amendment

10. **The Miranda rights are protections that primarily fall under which constitutional amendment?**

    a. the Third Amendment

    b. the Fourth Amendment

    c. the Fifth Amendment

    d. the Seventh Amendment

    e. the Eighth Amendment

11. In 1972, the Supreme Court banned the death penalty for what reason?

   a. It deprived individuals of their rights to "life, liberty, or property."

   b. It was cruel and unusual.

   c. It was being inconsistently applied and violated the due process of law.

   d. It was racially biased.

   e. It was inconsistent with international law.

Privacy rights

Explain why the rights associated with privacy are often controversial. (Pages 115–118)

Summary

The term "privacy rights" is not found in the Constitution—rather, it was established in a 1965 Supreme Court case—but it may be implied in several amendments in the Bill of Rights. The right to privacy is controversial because of the lack of explicit language in the Constitution and the lack of consensus on exactly what the right to privacy means. It has remained a hot-button issue because recognition of the right to privacy is an important facet of the contemporary debate on abortion.

Key term
privacy rights (p. 115)

Practice Quiz Questions

12. Which of the following freedoms guaranteed in the Bill of Rights is thought to imply a right to privacy?

   a. right to bear arms

   b. right to refuse to quarter soldiers

   c. right to secure legal counsel

   d. right to request a jury trial

   e. freedom of speech

13. In what case did the Supreme Court first establish the right to privacy?

   a. *Roe v. Wade*

   b. *Lawrence v. Texas*

   c. *Griswold v. Connecticut*

   d. *Gonzales v. Oregon*

   e. *Lemon v. Kurtzman*

Suggested Reading

Abraham, Henry J., and Barbara A. Perry. *Freedom and the Court: Civil Rights and Liberties in the United States*, 8th ed. Lawrence: University Press of Kansas, 2003.

Amar, Akhil Reed. *The Bill of Rights*. New Haven, CT: Yale University Press, 1998.

Bondenhamer, David J., and James W. Ely, eds. *The Bill of Rights in Modern America*. Bloomington: Indiana University Press, 2008.

Lewis, Anthony. *Gideon's Trumpet*. New York: Random House, 1964.

Moynihan, Daniel Patrick. *Secrecy: The American Experience*. New Haven, CT: Yale University Press, 1998.

Posner, Richard A. *Not a Suicide Pact: The Constitution in a Time of National Emergency*. New York: Oxford University Press, 2006.

Pritchett, C. Herman. *Constitutional Civil Liberties*. Englewood Cliffs, NJ: Prentice Hall, 1984.

Schweber, Howard. *Speech, Conduct, and the First Amendment*. New York: Peter Lang, 2003.

Walker, Samuel. *Presidents and Civil Liberties from Wilson to Obama: A Story of Poor Custodians*. New York: Cambridge University Press, 2014.

5

Civil Rights

You can't discriminate against me . . . right?

Joe Arpaio, of Phoenix, Arizona, is the self-described "toughest sheriff in America." He was also the target of a U.S. Justice Department investigation of discriminatory practices in the enforcement of immigration laws. He is either a hero or a villain, depending on one's views concerning illegal immigration. Supporters see him as a courageous fighter who enforces the law that the federal government seems unable or unwilling to enforce. Critics see him as a bigoted publicity hound who abuses the civil rights of nonwhites.

A lawsuit brought by the Justice Department concluded: "As a result of the pattern or practice of unlawful discrimination, Latinos in Maricopa County are systematically denied their constitutional rights ."[1] In an example of "egregious racial profiling," Latino drivers were four to nine times more likely to be stopped than non-Latino drivers.[2] Sheriffs used minor traffic violations, such as failure to signal a lane change, to pull over Latinos and ask for their documents. One incident that drew international attention was a sweep of a town of about 6,000 Yaqui Indians and Latinos outside Phoenix. Over two days, more than 100 deputies conducted hundreds of searches, netting nine undocumented immigrants. Subsequently one report said: "The community was so scarred by the event that families are still terrified to leave their homes when they see the sheriff's patrol cars."[3] This case was settled in 2015 and Arpaio agreed to stop the raids. In a separate federal case, district court judge Murray Snow issued two injunctions barring the sheriff's office from continuing the pattern of discrimination and establishing an elaborate system of monitoring and reporting to make sure the abuse did not continue.[4] Sheriff Arpaio defended his office, saying, "We don't racially profile, I don't care what everybody says," while his deputy called the court order "ludicrous crap."[5] In 2016, Judge Snow found Arpaio in civil contempt of court and in October 2016 federal prosecutors charged Arpaio with criminal contempt of court for ignoring those injunctions.[6] In November, his constituents voted him out of office.

Enforcing immigration law is an extremely conflictual issue. Hard-liners on immigration, such as Sheriff Arpaio, see illegal immigrants as a threat to the country and want to make securing our borders the top priority of immigration

Joe Arpaio, former sheriff of Maricopa
County (which includes Phoenix),
Arizona, argued that strong measures
were necessary to discourage illegal
immigration. Here, Arpaio stands in front of
Maricopa County jail the day the County's
controversial measures went into effect.

policy (while deporting all illegal immigrants). The alternative perspective emphasizes controlling illegal immigration, while protecting the civil rights of citizens and legal residents, and providing a path to citizenship for illegal residents who are productive and law-abiding. It would seem that such a conflictual issue would not be very amenable to compromise. Indeed, both President George W. Bush and President Barack Obama tried and failed to enact comprehensive immigration reform. Frustrated with Congress's inactivity on the DREAM Act, which would have given legal status to young immigrants who came to the United States as children, Obama took steps in June 2012 to halt the deportation of "dreamers," and then in April 2014 he issued an executive order aimed at curbing deportations.[7] This order was struck down by the Supreme Court in June 2016. The issue was prominent throughout the presidential campaign, as Donald Trump promised to build a wall between Mexico and the United States (and make Mexico pay for it) and to deport all 12 million illegal residents in the United States. President Trump has since backed away from the latter pledge and the fate of the wall is in question. Any reform that secures our borders while protecting the civil rights of law-abiding people will involve compromise.

The concept of civil rights encompasses much more than immigration policy. Civil rights are one of the best examples of the idea that politics is everywhere: policies concerning discrimination in the workplace, in housing, and against women, minorities, gay men and lesbians, and the disabled affect millions of Americans every day. To see how civil rights may affect you, consider the following scenarios:

- Scenario 1: You are driving home with friends after a party. You have not had anything to drink and are following all traffic laws. Suddenly flashing lights signal you to pull over. As the police officer approaches, you wonder if this happened because you and your friends are African Americans driving in an all-white neighborhood. Have your civil rights been violated? Now imagine a car full of white teenagers with all the other facts the same. Can an officer pull you over just because he or she thinks that teenagers are more likely to be engaging in criminal activity than older people?
- Scenario 2: You are a 21-year-old Asian-American woman applying for your first job out of college. After being turned down for a job at an engineering firm, you suspect that you didn't get the job because you are a woman and because management thought that you would not fit in with the "good ol' boy" atmosphere of the firm. Have your civil rights been violated?
- Scenario 3: You and your gay partner are told that "your kind" are not welcome in the apartment complex where you would like to live. Should you call a lawyer?
- Scenario 4: You are a white male graduating from high school. After you receive a rejection letter from the college that was your first choice, a friend tells you that one of your classmates got into the same school even though he had the same grades as you and his SAT scores were slightly lower. Your friend says that it is probably because of the school's affirmative action policy—the classmate who was accepted is Latino. Are you a victim of "reverse discrimination"? Have your civil rights been violated?

All these scenarios seem to be civil rights violations. However, some are, some are not, and some depend on additional considerations (we will return to these examples in the chapter's conclusion). What is discrimination? When is discrimination legal, and when is it not? How are civil rights in the United States defined today?

The context of civil rights

In general, **civil rights** are rights that guarantee individuals freedom from discrimination. The terms "civil rights" and "civil liberties" are often used interchangeably, but there are important differences. Civil liberties are the freedoms guaranteed in the Bill of Rights, such as freedom of speech, religious expression, and the press, as well as the "due process" protection of the Fourteenth Amendment. In contrast, civil rights protect all persons from discrimination and are rooted in laws and the equal protection clause of the Fourteenth Amendment. Moreover, civil liberties primarily limit what the government can do to you ("*Congress* shall make no law ... abridging the freedom of speech"), whereas civil rights protect you from discrimination both by the government and by individuals. As noted in the previous chapter, to oversimplify, civil liberties are about freedom and civil rights are about equality.

Neither civil liberties nor civil rights figured prominently at the Constitutional Convention. Equality is not even mentioned in the Constitution or the Bill of Rights. However, equality was very much on the Founders' minds, as is evident in this ringing passage from the Declaration of Independence: "We hold these truths to be self evident, that all men are created equal, that they are endowed by their Creator with certain unalienable rights, that among these are life, liberty, and the pursuit of happiness." Despite the broad language, this was a limited conception of equality, because women had no political or economic rights at that time. Similarly, equality did not apply to slaves or to Native Americans. Even propertyless white men did not have full political rights until several decades after the Constitution was ratified. Indeed, equality and civil rights in the United States have been a continually evolving work in progress.

civil rights
Rights that guarantee individuals freedom from discrimination. These rights are generally grounded in the equal protection clause of the Fourteenth Amendment and more specifically laid out in laws passed by Congress, such as the 1964 Civil Rights Act.

African Americans

From the early nineteenth century and the movement for the abolition of slavery until the mid-twentieth century and the civil rights movement, the central focus of civil rights was on African Americans. Other groups received attention more gradually. For example, starting in the mid-nineteenth century women began their fight for equal rights and over the next century the civil rights movement expanded to include groups such as Native Americans, Latinos, and Asian Americans. Most recently, attention has turned to the elderly, the disabled, and the LGBTQ community (lesbian, gay, bisexual, transgender, and queer/questioning people). The most divisive civil rights issue with the greatest long-term impact, however, has been slavery and its legacy.

Slavery and Its Impact Slavery was part of the American economy from nearly the beginning of the nation's history. Dutch traders brought 20 slaves to Jamestown, Virginia, in 1619, a year before the Puritans landed at Plymouth Rock. Between 1619 and 1808, when the importation of slaves was banned, about 600,000 to 650,000 slaves were forcibly brought from Africa to the United States (and about 75,000 to 100,000 more were brought from Africa but died in transit).[8]

It is impossible to overstate the importance of slaves to the southern economy. The 1860 census shows that there were 2.3 million slaves in the Deep South, constituting 47 percent of its population, and nearly 4 million slaves in the South overall. Most slaves worked on plantations, but others labored as shipyard workers, carpenters, bakers, stonemasons, millers, spinners, weavers, and domestic servants. In the states that later seceded from the Union, 30.8 percent of households owned slaves. The economic benefits of slavery for the owners were clear. By 1860, the per capita income for whites in

📷

Slavery was part of the American economy from the 1600s until it was abolished by the Thirteenth Amendment in 1865. The system of slavery in the South created a highly unequal society in which African Americans were denied virtually all rights. Abolitionists worked to undermine and abolish slavery. Harriet Tubman was instrumental in the success of the Underground Railroad, which brought countless slaves to freedom.

"

A house divided against itself cannot stand. I believe this government cannot endure permanently half-slave and half-free.

—President Abraham Lincoln

the South was $3,978; in the North it was $2,040. The South had only 30 percent of the nation's free population, but it had 60 percent of the wealthiest men.[9]

Abolitionists worked to rid the nation of slavery as its importance to the South grew, setting the nation on a collision course that would not be resolved until the Civil War. The Founders largely ducked the issue (see Chapter 2), and subsequent legislatures and courts did not come any closer to resolving the impasse between the North and South over slavery. The Missouri Compromise of 1820, which limited the expansion of slavery and kept the overall balance between slave states and free states, eased tensions for a while, but the issue persisted. Slave owners became increasingly frustrated with the success of the Underground Railroad, which helped some slaves escape to the North. The debate over admitting California as a free state or a slave state (or making it half-free and half-slave) threatened to split the nation once again. Southern states agreed to admit California as a free state, but only if Congress passed the Fugitive Slave Act, which required northern states to treat escaped slaves as property and return them to their owners. Soon after, Congress enacted the Compromise of 1850, which overturned the Missouri Compromise and allowed each new state to decide for itself whether to be a slave state or a free state.

All possibility of further compromise ended when the misguided *Dred Scott v. Sandford* decision of 1857 ruled that states could not be prevented from allowing slavery. It also held that slaves were property rather than citizens and, as such, had no legal rights. But believing that slavery was in jeopardy when Abraham Lincoln won the 1860 presidential election, the southern states seceded from the Union and formed the Confederacy.

The outcome of the Civil War restored national unity and ended slavery, but the price was very high. About 528,000 Americans died in the war, with an astonishingly high casualty rate (25 percent).[10] After the war, Republicans moved quickly to ensure that the changes accomplished by the war could not be easily undone: they promptly adopted the Civil War amendments to the Constitution. The Thirteenth Amendment banned slavery, the Fourteenth guaranteed that states could not deny newly freed slaves the equal protection of the laws and provided citizenship to anyone born in the United States, and the Fifteenth Amendment gave African-American men the right to vote. These amendments were ratified within five years, although southern states resisted giving freed slaves and their descendants "equal protection of the laws" over the next 100 years.

Slow Progress after Reconstruction During Reconstruction (1866–1877), blacks in the South gained political power through institutions such as the Freedmen's Bureau and the Union League. With the protection of the occupying northern army, blacks were able to vote and even hold public office. However, when federal troops withdrew and the Republican Party abandoned the South, blacks were almost completely disenfranchised through the imposition of residency requirements, poll taxes, literacy tests, the grandfather clause, physical intimidation, and other forms of disqualification. Later the practice known as the "white primary" allowed only whites to vote in Democratic primary elections and, given that the Republican Party did not exist in most southern states, blacks were effectively disenfranchised. Although most of these provisions claimed to be race neutral, their impact fell disproportionately on black voters and virtually eliminated black voting. Despite the constitutional guarantees of the Fourteenth and Fifteenth Amendments, blacks had little access to the political system in the South and they had little success in winning office at any level in the rest of the nation.[11]

The social and economic position of blacks in the South followed a path similar to their political fortunes. When Reconstruction ended in 1877, the southern states enacted "black codes," or **Jim Crow laws**, that led to complete segregation of the races. Jim Crow laws forbade interracial marriage and mandated the separation of the races in neighborhoods, hotels, apartments, hospitals, schools, and restrooms, at drinking fountains, and in restaurants, elevators, and even cemetery plots. In cases where it would have been inconvenient to completely separate the races, as in public transportation, blacks had to sit in the back of the bus or in separate cars on the train and give up their seats to whites if asked. The Supreme Court validated these practices in *Plessy v. Ferguson* (1896) in establishing the **"separate but equal" doctrine**, officially permitting segregation as long as blacks had equal facilities.

Initially after Reconstruction, the rest of the nation mostly ignored the status of blacks, because 90 percent of all African Americans lived in the South. But as blacks' northward migration gradually transformed the nation's demographic profile and its racial politics, America's "race problem" was no longer a southern problem. Although conditions for blacks were generally better outside the South, they still faced discrimination and lived largely segregated lives throughout the nation. In World Wars I and II, black soldiers fought and died for their country in segregated units. Professional sports teams were segregated, and black musicians and artists could not perform in many of the nation's leading theaters. Moreover, blacks largely were hired for the lowest-paying menial jobs.

Real progress began in the 1940s. The Supreme Court struck down the white primary in 1944, Jackie Robinson broke the color line in Major League Baseball in 1947, and President Harry Truman issued an executive order integrating the U.S. armed services in 1948. Then came the landmark decision *Brown v. Board of Education* (1954), which rejected the "separate but equal" doctrine, followed by *Brown v. Board of Education II* (1955), which ordered that public schools be desegregated "with all deliberate speed." These events set the stage for the growing success of the civil rights movement, discussed later in this chapter.

Native Americans, Asians, and Latinos

The legacy of slavery and racial segregation has been the dominant focus of U.S. civil rights policies, but many other groups have also fought for equal rights. Understanding

Jim Crow laws
State and local laws that mandated racial segregation in all public facilities in the South, many border states, and some northern communities between 1876 and 1964.

"separate but equal" doctrine
The idea that racial segregation was acceptable as long as the separate facilities were of equal quality; supported by *Plessy v. Ferguson* and struck down by *Brown v. Board of Education*.

the history of these struggles is also necessary to understanding today's civil rights policies.

Native Americans were the first group to come in contact with the European immigrants. Although initial relations were good, the settlers' appetite for more land and their insensitivity to Native-American culture fostered continual conflict. Native Americans were systematically pushed from their land and placed on reservations. The most infamous example was the removal of 46,000 members of the "Five Civilized Tribes" from the southeastern United States under the Indian Removal Act of 1830. Thousands of Native Americans died on the Trail of Tears on their way to reservations in Oklahoma.[12] Native Americans had no political rights; the U.S. government considered them "savages" to be eliminated. They did not gain the right to vote until 1924, just after women and well after black men. Although the U.S. government signed treaties with Native-American tribes that recognized them as sovereign nations (not as foreign nations but as "domestic dependent nations"),[13] in practice the government ignored most of the agreements. Only recently has the government started to uphold its obligations, although compliance remains spotty. Native Americans have struggled to maintain their cultural history and autonomy in the face of widespread poverty and unemployment.

Latinos also have struggled for political and economic equality. The early history of Latinos in the United States is rooted in the Mexican-American War (1846–1848) and the conquest by the United States of the territory that today makes up most of the southwestern states. Although Latinos had long experienced prejudice and discrimination, one of their first major political successes was Cesar Chavez's effort to organize farmworkers in the 1960s and 1970s. He established the United Farm Workers Union and forced growers to bargain with 50,000 mostly Mexican-American fieldworkers in California and Florida. While many Mexican Americans have roots that go back centuries, most Latinos have been in the United States for less than two generations and have become a political force only recently, despite now constituting the nation's largest minority.

Latinos' relative lack of political clout when compared with African Americans derives from two factors. First, Latinos vote at a much lower rate than African Americans because of language barriers and because about one-third of Latinos are not U.S. citizens and therefore cannot vote in national elections. Second, unlike African Americans, Latinos are a relatively diverse group politically, including people from many Latin American nations. Most Latino voters are loyal to the Democratic Party, but a majority of Cuban Americans are Republicans. Although this diversity means that Latino voters do not speak with one voice, it brings opportunity for increased political clout in the future, because both parties are eager to attract them as new voters. In 2016, Donald Trump surprised many experts by winning a higher percentage of the Latino vote (29 percent) than Mitt Romney did in 2012 (27 percent).

Asian Americans have experienced discrimination since their arrival in the United States in the nineteenth century. The first wave of Chinese immigrants came with the 1848 California gold rush and staked out their claims along with Americans. But by 1850, when the easy-to-find gold was gone, Americans tried to drive out the Chinese through violence and the Foreign Miners Tax. Subsequently, Chinese immigrants worked on building the intercontinental railroad between 1865 and 1869. However, because they were given the more dangerous jobs, many lost their lives. After the railroad was completed, Chinese workers returned to the West Coast, where they experienced increasing discrimination and violence. When Congress passed the Chinese Exclusion Act of 1882, Chinese already in the United States were prevented from becoming U.S. citizens—although the Supreme Court later granted their American-born children automatic citizenship under the Fourteenth Amendment.[14] The Chinese Exclusion Act also barred virtually all immigration from China—the first time in U.S. history that a specific ethnic group was singled out in this way. Later,

In the 1960s and 1970s, Cesar Chavez and the United Farm Workers Union successfully organized mostly Mexican-American farmworkers, first in California and then in other parts of the country. Here, Chavez speaks to a group in Texas.

during World War II, more than 110,000 Japanese Americans were singled out and placed in internment camps for fear that they were enemy supporters. Despite the internment being upheld by the Supreme Court at the time, a 1980 congressional commission determined that it was a "grave injustice" motivated by "racial prejudice, war hysteria and the failure of political leadership." Eight years later, President Ronald Reagan signed into law the Civil Liberties Act, which paid more than $1.6 billion in reparations to the survivors of the camps and their heirs.[15] In recent decades, a much broader range of Asians have immigrated to the United States, including Koreans, Filipinos, Hmong, Vietnamese, and Asian Indians; their diversity in culture means that they display equally diverse political views and voting patterns.

Women and civil rights

On the eve of the United States' declaration of independence in 1776, John Adams's wife, Abigail, advised him not to "put such unlimited power in the hands of the husbands. Remember, all men would be tyrants if they could.... If particular care and attention is not paid to the ladies, we ... will not hold ourselves bound by any laws in which we have no voice or representation."[16] John Adams did not listen to his wife. The Constitution did not give women the right to vote, and they were not guaranteed that civil right until the Nineteenth Amendment was ratified in 1920. Until the early twentieth century, women in most parts of the country could not hold office, serve on juries, bring lawsuits in their own name, own property, or serve as legal guardians for their children. A woman's identity was so closely tied to her husband that if she married a noncitizen she automatically gave up her citizenship. The rationale for these policies was called **protectionism**: women were considered too frail to compete in the business world and were seen as needing to be protected by men.

While protectionist sentiment waned by the mid-twentieth century, as recently as 1961 a Court upheld a Florida law that automatically exempted women but not men from compulsory jury duty. Later in this chapter, we describe how the Supreme Court has moved away from this discriminatory position and rejected protectionist thinking toward women.

protectionism
The idea under which some people have tried to rationalize discriminatory policies by claiming that some groups, like women or African Americans, should be denied certain rights for their own safety or well-being.

Gay men and lesbians

The most recent group in the struggle for civil rights is the LGBTQ community. For most of American history, gay men and lesbians lived secret lives and faced abuse and discrimination if they came out. The critical moment that spurred the gay rights movement occurred in 1969, during a police raid on the Stonewall Inn in New York City. (Police often raided gay bars to harass patrons and selectively enforce liquor laws.)[17] Rather than submitting to the arrests, the customers fought back, throwing stones and beer bottles, breaking windows, and starting small fires. Several hundred people gathered, and the fighting raged for three nights. The Stonewall Rebellion galvanized the gay community by demonstrating the power of collective action.

Since Stonewall, the gay rights movement has made progress through political mobilization and protest, legislative action, and legal action. Public support for gay rights has increased dramatically in recent years. In fact, an ABC News poll showed that 63 percent of Americans believe that same-sex couples should be entitled to the same benefits as heterosexual couples, whereas only 32 percent think they should not.[18] In May 2012, President Obama endorsed same-sex marriage for the first time, completing his gradual evolution on the issue. In 2015, the Supreme Court ruled that same-sex marriage is legal in all 50 states.[19]

In 2016, President Obama designated the historic site of the Stonewall uprising in New York City as a national monument to honor the LGBTQ equality movement.

"Why Should I Care?"

Why does this history matter for politics today? First, the effects of slavery and Jim Crow laws are still quite evident: legal racial segregation ended 50 years ago, but its legacy—especially evident in the difference that exists in the relative quality of education available to most whites and blacks—remains. Second, active discrimination based on race, gender, and sexual orientation is still evident in our society. Given the importance of race in the everyday lives of millions of Americans and in gaining an understanding of American politics, a grasp of the history that got us to where we are today is an important starting point.

★

ANALYZE INEQUALITY AMONG RACIAL, ETHNIC, AND SOCIAL GROUPS TODAY

The racial divide today

The racial divide today begins with the unequal treatment of racial minorities, women, gays, and lesbians and is rooted in a gulf that remains between the objective condition of minorities and that of whites as well as between the political views that they hold. Although substantial progress has been made in bridging that gulf, inequalities in political, social, and economic conditions remain.

Differences in voting access

The United States has a long history of discriminating against racial and ethnic minorities in the election process. Although African Americans voted at a rate that was quite similar to that of whites in presidential elections from 2008–2016, their turnout was somewhat lower than that of whites in midterm elections and other racial and ethnic minorities have generally lower turnouts (see Figure 5.1). Much of the difference in

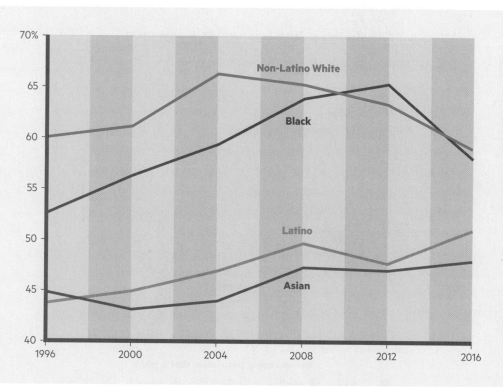

FIGURE 5.1

Turnout in Presidential Elections by Race

Turnout among African Americans has risen steadily over the last 20 years, while turnout of other groups has remained relatively flat. What do you think accounts for these trends? What could state governments do to increase voter turnout?

Source: The Diversifying Electorate—Voting Rates by Race and Hispanic Origin in 2012 (and Other Recent Elections), from Current Population Survey, www.census.gov (accessed 5/19/14); 2016 data aggregated by author from various sources.

voter turnout can be accounted for by education and income, but there still are practices and institutions that specifically depress minority-voter turnout. And many of these deterrents are intentional. The National Association for the Advancement of Colored People (NAACP), the U.S. Commission on Civil Rights, and the Brennan Center for Justice have all documented such practices in elections going back to 2000, including moving and reducing the number of polling places in areas with predominantly minority voters, changing from district-based to at-large elections, using voter challenges to target minority voters, redistricting that dilutes minority voting power, withholding information about registration and voting procedures from blacks, and "causing or taking advantage of Election Day irregularities."[20]

In 2016, these were 14 changes in state laws that restricted access to voting. These laws included requiring a photo ID to vote (which has a disproportionate impact on minorities because they are less likely to have a photo ID), proof of citizenship before being allowed to vote, cutbacks in early voting days and times, and making it more difficult to register people to vote. In addition, as we will discuss later, in 2013 the Supreme Court struck down an important provision of the Voting Rights Act of 1965 (VRA), making it easier for the nine states that had been covered by this provision of the law to implement discriminatory practices. In 2016, there were lawsuits in 11 states challenging limits on early voting and strict voter ID laws. Those supporting voting rights won at least partial victories in eight states, and cases were still pending in three states. Also, several states passed laws to automatically register voters and restore the right to vote for those with past criminal convictions.[21]

Socioeconomic indicators

The racial divide is also evident in social and economic terms. Nearly three times as many black families are below the poverty line as white families: 24.1 percent compared with 9.1 percent in 2015. The poverty rate of 21.4 percent for Hispanic families

Despite the removal of most formal barriers to voting, Latinos are less likely to vote and participate in politics than whites, blacks, and Asian Americans. Latino advocacy groups like Mi Familia Vota work to engage and register voters in their local communities.

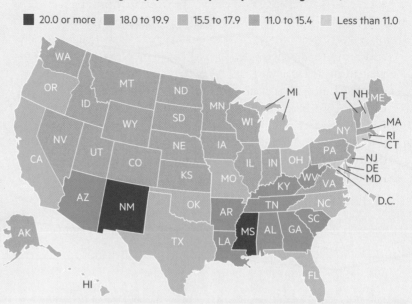

FIGURE 5.2

Poverty and Race, 2014

Carefully examine these maps. What is the relationship between poverty and minority population? How do you think these patterns might affect the politics of civil rights policies aimed at reducing discrimination in the workplace or housing?

Sources: Poverty data from U.S. Census Bureau, 2014 American Community Survey, www.census.gov/acs; race data from U.S. Census Bureau, *2012 Statistical Abstract*, Population Table 18, "Resident Population by Hispanic Origin and State: 2010," www.census.gov/compendia/statab/2012/tables/12s0018.pdf (accessed 11/3/12).

Percentage of population in poverty (U.S. average = 15.5)

- 20.0 or more
- 18.0 to 19.9
- 15.5 to 17.9
- 11.0 to 15.4
- Less than 11.0

Percentage of population that is white

- 90–94.4
- 80–89.9
- 70–79.9
- 45–69.9
- 22.7–44.9

in 2015 was similar to that of black families. While white median household income (that is, income from wages, salaries, interest, and disability and unemployment payments) was $62,950 in 2015, black median household income was $36,898 (58.6 percent of white family income) and Hispanic median household income was $45,148 (71.7 percent of white family income).[22] Moreover, the gap in overall wealth is much more dramatic. The average white household has more than six times the assets of the typical nonwhite family. In 2013, the median household net worth (that is, the sum of all assets, including houses, cars, and stock) was $142,000 for whites and $18,100 for nonwhites.[23] Poverty is not distributed equally throughout the United States but rather is concentrated in areas where the minority population is the highest (see Figure 5.2).

Other indicators show similar patterns. For example, the rate of black adult male unemployment has been about twice as high as that of white adult male unemployment for the past 45 years. On every measure of health—life expectancy, infectious diseases, infant mortality, cancer rates, heart disease, and strokes—the gaps between whites and blacks are large and, in some cases, increasing.[24] Current research suggests that racial disparities in health outcomes may be caused in part by government policies and business-related decisions. Broadly labeled "environmental racism," these practices mean that minority groups are much more likely to live in areas affected by pollution, toxic waste, and hazardous chemical sites.[25] One of the most extreme examples of this came to light in late 2015 and early 2016 in Flint, Michigan. In 2014, to save money, the city switched the public water supply from Lake Huron to the Flint River. The poor, majority-black residents of Flint soon reported discolored, foul-looking water, but city and state officials ignored their complaints. Researchers demonstrated that levels of lead in the water far exceeded safe levels. Many residents had elevated levels of lead in their blood, among other serious health issues. President Obama declared the city a disaster area and aid was provided in early 2016, but permanent damage had already been done.[26]

Criminal justice and hate crimes

The greatest disparity between racial minorities and whites may be in the criminal justice system. Recently, tensions have been high between minority communities and the police in the wake of dozens of cases of police shooting unarmed black men. In 2015, police killed 1,139 people in the United States; of those, 223 were unarmed and 75 were African Americans (see What Do the Numbers Say?).[27] Most of these involved tragic circumstances in which police were acting appropriately given existing protocol. But several highly publicized cases reveal negligent and, in some cases, criminal behavior by police officers. In 2013, following the acquittal of a neighborhood watch member, George Zimmerman, for shooting an unarmed 17-year-old African American, Trayvon Martin, a group called Black Lives Matter was formed.[28] The next year in Ferguson, Missouri, thousands of protesters gathered to call attention to the killing of an unarmed man, Michael Brown, by a police officer. The officer was acquitted, but an investigation by the Department of Justice found patterns of discriminatory behavior by the Ferguson Police Department. In 2015 and 2016, other high-profile cases of unarmed African Americans being killed by officers happened in Cleveland, Baltimore, Chicago, Staten Island, Baton Rouge, and Minneapolis–St. Paul. One case in North Charleston, South Carolina, led to the officer being charged with murder. Following a daytime traffic stop

Dylann Roof is shown here after his arrest for shooting and killing nine people during a prayer service in a church in Charleston, South Carolina. A mourner outside the church is overcome with grief.

There have been dozens of high-profile cases in recent years of police officers shooting unarmed black men. Michael Slager, a North Charleston, South Carolina, police officer, is shown here shooting Walter Scott following a traffic stop for a broken taillight.

> There are very few African-American men in this country who haven't had the experience of being followed when they were shopping in a department store. That includes me.
>
> —President Barack Obama

for a broken taillight, Officer Michael Slager shot Walter Scott in the back eight times from 15 to 20 feet away as Scott was running away, and lied about what happened to cover up his crime. A bystander's video showed the murder and led to his arrest. Slager's trial was underway as this edition went to press (November 2016).

Racial profiling subjects many innocent blacks to intrusive searches. In addition, blacks are not only more likely than whites to be convicted for the same crimes but also likely to serve longer sentences.[29] And African Americans and other minorities are subjected to hate crimes much more frequently than whites. According to the FBI hate-crime statistics, in 2014 nearly two-thirds of race-related hate crimes in the United States were "anti-black," while only 23 percent were "anti-white" (just under half of all hate crimes are race based). This means that the rate of anti-black hate crimes is nearly five times what would be expected based on the percentage of African Americans in the United States, while the rate of anti-white hate crimes is about one-third as high as would be expected.[30] One of the most extreme hate crimes in recent years happened in 2015 when Dylann Roof, a 21-year-old white supremacist, shot and killed nine people at a Bible study in the historic Emanuel African Methodist Episcopal Church in Charleston, South Carolina. Roof later confessed that he was trying to ignite a race war.

This backdrop of racial inequality, discrimination, and violence drives civil rights activists to push their agenda in the three branches of government: legislative, executive, and judicial. In some instances, activists work in several arenas simultaneously; in others, they seek redress in one arena after exhausting alternatives in the others. The civil rights movement, which was crucial in the early policy successes, also continues to mobilize from the grass roots.

EXPLAIN THE APPROACHES USED TO BRING ABOUT CHANGE IN CIVIL RIGHTS POLICIES

The policy-making process and civil rights

Our civil rights policies are produced by several key players. First, the public becomes involved through social movements to put pressure on the political system to change. But Congress, the president, and the courts all also exert their own influence on policies that define civil rights.

Social movements

From the early women's rights movement and abolitionists of the nineteenth century to the gay rights and civil rights movements of the mid-twentieth century, activists have

Total People Killed by Police in 2015, by Race

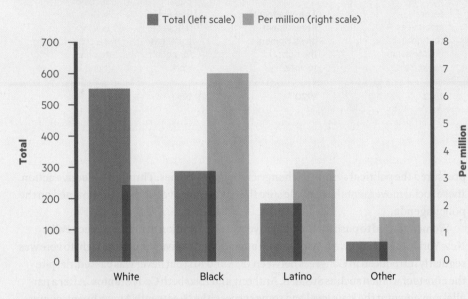

Legend: Total (left scale) ■ Per million (right scale)

Unarmed People Killed by Police in 2015, by Race

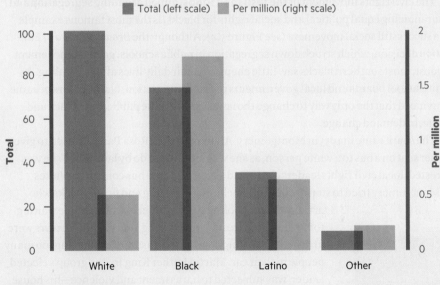

Legend: Total (left scale) ■ Per million (right scale)

Racial Inequality in Law Enforcement

Recent events in Ferguson, Missouri, Baltimore, Maryland, and Staten Island, New York, among other places, have touched off a nationwide debate about fairness in law enforcement. Do racial inequalities exist in law enforcement? What do the numbers say?

Source: "The Counted: People Killed by Police in the US," *The Guardian*, www.theguardian.com/us-news/ng-interactive/2015/jun/01/the-counted-police-killings-us-database# (accessed 8/15/16).

Think about it

- For all victims (total and unarmed), what racial category had the highest number of deaths? What racial category had the highest number per million people? What do you think accounts for this difference?
- Is there a greater racial disparity in the first chart that shows all people killed by police, or the second chart that shows unarmed people?
- What, if anything, surprises you about these numbers? Why?

FIGURE
5.3

Women's Rights Time Line

First women's rights convention held in Seneca Falls, New York.	Territory of Wyoming gives women the right to vote.	Congress requires equal pay for equal work for federal employees (but not for private sector workers).	The Nineteenth Amendment gives women the right to vote.	Equal Pay Act requires equal pay for equal work.	Title VII of the Civil Rights Act bars employment discrimination based on race, sex, and other grounds.
1848	1869	1872	1920	1963	1964

pressured the political system to change civil rights policies. Through collective action, these social movements have made sure that such controversial issues remained on the policy agenda.

Women started to push for the right to vote at a convention in 1848 at Seneca Falls, New York. Subsequently, a constitutional amendment to give women the right to vote was regularly introduced in Congress between 1878 and 1913 but never was passed, despite the efforts of women such as Susan B. Anthony and Elizabeth Cady Stanton. After a parallel movement at the state level had some success, the Nineteenth Amendment, giving women the right to vote, was finally passed in 1919 and ratified in 1920 (see Figure 5.3).

The civil rights movement of the 1950s and 1960s, aimed at ending segregation and guaranteeing equal political and social rights for blacks, is the most famous example of a successful social movement (see Figure 5.4). Although the *Brown v. Board of Education* decision, which struck down segregation in public schools, gave the movement a boost, most southern blacks saw little change in their daily lives after the ruling. As white school boards and local governments resisted integration, black leaders became convinced that the only way to change the laws was to get the public, both black and white, to demand change.

The spark came in 1955 in Montgomery, Alabama, when Rosa Parks refused to give up her seat on a bus to a white person, as she was required to do by law. When she was arrested, local civil rights leaders organized a boycott of the bus company. Whites in Montgomery tried to stop the boycott, including arresting and fining blacks who arranged a car pooling system to get to work: people waiting for a ride were arrested for loitering, and car pool drivers were arrested for lacking appropriate insurance or having too many people in their car. Martin Luther King Jr., the group's elected leader, was subjected to harassment and violence—his house was firebombed, and he was arrested several times. Finally, a federal district court ruled that the segregation policy was unconstitutional and the Supreme Court upheld the ruling.

Nonviolent Protest In 1960, four black students in Greensboro, North Carolina, went to a segregated lunch counter at a local Woolworth's and asked to be served. They waited for an hour without being served and had to leave when the store closed. When 20 students returned the next day, national wire

Four African-American college students protest at a whites-only lunch counter in Greensboro, North Carolina. These sit-ins spread throughout the South in 1960 as civil rights activists were able to put pressure through their nonviolent protests on businesses to integrate.

1965	1967	1972	1973	1982	2009
Griswold v. Connecticut legalizes the use of contraceptives by married couples.	Federal affirmative action policies are extended to women by an executive order.	Title IX of the Education Amendments of 1972 requires equal access to programs for men and women in higher education.	*Roe v. Wade* establishes a constitutional right to abortion.	Thirty-five states ratify the Equal Rights Amendment, passed by Congress in 1971–1972, falling three states short of the number needed to add the amendment to the Constitution.	Lilly Ledbetter Fair Pay Act makes it easier to sue for gender-based pay discrimination.

services picked up the story. Within two weeks, the sit-ins spread to 11 cities. In some cases, the students encountered violence; in others, they were simply arrested. However, they continued to respond with passive resistance, and new waves of protesters replaced those who had been arrested. The Student Nonviolent Coordinating Committee (SNCC) was created to coordinate the protests. The Greensboro Woolworth's was integrated on July 26, 1961, but the protests continued in other cities. By August 1961, the sit-ins had 70,000 participants and there had been 3,000 arrests.[31] The sit-ins marked an important shift in the tactics of the civil rights movement away from the court-based approach and toward the nonviolent civil disobedience that had been successful in Montgomery.

The next significant events occurred in Birmingham, Alabama, which experienced 18 unsolved bombings of black churches and homes in a six-year period. During a peaceful protest in 1963, Martin Luther King Jr. and many others were arrested. While in solitary confinement, King wrote his "Letter from the Birmingham Jail," an eloquent statement of the principles of nonviolent civil disobedience. Responding to white religious leaders who said that King's actions were "unwise and untimely" and that "when rights are consistently denied, a cause should be pressed in the courts and in negotiations among local leaders, and not in the streets," King wrote a justification for civil disobedience, asserting that everyone had an obligation to follow just laws but an equal obligation to break unjust laws.

Public Opinion and Legislative Action Following King's release from jail, the situation escalated. The protest leaders decided to use children in the next round of demonstrations. After more than 1,000 children were arrested and the jails were overflowing, the police turned fire hoses and police dogs on children trying to continue their march. Media coverage turned public opinion in favor of the marchers as the country expressed outrage over the violence in Birmingham. Similar protests occurred in over 100 southern cities.

Mass protest became the preferred tool of many other social movements for civil rights and other causes. Vietnam War protesters marched on Washington by the hundreds of thousands in the late 1960s and early 1970s. Likewise, the women's rights, gay rights, and environmental movements have staged many mass demonstrations in Washington and other major cities.

Most recently, large-scale demonstrations against Wall Street and international organizations, such as the International Monetary Fund and the World Trade Organization, have swept the nation. The Occupy Wall Street movement, which started in

FIGURE
5.4

African American Civil Rights Time Line

Government Action

May 17
U.S. Supreme Court rules segregated schools are unconstitutional in the *Brown v. Board of Education* decision.

September 9
The Federal Civil Rights Act prohibits discrimination.

September 23
President Eisenhower sends troops to escort black students into a white high school in Little Rock, Arkansas.

1954   1957

Social Movement

December 1
Rosa Parks is arrested for refusing to move to the back of a bus in Montgomery, Alabama.

February 1
Black college students, refused service at a lunch counter in Greensboro, North Carolina, launch a sit-in.

May 4
Freedom Riders test a Supreme Court decision that integrated interstate bus travel, sparking violence.

1955   1960   1961

Source: Adapted from "Key Moments in Civil Rights History," *Ann Arbor News*, January 11, 2004, www.mlive.com.

September 2011, spread to more than 1,500 cities in 82 nations. Modeling their actions after the nonviolent protests of the civil rights era, protesters occupied public spaces to make their views known. The Occupy movement's slogan "We are the 99%" drew attention to income inequality and helped set the tone for the 2012 presidential election. Conservative activists, such as those in the pro-life movement, have also used nonviolent protest, sit-ins, and mass demonstrations. Protests against President Obama's policies early in 2009 evolved into the "Tea Party" movement (evoking the Boston Tea Party of the American Revolution). Rooted in an opposition to high taxes and activist government, the Tea Party movement organized protests on Tax Day (April 15, 2009) that drew more than 300,000 people in 346 cities.[32] Clearly, the legacy of the civil rights movement has been not only to help change unjust laws but also to provide a new tool for political action across a broad range of policy areas.

This tool has evolved in the most recent period to combine the power of social media and mass protest. #BlackLivesMatter started in 2013 on social media, but expanded in 2014–2016 to organize mass protests against police killings in many cities across the country.

July 2
President Johnson
signs the Civil
Rights Act.

August 6
The Federal Voting Rights Act
prohibits denying anyone the
vote on the basis of color or race.

1964

1965

April 16
Martin Luther King Jr. writes his
"Letter from the Birmingham Jail,"
defending nonviolent civil
disobedience against unjust laws.

February 21
Malcolm X is shot and
killed in New York.

August 28
Martin Luther King Jr. delivers
his "I Have a Dream" speech
at the March on Washington.

March 7
Six hundred voting rights
marchers are attacked by
police with clubs and whips
on the Edmund Pettus
Bridge outside Selma,
Alabama. On March 21,
about 3,200 marchers
head out again on a
four-day march to
Montgomery in support
of voting rights.

September 15
Four girls are killed when
a Baptist church in
Birmingham, Alabama,
is bombed.

June 21
Three civil rights workers
are murdered outside
Philadelphia, Mississippi.

April 4
Martin Luther King
Jr. is slain in Memphis,
Tennessee.

1963

1964

1965

1968

The Courts

The Supreme Court has played an important role in defining civil rights. In the mid-twentieth century, the justices moved away from the "separate but equal" doctrine, required the desegregation of public schools, and upheld landmark civil rights legislation passed by Congress. More recently, they have expanded civil rights for women and the LGBTQ community, but they also have endorsed a "color-blind" position that some see as a movement away from protecting civil rights.

Challenging "Separate but Equal" in Education In the 1930s, the NAACP, which was established to fight for equal rights for black people, started a concerted effort to nibble away at the "separate but equal" doctrine. Rather than tackling segregation head-on, the NAACP challenged an aspect of segregation that would be familiar to the Supreme Court justices: the ways in which states kept blacks out of all-white law schools.

A 15-year-old is attacked by a police dog during a civil rights demonstration in Birmingham, Alabama, on May 3, 1963. The next day, during a meeting at the White House, President Kennedy discussed this photo, which had appeared on the front page of the *New York Times*. Reaction against police brutality helped spur Congress and the president to enact civil rights legislation.

The Court's first ruling in this area came in 1938, in a case from Missouri. Here the state paid black students' tuition to attend an out-of-state school, while white students attended the in-state school tuition-free. The state defended the practice under the "separate but equal" doctrine, but the Court rejected these arguments. The bottom line was that white students could attend law school in the state and similarly qualified black students could not, which violated the Fourteenth Amendment's equal protection of the laws.[33]

Another case chipped away at the principle of "separate but equal" itself. In 1950, Texas had a separate law school for black students, but this school had only four part-time faculty, no librarian in the law library, and a library with few of the promised books. The situation had started to improve after the case was under way, but the Court ruled that this was not good enough. There were intangible aspects of the quality of law school, such as the school's reputation, the "position and influence of the alumni," and "traditions and prestige." This ruling came very close to saying that "separate but equal" was a contradiction in terms, but the Court stopped just short of reaching that conclusion.[34]

After these victories, the signals increasingly indicated that the Supreme Court was ready to strike down the "separate but equal" doctrine. As background, in addition to the law school cases, in 1948 the Court had ruled that "restrictive covenants"—clauses in real estate contracts that prevented a property owner from selling to an African American—could not be enforced by state or local courts because of the Fourteenth Amendment's prohibition against a state denying blacks the "equal protection of the laws." This application of the Fourteenth Amendment was expanded in the landmark ruling *Brown v. Board of Education*.

The *Brown* case arrived on the Court's docket in 1951, was postponed for argument until after the 1952 elections, and was re-argued in December 1953. The postponement was intentional, because the Court knew that a firestorm would ensue. In its unanimous decision the Court ruled: "In the field of public education, the doctrine of separate but equal has no place. Separate educational facilities are inherently unequal, depriving the plaintiffs of the equal protection of the laws."[35] The case was significant not only because it required all public schools to desegregate but also because it used the equal protection clause of the Fourteenth Amendment in a way that had potentially far-reaching consequences. Also, even though the decision did not rule segregation unconstitutional in all contexts, *Brown* provided an important boost to the civil rights movement.

DID YOU KNOW?

75%

of African-American students and 79 percent of Latino students attend schools that are majority minority.
Source: *U.S. News & World Report*

The Push to Desegregate Schools In 1955, *Brown v. Board of Education II* addressed the implementation of desegregation and required the states to "desegregate with all deliberate speed."[36] The odd choice of words, "all deliberate speed," was read as a signal by southerners that they could take their time with desegregation. The phrase does seem to be contradictory: being deliberate does not usually involve being speedy. Southern states engaged in "massive resistance" to the desegregation order. In some cases, they even closed public schools rather than integrate them—and then reopened the schools as "private," segregated schools for which the white students received government vouchers. However, Maryland, Kentucky, Tennessee, Missouri, and the District of Columbia desegregated their schools within two years.

Eight years after *Brown I*, little had changed in the Deep South: fewer than 1 percent of black children attended school with white children.[37] Through the 1960s, the courts had to battle against the continued resistance to integration. In 1971, the Court shifted its focus from **de jure** segregation (segregation mandated by law) to **de facto** segregation (segregation that existed because of segregated housing patterns) and approved school busing as a tool to integrate schools.[38] This approach was extremely controversial. The Court almost immediately limited the application of busing by ruling in a Detroit case that busing could not go beyond the boundaries of a city's school district: students did not have to be bused from suburbs to cities unless it could be shown that the school district's lines were drawn in an intentionally discriminatory way.[39] This rule encouraged "white flight" from the cities to the suburbs in response to court-ordered busing.

The Supreme Court retreated further from enforcing desegregation in 1991 when it ruled that a school district could be released from a court-ordered desegregation plan if the district had taken "all practicable steps" to desegregate. Furthermore, districts do not have to address segregation in public schools that is caused by segregated housing.[40] The Court ruled in 1995 that low minority achievement scores are not evidence of a district's failure to desegregate, and it said that school districts cannot be forced by the courts to spend money to establish magnet schools with special programs that could attract white students from the suburbs.[41] In a significant recent decision, in 2007 the Court invalidated voluntary desegregation plans implemented by public school districts in Seattle and Louisville. Both districts set goals for racial diversity and denied assignment requests if they tipped the racial balance above or below certain thresholds. In these cases, the discrimination was against white students who wanted to be in schools with few minority students, rather than black students who wanted to be in integrated schools.[42]

Expanding Civil Rights Other significant rulings in the 1960s struck down state laws that forbid interracial marriages (16 states had such laws), upheld all significant parts of the Civil Rights Act, and expanded the scope of the VRA. In central cases, the justices ruled that Congress had the power to eliminate segregation in public places, such as restaurants and hotels, under the commerce clause of the Constitution.

One important area of cases was in employment law. In 1971, the Court ruled that employment tests, such as written exams or general aptitude tests, that are not related to job performance and that discriminate against blacks violate the 1964 Civil Rights Act.[43] This meant that if the employment practice had a bad *effect* on a racial group it didn't matter whether or not the discrimination was *intended*. The Supreme Court and Congress have gone back and forth in defining this concept, but it is still important in workplace discrimination suits. (See also Nuts & Bolts 5.1.)

The Color-Blind Court and Judicial Activism Recently, the Supreme Court has been gradually imposing a "color-blind jurisprudence" over numerous issues. One

de jure
Relating to actions or circumstances that occur "by law," such as the legally enforced segregation of schools in the American South before the 1960s.

de facto
Relating to actions or circumstances that occur outside the law or "by fact," such as the segregation of schools that resulted from housing patterns and other factors rather than from laws.

Busing students from one school district to another in the interest of desegregation has been controversial since the 1960s. In 2007, the Supreme Court invalidated voluntary desegregation plans in Louisville and Seattle school districts.

Race-Related Discrimination as Defined by the Equal Employment Opportunity Commission

Race/Color Discrimination

Race discrimination involves treating someone (an applicant or employee) unfavorably because he/she is of a certain race or because of personal characteristics associated with race (such as hair texture, skin color, or certain facial features). Color discrimination involves treating someone unfavorably because of skin color complexion.... Discrimination can occur when the victim and the person who inflicted the discrimination are the same race or color.

Race/Color Discrimination and Work Situations

The law forbids discrimination when it comes to any aspect of employment, including hiring, firing, pay, job assignments, promotions, layoff, training, fringe benefits, and any other term or condition of employment.

Race/Color Discrimination and Harassment

It is unlawful to harass a person because of that person's race or color. Harassment can include, for example, racial slurs, offensive or derogatory remarks about a person's race or color, or the display of racially offensive symbols. Although the law doesn't prohibit simple teasing, offhand comments, or isolated incidents that are not very serious, harassment is illegal when it is so frequent or severe that it creates a hostile or offensive work environment or when it results in an adverse employment decision (such as the victim being fired or demoted). The harasser can be the victim's supervisor, a supervisor in another area, a coworker, or someone who is not an employee of the employer, such as a client or customer.

Race/Color Discrimination and Employment Policies/Practices

An employment policy or practice that applies to everyone, regardless of race or color, can be illegal if it has a negative impact on the employment of people of a particular race or color and is not job-related and necessary to the operation of the business.

Source: U.S. Equal Employment Opportunity Commission, "Race/Color Discrimination," www.eeoc.gov (accessed 10/4/12).

significant area was the 1992 racial redistricting in which 15 new U.S. House districts were drawn to help elect African Americans and 10 districts were drawn to help elect Latino members. The resulting dramatic change in the number of minorities in Congress (more than 50 percent) was rooted in the 1982 amendments to the VRA. Instead of mandating a fair *process*, this law and subsequent interpretation by the Supreme Court mandated that minorities be able to "elect representatives of their choice" when their numbers and configuration permit. As a result, the legislative redistricting process now had to avoid discriminatory *results* rather than being concerned only with discriminatory *intent*.

However, in several decisions, starting with the 1993 case *Shaw v. Reno*, the Supreme Court's adherence to a color-blind jurisprudence has thrown the constitutionality of black-majority districts into doubt. The Court has ruled that black-majority districts are legal as long as they are "done right,"[44] but it has consistently held that if race is the predominant factor in drawing district lines the districts are unconstitutional because they violate the equal protection clause of the Fourteenth Amendment. Based on this reasoning, black-majority districts in North Carolina, Georgia, Louisiana, Virginia, Texas, and Florida were found to be unconstitutional. In the most recent case, in 2001, the Court upheld the re-drawn 12th District in North Carolina, which no longer was a black majority, arguing that when race and partisanship are so intertwined—as they are when 90 percent of African Americans vote for a Democratic candidate—plaintiffs cannot assume that African Americans were placed together for racial reasons. This ruling opens the door for a greater consideration of race than had been allowed in the previous cases. However, racial redistricting is an unsettled area of the law.[45]

The Court also struck down an important part of the 1965 VRA in a 2013 ruling. This case concerned the "coverage formula" that determines which states have to get approval from the Justice Department before implementing changes in an election law or practice (such as redistricting or moving the location of a polling place). This "preclearance" provision of the law was viewed as one of the best ways to stop discriminatory voting practices because it could prevent them before they were implemented, rather than having to wait until they went into effect. The Court ruled that the coverage formula was an unconstitutional burden on the covered states and was a violation of the Tenth Amendment.[46]

The racial redistricting and voting rights cases illustrate that the Supreme Court is increasingly activist in civil rights. It is generally unwilling to defer to any other branch of government that disagrees with its view of discrimination and equal protection (see Chapter 13 for a discussion of judicial activism). In some periods, judicial activism may serve to further civil rights, as in the 1950s and 1960s, or to limit them, as in the recent period.

Women's Rights The Supreme Court has also been central in shaping women's civil rights. Until relatively recently, the Court did not apply the Constitution to women, despite the Fourteenth Amendment's language that states may not deny any *person* the equal protection of the laws. Apparently, women were not regarded as people when it came to political and economic rights in the nineteenth and early twentieth centuries. These protectionist notions were finally rejected in three cases between 1971 and 1976, when the Court made it much more difficult for states to treat men and women differently.

The first case involved an Idaho state law that gave a man priority over a woman when they were otherwise equally entitled to execute a person's estate. This law was justified on the "reasonable" grounds that it reduced the state courts' workload by having an automatic rule that would limit challenges. But the Court ruled that the law was arbitrary, did not meet the "reasonableness" test, and therefore violated the woman's equal protection rights under the Fourteenth Amendment.[47] The second case involved a female air force officer who wanted to count her husband as a dependent for purposes of health and housing benefits. Under the law at the time, a military man could automatically count his wife as a dependent, but a woman could claim her husband only if she brought in more than half the family income. The Court struck down this practice, saying that protectionist laws, "in practical effect, put women not on a pedestal, but in a cage."[48]

These two cases still relied on the **rational basis test** for discrimination between men and women. It wasn't until 1976 that the Court established the intermediate scrutiny test (see Chapter 4) in a case involving the drinking age. In the early 1970s, some states had a lower drinking age for women than for men on the "reasonable (or rational) basis" that 18- to 20-year-old women are more mature than men of that age (and thus less likely to abuse alcohol). The new intermediate scrutiny standard meant that the government's policy must be "substantially related" to an "important government objective" to justify the unequal treatment of men and women, so the law was struck down.[49]

Before this case, only two standards served to apply the Fourteenth Amendment to different categories of people: the rational basis test and the strict scrutiny test. The strict scrutiny test gave racial minorities the strongest protection as the "suspect classification" under the Fourteenth Amendment, and stipulated that there must be a "compelling state interest" to discriminate among people if race is involved. The other standard, the rational basis test, said that it was acceptable to discriminate against

rational basis test
The use of evidence to suggest that differences in the behavior of two groups can rationalize unequal treatment of these groups.

a group of people as long as there was a "rational basis" for that state law. Today, for example, states can pass drinking laws that allow only those who are 21 and older to drink on the grounds that traffic fatalities will be lower with that drinking age rather than under a law that allows 18-year-olds to drink (see How It Works: Civil Rights in this chapter). The intermediate scrutiny standard gives women stronger protections than the rational basis test, but this standerd is not as strong as strict scrutiny.

The more aggressive application of the Fourteenth Amendment for women helped in providing them the equal protection of the laws, as shown in a Court decision that struck down the Virginia Military Institute (VMI) male-only admission policy. The ruling stated that VMI violated the Fourteenth Amendment's equal protection clause because it failed to show an "exceedingly persuasive justification" for its sex-biased admissions policy.[50]

Two other areas where the Court helped advance women's rights were affirmative action and protection against sexual harassment. In 1987, the Court approved affirmative action in a case involving a woman who was promoted over a man despite the fact that he scored slightly higher than she did on a test. The Court ruled that this was acceptable to make up for past discrimination.[51] The Court made it easier to sue employers for sexual harassment in 1993, saying that a woman did not have to reach the point of a nervous breakdown before claiming that she was harassed; it was enough to demonstrate a pattern of "repeated and unwanted" behavior that created a "hostile workplace environment."[52] Later rulings stated that if a single act is flagrant the conduct did not have to be repeated to create a hostile environment.

The Court has also restricted the rights of women in some instances. In 1984, it ruled that Title IX of the Education Amendments of 1972, which prohibits sex discrimination in "any education program or activity receiving Federal financial assistance," applied to private colleges and universities in which students received federal financial aid. However, in a blow to equal treatment for women, the Court said that only the programs receiving federal funds could not discriminate, rather than the institution as a whole. This ruling released many athletic programs from their obligation to provide equal opportunity for women athletes.[53] Congress overturned the ruling with the Civil Rights Restoration Act in 1988.

More recently, Lilly Ledbetter sued Goodyear Tire & Rubber Company because she had received lower pay than men doing the same work over a 20-year period, which she claimed was gender discrimination. However, the Court rejected her claim, saying that she did not meet the time limit required by the law, as the discrimination must have occurred within 180 days of the claim; this overturned the long-standing policy of the EEOC—the Equal Employment Opportunity Commission—which held that each new paycheck restarted the 180-day clock as a new act of discrimination.[54] Dissenters pointed out that pay discrimination usually occurs in increments over long periods, so it would be impossible to recognize unequal pay within 180 days of an initial paycheck. Congress overturned the Court's decision and restored the old standard in January 2009 by passing the Lilly Ledbetter Fair Pay Act. But as Figure 5.5 shows, significant pay disparities between men and women remain throughout much of the United States. Early in 2016, President Obama issued an executive order requiring companies to report to the federal government what they pay employees by race, gender, and ethnicity. He said, "Women are not getting the fair shot that we believe every single American deserves."[55]

Gay Rights The Supreme Court has a similarly mixed record on gay rights. The Court's decisions in early cases were not supportive of gay rights. One of the first cases concerned Georgia's law banning sodomy. The Supreme Court ruled in *Bowers v. Hardwick* (1986) that homosexual behavior was not protected by the Constitution

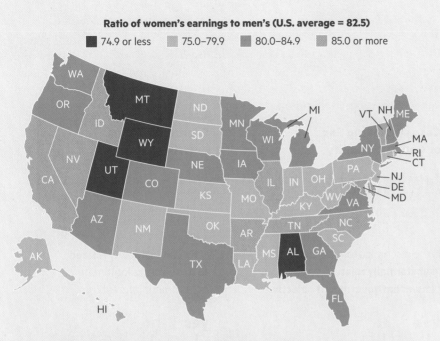

Ratio of women's earnings to men's (U.S. average = 82.5)

■ 74.9 or less ▨ 75.0–79.9 ▨ 80.0–84.9 ▨ 85.0 or more

Sources: Data from "Highlight of Women's Earnings in 2014," *BLA Reports*, U.S. Bureau of Labor Statistics, November 2015, Table 3, p. 26, www.bls.gov (accessed 1/29/16); map taken from U.S. Bureau of Labor Statistics, "Women's Earnings in Texas—2014," Chart 3, www.bls.gov (accessed 1/29/16).

FIGURE 5.5

Women's Earnings as a Percentage of Men's Earnings, 2014

There is a substantial difference between women's and men's earnings in the United States. What could account for this variation? How much do you think it has to do with levels of discrimination and how much with differences in the nature of the jobs that men and women hold?

and that state laws banning it could be justified under the most lenient "rational basis" test.[56]

After cases where it sidestepped the issue, the Court first endorsed civil rights for gays in 1996. Here the Court struck down an amendment to the Colorado state constitution that prevented them from suing for discrimination in employment or housing. The Court said that the amendment violated gays' equal protection rights because it "withdrew from homosexuals, but no others, specific legal protection from the injuries caused by discrimination."[57] An important ruling came in 2003 in a case involving two Houston men. As we discussed in Chapter 4, John Geddes Lawrence and Tyron Garner were prosecuted for same-sex sodomy (which was illegal in Texas) after police found them having sex in Lawrence's apartment. The Supreme Court ruled in a historic 6–3 decision that the due process clause of the Fourteenth Amendment guarantees freedom of not only thought, belief, and expression but also certain intimate conduct (including homosexual relations).[58]

The Supreme Court issued two important rulings on same-sex marriage in 2013. The first case was a narrow ruling that reinstated same-sex marriage in California but did not affect any other state. The second case was a more far-reaching decision that struck down the Defense of Marriage Act (DOMA) as a violation of the Fifth Amendment's due process clause. The majority opinion said that the federal government cannot deny benefits to same-sex couples who are legally married under state law. The gradual movement toward endorsing same-sex marriage culminated in 2015 in the landmark ruling *Obergefell v. Hodges*, which legalized same-sex marriage in all 50 states (for more on the Supreme Court's ruling in this case, see How It Works: The Court System in Chapter 13).[59] The 5–4 ruling said that the fundamental right to marry is guaranteed by both the due process clause and the equal protection clause of the Fourteenth Amendment.

> The Constitution promises liberty to all within its reach ... [and] extend[s] to certain personal choices central to individual dignity and autonomy, including intimate choices that define personal identity and beliefs.
>
> —Supreme Court's majority opinion in *Obergefell v. Hodges*

Civil Rights

Cases Involving "Suspect Classification" (race, ethnicity, creed, or national origin)

Strict Scrutiny Test

1. Is unequal treatment justified by a **"compelling state interest"**?

yes   **no**

↓

discrimination is illegal

2. Is unequal treatment the **"least restrictive"** option?

yes   **no**

↓

discrimination is illegal

Very few cases meet this standard.

Cases Involving Sex or Gender Equality

Intermediate Scrutiny Test

1. Is the discriminatory policy **"substantially related"** to an **"important government objective"**?

yes   **no**

↓

discrimination is illegal

2. Is the discrimination **not substantially broader** than it needs to be to protect the important government interest?

yes   **no**

↓

discrimination is illegal

Some discrimination based on gender is permitted, but this test is harder to pass than the rational basis test applied to gender cases in the past.

Cases Involving Age, Economic Status, or Other Criteria

Rational Basis Test

1. Is the law **rationally related to furthering** a legitimate government interest?

yes   **no**

↓

discrimination is illegal

2. Does the policy avoid **"arbitrary, capricious, or deliberate"** discrimination?

yes   **no**

↓

discrimination is illegal

This is the easiest hurdle for a law or policy to pass.

→ **discrimination is legal** ←

Evaluating Discrimination Cases

 ## Strict Scrutiny Test

Case 1:

The University of Michigan Law School's "holistic" race-conscious admissions policy is designed to promote diversity.

Case 2:

The University of Michigan's more rigid race-conscious undergraduate admissions policy was designed to promote diversity.

The Court asked...

1. Is unequal treatment justified by a "compelling state interest"?
2. Is unequal treatment the "least restrictive" option?

The Court said...

In Case 1, discrimination is OK. In *Grutter v. Bollinger* (2003), the Court ruled that the state's interest in **racial diversity in higher education was compelling,** and that this specific admissions policy was narrowly tailored. This was affirmed in *Fisher v. Univ. of Texas* (2016).

In Case 2, discrimination is not OK. In *Gratz v. Bollinger* (2003), the Court **struck down Michigan's undergraduate admissions policy** for not being narrowly tailored.

 ## Intermediate Scrutiny Test

Case 1:

A California state law says that men—but not women—can be guilty of statutory rape.

Case 2:

The Virginia Military Institute maintained a male-only admissions policy.

The Court asked...

1. Is the discriminatory policy "substantially related" to an "important government objective"?
2. Is the discrimination not substantially broader than it needs to be to to protect the important government interest?

The Court said...

In Case 1, discrimination is OK. In *Michael M. v. Superior Court* (1981), the Court found that the state had a **strong interest in preventing illegitimate pregnancy** and in punishing only the participant who, by nature, suffers few of the consequences of his conduct.

In Case 2, discrimination is not OK. In *United States v. Virginia* (1996), the Court **struck down the Virginia Military Institute's policy** as a violation of the equal protection clause of the Fourteenth Amendment.

Rational Basis Test

Case 1:

States have a 21-year-old drinking age that applies equally to men and women.

Case 2:

An Oklahoma law allowed 18- to 20-year-old women—but not men—to buy 3.2% beer.

The Court asked...

1. Is the law rationally related to furthering a legitimate government interest?
2. Does the policy avoid "arbitrary, capricious, or deliberate" discrimination?

The Court said...

In Case 1, discrimination is OK. Various state supreme courts have upheld these laws on the rational basis that **the laws may prevent drunk driving among 18- to 20-year-olds.**

In Case 2, discrimination is not OK. In *Craig v. Boren* (1976), the Court **struck down this law,** rejecting the rational basis that Oklahoma had claimed and instead applying intermediate scrutiny.

?

Critical Thinking

1. **Is it easier for the government to discriminate against** someone based on age or race? Why?

2. **What is the standard used by the Court if the state wants** to make distinctions between people based on race? Under what circumstances and in what scenarios is discrimination based on race legal?

This summary of cases demonstrates that the courts can be both a strong advocate of and an impediment to civil rights. In general, however, the courts have a limited *independent* impact on policy. Indeed, the Supreme Court must rely on the other branches of government to carry out its policy decisions.

Congress

Congress has provided the basis for protection of civil rights through laws enacted starting in the 1960s. Applying to racial and ethnic minorities and women, these laws attempted to ensure a "level playing field" of equal opportunity.

Key Early Legislation The bedrock of equal protection that exists today stems from the 1964 Civil Rights Act, the 1965 VRA, and the 1968 Fair Housing Act. President Lyndon Johnson, a former segregationist, helped push through the Civil Rights Act when he became president. The act barred discrimination in employment based on race, sex, religion, or national origin; banned segregation in public places; and established the EEOC as the enforcement agency for the legislation.

The VRA eliminated direct obstacles to minority voting in the South, such as discriminatory literacy tests and other voter registration tests, and provided the means to enforce the law: federal marshals were charged with overseeing elections in the South. The VRA, often cited as one of the most significant pieces of civil rights legislation,[60] precipitated an explosion in black political participation in the South. The most dramatic gains came in Mississippi, where black registration increased from 6.7 percent before the VRA to 59.8 percent in 1967.

The Fair Housing Act of 1968 barred discrimination in the rental or sale of a home based on race, sex, religion, or national origin. Important amendments to the law enacted in 1988 added disability and familial status (having children under age 18), provided new administrative enforcement mechanisms, and expanded Justice Department jurisdiction to bring suit on behalf of victims in federal district courts.[61]

Among other amendments to civil rights laws, most important were the 1975 amendments to the VRA that extended coverage of many of the law's provisions to language minorities (that is, guaranteeing in certain districts with large numbers of citizens who are not proficient in English that registration and voting materials would be made available to them in their native language); the 1982 VRA amendments, which extended important provisions of the law for 25 years and made it easier to bring a lawsuit under the act; the 1991 Civil Rights Act; and the 2006 extension of the VRA for another 25 years. The 1991 law overruled or altered parts of 12 Supreme Court decisions that had eroded the intent of Congress when it passed the civil rights legislation. It expanded earlier legislation and increased the costs to employers for intentional, illegal discrimination.

Protections for Women Women have also received extensive protection through legislation. In 1966, the National Organization for Women (NOW) was formed to push for enforcement of Title VII of the Civil Rights Act, which barred discrimination based on gender. NOW's members convinced President Johnson to sign an executive order that eliminated sex discrimination in federal agencies and among federal contractors, but it was difficult to enforce. Finally, in 1970 the EEOC started enforcing the law. Before long, one-third of civil rights cases involved sex discrimination, and those numbers remain high.

In 1972, Congress passed Title IX of the Education Amendments, which prohibits sex discrimination in institutions that receive federal funds. The law has had the

DID YOU KNOW?

66.2%

of African Americans voted in 2012 compared with 64.1 percent of whites (but African-American turnout was slightly lower than whites' turnout in 2016).

Source: Pew Research Center

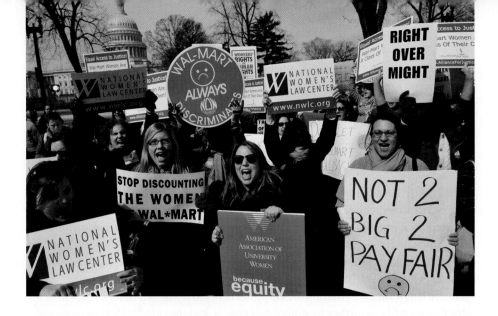

📷

Demonstrators rallied in support of female workers who had filed a sexual discrimination lawsuit against Walmart. Betty Dukes (the lead plaintiff in the case) and a class of 1.6 million women who worked for Walmart filed a class-action suit against Walmart, claiming that Walmart paid men more than women and favored men over women when deciding on promotions. In 2011, the Supreme Court ruled in favor of Walmart, saying that women would have to prove discrimination individually rather than in a class-action lawsuit.

> **No person in the United States shall, on the basis of sex, be excluded from participation in, be denied the benefits of, or be subjected to discrimination under any educational program or activity receiving Federal financial assistance.**
>
> **—Full text of Title IX**

greatest impact in women's sports. In the 1960s and 1970s, opportunities for women to play sports in college or high school were limited because of few scholarships and small budgets for women's sports. Although it took nearly 30 years to reach parity between men and women, most universities are now in compliance with Title IX. Nonetheless, many men's sports, such as baseball, tennis, wrestling, and gymnastics, were cut at universities that had to bring the number of student athletes into rough parity and critics argued that such cuts were unfair, especially as the interest in women's sports was not as high as for men's sports. Defenders of the law argue that the gap in interest in women's and men's sports will not change until there is equal opportunity. There is some evidence to support that claim, as interest is increasing in professional women's soccer with the NWSL (National Women's Soccer League) and professional women's basketball with the WNBA (Women's National Basketball Association), as well as in well-established women's professional sports such as golf and tennis.

Another significant effort was the failed Equal Rights Amendment. It was approved by Congress in 1972 with simple wording: "Equality of rights under the law shall not be denied or abridged by the United States or any state on the account of sex." Many states passed it within months, but the process lost momentum and after seven years (the deadline set by Congress for ratification by the states) the amendment fell 3 states short of the required 38 states. The amendment received a three-year extension from Congress, but it still did not get passage by the additional three states.

In 1994, Congress passed the Violence against Women Act, which allowed women who were the victims of physical abuse and violence to sue in federal court and provided funding for investigating and prosecuting violent crimes against women, for helping the victims of such crimes, and for prevention programs. In 2000, part of this law was overturned by the Supreme Court, which ruled that Congress had exceeded its powers under the commerce clause.[62] Nonetheless, the funding provisions of the act were reauthorized and expanded by Congress in 2000, 2005, and 2013.

Protections for the Disabled and for Gay Rights Other important civil rights legislation included the 1990 Americans with Disabilities Act, which provided federal protections for disabled Americans in terms of workplace discrimination and access to public facilities. This law produced the curb cuts in sidewalks, access for wheelchairs to public buses and trains, special seating in sports stadiums, and many other changes that provide the disabled an equal opportunity to participate more fully in society.[63]

Congress's track record in protecting gay rights has not been as strong. In fact, most of the steps taken by Congress have been to restrict gay rights. In 1996, Congress reacted to the possibility that some liberal states would allow same-sex marriage by passing DOMA. This act defined marriage as only between a man and woman and barred couples in same-sex marriages from receiving federal insurance or Social Security spousal benefits and from filing joint federal tax returns. (However, as we noted earlier, this law was struck down by the Supreme Court in 2013, and the entire law was overturned in 2015.)

In a possible change of course, in 2009 Congress passed the Matthew Shepard and James Byrd Jr. Hate Crimes Prevention Act. This legislation expanded the hate-crime laws based on race, color, religion, or national origin to include attacks based on sexual orientation, gender identity, or mental or physical disability. The law also lifted a requirement that a victim had to be attacked while engaged in a federally protected activity, such as attending school, for it to be a federal hate crime. In signing the bill, President Obama said, "After more than a decade of opposition and delay, we've passed inclusive hate-crimes legislation to help protect our citizens from violence based on what they look like, who they love, how they pray or who they are."[64] The law commemorates the murders of James Byrd Jr., who in 1998 was dragged behind a pickup truck by white supremacists for three miles until his head and right arm were severed, and Matthew Shepard, a gay teenager who in 1998 was beaten by two men, tied to a fence, and left to die. Also, the Employment Non-Discrimination Act, which would prohibit discrimination in employment based on sexual orientation, has been proposed in nearly every Congress since 1994. A version of the bill passed the House in 2007 but died in the Senate.

The president

The civil rights movement has benefited greatly from presidential action, such as President Truman's integration of the armed services in 1948 and President Eisenhower's use of the National Guard to enforce a court order to integrate a school in Arkansas in 1957. Executive orders by President Kennedy in 1961 and President Johnson in 1965 established affirmative action, and in 1969 Richard Nixon expanded the "goals and numerical ranges" for hiring minorities in the federal government.

The most significant action by a president in the area of civil rights for gay men and lesbians was President Bill Clinton's effort to end the ban on homosexuals in the military. Under his policy of "don't ask, don't tell," the military would stop actively searching for and discharging homosexuals from the military ranks, and recruits would not need to reveal their sexual orientation. But if the military did find out (without conducting an investigation) that a person was gay, he or she still could be disciplined or discharged. Subsequently, President Obama promised to repeal "don't ask, don't tell" and under his administration Congress passed the Don't Ask, Don't Tell Repeal Act of 2010. The repeal went into effect on September 20, 2011. Minutes afterward, navy lieutenant Gary Ross and his longtime partner were married in Vermont and Ross became the first openly gay married person in the military.[65]

The low priority that recent presidential candidates have given to civil rights policy more generally means that it is less likely that significant and dramatic change will come from unilateral action by the president. Instead, attention to civil rights concerns in the executive branch has primarily been in two areas since 1993: racial diversity in presidential appointments and use of the bully pulpit to promote racial concerns and interests.

President Bill Clinton was active in both areas. His cabinet, subcabinet, and judicial appointments achieved the greatest gender and racial balance in history. Fourteen percent of Clinton's first-year presidential appointments were African American

You do not take a person who, for years, has been hobbled by chains and liberate him, bring him up to the starting line of a race and then say you are free to compete with all the others, and still just believe that you have been completely fair.

—President Lyndon Johnson
on affirmative action

The controversial "don't ask, don't tell" policy of the U.S. military had prevented gay men and lesbians from serving openly in the armed forces. Congress passed the Don't Ask, Don't Tell Repeal Act of 2010, which went into effect on September 20, 2011. Once gays and lesbians in the military did not have to hide their sexual affiliation, they were free to marry in states that permitted same-sex marriage. #DADT

(compared with 12 percent of the country's population in 1992), 6 percent were Latino (compared with 9.5 percent of the country's population), and the percentages of Asian-American and Native-American appointees were identical to their proportions in the population. (The proportion of women appointees—27 percent—was well short of their proportion in the population, but it still was a record high.) Clinton also used the bully pulpit to advocate a civil rights agenda focusing on problems faced by minorities.

President George W. Bush did not achieve the same level of diversity in his appointments as had Clinton, but his administration was more diverse than those of other Republican presidents. Moreover, Bush made serious overtures to minorities, especially Latinos, in his effort to expand the Republican Party base. In terms of Barack Obama's presidency, the historical significance of his successful campaign as a minority candidate is clear. And like his predecessors, Obama nominated a diverse cabinet—with 14 men, 7 women, and 7 racial minorities. Eric Holder was the first African American to serve as attorney general, and Sonia Sotomayor is the first Latina on the Supreme Court. Obama also nominated Elena Kagan to the Supreme Court, putting three women on the Court for the first time.

Donald Trump was elected with racially divisive positions, such as building a wall with Mexico and deporting 12 million illegal residents. In his election night victory speech he emphasized the importance of representing all Americans and uniting the country. It will be interesting to watch how his administration deals with these seemingly divergent viewpoints.

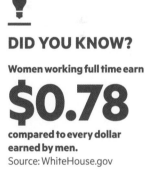

DID YOU KNOW?

Women working full time earn

$0.78

compared to every dollar earned by men.

Source: WhiteHouse.gov

"Why Should I Care?"

Why is it important for us to know about who the key players are in civil rights? At various times in our history, different branches of government took the lead in promoting civil rights: Congress in the 1960s with the Civil Rights Act and the VRA, Presidents Clinton and Obama with promoting diversity in presidential appointments, and the Supreme Court in endorsing same-sex marriage. If we want to see policies around these kind of issues change, knowing who is involved, and what impact they can have, is critical.

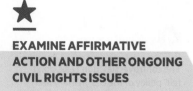
Civil rights issues today

There is vigorous debate over the likely direction of the civil rights movement in the twenty-first century. These debates play out over a broad range of issues, several of which are outlined in this section.

Affirmative action

Even though the Civil Rights Act of 1964 ensured that all Americans would enjoy equality of opportunity, blacks continued to lag behind whites in socioeconomic status. In 1965, President Johnson required all federal agencies and government contractors to submit written proposals to provide an equal opportunity for employment of blacks, women, Asian Americans, and Native Americans within various job categories and to outline programs to achieve those goals. The policy was expanded under President Richard Nixon, and throughout the 1970s and 1980s affirmative action programs grew in the private sector, higher education, and government contracting. Through such programs, employers and universities gave special opportunities to minorities and women.

Affirmative action takes many forms. The most passive type involves recruiting women and minorities for employment or college admission by placing ads in newspapers and magazines, visiting inner-city schools, or sending out targeted mailings. A more active form involves including race or gender as a "plus factor" in the admissions or hiring decision. That is, in a pool of qualified candidates a minority applicant may receive an advantage over white applicants. (Women generally do not receive special consideration in admissions decisions, but gender may be a "plus factor" in some employment decisions.) The strongest form of affirmative action is the use of quotas—strict numerical targets to hire or admit a specific number of applicants from underrepresented groups.

Affirmative action has been a controversial policy. Polls indicate that minorities are much more supportive of the practice than whites. Many whites view it as "preferential treatment" and "reverse discrimination." A majority of whites support passive forms of affirmative action, such as "education programs to assist minorities in competing for college admissions," but draw the line at preferences, even when they are intended to make up for past discrimination.[66]

The Supreme Court has helped define the boundaries of this policy debate. The earliest cases concerning affirmative action in employment upheld preferential treatment and rigid quotas when the policies were necessary to make up for past discrimination.[67] In each instance, there had been a previous pattern of discrimination and exclusion. Then, in 1989, the Court started moving in a "color-blind" direction concerning "set-aside" programs in government contracting. In 1983, Richmond, Virginia, began requiring contractors who had won city construction contracts to subcontract at least 30 percent of the work to minority-owned businesses. After a white business owner sued, the Court ruled that set-asides were unconstitutional without evidence of discrimination against minorities and that any such programs had to be "narrowly tailored to meet a compelling state interest."[68] The same reasoning was applied to federal contracting set-aside programs in 1995.[69]

The Court moved in a more color-blind direction in an important reverse-discrimination employment case in 2009. In that case, 17 white firefighters and 1 Hispanic firefighter sued the city of New Haven, Connecticut, for throwing out the results of a test that would have been used to promote them. The city tried to ignore

Affirmative Action in College Admissions

Since 1978, the Supreme Court has endorsed the idea of race as a "plus factor" in college admissions while rejecting the idea of strict quotas or point systems. This approach was affirmed in a 2003 case involving the University of Michigan's law school, but many Court-watchers believed that affirmative action would be struck down in the 2016 case *Fisher v. University of Texas, Austin*.[a] Instead, Justice Kennedy sided with the liberals and upheld the practice.

UT Austin's college admissions process has two parts. First, anyone in the top 10 percent of a Texas public high school is guaranteed admission to UT (in recent years this has been closer to the top 8 percent). Because most high schools in Texas are somewhat segregated by race, the 10 percent plan automatically creates diversity for the entering class. Second, the remaining 25 percent of in-state students are admitted by a "holistic" program that evaluates their entire record and includes race as a "plus factor." It was this second part that Abigail Fisher challenged after being denied admission to UT. The legal question that the Court had to decide was whether the university's affirmative action program violated the equal protection clause of the Fourteenth Amendment and civil rights laws barring discrimination on the basis of race or could be justified as serving a "compelling state interest" under the strict scrutiny standard.

Diversity deserves consideration.

Advocates of affirmative action argue that a diverse student body promotes viewpoint diversity that is essential to learning. Having racial diversity in the student body is likely to produce more viewpoint diversity in classroom

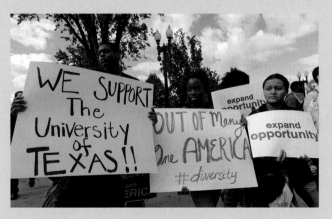

📷 Students protest outside the Supreme Court in support of diversity at the University of Texas.

discussions than would occur with a mostly white student body. The majority opinion in the Texas case also argued that a more diverse student body leads to "the destruction of stereotypes," promotes "cross-racial understanding," and prepares students "for an increasingly diverse work force and society." Furthermore, proponents argue, the courts are not the proper place to decide these issues. Instead, as with the complex and highly charged topic of racial redistricting, the political branches of government are where these decisions should be made. The Court endorsed this position of judicial restraint in a 2014 case involving a ban on affirmative action in Michigan.[b]

The Court argued that the Texas approach was "narrowly tailored" to serve the compelling state interest of viewpoint diversity because the 10 percent plan, by itself, did not produce the desired level of diversity and would create perverse incentives. Justice Kennedy wrote, "Percentage plans encourage parents to keep their children in low-performing segregated schools, and discourage students from taking challenging classes that might lower their grade point averages."

Affirmative action is just another kind of discrimination.

Opponents reply that supporters of affirmative action have not provided convincing evidence that racial diversity in colleges has any beneficial effects. They also argue that "viewpoint diversity" arguments assume that members of all racial minorities think alike, drawing a comparison to racial profiling in law enforcement. It is just as offensive, they say, that an admissions committee thinks that one black student has the same views as another black student as it is that a police officer may pull over a black teenage male just because he fits a certain criminal profile.

Opponents also argue that affirmative action amounts to "reverse discrimination" and that any racial classification is harmful. Justice Alito's scathing dissent in the Texas case said, "[. . .] U.T. has never provided any coherent explanation for its asserted need to discriminate on the basis of race, and [. . .] U.T.'s position relies on a series of unsupported and noxious racial assumptions." Alito also argued that concepts such as viewpoint diversity and "cross-cultural understanding" are "slippery" and difficult to analyze systematically.

The Texas case will not be the end of the debate concerning affirmative action in higher education. A pending suit challenges Harvard University's affirmative action program as discriminating against Asian Americans. If you had to rule on the Texas case, how would you have decided? Take a stand.

take a stand

1. To what extent should race be used as a "plus factor" to promote racial diversity and viewpoint diversity, if at all? Is the "top 10 percent" plan a better approach?

2. Think of your own experiences in high school and college. Has racial diversity contributed to viewpoint diversity?

the test results because no African-American firefighters would have qualified for promotion and the city feared a "disparate impact" lawsuit. However, the Court ruled that the exam did appear to be "job related and consistent with business necessity" (as required by Section VII of the Civil Rights Act) and that unless the city could provide a "strong basis in evidence" that it would have been sued it had to consider the results of the exam.[70]

The landmark decision for affirmative action in higher education was Regents of the *University of California v. Bakke* (1978).[71] Allan Bakke, a white student, sued when he was denied admission to medical school at the University of California, Davis, in successive years. Bakke's test scores and GPA were significantly higher than those of some minority students who were admitted under the school's affirmative action program. The Supreme Court agreed with Bakke that rigid racial quotas were unconstitutional but allowed race to be used in admissions decisions as a "plus factor" to promote diversity in the student body.

In two 2003 cases from the University of Michigan, the Court's rulings were consistent with *Bakke*, saying that the law school's "holistic approach" that considered race as one of the factors in the admission decision was acceptable but that the more rigid approach for undergraduate admissions at Michigan, which automatically gave minority students 20 of the 100 points needed to guarantee admission, was unacceptable.[72] Though these two decisions affirmed *Bakke*, it was the first time that a majority of the Court clearly stated that "student body diversity is a compelling state interest that can justify the use of race in university admissions."[73] In 2006, voters in Michigan passed Proposal 2, an initiative to make it illegal for state bodies to consider race in admissions and hiring decisions; this policy was upheld by the Supreme Court in 2014.[74] This means that states will be able to decide whether to consider affirmative action in higher education, because the policy is neither prohibited nor required by the Constitution.

In 2008, the University of Texas at Austin was sued by a white student who claimed she was a victim of reverse discrimination. Texas had achieved a racially diverse student body by giving admission to the top 10 percent of every graduating high school class (in recent years, this policy was changed to the top 7 percent). This approach worked because most high schools in Texas were still segregated. In 2013, the Court affirmed that diversity could be a legitimate goal for the state but that the appeals court that upheld the admissions policy had failed to apply the strict scrutiny standard. Therefore, the case was sent back to the appeals court, which upheld Texas's affirmative action policy in July 2014. In June 2016, the Court affirmed that decision by a 4–3 vote.[75] For more on affirmative action in college admissions, see the Take a Stand feature.

Abigail Fisher sued the University of Texas over their affirmative action policy. She is shown talking to reporters outside the Supreme Court after the case was heard in 2016.

Multicultural issues

Issues involving the multicultural, multiracial nature of American society will become more important as whites cease to be the majority of the population by midcentury. Two key issues are English as the official language and immigration.

Decisions to establish English as the official language in many states have had wide-reaching consequences. For example, the Supreme Court upheld an Alabama state law requiring that the state driver's license test be conducted only in English. A

Mexican immigrant sued under Title VI of the 1964 Civil Rights Act, claiming that the Alabama law had a disparate impact on non-English-speaking residents. However, the Court held in *Alexander v. Sandoval* (2001) that individuals may not sue federally funded state agencies over policies that have a discriminatory effect on minorities under Title VI.[76] This decision has far-reaching consequences for the use of the Civil Rights Act to fight patterns of discrimination, especially in education policy (for example, civil rights advocates have challenged the use of standardized testing because of its disparate impact on minorities) and environmental policy (lawsuits brought under Title VI have alleged "environmental racism" in decisions to place hazardous waste dumps in predominantly minority areas).

Immigration regained center stage after the September 11 terrorist attacks, when some people saw immigration as a threat that must be curtailed. The government asserted that it would not engage in racial profiling of Arab Americans—for example, subjecting them to stricter screening at airports—but many commentators argued that such profiling would be justified, and there was at least anecdotal evidence of increased discrimination against people of Middle Eastern descent. After the terrorist attacks in Paris and San Bernardino, California, in 2016 the debate in the presidential campaign shifted to a strongly anti-immigrant tone. Donald Trump proposed preventing all Muslims from entering the United States until we could make sure there was no terrorist threat. Other Republican presidential candidates endorsed the idea of preventing all emigrants from Syria, who were flooding into Europe, from entering the United States, but Hillary Clinton strongly resisted the idea, pointing out that the United States is a nation of immigrants and that precautions can be taken to make sure that terrorists do not slip into the country.

Over the past two decades, immigration has been central in many political debates. This intensified in 2010, when Arizona enacted an anti-immigration law that requires local law-enforcement officials to check the immigration status of a person in a "lawful stop, detention, or arrest" if there is a "reasonable suspicion" that the person is an illegal alien. The law also requires immigrants to always carry papers and bans people without proper documents from seeking work in public places. The chapter opener noted some of the violations in civil rights that occurred when local law-enforcement officials started enforcing this law. Opponents of the law argue that it requires illegal

Border patrol agents detain undocumented immigrants apprehended near the Mexican border outside McAllen, Texas. Illegal immigration continues to be a hot-button issue in national electoral and legislative politics.

racial profiling and that the federal government has the sole responsibility for deciding immigration law. The Supreme Court struck down three of the four main provisions of the law, citing the supremacy clause of the Constitution. This decision meant that Congress, not the states, determines immigration law when the two laws conflict. The Court upheld the controversial "show me your papers" part of the law, saying that the state was simply enforcing the federal law. However, the Court indicated that the law must be applied in a race-neutral way and could be struck down if there was clear evidence of racial profiling.[77] Several months later, a federal district court judge cleared the way for implementation of the "show me your papers" law, saying that the Supreme Court wanted to see actual evidence of discrimination rather than speculation that the law could have a discriminatory effect.[78]

As noted in the introduction, the immigration system is widely viewed as broken and in need of reform. However, neither President Bush nor President Obama was able to get Congress to approve their proposals to provide a "path to citizenship" for undocumented immigrants. In 2015, President Obama used executive orders to implement part of his immigration policy (concerning the deportation of young adults who were brought to the United States illegally by their parents and the parents of children who are citizens). The Supreme Court deadlocked 4–4 in a June 2016 case, upholding the lower court's ruling that struck down the executive order. More than 4 million immigrants had to await the results of the election. President Trump has vowed to cancel this program, but it is less clear that he will be able to implement the massive deportation program that he endorsed during the campaign.

The debates over affirmative action, English as the country's official language, and immigration reform clearly illustrate the conflictual nature of civil rights policy. However, history has shown that when public opinion strongly supports a given application of civil rights—for example, the integration of African Americans in the South in the 1960s and, more recently, allowing gays to openly serve in the military and recognizing same-sex marriage—public policy soon reflects those views. Although it is impossible to say when there will be comprehensive immigration reform that includes a path to citizenship, policy appears to be headed in that direction, given the trends in public opinion.

Conclusion

Enforcing civil rights means providing equal protection of the law to individuals and groups that are discriminated against, which may include noncitizens and illegal immigrants. But figuring out exactly when an individual's civil rights have been violated can be tricky. When does a routine traffic stop by a police officer turn into racial profiling? To help figure that out, we now can answer the questions about possible civil rights violations that introduced this chapter.

- Scenario 1: On the one hand, the African-American teenagers who were pulled over by the police may or may not have had their civil rights violated, depending on the laws in their state. In Massachusetts, for example, it is prohibited to consider the "race, gender, national or ethnic origin of members of the public in deciding to detain a person or stop a motor vehicle" except in "suspect specific incidents."[79] On the other hand, in the scenario in which the police pulled over white teenagers the traffic stop would have been acceptable as long as there had been "probable cause" to justify the stop.

- Scenario 2: The Asian-American woman who did not get the job could certainly talk to a lawyer about filing a "disparate impact" discrimination suit. Under the 1991 Civil Rights Act, the employer would have the burden of proof to show that she was not a victim of the "good ol' boy" network.
- Scenario 3: The gay couple who could not rent the apartment because of their sexual orientation might have a basis for a civil rights lawsuit based on the Fourteenth Amendment; however, this would depend on where they live, given that there is no federal protection against discrimination against gay men and lesbians (and the Supreme Court has not applied the Fourteenth Amendment in this context).
- Scenario 4: Court decisions concerning affirmative action in Michigan and Texas show that the white student who was not admitted to the university of his choice would have to take his lumps, as long as the affirmative action program considered race as a general "plus factor" rather than assigning more or fewer points for it (and the practice was allowed by his state).

This review of civil rights in the United States has highlighted only some of the most important issues, but a significant agenda remains. The civil rights movement will continue to use the multiple avenues of the legislative, executive, and judicial branches to secure equal rights for all Americans. Although this process may take many years, history demonstrates that when public opinion becomes more supportive of diversity and stronger civil rights our political institutions support the views of the people.

STUDY GUIDE

The context of civil rights

Describe the historical struggles groups have faced in winning civil rights. (Pages 125–130)

Summary

Civil rights are protections from discrimination both by the government and by individuals and are rooted in laws and the equal protection clause of the Fourteenth Amendment. The concept of equality has evolved over time, with protections now for the LGBTQ community, women, African Americans, Native Americans, Asian Americans, and Latinos. Despite our attempts to live in a color-blind society, awareness of race still influences many people's opinions and behavior.

Key terms

civil rights (p. 125)

Jim Crow laws (p. 127)

"separate but equal" doctrine (p. 127)

protectionism (p. 129)

Practice Quiz Questions

1. **The distinction between civil rights and civil liberties is that civil rights _____ while civil liberties _____ .**
   a. protect against discrimination; are guaranteed in the Bill of Rights
   b. are guaranteed in the Bill of Rights; protect against discrimination
   c. are guaranteed in the Bill of Rights; limit what the government can do to you
   d. limit what the government can do to you; protect against discrimination
   e. limit what the government can do to you; are guaranteed in the Bill of Rights

2. **The Missouri Compromise _____ .**
   a. ruled that people held as slaves are not protected by the Constitution
   b. established that three-fifths of the slaves could count in a state's population
   c. limited the expansion of slavery while maintaining the balance of slave states
   d. gave slaves the right to vote
   e. ended slavery in the South

3. **Plessy v. Ferguson established _____ .**
   a. the legitimacy of poll taxes
   b. the "separate but equal" doctrine
   c. that Jim Crow laws were illegal
   d. the process of desegregation in the South
   e. the legality of slavery

4. **The principle of _____ was used in many court cases to deny women equal rights.**
   a. matriarchy
   b. "separate but equal"
   c. sectionalism
   d. misandry
   e. protectionism

The racial divide today

Analyze inequality among racial, ethnic, and social groups today. (Pages 130–134)

Summary

Beyond the unequal treatment of racial minorities, women, and LGBTQ individuals, inequalities in political, social, and economic conditions also persist. Whites are able to participate in politics at a higher rate, enjoy a better standard of living, and avoid prejudice in the criminal justice system.

Practice Quiz Questions

5. **Most of the differences in voter turnout among whites relative to racial minorities can be accounted for by _____ .**
   a. contemporary Jim Crow laws
   b. voter purge lists
   c. voter ID laws
   d. poll taxes
   e. education and income

6. **The gaps between whites and blacks on health measures are _____ and in many cases _____ .**
   a. large; decreasing
   b. large; increasing
   c. small; decreasing
   d. small; increasing
   e. small; staying the same

The policy-making process and civil rights

Explain the approaches used to bring about change in civil rights policies. (Pages 134–151)

Summary

Depending on the political context, each branch of government has played a role in the expansion of civil rights. Moreover, federalism has played a role in this process. Although the state governments often lagged behind the federal government in African Americans' civil rights, they have been on the forefront in protecting the rights of gays and lesbians.

Key terms

de jure (p. 141)   rational basis test (p. 143)
de facto (p. 141)

Practice Quiz Questions

7. Early in the nation's history, civil rights activism was focused on ____.

 a. women

 b. gays and lesbians

 c. African Americans

 d. Latinos

 e. Native Americans

8. Early in the civil rights movement (before the 1960s), which branch provided most of the successes?

 a. state governments

 b. Congress

 c. the presidency

 d. the bureaucracy

 e. the Supreme Court

9. The difference between de facto segregation and de jure segregation is that de facto segregation ____, while de jure segregation ____.

 a. is the result of circumstances; is mandated by law

 b. is mandated by law; is the result of circumstances

 c. applies to racial minorities; applies to women

 d. applies to women; applies to racial minorities

 e. applies to all groups; applies to racial minorities

10. The strongest protection as the "suspect classification" applies which test?

 a. rational basis

 b. strict scrutiny

 c. intermediate scrutiny

 d. privileged interest

 e. disparate impact

11. The VRA ____.

 a. established "majority-minority" districts

 b. established compulsory voter registration for African Americans

 c. eliminated direct obstacles to minority voting in the South

 d. barred discrimination in the rental or sale of a home

 e. reduced participation by African Americans in the South

12. Relative to the protection of individuals with disabilities, Congress's track record in protecting gay rights is ____.

 a. stronger

 b. about the same

 c. weaker

 d. nonexistent

 e. more focused on job discrimination

Civil rights issues today

Examine affirmative action and other ongoing civil rights issues. (Pages 152–156)

Summary

The public is divided on the appropriateness of civil rights policies, with some groups preferring a "color-blind" and some groups preferring a "color-conscious" approach. Furthermore, the debates over issues such as affirmative action, immigration reform, and establishing English as the official language in many states indicate the level of conflict over civil rights policy. Nonetheless, when public opinion does strongly support the application of civil rights in a particular arena, policy makers generally respond to these views.

Practice Quiz Question

13. What did the case *Regents of the University of California v. Bakke* establish?

 a. that race could play no role in the college admissions process

 b. that gender could play no role in the college admissions process

 c. that strict racial quotas in the admissions process were legal

 d. that race could be used as a "plus factor" in the admissions process

 e. that gender could be used as a "plus factor" in the admissions process

Suggested Reading

Berman, Ari. *Give Us the Ballot: The Modern Struggle for Voting Rights in America*. New York: Farrar, Straus and Giroux, 2015.

Canon, David T. *Race, Redistricting, and Representation: The Unintended Consequences of Black-Majority Districts*. Chicago: University of Chicago Press, 1999.

Dawson, Michael C. *Behind the Mule: Race and Class in African-American Politics*. Princeton, NJ: Princeton University Press, 1994.

Hochschild, Jennifer L., Vesla M. Weaver, and Traci R. Burch. *Creating a New Racial Order: How Immigration, Multiracialism, Genomics, and the Young Can Remake Race in America*. Princeton, NJ: Princeton University Press, 2012.

Katznelson, Ira. *When Affirmative Action Was White: An Untold History of Racial Inequality in Twentieth-Century America*. New York: W. W. Norton, 2005.

Kennedy, Randall. *For Discrimination: Race, Affirmative Action, and the Law*. New York: Vintage Books, 2015

Kousser, J. Morgan. *Colorblind Injustice: Minority Voting Rights and the Undoing of the Second Reconstruction*. Chapel Hill: University of North Carolina Press, 1999.

Tate, Katherine. *Black Lawmaking in the U.S. Congress from Carter to Obama*. Ann Arbor: University of Michigan Press, 2014.

Thernstrom, Stephan, and Abigail Thernstrom. *America in Black and White: One Nation, Indivisible—Race in Modern America*. New York: Simon and Schuster, 1997.

6

Public Opinion and the Media

Do politicians listen to the people? Should they?

At first glance, it seems clear that Americans demand stricter controls on gun ownership. Even before the Orlando shooting in June 2016, polls showed that strong majorities favored background checks for gun purchasers, prohibiting people on the federal "no fly" list from purchasing guns, and constructing a federal database of gun owners. At the same time, however, no observer of Washington politics believed that these measures had any chance of becoming law. This discrepancy between apparent citizen demands and policy outcomes suggested to some that House members and senators feared that a vote for gun control would prompt the National Rifle Association and other groups to run campaign ads against them. If so, wasn't this a case of politicians not listening to the people and instead giving in to the pressure of a well-funded special interest group?

Before we blame elected officials, we need to examine public opinion itself. What does it mean when someone expresses a political opinion—for example, support for a gun control proposal or disapproval of the president's performance? Where do these sentiments come from? Are they long held or fleeting? Are these sentiments real, in the sense that they reflect judgments that shape the person's behavior, or are they just something that a person says without really believing it? Candidates, political parties, journalists, and political scientists take thousands of polls to determine who is likely to vote; what sorts of arguments, slogans, and platforms would appeal to these voters; and which policies are in demand by the electorate. Yet some evidence suggests that most Americans improvise their responses to poll questions; have no firm opinions

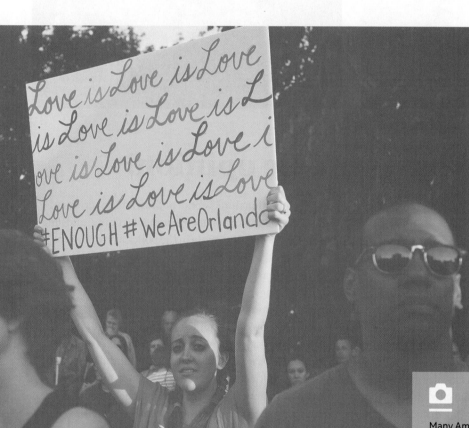

★
CHAPTER GOALS

Define *public opinion* and explain why it matters in American politics.
pages 162–165

Explain how people form political attitudes and opinions.
pages 166–169

Describe basic survey methods and potential issues affecting accuracy.
pages 170–175

Present findings on what Americans think about government and why it matters.
pages 176–182

Describe the major types of news sources and the role they play in American politics.
pages 182–186

📷

Many Americans have attended or seen pictures of memorials to victims of gun violence. Strong majorities favor some limits on gun ownership. Why, then, have such proposals failed to be enacted?
#WeAreOrlando #PulseOrlando

Public Opinion and the Media **161**

Are Americans poorly informed about politics? One survey found that more Americans could identify characters on *The Simpsons* than could list which liberties the Bill of Rights guarantees, and another found most respondents unable to name any Supreme Court justices. #SCOTUS

about government policy; are easily swayed by candidates, advocacy groups, or the media; and may respond inconsistently to questions that ask the same thing but are worded differently. If those studies are correct, how do we know what people think and how the media shape their opinions? How should we expect politicians to react? How does public opinion work?

DEFINE *PUBLIC OPINION* AND EXPLAIN WHY IT MATTERS IN AMERICAN POLITICS

public opinion
Citizens' views on politics and government actions.

Whoever can change public opinion can change the government.

—President Abraham Lincoln

What is public opinion?

Public opinion describes what the population thinks about politics and government—what government should be doing, evaluations of what government *is* doing, and judgments about elected officials and others who participate in the political process—as well as the wider set of beliefs that shape these opinions.

Public opinion matters for three reasons. First, citizens' political actions—including voting, contributing to campaigns, writing letters to senators, and undertaking other kinds of activism—are driven by their opinions.[1] Therefore, if we want to either understand an individual's behavior or analyze broader political outcomes, such as who wins an election or the fate of a legislative proposal, we need good data on public opinion.

Second, examining public opinion helps explain the behavior of candidates, political parties, and other political actors. Politicians look to public opinion to determine what citizens want them to do and how happy citizens are with their behavior in office.

Third, because public opinion is a key to understanding what motivates citizens and political officials, it can shed light on the reasons for specific policy outcomes. For example, changes in the policy mood—the public's demand for new policies—are linked to changes in government spending.[2] When people want government to do more, spending increases more rapidly; when people want less from government, spending goes down (or increases more slowly).

Describing public opinion

Modern theories of public opinion distinguish between two types of opinions: opinions that are preformed as well as opinions that are formed on the spot as needed. The first type includes broad expressions such as how a person thinks about politics, what he or she wants from government, or principles that apply across a range of issues. These

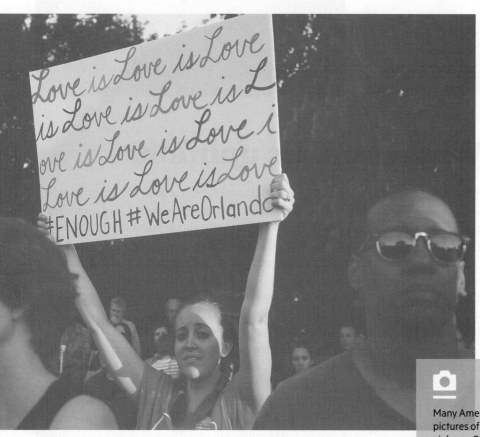

📷

Many Americans have attended or seen
pictures of memorials to victims of gun
violence. Strong majorities favor some limits
on gun ownership. Why, then, have such
proposals failed to be enacted?
#WeAreOrlando #PulseOrlando

Are Americans poorly informed about politics? One survey found that more Americans could identify characters on *The Simpsons* than could list which liberties the Bill of Rights guarantees, and another found most respondents unable to name any Supreme Court justices. #SCOTUS

about government policy; are easily swayed by candidates, advocacy groups, or the media; and may respond inconsistently to questions that ask the same thing but are worded differently. If those studies are correct, how do we know what people think and how the media shape their opinions? How should we expect politicians to react? How does public opinion work?

★

DEFINE *PUBLIC OPINION* AND EXPLAIN WHY IT MATTERS IN AMERICAN POLITICS

public opinion
Citizens' views on politics and government actions.

Whoever can change public opinion can change the government.

—President Abraham Lincoln

What is public opinion?

Public opinion describes what the population thinks about politics and government—what government should be doing, evaluations of what government *is* doing, and judgments about elected officials and others who participate in the political process—as well as the wider set of beliefs that shape these opinions.

Public opinion matters for three reasons. First, citizens' political actions—including voting, contributing to campaigns, writing letters to senators, and undertaking other kinds of activism—are driven by their opinions.[1] Therefore, if we want to either understand an individual's behavior or analyze broader political outcomes, such as who wins an election or the fate of a legislative proposal, we need good data on public opinion.

Second, examining public opinion helps explain the behavior of candidates, political parties, and other political actors. Politicians look to public opinion to determine what citizens want them to do and how happy citizens are with their behavior in office.

Third, because public opinion is a key to understanding what motivates citizens and political officials, it can shed light on the reasons for specific policy outcomes. For example, changes in the policy mood—the public's demand for new policies—are linked to changes in government spending.[2] When people want government to do more, spending increases more rapidly; when people want less from government, spending goes down (or increases more slowly).

Describing public opinion

Modern theories of public opinion distinguish between two types of opinions: opinions that are preformed as well as opinions that are formed on the spot as needed. The first type includes broad expressions such as how a person thinks about politics, what he or she wants from government, or principles that apply across a range of issues. These kinds of beliefs typically form early in life and remain stable over time. Some of these beliefs are obviously political, such as party identification, ideology (liberal or conservative), and judgments about whether elected officials lose touch with citizens. The second, more specific type of opinion, such as beliefs about homosexuality or religion, may seem irrelevant to politics, but in fact a wide range of seemingly nonpolitical beliefs directly shape Americans' political opinions.

Liberal or conservative ideology is a good example of a stable opinion: the best way to predict an American's ideology at age 40 is to assume it will match his or her ideology at age 20. The same is true for party identification. However, even fundamental opinions like these sometimes change in response to events. In a later section, we look more closely at how such opinions form and why they change.

Many opinions are latent

One important thing to understand about public opinion is that although ideology and party identification are largely consistent over time, they are exceptions to the rule.[3] The average person does not maintain a set of fully formed opinions on all political topics. Instead, most Americans' political judgments are **latent opinions**: they are constructed only as needed, such as when answering a survey question or deciding on Election Day how to vote. For example, when most people are asked about climate change they probably do not have a specific response in mind simply because they have not thought much about the question. Their opinions become concrete only when they are asked about those opinions.

People who follow politics closely have more preformed opinions than the average American, whose interest in politics is relatively low. But very few people are so well informed that they have ready opinions on a wide range of political and policy questions. Moreover, even when people do form opinions in advance they may not remember every factor that influenced their opinions. Thus, an individual may identify as a liberal or a conservative, or as a supporter of a particular party, but may be unable to explain the reasons behind these ideological leanings.[4]

How people form opinions

When people form opinions on the spot, they are based on **considerations**, which are the pieces of relevant information—such as ideology, party identification, religious beliefs, recent events, and personal circumstances—that come to mind when the opinion is requested.[5] The process of forming an opinion usually is not thorough or systematic, since most people don't take into account everything they know about an issue.[6] Rather, they use only considerations that come to mind immediately.[7] Highly informed people who follow politics use this process, as do those with low levels of political interest and knowledge.[8]

Many studies of public opinion support the idea that most people form opinions on the spot using a wide range of considerations. Consider the following research findings: Attitudes about immigration are shaped by evaluations of the state of the economy.[9] (See the Take a Stand feature.) People judge government spending proposals differently depending on whether a Republican or a Democrat made the proposal, using their own party identification as a consideration.[10] Evaluations of affirmative action programs vary depending on whether the survey question reminds respondents that such programs might hurt their own economic well-being.[11] Voters' party identification and ideology influence their evaluations of candidates.[12] Individuals' willingness to allow protests and other expressions of opinions they disagree with depends on their belief in tolerance.[13] And if people feel obligated to help others in need, they are more likely

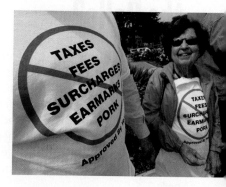

A person's ideological perspective is relatively stable over time. People who have a conservative ideology generally oppose increasing government spending and taxes.

latent opinion
An opinion formed on the spot, when it is needed (as distinct from a deeply held opinion that is stable over time).

considerations
The many pieces of information a person uses to form an opinion.

Should Politicians Follow the Polls?

Elected officials in America work hard to cast votes and take other actions that their constituents will like. At first glance, this behavior seems easy. All a politician needs to do is take a poll, measure public opinion in his or her state or district, and comply with the demands expressed in the survey responses. The problem is, poll results need interpretation. Small differences in question wording can produce very different responses, or public opinion can remain vague, despite the polls.

Imagine that a survey on immigration was conducted in your congressional district, asking voters if they favored allowing illegal immigrants to stay in the country or if people here illegally should be deported as soon as possible. Suppose that the poll results indicate strong support for one of the two options, and that you yourself have no strong feelings about illegal immigrants. The decision you face is: Should you demand that Congress enact immigration reform consistent with the poll results or should you quietly ask that immigration reform be kept off the agenda?

Follow the poll.
Elected officials often have strong incentives to do what constituents demand—in this case, to push for immigration reform measures that are consistent with the demands expressed in the poll. By this logic, if most constituents want immigrants to gain legal status then you'd ask for a reform proposal that made legal status possible. Conversely, if the poll indicated that most constituents favored deportation you would push for legislation that funded a program to achieve this goal. Doing so would allow you to claim some credit for the specifics of the bill, as well as for your vote, which in theory would please most of your constituents and increase your chances of reelection.

Stay quiet.
As we discuss throughout the chapter, poll results are highly sensitive to question wording, timing, and other factors, making it hard to interpret even seemingly clear findings. Suppose, for example, the poll indicates support for allowing illegal immigrants to gain legal status. However, the survey did not ask whether legal status would require learning English, holding a stable job, paying back taxes, or other conditions. Even though none of these conditions were in the question, most of your constituents probably had some of them in mind when they thought about how they wanted to answer the question. In other words, even if nothing changes, your constituents' support of immigration reform depends on what the reforms look like.

The situation is no easier if your poll indicates support for deportation. Would the government search for illegals to deport or just deport people they happen to find? What would happen to children whose parents entered the country illegally but who were born in the United States and are therefore citizens? For some respondents, the solution is a nationwide house-to-house search, with children deported with their parents. But others would reject a deportation process that did either of these things. So here again, the poll results, one-sided as they are, don't provide you with foolproof guidance about how to vote.

Americans in both parties agree on the need for immigration reform but differ as to what they think the new immigration policies should be.

take a stand

1. Suppose you are a politician who feels that changes in immigration policy are needed but are faced with the quandary described earlier. Would you do nothing, so as to avoid alienating your constituency, or would you force a policy change and accept the political consequence—possible removal from office?

2. What poll questions would you use to get a clearer picture of public opinion on immigration?

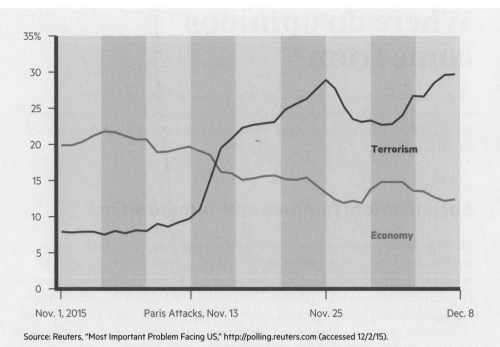

Source: Reuters, "Most Important Problem Facing US," http://polling.reuters.com (accessed 12/2/15).

FIGURE 6.1

Views on Terrorism before and after Paris Attacks

Opinions are sensitive to recent events; when asked to name the most important problem facing the United States today, the percentage of respondents who answered "terrorism" increased sharply after the 2015 attacks in Paris, France. Rahm Emanuel (President Obama's first Chief of Staff) once said, "You never let a serious crisis go to waste." Based on this argument, how would a politician respond to the Paris attacks?

to support government programs that benefit the poor.[14] As all these examples show, diverse considerations play a significant role in influencing citizens' political opinions.

Sometimes competing or contradictory considerations influence the opinion-formation process. In the case of abortion laws, many people believe in protecting human life but also in allowing women to make their own medical decisions.[15] When a survey asks people with both beliefs for their opinion about abortion laws, their response will depend on which consideration comes to mind and seems most relevant as they are answering the question. Opinions about other morally complex issues such as right-to-die legislation, or about race-related issues such as affirmative action, also often involve competing considerations.[16]

Even events can influence considerations. Consider Figure 6.1, which shows Reuters poll data from surveys conducted in the weeks before and after the November 2015 ISIS terrorist attacks against civilians in Paris, France. As you see, the percentage of Americans who saw terrorism as the most important problem jumped upward in the week after the attack from about 10 percent to about 30 percent, moving ahead of the percentage who saw the economy as the most important problem. What other events can you think of that have galvanized American public opinion?

"Why Should I Care?"

In a democracy, elected officials stay in office by keeping their constituents happy. As a result, knowing what public opinion looks like—what citizens believe, what they want government to do—helps us to understand the choices elected officials make. New policy initiatives such as stricter gun control laws are unlikely to be enacted in the absence of strong, sustained public support. Conversely, even controversial proposals such as Obamacare can be enacted over strong opposition, as long as there are enough enthusiastic supporters. Public opinion both motivates and constrains elected officials. And understanding what goes into people's opinions—whether they are deep and well considered or shallow and formed in the moment—can help you evaluate claims by politicians and the media, and better predict which policies are likely to be enacted and which will fail.

Where do opinions come from?

There are numerous sources of public opinion. Some arise from early life experiences, such as exposure to the beliefs of parents, relatives, or teachers; others result from later life events. Politicians and other political actors also play a critical role in the opinion-formation process.

Socialization: families and communities

political socialization
The process by which an individual's political opinions are shaped by other people and the surrounding culture.

Theories of **political socialization** show that many people's political opinions start with what they learned from their parents, including liberal or conservative ideology, level of trust in others, and class, racial, and ethnic identity.[17] Although people sometimes respond to events by modifying their opinions, for many individuals the ideas learned during childhood shape their political opinions throughout their lives.[18]

Beyond the influence of parents and family, research finds broader aspects of socialization that shape political opinions. Consider the following examples: People are socialized by their communities—by the people they interact with while growing up, such as neighbors, teachers, clergy, and others.[19] Support for democracy as a system of government and for American political institutions is higher for individuals who take a civics class in high school.[20] Growing up in a homogeneous community, where many people share the same cultural, ethnic, or political beliefs, increases an adult's sense of civic duty—his or her belief that voting or other forms of political participation are important social obligations.[21] Volunteering in community organizations as a child shapes political beliefs and participation in later life.[22] Engaging in political activity as a teenager, such as volunteering in a presidential campaign, generates higher levels of political interest as an adult; it also strengthens the belief that people should care about politics and participate in political activities.[23] As indicated by the range of activities and interactions summarized here, many aspects of socialization can influence one's political outlook.

Events

Although socialization often influences individuals' fairly stable core beliefs, public opinion is not fixed. All kinds of events—from everyday interactions to traumatic, life-changing disasters—can capture people's attention and cause them to revise their understanding of politics and the role of government. For example, although an individual's initial partisan affiliation likely reflects his or her parents' leanings, it may change in response to subsequent events such as who runs for office, what platforms they campaign on, and their performance in office—especially if those factors affect the individual directly.[24]

Some events that shape beliefs are specific, individual experiences. For example, someone who believes that he or she managed to get a college degree only because of government grants and guaranteed student loans might favor a large, activist government that provides numerous benefits to its citizens. And individuals' support for same-sex marriage is strongly influenced by the number of people they know who are

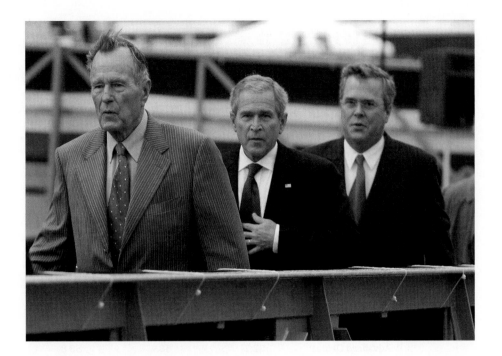

In general, children tend to adopt their parents' ideology and party affiliation. Former president George H. W. Bush and his sons, former president George W. Bush and former governor of Florida (and presidential candidate) Jeb Bush, are all Republicans.

gay or lesbian.[25] Beliefs are also shaped by major national or world events. After the September 11 terrorist attacks, many citizens became more willing to restrict civil liberties to reduce the chances of future attacks.[26] Support for restrictions remained elevated 15 years later, suggesting a long-term change in public opinion.[27] Less specific events such as changes in the economy hold a similar sway over opinions, such as presidential approval. Presidents are more likely to have high approval ratings when economic growth is high and inflation and unemployment are low, whereas their ratings fall when growth is sluggish or negative and unemployment and inflation are high. A president's popularity is also affected by scandals involving his or her administration. For example, the slight dip in President Obama's popularity during 2013 was in part due to revelations about NSA monitoring of Americans' cell phone conversations.

Group identity

Individuals' opinions are also influenced by social categories or groups, such as gender, race, and education level. These characteristics might shape opinions in three ways. The first two ways relate to the fact that individuals learn about politics from the people around them. Therefore, those who live in the same region or who were born in the same era might have similar beliefs because (1) they experienced the same historical events at similar points in their lives or (2) they learned political viewpoints from one another. In the United States, opinions on many issues are highly correlated with the state or region where a person grew up.[28]

Third, individuals may rely on others who "look like" them as a source of opinions. Some political scientists, for example, argue that group identities shape partisanship: when people decide between being a Republican or a Democrat, they think about which demographic groups are associated with each party and pick the party that has more members from the groups they feel they are a part of.[29]

TABLE
6.1

The Importance of Groups

The General Social Survey (GSS) has been conducted since 1972 to assess the opinions of Americans on certain key issues. Those who take the surveys are asked to indicate if they agree or disagree with statements such as those shown in the table. The percentages indicate those who agree with the statements. Group differences based on such factors as gender, age, race, and family income have been shown to affect the answers given by the respondents.

Source: 2014 Data from General Social Survey 1972–2014, Cumulative Datafile, Survey Documentation and Analysis (SDA) at UC Berkeley, http://sda.berkeley.edu (accessed 10/30/15).

		"Favor preferences in hiring blacks" (percentage who strongly support or support)	"Abortions OK if woman wants one for any reason" (percentage who agree)	"OK to allow anti-American Muslim cleric to speak" (percentage who agree)
Gender	Male	18.5%	47.1%	49.1%
	Female	18.8	43.5	36.6
Age	18–30	25.1	49.4	39.2
	31–40	13.6	42.3	41.3
	41–55	20.8	40.3	46.3
	56–89	16.1	45.2	41.4
Education	Less than High School	28.1	21.8	26.3
	High School	17.9	40.8	39.0
	Bachelor's Degree	17.2	61.9	58.9
	Advanced Degree	22.2	58.9	58.8
Race	White	12.2	46.5	50.0
	African-American	38.9	46.7	30.9
	Hispanic	23.9	34.5	26.2
	Other	30.1	62.0	31.1
Family Income	Low	25.0	35.6	30.6
	Lower Middle	21.0	42.5	40.9
	Higher Middle	10.9	45.7	44.0
	High	17.3	57.9	55.7

DID YOU KNOW?

The probability that you will be contacted to participate in a typical national poll is

.001%

Source: General Social Survey Data Archive

One reason for looking at group variations in public opinion is that candidates and political consultants often formulate their campaign strategies in terms of groups. For example, analyses of the three previous presidential elections show that Barack Obama's and Hillary Clinton's electoral strategies were shaped by the goal of attracting support from young Americans, African Americans, Hispanics, and women.[30] Table 6.1 includes data on the variation in opinions across different groups of Americans. There are sharp differences among groups on some questions. For example, people of different education levels respond very differently to both questions about abortion and free speech. However, education has little to do with opinions about affirmative action. Moreover, even with these differences across groups, political scientists Jack Citrin and David O. Sears have found that most people think of themselves as Americans rather than as part of an ethnic, racial, or age-based group.[31]

These data indicate that group characteristics can be important predictors of some of an individual's opinions, but they are not the whole story.[32] Americans' opinions are a product of their socialization and life experiences as well as their group characteristics.

Politicians and other political actors

Opinions and changes in opinion are also subject to influence by politicians and other political actors (such as political parties and party leaders, interest groups, and leaders of religious, civic, and other large organizations). In part, this link exists because Americans look to these individuals for information because of their presumed expertise. For example, if you do not know what to think about gun control you might seek out someone who appears to know more about the issues than you do. If his or her opinions seem reasonable, you might adopt them as your own.[33] Of course, most people take account of an expert's opinions only when they generally agree with the expert—perhaps because they hold matching conservative or liberal views or because they have some other basis for thinking their preferences match the expert's. Thus, during the general election, Donald Trump's claims that the electoral process was rigged against him contributed to his supporters' high levels of distrust of government.

Politicians and other political actors also work to shape public opinion. Some political scientists argue that politicians describe proposals through arguments and images designed to tap the public's strong opinions, with the goal of winning support for these proposals.[34] While President Obama and his staff expended much effort to promote health care reform, giving dozens of speeches, holding rallies, and briefing legislators, opponents managed to shape many Americans' opinions by making dire pronouncements of the proposal's potentially negative outcomes.[35] Even though health care reform was eventually enacted, these opposition efforts turned initial majority public support into a dead heat. However, in the years after enactment, as none of these dire predictions have come true, support for Obamacare gradually increased, confirming that the success of efforts to shape public opinion depends on facts as well as argument.[36]

In sum, public opinion at the individual level is driven by many factors—most notably life experiences, including current events as we perceive them. In the case of gun control, for example, beliefs are likely to depend on individuals' background—whether they own a gun, hunt, or know someone who does; their political beliefs, including how tolerant they are of government regulation of individual behavior; as well as events involving guns. Thus, while public opinion may shift somewhat in response to events such as the Orlando shooting, such events are only one factor that shapes opinion. As a result, the shift in opinion may be quite small.

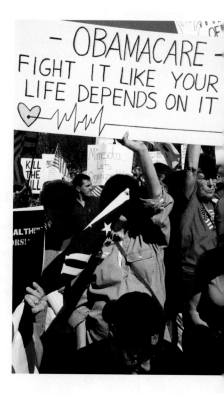

Politicians on both sides of the debate tried to influence public opinion about health care reform. While Obama and the Democrats sought to convince Americans that the new plan was necessary, opponents played up the possible disadvantages, with references to costs, "death panels," and bureaucratic incompetence. #ACA #Obamacare

How people form opinions matters because understanding what people say about politics on the news, or in the classroom, or around the dinner table depends on where they are coming from. Perhaps an important event has shaped their opinion, maybe their parents or connection to a social or generational group has influenced them, or maybe a combination of all of these and more. Knowing what's behind someone's opinions and arguments on an issue can help you decide how you feel about that issue and whether or not that argument carries weight.

"Why Should I Care?"

mass survey
A way to measure public opinion by interviewing a large sample of the population.

population
The group of people whom a researcher or pollster wants to study, such as evangelicals, senior citizens, or Americans.

Measuring public opinion

For the most part, information about public opinion comes from **mass surveys**—face-to-face or telephone interviews with hundreds or thousands of voters. A mass survey seeks to measure the attitudes of a particular **population** or group of people, such as the residents of a specific congressional district, evangelicals, senior citizens, or even the nation's entire adult population (see How It Works: Measuring What a Nation of 320 Million Thinks: A Checklist). For large groups such as these, it would be impossible to survey everyone. So surveys typically involve **samples** of between a few hundred and several thousand individuals.

Mass surveys

One of the principal attractions of mass surveys is that they can in theory provide very accurate estimates of public opinion for a large population by using relatively small samples (see Nuts & Bolts 6.1). For example, while polls taken very early in a

---

◆ **NUTS & BOLTS 6.1**

Sampling Error in Mass Surveys

The **sampling error** in a survey (the predicted difference between the average opinion expressed by survey respondents and the average opinion in the population, sometimes called the *margin of error*) using a random sample depends on the sample size. Sampling error is large for small samples of around 200 or fewer but decreases rapidly as sample size increases.

Sample size

sampling error
The predicted difference between the average opinion expressed by survey respondents and the average opinion in the population, sometimes called the *margin of error*. Increasing the number of respondents lowers the sampling error.

The graph shows how the sampling error for a random sample decreases as sample size increases. For example, in surveys with 1,000 respondents the sampling error is 3 percent, meaning that 95 percent of the time the results of a 1,000-person survey will fall within the range of 3 percentage points above or below the actual percentage in the population that holds a particular opinion surveyed. If the sample size was increased to 5,000 people, the sampling error would decline to 1.4 percent.

Sampling errors need to be taken into account in interpreting what a poll says about public opinion. For example, a June 2016 YouGov poll of 1,300 Americans found that 66 percent gave an unfavorable rating of Donald Trump, and 33 percent rated him favorably. Because the difference in the percentages (33 points) exceeds the sampling error (about 2.5 points), it is reasonable to conclude that, at the time the poll was conducted, more Americans saw Trump unfavorably than favorably.

In contrast, suppose the poll found a narrow 51 to 49 percent split slightly favoring approval. Because the difference in support is smaller than the sampling error, it would be a mistake to conclude that the majority of Americans have a favorable opinion of Trump. Even though more people in the sample express this opinion, there is a good chance that the opposite is true in the overall population.

You don't need to calculate sampling errors to make sense of political polls—just keep two things in mind. First, large samples (1,000 or more) are much more likely to provide accurate information about population opinions than small ones (fewer than 500). Second, be cautious when you read about small differences in survey responses, as these patterns are unlikely to hold true in the entire population.

---

presidential campaign (such as a year in advance of the general election) are poor predictors of the ultimate outcome, polls taken after the campaign has gotten started, when both parties' nominees are known, provide very good predictions of who will win the election and how many votes that candidate will receive.[37]

Large-scale surveys such as the American National Election Study (ANES), conducted every election year (typically both before and after the general election), use various types of questions to measure citizens' opinions. In presidential election years, participants in the ANES are first asked whether they voted for president. If they say yes, they are asked which candidate they voted for: a major-party candidate (for example, Hillary Clinton or Donald Trump in 2016), an Independent candidate, or some other candidate.

Another kind of survey question uses an issue scale. For example, respondents might be asked about the government's role in protecting morality or their own liberal or conservative ideology. Two opposing statements are given for each topic, and respondents are asked to agree with the one that comes closest to their views, including options in the middle of the two extremes.

A typical survey like the General Social Survey or the ANES will ask about a hundred questions related to issues and candidates, along with additional questions about the respondents' age, education, and marital status. Some surveys conducted by media sources, candidates, or political parties are shorter, focusing on voter evaluations of specific candidates and the reasons for these evaluations. In the main, the length of a survey reflects the fact that people have limited attention spans, so there is a trade-off between learning more about each respondent's opinions and getting them to agree to be surveyed in the first place (shorter surveys can also be less expensive).

Problems in measuring public opinion

Although measuring public opinion might seem an easy task—just find some people and ask them questions!—it is actually very complicated. The problems begin with determining and gathering an appropriate, representative sample of subjects. These difficulties are compounded by issues pertaining to the wording of the questions and further complicated by the very nature of public opinion itself. Consequently, survey results must be read carefully, taking into account who is being surveyed, when they are being surveyed, what opinions people are being asked about, and what mechanism is used to ask survey questions.

Issues with Survey Methods Building a random sample of respondents is not easy. One strategy is to choose households at random from census data and send interviewers out for face-to-face meetings. Another strategy involves contacting people by telephone using random digit dialing, which allows surveyors to find people who have unlisted phone numbers or who just use a cell phone. While each technique in theory produces a random sample, in practice they both may deviate from this ideal. Face-to-face interviews of people in their homes during work hours won't include adults who work during the day and are not home. Even with phone surveys, many people refuse to participate. Pollsters must adjust their survey results to account for these and other potential biases. Sometimes these corrections can introduce new errors. For example, in the 2016 presidential race, attempts to account for likely voters appear to have led to underestimates of support for Donald Trump, the ultimate winner.

To keep costs down, many organizations use Internet polling, in which volunteer respondents log on to a website to participate in a survey, or robo-polls, in which a computer program phones people and interviews them. While these techniques are less expensive, there are often doubts about the quality of the samples they produce.[38]

sample
Within a population, the group of people surveyed in order to gauge the whole population's opinion. Researchers use samples because it would be impossible to interview the entire population.

DID YOU KNOW?

45

state- and national-level polls of the presidential race were released in the last two weeks of the 2016 campaign.
Source: Pollster.com

On average, people should be more skeptical when they see numbers. They should be more willing to play around with the data themselves.

—**Nate Silver,** FiveThirtyEight.com

DID YOU KNOW?

90%

of people contacted by phone to participate in a political survey either don't answer or refuse to participate.
Source: Pew Research Center

Measuring What a Nation of 320 Million Thinks: A Checklist

✓ **A Random Sample:**
Were the people who participated in the survey selected randomly, such that any member of the population had an equal chance of being selected?

✓ **Sample Size:**
How many people do researchers need to survey to know what 320 million Americans think? Major national surveys usually use a sample of 1,000–2,000 respondents.

± 2%

✓ **Sampling Error:**
For a group of any size (even 320 million), 95 percent of the time a survey of 1,000 randomly selected respondents will measure the average opinion in a population within 2 percentage points. Reputable surveys will usually give the sampling error (sometimes also called "margin of error").

✓ **Question Wording:**
Did the way the question was worded influence the results? Scientific surveys try to phrase questions in a neutral way, but even in reputable polls, differences in question wording can influence answers.

✓ **Reliable Respondents:** Respondents often give socially acceptable answers rather than truthful ones—or invent opinions on the spot. Is there a reason to think people may not have answered a survey honestly and thoughtfully?

How it works: in practice

Surveying the 2016 Elections: Two Approaches

To illustrate how these requirements for good survey design play out in real life, we examine how two well-known polling organizations, the Pew Research Center and Rasmussen Reports, designed polls to measure presidential preference during the 2016 campaign.

Rasmussen Reports

Land-line only.

A random sample: Use a **land-line-only sample.**

Sample size: Survey the **first person who answers the phone.**

Adjust results.

Sampling error: If there are more Democrats in your sample than you expect, **adjust your results** to reduce support for Clinton.

Use a script to call.

Reliable respondents: Use a computer script, and only call once. Do the survey in a **short time period (hours).**

Pew Research Center

Include cell phones.

A random sample: Generate a **random sample of Americans,** including people who only have cell phones.

Sample size: When you call a residence, only **talk to the person who's in your sample.**

Don't adjust results.

Sampling error: If the partisan divide in the sample is not what you expect, **treat it as a finding**—people may be changing their party ID.

Use a person to call.

Reliable respondents: Use a live interviewer, and call back people you miss the first time. **Implement the survey over several days.**

❓ Critical Thinking

1. **When evaluating these two polling organizations, how would you respond to someone who said he still** preferred Rasmussen's polls because they correctly predicted the outcome of a Senate race in his state in 2014?

2. **Which kinds of respondents are likely to be put off by polls** that the computer scripts? How might this affect the findings of the survey?

Outcome

Rasmussen data are incomplete...

A random sample: **Rasmussen misses people who only use cell phones** (many of whom are younger and are Democrats).

Sample size: Rasmussen is **biased toward people likely to answer the phone.** These people tend to be older and include more men than average.

and assume nothing has changed.

Sampling error: Adjusting for partisanship **assumes that no changes in party ID have occurred** since the last election.

Reliable respondents: Rasmussen tactic **lowers response rate.** Rasmussen tactic makes poll results sensitive to short-term events.

Pew is more reliable.

Pew's results were generally regarded as more reliable than Rasmussen's—and ultimately **made more accurate predictions about the 2016 results.** Furthermore, Rasmussen kept its data largely private, while Pew released its questionnaire. This made Pew's survey verifiable and provided an opportunity for further analysis.

TABLE 6.2

The Impact of Question Wording on Opinions

How questions are worded can affect survey results. These surveys all ask about immigration reform but differ in the number of requirements that noncitizens would have to satisfy. In light of how the responses to survey questions are shaped by the precise wording of these questions, what sort of question would you ask if your goal was to show that Americans favored immigration reform? What if you wanted to show high levels of opposition?

% Support or Favor	Question	Pollster	Poll Date
81	Here are some questions about how the U.S. government should treat illegal immigrants who have **been in the country for a number of years, hold a job, speak English and are willing to pay any back taxes they owe**. Would you favor or oppose a bill that allowed immigrants to stay in this country rather than being deported and eventually allow them to apply for U.S. citizenship?	CNN/ORC	2/2/2014
78	Do you favor or oppose allowing illegal immigrants to remain in the country and eventually qualify for U.S. citizenship, **as long as they meet certain requirements like paying back taxes, learning English, and passing a background check**?	Fox News	4/22/2013
77	Would you favor or oppose providing a path to citizenship for illegal immigrants in the U.S. if they met certain requirements including a **waiting period, paying fines and back taxes, passing criminal background checks, and learning English**?	CBS News	10/21/2013
51	The U.S. Senate is considering an immigration bill that would attempt to **increase border security and create a path to citizenship for many immigrants who are in this country without permission** from the U.S. government. Based on what you have read or heard about this bill, do you favor or oppose it?	CNN/ORC	6/13/2013
46	As you may know, the U.S. Senate passed an immigration law that includes **a path to citizenship for undocumented immigrants now living in the United States, and stricter border control at a cost of $46 billion**. Do you support or oppose this proposal?	*Post*/ABC	7/21/2013
46	Congress is debating changing immigration laws. Do you support or oppose a revision of immigration policies that would provide **a path to citizenship for 11 million undocumented immigrants in the United States**?	Bloomberg	6/3/2013

Source: Scott Clemet, "Immigration Reform Is Super Popular. Here's Why Congress Isn't Listening," *Washington Post*, July 2, 2014 (accessed 11/2/15).

The wording of questions can also influence survey results. Table 6.2 shows different questions asked during 2013–2014 to measure opinions about providing citizenship to illegal aliens. As you can see, support depends on the requirements that people would need to fulfill in order to become citizens. As a result, support for immigration reform is much higher in the top three polls compared with the bottom three. These issues shouldn't make you suspicious that pollsters are trying to skew their findings—rather, it shows just how hard it is to accurately measure opinions.

Unreliable Responses People are sometimes reluctant to reveal their opinions. Rather than speaking truthfully, they often give socially acceptable answers or the ones that they think the interviewers want to hear. In the case of voter turnout in elections, up to one-fourth of respondents who say they voted when surveyed actually did not vote at all.[39] Political scientists refer to this behavior as the social desirability bias, meaning that people are less willing to admit actions or express opinions (such as racial prejudice) that they think their neighbors or society at large will disapprove of.[40] In 2016, a small percentage of poll respondents, labeled "shy Trump voters," refused to express their true support for candidate Donald Trump. Pollsters use various techniques to address this problem, such as framing a question in terms of the entire country rather than the respondent's own beliefs.

The Accuracy of Public Opinion Early theories of public opinion held that the average American's opinions about politics were incomplete at best and wildly inaccurate at worst. Modern theories have revised these conclusions. It is true that many Americans have significant gaps in factual information, such as which party controls the House or the Senate,[41] and routinely overestimate the amount of federal money spent on government programs such as foreign aid. However, rather than reflecting ignorance, these misperceptions often result from poor survey design or the respondents' misinterpretation of survey questions.

Claims about Obamacare reform are a good example. A 2015 poll asked people whether health care spending by the federal government was higher or lower than estimates made at the time the program was enacted in 2010. Forty-two percent said spending was higher, 40 percent did not know—and only 5 percent of respondents gave the correct answer, that spending was less than expected.[42] How can we explain these findings?

We can offer four explanations: (1) Many respondents likely had not thought about the questions beforehand. When they were asked for an opinion as part of a survey, there was no time to do research or think things through. (2) Incomplete or inaccurate responses to survey questions may reflect respondents' unwillingness to admit they don't know about something: survey participants sometimes make up responses to avoid appearing ill informed.[43] In the main, people are more likely to express sensible, thoughtful, and accurate opinions when asked about an issue or question that they have personal experience with—for example, whether their own spending on health care had increased rather than their assessment of Obamacare. (3) Because opinions are subject to influence by politicians and others, survey respondents might have evaluated Obamacare negatively because they formed their opinions after hearing certain public figures repeatedly describe the program in highly negative terms. (4) Many supposed facts are "contested truths," meaning that it is reasonable for individuals to hold a range of views.[44]

Such problems do not arise in all areas of public opinion. Respondents' ability to express specific opinions, as well as the accuracy of their opinions, rises if the survey questions relate to their everyday life.[45] Thus, the average American would be more likely to have an accurate sense of the state of the economy or his or her own personal economic condition than of the situation in Syria or the Ukraine. Everyday life gives us information about the economy; in contrast, we learn about Syria or the Ukraine only if we take the time to gather information.

"

As always, keep in mind that the poll does not, and cannot, predict the outcome of the election in November.

—Disclaimer on CNN preelection poll

New technologies have made surveys cheaper and easier, allowing groups to poll more often and ask a much wider range of questions. However, just reading more polls doesn't automatically make you better informed about American politics. You have to consider how the poll was administered in order to make sense of its findings.

"Why Should I Care?"

What Americans think about politics

American public opinion encompasses what people think of the federal government and their ideological beliefs. These opinions drive overall support for government action and serve as the basis for opinions on more specific policy questions. So to understand what America's national government does and why, we have to determine what Americans ask of it.

Ideological polarization

ideological polarization
The effect on public opinion when many citizens move away from moderate positions and toward either end of the political spectrum, identifying themselves as either liberals or conservatives.

We begin by examining liberal and conservative ideology and party identification to see if historical data show evidence of polarization. Are there fewer moderates and more strong liberals and conservatives today than a generation ago? The What Do the Numbers Say? feature shows two kinds of survey data: responses to a question measuring ideology (liberal, moderate, or conservative), and a question that taps a respondent's party identification (Republican, Independent, or Democrat). The trends show no evidence of **ideological polarization**. It is hard to look at these data and think in terms of sharp divisions.

Looking more closely at opinion polarization, the third part of the What Do the Numbers Say? feature divides the electorate into eight groups based on answers to questions that tap important principles, from foreign policy to domestic issues, civil liberties, and morality. Principles such as these are a kind of consideration—they form the basis for opinions that people express in surveys or act on when they vote or engage in other political behavior. The figure shows, first, that only about a third of the electorate (Steadfast Conservatives, Business Conservatives, and Solid Liberals) hold consistent ideological beliefs—meaning that they generally give one kind of answer (conservative or liberal) when asked questions that tap their underlying principles. Even then, the data show that there are two broad groups of conservatives, one focused more on social issues, the other oriented more toward Wall Street and pro–immigration reform. Moreover, most people fall into one of the intermediate groups, meaning that they express a mix of liberal and conservative issue positions.

While these data confirm that Americans disagree on important policy questions, they argue against the conception of a polarized America, with a large group of secular liberals opposing another large group of religious conservatives, with few people in the middle. Public opinion is much more complex. Most people could be labeled as liberals or as conservatives, secular or religious, depending on which issues they are asked about. Thus, even though people say they are liberals (or conservatives), this response does not mean that they hold liberal (or conservative) preferences on all issues. In addition, self-professed moderates may hold relatively extreme preferences on certain policy questions. Thus, understanding what Americans think and what they want from government often requires data on specific policy questions rather than broad judgments about the liberal or conservative nature of American public opinion.

Evaluations of government and officeholders

Another set of opinions addresses how people view the government: how well or poorly they think it is doing, whether they trust it, and their evaluations of individual politicians. These opinions matter for several reasons. First, citizens' judgments about the

Liberal or Conservative Ideology in America

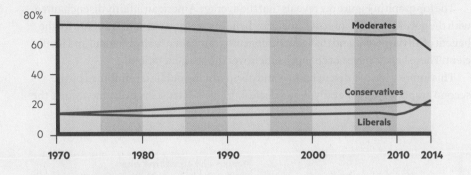

Party Identification in America

| Democrat 32% | Independent 39% | Republican 23% | Other 6% |

Political Typology

Reliable Republicans
Steadfast conservatives (*socially conservative, populist*)
Business conservatives (*pro–Wall Street, pro-immigrant*)

Less partisan, less predictable
Young outsiders (*conservative on government, liberal on social issues*)
Hard-pressed skeptics (*financially stressed, pessimistic*)
Bystanders (*young, on the sidelines*)
Next generation left (*young, liberal on social issues, less liberal on social safety net*)
Faith and family left (*racially diverse and religious*)

Reliable Democrats
Solid liberals (*liberal across-the-board*)

0 2 4 6 8 10 12 14 16%

Sources: Data from General Social Survey 1972–2014, Cumulative Datafile, Survey Documentation and Analysis (SDA) at UC Berkeley, http://sda.berkeley.edu (accessed 11/5/15); Pew Research Center, "Trends in Party Identification, 1939–2014," www. people-press.org, April 5, 2015 (accessed 11/5/2015); Pew Research Center, "Beyond Red vs. Blue: The Political Typology," June 26, 2014, www.people-press.org (accessed 12/9/15).

Are the American People Polarized?

Many commentators describe politics in America as highly conflictual, with most Americans holding either liberal or conservative points of view and identifying with one of the two major parties. Is polarization as strong as these commentators think? What do the numbers say?

Think about it

- According to the top figure, how have levels of polarization changed since the 1970s?
- What does the political typology reveal about divisions within each political party?

government's overall performance may shape their evaluations of specific policies, especially if they do not know much about the policies.[46] Also, evaluations of specific policies may be shaped by how much a citizen trusts the government; more trust brings higher evaluations.[47] Finally, trust in government and overall evaluations of it might influence a citizen's willingness to vote for incumbent congressional representatives or a president seeking reelection.[48] In fact, the chances that someone voted for Donald Trump in 2016 were much higher given low trust in government.

The top graph in Figure 6.2 reveals that the average American is fairly disenchanted with the government. As of 2015, a majority believes that government is not run for the benefit of all the people and that government programs are usually wasteful and inefficient. These beliefs have not changed much over the last generation.

This impression of a disenchanted and disapproving public is reinforced by the second graph, which generally shows declining levels of trust in government since the

FIGURE 6.2

What Do Americans Think about Government?

A significant percentage of Americans have always been distrustful and disparaging of the federal government—and the percentage of people holding such views has increased markedly in the last generation. Does the perception that government is wasteful and inefficient make it easier or harder to enact new policies? How might the decline in trust explain the rise of the Tea Party organization and candidates like Donald Trump and Bernie Sanders?

Sources: Pew Research Center, "A Wider Ideological Gap Between More and Less Educated Adults," April 26, 2016, www. people-press.org (accessed 8/24/16); Pew Research Center, "Beyond Distrust: How Americans View Their Government," November 25, 2016, www.people-press.org (accessed 8/25/16).

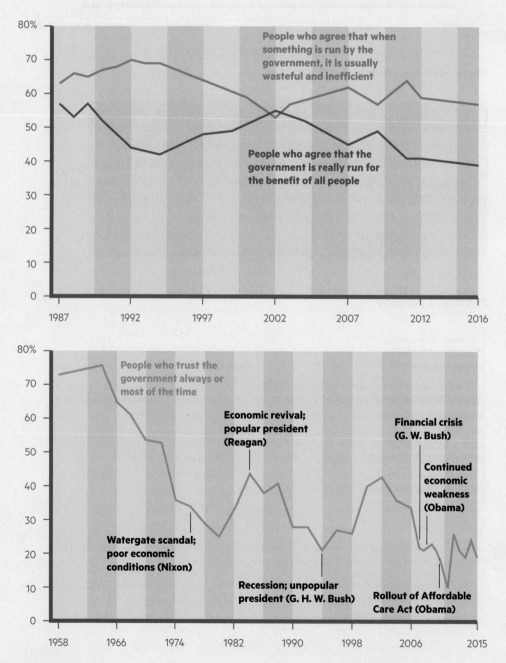

1960s. Many scholars have argued that low levels of trust make it harder for elected officials to enact new policies, especially those involving large expenditures.[49] Some scholars even argue that low levels of trust raise questions about the future of democracy in America.[50] How can we say that American democracy is a good or popular form of government when so many people are unhappy with the performance of elected officials and bureaucrats and so few people trust the government?

One important insight is that although Americans don't like the government in general, they tend to be more satisfied with their own representatives in Washington (see Chapter 10). For example, when a survey question asks about "the government" it may cause respondents to picture a roomful of bureaucrats pushing paperwork, whereas asking about "your representative" may lead respondents to think of someone working on their behalf. Also, as we discuss in Chapter 10, members of Congress work hard to convince their constituents that they are doing everything possible to satisfy constituents' demands. Sometimes members blame the institution of Congress and the government bureaucracy for shortcomings, portraying themselves as standing between their constituents and an inefficient government.

Policy preferences

In a diverse country of more than 320 million, people care about a wide range of policies. One useful measure of Americans' policy preferences is the **policy mood**, which captures the public's collective demands for government action on domestic policies.[51] Policy mood measures are constructed from surveys that address a wide range of policy questions.[52]

Fluctuations in the policy mood in America have led to changes in defense spending, environmental policy, and civil rights, among others—and have influenced elections.[53] Figure 6.3 shows that when the policy mood leans in an activist direction (Americans

policy mood
The level of public support for expanding the government's role in society; whether the public wants government action on a specific issue.

FIGURE 6.3

Policy Mood

Surveys assess the public's policy mood by asking questions about specific policy questions such as levels of taxation and government spending and the role of government. The level of conservatism (for example, support for smaller, less-active government) was at a high in 1952 and 1980. Could you have used the policy mood prior to the election to predict the outcomes of the 2012 presidential and 2012 and 2014 congressional elections?

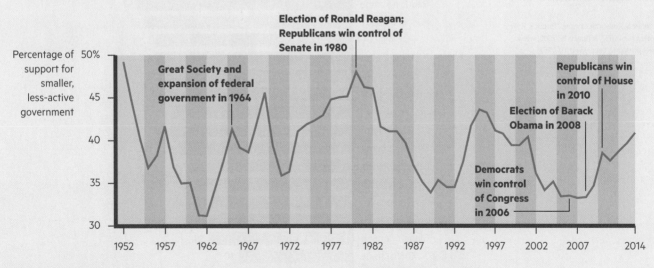

Source: Policy Mood data available at http://stimson.web.unc.edu/data/, additional calculations by authors (accessed 11/7/2015).

want government to do more, corresponding to lower values on the vertical axis), such as in the early 1960s, conditions are ripe for an expansion of the federal government involving more spending and new programs. But when the policy mood leans in the opposite direction (Americans want a smaller, less-active government; higher values on the vertical axis), officials generally enact smaller increases in government spending and fewer new programs—or, as in 2010, 2012, and 2014, candidates who support a more active government are more likely to be defeated. At present, opposition to government action is at nearly its highest level since the late 1980s. Given these opinions, we should not expect major expansion in the size and scope of the government, at least not until the public policy mood moves in a more activist direction.

Regarding more specific policy preferences, everything we have said in this chapter reinforces the idea that public opinion is often a moving target. While some beliefs and preferences are stable over time, opinions about specific policies can change from year to year, month to month, or even day to day. One of the best ways to take a snapshot of these beliefs is to ask citizens what they see as the top policy priorities facing the nation. Figure 6.4 shows responses to a 2015 survey.

The top priorities—terrorism, the economy (including jobs), education, Social Security, the budget deficit, and health care costs—have not changed very much over the last several decades. The only difference is that terrorism appeared on the list only after the September 11 attacks in 2001. It is no exaggeration to say that Americans are always worried about the economy. Even when other pressing issues, such as terrorism, surpass the economy as the most important problem to Americans, the economy is typically listed second or third. In general, as the state of the economy declines, more and more people

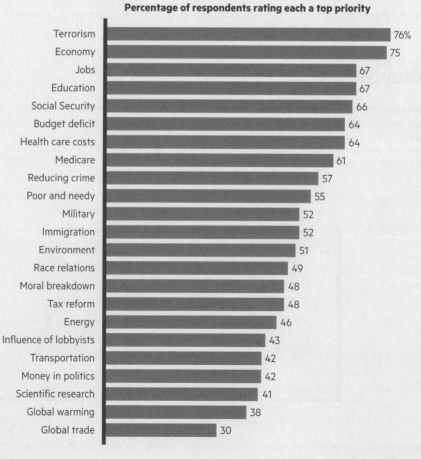

FIGURE 6.4

The American Public's Policy Priorities, 2015

Given this data on policy priorities, what legislation will likely be proposed by incoming president Donald Trump?

Source: Pew Research Center, "Public's Policy Priorities for 2015," January 15, 2015, www. people-press.org (accessed 11/7/15).

Percentage of respondents rating each a top priority

Terrorism	76%
Economy	75
Jobs	67
Education	67
Social Security	66
Budget deficit	64
Health care costs	64
Medicare	61
Reducing crime	57
Poor and needy	55
Military	52
Immigration	52
Environment	51
Race relations	49
Moral breakdown	48
Tax reform	48
Energy	46
Influence of lobbyists	43
Transportation	42
Money in politics	42
Scientific research	41
Global warming	38
Global trade	30

© 1994 Watterson/Dist. by Universal Press Syndicate

Politicians read public opinion polls closely to gauge whether their behavior will anger or please constituents. Few politicians always follow survey results—but virtually none would agree with Calvin's father that polls should be ignored entirely.

rate the economy as their greatest concern. Moreover, the percentage of people who make reference to their personal economic concerns—for example, unemployment or worries about retirement—also increases.

These policy priorities frame contemporary political debates and divide the political parties. Think about what Republicans and Democrats in Washington argue about: how best to fight terrorism and secure the United States from attack, how to increase economic growth and reduce the unemployment rate, what the government's role should be in providing health care and making sure that Americans have secure retirements. In a very fundamental way, then, this list confirms that American politicians are intimately connected to their constituents—the issues that they debate and legislate on are the ones that many people care about.

The list of policy priorities also explains government inaction on some issues. For example, only 38 percent of Americans see global warming as a top policy priority—and gun control doesn't even appear on the list. Thus, the fact that Congress has not legislated on either of these issues in recent years is actually consistent with public opinion. For better or worse, the average American has other priorities for government action.

Public Opinion Is Relevant We can say with confidence that public opinion remains highly relevant in American politics today. One key piece of evidence is the amount of time and effort politicians, journalists, and political scientists spend trying to find out what Americans think. Of course, it is easy to find examples in which the political process appears to ignore public opinion in cases in which policy has stayed the same despite a majority supporting change. In other cases, new policies have been enacted even though a majority preferred the status quo. But these examples do not mean that public opinion is irrelevant. It is not always possible to please a majority of citizens. Politicians' willingness to do so depends on whether the majority is organized into interest groups, how much they care about the issue (and the intensity of the opposition), and, most important, the details of their preferences.

Public Opinion Can Influence Government Despite all the difficulties described, public opinion exerts a conspicuous influence in widespread areas of government. We mention this broad influence repeatedly throughout this book. In Chapter 10, we describe how legislators endeavor to determine what their constituents want and how their constituents will respond to different actions. In Chapter 8, we see how voters use retrospective evaluations to form opinions about whom to vote for and how candidates incorporate the public's views into campaign platforms that will attract widespread support. And in Chapter 7, we discuss how voters use candidates' party affiliations like brand names to determine how candidates will behave if elected. Scholars have found that congressional actions on a wide range of issues, from votes on defense policy to the confirmation of Supreme Court nominees, are shaped by constituent opinion.[54] Moreover, careful analysis of the connection between opinions and actions shows that this linkage does not exist because politicians are able to shape public opinion in line with what they want to do; rather, politicians behave in line with their constituents' opinions because to do otherwise would place the politicians in jeopardy of losing the next election.[55]

Recent events also speak to the influence of public opinion. Think about the failure of elected officials over the last few years to repeal Obamacare, enact immigration reform, or pass new limits on the ownership of handguns and assault rifles. In all of these cases, a significant portion of Americans wanted policy change, but a substantial percentage were opposed and even the supporters disagreed on what kinds of changes were best. Congressional inaction on these measures does not reflect a willful ignorance of public opinion. Rather, it reflects the lack of a public consensus about what government should do. Inaction on these issues is exactly what we should expect if public opinion is real and relevant to what happens in politics.

"Why Should I Care?"

Political scientists and pollsters spend so much time trying to measure public opinion because it shapes election outcomes and policy changes in Washington. If you want to know what the federal government is going to do over the next four years, spend some time trying to determine what people want.

★

DESCRIBE THE MAJOR TYPES OF NEWS SOURCES AND THE ROLE THEY PLAY IN AMERICAN POLITICS

mass media
Sources that provide information to the average citizen, such as newspapers, television networks, radio stations, and websites.

The news media

Closely related to our discussion of public opinion is the role of the news media, for it is generally through the media that Americans receive political information. This section describes the **mass media**, the many sources of political information available to Americans, and how people use (or don't use) this information. Finally, we consider how the media may influence public opinion and politics. The development of the Internet over the last generation has dramatically increased the number of media sources and the range of information available to the average American. With this change, it is less important to describe each source and what kinds of information they can (and cannot) provide. In contemporary America, there are so many sources and so much information that Americans can become experts on virtually any aspect of politics or public policy—if they are willing to search for information and put together what they find.

Media sources in the twenty-first century

Over the last two decades, the Internet has become a major and often dominant source for information about American politics. Most American newspapers, television networks, radio stations, and cable stations offer free access to most or all of their daily news via websites and mobile apps as well as providing some Web-only information. They also post blogs written by their reporters. One of the most influential conservative weekly magazines, *National Review*, has a Web version, National Review Online, where many of the magazine's reporters publish Web-exclusive stories.[56]

There are also many Internet-only sites that offer a combination of rumor, inside information, and deep analysis of American politics. Some, such as Politico, Vox, and FiveThirtyEight, have paid staff and report on a wide range of topics. Others have a narrower focus: SCOTUSblog (the Supreme Court of the United States blog) analyzes Supreme Court decisions, judicial nominations, and other legal questions.[57] Other blogs such as The Monkey Cage (now affiliated with the *Washington Post*) and the Mischiefs of Faction (now part of Vox) use political science research to explain contemporary American politics.[58] And many websites, some run by ordinary citizens, provide their own insights and information about American politics. Finally, even Facebook offers news about politics through its news feed and trending stories menu.

The creation of the Internet, along with increases in the number of mainstream media sources, has dramatically increased the amount of information about politics that is available to the average American. Imagine yourself in the late 1940s. Suppose you wanted to learn about President Truman's State of the Union address. If you couldn't go to Washington to hear it in person, where could you have gotten information about the speech? If you lived in a big city, the speech would probably be covered in the next day's newspaper. If you lived in a small town, your local paper might or might not run the story. If it didn't, you would need a subscription to either a big-city paper (which would arrive a week after the fact) or a weekly or monthly news magazine or you would need to have access to a radio that could pick up a station broadcasting the speech.

Now consider the modern era, in which major political events saturate the media. Suppose it's a day in early 2016, right before the Iowa Caucuses, and you want to know what Donald Trump said during a campaign appearance yesterday. You can tune in to one of the four major television networks, numerous cable news channels, public television stations, or radio stations, or watch video clips on many websites. Most television stations will feature pundits' commentaries on the race and will interview prominent politicians and commentators. Jimmy Fallon and other late-night hosts will probably make jokes about Trump and the other candidates on late-night television, and John Oliver will skewer them on his Sunday show. Tomorrow the race will be front-page news and larger papers will publish the full text of Trump's speech. Countless Internet sites will offer information and analyses. And you will be able to watch a video of the speech on YouTube and many other sites. The point is, there are many places to get information; you would have to work to avoid them.

The Internet has created more opportunities for homegrown media, allowing a would-be citizen journalist or subject expert to easily set up a website, Facebook page, YouTube channel, or some other way to present information. Such reporting has the potential to shape elections or at least to distract politicians from their desired message. During the last month of the 2016 presidential election, someone sent the *Washington Post* outtakes from a 2005 episode of *Access Hollywood* in which Donald Trump discussed "kissing, groping, and trying to have sex with women" (in the *Post*'s terms). After the story became public, many other women came forward to claim that Trump had sexually harassed or sexually assaulted them. Of course, Trump won the election—but these revelations cost him significant support from women voters.

The Internet creates new opportunities for two-way interaction between citizens, reporters, and government officials. Many reporters and politicians host live chat sessions, allowing people to ask follow-up questions about published stories, or interact with their audience through a variety of social media sites, including Facebook, Twitter, and reddit. While there is much more information available today than a generation ago, these sources are constantly in flux. Websites and Web pages come and go. Even well-established media sources can quickly change. For example, recent years have seen sizable declines in magazine and newspaper readership. Companies that once owned newspapers in Chicago, Philadelphia, and Minneapolis have gone bankrupt, whereas several major U.S. cities, including Seattle, Birmingham, and New Orleans, have a hometown daily newspaper that appears in print form. Other newspapers have cut foreign bureaus, reduced their staff, and thinned the amount of news in every edition.[59] At the same time, the major television networks as well as cable television sources have also seen declines in viewership.

DID YOU KNOW?

65%

of American adults use Facebook, and about half of these people say they get their news from Facebook.
Source: Pew Research Center

Information and coverage of important events becomes instantaneously available through Internet sources like Twitter feeds and blogs. Clinton's campaign announcement was followed by commentary and analysis. @HillaryClinton #I'mWithHer

DID YOU KNOW?

Newspaper revenue has declined

50%

over the last 10 years.
Source: Pew Research Center

Regulating the media

Federal Communications Commission (FCC)
A government agency created in 1934 to regulate American radio stations and later expanded to regulate television, wireless communications technologies, and other broadcast media.

broadcast media
Communications technologies, such as television and radio, that transmit information over airwaves.

equal time provision
An FCC regulation requiring broadcast media to provide equal air time on any non-news programming to all candidates running for an office.

media conglomerates
Companies that control a large number of media sources across several types of media outlets.

media effects
The influence of media coverage on average citizens' opinions and actions.

Federal regulation of the news media was driven by the fact that many media sources are profit-seeking businesses—as well as concerns over the media's potential to shape public opinion. For example, the **Federal Communications Commission (FCC)** regulates **broadcast media**, such as radio stations, as well as broadcast and cable television.

Limits on Ownership and Content Until very recently, a central concern of the FCC was that one company or organization might buy enough stations to dominate the airwaves in an area and become a monopoly, offering only one set of programs or point of view. For many years, FCC regulations limited the number of radio and television stations a company could own in a community and the total nationwide audience that a company's television stations could reach.[60]

The FCC also created the **equal time provision**, which states that if a radio or television station gives air time to a candidate outside its news coverage—such as during an entertainment show—it has to give an equivalent amount of time to other candidates running for the same office.

Deregulation The FCC's limits on ownership and content have been eliminated because of the development of cable television, satellite television, and the Internet. The logic is that with so many sources of information, if one broadcaster ignores a candidate, an issue, or a viewpoint citizens can still find what they want from another source. Pressure for deregulation also came from the owners of media companies, who wanted to buy more television, radio, and cable stations, as well as from book and magazine publishers, Internet service providers, and newspapers.[61]

These regulatory changes have shaped the current media landscape in two ways. First, concentration: many media companies own multiple media sources in a town or community. For example, ClearChannel Communications owns multiple AM and FM radio stations in more than 30 cities. The second trend is cross-ownership, which involves one company owning several different kinds of media outlets, often in the same community. For example, the Tribune Company in Chicago owns the WGN radio station, the WGN television station, and the *Chicago Tribune* daily newspaper. These trends have given rise to **media conglomerates**, companies that control a wide range of news sources.[62] Nuts & Bolts 6.2 shows the diverse holdings of one such company, News Corp/21st Century Fox.

Media effects on citizens and government

The study of **media effects** explores whether exposure to media coverage of politics changes what people think or do. There is considerable evidence that media coverage influences its audience—in simple terms, much of what Americans know about politics comes from the stories they read, watch, or listen to. In part, these effects arise because people exposed to stories that describe a particular event learn new facts as a result of their exposure. However, some of the impact of media coverage stems not from what such stories contain but from how they present certain information or even whether a story is reported at all.[63]

Many studies have found that exposure to political coverage changes what citizens know: at the most basic level; people who watch, read, or listen to more coverage about politics know more than people with less exposure.[64] What people learn can shape the demands they place on politicians.[65] However, at least part of this effect arises because of underlying interest: people who are interested in politics know more in the first place and, because of their interest, watch more media coverage of events as they happen. Moreover, because people can pick and choose which coverage to watch, read, or listen

Holdings of News Corp/21st Century Fox

NUTS
& BOLTS
6.2

News Corp/21st Century Fox* is an example of a media conglomerate, a company that controls a variety of media outlets throughout the world. It owns cable television networks, television and radio stations, newspapers, movie-production companies, magazines, and even sports teams. This structure allows the company to rebroadcast or reprint stories in different outlets and thus operate more efficiently, but opponents are concerned that conglomerates might expand to control most—or even all—of the sources that are available to the average citizen, making it impossible to access alternate points of view.

Fox Television Stations	Film Companies	Books and Magazines
31 U.S. stations	21st Century Fox Fox Searchlight Pictures Fox Television Studios Blue Sky Studios 11 other film companies	45 book publishers (including HarperCollins) worldwide 3 magazines

Satellite and Cable Holdings	Newspapers	Other Holdings
Fox News Channel More than 60 other cable channels in and outside United States 6 satellite television channels	*New York Post* *Wall Street Journal* 3 UK newspapers 19 Australian newspapers 30 local U.S. newspapers	AmericanIdol.com Over 50 news and entertainment websites Many other businesses

* These two companies were created in 2013 by dividing the operations of the News Corporation. However, the founder of the News Corporation, Rupert Murdoch, is the chairman and CEO of 21st Century Fox and the executive chairman of News Corp, and his family trust still holds a controlling interest in both corporations.

to, what they learn from the media tends to reinforce their preexisting beliefs. That is, a conservative might listen to Sean Hannity, while a liberal would opt for watching MSNBC. Both people may learn something from the coverage, but the most likely result is that they will only grow more certain in their opinions.[66] Finally, changes caused by media coverage are usually (but not always) short-lived.

Given this evidence of media effects, one of the central questions is whether reporters and editors have a discernable bias: that is, do their decisions about which events to report on and how they report on them reflect a conscious effort to shape public opinion in a liberal, conservative, or other direction? Surveys of the American electorate have found a **hostile media** effect: Democrats generally think the media favor Republicans, whereas Republicans have the opposite belief. That is, everyone seeks to think that the media are biased against the candidates and policies they prefer.[67] It is easy to find examples of suspicious decisions by reporters and their editors that suggest some sort of overt bias in coverage, and many journalists and commentators admit that they take an ideological or partisan perspective.

It is also no surprise that politicians complain about media coverage: the stakes for them are very high. For example, during the final weeks of the 2016 election, Donald Trump's campaign wanted more attention paid to their claims about the need for trade reform and their claims that Hillary Clinton was a corrupt politician, instead of the media's focus on several harassment claims against Trump and his poor performance in the presidential debates. While Trump's campaign argued that media coverage was biased against their candidate, the simpler explanation for their anger is that they wanted Trump to win, and that a fair accounting of the campaign (which is what the mainstream media provided, by and large) would be harmful to their candidate.

In fact, while it is easy to find media coverage of politics that is incomplete, or cases where reporters made predictions that later turned out to be false, it is hard to find cases of systematic bias in media coverage. It is also hard to find a scholarly study that

hostile media
The tendency of people to see neutral media coverage of an event as biased against their point of view.

presents strong evidence of systematic media bias in a liberal or conservative direction. Part of the problem is that it is hard to measure media bias. For example, one study found that when the Fox News Network began broadcasting in a community, voting for Republican candidates in the next election increased significantly.[68] Does this mean that some viewers became pro-Republican after listening to allegedly pro-Republican broadcasts on Fox News? Perhaps, but the study did not directly measure the behavior of individuals in these communities, so there was no way to be sure that new Republican supporters were actually Fox News viewers. Even if they were, it may be that watching Fox News had no effect on voting but that Fox News executives were looking for communities that were trending Republican when deciding which new markets to enter. Untangling these effects is difficult, and if media bias were as pronounced as some critics claim it would likely be easier to measure.

filtering
The influence on public opinion that results from journalists' and editors' decisions about which of many potential news stories to report.

framing
The influence on public opinion caused by the way a story is presented or covered, including the details, explanations, and context offered in the report.

Filtering and Framing Compared with overt bias, filtering and framing could produce subtler but stronger impacts on public opinion. **Filtering** (also called agenda-setting) results from journalists' and editors' decisions about which stories to report. **Framing** refers to how the description or presentation of a story, including the details, explanations, and context, changes the reaction people have to the information. Space limitations mean that some filtering is inevitable as reporters and editors decide which stories to cover. Similar decisions about what to report and how to present the information lead to framing effects. Even if everyone in the political media adhered to the highest standards of accuracy, these influences would still exist.

"Why Should I Care?"

It's important to have a clear and accurate understanding of today's media sources. If you're looking for someone to blame for Americans' lack of knowledge about politics, the mass media is not a good candidate. While most sources fall short in one way or another, there is a wealth of information available, most of it for free. But most people never search for political information and ignore much of what they encounter. Journalists can do the most effective reporting possible—providing in-depth, balanced coverage of critical events—but unless people take time to read or view that coverage, they will remain uninformed.

Conclusion

Public opinion and the media matter in American politics. Our nation's citizens have ideas about what they want government to do, and they use these ideas to guide their political choices. Most of the time, these beliefs are formed only when needed, so they are sensitive to recent events. In a country as large and diverse as the United States, disagreements over government policy are inevitable. However, even though public opinion data show disagreement in many areas, they also show areas where compromise is possible.

News media are Americans' primary source of public information about politics and policy. Although journalists can shape public opinion, media coverage is also substantially influenced by the need to attract an audience. There is little evidence, however, to support claims of an ideological bias in media coverage.

The average American is not an expert on government policies and knows relatively little about possible alternatives. But even a small amount of information is enough to inform his or her beliefs about what policies should be enacted. Politicians, moreover, generally take care to behave in accordance with the public's demands. Changes in the last few years in government policy, politicians' statements, and election outcomes all reflect changes in the policy mood.

STUDY GUIDE

What is public opinion?

Define *public opinion* and explain why it matters in American politics. (Pages 162–165)

Summary

What the population thinks about politics and government matters for three reasons: people's political actions are driven by their opinions; there is a strong linkage between people's opinions and political actors' behavior; and public opinion helps us understand how specific policy outcomes are achieved.

Key terms

public opinion (p. 162)   considerations (p. 163)
latent opinion (p. 163)

Practice Quiz Questions

1. **What does it mean that most political judgments are latent opinions?**
    a. Most Americans have preformed opinions.
    b. Most Americans have well-thought-out reasons for preferring a policy.
    c. Most Americans do not have any meaningful political attitudes.
    d. Most Americans form their opinions only as needed.
    e. Most opinions are not accurate.

2. **Which of the following is *not* true regarding considerations?**
    a. Well-informed and poorly informed people use them in forming opinions.
    b. Opinions on morally complex issues do not involve considerations.
    c. Political events can become considerations.
    d. They may be contradictory.
    e. Party identification is often used in considerations.

Where do opinions come from?

Explain how people form political attitudes and opinions. (Pages 166–169)

Summary

Political opinions are influenced by a wide range of factors. The belief systems of our parents and relatives influence our opinions early on, and our social groups influence our perspectives later in life. Personal events such as attending college or moving to a new city may influence how we think about politics, as do national events such as the attacks on September 11. Even political debates by political elites and party leaders shape our political attitudes.

Key term

political socialization (p. 166)

Practice Quiz Questions

3. **Theories of political socialization say that people's opinions are influenced first by _____.**
    a. what they learned from their parents
    b. the way political parties change over time
    c. their genetic and biological factors
    d. their personality traits
    e. politicians

4. **The idea that individuals will rely on others who "look like" them for opinions relates to _____.**
    a. political socialization
    b. group identity
    c. political events
    d. generational effects
    e. time-series effects

5. **Which phrase best completes the following statement regarding the sources of public opinion? "Politicians and other political actors work to _____ public opinion."**
    a. respond to
    b. ignore
    c. disregard
    d. stabilize
    e. shape

Measuring public opinion

Describe basic survey methods and potential issues affecting accuracy. (Pages 170–175)

Summary

Most information about public opinion comes from mass surveys involving hundreds or thousands of respondents. The accuracy of surveys is influenced by several factors, including the size of the sample and whether the people in the sample are randomly selected. Using a randomly selected sample, researchers can draw conclusions about public opinion across the American population.

Key terms

mass survey (p. 170)	**sampling error** (p. 170)
population (p. 170)	**sample** (p. 171)

Practice Quiz Question

6. Why is it important to get a large random survey sample?

  a. to keep costs down

  b. to provide deep insights into why people hold their opinions

  c. to help candidates fine-tune their campaign messages

  d. to be able to generalize about the broad population

  e. to prevent question wording from biasing survey results

What Americans think about politics

Present findings on what Americans think about government and why it matters. (Pages 176–182)

Summary

As a whole, the American electorate is ideologically moderate, with relatively little ideological polarization. Paradoxically, while trust in the government has declined steadily since the 1960s, people are still generally rather happy with their own representatives in Washington, D.C., and low trust in government does not preclude Americans from approving of specific government programs and activities. Government policy and congressional outcomes are responsive to changes in public mood, and most policy decisions (and arguments) reflect the priorities of a majority of Americans.

Key terms

ideological polarization (p. 176)	**policy mood** (p. 179)

Practice Quiz Questions

7. In the 1970s, the majority of people identified themselves as ideologically _____; in the 2000s, most people identified as _____.

  a. moderate; conservative

  b. moderate; moderate

  c. moderate; liberal

  d. conservative; moderate

  e. conservative; conservative

8. Americans generally _____ of the government; Americans generally _____ of their own representatives.

  a. approve; approve

  b. approve; disapprove

  c. disapprove; approve

  d. disapprove; disapprove

9. What is policy mood?

  a. public support for Congress

  b. presidential approval rating

  c. public demand for government action on domestic policies

  d. public demand for government action on international policies

  e. public demand for government action on alienation

10. Which policy area is always near the top of Americans' concerns?

  a. economic conditions

  b. health care

  c. gay rights

  d. immigration

  e. the environment

The news media

Describe the major types of news sources and the role they play in American politics. (Pages 182–186)

Summary

While the term "media" traditionally referred only to print sources, technological advances allowed political information to be spread through radio, television, and the Internet. The creation of the Internet and the proliferation of media sources more generally have drastically increased the amount of information about politics that is available to the average American. Much of what Americans know about politics comes not only from the stories that they are exposed to in the news but also from the way these stories are presented (or if stories are reported at all). Potential media bias, filtering, and framing all may influence the type and scope of information that reporters choose to disseminate.

Key terms

mass media (p. 182)
Federal Communications Commission (FCC) (p. 184)
broadcast media (p. 184)
equal time provision (p. 184)
media conglomerates (p. 184)
media effects (p. 184)
hostile media (p. 185)
filtering (p. 186)
framing (p. 186)

Practice Quiz Questions

11. What is one result of the decreased barriers to publication on the Internet?

a. Few opportunities exist for citizens to interact with reporters or government officials.

b. People with no official connection to candidates can have significant influence on elections.

c. The accuracy of political information has improved.

d. Few average citizens report on events as they happen.

e. Like-minded political supporters have difficulty organizing and staying informed on issues.

12. The deregulation of the media has resulted in _____ .

a. increasing enforcement of the equal time provision

b. increasing enforcement of the fairness doctrine

c. increasing use of the Internet

d. increasing scrutiny of media concentration

e. increasing frequency of cross-ownership

13. What is one problem with research on media bias?

a. Few scholars are interested in studying media bias.

b. It is difficult to measure bias.

c. No journalist will admit that bias exists.

d. There's little chance that media sources are biased.

e. There are not enough media sources to create a sample.

14. Space limitations mean that some _____ is inevitable.

a. filtering

b. slant

c. priming

d. framing

e. soft news

Suggested Reading

Campbell, David. *Why We Vote: How Schools and Communities Shape Our Civic Life*. Princeton, NJ: Princeton University Press, 2006.

Cappella, J. N., and K. H. Jamieson. *Spiral of Cynicism: The Press and the Public Good*. New York: Oxford University Press, 1997.

Carmines, Edward G., and James A. Stimson. *Issue Evolution: Race and the Transformation of American Politics*. Princeton, NJ: Princeton University Press, 1990.

Converse, Phillip E. "The Nature of Belief Systems in Mass Publics." In *Ideology and Discontent*, edited by David E. Apter, 206–61. Glencoe, IL: Free Press of Glencoe, 1964.

Davenport, Christian. *Media Bias, Perspective, and State Repression: The Black Panther Party*. New York: Cambridge University Press, 2010.

Delli Carpini, Michael X., and Scott Keeter. *What Americans Know about Politics and Why It Matters*. New Haven, CT: Yale University Press, 1997.

Green, Donald P., Bradley Palmquist, and Eric Schickler. *Partisan Hearts and Minds*. New Haven, CT: Yale University Press, 2002.

Hibbing, John R., and Elizabeth Theiss-Morse. *Congress as Public Enemy: Public Attitudes toward American Political Institutions*. New York: Cambridge University Press, 1995.

Iyengar, Shanto. *Is Anyone Responsible? How Television Frames Political Issues*. Chicago: University of Chicago Press, 1991.

Jacobs, Lawrence R., and Robert Y. Shapiro. *Politicians Don't Pander: Political Manipulation and the Loss of Democratic Responsiveness*. Chicago: University of Chicago Press, 2000.

Lippman, Walter. *Public Opinion*. 1922. Reprint, New York: Free Press, 1997.

Lupia, Arthur, and Mathew D. McCubbins. *The Democratic Dilemma*. New York: Cambridge University Press, 1998.

Marcus, George E., John L. Sullivan, Elizabeth Theiss-Morse, and Sandra L. Wood. *With Malice toward Some: How People Make Civil Liberties Judgments*. New York: Cambridge University Press, 1995.

Patterson, Thomas. *Out of Order*. New York: Knopf, 1993.

Peffley, Mark, and Jon Hurwitz. *Justice in America: The Separate Realities of Blacks and Whites*. New York: Cambridge University Press, 2010.

Prior, Markus. *Post-Broadcast Democracy: How Media Choice Increases Inequality in Political Involvement and Polarizes Elections*. New York: Cambridge University Press, 2007.

Zaller, John. *The Nature and Origins of Mass Opinion*. New York: Cambridge University Press, 1992.

7

Political Parties

How do political parties organize American politics?

Anyone paying attention during the 2016 elections might easily conclude that American political parties were beset with internal conflicts and subordinate to candidates and officeholders. Citizens' confidence in the two parties was at an all-time low. Both parties had contentious presidential nomination contests, complete with charges that party leaders were biased and that the rules were rigged. While Democrats ultimately united behind their general-election nominee, Hillary Clinton, many Republicans refused to endorse or campaign with their party's nominee, Donald Trump. Republican Senate Majority Leader Mitch McConnell refused to say anything about Trump, and Speaker of the House of Representatives Paul Ryan told his colleagues in the Republican caucus that he would focus on helping them get reelected, ignoring requests by Republican National Committee Chair Reince Priebus for Ryan to get involved in the presidential campaign. After the election, Republican members of Congress congratulated Trump on his victory, but refused to commit to enacting his agenda.

Though parties appear fractured, unpopular, and leaderless, political scientists argue that parties play a critical role in American politics. Decades of public opinion research have shown that most Americans have a long-term attachment to one of the major parties and that this attachment shapes whom they vote for and how they interpret events. One of the best explanations of the modern presidential nomination process, *The Party Decides*, argues that endorsements from politicians and party officials are essential to a nominee's success.[1] And a key theory that scholars use to explain the legislative process says that parties are the key players in the legislative process.

This chapter explains the complex role of American political parties. Political parties embody some of the most fundamental conflicts that underlie American politics. Parties help shape the way Americans think about candidates, policies, and vote decisions. Parties also impact elections by recruiting candidates, paying for campaign ads, and mobilizing supporters. After elections, the winning party's candidates implement their vision, while the losers try to derail these efforts and develop an alternative vision that will attract support. In so doing,

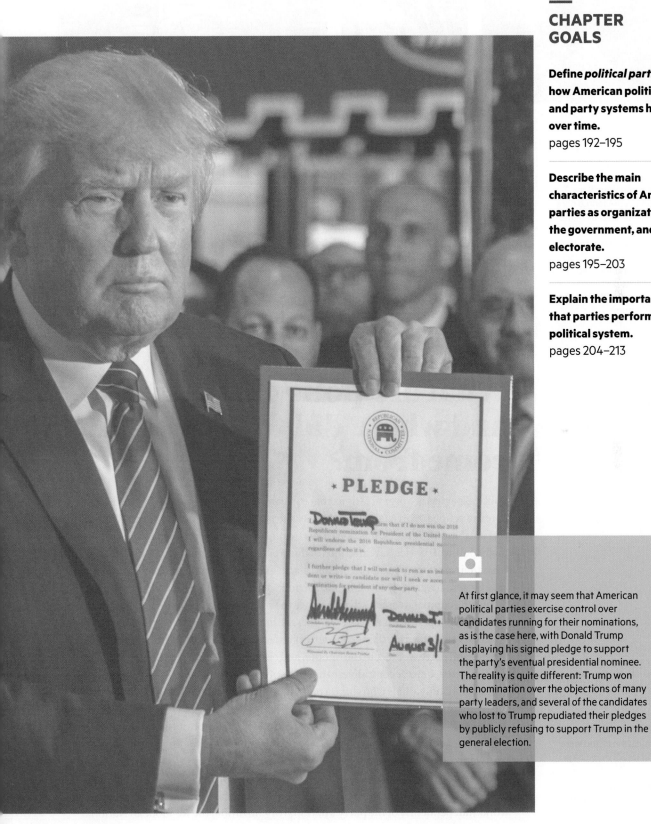

Define *political parties* **and show how American political parties and party systems have evolved over time.**
pages 192–195

Describe the main characteristics of American parties as organizations, in the government, and in the electorate.
pages 195–203

Explain the important functions that parties perform in the political system.
pages 204–213

📷

At first glance, it may seem that American political parties exercise control over candidates running for their nominations, as is the case here, with Donald Trump displaying his signed pledge to support the party's eventual presidential nominee. The reality is quite different: Trump won the nomination over the objections of many party leaders, and several of the candidates who lost to Trump repudiated their pledges by publicly refusing to support Trump in the general election.

American political parties have three largely separate components: the party organization, represented here by Donna Brazile, interim chair of the Democratic National Committee; the party in government, represented by House Minority Leader Nancy Pelosi (D-CA) and House Minority Whip Steny Hoyer (D-MD); and the party in the electorate, exemplified by the crowd at a rally for Hillary Clinton.
#DNC @TheDemocrats

DEFINE *POLITICAL PARTIES* AND SHOW HOW AMERICAN POLITICAL PARTIES AND PARTY SYSTEMS HAVE EVOLVED OVER TIME

party organization
A specific political party's leaders and workers at the national, state, and local levels.

party in government
The group of officeholders who belong to a specific political party and were elected as candidates of that party.

party in the electorate
The group of citizens who identify with a specific political party.

parties unify and mobilize disparate groups, simplify the choices that voters face, and bring efficiency and coherence to government policy making.

Although American political parties often have an impact on elections and policy, the same organizations can sometimes seem inept, irrelevant, and paralyzed by conflict. Our task in this chapter is to explain this variation using two of our main themes—conflict is natural and the rules of the political games matter. While American political parties are the product of disagreements about what government should do, these differences sometimes split politicians and activists within an established party organization—making it all but impossible for these individuals to work together. Why—and when—do parties matter?

What are political parties and where did today's parties come from?

Political parties are organizations that run candidates for political office and coordinate the actions of officials elected under the party banner. Looking around the world, we find many different kinds of parties. In numerous western European countries, the major political parties have millions of dues-paying members and party leaders control what their elected officials do. In contrast, in many new democracies, candidates run as representatives of a party, but party leaders have no control over what candidates say during the campaign or how they act once they win office. America's major political parties, the Republicans and the Democrats, lie somewhere between these extremes.

However, rather than being unified organizations with party leaders at the top, candidates and party workers in the middle, and citizen-members at the bottom, American political parties are decentralized: they constitute a loose network of organizations, groups, and individuals who share a party label but are under no obligation to work together.[2]

The **party organization** is the structure of national, state, and local parties, including party leaders and workers. The **party in government** is made up of the politicians who were elected as candidates of the party. And the **party in the electorate** includes all the citizens who identify with the party. For example, the Speaker of the House of Representatives, Paul Ryan, is the leader of Republican House members, but he works independently of the party's national organization, the Republican National

Committee (RNC); neither one is in charge of the other. Ryan is also not in charge of other Republican groups in Congress, such as the Freedom Caucus (a group of conservative Republicans)—and although Caucus members may be somewhat sympathetic to Ryan's arguments, they are under no obligation to do what he asks. Similarly, the RNC cannot command state and local Republican Party organizations to take some actions and not others. Moreover, while many Americans think of themselves as members of a political party, someone who identifies with the Republican Party is not obligated to work for or give money to the party or to vote for its candidates. As you will see, organization matters: the fact that American political parties are split into three parts has important implications for what they do and for their impact on the nation's politics.

Political scientists use the term "**party system**" to describe periods in which the major parties' names, their groups of supporters, and the issues dividing them have all been constant. As Table 7.1 shows, there have been six party systems in America.[3] For each party system, the table gives the names of the two major parties, indicates which party dominated (that is, won the most presidential elections or controlled Congress), and describes the principal issues dividing the parties.

The evolution of American political parties

Political parties formed soon after the Founding of the United States. The first American parties, the Federalists and the Democratic-Republicans, were primarily parties in government. Federalists wanted a strong central government and a national bank, and they favored assumption of state war debts by the national government; Democratic-Republicans took the opposite positions based on their preference for concentrating power at the state level. These political parties were quite different from their modern counterparts. In particular, there were no national party organizations, few citizens thought of themselves as party members, and candidates for office did not campaign as representatives of a political party.

For two decades, the two parties were more or less evenly matched in Congress, although the Federalists did not win a presidential contest after 1800. However, during the 1814 elections the Federalist Party lost most of its congressional seats due to Federalist legislators' opposition to the War of 1812 and their support for a pay raise for members of Congress. These defeats led to the Era of Good Feelings, when there was only one political party, the Democratic-Republicans. Following the election of President Andrew Jackson in 1828, the organization that elected Jackson became known as the Democratic Party. At the same time, another new party, the Whig Party, was formed and the second party system came into existence.

The new Democratic Party cultivated electoral support by building organizations to mobilize citizens and bind them to the party. The party also implemented the **party principle**, the idea that a party is not just a group of elected officials but an organization that exists apart from its candidates, and the **spoils system**, whereby party workers were rewarded with benefits such as federal jobs.[4]

In the 1840s, the issue of slavery split the second party system, leading to a third party system. Most Democratic politicians either supported slavery outright or wanted to avoid debating the issue.[5] The Whig Party was split between (1) politicians who agreed with the Democrats and (2) abolitionists, who wanted to end slavery. Ultimately, antislavery Whigs left the party and formed the Republican Party, which also attracted antislavery Democrats, leading to the demise of the Whig Party. This move divided the country into a largely Republican Northeast, a largely Democratic South, and politically split Midwestern and border states.[6]

party system
Periods in which the names of the major political parties, their supporters, and the issues dividing them have remained relatively stable.

The Tammany Hall political machine, depicted here as a rotund version of one of its leaders, William "Boss" Tweed, controlled New York City politics for most of the nineteenth and early twentieth centuries. Its strategy was "honest graft," rewarding party workers, contributors, and voters for their efforts to keep the machine's candidates in office.

"THAT'S WHAT'S THE MATTER."
Boss Tweed. "As long as I count the Votes, what are you going to do about it?

party principle
The idea that a political party exists as an organization distinct from its elected officials or party leaders.

spoils system
The practice of rewarding party supporters with benefits like federal government positions.

American Party Systems

There have been six party systems in the United States since 1789.

Party System	Major Parties (dominant party in boldface)	Key Issues
First (1789–1828)	Federalists, Democratic-Republicans (neither party was dominant)	Location of the capital, financial issues (e.g., national bank)
Second (1829–1856)	**Democrats**, Whigs	Tariffs (farmers vs. merchants), slavery
Third (1857–1896)	Democrats, **Republicans**	Slavery (pre–Civil War), Reconstruction (post–Civil War), industrialization
Fourth (1897–1932)	Democrats, **Republicans**	Industrialization, immigration
Fifth (1933–1968)	**Democrats**, Republicans	Size and scope of the federal government
Sixth (1969–present)	Democrats, Republicans (neither party is dominant)	Size and scope of the federal government, civil rights, social issues, foreign policy

📷

Debate over Roosevelt's New Deal programs established the basic divide between Democrats and Republicans that continues to this day: in the main, Democrats favor a larger federal government that takes an active role in managing the economy; Republicans prefer a smaller federal government and fewer programs and regulations.

Even after the Civil War, the Republicans and Democrats remained the two prominent, national parties. The parties were divided over the size and scope of the federal government: should the federal government help farmers and rural residents or inhabitants of rapidly expanding cities, and should it regulate America's rapidly growing industrial base? Democrats built a coalition of rural and urban voters by proposing a larger, more active federal government and other policies that would help both groups.

The fifth party system was born out of the Great Depression. Many Republicans argued that conditions would improve over time and that government intervention would do little good, while Democrats proposed new government programs that would help people in need and spur economic growth. The Democratic landslide in the 1932 elections led to the New Deal, a series of federal programs designed to stimulate the national economy, help needy people, and impose a variety of new regulations.

Debate over the New Deal brought together the New Deal coalition of African Americans, Catholics, Jewish people, union members, and white southerners, who became strong supporters of Democratic candidates over the next generation.[7] This transformation established the basic division between the parties that exists to the present day: Democrats generally favor a large federal government that takes an active role in managing the economy and regulating behavior, while Republicans believe that many such programs should be provided by state and local governments or not provided at all.

A sixth party system emerged as new political questions and debates divided the parties.[8] Beginning in the late 1940s, many Democratic candidates and party leaders, particularly outside the South, came out against the "separate but equal" system of racial discrimination in southern states and in favor of programs designed to ensure equal opportunity for minority citizens.

At the same time, Democratic politicians argued for expanding the role of the federal government into health care, antipoverty programs, and education. Most Republicans opposed these initiatives, although a significant portion did not. At the same time, these new issues also began to divide American citizens and organized groups.[9]

These developments produced a gradual but significant shift in the groups that identified with each party. White southerners and some Catholics moved to the Republican

Party, and minorities, particularly African Americans, started identifying more strongly as Democrats. Democrats also gained supporters in New England and West Coast states. By the late 1980s, all three elements of the Republican and Democratic parties (organization, government, and electorate) were much more like-minded than they had been a generation earlier.

Realignments Each party system is separated from the next by a realignment—a change in one or more of the factors that define a party system. These factors include the issues that divide the parties, the nature and function of the party organizations, the composition of the party coalitions, and the specifics of government policy.

In most cases, a realignment begins with the emergence of a new question or issue debate that captures the attention of large numbers of ordinary citizens, activists, and politicians. For example, as noted, the fifth party system (1933–1968) was born during the Great Depression, when the parties were primarily divided by their positions on the appropriate size of the federal government.

realignment
A change in the size or composition of the party coalitions or in the nature of the issues that divide the parties. Realignments typically occur within an election cycle or two, but they can also occur gradually over the course of a decade or longer.

Looking at American political parties today, you might think that Democratic and Republican parties have been around forever, that they are evenly split in party identifiers and officeholders, and that their main disagreement has always concerned the size and scope of government. None of these ideas is true. Moreover, the changes over time in the Republican and Democratic parties illustrate how these organizations adapt to shifts in public opinion. Thus, American political parties may look very different 10 years from now than they do today.

"Why Should I Care?"

American political parties today

★

DESCRIBE THE MAIN CHARACTERISTICS OF AMERICAN PARTIES AS ORGANIZATIONS, IN THE GOVERNMENT, AND IN THE ELECTORATE

We've seen that from the beginning political parties have been a central feature of American politics. The next steps are to examine the different aspects (the party organization, the party in government, and the party in the electorate) of American political parties, describe the role they play in elections and in government, and compare their behavior in practice with the job description presented earlier in this chapter.

The party organization

The principal body in each party organization is the national committee, which consists of representatives from state party organizations, usually one man and one woman per state. The state party organizations in turn are made up of professional staff plus thousands of party organizations at the county, city, and town levels. The job of these organizations is to run the party's day-to-day operations, recruit candidates and supporters, raise money for future campaigns, and work to build a consensus on major issues.

Both major parties also include a number of constituency groups (the Democrats' term) or teams (the Republicans' term). These organizations within the party work to attract the support of demographic groups considered likely to share the party's issue

national committee
An American political party's principal organization, comprising party representatives from each state.

concerns—such as specific racial or ethnic groups, people with strong religious beliefs, senior citizens, women, and many others—and assist in fund-raising.[10]

Each party organization also includes groups designed to build support for, or coordinate the efforts of, particular individuals or politicians. These groups include the Democratic and the Republican Governors' Associations, the Young Democrats, the Young Republicans, and more specialized groups such as the Republican Lawyers' Organization or the Democratic Leadership Council (DLC), an organization of moderate Democratic politicians.[11]

Other Allied Groups Many other groups, such as **political action committees (PACs)** or **527 organizations**, labor unions, and other interest groups and organizations, are loosely affiliated with one of the major parties. For example, the organization MoveOn.org typically supports Democratic candidates. Similar organizations on the Republican side include the Club for Growth, Americans for Prosperity, Crossroads GPS, and many evangelical groups. Most groups that use the "Tea Party" label to describe themselves generally have some connection to the national or local Republican Party.[12] Though these groups often favor one party over the other, they are not part of the party organization and do not always agree with the party's positions or support its candidates—in fact, many have to operate independently of the parties and their candidates in order to preserve their tax-exempt status. (For more details on campaign finance see Chapters 8 and 9.)

As this description suggests, the party organization has a fluid structure rather than a rigid hierarchy.[13] Individuals and groups work with a party's leaders and candidates when they share the same goals, but unless they are paid party employees, they are under no obligation to do so (even paid party workers can quit rather than work for a candidate or a cause they oppose).

Party Brand Names The Republican and Democratic party organizations have well-established brand names. Because the parties stand for different things, both in terms of their preferred government policies and in terms of their ideological leanings, the party names themselves become a shorthand way of providing information to voters about the parties' candidates.[14] Hearing the term "Democrat" or "Republican" calls to mind ideas about what kinds of positions the members of each party support, what kinds of candidates each party runs, and how these candidates will probably vote if they are elected to office. Citizens can use these brand names as a cue to decide whom to vote for in an election. (See Chapter 8 for more information about voting cues.)

Limits of the Party Organization One critical thing to understand about the Democratic and Republican party organizations is that they are not hierarchies. No one person or group in charge determines what either organization does—which often makes them look disorganized, as the Will Rogers quote indicates. Within the RNC and Democratic National Committee (DNC), the party organization's issue positions are set not by the committee chair but by DNC or RNC members from all 50 states. If the committee chair and the committee disagree, the chair cannot force the committee members to do what he or she wants.

The national party organization is also unable to force state and local parties to share its positions on issues or comply with other requests. State and local parties make their own decisions about state- and local-level candidates and issue positions. The national committee can ask nicely, cajole, or even threaten to withhold funds (although such threats are rare), but if a state party organization, an independent group, or even an individual candidate disagrees with the national committee, there's little the national committee can do to force compliance.

---

political action committee (PAC)
An interest group or a division of an interest group that can raise money to contribute to campaigns or to spend on ads in support of candidates. The amount a PAC can receive from each of its donors and the amount it can spend on federal electioneering are strictly limited.

527 organization
A tax-exempt group formed primarily to influence elections through voter mobilization efforts and to issue ads that do not directly endorse or oppose a candidate. Unlike PACs, they are not subject to contribution limits and spending caps.

99

I am not a member of an organized political party. I am a Democrat.

—Will Rogers

The party in government

The party in government consists of elected officials holding national, state, and local offices who have taken office as candidates of a particular party. They are the public face of the party, somewhat like the players on a sports team. Although players are only one part of a sports franchise—along with owners, coaches, trainers, and support staff—the players' identities are what most people call to mind when they think of the team. Because the party in government is made up of officeholders, it has a direct impact on government policy. Members of the party organization can recruit candidates, write platforms, and pay for campaign ads, but only those who win elections—that is, the party in government—get to serve as members of Congress or as executive officials and actually propose, debate, vote on, and sign the legislation that determines what government does.

Caucuses and Conferences In the House and Senate, the Democratic and Republican parties are organized around working groups called a **caucus** (Democrats) or a **conference** (Republicans). The party caucus or conference serves as a forum for debate, compromise, and strategizing among a party's elected officials. Under unified government (when the same party controls Congress and the presidency) these discussions focus on finding common ground within the party—such as the negotiations that led to the enactment of Obamacare in 2010 without any support from Republicans. Under divided government or when a party is in the minority, the focus changes to finding opportunities to work with the other party, or strategizing on how to block the other party's initiatives.

Each party's caucus or conference also meets to decide legislative committee assignments, leadership positions on committees, and leadership positions within the caucus or conference.[15] Caucus or conference leaders serve as spokespeople for their respective parties, particularly when the president is from the other party. The party in government also contains groups that recruit and support candidates for political office, the Democratic Congressional Campaign Committee (DCCC), the Democratic Senatorial Campaign Committee (DSCC), the National Republican Congressional Committee (NRCC), and the National Republican Senatorial Committee (NRSC).

Policy Positions The modern Congress is polarized: in both the House and the Senate, Republicans and Democrats hold different views on government policy (see What Do the Numbers Say? on p.199). Figure 7.1 compares legislators on the basis of their ideology or their general feelings about government policy, as measured by a liberal-conservative scale. The data reflect two House sessions: the 83rd House of 60 years ago (elected in 1952) and the 114th House (elected in 2014).

These graphs tell us two things. First, over the last 60 years the magnitude of ideological differences between the parties in Congress has increased. In the 83rd House there was some overlap between the positions of Democrats and Republicans, but it had disappeared by the 113th House.[16]

Second, Figure 7.1 reveals that both parties in government include a mixture of ideologies, not a uniform consensus opinion. In the 83rd House plot, for example, Democrats vary from the relatively liberal left end of the scale to the moderate (middle) and even somewhat conservative right side. Democrats in the 114th House were, on average, more liberal than their colleagues in the 83rd, but a wide range of ideologies was still represented in the Democratic Caucus. The same is true for Republicans, who leaned in the conservative direction in both the 114th and the 83rd Houses.

The ideological diversity within each party in government can create situations in which a caucus or conference is divided on a policy question. Compromise within a

caucus (congressional)
The organization of Democrats within the House and Senate that meets to discuss and debate the party's positions on various issues in order to reach a consensus and to assign leadership positions.

conference
The organization of Republicans within the House and Senate that meets to discuss and debate the party's positions on various issues in order to reach a consensus and to assign leadership positions.

FIGURE 7.1

Ideology of the Parties in Government: 83rd House and 114th House

Over the last several decades, ideological differences between Democrats and Republicans in Congress have increased significantly. However, even in the 114th House both parties still included a wide range of views. In light of these data, would you expect more or less partisan conflict in the modern Congress than there was in the early 1950s? According to these data, would you expect House members in each party to agree on what policies to pursue?

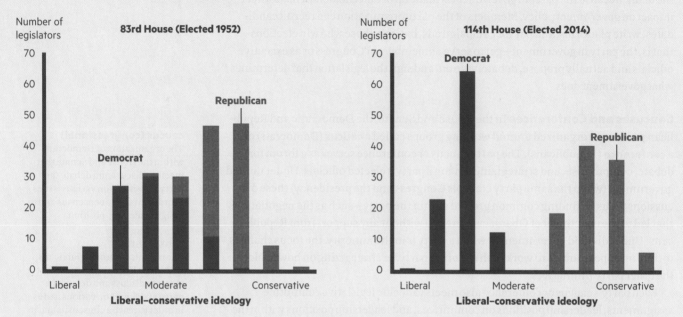

Source: "Constant Space DW-NOMINATE Scores," December 19, 2015, http://voteview.com (accessed 1/19/16).

DID YOU KNOW?

7%

of Americans say they worked for a political candidate or issue campaign during the last year.

party identification (party ID)
A citizen's loyalty to a specific political party.

party's working group is not inevitable—even though legislators share a party label, they may not be able to find common ground. In the last few years, congressional Republicans have been divided on issues such as immigration, spending levels, and the federal debt limit.[17]

The party in the electorate

The party in the electorate consists of citizens who identify with a particular political party. Most Americans say they are either Democrats or Republicans, although the percentage has declined over the last two generations. **Party identification (party ID)** is a critical variable in understanding votes and other forms of political participation.

Party ID Party ID is different from formal membership in a political party. Although the Republicans and the Democrats have websites where people can sign up to receive e-mail alerts and contribute online to party causes, joining a party does not give a citizen any direct influence over what the party does. Rather, the party leaders and the candidates themselves make the day-to-day decisions. These individuals often heed citizens' demands, but there is no requirement that they do so. Real participation in party operations is open to citizens who become activists by working for a party organization or one of its candidates. Activists' contributions vary from stuffing envelopes to

Are the Parties More Polarized than Ever?

For the last twenty years, it seems as though all the news about political parties has been about conflict and stalemate. It seems as though political campaigns are increasingly negative, compromise on issues is rare, and Republicans and Democrats have divided into camps that are never likely to agree on anything. Is this trend new? What do the numbers say?

Ideological Polarization in Congress

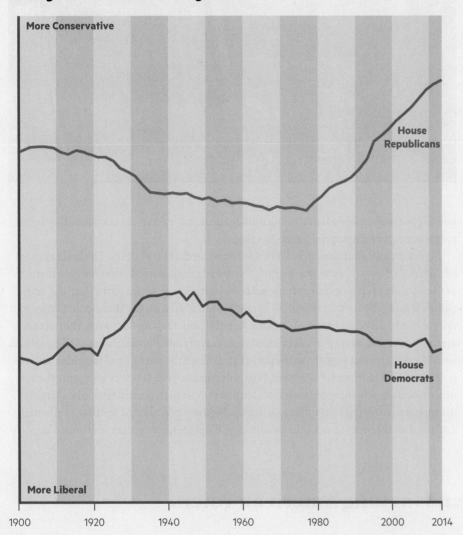

Think about it

- This graph uses voting behavior to measure the average ideology (liberal–conservative) of House Democrats and Republicans. Since the 1980s, have Republicans gotten more conservative, have Democrats become more liberal, or both?
- How might these changes make it harder for members of the contemporary Congress to enact major changes in government policy? What is more likely: compromise or gridlock?

Activist volunteers undertake most of the one-on-one efforts to mobilize support for a party and its candidates.

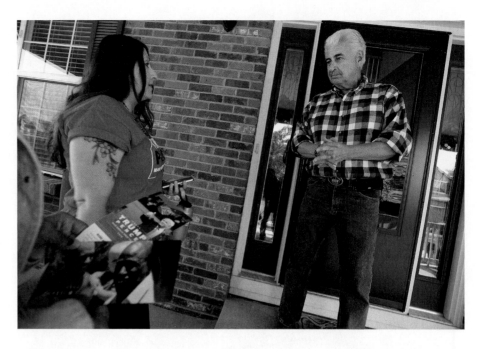

helping out with a phone bank, being a delegate to a party convention, attending campaign rallies, or campaigning door-to-door.

Figure 7.2 gives data on party ID in America over the last 75 years. The first segment of the graph shows that the Democratic Party had a considerable advantage in terms of the number of citizens identifying with the party from the late 1930s until the late 1980s. During the 1970s, nearly half of adults identified with the Democratic Party and only about 20 percent identified with the Republicans. During the 1990s, the percentage of Democratic identifiers decreased significantly and the percentage of Republican identifiers increased slightly, to the point that in 2002 the parties had roughly the same percentage of identifiers.[18] However, beginning in 2003 the Democrats again opened up a significant advantage in terms of identifiers, although the difference has largely disappeared in recent years. The two lines in Figure 7.2 do not add up to 100 percent, and the difference represents the percentage of independent voters who do not identify

FIGURE 7.2   Party ID Trends among American Voters

In terms of party ID, the parties have moved from rough parity in the late 1930s and 1940s to a period of Democratic advantage that lasted from the 1950s to the 1980s. Beginning in 2003, Democrats appeared to be opening up another advantage, although this change has eroded in recent years. What events might have caused these changes in party ID?

Source: Pew Research Center, "A Deep Dive into Party Affiliation," April 7, 2015, www.people-press.org (accessed 12/20/15).

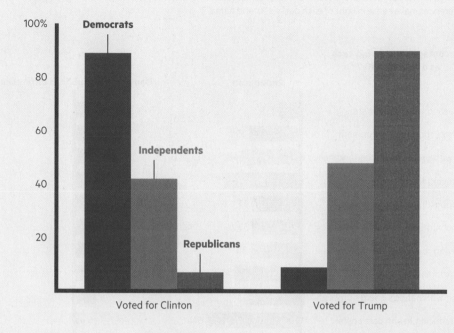

FIGURE
7.3

The Impact of Party ID on Voting Decisions in the 2016 Presidential Election

Americans are much more likely to vote for candidates who share their party affiliation. What does this relationship tell us about the impact of campaign events (including speeches, debates, and gaffes) on voting decisions?

Source: Data compiled from CNN Exit Poll, www.cnn.com/election/results/exit-polls/national/president (accessed 11/9/16).

with either party. Just like the percentages of Republican and Democratic identifiers, the percentage of Independents fluctuates over time.

Looking more closely at vote decisions, we see that Figure 7.3 shows how Democrats, Republicans, and Independents voted in the 2016 presidential election ("closet partisan" Independents are grouped with the party they actually affiliate with). This figure shows that if you are trying to predict how someone will vote the most important thing to know is his or her party ID.[19] Almost 90 percent of Democrats voted for Hillary Clinton, the Democratic nominee; and about the same percentage of Republicans voted for Donald Trump. Trump's victory was due to his slightly higher margin among independents.

Party Coalitions Data on party ID enable scholars to determine the **party coalitions**, or groups of citizens who identify with each party as well as the nature of disagreements between the parties.

The contemporary Republican and Democratic party coalitions differ systematically in terms of their policy preferences—what they want government to do—as shown in Figure 7.4. This data indicates the extent to which partisans disagree about the relative importance of issues such as providing health insurance to the uninsured, addressing global warming, and strengthening the military. These differences hammer home the idea that party labels are meaningful: if you know someone is a Republican (or a Democrat), this information tells you something about what that person probably wants government to do and how he or she will likely vote in the next election. These differences also create opportunities for **issue ownership**: candidates from a party tend to concentrate their campaigns on issues that are priorities for members of their party in the electorate and ignore issues that their party in the electorate considers unimportant.[20]

> **There's no evidence from decades of Pew Research surveys that public opinion, in the aggregate, is more extreme now than in the past. But what has changed—and pretty dramatically—is the growing tendency of people to sort themselves into political parties based on their ideological differences.**
>
> —Pew Research Center

party coalitions
The groups that identify with a political party, usually described in demographic terms such as African-American Democrats or evangelical Republicans.

issue ownership
The theory that voters associate certain issues or issue positions with certain parties (like Democrats and support for government-provided health insurance).

FIGURE
7.4

Democrats' and Republicans' Top Priorities

The Republican and Democratic party coalitions have different priorities on many issues, ranging from environmental protection to deficit reduction—and on a few issues their differences are small, such as reforming the tax system and reducing the influence of lobbyists. Do these differences make sense in light of each party's "brand name"?

Percentage considering each as a "top priority"

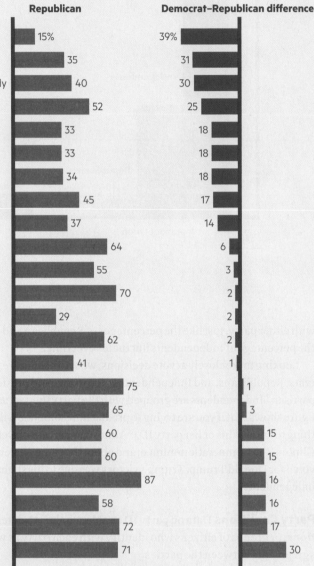

Democrat		Republican	Democrat–Republican difference
54%	Dealing with global warming	15%	39%
66	Protecting the environment	35	31
70	Dealing with problems of poor and needy	40	30
77	Improving the educational system	52	25
51	Supporting scientific research	33	18
51	Dealing with role of money in politics	33	18
52	Improving roads, bridges, and transit	34	18
62	Addressing race relations	45	17
51	Dealing with nation's energy problem	37	14
70	Reducing health care costs	64	6
58	Making Medicare system sound	55	3
72	Improving the job situation	70	2
31	Dealing with global trade issues	29	2
64	Reducing crime	62	2
42	Reducing the influence of lobbyists	41	1
74	Strengthening the nation's economy	75	1
62	Making Social Security system sound	65	3
45	Reforming the nation's tax system	60	15
45	Dealing with issue of immigration	60	15
71	Defending country from terrorism	87	16
42	Dealing with moral breakdown	58	16
55	Reducing the budget deficit	72	17
41	Strengthening the U.S. military	71	30

Source: Pew Research Center, "Public's Policy Priorities Reflect Changing Conditions at Home and Abroad," January 15, 2015, www.people-press.org (accessed 12/20/15).

The Party Coalitions

Many groups, such as African Americans and white evangelicals, are much more likely to affiliate with one party than the other. What are the implications of these differences for the positions taken by each party's candidates?

**FIGURE
7.5**

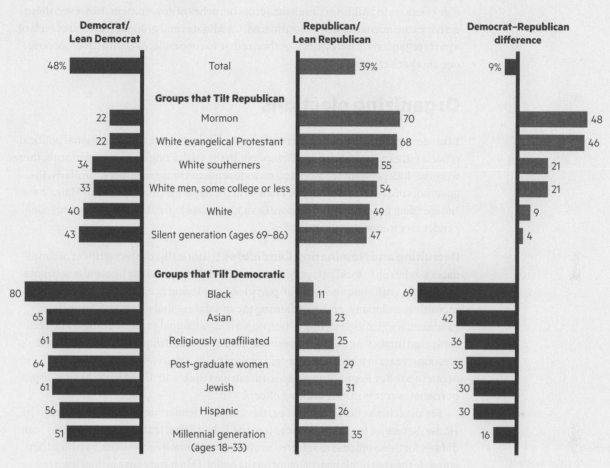

	Democrat/ Lean Democrat		Republican/ Lean Republican	Democrat–Republican difference
Total	48%		39%	9%
Groups that Tilt Republican				
Mormon	22		70	48
White evangelical Protestant	22		68	46
White southerners	34		55	21
White men, some college or less	33		54	21
White	40		49	9
Silent generation (ages 69–86)	43		47	4
Groups that Tilt Democratic				
Black	80		11	69
Asian	65		23	42
Religiously unaffiliated	61		25	36
Post-graduate women	64		29	35
Jewish	61		31	30
Hispanic	56		26	30
Millennial generation (ages 18–33)	51		35	16

Source: Pew Research Center, "A Deep Dive into Party Affiliation," April 7, 2015, www.people-press.org (accessed 12/20/15).

These policy disagreements reflect sharp differences in the composition of the party coalitions, as shown in Figure 7.5. As you can see, some groups are disproportionately likely to identify as Democrats (African Americans), some are disproportionately likely to identify as Republicans (white evangelicals), and other groups have no clear favorite party (people born in 1945 and earlier). Again, these coalitions have shifted over time. For example, the Republican advantage among white southerners and white evangelical Protestants has existed only since the 1980s.[21]

Knowing that someone is a Democrat or a Republican tells you a lot about the issues that person cares about, whether he or she will like or dislike different candidates, and whom he or she will vote for in an election. Taken together, information about the kinds of people who identify with each party tells you a lot about the kinds of candidates who will run under the party banner and the platforms they will campaign on.

"Why Should I Care?"

The role of political parties in American politics

Political parties play an important dual role in American politics, from helping to organize elections to building consensus across branches of government. However, these activities are not necessarily coordinated. Candidates and groups at different levels of a party organization may work together, refuse to cooperate, or even actively oppose one another's efforts.

Organizing elections

In modern American politics, virtually everyone elected to a state or national political office is either a Republican or a Democrat. In the 115th Congress, elected in 2016, there were two Independent senators and no Independent House members. Similarly, the governors of 48 states were either Democrats or Republicans (Alaska and Maine have Independent governors) and of more than 7,300 state legislators very few were Independents or minor-party candidates.

Recruiting and Nominating Candidates Historically, the recruitment of candidates was left up to local party organizations. But the process has become much more systematic, with state and national party leaders playing a central role in finding and recruiting, endorsing, and contributing to candidates—and often promising those candidates help in assembling a staff, organizing a campaign, and raising additional campaign funds.[22] Actions like these can have a profound impact on congressional elections; years in which one party gains significant congressional seats (such as Democrats in 2008 or Republicans in 2010) are in part the result of one party having disproportionate success in its recruiting efforts.

For all of these efforts, though, parties and their leaders do not control who runs in House, Senate, or presidential races (see the Take a Stand feature). In most states, candidates for these offices are selected in a **primary election** or a **caucus**, in which they compete for a particular party's spot on the ballot. (Most states use primaries; a few state parties use conventions to select candidates.) Nuts & Bolts 7.1 further explains the different ways that the parties select candidates. Most notably, Donald Trump won the 2016 Republican presidential nomination by virtue of his victories in the party's primaries and caucuses over the objections of many party leaders. Trump's victory demonstrates that party endorsements, while significant, are not the only factor in shaping nomination contests.

Running as a major party's congressional nominee, as opposed to running as an Independent, is almost always the easiest way to get on the general-election ballot. Some states give the Republican and Democratic nominees an automatic spot on the ballot. Even in states that don't automatically allocate ballot slots this way, the requirements for the major parties to get a candidate on the ballot are much less onerous than those for minor parties and Independents. In California, for example, a party and its candidates automatically qualify for a position on the ballot if any of the party's candidates for statewide office received more than 2 percent of the vote in the previous election. In contrast, Independent candidates need to file petitions with more than 150,000 signatures to get on the ballot without a major-party label—an expensive, time-consuming task.[23] These advantages help explain why virtually all prominent candidates for Congress and the presidency run as Democrats or Republicans.

National parties also manage the nomination process for presidential candidates. This process involves a series of primaries and caucuses held over a six-month period

primary election
A ballot vote in which citizens select a party's nominee for the general election.

caucus (electoral)
A local meeting in which party members select a party's nominee for the general election.

Should Parties Choose Their Candidates?

One of the facts of life for the leaders of the Democratic and Republican parties is that they cannot determine who runs as their party's candidate for political office. They can encourage some candidates to run and attempt to discourage others by endorsing their favorites and funneling money, staff support, and other forms of assistance to the candidates they prefer. But in the end, congressional candidates get on the ballot by winning a primary or a vote at a state party convention; presidential candidates compete in a series of primaries and caucuses. Is this system a good one?

Let the party decide.

Many scholars have argued that letting parties choose their candidates increases the chances of getting experienced, talented candidates on the ballot.[a] After all, party leaders probably know more than the average voter about who would make a good candidate or elected official. Plus, party leaders have a strong incentive to find good candidates and convince them to run: their party's influence over government policy increases with the number of people they can elect to political office. And finally, in states that have no party registration or day-of-election registration, giving the nomination power to party leaders would ensure that a group of outsiders could not hijack a party primary to nominate a candidate who disagreed with a party's platform or who was unqualified to serve in office.

While cases of outright hijacking of party nominations are fairly rare, political parties don't always get the nominees their leaders want, and party leaders cannot force candidates out of a race. In the 2016 election cycle, for example, many Republican Party leaders believed that Donald Trump was not the party's strongest nominee. Trump gained the nomination over their objections by winning the party's caucus and primary contests.

Let the people decide.

One argument in favor of giving the nomination power to the people is that party leaders have not always shown good judgment in picking either electable or qualified candidates. Many of the same Republican leaders who opposed Trump had supported party nominees John McCain in 2008 and Mitt Romney in 2012, both of whom went on to lose in the general-election contest. This track record suggests that party leaders are far from infallible.

The second argument for letting the people decide hinges on a judgment about whose wishes should prevail in nomination contests: the people who make up the party in the electorate or the people in the party organization. What right does the party organization have to select nominees, given that support from the party in the electorate (their contributions and votes in elections) is essential for electoral success? Moreover, shouldn't voters have a say in determining what their electoral choices look like? If party leaders choose, voters may not like any of the options put before them.

Why, then, do voters in America get to pick party nominees in primaries? Direct primaries were introduced in American politics during the late 1800s and early 1900s.[b] The goal was explicit: reform-minded party activists wanted to take the choice of nominees out of the hands of party leaders and give it to the electorate, with the assumption that voters should be able to influence the choice of candidates for the general election. Moreover, reformers believed that this goal outweighed the expertise held by party leaders.

Here is the trade-off: If party leaders select nominees, they would likely choose electable candidates who share the policy goals held by party leaders. If voters choose nominees, they can pick whomever they want, using whatever criteria they like—but there is no guarantee that these candidates will be skilled general-election campaigners or effective in office.

In the end, some groups must be given control over the selection of a party's nominees. Should this power be given to party leaders or to the people? Take a stand.

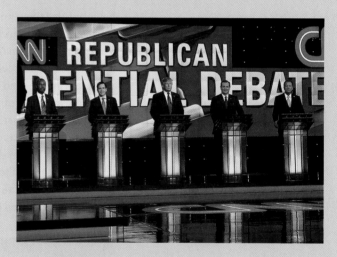

Both political parties organize a series of candidate debates during their presidential nomination contests, giving candidates a chance to present themselves before a national audience.

take a stand

1. One reform proposal would increase the importance of the parties as sources of campaign funds. Would this change have made much of a difference in the 2016 Republican presidential contest?

2. What kind of nomination procedure would be favored by insurgent groups such as the various Tea Party organizations?

Types of Primaries and Caucuses

Primary Election	An election in which voters choose the major-party nominees for political office, who subsequently compete in a general election.
Closed primary	A primary election system in which only registered party members can vote in their party's primary.
Nonpartisan primary	A primary election system in which candidates from both parties are listed on the same primary ballot. Following a nonpartisan primary, the two candidates who receive the most votes in the primary compete in the general election, even if they are from the same party.
Open primary	A primary election system in which any registered voter can participate in either party's primary, regardless of the voter's party affiliation.
Semi-closed primary	A primary election system where voters registered as party members must vote in their party's primary, but registered Independents can vote in either party's primary.
Caucus Election	A series of local meetings at which registered voters select a particular candidate's supporters as delegates who will vote for the candidate in a later, state-level convention. (In national elections, the state-convention delegates select delegates to the national convention.) Caucuses are used in some states to select delegates to the major parties' presidential nominating conventions. Some states' caucuses are open to members of any party, while others are closed.

beginning in January of a presidential election year. The type of election (primary or caucus; about two-thirds of states use primaries) and its date are determined by state legislatures, although national party committees can limit the allowable dates, using their control over seating delegates at the party conventions to motivate compliance. Voters in these primaries and caucuses don't directly select the parties' nominees. Instead, citizens' votes are used to determine how many of each candidate's supporters become delegates to the party's national **nominating convention**, where delegates vote to choose the party's presidential and vice-presidential nominees. The national party organizations determine how many delegates each state sends to the convention based on factors such as state population, the number of votes the party's candidate received in each state in the last presidential election, and the number of House members and senators from the party that each state elected (see How It Works: Nominating Presidential Candidates).

nominating convention
A meeting held by each party every four years at which states' delegates select the party's presidential and vice-presidential nominees and approve the party platform.

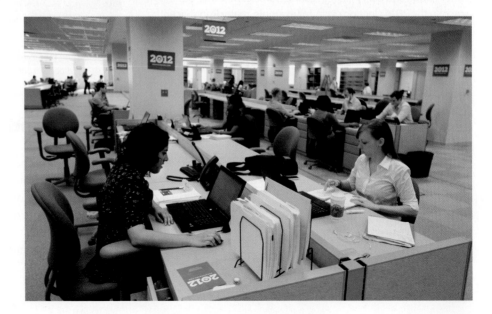

One of the most important ways parties help candidates is by raising money to fund campaigns. In 2012, the DNC raised nearly a billion dollars to help reelect President Obama and to support other Democratic candidates. The RNC raised a similar amount. #DNC #RNC

Campaign Assistance One of the most visible ways that the political parties support candidates is by contributing to and spending money on campaign activities. By and large, federal law mandates that these funds be spent by the organization that raised them; the national party, for example, is limited in the amount of money it can contribute to congressional and presidential candidates or to state party organizations. As we discuss in Chapter 8, however, party organizations that raise campaign funds can use them to help candidates get elected through independent expenditures—by running their own ads in a candidate's district or state.

Figure 7.6 shows the amount of money raised by the top groups within the Republican and Democratic parties for the 2016 election (through November 4). The final figures show that the parties and their various committees raised over a billion dollars. The DNC and RNC raised the most money, but the congressional campaign committees also raised significant sums. Congressional Democratic committees outraised their Republican counterparts. And congressional leaders raised almost $50 million for the campaigns of their colleagues.[24]

Along with supplying campaign funds, party organizations give candidates other assistance, ranging from offering campaign advice (including which issues to emphasize, how to deal with the press, and the like) to conducting polls. Party organizations at all levels also undertake get-out-the-vote activities, encouraging supporters to get to the polls.

Party Platforms The **party platform** is a set of promises about what candidates from the party will do if they are elected. The most visible party platform is the one approved at each party's presidential nominating convention, but the party organizations in the House and Senate also release platforms, as do other groups in the major parties. Party platforms generally reflect the brand name differences between the parties discussed earlier. For example, in the case of abortion rights, the 2016 Republican presidential platform favored a total ban on abortions, while the Democratic presidential platform

party platform
A set of objectives outlining the party's issue positions and priorities. Candidates are not required to support their party's platform.

FIGURE 7.6

Democratic and Republican Fund-Raising in the 2015–2016 Election Cycle

In the 2015–2016 election cycle, party and leadership committees raised more than $1 billion in campaign funds. Although most of this money was raised by the national committees, the state, local, and candidate committees also raised significant sums. To what extent might these funds allow the national committees to force candidates to run on the party platform?

Source: Calculated by the authors from data at www.fec.gov and www.opensecrets.org (accessed 11/6/16).

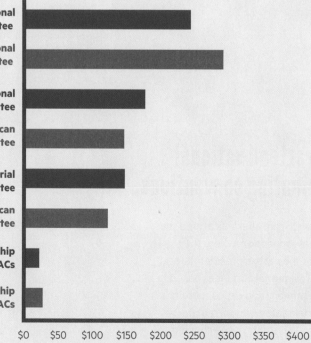

Nominating Presidential Candidates

Primaries and caucuses...

Closed Primaries
Only voters registered with party vote

Open Primaries
Open to voters from any political party and Independents

Caucus or Local Convention
Party members meet in groups to select delegates

are used to select delegates...

Republican Party
States can award all delegates to the winning candidate

or award delegates proportionally.

Democratic Party
The state's delegates are divided proportionally.

who attend national nominating conventions.

Delegates from all states attend the national convention, where they vote for the party's presidential and vice-presidential nominees based on the primary and caucus results. Superdelegates—important party leaders—also vote at the convention.

The Nomination of Donald Trump for President, 2016

While Donald Trump was the clear winner in the 2016 Republican presidential nomination contest, his campaign benefitted from the rules used in some of the early contests, particularly the use of primary elections rather than caucuses.

☐ Winner-take-all delegate allocation
☐ Proportional delegate allocation
% Percentage of popular vote won
ǂ Delegates allocated

		Trump	Rubio	Cruz	Kasich	Caucus/ Primary	Winner Take All?
Feb. 1	Iowa	24%	23%	28%	2%	Caucus	NO
Feb. 9	New Hampshire	35%	12%	11%	16%	Primary	NO
Feb. 20	South Carolina	33%	23%	23%	8%	Primary	YES
Feb. 23	Nevada	46%	24%	21%	4%	Caucus	NO
Mar. 1	Alabama	43%	19%	21%	4%	Primary	NO
	Alaska	34%	15%	36%	4%	Caucus	NO
	Arkansas	33%	25%	31%	4%	Primary	NO
	Georgia	39%	24%	24%	6%	Primary	NO
	Massachusetts	49%	18%	10%	18%	Primary	NO
	Minnesota	21%	37%	29%	6%	Caucus	NO
	Oklahoma	28%	26%	34%	4%	Primary	NO
	Tennessee	39%	21%	24%	5%	Primary	NO
	Texas	27%	19%	44%	4%	Primary	NO
	Vermont	33%	19%	10%	30%	Primary	NO
	Virginia	35%	32%	17%	9%	Primary	NO
Total delegates		**340**	**116**	**230**	**27**		

Note: Colorado has been omitted because its caucus did not allocate delegates.
Source: Data compiled by the authors.

Critical Thinking

1. **Which states used winner-take-all rules in 2016?** How much did Trump benefit from this rule in terms of delegate counts? Would his delegate count have improved if more states used winner-take-all?

2. **One argument about caucuses is that they allow** lesser-known candidates (such as John Kasich) to build support. Did this rule hold for Kasich in 2016?

expressed support for a woman's right to choose, meaning that abortion would be legal under a wider range of conditions.

In theory, party platforms describe differences between the major parties, capture each party's diagnosis of the problems facing the country, and present the party's plan for solving those problems. In this way, party platforms give citizens an easy way to evaluate candidates. However, candidates are not obligated to support their party's platform and many take divergent stances on some issues. For example, notwithstanding the consistently strong pro-choice position on abortion in the Democratic Party's presidential platforms over the last generation, some Democratic members of Congress, such as Illinois representative Dan Lipinski, have promised to vote to restrict abortions if elected—a position closer to the Republican platform.[25] For some of these candidates, this position has reflected personal or religious beliefs; for others, it has been driven by the desire to reflect the opinion of voters in their district or state.

Parties don't exert total control over their members. Republican Party leaders could not stop then–freshman senator Ted Cruz (R-TX) from filibustering for 23 hours in an attempt to stop a budget compromise. @TedCruz

Cooperation in government

Parties also play an important role in enabling like-minded politicians to cooperate on policy plans and strategies for enacting their proposals. Parties in government develop agendas, coordinate the actions of members across branches of government, and provide accountability to voters.

Agenda-Setting Throughout the year, the parties in government meet to devise strategies for legislative action—that is, to set agendas. What proposals should they offer and in what order should these proposals be considered? Should the parties try to make a deal with the president or with legislators from the other party?

However, the party in government can act collectively this way only when its members can agree on what they want. Such agreement is not always possible or may require extensive negotiation and compromise. Even with unified Republican control of Congress and the presidency after the 2016 election, disagreements within the party on issues such as trade, immigration reform, and infrastructure spending may delay or deter legislative action.

Coordination Political parties play an important role in coordinating the actions taken in different branches of government. Such coordination is extremely important for enacting new laws, because unless supporters in Congress can amass a two-thirds majority to override a veto they need the president's support. Similarly, the president needs congressional support to enact the proposals he or she favors. To these ends, the president routinely meets with congressional leaders from his or her party and occasionally meets with the entire caucus or conference. Various members of the president's staff also meet with House and Senate members to present the president's proposals and hear what members of Congress from both parties want to enact.

During 2009, President Obama held many meetings with Democratic members of Congress to lobby them to support his proposals for health care reform. Although many congressional Democrats supported Obama's proposals, enactment was nearly derailed by several Democratic representatives and senators who demanded amendments to restrict government payment for abortions. Obama opposed these efforts but was powerless to stop them. In fact, getting the last few votes needed for enactment required Obama to promise to issue an executive order that had essentially the same effect as the proposed amendments.

Coordination can also occur between caucuses or conferences in the House and Senate. At the same time that President Obama and Democrats in Congress were negotiating over health care reform, congressional Republicans were devising strategies for delaying and defeating these proposals. Although their efforts did not prevent the enactment of reform legislation, their strong opposition required the president and congressional leaders to accept many changes favored by moderate and conservative Democrats in order to enact the legislation without Republican support. Such coordination efforts require real work and compromise, as party leaders in the House and the Senate do not have authority over each other or over the elected members of their party. Nor can the president order a House member or senator to do anything, even if the legislator is from the president's own party.

Accountability One of the most important functions political parties play in a democracy is to give citizens identifiable groups to reward or punish for government action or inaction. Using the ballot box, voters will reward and punish elected officials, often based on their party affiliation and on the behavior of that party's members in office. In this way, the electorate uses the party system to hold officials accountable for outcomes such as the state of the economy or America's relations with other nations.

During periods of **unified government**, when one party holds majorities in both the House and the Senate *and* controls the presidency, that party is the party in power. It has enough votes to enact policies in Congress and a good chance of having them signed into law by the president. During times of **divided government**, when one party controls Congress but not the presidency or when different parties control the House and Senate, the president's party is considered the party in power. Focusing on parties makes it easy for a citizen to issue rewards and punishments. Is the economy doing well? Then that citizen is likely to vote for the candidates from the party in power. But if the economy is doing poorly or if the citizen feels that government is wasting tax money or enacting bad policies, she or he can vote for candidates from the party that is currently out of power. When citizens behave this way, they strengthen the incentive for elected officials from the party in power to work together to develop policies that address voters' concerns—on the premise that if they do, voters will reward them with another term in office.

Consider the 2010 midterm election, when many Americans voted against Democratic candidates because of poor economic conditions. While Democrats lost seats in both the House and the Senate, most Democratic incumbents were returned to office. Why? Some were elected from states or districts dominated by Democratic identifiers. But many others were reelected because they campaigned on a platform of changing policy or because of their efforts to help local businesses, saying in effect, "Instead of punishing me for my party affiliation, reward me for working on your behalf." In sum, while parties in government can do all of these things, there is no guarantee that

unified government
A situation in which one party holds a majority of seats in the House and Senate and the president is a member of that same party.

divided government
A situation in which the House, Senate, and presidency are not controlled by the same party—for example, when Democrats hold the majority of House and Senate seats and the president is a Republican.

In 2016, Representative Stephanie Murphy (D-FL) defeated 12-term Republican incumbent John Mica on the strength of a campaign that emphasized Mica's support for Donald Trump's views on women's health and gun policy.

Minor-party presidential candidates, such as Ralph Nader in 2000, sometimes attract considerable press attention because of their distinctive, often-extreme policy preferences—but they rarely affect election outcomes. Nader ran again, as an Independent, in 2004 and 2008.

individuals elected under a party's banner will agree to do so. For example, candidates may refuse to endorse their party's platform because it conflicts with their own policy goals or because it would be unpopular with their constituents. Accordingly, one of the biggest problems for party leaders is to forge compromise among their candidates and elected members—to ensure that the party can act as a unified, disciplined organization.

Minor parties

So far, this chapter has focused on the major American political parties—the Republicans and the Democrats—and paid less attention to other party organizations. The reason is that minor political parties in America are *so* minor that they are generally not significant players on the political stage. Many such parties exist, but few run candidates in more than a handful of races and very few minor-party candidates win political office. Few Americans identify with minor parties, and most exist for only a relatively short period.

Effects on Election Outcomes Even so, you may think we are giving minor parties too little attention. Consider Ralph Nader, who ran as the Green Party nominee for president in 2000, winning almost 5 percent of the vote. In some states, the number of votes Nader received exceeded the margin separating Democrat Al Gore from Republican George Bush. In particular, in Florida, where Bush won by only a few hundred votes after a disputed recount, Nader received almost 100,000 votes. These votes would have been enough to swing the state, and the election, to Gore.

However, the outcome of Nader's 2000 presidential campaign doesn't so much highlight the importance of minor parties as it illustrates the closeness of the 2000 presidential election. If Nader had not run, Gore might have received enough additional support to win. But given that Bush's margin of victory in Florida was so small, any number of seemingly minor events (a polling station closing early or rain in some areas and sunshine in others) could have changed the outcome.

Minor parties did not play a decisive role in the 2016 presidential election, but in several swing states (for example, Florida, Pennsylvania, Wisconsin, and Michigan) they received more votes than the margin of difference between Donald Trump and Hillary Clinton. The most successful were the Green Party (1.4 million votes) and the Libertarian Party (over 4 million votes). In all, minor parties won about 6.5 million votes in the 2016 presidential race, about 4.5 percent of the total.

Even in terms of lower offices, minor-party candidates typically attract only meager support. While the Libertarian Party claims to have over a dozen officeholders, many of these officials held unelected positions such as seats on county planning boards or ran unopposed for relatively minor offices such as justice of the peace.[26]

Looking back in history, we see that some minor-party candidates for president have attracted a substantial percentage of citizens' votes. George Wallace (governor of Alabama at the time) ran as the candidate of the American Independent Party in 1968, receiving about 13 percent of the popular vote nationwide. Texas millionaire Ross Perot, the Reform Party candidate for president in 1996, won 8.4 percent of the popular vote. Perot also ran as an Independent in 1992, winning 18.2 percent of the popular vote.

Structural and Issue Differences The differences between major and minor political parties in contemporary American politics grow even more substantial when considered in terms other than election outcomes. For most minor parties, the party in government does not exist, as few of their candidates win office. Many minor parties have virtually no organization beyond a small party headquarters and a website. Some minor parties, such as the Green Party, the Libertarian Party, and the Reform Party, have local chapters that meet on a regular basis. But these modest efforts pale in comparison with the nationwide network of offices, thousands of workers, and hundreds of millions of dollars deployed by Republican and Democratic party organizations. Nonetheless, research shows that some people vote for minor-party candidates in order to show their support of these candidates' positions and to express their belief that neither major party can govern effectively.[27]

The issues and issue positions taken by minor parties and their candidates are almost always very different from those espoused by the major parties. The Constitution Party, for example, advocates an end to government civil service regulations; a ban on compulsory school attendance laws; withdrawal of the United States from the UN and all international trade agreements; abolishing foreign aid, the income tax, the Internal Revenue Service (IRS), and all federal welfare programs; and repealing all campaign finance legislation, the Endangered Species Act, and federal firearms regulations.[28] These positions are extreme, not in the sense of being silly or dangerous but in the sense that relatively few Americans feel the same way.

"Why Should I Care?"

You may dislike political parties or party leaders in Congress, but the fact is, the parties are key players in congressional policy making and in negotiations between Congress and the president. If you are trying to decide whether a new program (or nominee) has a chance of being approved, one of the first things you need to consider is whether the party caucuses in the House and Senate (particularly the majority-party caucuses) are in favor or opposed.

Conclusion

American political parties help organize elections, unify disparate social groups, simplify the choices facing voters, and build compromises around party members' shared concerns—all with the goals of winning elections and setting government policy. However, recent events demonstrate that the success of political parties depends on whether individual party members—candidates, citizens, and party leaders—are willing to take the actions necessary to achieve electoral and policy goals. In recent years, congressional Republicans have campaigned on a platform of making substantial changes in the size and scope of the federal government. However, their apparent consensus disappeared once in office, as legislators disagreed on which programs should be cut, constituents demanded that their favorite programs be saved, and party leaders worried that taking a hard line would lead to electoral defeat. Ultimately, the party's budget-cutting goals were not achieved. Similarly, Trump's victory masks deep disagreements within the current Republican party in government.

Of course, these difficulties do not reflect a problem with the Republican Party per se. The Democrats' success at enacting Obamacare and other significant proposals in Obama's first term masked significant differences of opinion among the party's elected officials, activists, and citizen supporters. And Hillary Clinton's loss in the 2016 election will no doubt push Democrats to examine weaknesses in their party's message. They will have to decide how much to compromise with—or block—President Trump as he tries to enact his policy agenda. As we have seen, parties try to find a way to bridge such differences in order for members to act together to accomplish common goals. However, the parties' ability to bring people together is not absolute. Individual party members respond to constituents, party leaders, and public opinion in many ways, sometimes taking actions in line with party goals and other times acting in ways that help themselves and that defy the party.

STUDY GUIDE

What are political parties and where did today's parties come from?

Define *political parties* and show how American political parties and party systems have evolved over time. (Pages 192–195)

Summary

Political parties are a central feature of American politics, although they look and act very differently today than they have in the past. Political scientists use the term "party system" to refer to a period of party stability; in all, there have been six different party systems in the country's history. Party systems have been separated by realignments, which occur when some of the defining factors of the party system are changed or specified and when rifts in the group develop because of these changes.

Key terms

party organization (p. 192) party principle (p. 193)
party in government (p. 192) spoils system (p. 193)
party in the electorate (p. 192) realignment (p. 195)
party system (p. 193)

Practice Quiz Questions

1. Which were the first well-known parties in the United States?

a. Federalists and Democratic-Republicans
b. Democrats and Republicans
c. Whigs and Federalists
d. Democrats and Whigs
e. Whigs and Republicans

2. The idea that a party is not just a group but an organization that exists apart from its candidate is called the _____.

a. party system
b. spoils system
c. conditional party government

d. party ID
e. party principle

American political parties today

Describe the main characteristics of American parties as organizations, in the government, and in the electorate. (Pages 195–203)

Summary

The modern party is composed of three parts. The party organization is a loosely defined group of individuals and organizations that are focused on supporting political candidates when they share the same policy goals. The party in the government consists of elected officials who are the members of a particular party. The party in the electorate consists of citizens who identify with a particular political party.

Key terms

national committee (p. 195) conference (p. 197)
political action committee party identification (party
(PAC) (p. 196) ID) (p. 198)
527 organization (p. 196) party coalitions (p. 201)
caucus (congressional) (p. 197) issue ownership (p. 201)

Practice Quiz Questions

3. The Democratic and Republican party organizations _____ hierarchical; they are _____ to force state and local parties to share their positions on issues.

a. are not; able
b. are not; unable
c. are; able
d. are; unable
e. are; sometimes able

4. A group of elected officials of the same party who come together to organize and strategize is called a _____.

a. cabal
b. conditional party government
c. primary
d. PAC
e. caucus

5. The modern Congress is _____; the distance between the parties has _____ over the past 60 years.

a. polarized; increased
b. polarized; stayed the same
c. not polarized; decreased
d. not polarized; stayed the same
e. not polarized; increased

The role of political parties in American politics

Explain the important functions that parties perform in the political system. (Pages 204–213)

Summary

Political parties serve two major roles in the political system. First, they contest elections by recruiting and nominating candidates and supporting candidate campaigns. Second, they facilitate cooperation in government by providing a framework for agenda-setting, coordination, and accountability among members of the same party. There are many different minor political parties, and while they rarely make a significant impact on the political stage, they do occasionally influence election outcomes. The two big issues facing minor parties are that their platforms do not appeal to a large portion of Americans and that the electoral system makes it hard for minor parties to win elections.

Key terms

primary election (p. 204)   **party platform** (p. 207)
caucus (electoral) (p. 204)   **unified government** (p. 211)
nominating convention (p. 206)   **divided government** (p. 211)

Practice Quiz Questions

6. **Which is *not* one of the ways political party organizations support candidates?**
   a. by controlling who runs in House and Senate races
   b. by contributing money to campaign activities
   c. by offering advice on how to deal with the press
   d. by organizing get-out-the-vote activities
   e. by offering advice on which issues to emphasize

7. **Why do most candidates support their party platforms?**
   a. because candidates are required to support the platforms
   b. because all candidates vote on the platforms that are written
   c. because candidates get kicked out of the party for not doing so
   d. because both major parties' platforms are essentially the same
   e. because most candidates and their constituents generally agree with the platform

8. **When the president, House, and Senate are controlled by the same party, this is called:**
   a. party in government
   b. responsible party government
   c. unified government
   d. divided government
   e. conditional party government

9. **In American politics, minor parties _____.**
   a. are very prominent at the state and local levels
   b. are prominent only in congressional elections
   c. win few offices at any level of government
   d. win a significant number of offices at all levels
   e. are more influential today than in the past

10. **The issue positions of minor parties are usually _____.**
   a. very different from those of the major parties and most Americans
   b. very similar to those of the major parties and most Americans
   c. developed with input from a national network
   d. based on the preferences of the party's members in government
   e. not the reason people vote for minor-party candidates

Suggested Reading

Aldrich, John. *Why Parties?*, 2nd ed. Chicago: University of Chicago Press, 2014.

Bartels, Larry M. *Unequal Democracy: The Political Economy of the New Gilded Age*. New York: Russell Sage Foundation, 2008.

Carmines, Edward G., and James A. Stimson. *Issue Evolution: Race and the Transformation of American Politics*. Princeton, NJ: Princeton University Press, 1989.

Cohen, Marty, David Karol, Hans Noel, and John Zaller. *The Party Decides: Presidential Nominations before and after Reform*. Chicago: University of Chicago Press, 2008.

Cox, Gary, and Mathew McCubbins. *Setting the Agenda: Party Government in the U.S. House of Representatives*. New York: Cambridge University Press, 2005.

Fiorina, Morris. *Retrospective Voting in American National Elections*. New Haven, CT: Yale University Press, 1981.

Green, Donald, Bradley Palmquist, and Eric Schickler. *Partisan Hearts and Minds*. New Haven, CT: Yale University Press, 2004.

Noel, Hans. *Political Ideologies and Political Parties in America*. New York: Cambridge University Press, 2014.

Polsby, Nelson. *Consequences of Party Reform*. New York: Oxford University Press, 1983.

Rohde, David. *Parties and Leaders in the Post-reform House*. Chicago: University of Chicago Press, 1991.

Schattschneider, E. E. *Party Government*. New York: McGraw-Hill, 1942.

8

Elections

Who wins? Who loses? And why?

Every two years, Americans elect 435 House members and 33 or so senators; every four years, we elect a president. Out of these many separate contests, a few races attract disproportionate interest because they provide insights into what voters are thinking, because they reveal the usefulness of different campaign strategies, or simply because of what's at stake. In 2016, the election to watch was the battle for the presidency, Republican Donald Trump versus Democrat Hillary Clinton. It is hard to imagine a starker choice: Trump, the political newcomer who had never held elected office or served in government, against Clinton, the Washington insider and the first female general-election presidential candidate; Trump's promise to "make America great again" with a combination of tax cuts, renegotiating trade deals, more military spending, and threats of mass deportations against Clinton's platform of increasing funding for a wide range of initiatives, from curing Alzheimer's to helping displaced workers, and putting government squarely on the side of LGBTQ equality, disability rights, racial justice, and preventing gun violence. Regardless of what you think of these candidates and their promises, it is clear that this election mattered. Over the next four years (and beyond), America will be a different place with Donald Trump in the White House than if Hillary Clinton had won.

The 2016 presidential elections are also a good example of the central themes of this text. Candidates compete for political office, offering the people distinct, competing visions of what the federal government should do, from what the tax code should look like, to how government should spend the tax money it collects, to what regulations the government should impose on individuals and corporations. These considerations mattered even in 2016, when Donald Trump's qualifications, temperament, and behavior toward women became central issues in the campaign.

American elections are also about rules. The fact that Donald Trump won the Republican nomination reflects his popularity with Republican primary voters but also the way the party chooses its candidate. Moreover, Trump won

**Present the major rules and
procedures of American
elections.**
pages 218–227

**Describe the features,
strategies, and funding of
campaigns for federal office.**
pages 227–237

**Explain the key factors that
influence voters' choices.**
pages 237–240

**Analyze the issues and outcomes
in the 2016 election.**
pages 241–246

STRONGER
TOGETHER

The 2016 presidential election between
Secretary of State Hillary Clinton and
billionaire businessman Donald Trump
reflected the country's deep divisions
over policy, race, gender, class, and even
geography. And this election showed how
electoral rules and processes—even when
things seem unique and unpredictable—
can greatly affect the outcome.

the general election by winning a majority of votes in the electoral college (awarded by winning the most votes in different states), despite losing the popular vote to Clinton. More generally, candidates in American elections are elected for different periods of time to represent districts, states, or the entire nation—places that vary tremendously in terms of what constituents want from government. A variety of rules determine who runs, who votes, and how candidates campaign. Even ballot layouts and how votes are cast and counted vary across states. Elections also differ in the amount of media coverage they receive, the level of involvement of political parties and other organizations, and how much attention citizens pay to the contests. All these aspects of the election process—who runs, how candidates campaign, and how voters respond—shape who wins and who loses, what happens in Washington, and ultimately the policies that affect people's everyday lives. Why do some candidates win and others lose—and why do these outcomes matter in American politics?

★

PRESENT THE MAJOR RULES AND PROCEDURES OF AMERICAN ELECTIONS

incumbent
A politician running for reelection to the office he or she currently holds.

Though incumbents fared very well in 2016's congressional elections, some still lost, like Nevada Republican Crescent Hardy.

How do American elections work?

The American political system is a representative democracy: Americans do not make policy choices themselves, but they vote for individuals who make these choices on their behalf. Thus, we begin by describing the rules and procedures that define American national elections. Our working assumption for explaining the rules and processes of elections as well as the behavior of candidates and voters is that they are tied directly to what elections do: selecting representatives, giving citizens the ability to influence the direction of government policy, and providing citizens with the opportunity to reward and punish officeholders seeking reelection.

The most visible function of American national elections is the selection of officeholders: members of the House and Senate and the president and vice president. Candidates can be **incumbents** or challengers. America has a representative democracy, which means that by voting in elections Americans have an indirect effect on government policy. Although citizens do not make policy choices themselves, they determine which individuals get to make these choices. In this way, elections connect citizen preferences and government actions.

The fundamental choice in an election is between two or more candidates running for some political office—in national elections this means a seat in the House or the Senate or the presidency. But elections also involve a choice between candidates' policy platforms, the set of policies and programs they promise to carry out if elected. By investigating candidates' platforms, citizens learn about the range of options for government policy. Moreover, their voting decisions determine who gets to make choices about future government policy and thereby shape policy itself. This description is particularly true for the 2016 Senate elections, where Trump's victory and Republican victories in House and Senate elections gave Republicans unified control of the federal government.

The election process also creates a way to hold incumbents accountable. When citizens choose between voting for an incumbent or a challenger, they can consider the incumbent's performance, asking, "Has he [or she] done a good job on the issues I care about?"[1] Citizens who answer yes typically vote for the incumbent, and those who say no typically vote for the challenger. These evaluations are significant because they make incumbents responsive to their constituents' demands.[2] If an elected official anticipates that some constituents will consider his or her performance when making their decision, the official will try to take actions that these constituents will like. Otherwise, voters can opt to remove the official from office because they disapprove of his or her performance and believe the country will fare better if a different candidate wins.

Two stages of elections

House and Senate candidates face a two-step procedure. First, if prospective candidates want to run on behalf of a political party, they must win the party's nomination in a primary election. If the would-be candidates want to run as Independents, they need to gather signatures on a petition to secure a spot on the ballot. Different states hold either **open primaries**, **semi-closed primaries**, or **closed primaries**, and state law sets the timing of these elections. A few states hold single primaries, in which there is one election involving candidates from both parties, with the top two finalists (regardless of party) receiving nominations to the general election.

The second step in the election process, the **general election**, is held throughout the nation on the first Tuesday after the first Monday in November. Federal law designates this day as Election Day. General elections determine who wins elected positions in government. The offices at stake vary depending on the year. Presidential elections occur every four years (2008, 2012, 2016, ...). In a presidential election year, Americans elect the entire House of Representatives, one-third of the Senate, and a president and vice president. During midterm elections (2006, 2010, 2014, ...), there is no presidential contest, but the entire House and another one-third of the Senate are up for election.

The Constitution limits voting rights to American citizens who are at least 18 years old. There are also restrictions on voter eligibility; these vary across states, including residency requirements (usually 30 days) and whether people convicted of a major crime can vote. A recent development in American elections is an increase in the practice of no-excuse absentee voting as well as early voting, or casting a general-election vote prior to Election Day.[3]

Constituencies: who chooses representatives?

In American elections, officeholders are elected in single-member districts in which only the winner of the most votes takes office. (Although each state's senators both represent the whole state, they are elected separately, usually in different years.) Senate candidates compete throughout the state; House candidates compete in congressional districts. In most states, the congressional district lines are drawn by state legislatures. In a few states, nonpartisan commissions or committees of judges perform this function. (For details on redistricting, see Chapter 10.)

Because members of the House and Senate are elected from specific geographic areas, they often represent very different kinds of people. Their constituents differ in terms of age, race, income level, occupation, and political leaning, including party affiliation and ideology. Therefore, legislators from different areas of the country face highly diverse demands from their constituents—leading them to pursue very dissimilar kinds of policies. For example, Democratic senator Charles Schumer, one of the senators from New York, represents a fairly liberal state where most people take some sort of pro-choice position on abortion rights, while Republican senator Richard Shelby

DID YOU KNOW?

510,000

The total number of federal, state, and local elected offices in the United States.
Source: Jennifer Lawless, *Becoming a Candidate*

open primary
A primary election in which any registered voter can participate in the contest, regardless of party affiliation.

semi-closed primary
A primary where anyone who is a registered member of the party or registered as an Independent can vote.

closed primary
A primary election in which only registered members of a particular political party can vote.

general election
The election in which voters cast ballots for House members, senators, and (every four years) a president and vice president.

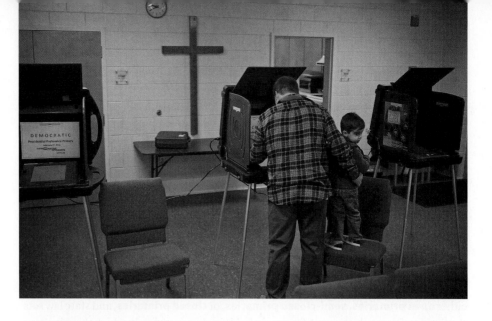

Americans vote in all sorts of places, including libraries, fire stations, schools, private homes, and sometimes churches, as shown in this photo of a polling station in the 2016 South Carolina primary.

is one of the senators from the conservative state of Alabama, where most voters have long been opposed to abortions. Suppose the Senate votes on a proposal to ban all abortions after the twelfth week of pregnancy. Shelby knows that most of his constituents would probably want him to vote for the proposal, and Schumer knows that most of his constituents would probably want him to vote against it. This example illustrates that congressional conflicts over policy often reflect differences in constituents' demands. Schumer and Shelby themselves may hold different views on abortion rights, but even if they agreed, their constituents' distinct demands would make it likely that as legislators they would vote differently.

Determining who wins

Most House and Senate contests involve **plurality voting**: the candidate who gets the most votes wins. However, some states use **majority voting**, meaning that a candidate needs more than 50 percent of the vote to win. In these states, if no candidate has a majority a **runoff election** takes place between the top two finishers.

The two-step process of primary and general elections can have a similar effect on the election's outcome. Sometimes the winner of a primary is not a party's best candidate for the general election. For example, in the 2016 presidential race, one of the principal arguments for choosing someone other than Hillary Clinton as the Democratic nominee (such as Senator Bernie Sanders, Vice President Joe Biden, or some other Democratic senator or governor) was that these candidates would have a better chance of winning the general election. While Clinton had many enthusiastic volunteers, a first-rate campaign organization, and considerable Washington experience as First Lady, senator, and secretary of state, she was also strongly disliked by a sizable fraction of the American electorate—partly because of her status as a Washington insider, and partly because of issues such as her use of a private e-mail server while secretary of state. In the end, despite beating Sanders in the primaries and discouraging other Democrats from entering the nomination contest, Clinton lost the general election to Donald Trump. Given the closeness of the 2016 election, another Democrat, someone who did not have Clinton's disadvantages, might well have gone on to defeat Trump.

The Ballot Americans vote by using a variety of machines and ballot structures based on where they live. Over the last decade, electronic touch screen voting machines have replaced paper ballots and mechanical voting machines, usually with some sort of paper receipt to allow manual recounts. The Help America Vote Act of 2002 provided

plurality voting
A voting system in which the candidate who receives the most votes within a geographic area wins the election, regardless of whether that candidate wins a majority (more than half) of the votes.

majority voting
A voting system in which a candidate must win more than 50 percent of votes to win the election. If no candidate wins enough votes to take office, a runoff election is held between the top two vote-getters.

runoff election
Under a majority voting system, a second election held only if no candidate wins a majority of the votes in the first general election. Only the top two vote-getters in the first election compete in the runoff.

funds to local communities to purchase new electronic voting machines. At the same time, political scientists have researched which ballot structures minimize the chances that individuals will vote for the wrong candidate, as well as how to ensure that electronic voting is free of fraud and mistakes.[4]

Ballot counting itself adds more complexities. Most states have laws that allow vote recounts if a race is sufficiently close (typically within 1 percent or less). Even when a recount occurs, it may be impossible to definitively determine who won a particular election, as the statutes that determine which ballots are valid are often open to interpretation.

What *is* clear is that election rules can affect results. Particularly in close races, small changes in the rules governing elections can easily change outcomes.

Presidential elections

Many of the rules governing elections, such as who is eligible to vote, are the same for both presidential and congressional elections. However, presidential contests have several unique rules regarding how nominees are determined and how votes are counted. Moreover, the constitutional requirements for presidential candidates are also somewhat stricter than those for congressional candidates (see Nuts & Bolts 8.1).

The Nomination: Primaries and Caucuses Presidential nominees from the Democratic and Republican parties are determined by state-level **primaries** and **caucuses** over a five-month period beginning in January of an election year.[5] Voters in these elections select delegates to attend the nominating conventions that take place during the summer. There the delegates cast the votes that determine their party's presidential and vice-presidential nominees. The format of these elections, including their timing and the number of delegates selected per state, is determined on a state-by-state basis by the state and national party organizations.[6] A candidate's principal goal is to win as many delegates as possible.

The details of translating primary and caucus votes into convention delegates vary from state to state, but some general rules apply. All Democratic primaries and caucuses use **proportional allocation** to divide each state's delegate seats between the candidates; thus, if a candidate receives 40 percent of the votes in a state's primary the candidate gets roughly 40 percent of the convention delegates from that state. Some Republican contests use proportional allocation, but others are **winner-take-all**. In these, the candidate who receives the most votes gets all of the state's convention delegates. These rules can have a significant effect on candidates' campaign strategies and the outcome of the nomination process. (See How It Works: Nominating Presidential Candidates in Chapter 7.)

primary
A ballot vote in which citizens select a party's nominee for the general election.

caucus
A local meeting in which party members select a party's nominee for the general election.

proportional allocation
During the presidential primaries, the practice of determining the number of convention delegates allotted to each candidate based on the percentage of the popular vote cast for each candidate. All Democratic primaries and caucuses use this system, as do some states' Republican primaries and caucuses.

winner-take-all
During the presidential primaries, the practice of assigning all of a given state's delegates to the candidate who receives the most popular votes. Some states' Republican primaries and caucuses use this system.

Office	Minimum Age	Residency Requirement
President	35	Natural-born citizen (born in the United States or on U.S. territory, or child of citizen parent)
Senator	30	Resident of state; U.S. citizen for at least nine years
Representative	25	Resident of state; U.S. citizen for at least seven years

NUTS & BOLTS 8.1

Constitutional Requirements for Candidates

> Campaigns don't end—they run out of money.
>
> —**Richard Gephardt,** former Speaker of the House and presidential candidate

The order in which the primaries and caucuses in different states take place is another important factor, because many candidacies do not survive beyond the early contests.[7] Most presidential candidates pour everything they have into the first few contests. Candidates who do well early on attract financial contributions, campaign workers, endorsements, and additional media coverage, all of which enables them to move on to subsequent primaries or caucuses. But for candidates who do poorly in the first contests, contributions and coverage dry up, leaving these candidates with no alternative but to drop out of the race. For example, a total of 17 candidates entered the race for the 2016 Republican presidential nomination. Five withdrew before any convention delegates were selected. By mid-March, two months into the process and six months before the convention where the nominee was actually selected, the race was down to only three candidates.

For many years, Iowa and New Hampshire have held the first presidential nomination contests, with the Iowa caucus taking place a week before the New Hampshire primary. These states' position at the beginning of the process is largely a historical accident, but party officials from other states often complain about the disproportionate influence of these states.

The parties' national committees can issue rules and requirements about the timing of state presidential primaries, but state law sets the election dates, meaning that a national committee's directives may not be followed. As a result, the 2016 nomination process was roughly the same as in previous years, with Iowa and New Hampshire holding the initial contests, in early February 2016, followed by a primary in South Carolina and a caucus in Nevada later in the month and the remaining contests beginning in March and continuing to June. One recent trend is regional primaries, where all of the states in a given area (such as southern states) hold their primaries or caucuses on the same date.

The National Convention Presidential nominating conventions happen late in the summer of an election year. Their main task is to select the party's presidential nominee, although usually the vote at the convention is a formality; in most recent contests one candidate has emerged from the nomination process going into the convention with a clear majority of delegates and was able to win the nomination on the first ballot. To get the nomination, a candidate needs the support of a majority of the delegates. If no candidate receives a majority after the first round of voting at the convention, the voting continues until someone does. When a sitting president runs for reelection, as Barack Obama did in 2012, he or she typically faces little opposition for the party's general-election nomination.

After the delegates nominate a presidential candidate, they nominate a vice-presidential candidate. The presidential nominee chooses this running mate (generally before the convention), and the delegates almost always ratify this choice without much debate. Convention delegates also vote on the party platform, which describes what kinds of policies its candidates will supposedly seek to enact if they are elected.

The final purpose of a convention is to attract public attention to the party and its nominees. Public figures give speeches during the evening sessions when all major television networks have live coverage. At some recent conventions, both parties have drawn press attention by recruiting speakers who support their political goals despite being associated with the opposing party.

Once presidential candidates are nominated, the general-election campaign officially begins—although it often unofficially

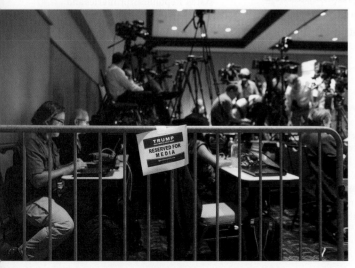

Presidential campaign appearances almost always involve extensive print and electronic media coverage, reporting on virtually everything the candidates say or do.

starts much earlier, as soon as the presumptive nominees are known. We say more about presidential campaigns in a later section.

Counting Presidential Votes Let's assume for a moment that the campaigning is over and that Election Day has arrived. Even though in the voting booth you choose between the candidates by name, you actually don't vote directly for a presidential candidate. Rather, when you select your preferred candidate's name you are choosing that person's slate of pledged supporters from your state to serve as electors, who will then vote to elect the president. The number of electors for each state equals the state's number of House members (which varies by state population) plus the number of senators (two per state). Altogether, the electors chosen by the citizens of each state constitute the **electoral college**, the body that formally selects the president.

In most states, the electoral votes are allocated on a winner-take-all basis: the candidate who receives the most votes from a given state's citizens gets all of that state's electoral votes. But two states, Maine and Nebraska, allocate most of their electoral votes at the congressional district level: in those states, the candidate who wins the most votes in each congressional district wins that district's single electoral vote. Then the remaining two electoral votes go to the candidate who gets the most votes statewide.[8] (See Nuts & Bolts 8.2 for state-by-state electoral vote totals.)

The winner-take-all method of allocating most states' electoral votes makes candidates focus their attention on two kinds of states: high-population states with lots of electoral votes and so-called swing states, where the contest is relatively close. It's better for a candidate to spend a day campaigning in California (55 electoral votes) than in Montana (3 electoral votes). However, if one candidate is sure to win a particular state both candidates will direct their efforts elsewhere. This explains why both campaigns in 2016 spent so much time and campaign funds on states such as Ohio and Florida (swing states with a large number of electoral votes)—and why they largely ignored states such as Delaware (small state, one-party-dominates category). (See How It Works: The Electoral College.)

> You win some, you lose some. And then there's that little-known third category.
>
> —**Al Gore,** who lost the 2000 presidential vote in the electoral college despite winning the most votes on Election Day

electoral college
The body that votes to select America's president and vice president based on the popular vote in each state. Each candidate nominates a slate of electors who are selected to attend the meeting of the college if their candidate wins the most votes in a state or district.

NUTS
& BOLTS
8.2

Electoral Votes and Swing States

Presidential campaigns focus their attention on states with high electoral votes and swing states, those where each candidate has a good chance of winning. In this box, we group states into categories based on their number of electoral votes and on whether one party always won the state in recent presidential elections.

Number of Electoral Votes	One Party Dominates in Recent Elections?	
	Yes (Not a Swing State)	**No** (Swing State)
3–5	D.C., Delaware, Alaska, Montana, North Dakota, South Dakota, Vermont, Wyoming, Hawaii, Maine, Rhode Island, Idaho, Nebraska, West Virginia	New Hampshire, New Mexico
6–10	Arkansas, Kansas, Utah, Connecticut, Oregon, Oklahoma, Kentucky, Louisiana, Alabama, South Carolina, Maryland, Mississippi, Missouri, Minnesota	Iowa, Nevada, Colorado, Wisconsin
More than 10	Massachusetts, Arizona, Tennessee, Washington, New Jersey, Georgia, Illinois, New York, Texas, California	Indiana, Virginia, North Carolina, Ohio, Florida, Michigan, Pennsylvania

The Electoral College

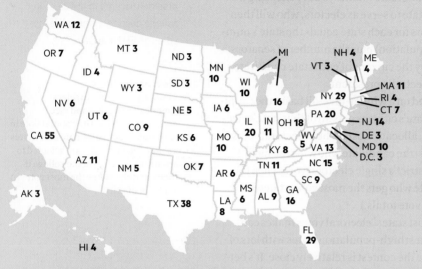

Electoral Votes per State

The number of electors from each state equals the state's number of House members (which varies based on state population) plus the number of senators (two per state). Each elector has one vote in the electoral college.

Who Are the Electors?

Candidates to be electors are nominated by their political parties. They pledge to support a certain candidate if they are elected to the electoral college. When you cast your vote for a presidential candidate, you are in fact voting for the slate of potential electors who support that candidate.

Delaware Idaho Nebraska South Dakota

Washington West Virginia

California Popular Vote

40%

60%

California Electoral Votes (55)

100%

Winning a State

Most states give all of their electoral college votes to the candidate who wins the most votes in that state. So, even if a candidate only gets 51 percent of the vote in the state, his or her entire slate of electors is elected, and he or she gets all of the state's votes in the electoral college.

100% of electoral votes go to winner

Donald Trump's Electoral College Strategy, 2016

Solid Republican States (164)
Core Four States (68)

Trump's campaign started by identifying "solid Republican" states—ones with a history of strong Republican support—which gave them a start of 164 electoral votes. Then, they focused on what campaign manager Kellyanne Conway called their "core four" states—ones they knew they needed in order to have a chance at victory: Florida, North Carolina, Ohio, and Iowa. This would bring them to 232 electoral votes. Where would they go to get the additional 38 electoral votes needed for victory?

164+68
232

Target the Rust Belt: *Michigan, Minnesota, Pennsylvania, and Wisconsin* These states have relatively weak economies and few minority voters.

MN **10**
WI **10**
MI **16**
PA **20**

164+68+56
288

Hold off Growing Minority Populations: *Arizona, Georgia, Nevada, Colorado* Though Democrats hoped to win all these states because of their high minority populations, only Nevada and Colorado have been swing states in recent elections, and many people felt that Georgia and Arizona had been trending toward Democrats.

NV **6**
AZ **11**
CO **9**
GA **16**

164+68+42
274

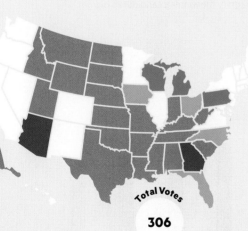

Total Votes
306

2016 Results

Trump used **a combination of these strategies** to win 306 electoral votes, and the presidency.[†]

Trump's Final Winning Electoral College Map

AL **9**	IN **11**	MS **6**	OK **7**	WV **5**
AK **3**	IA **6**	MO **10**	PA **20**	WI **10**
AZ **11**	KS **6**	MT **3**	SC **9**	WY **3**
AR **6**	KY **8**	NE **5**	SD **3**	
FL **29**	LA **8**	NC **15**	TN **11**	
GA **16**	ME **1***	ND **3**	TX **38**	
ID **4**	MI **16**	OH **18**	UT **6**	

Critical Thinking

1. **Why didn't the Trump campaign** focus on some delegate-rich states like California and New York?

2. **In what state do you think the Trump campaign** spent the most money? Where do you think Trump made the most personal appearances? Why?

* Maine splits its electoral votes; Trump received 1, Clinton 3.

† Ultimately, Trump won the electoral college with 304 votes to Hillary Clinton's 227. Seven electors voted for someone other than their party's candidate.

While most Americans believe that the winner of the presidential election is decided on Election Day, this outcome is actually just the first step in a process that determines the winner. After citizens' votes are counted in each state, the slates of electors meet in December in the state capitals. At their meetings, the electors almost always vote for the presidential candidate they have pledged to support. After the votes are certified by a joint session of Congress, the candidate who wins a majority of the nation's electoral votes (at least 270) is the new president. If no candidate receives a majority of the electoral college votes, the members of the House of Representatives choose the winner. They follow a procedure in which the members from each state decide which candidate to support and then cast one collective vote per state, with the winner needing a majority of these state-level votes to win. This procedure has not been used since 1824, although it might be required if a third-party candidate wins a significant number of electoral votes or if a state's electors refuse to cast their votes.[9]

A presidential candidate can win the electoral college vote, and thus the election, without receiving a majority of the votes cast by citizens. When a third-party candidate for president receives a substantial number of votes, the winner can easily end up receiving more votes than any other candidate without winning a majority of the popular vote. Bill Clinton won a substantial electoral college majority in 1992, while receiving only 43 percent of the popular vote. This was due to the fact that Ross Perot, a third-party candidate, received almost 19 percent of the national popular vote but not enough support in any one state to win electoral votes. In 2012, Barack Obama won about 50 percent of the popular vote but nearly 62 percent of the electoral votes.

FIGURE 8.1

Popular Vote versus Electoral Vote Percentages, 2000–2016

Political scientists argue that the electoral college system tends to magnify the winning candidate's margin of victory. Do the data presented here support this view?

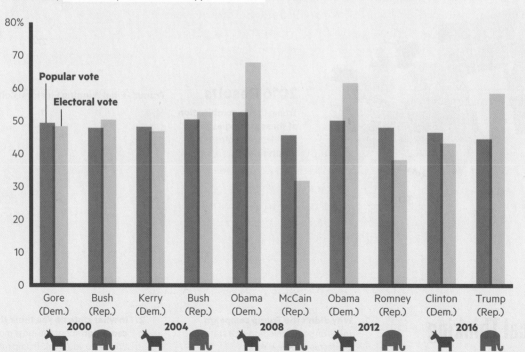

Source: U.S. National Archives and Records Administration, www.archives.gov/federal-register/electoral-college/historical.html (accessed 11/12/12).

It is also possible for a candidate who loses the popular vote to receive the majority of electoral votes and win the election. This outcome occurred in 2016 and 2000. (See Figure 8.1 for a comparison of electoral and popular vote totals in recent presidential elections.)

American elections incorporate a complex set of laws, rules, and procedures. And these rules matter—the candidates who win under current rules might lose given other reasonable ways to conduct elections. Put another way, one key to winning elections (just like any other game of strategy) is to know the rules.

Electoral campaigns

★

DESCRIBE THE FEATURES, STRATEGIES, AND FUNDING OF CAMPAIGNS FOR FEDERAL OFFICE

Now that we have reviewed the main steps of how American elections work, we will focus in this section on the campaign process and what candidates do to convince people to vote for them on Election Day. Our emphasis is on things that candidates do regardless of the office they are running for, across the entire **election cycle**, the two-year period between general elections.

election cycle
The two-year period between general elections.

The "fundamentals"

Before talking about all the things candidates and their supporters do to shape election outcomes, it is crucial to understand that many important factors are beyond their control. Political scientists call these factors the *fundamentals*. In part, the fundamentals include the rules that govern elections, such as photo ID requirements for voting, which in turn shape voter turnout in ways that hurt some candidates (usually Democrats) and help others. Another fundamental is how many people in a candidate's district share his or her party ID. As we showed in Chapter 7 ("Political Parties"), an individual's party ID is a strong influence on his or her voting decisions. Particularly in presidential elections, economic conditions also have a strong effect on who wins. As you see in the What Do the Numbers Say? feature, a stronger economy benefits incumbent presidents running for reelection (for example, Obama in 2012), while a weak economy hurts incumbents (Jimmy Carter in 1980) and their successors (Hillary Clinton in 2016).

The impact of party ID and economic conditions, along with many of the electoral rules we discussed earlier, illustrates another important fact about elections in America: many of the factors that shape election outcomes are out of the candidates' control. Candidates might like to think that they can convince people to vote for them regardless of circumstances. But the fundamentals tell us which candidates face an uphill fight or an easy ride—either because voters are well aware of these factors before the campaign begins or because campaigns are mechanisms by which voters become informed.[10] It may not be fair to reward or blame candidates for the state of the economy, as even presidents have only limited control over economic growth or unemployment levels. For better or worse, however, a significant fraction of American voters behave this way[11]

📷

Each term, members of Congress decide whether to retire or run for another term. Rep. Dan Benishek (R-MI) announced his decision not to seek reelection in 2016 in late 2015, leaving his seat in the House open. Retirement decisions, which create open-seat races, are an opportunity for one party to gain seats from the other.

open seat
An elected position for which there is no incumbent.

📷

Most officeholders are always campaigning—traveling around their states or districts, talking with constituents, and explaining their actions in office—all in the hope of winning and keeping support for the next election. Here, Representative Beto O'Rourke (D-TX) meets with constituents on the Paso del Norte bridge, which crosses into the U.S. from Mexico. @RepBetoORourke

Setting the stage

On the day after any election, candidates, party officials, and interest groups all start thinking about the next election cycle. They consider who won and who lost, which incumbents look like safe bets for reelection and which ones might be vulnerable, who might retire soon or run for another office in the next election, and whether the election returns reveal new information about the kinds of campaigns or issues that might increase voter turnout or support the next time.

Party committees and candidates have particular interest in the likelihood that incumbents might retire, thereby creating an **open seat**. Open seats are of special interest because incumbents generally hold an election advantage.[12] So, when a seat opens, candidates from the party that does not control the seat know that they might have a better chance to win because they will not have to run against an incumbent.

Presidential campaigns work the same way. Virtually all first-term presidents run for reelection. Potential challengers in the opposing party study the results of the last election to see how many votes the president received and how this support was distributed across the states to determine their own chances of winning against the incumbent. Candidates in the president's party make the same calculations, although no sitting president in the twentieth century was denied renomination. Nonetheless, some presidents (Harry Truman in 1952, Lyndon Johnson in 1968) retired because their chances of being renominated were not good, while others (Gerald Ford in 1976, Jimmy Carter in 1980) faced tough primary contests.[13]

Before the campaign

Most incumbent House members, senators, and presidents work throughout the election cycle to secure their reelection. Political scientists label this activity the permanent campaign[14]: it involves keeping the constituents happy and raising money for the campaign. As we will see in Chapter 10, congressional incumbents try to keep their constituents happy by taking actions that ensure the voters can identify something good that the incumbent has done.[15] Incumbent presidents make the same calculations. During

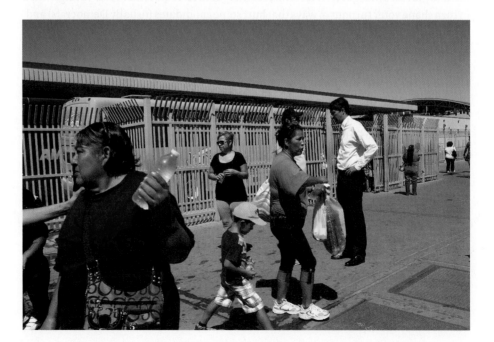

Vote Share for President's Party vs. Economic Growth

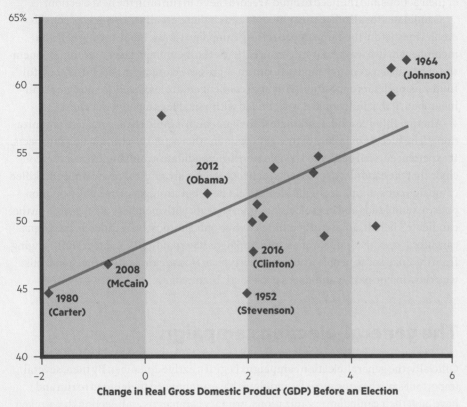

"The Fundamentals" and Presidential Elections

Political scientists argue that "the fundamentals" play a key role in American elections. For example, the state of the economy is thought to influence vote decisions in presidential elections—a strong economy benefits incumbent presidents or their successors. However, most candidates (and journalists) argue that the things candidates say and do during the campaign determine who wins and who loses. What do the numbers say?

To answer this question, let's examine this figure, which shows the relationship between presidential election outcomes (vote for the incumbent president or the candidate from their party) and economic conditions (the growth in real personal income in the year before the election).

Think about it

- Do incumbent presidents do better when the economy is strong than when it is weak?
- Candidates who lose, such as Clinton in 2016 or Romney in 2012, are criticized for running poor campaigns. Look at the data points that describe economic conditions in these elections and the percentage of the popular vote received by Obama in 2012 and Clinton in 2016. Given the state of the economy in these years, is there any evidence that Romney or Clinton did worse than you would expect?
- What signs are there in the chart that other factors besides "the fundamentals" might influence presidential election outcomes?

DID YOU KNOW?

The 2016 Clinton campaign had

200,000

volunteers and 4,000 paid staff (including people working in Democratic party organizations).

Barack Obama's first months in office, many of his advisers argued that he had to offer an economic stimulus plan in light of polls showing that the economy was an overriding concern to most Americans. Obama did so—a decision driven by political as well as policy concerns. Of course, many presidential actions are taken in response to events rather than initiated to gain voter support. Particularly in the case of wars and other conflicts, it is far-fetched to say that presidents initiate hostilities for political gain. Even so, presidents, just like other politicians, are keenly aware of the political consequences of their actions and the need to build a record they can run on in the next election.

Candidates for all offices, incumbents and challengers alike, also devote considerable time before the campaign to raising campaign funds. Fund-raising helps an incumbent in two ways.[16] First, it ensures that if the incumbent faces a strong opponent she or he will have enough money to run an aggressive campaign. Second, successful fund-raising deters opposition. Potential challengers are less likely to run against an incumbent if that individual is well funded with a sizable campaign war chest.[17]

Another thing candidates do before the campaign is build their campaign organization.[18] The success or failure of these efforts is another signal of a candidate's prospects. If experienced, well-respected people work in a candidate's campaign, observers conclude that the candidate's prospects for being elected are probably good. Indeed, skilled campaign consultants are highly desirable. They plan strategies, run public-opinion polls, assemble ads and buy television time, and talk with members of the media on the candidate's behalf, among other things. While only the most well-funded campaigns can afford top consultants, almost all campaigns have paid and volunteer staff, ranging from the dozen or so people who work for a typical House candidate to the thousands who run a major-party candidate's presidential campaign.

The general-election campaign

Officially, the general-election campaigns begin in early September. By then, several important steps have occurred: candidates have announced their intent to run and have built their campaign organizations, primary campaigns and elections have taken place, and both parties have chosen their presidential nominees and their congressional candidates. Interest groups, candidates, and party committees have raised most of the funds they will use or donate in the campaign. The race is on.

Name Recognition One fundamental campaign strategy, particularly in congressional campaigns, is to build name recognition. Since many citizens know fairly little about congressional candidates, efforts to increase a candidate's name recognition can deliver a few extra percentage points of support—enough to turn a close defeat into a victory. (Practically all voters can identify the major-party presidential candidates, so name recognition efforts are not as central to these elections.)

GOTV ("get out the vote") or the ground game
A campaign's efforts to "get out the vote" or make sure their supporters vote on Election Day.

Getting Out the Vote A second basic strategy is mobilization. Turnout is not automatic: candidates have to make sure that their supporters actually go to the polls and vote (or make sure they have an absentee ballot). Campaign professionals refer to voter mobilization efforts as GOTV ("get out the vote") or the ground game.[19] Most campaigns for Congress or the presidency use extensive door-to-door canvassing, as well as phone banks and e-mail. Both Republican and Democratic campaigns use sophisticated databases, combining voter registration data with demographic information to determine who their potential supporters are and how best to reach them and convince them to vote.[20] Sometimes these contacts are made through social media, but many campaigns still use volunteers to knock on doors and present their candidate's messages to voters one at a time.

Promises and Party Positions Issues matter in American elections. A candidate's issue positions help to mobilize supporters and attract volunteers, activists, interest-group endorsements, and contributions. Issue positions also define what a government will seek to do differently depending on who gets elected. Thus, another important set of campaign decisions involves the candidate's campaign platform, which presents his or her stances on issues and promises about how the candidate will act in office.

In writing their platform, candidates may be constrained by positions they have taken in the past or by their party affiliation. For one thing, candidates whose positions vary from one election to another or between the primary and general elections often lose support from voters who see the changes as a sign of manipulation.[21] Also, Chapter 7 showed that the parties have strong brand identities that lead many citizens to associate Democrats with liberal policies and Republicans with conservative ones; as a result, candidates often find it difficult to make campaign promises that contradict these perceptions. Also influencing a candidate's positions are demands from potential supporters. For example, in a state or district with many conservative or Republican voters, opposition to health care reform legislation or to amnesty for illegal immigrants might be a winning electoral strategy—just as support for these proposals would generally be helpful for candidates running in states or districts where most voters are moderate to liberal or Democrats.

The two-step electoral process in American elections also influences candidate positions. To win office, candidates have to campaign three times, first to build a staff and gain contributors and volunteers (the so-called silent primary or money primary), then in a primary to get on the ballot, and then in a general election. This process gives candidates an incentive to take relatively extreme policy positions—and encourages the entry of relatively extreme candidates. The reason is that party activists, contributors, and primary voters (the people whose support candidates need to attract in the first two steps) hold more extreme positions than voters in the general election. Thus, in the typical congressional district, Republican candidates win primaries by taking conservative positions, while Democratic candidates win primaries by upholding liberal views. However, a position or promise that attracts votes in a primary election might not work so well in the general election, or vice versa. For example, during the 2016

Candidates may gain media attention and name recognition by hosting campaign events alongside well-known "surrogates." Here, senator and former presidential candidate John McCain (R-AZ) speaks at an event supporting incumbent Senator Pat Toomey (R-PA).

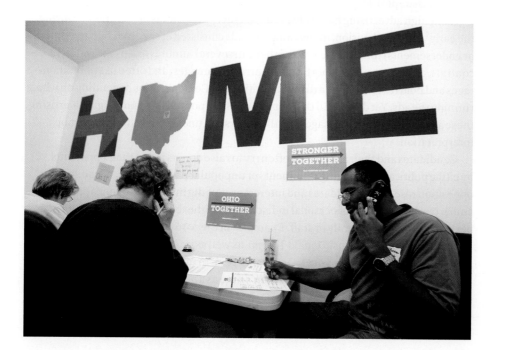

American presidential campaigns depend on thousands of paid and volunteer staff. Here, volunteers for Democratic candidate Hillary Clinton make phone calls to potential supporters from a Clinton campaign office in Newark, Ohio.

Democratic presidential nomination campaign, challenger Bernie Sanders attracted support by promising to expand government health insurance programs. While this promise was popular among Democratic activists, contributors, and primary voters and helped Sanders compete in a close race against Hillary Clinton for the nomination, it would likely have cost Sanders considerable support in the general election.

Debates Candidates often contrast their own records or positions with those of opposing candidates or make claims designed to lower voters' opinions of their opponents. Sometimes these interactions occur during a formal debate. Most congressional campaigns involve debates in front of an audience of likely voters, a group of reporters, or the editorial board of a local newspaper. Typically candidates take questions from reporters, although sometimes candidates question each other or answer questions from the audience.

Presidential campaigns involve multiple debates during the primary and caucus season. Throughout the months before the first primaries and caucuses, each party's candidates gather for many single-party debates using a variety of formats. During the general election, the Republican and Democratic nominees meet for several debates. (The number and format are negotiated between the campaigns and the Commission on Presidential Debates, a nonpartisan organization that organizes the debates.)[22] The 2016 presidential campaign featured three debates between the presidential nominees and one between the vice-presidential nominees. The debates offer valuable free exposure: given a relatively uninterested electorate, candidates must present themselves in a way that captures voters' attention and gains their support.

Campaign Advertising: Getting the Word Out One of the realities of modern American electoral campaigns is that they are, for the most part, conducted indirectly—through social media, through news coverage of events, and (most important) through paid campaign advertising. Candidates, party committees, and interest groups spend more than several billion dollars during each election cycle for federal office. Most of that money is spent on 30-second television spots. Such advertising is critical because, as we discussed in Chapter 6, candidates cannot assume that citizens will take the time to learn from other sources about the candidates, their qualifications, and their issue positions.

Campaign advertising has evolved considerably over the last generation.[23] During the early years of television, many campaign ads consisted of speeches by candidates or endorsements from supporters and they ran several minutes in length. Today, in contrast, campaign ads are short, feature arresting images, and often use photomontages and bold text to engage a distracted citizenry. Content varies depending on who is running the ads. Yet despite all the money and effort poured into campaign advertising, these ads must deliver a message that all viewers can understand without too much interpretation.

Candidates and their supporters often try to raise doubts about their opponents by citing politically damaging statements or unpopular past behavior. In conducting opposition research, candidates and interest groups dig into an opponent's past for embarrassing incidents or personal indiscretions, either by the candidate or by a member of the candidate's family or staff. Examples in the 2016 campaign include sexual assault claims made against Donald Trump, as well as information suggesting he paid no federal income taxes over a 20-year period. In turn, Trump's campaign highlighted the fact that during Hillary Clinton's time as a public defender in Arkansas she defended a client accused of forcible rape.

Another way that candidates may confront one another involves the use of attack ads, which are campaign ads that criticize the opponent. Many such ads stretch the truth (or break it outright), trying to get voters to stop and think—or to get the opposing candidate to spend time and money denying the ads' claims. One of Trump's central campaign themes was to emphasize the economic and security dangers facing America, then argue that he was the only candidate who could mitigate these dangers. Trump's strategy played an important role in motivating his core supporters to turn out on Election Day.

One critical question about campaign advertising is whether the ads work: whether they shape what people know or influence their vote decisions or other forms of participation. Some observers have complained that campaign ads—especially attack ads and negative campaigning—depress voter turnout and reinforce citizens' negative perceptions of government.[24] However, perhaps because Americans tend to pay little attention to politics, many of these ads have little to no effect on what voters think or how they behave.

Other evidence suggests that campaign advertising has several beneficial effects. Scholars have found that people who are exposed to campaign ads tend to be more interested in the campaign and know more about the candidates.[25] Moreover, many campaign ads highlight real differences between the candidates and the parties.[26] Even so, average citizens know that they cannot believe everything they see on television, so campaign advertising, if it does anything at all, captures their attention without necessarily changing their minds.[27]

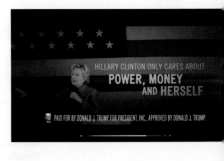

In the 2016 presidential race, many of the ads aired by the Trump campaign and Republican groups criticized Hillary Clinton, focusing on what they deemed to be her corrupt political associations.

Campaign finance

"Campaign finance" refers to money collected for and spent on campaigns and elections by candidates, political parties, and other organizations and individuals. The **Federal Election Commission** is in charge of administering election laws, including the complex regulations pertaining to how campaigns can spend money. The most recent changes in campaign finance rules, which were passed as the Bipartisan Campaign Reform Act (BCRA), took effect after the 2002 elections and have been modified by subsequent Supreme Court decisions—most notably, *Citizens United v. Federal Election Commission* (2010), which removed all restrictions on campaign funding by corporations and labor unions.

Federal Election Commission
The government agency that enforces and regulates election laws; made up of six presidential appointees, of whom no more than three can be members of the same party.

While campaign finance law is complex, most Americans believe the effects of campaign finance are simple: candidates cannot win without spending money, victory goes to the candidate with the larger budget, and, as a result, candidates listen to large donors and ignore average citizens. They also believe that elections cost too much. The reality is much more complex. Candidates need money to run effective campaigns (and particularly to pay for campaign advertising), but spending does not guarantee victory. And while candidates court large donors, they are even more obsessed with winning the support of ordinary citizens, because in the end, elections are about votes, not money.

Types of Funding Organizations The limits on campaign contributions in the BCRA—also known as the McCain–Feingold Act—vary depending on whether contributions are made by an individual or a group and by the type of group, as Table 8.1 shows. These contributions are called **hard money**, meaning funds that can be used to help elect or defeat a specific candidate (donations made during the primaries and general elections count separately).

Contributions that are not used to help a specific candidate are called **soft money** and are not subject to the limits imposed on hard money. A 527 organization (the number refers to a provision in IRS regulations) can raise unlimited soft money from

hard money
Donations that are used to help elect or defeat a specific candidate.

soft money
Contributions that can be used for voter mobilization or to promote a policy proposal or point of view as long as these efforts are not tied to supporting or opposing a particular candidate.

TABLE
8.1

Contribution Limits in the 2016 Election

The BCRA of 2002 put into effect limits on how much individuals, organizations, and corporations could contribute to candidates' campaigns. The limits were changed based on Supreme Court decisions in 2010 and 2014. At present, although there are still limits on contributions that individuals and PACs can make to each individual candidate, there are no limits on total overall contributions to multiple candidates by individuals and PACs.

	Individual Candidates	National Party Committees	State, District, and Local Parties	PACs	Limit on Total Contributions
Individuals	$2,700	$33,400	$10,000 (combined limit)	$5,000	No limit
PACs	$5,000	$15,000	$5,000 (combined limit)	$5,000	No limit
National Party Committees	$5,000	No limit	No limit	$5,000	$45,400 to Senate candidate per campaign
State, District, and Local Party Committees	$5,000 (combined limit)	No limit	No limit	$5,000 (combined limit)	No limit

Source: Federal Election Commission, "Contribution Limits for 2015–2016," www.fec.gov/pages/brochures/contriblimits.shtml (accessed 3/13/16).

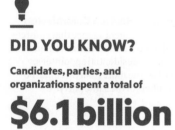

DID YOU KNOW?

Candidates, parties, and organizations spent a total of

$6.1 billion

during the 2015–2016 election cycle.

individuals or corporations for voter mobilization and for issue advocacy, but these expenditures must not be coordinated with a candidate or a party. Ads by 527s cannot advocate the election or defeat of a particular candidate or political party.[28] Another type of organization, described using the IRS code as a 501(c)(4), has been active in recent elections. The principal difference between 527s and 501(c)(4)s is that the latter type of organization does not have to disclose the names of its contributors. Chapter 9 looks more closely at PACs, 527s, and 501(c)(4)s.

Political action committees (PACs) are groups that aim to elect or defeat particular candidates or political parties. A company or an organization can form a PAC and solicit contributions from employees or group members. As Table 8.1 shows, the amount PACs can give to each candidate in an election is limited, but these limits pertain only to hard money. PACs can also form a 527, which can then accept unlimited amounts of soft money. As discussed in Chapter 7, political party committees are entities within the Republican and Democratic parties. Both major parties have a national committee and a campaign committee in each house of Congress. Party committees are limited in the amount of hard money they can give to a candidate's campaign and in the amount they can spend on behalf of the candidate as a coordinated expenditure. However, a party committee (and, after *Citizens United*, corporations and labor unions) can spend an unlimited amount in independent expenditures to elect a candidate or candidates. To be considered independent, expenditures must not be controlled, directed, or approved by any candidate's campaign. Independent expenditures can pay for campaign advertising, but the candidate or candidates cannot be consulted on the content.

Current law gives presidential candidates the ability to receive federal campaign funding for the primary and general-election campaign (in the primary, these are matching funds; in the general, they are a block grant). These federal funds are generated, in part, by money that taxpayers voluntarily allocate out of their federal taxes by

TABLE
8.2

	2014	2016
Presidential Candidates*		
Republican	—	$562,047,053
Democrat	—	$734,118,418
Congressional Candidates		
House incumbents	$614,461,886	$627,192,004
House challengers	$154,056,805	$135,688,346
House open-seat candidates	$188,948,198	$197,293,425
Senate incumbents	$330,229,985	$356,227,722
Senate challengers	$144,176,116	$177,561,478
Senate open-seat candidates	$140,150,238	$97,993,147
Political Parties		
Republicans	$574,483,784	$756,931,035
Democrats	$731,318,780	$985,956,892
Independent Expenditures	$781,690,240	$1,482,375,912
Totals	$3,659,516,032	$6,113,385,432

Candidate, Party, and Interest-Group Election Fund-Raising, 2014–2016

Candidates and political parties raise and spend a great deal of money in their campaigns. Do these numbers help to explain the high reelection rates for members of Congress?

*Presidential spending includes federal matching funds for the general election.

Source: Calculated by the authors from data at www.opensecrets.org (accessed 11/6/16).

checking off a box on their tax return form. However, in order to accept federal funds, candidates must abide by overall spending limits (and, during the nomination, by state-by-state spending caps). During the last two presidential campaigns, all of the major candidates decided against accepting these funds during the nomination and general-election campaign, which meant that they were not bound by the spending caps (although individual contributors were still limited to the amounts shown in Table 8.1).

These complex campaign finance regulations reflect two simple truths. First, any limits on campaign activities involve balancing the right to free speech about candidates and issues with the idea that rich people or well-funded organizations should not be allowed to dominate what voters hear during the campaign. Second, an enormous amount of money is spent on American elections (see Table 8.2).

The Effects of Money in Politics The raw data on campaign finance do not always tell the whole story. For example, the total amount spent on electioneering represents all funding for the 435 House contests, 33 or 34 Senate races, a presidential election, and state and local races. Moreover, in terms of television advertising alone, a 30-second ad on a major network can cost tens or hundreds of thousands of dollars.[29] Given that even House campaigns may run hundreds of ads and presidential campaigns run tens of thousands, it is easy to see why campaign costs pile up so quickly.

The principal concern about all this campaign cash is that the amount of money spent on a candidate's campaign might matter more than the candidate's qualifications or issue positions. That is, candidates—in particular, wealthy ones who can self-fund their campaigns—could get elected regardless of how good a job they would do, simply

Political action committees spend millions on campaign advertising. Often, their ads are highly negative. This one attacks Donald Trump for being homophobic in his rhetoric.

Is There Too Much Money in Politics?

Campaign finance regulations place restrictions on what Americans can do to influence election outcomes—but should they? Suppose you are a wealthy person or the head of a corporation with deep pockets. Under current law, you and your corporation can only donate about $15,000 to a candidate's campaign; corporations have to form a PAC to do so and cannot pay for the contribution with business revenues. You can also form one of several types of organizations that can spend unlimited money to run campaign ads designed to help elect your preferred candidates or donate to an existing organization. Clearly, having money gives you options for participation in American elections that are not open to the average citizen. Is that a good thing?

It's a free country, and spending money on politics is part of that freedom.
Limits on campaign spending conflict with fundamental tenets of American democracy. The Bill of Rights states that Congress cannot abridge "freedom of speech, or of the press; or the right of the people peaceably to assemble, and to petition the Government for a redress of grievances." One interpretation of the First Amendment that has shaped recent Supreme Court decisions on campaign finance is that people should be free to spend whatever they want on contesting elections—excluding bribes, threats, and other illegal actions, of course. Also, given that campaign spending is no guarantee of electoral success, it is not clear that eliminating spending limits would give big donors control over election outcomes.

Another argument for eliminating limits on political activities is that with one exception (donations to 501[c][4] organizations), donors and political activists are required to file quarterly reports on their campaign activities. Therefore, other activists and even ordinary citizens would quickly learn of any large-scale attempts to manipulate election outcomes and could decide to work for the other side or simply vote against a big donor's preferred candidates.

Campaign contributions need to be constrained.
Even if there's no evidence that money buys elections, there is also no guarantee that under the right circumstances a big donation or ad campaign would not make the difference for one or more candidates. With this possibility in mind, it makes sense to place broad limits on campaign contributions and independent expenditures, to level the playing field between ordinary citizens and political activists with deep pockets.

Just because someone is rich shouldn't give him or her additional ways to influence election outcomes.

Moreover, while it is true that limiting campaign activities requires imposing limits on speech rights, limitations on civil liberties are nothing new. All of the individual rights set out in the Bill of Rights are limited in one way or the other. Even freedom of speech is limited in areas such as hate speech and statements that pose a clear and present danger. Imposing limits on campaign activities could be justified on grounds that maintaining free and fair elections is important enough to justify a modest limitation on what individuals and organizations can do to influence election outcomes.

📷 Does money equal speech or should campaign contributions be limited?

Because money for ads is a necessary component of a political campaign, the possibility remains that a rich donor could change election outcomes by giving large sums to challengers in congressional elections. And in close races, giving a candidate extra funds to increase his or her GOTV efforts or to run additional campaign ads might be enough to change the outcome.

Does the risk of allowing rich donors disproportionate power over elections outweigh the dangers associated with restricting their speech rights? Take a stand.

take a stand

1. Limits on individual campaign contributions guard against allowing wealthy people to dominate elections. What are some of the possible drawbacks of such regulations?

2. Under current law, corporations and unions (not just individuals) are allowed unlimited political expenditures as long as they are independent of a candidate's campaign organization. Why do you think independent expenditures are less regulated than direct contributions to campaigns?

because they have more money than competing candidates to pay for ads, polls, a large staff, and mobilization efforts. Another concern is that individuals and organizations or corporations that can afford to make large contributions (or fund their own election-eering efforts) might be able to dictate election outcomes or, by funding certain candi-dates' campaigns, garner disproportionate influence over the subsequent behavior of elected officials. (The Take a Stand feature discusses these issues further.)

However, there is little evidence that campaign contributions alter legislators' behavior or that contributors are rewarded with votes supporting their causes or favor-able policies.[30] Contributions may also help with access, getting an appointment to present arguments to a politician or his or her staff. But people and organizations who contribute are already friendly with the politicians they support, and the politicians would likely hear their arguments in any case.

It's also clear that having a lot of campaign cash doesn't make a candidate into a winner—and that winners don't always outspend their opponents. Consider the 2016 Republican presidential primaries: the campaigns of Jeb Bush, Chris Christie, and Marco Rubio had large budgets and the support of outside groups with deep pockets. Even so, they all lost. The winner of the election, Donald Trump, spent substantially less than his opponents in both the nomination and general-election campaigns. Of course, Trump entered the campaign with high levels of name recognition and his cam-paign message resonated with Republican primary voters. But that is exactly the point: victories aren't bought with campaign cash. Candidates need a base level of funding to hire staff, travel, and run some campaign ads. Beyond that point, success is a function of what candidates say and do, not the amount of contributions they receive or ads run on their behalf.[31]

"Why Should I Care?"

When you follow the news about political campaigns, pay attention to the money candidates raise (and spend), where they campaign (and to whom they appeal), the tone and message of their campaigns, and larger fundamentals, such as the strength of the economy. These factors can provide strong clues about who is likely to win (or lose). Remember, though, that politicians don't win elections just by spending a lot of money. Sometimes candidates win despite lower budgets. The other factors listed here and examined in this chapter often have stronger effects on the outcome than money alone.

How do voters decide?

★
EXPLAIN THE KEY FACTORS THAT INFLUENCE VOTERS' CHOICES

All the electoral activities we have considered so far are directed at citizens: making sure they are registered to vote, influencing their voting decisions, and getting them to the polls. Now we examine how citizens respond to these influences. The first things to understand are that only a minority of citizens report high levels of interest in cam-paigns, many people know little about the candidates or the issues, and many people do not vote.[32]

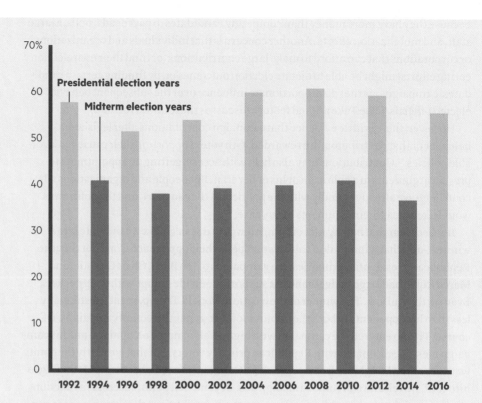

FIGURE 8.2

Turnout in Presidential and Midterm Elections, 1992–2016

The figure shows how turnout of registered voters varies both over time and between presidential and midterm elections. Why don't more people vote in midterm election years? Why don't more people vote in any given year?

Source: United States Election Project, www. election project.org (accessed 11/9/16).

paradox of voting
The question of why citizens vote even though their individual votes stand little chance of changing the election outcome.

DID YOU KNOW?

61.2%

Voter turnout for African Americans in the 2016 presidential election.
Source: Calculated by author from exit polls and historical data.

Who votes, and why?

Politics is everywhere, but getting involved is your choice. Voting and other forms of political participation are optional. Even a strong preference between two candidates may not drive a citizen to the polls because each person's vote is just one of many.[33] The only time a vote "counts," in the sense that it changes the outcome, is when the other votes are split evenly so that one vote breaks the tie. Moreover, voting involves costs. Even if you don't learn about the candidates but vote anyway, you still have to get to the polls on Election Day. Thus, the **paradox of voting** is this: Why does anyone vote, given that voting involves costs and the chances of affecting the outcome are small?

Figure 8.2 shows that among Americans the percentage of registered voters who actually voted has been, in recent presidential elections, around 60 percent, although the actual turnout (votes as a percentage of the total adult population) has been closer to 50 percent.[34] As the figure shows, turnout is significantly higher in presidential elections than in midterm elections. Turnout is even lower in primaries and caucuses.

In the main, turnout is higher for whites than for nonwhites (African Americans have been an exception in recent elections), and among older Americans compared with younger cohorts, and for college graduates relative to people with a high school education or less. Men and women, however, say they vote at roughly the same rate. Many factors explain variation in turnout. People who vote regularly are more likely to see it as an obligation of citizenship, to feel guilty when they do not vote, and to think that the election matters. In contrast, turnout is much lower among those who are angry with the government, think that government actions do not affect them, or think that voting will have no impact on government policy.[35]

These findings demonstrate the importance of mobilization in elections. As discussed earlier, many candidates for political office spend at least as much time trying to convince their supporters to vote as they do attempting to persuade others to become supporters in the first place. Because many Americans either do not vote or vote only sporadically, mobilization is vital for winning elections.

How do people vote?

Although candidates, parties, and other organizations release a blizzard of endorsements, reports, and press releases throughout the campaign, much of this information may be difficult to interpret. It is a daunting task, even for the rare, highly motivated voter.

Voting Cues The combination of a lack of interest and a relatively complex task leads most Americans to base their voting decisions on easily interpretable pieces of information, or **voting cues**.[36] Voters in American national elections use many kinds of cues, such as party ID (voting for the incumbent candidate who shares your party ID), the personal vote (voting for a candidate who has helped you get assistance from a government agency or has helped your community benefit from desirable government projects), personal characteristics (voting for the candidate whose personal characteristics such as age, race, gender, ethnicity, religious beliefs, or background match your own), or pocketbook voting (voting for the incumbent if the economy is strong and for the challenger otherwise, as illustrated by the quote from Ronald Reagan).

Voters can also use multiple cues. Cues give people a low-effort way to cast a vote that, more likely than not, is consistent with the voter's true preference among candidates.[37] Studies have found that citizens who use cues and are politically well informed are more likely to cast a reasonable vote (one that's consistent with their underlying policy preferences relative to candidates' positions) than those who use cues but are otherwise relatively politically ignorant. In essence, information helps people to select the right cue.[38]

All the strategies identified here for making voting decisions are used to some extent in every election. However, in normal elections, when congressional reelection rates are high and the seat shift between the parties is small, voters generally use cues that focus on the candidates themselves—such as incumbency, partisanship, a personal connection to a candidate, or the candidate's personal characteristics or past performance. This behavior is consistent with the saying that "all politics is local": many congressional elections are independent, local contests in which a candidate's chances of winning depend on what voters think of the candidate in particular—not the president, Congress, or national issues. It also explains why electoral **coattails** are typically very weak in American elections and why so many Americans cast **split tickets** rather than **straight tickets**. In the main, voting decisions in presidential and congressional elections are made independently of each other.

Voting in wave elections

"Wave" elections generally occur when a large number of voters vote against incumbents because of poor economic conditions, political scandal, or a costly, unpopular war. In 2006, many voters disapproved of how the war in Iraq was being conducted.[39] And in 2010 many voters disapproved of economic conditions in general as well as corporate bailouts, economic stimulus legislation, and health care reform.

Under these conditions many voters look for someone to blame, focusing on members of Congress from the party in power. They then vote against these members, either as a protest vote or because they want to put different individuals in charge in the hope that conditions will improve.

Voting is costly in terms of time and effort. After registering and informing themselves about the election, voters have to take the time to go to the polls and possibly wait in line.

voting cues
Pieces of information about a candidate that are readily available, easy to interpret, and lead a citizen to decide to vote for a particular candidate.

"

Are you better off than you were four years ago?

—**Ronald Reagan,** running for president against incumbent Jimmy Carter

coattails
The idea that a popular president can generate additional support for candidates affiliated with his or her party. Coattails are weak or nonexistent in most American elections.

split ticket
A ballot on which a voter selects candidates from more than one political party.

straight ticket
A ballot on which a voter selects candidates from only one political party.

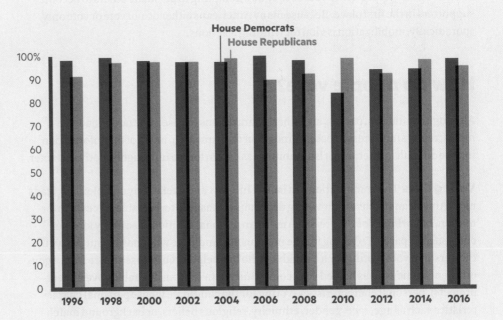

FIGURE 8.3

Percentage of House Incumbents Reelected

The figure shows that, despite public dissatisfaction with Congress, incumbents still tend to be reelected in their respective districts. According to the chart, which congressional elections were wave elections? Which were normal elections?

Source: Calculated by the authors from election results.

During campaigns, candidates often seek to strengthen the perception that they share (or at least are sympathetic to) average Americans' beliefs and interests. Hillary Clinton meets with voters over coffee and pastries at a campaign stop in Stone Ridge, Virginia.

Even in wave elections, reelection rates for members of Congress (the percentage of incumbents who successfully run for reelection) are generally high, as Figure 8.3 shows for the House of Representatives over the last generation. During that period, neither party had a House reelection rate of less than 80 percent, even in 2006, when 100 percent of Democratic House incumbents running for reelection were reelected, the reelection rate for House Republican incumbents was almost 90 percent.

Reelection rates for members of Congress are so high because senators and representatives work to insulate themselves from electoral challenges through tactics we discuss in this chapter and will discuss further in Chapter 10. Even so, congressional incumbents are not necessarily safe from electoral defeat. Rather, their high reelection rates result from the actions they take every day, which are calculated to win favor with their constituents. In normal elections, these strategies are generally enough to ensure reelection. In wave elections, however, they are not enough to protect some legislators from protest votes against the disadvantaged party, as the Democrats learned in 2010.

"Why Should I Care?"

After each election, people look at the results and try to figure out what the election was about—why some candidates won and others lost. Before each election, would-be candidates wonder whether this is "the year" to run for office (you may be one of these candidates someday). The most important thing to understand is that there are no easy explanations and no guarantees. The problem is not that voters are fickle or clueless or that the rules are too complex. Rather, elections boil down to voters and the many different ways they decide how to vote. Knowing what is likely to influence voters can help you make predictions about who will win elections and thus what policies and issues government will tackle.

Understanding the 2016 election

The 2016 contest is an excellent example of how and why elections matter. When the campaigns began, it seemed as though several critical issues hung in the balance. America's next president would likely appoint at least one (and probably two or three) Supreme Court justices. This had the potential to change the ideological balance of the Court, making recent decisions on campaign finance, affirmative action, same-sex marriage, and abortion rights open for revision. Republican control of the presidency would make it easier to repeal President Obama's health care and financial reforms. All of Obama's executive orders, ranging from limits on deporting undocumented aliens to measures restoring commercial and diplomatic ties with Cuba, could be abolished by the new president on his or her first day in office. Finally, the next president—if they chose—could work to resolve policy gridlock in areas such as gun control, reducing the federal deficit, making changes to Social Security and Medicare, entitlement reform, and immigration law.

The first thing to understand about the 2016 elections is their uniqueness. For the first time in 50 years, a major party nominated a presidential candidate with no prior political experience, Republican Donald Trump. It is hard to think of another candidate in American politics who even comes close to Trump and his willingness to say completely outlandish things. Trump also ran a unique campaign, with limited advertising, a weak ground game, and a willingness to deviate from the standard Republican platform on issues such as trade, civil liberties, and foreign policy. Trump was the least popular major-party presidential nominee of all time, and many Republican elected officials and party leaders refused to support Trump in the general election.

Democrats in 2016 selected Hillary Clinton, a former First Lady, senator, and secretary of state, as their nominee. This choice was historic: Clinton was the first woman to lead a major-party presidential ticket in America. Notwithstanding this distinction, Clinton's popularity was only somewhat higher than Trump's. Clinton also faced a surprisingly strong challenge in the Democratic primaries from Senator Bernie Sanders, and was only narrowly ahead of Trump during most of the general-election campaign.

All of these factors make the 2016 election a crucial test of many of the theories we have offered throughout this text. How could Trump win the Republican nomination in light of our assertion that "the party decides"? How did Clinton win the nomination despite the many arguments made against her candidacy—or, why did Trump win despite his political baggage and an under-financed campaign? You will see that for all its uniqueness, much of what happened in the 2016 election fits our description of how campaigns work and why some candidates win while others lose.

The path to 2016: the 2012 and 2014 elections

At first glance, the 2012 and 2014 elections were mirror-image contests: Democrat Barack Obama won reelection in 2012 and his party gained seats in both houses of Congress, but in 2014, Republicans regained control of the Senate and enlarged their House majority. These outcomes illustrate the essence of contemporary American politics: Americans are sharply divided on many issues, no party has an enduring advantage, and election outcomes hinge on factors such as the state of the economy, the number of seats each party has to defend, and the candidates that each party runs for office.

The 2012 Presidential and Congressional Elections The economy was the central issue in the 2012 campaign. Unemployment remained relatively high and economic growth was relatively low. At first glance, the data appeared to pose a serious threat to President

Obama's reelection chances. But many Americans seemed to hold Obama only partially responsible for the economy, believing that he had inherited many of the problems from the previous administration, and gave him some credit for his economic stimulus legislation.

In the presidential race, Mitt Romney was the front-runner on the Republican side from the beginning of the nomination process, although he faced serious opposition for most of the primary season. Nonetheless, it was not a surprise that Romney won the nomination: he was an experienced candidate who had run for president in 2008 and had served as governor of Massachusetts from 2003 until 2007. His record as a businessman appealed to voters who thought that government should be run more efficiently. In contrast to Romney and the Republicans, President Obama won renomination with no significant opposition, as is usual for incumbent presidents.

Early in the general-election campaign, with most states squarely in one candidate's camp or the other, attention focused on nine swing states where neither candidate was significantly ahead: North Carolina, Ohio, Virginia, Florida, New Hampshire, Nevada, Wisconsin, Colorado, and Iowa. Most Americans had largely made up their minds fairly early in the campaign, and few were open to persuasion. Under these conditions, voter mobilization played a crucial role, and Obama's campaign was much better organized to get people to the polls, both for early voting and on Election Day. In the end, Obama defeated Romney by a slight margin in the popular vote and by a somewhat larger margin in the electoral college.

At the congressional level, many Republican candidates in 2012 ran on platforms emphasizing the need to reduce government spending and regulations, generally saying that they would make the repeal of President Obama's health care reforms a central priority if they were elected or reelected. Most Democrats either championed the health care reforms or, in swing districts and states, talked about them as little as possible. On Election Day, Democrats won one additional Senate seat (counting two Independents who were expected to caucus with the Democrats) and eight House seats.

The 2014 Congressional Elections On one level, the 2014 midterm election was among the least exciting in recent years. Various Tea Party organizations remained active, but had limited success in electing their preferred candidates. No single overarching issue, such as fears of an economic collapse or the costs of a protracted war in Iraq, informed voters' choices or debates between candidates. Many stories described 2014 as "an election about nothing," meaning that the issues motivating voters varied somewhat from state to state.

National conditions in 2014 favored the Republican Party and its candidates. President Obama's approval rating had declined steadily since his reelection, enough so that he did not campaign with many Democratic candidates to avoid hurting their election efforts. These factors, combined with fears about Ebola and the ISIL terrorist organization, contributed to a small but discernible advantage for Republican candidates in most areas of the country.

Democrats were also disadvantaged because they had more Senate seats to defend: of the 35 seats being contested, Democrats controlled 21 and Republicans only 15. More important, many of the Democratic seats were in states where the party was weak. These conditions, coupled with the Republican Party's success in helping their incumbents and strong challengers to win primaries and caucuses, meant that, even before the general-election campaign began, Republicans stood an excellent chance to gain control of the Senate. Control of the House was not at stake, as the 2010 and 2012 elections had left relatively few vulnerable Democratic or Republican incumbents. In the end, the narrow Republican advantage translated into modest gains for the party in the House and larger gains in the Senate where Republicans gained nine seats and took control of the chamber with a 53 to 46 advantage over Democrats.

The 2016 elections: the nomination process

When Donald Trump entered the race for the Republican presidential nomination in the summer of 2015, many analysts (and some political scientists) argued that he would

Elections matter, especially when they determine who controls the congressional agenda. Republican gains in the Senate in 2014 led to Mitch McConnell (R-KY) taking over as Senate Majority Leader.

have little chance of winning. How could a twice-divorced political amateur, reality TV star with moderate positions on LGBTQ rights and a reputation for saying and doing controversial things, hope to win the nomination from a party dominated by social conservatives, much less a general election?

In retrospect, the conditions of the 2016 Republican nomination were ideal for a candidate like Trump. Seventeen candidates competed for the Republican nomination—many were current or former senators or governors, or had successful careers outside politics. However, none of the other candidates had the combination of organization, campaign funds, and voter appeal needed to claim the status of front-runner or gather endorsements from party leaders. Among these candidates, Trump stood out because of his preexisting high name recognition, his popularity among a large group of Republican primary voters, and his ability to largely self-fund a campaign. It is possible (but not certain) that Trump would have lost the nomination if party leaders had moved early in the process to unify behind one of the other challengers—but they did not. Trump went to the Republican Convention in July 2016 with solid support from Republican identifiers.

After the Republican Convention, there were clear signs that the general election was going to be an uphill fight. Trump had not built the large organization needed to run a national campaign or mobilize supports on Election Day. His campaign fund-raising lagged far behind Clinton's. Many Republican politicians (including many of Trump's former opponents) either skipped the Convention or came out against Trump. The central themes of the Convention, particularly Trump's vow to "make America great again," the focus on security, the depiction of Clinton and her fellow Democrats as corrupt and dangerous, and Trump's claim that "only I can fix" a troubled economy, nation, and world, were aimed at motivating Trump's core supporters rather than at converting wayward Republicans and independents.

On the Democratic side of the presidential race, many potential candidates decided against entering the race in 2016, believing that Hillary Clinton was likely to run, and would be the odds-on favorite if she did. Vice President Joe Biden considered running, but decided not to in the wake of his son's death from a brain tumor. Ultimately, the race boiled down to a contest between Clinton and Senator Bernie Sanders. At first, Sanders was not expected to present much of a challenge to Clinton, as he held relatively liberal positions on many issues and had spent most of his career in Congress as an Independent, officially joining the Democratic Party at the same time that he announced his presidential campaign. However, while Clinton's center-left positions on many issues were well-suited to a general-election campaign, Sanders's positions were attractive to the more liberal Democratic base and to young voters. After a long, drawn-out, sometimes heated contest, Clinton won the Democratic nomination because of steadfast support from minority Democrats, because she was seen as more electable by many voters, and because of overwhelming support from Democratic party leaders.

In congressional elections, attention focused largely on Senate races, as Democrats needed to gain only five Senate seats to take majority control of the chamber (four if a Democrat won the presidency). In a reverse of 2014, the fundamentals in 2016 favored Democrats, who had only 10 seats to defend. Democrats also had considerable success in convincing good candidates to enter these Senate races and discouraging competitive primaries. In contrast, 22 Republican senators were up for reelection (plus two open seats), about a third in states won by Obama in 2012. However, Republican control of the House was thought to be largely secure, given their substantial 32-seat majority and a relatively low number of electorally vulnerable members on both sides.

The 2016 general election

Trump's high point in the polls was immediately after the Republican Convention, when polling averages showed him drawing even with Clinton and perhaps even a

FIGURE 8.4

Groups and Votes in the 2016 Election

This figure shows variation in group support for Democrats and Republicans in the 2016 elections. How did the positions and issues emphasized by candidates in the two parties create or strengthen these differences?

Source: Exit poll data at www.elections.nytimes.com (accessed 11/6/14).

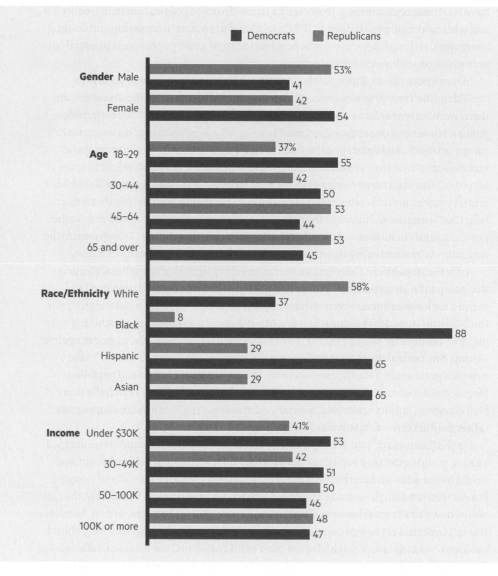

■ Democrats ■ Republicans

	Democrats	Republicans
Gender Male	41	53%
Female	54	42
Age 18–29	55	37%
30–44	50	42
45–64	44	53
65 and over	45	53
Race/Ethnicity White	37	58%
Black	88	8
Hispanic	65	29
Asian	65	29
Income Under $30K	53	41%
30–49K	51	42
50–100K	46	50
100K or more	47	48

little ahead. After that point in the campaign, these averages always showed Clinton in front, although the margin varied over the course of the campaign and some individual surveys produced results showing Trump with a narrow lead. Even so, the consistently high percentage of undecided voters, relatively large support for minor-party candidates, and Clinton's low popularity ratings suggested the race was far from over.

As we discussed earlier, there were clear differences between the presidential candidates on issues ranging from immigration reform to gun control. However, there was an even bigger difference in the candidates' diagnoses of what was needed to effect policy change in Washington. The message from Clinton's campaign was that partisan conflict reflects sincere differences of opinion, differences that often cannot be compromised. In contrast, Donald Trump argued that his management experience and deal-making talents gave him a unique ability to broker policy change, even given deep-set differences between Republicans and Democrats. Trump also referred to Clinton as "Crooked Hillary," arguing that because Clinton had worked as a senator and secretary of state, she was at least partly responsible for policy failures and gridlock in Washington. By mid-October Trump had lost significant support from independents and Republicans because of more than a dozen allegations of sexual harassment and assault, and because of his relatively poor performance during the three debates, where he seemed unprepared and unwilling to provide specifics of how he would implement his campaign promises. Trump also dropped in the polls because of many inflammatory statements, such as his refusal to commit to conceding the election if he lost.

In the last two weeks of the campaign, the polling gap between Trump and Clinton narrowed considerably, partly driven by a reopening of the FBI investigation into Clinton's use of a private e-mail server. (The investigation was closed on the weekend before the election.) While the Clinton campaign continued extensive campaign advertising, the Trump campaign ramped up spending in its own advertising effort. Days before the election, most campaign experts expected Clinton to win, based on her narrow lead and the Democrats' expected advantage in early voting and Election Day mobilization.

However, on Election Day, Trump benefitted from significantly higher than expected turnout in rural communities, which helped him win recent Democratic strongholds of Michigan, Pennsylvania, and Wisconsin. And while Clinton received strong support from African-American, Latino, and younger voters (see Figure 8.4), lower than expected turnout from these groups cost Clinton support in the crucial swing states of North Carolina and Florida, especially in light of Trump's strong support from rural, white, and older voters. The results also show a much larger gender gap than in previous elections—women, especially those with a college degree, were much more likely to vote for Clinton over Trump. Clinton won more votes overall, but Trump prevailed in the electoral college (see Figure 8.5). Notably, Trump won the election despite receiving fewer votes than losing 2012 Republican candidate Mitt Romney—however, Clinton lost even more votes compared to Barack Obama in 2012. In congressional races, Democrats gained only two Senate seats, and five House seats.

What drove the election results? One important factor was turnout, especially the apparent failure of the Democrats' get-out-the-vote drive compared to the much more modest Republican effort. Trump did not improve on Mitt Romney's poor showing with minority voters in 2012, but lower turnout from these groups compared to 2012 and 2008 was a key factor in Clinton's defeat. In addition, there were clear policy differences between Clinton and Trump supporters, especially on immigration reform and the economy. Vote decisions in 2016 were also highly correlated with evaluations of President Obama (people who were critical of Obama's presidency were more likely to vote for Trump), which makes sense given the importance of party identification in shaping presidential approval.

Donald Trump's victory in the 2016 presidential campaign was a shock to many, even his supporters.

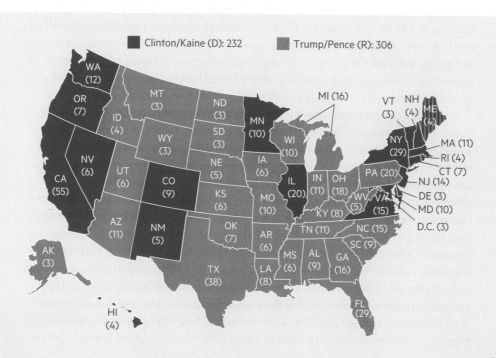

Clinton/Kaine (D): 232   Trump/Pence (R): 306

WA (12), OR (7), MT (3), ND (3), MN (10), MI (16), VT (3), NH (4), ME (4), ID (4), SD (3), WI (10), NY (29), MA (11), RI (4), WY (3), IA (6), PA (20), CT (7), NV (6), UT (6), NE (5), IL (20), IN (11), OH (18), NJ (14), DE (3), CA (55), CO (9), KS (6), MO (10), WV (5), VA (15), MD (10), AZ (11), NM (5), OK (7), KY (8), TN (11), NC (15), D.C. (3), AK (3), AR (6), SC (9), MS (6), AL (9), GA (16), TX (38), LA (8), FL (29), HI (4)

FIGURE 8.5

The 2016 Presidential Election: State-by-State

Note: Donald Trump won the electoral college with 304 votes to Hillary Clinton's 227. Seven electors voted for someone other than their party's candidate.

Though Hillary Clinton fell short in her effort to become America's first female president, she was able to win over 65 million votes—more than any candidate besides Barack Obama.

Consequences of the 2016 elections

The 2016 elections move America from divided government to unified Republican control of the presidency and Congress. At least for the next two years, this change should reduce the level of policy gridlock in Washington, and move policy in a firmly conservative direction. Thus, instead of focusing on inaction on issues such as gun control, the country may well watch as President Trump and the Republican Congress loosen federal restrictions on gun purchase and ownership, or shift the ideological composition of the Supreme Court for years to come.

Even so, it is important to remember that Trump and his fellow Republicans will face the same policy constraints that shaped policy under the Obama administration and previous presidents. In the first weeks after his election, for example, Trump moved away from proposing a full-scale repeal of Obamacare, offering to keep in place popular provisions such as allowing children to remain on their parents' health insurance until they are 26. And while Trump vowed to destroy ISIL, the reality is that this goal has been America's policy for several years, and it is not clear what new initiatives Trump's administration could implement to achieve this goal. Finally, as a political outsider with many advisers from outside Washington, Trump is at a disadvantage in understanding how the bureaucracy works and the limits to his ability to force compliance with his directives.

In sum, while the easy prediction following the 2016 elections was that everything about American politics is about to change, the reality is that there are many constraints on the policy process, from public opinion to the limited amount of time and energy that presidents and their advisers have to formulate new policy proposals. The 2016 elections have put many policy questions back into play, and revealed ideological splits in both parties. Over the next four years (two until the 2018 midterm elections), we will watch how President Trump and the Republican Congress determine their agenda, arrive at compromises, and work to enact their policy proposals—working inside the rules and institutions that define American politics, and acting in light of the fundamental divisions in American society over the size and scope of the federal government.

Conclusion

Candidates in American national elections compete for different offices using a variety of rules that determine who can run for office, who can vote, and how ballots are counted and winners determined. Election outcomes are shaped by who runs for office and how they campaign, who decides to vote, and how they decide whom to support, but also by the rules that govern electoral competition. By taking these factors into account, we can explain why Donald Trump defeated Hillary Clinton in 2016—or why these candidates won their party's nominations rather than someone else.

It is easy to complain about American elections. Citizens are not experts about public policy. They often know little about the candidates running for office. Candidates sensationalize, attack, and dissemble rather than giving details about what they would do if elected. Even so, there are clear, systematic differences between Democratic and Republican candidates that translate into different government policies depending on who holds office. It matters that Trump was elected in 2016 and Republicans held onto control of the House and the Senate. Moreover, the criteria that average Americans use to make voting decisions reflect these differences. In addition, many examples of seemingly strange behavior in American elections make more sense once you examine them. It is understandable that so few Americans are issue voters and that many people decide to not vote. It also makes sense that candidates seeking the attention of distracted voters tend to emphasize sensationalism over sober discussion of policies, or that attack ads often succeed. The outcome of every election is the result of all these individual-level choices added together. In that sense, election outcomes reflect the preferences of the American people.

STUDY GUIDE

How do American elections work?

Present the major rules and procedures of American elections. (Pages 218–227)

Summary

Elections in America generally have two steps. Primary elections select candidates for each party, and general elections determine who wins the office. Some of the rules for presidential elections differ from those of other elections; notably, the Electoral College system determines the winner of the general election.

Key terms

incumbent (p. 218)
open primary (p. 219)
semi-closed primary (p. 219)
closed primary (p. 219)
general election (p. 219)
plurality voting (p. 220)
majority voting (p. 220)

runoff election (p. 220)
primary (p. 221)
caucus (p. 221)
proportional allocation (p. 221)
winner-take-all (p. 221)
electoral college (p. 223)

Practice Quiz Questions

1. **Runoff elections occur only in states that use _____.**
   a. majority voting
   b. primary elections
   c. plurality voting
   d. absentee ballots
   e. proportional allocation

2. **The winner-take-all method of allocating most states' electoral votes results in candidates focusing on _____ states and _____ states.**
   a. low-population; safe
   b. high-population; safe
   c. low-population; swing
   d. high-population; swing
   e. safe; swing

Electoral campaigns

Describe the features, strategies, and funding of campaigns for federal office. (Pages 227–237)

Summary

Party organizations and candidates begin preparing for the next election the day after the last election ends. They focus on fund-raising and determining which races are likely to be competitive. Incumbents work throughout the election cycle to maintain their good standing among the voters and secure their reelection bids. During a campaign, candidates work hard, particularly through the use of advertisements, to increase their name recognition and mobilize their supporters.

Key terms

election cycle (p. 227)
open seat (p. 228)
GOTV ("get out the vote") or the ground game (p. 230)

Federal Election Commission (p. 233)
hard money (p. 233)
soft money (p. 233)

Practice Quiz Questions

3. **An open-seat election is one where _____.**
   a. there is no challenger in the race
   b. there is no incumbent in the race
   c. an incumbent loses his/her seat due to redistricting
   d. an incumbent faces a challenger in his/her own primary
   e. an incumbent faces a challenger in the general election

4. **What effect does fund-raising have for incumbents?**
   a. It ensures the potential for an aggressive campaign, but it has no effect on opposition.
   b. It ensures the potential for an aggressive campaign, and it deters opposition.
   c. It ensures the potential for an aggressive campaign, and it encourages opposition.
   d. It has no effect on the potential for an aggressive campaign, but it does deter opposition.
   e. It has no effect on the potential for an aggressive campaign, nor does it deter opposition.

5. **"GOTV" and "ground game" refer to a candidate's attempts to _____.**
   a. boost name recognition
   b. mobilize supporters
   c. increase fund-raising
   d. deter opposition
   e. win endorsements

6. **Research shows that modern campaign ads are likely to _____.**
   a. change voters' minds
   b. feature speeches by the candidate
   c. have beneficial effects, such as informing voters

d. run several minutes in length

e. increase turnout

7. What is soft money?

a. money that can be given directly to a candidate

b. money that is given by members of the opposing party

c. money that can be spent to mobilize voters for a specific candidate

d. money that candidates spend to boost the party's reputation

e. money that is not tied to a specific candidate

How do voters decide?

Explain the key factors that influence voters' choices.
(Pages 237–240)

Summary

Despite the fact that politics is everywhere, ordinary voters don't pay much attention to politics. Turnout rates are modest, and people know relatively little about the candidates and their positions. While some voters are highly interested in politics and collect all the information they can about the candidates, most voters make their decision based on voting cues.

Key terms

paradox of voting (p. 238)

voting cues (p. 239)

coattails (p. 239)

split ticket (p. 239)

straight ticket (p. 239)

Practice Quiz Questions

8. What is the paradox of voting?

a. Voting is costly, and the chances of affecting the election outcome are small.

b. Voting is costly, and approval for government is high.

c. Voting is easy, and the chances of affecting the election outcome are large.

d. Voting is easy, but informing yourself about the candidates takes time.

e. Approval for government is low, but voter turnout rates are high.

9. Voters who rely on voting cues to determine their voting choice are _____.

a. likely to cast a reasonable vote, regardless of their information level

b. unlikely to cast a reasonable vote, regardless of their information level

c. likely to cast a reasonable vote, and more so if they are informed

d. unlikely to cast a reasonable vote, and less so if they are informed

e. neither more nor less likely to cast a reasonable vote than voters who ignore cues

10. Weak coattails and split tickets serve as indicators that _____.

a. most voters don't know anything about the candidates

b. most elections are determined by local issues

c. most elections are determined by national issues

d. most voters use political parties as their dominant voting cue

e. most voters use incumbency as their dominant voting cue

Understanding the 2016 election

Analyze the issues and outcomes in the 2016 election.
(Pages 241–246)

Summary

The 2016 elections were a significant victory for Republicans: they held on to majorities in the House and Senate, and the presidential election was won by the Republican candidate, Donald Trump. These Republican victories created unified government in Washington for the first time since 2009, although the expectation that Republicans would be able to enact significant policy changes must be tempered by the reality of significant differences among Republican elected officials on many issues, disagreements between Republican members of Congress and their new president, and the fact that Democratic senators can still filibuster Republican initiatives.

Practice Quiz Questions

11. What is the most accurate statement about the role of economic conditions in the 2016 election?

a. Looking across the entire nation, economic uncertainty shifted votes to Trump.

b. The Trump campaign's mobilization efforts offset the loss of support from a weak economy.

c. Hillary Clinton's campaign blamed President Obama for slow economic growth.

d. Economic conditions did not matter because most Americans based their vote on other issues.

e. The Clinton campaign convinced voters that Republican Senate leaders were to blame for the poor economy.

12. How did the electoral map favor Democratic Senate candidates in 2016?

a. Democratic efforts at redistricting gave them a sharp advantage in Senate contests.

b. Economic growth was uneven across the states, particularly in Senate seats controlled by the Democrats.

c. Republicans had to defend a disproportionate number of Senate seats, and many of these seats were in states where Democrats outnumbered Republicans.

d. Independent candidates drew votes away from Republican candidates.

e. Republican candidates were more likely to lose in states where a majority of voters supported Donald Trump.

13. **Which of the following is the most important factor in explaining Donald Trump's victory over Hillary Clinton in the 2016 election?**

    a. The fact that more Americans are Republicans than Democrats

    b. Perceptions of Trump as trustworthy and honest

    c. Reduced turnout by minority groups that supported Democrats in 2008 and 2012

    d. Widespread dislike of Barack Obama

    e. Decisions by President Obama and Senator Bernie Sanders to not campaign for Clinton

Suggested Reading

Abramson, Paul, John Aldrich, and David Rohde. *Change and Continuity in the 2012 and 2014 Elections.* Washington, DC: CQ Press, 2015.

Bartels, Larry M., and Christopher H. Achen. *Democracy for Realists: Why Elections Do Not Produce Responsive Government.* Princeton, NJ: Princeton University Press, 2016.

Cramer, Richard Ben. *What It Takes: The Way to the White House.* New York: Vintage Books, 1993.

Fiorina, Morris P. *Retrospective Voting in American National Elections.* New Haven, CT: Yale University Press, 1981.

Grimmer, Justin, Sean J. Westwood, and Solomon Messing. *The Impression of Influence: Legislator Communication, Representation, and Democratic Accountability.* Princeton, NJ: Princeton University Press, 2015.

Halperin, Mark, and John Heilemann. *Double Down: Game Change 2012.* New York; Penguin Books, 2013.

Key, V. O. *The Responsible Electorate.* New York: Vintage Books, 1966.

Popkin, Samuel. *The Reasoning Voter.* Chicago: University of Chicago Press, 1991.

Sides, John, and Lynn Vavreck. *The Gamble: Choice and Chance in the 2012 Presidential Election.* Princeton, NJ: Princeton University Press, 2013.

9

Interest Groups

Do interest groups serve the needs of the many, or the privileged few?

There are nearly 20 million college students in America today. Many of these students (or their parents) take on large student loans to fund their education. Over the last 20 years, there have been several proposals to change how these loans are made. These policy suggestions range from a system whereby banks and other financial institutions provide the money to a plan that has the federal government making the loans directly to students and their parents. Either of these proposals would reduce borrowing costs and free up billions of dollars for Pell grants and other programs benefiting college students.

At first glance, reducing the cost of student loans would be an easy sell—who would oppose making college more affordable? The answer is the companies and institutions that make money originating and managing these loans—financial institutions such as Sallie Mae, Citibank, and others. If the country were to move to direct loans, these financial institutions would lose a lucrative source of income. To avert this kind of legislation, these institutions spent millions on lobbyists to make their case before the public and Congress, emphasizing that a move to direct loans would put thousands of their employees out of work (and reminding politicians that many of those who work for the financial institutions live and work in political swing states like Florida).

For most Americans, this story looks all too common: organized, well-funded groups lobbying against changes that would benefit broader segments of the population. How can individuals have a voice in the policy process when they are fighting against organizations that have millions of dollars and extensive connections on their side? Even if individuals try to form new groups to advance their policy goals, their battle against well-entrenched and well-funded groups does not seem like a fair fight. Surprisingly, the case of student loans is one where David appears to have beaten Goliath. Despite intense, well-funded lobbying against direct loans, legislation implementing this change was enacted in 2010—meaning that you and your parents are now able to get lower-interest loans directly from the federal government. Placed against concerns about

★

CHAPTER GOALS

Define *interest groups* and describe the characteristics of different types of groups.
pages 252–260

Explore the ways interest groups try to influence government policies.
pages 260–269

Evaluate interest group influence.
pages 269–272

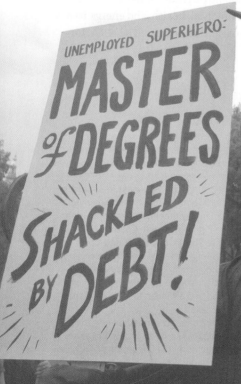

📷

The debate over federal direct student loans pitted well-funded banks and other financial institutions against millions of college students and their parents. Did the banks' ability to lobby members of Congress and bureaucrats translate into a policy victory?

interest group power, this example only deepens the mystery: if lobbying always works, how did the side with all the lobbyists lose the fight over direct loans?

This chapter surveys the wide range of interest groups in American politics—from large, powerful groups such as the National Rifle Association (NRA) to small organizations that lobby on issues that concern only a few Americans. Our aim is to get to the bottom of examples like student loan reform and the NRA's apparent control over gun control to understand what they really tell us about the power of interest groups in American politics. How do interest groups work? How often do they get what they want, and where does their influence come from? Do lobbying victories always go to the side with the most money?

★

DEFINE *INTEREST GROUPS* AND DESCRIBE THE CHARACTERISTICS OF DIFFERENT TYPES OF GROUPS

interest group
An organization of people who share common political interests and aim to influence public policy by electioneering and lobbying.

lobbying
Efforts to influence public policy through contact with public officials on behalf of an interest group.

What are interest groups?

Interest groups are organizations that seek to influence government policy by helping to elect candidates who support the organizations' policy goals and by **lobbying** elected officials and bureaucrats. Lobbying involves persuasion—using reports, protests, informal meetings, or other techniques to convince an elected official or bureaucrat to help enact a law, craft a regulation, or do something else that a group wants. The members of an interest group can be individual citizens, local governments, businesses, foundations or nonprofit organizations, churches, or virtually any other entity. An interest group's employees or members may lobby on the group's behalf, or a group may hire a lobbyist or lobbying firm to do the work for it. Nuts & Bolts 9.1 gives some examples of the types of interest groups found in contemporary American politics.

Sometimes interest groups are primarily political organizations. One such group is Public Citizen, which conducts research projects, lobbies legislators and bureaucrats, and tries to rally public opinion on a range of environmental, health, and energy issues. In some cases, lobbying is only one part of what an organization does. The NRA, for

NUTS & BOLTS 9.1

Types of Interest Groups

Scholars often divide interest groups into categories based on who their members are or the number or kinds of things they lobby for.

- **Businesses** are for-profit enterprises that aim to influence policy in ways that will increase profits or satisfy other goals. Many corporations such as Google, Exxon, Boeing, Facebook, Citibank, and Sallie Mae have lobbying operations that petition government for contracts or favorable regulations of their firm or industry.
- **Trade or peak associations** are groups of businesses (often in the same industry) that band together to lobby for policies that benefit all of them.
- **Professional associations** represent individuals who have a common interest such as a profession.
- **Labor organizations** lobby for regulations that make it easy for workers to form labor unions, as well as for a range of other policies. The largest of these is the American Federation of Labor and Congress of Industrial Organizations (AFL-CIO).

- **Citizen groups** range from those with mass membership (such as the Sierra Club) to those that have no members but claim to speak for large segments of the population. One such group is the Family Research Council (FRC), which describes itself as "promoting the Judeo-Christian worldview as the basis for a just, free, and stable society." FRC Action (the lobbying arm of the organization) promotes a range of policies, from legislation that defines marriage as between a man and a woman to legislation that would eliminate estate taxes.
- **Institutional interest groups** are formed by nonprofits such as universities, think tanks, or museums. For example, the Committee on Institutional Cooperation (CIC) is a group of universities including the Big 10 in the Midwest that prepares research that helps individual universities make the case for continued federal support.

example, endorses candidates, contributes to campaigns, and lobbies elected officials, but it also runs gun safety classes, holds competitions, and sells hardware to its members. In other cases, interest group activity is almost hidden within an organization. For example, most drivers know that the American Automobile Association (AAA) provides emergency roadside service and maps, but many people are not aware that AAA is also an interest group that lobbies for policies such as limiting new drivers to daylight-only hours.

As these descriptions suggest, interest groups and lobbying are ubiquitous in American politics. Many organizations have lobbying operations or hire lobbyists to work on their behalf. You may think that you don't belong to a group that lobbies the federal government, but the odds are that you do.

Organizational structures

Interest groups differ in how they are organized—whether the group is one body or made up of many smaller, local groups. How a group is organized makes a difference for the kinds of lobbying tactics it can use, as well as how decisions are made about what to lobby for.

Centralized Groups or Confederations There are two main models of interest group structure. Most large, well-known organizations are centralized groups: two examples are the NRA and the American Association of Retired Persons (AARP). National organizations like these typically have headquarters in Washington, D.C., operate field offices in large state capitals, and have members nationwide. Each organization's leadership is located in its headquarters, and these leaders determine the group's lobbying goals and tactics. The other structural model is a confederation, which comprises largely independent, local organizations. For example, the National Independent Automobile Dealers Association (NIADA) encompasses 50 state-level organizations that provide membership benefits to car dealers who join and that also raise much of the money that NIADA contributes to political candidates (several million dollars in recent elections).

Both organizational structures have advantages and disadvantages. A centralized organization controls all the group's resources and can deploy them efficiently, but it can be challenging for these groups to find out what their members want. In contrast, because confederations maintain independent chapters at the state and local levels, their national headquarters can easily learn what the members want simply by contacting the local groups. But this strength is related to a weakness: because state and local chapters mostly function independently of the national headquarters, confederated groups often experience conflict, as different local chapters disagree over what to lobby for and which candidates to support.

Mass Associations or Peak Associations Interest groups can also be distinguished according to the size of their membership and the members' role in the group's activities. Some are mass associations with many dues-paying members. One example is the Sierra Club, which has over 2 million members who pay annual dues of about $30 each. Besides keeping its members informed about the implementation of environmental policy in Washington, D.C., the Sierra Club endorses judicial nominees and candidates for elected positions, files lawsuits to increase environmental protection on government projects, and works with members of Congress to develop legislative proposals. The group's members elect the organization's board of directors.

centralized groups
Interest groups that have a headquarters, usually in Washington, D.C., as well as members and field offices throughout the country. In general, these groups' lobbying decisions are made at headquarters by the group leaders.

confederations
Interest groups made up of several independent, local organizations that provide much of their funding and hold most of the power.

mass associations
Interest groups that have a large number of dues-paying individuals as members.

Yet not all mass associations give members a say in selecting their leaders or determining their mission. For example, the AARP claims to lobby for policies its members favor, but members actually have no control over which legislative causes the group chooses. Moreover, the AARP does not poll members to determine its issue positions, nor do members pick AARP leadership.

Peak associations have a different type of membership,[1] exemplified by the Business-Industry Political Action Committee (BIPAC). This association of several hundred businesses and trade associations aims to elect "pro-business individuals" to Congress.[2] Individuals cannot join peak associations—they may work for member companies or organizations, but they cannot become dues-paying members on their own. The umbrella organization that led efforts to enact direct funding for student loans, the Student Aid Alliance, was another such peak association.

Membership: benefits and incentives

Attracting members is important for an interest group's success. Society is full of groups of like-minded people (such as college students) who do not organize to lobby or who choose to enjoy the benefits of organizations without participating. Therefore, most organizations develop mechanisms to promote participation. These mechanisms fall into three categories: benefits from participation, coercion, and selective incentives.

Studies of political parties and interest groups find that some individuals volunteer out of a sense of duty or because they enjoy working together toward a common goal. These benefits of participation are called either **solidary benefits**, which come from working with like-minded people, or **purposive benefits**, which come from working to achieve a desired policy goal.[3] When these benefits are not enough to prompt participation, groups try other measures to promote active membership.

A second mechanism is **coercion**, or required participation. Consider labor unions. They provide public goods to workers by negotiating with management on behalf of worker-members over pay issues and work requirements. In many cases, worker-members have to join the union: union shop laws require them to pay union dues as a condition of their employment.

Finally, **selective incentives** (also called material incentives) are benefits given only to the members of a given interest group. Thus, for example, AAA members can call AAA at any time for emergency service when they have car trouble. AAA also

peak associations
Interest groups whose members are businesses or other organizations rather than individuals.

solidary benefits
Satisfaction derived from the experience of working with like-minded people, even if the group's efforts do not achieve the desired impact.

purposive benefits
Satisfaction derived from the experience of working toward a desired policy goal, even if the goal is not achieved.

coercion
A method of eliminating nonparticipation or free riding by potential group members by requiring participation, as in many labor unions.

selective incentives
Benefits that can motivate participation in a group effort because they are available only to those who participate, such as member services offered by interest groups.

AAA (formerly the Automobile Association of America) is a well-known provider of emergency road service, yet few people are aware of its role as an interest group that lobbies for a wide range of policy changes and builds awareness of key transportation issues. #AAA

DUI	
IT COSTS MORE THAN YOU THINK!	
ESTIMATED COSTS FOR A FIRST DUI CONVICTION:	
Fine (minimum)	$390
Penalties	$1,245
Vehicle Tow/Storage	$350
Alcohol Education Class	$575
Victim Restitution Fund	$140
DMV License Re-Issue	$125
Booking	$170
Insurance Increase	$10,154
Legal Fees	$2,500
TOTAL COST	**$15,649**

provides its members with annotated maps and travel guides, discounts at hotels and restaurants, and other benefits. These services mask the interest group role of AAA. For example, its Foundation for Traffic Safety delivers research reports to legislators on topics ranging from lowering the blood alcohol level threshold that legally defines drunk driving to increasing the restrictions on driving by senior citizens.[4] It's unlikely that many AAA members—who join for the selective incentives—are aware of the organization's lobbying efforts. The inducements drive membership, which funds the organization's lobbying operation.

Resources

The resources that interest groups use to support their lobbying efforts are people (the members), money, and expertise. Although we examine interest group strategies in a later section, here we emphasize that a group's resources influence its available lobbying strategies. Some groups have sufficient funding and staff to pursue a wide range of strategies, while smaller groups with fewer resources have only a few lobbying options.

A crucial resource for most interest groups is the membership. Group members can write to or meet with elected officials, travel to Washington for demonstrations, and even offer expertise or advice to the group's leaders. When the "members" of a group are corporations, as is the case with trade associations, CEOs and other corporate staff can help with the group's lobbying efforts.

Money is another important resource. Virtually everything interest groups do, from meeting with elected officials to fighting for what they want in court, can be purchased as services. Money can also go toward campaign contributions or developing and running campaign ads. And, of course, money is necessary to fund interest groups' everyday operations. Well-funded interest groups and firms have a considerable advantage in the lobbying process. If they need an expert, a lobbyist, or a lawyer, they can hire one, or open a Washington office to increase contacts with legislators and bureaucrats. Also, they can pay for campaign ads and make contributions to candidates and parties, while groups with less cash cannot use these strategies. Smaller firms might join a trade association to lobby for policies that help all of the association's members.

Expertise is a third type of group resource. It takes many forms. Some lobbying firms (especially those that employ former members of Congress or congressional staff) have inside information on the kinds of policies that might be enacted in the House or Senate. Interest groups with dues-paying members (such as the AARP) can poll their membership to find out what they would like government to do. Groups can also employ staff (or can hire experts) to conduct research or develop policy proposals. A firm's in-house lobbyists can provide information about how a change in government policy will affect the firm's profits and employment. All of this information can be deployed to persuade elected officials or bureaucrats about the merits of a group's or a firm's demands (as well as the political consequences of inaction) and offer ready-made solutions to the problems the group has identified.

Staff

Interest group staff fall into two categories: experts on the group's main policy areas, and people with useful government connections and knowledge of procedures. The first group includes scientists, engineers, and others with advanced degrees; the second primarily comprises people who have worked inside government as elected officials, bureaucrats, or legislative staff.[5] Sometimes these former members of

revolving door
The movement of individuals from
government positions to jobs with
interest groups or lobbying firms, and
vice versa.

government are also policy experts, but their unique contribution is their knowledge of how government works and their already-existing relationships with officeholders and other former coworkers in government.

The practice of transitioning from government positions to working for interest groups or lobbying firms, or transitioning from lobbyist to officeholder, is often called the **revolving door**.[6] For example, as of 2016, over half of the members of Congress who retired at the end of the 113th Congress had moved to lobbying jobs.[7] The percentages are similar for congressional staff and bureaucrats. The concern is that past government employees might capitalize on personal ties with their former colleagues—or that someone working in government may favor a corporation that might hire them as a lobbyist in the future. These concerns have led to proposals to ban former elected officials, staff, and bureaucrats from working as lobbyists for some time period after they have left government service—and banning former lobbyists named to government positions from administering programs that they previously lobbied for.

The business of lobbying

Interest group lobbying is heavily regulated.[8] Such firms must file annual reports identifying their clients and specifying how much each client paid. Similarly, interest groups and corporations must file reports that list staff members who spent more than 20 percent of their time lobbying Congress and that detail expenditures to lobbying firms. Data from these sources and others offer insight into the extent of lobbying in American politics.

Today lobbying involves billions of dollars a year. Figure 9.1 (top) presents annual lobbying expenditures for 2000 through 2015. As the figure shows, a total of $3.2 billion was spent on lobbying in 2015. The amount spent as well as the number of groups lobbying government has increased significantly over the last decade, although it has declined slightly in the last few years.

Why are there so many interest groups and registered lobbyists, and why are their numbers increasing? Figure 9.1 (bottom) suggests that this proliferation is related to the large size and widespread influence of the federal government. Corporations lobby because they have a stake in what the government does: they want their company to get a government contract; they want a new regulation to favor their business sector. Individuals lobby to limit what citizens can do or relax restrictions on citizens' behavior—or to change corporate behavior. Simply put, the federal government does so many things and spends so much money that many individuals, organizations, and corporations have strong incentives for lobbying.[9] Moreover, as groups form on one side of a policy question and start to lobby, people who oppose them may form their own interest groups and start lobbying as well, either separately or together.[10]

The expenditures on lobbying pay for many things. For example, at the same time that engineers at the Lockheed Martin Corporation worked to build the new F-35 fighter-attack plane for the military, Lockheed's lobbyists were working to ensure that the program retained its government funding and Lockheed had government approval for exporting the plane to other countries. These meetings involved members of Congress, congressional staff, senior members of President George W. Bush's (and later President Obama's) staff, and the leaders of labor unions whose members worked for Lockheed.[11] Lockheed also ran ads in newspapers in Washington, D.C., promoting its new warplane. Thus, to support its goal of F-35 sales, Lockheed paid the salaries of its employees who planned and executed the lobbying effort, paid for outside lobbyists and their meetings on Capitol Hill, and spent additional money on broader publicity efforts.

DID YOU KNOW?

427

**former members of Congress were
registered lobbyists as of 2015.**

Source: Opensecrets.org

FIGURE
9.1

Growth in Spending on Lobbying and Total Federal Spending, 2000–2015

These data show that in recent years interest groups have spent several billion dollars lobbying the federal government. Does this amount seem surprisingly large or surprisingly small, given what lobbyists do and given the total federal outlays of money?

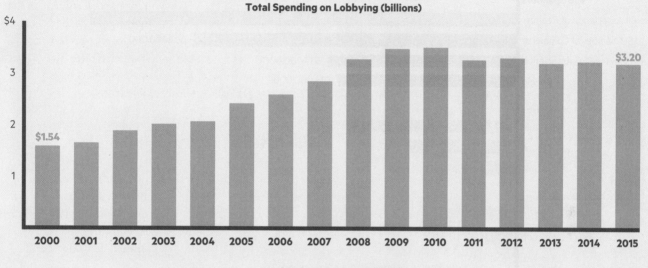

Total Spending on Lobbying (billions)

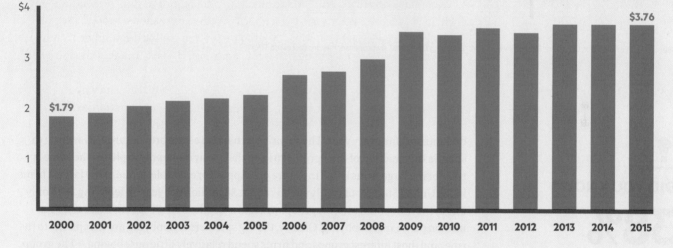

Total Federal Outlays (trillions)

Sources: Data available at Center for Responsive Politics, "Lobbying Database," www.opensecrets.org (accessed 2/7/16); Office of Management and Budget, Table 1.1, www.whitehouse.gov/omb/budget/historicals (accessed 2/1/16).

Figure 9.2 shows lobbying expenditures for several different firms and associations during the 2015–2016 election cycle. Members of the first group—three associations and one company—were the highest spenders on lobbying during this time. For each one, it's not hard to imagine why they devote so much efforts to lobbying: Realtors, for example, might be concerned about maintaining government policies that make it almost essential to hire a Realtor to help buy or sell a home. Even so, the fact that the National Association of Realtors spends only about $83 million on lobbying is something of a surprise. After all, over a million people work in real estate, generating billions of

> **If you can't eat their food, drink their booze, take their money and then vote against them, you've got no business being up here.**
>
> —**Jessie Unruh,** California state legislator

FIGURE 9.2

Variation in Lobbying Expenditures

Lobbying expenditures vary widely. Some influential groups (such as the U.S. Chamber of Commerce) spend hundreds of millions of dollars a year, but many other influential groups (such as the NARAL and the Family Research Council) spend relatively little. How can groups have influence over government policy despite spending almost nothing on lobbying?

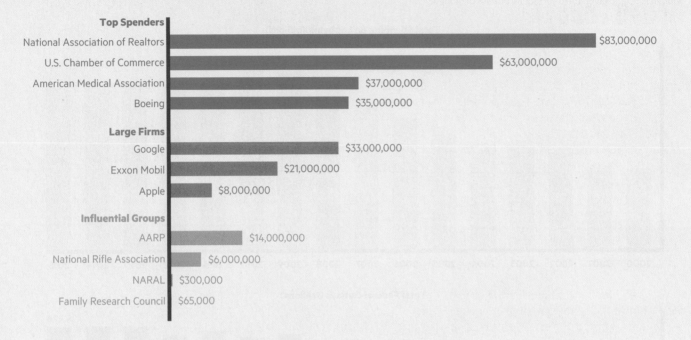

Top Spenders
- National Association of Realtors — $83,000,000
- U.S. Chamber of Commerce — $63,000,000
- American Medical Association — $37,000,000
- Boeing — $35,000,000

Large Firms
- Google — $33,000,000
- Exxon Mobil — $21,000,000
- Apple — $8,000,000

Influential Groups
- AARP — $14,000,000
- National Rifle Association — $6,000,000
- NARAL — $300,000
- Family Research Council — $65,000

Sources: Data available at Center for Responsive Politics, "Lobbying Database," www.opensecrets.org (accessed 11/6/16).

DID YOU KNOW?

38%

The percentage of total lobbying expenditures made by the top 100 interest groups

Source: Opensecrets.org

trade association
An interest group composed of companies in the same business or industry (the same "trade") that lobbies for policies that benefit members of the group.

dollars in profits every year. The surprise is that real estate brokers are only willing to spend a tiny fraction of their profits to keep their near monopoly in place. The same is true for the large firms listed in Figure 9.2. Apple, for example, is one of the largest firms in the United States, but it only spends about $8 million per year on lobbying. And only one of the influential interest groups in Figure 9.2 (the AARP) spends more than $10 million per year on lobbying. Clearly, the big spenders on lobbying are exceptions to the rule, and most interest groups and firms spend relatively little on lobbying.[12] The group that sends a turkey to the White House for a ceremonial pardon every year at Thanksgiving, the National Turkey Federation, spends less than a hundred thousand dollars every year to lobby the federal government on a relatively small range of issues. Many other groups spend even less, barely scraping together enough cash to send someone to plead their case in Washington. In fact, a few groups account for a substantial fraction of total lobbying expenditures.

Other companies lobby through their membership in **trade associations**. Consider the National Beer Wholesalers Association (NBWA), a nationwide group of local businesses that buy beer from brewers and resell it to stores and restaurants. NBWA's principal lobbying goal is to ensure that laws remain in place requiring intermediaries between beer producers and the stores, bars, and restaurants that sell beer to consumers. If the rules change to allow beer producers to deal with the end sellers directly, then NBWA's members would likely lose business.

Restrictions on Interest Group Lobbying

Under current congressional rules, members of Congress and their staffs are severely limited in the size of gifts they can receive from lobbyists. Similar restrictions had existed for decades but were tightened in the mid-2000s after it was revealed that former congressional staffer-turned-lobbyist Jack Abramoff had used "golf junkets, free meals at the restaurant he owned, seats at sporting events, and, in some cases, old-fashioned cash" to lobby members of Congress.[a] The current restrictions limit members and their staffs to accepting gifts only if they are valued at less than $50—moreover, the total worth of the gifts that any lobbyist can give to a particular member of Congress or staffer is limited to $100 per year. Are these restrictions fair? Do they help or hurt the political process?

When scandals surrounding Jack Abramoff came to light in 2005, many Americans considered him a typical lobbyist. Abramoff's actions were illegal, but the question remains: Are his tactics common in Washington, or was he a rare exception?

Keep the rules, and maybe tighten them.

Supporting this option seems like a no-brainer. These regulations are based on a sensible intuition that laws are needed to prevent well-funded, unscrupulous lobbyists from offering inducements to members of Congress and their staffs in return for policy change. Simply put, groups that can send people to Washington to wine and dine members of Congress, congressional staff, and bureaucrats might gain a significant advantage over those who are unable to do so. Even if a fancy lunch doesn't buy a legislator's vote, it might help with access—that is, give the group a chance to make their arguments and perhaps change some minds. In this way, rules that allow even small gifts create an advantage for some interest groups (those that can open a Washington office or hire lobbyists) and a disadvantage for others. As a result, many reform proposals would go further, preventing lobbyists from giving anything to a member of Congress, legislative staffer, or bureaucrat—even a cup of coffee.

Relax the rules (a little).

Some argue that worries about interest group influence seem a little overstated. Suppose an interest group takes some congressional staff out to lunch or invites them to an evening reception. Nice treatment might increase the chances that the staffers would meet with the group's lobbyists or look at the group's proposals. But congressional staff and the legislators they work for are going to support a group's proposals only if they help the member's constituents or if they move policy in a way the member favors, not just because of an interest group's free lunch. Also, the targets of lobbying know what's going on—they're not going to think a lobbyist is their new friend and ally just because of a small gift.

Finally, there are downsides to tight controls on these gifts and perks. The current rules on lobbyists' gifts create a lot of paperwork for members and their staffs, who have to file reports on just about anything they receive from a lobbyist, even if that individual is a former colleague, neighbor, or friend. The rules are also extremely complicated—for example, legislators are allowed to eat the hors d'oeuvres provided at a reception, but they cannot sit down to a full meal without violating the gift restrictions. The disclosure requirements are also a burden to smaller interest groups and firms, which have to document everything they do on complex forms. As a result, members of Congress, their staff, interest groups, and lobbying firms spend considerable time and effort on documenting small gifts that are unlikely to have any effect on policy outcomes.

take a stand

1. To what extent do you think current congressional rules limiting the size of gifts that members of Congress and their staffers can receive from lobbyists have curbed illegal behavior by interest groups?

2. Are these rules aimed at exceptional cases or average interest groups?

Although the amount of money spent on lobbying by interest groups may seem like a lot (and often leads to calls for restrictions on lobbying, as discussed in the Take a Stand feature), it is small compared with how much is at stake.[13] The federal government now spends more than $3 trillion every year. In recent years, spending by interest groups and by the lobbying arms of organizations and corporations has totaled $3 billion every year. That's a lot of money, but it's still only about 0.1 percent of total federal spending. This difference raises a critical question: If interest groups could control policy choices by spending money on lobbying, why aren't they spending more? We will address this question throughout the remainder of this chapter, focusing on how groups lobby and the limits of their influence over government policy.

"Why Should I Care?"

When you think of a lobbyist, don't imagine a guy in an expensive suit carrying a briefcase of cash (or a campaign contribution). More often, people become lobbyists because they believe in the goals of the group they represent. And they generally don't wear expensive suits. Understanding who lobbyists really are, and what they really do, is key to evaluating whether or not they have too much influence in American politics.

★

EXPLORE THE WAYS INTEREST GROUPS TRY TO INFLUENCE GOVERNMENT POLICIES

inside strategies
The tactics employed within Washington, D.C., by interest groups seeking to achieve their policy goals.

outside strategies
The tactics employed outside Washington, D.C., by interest groups seeking to achieve their policy goals.

direct lobbying
Attempts by interest group staff to influence policy by speaking with elected officials or bureaucrats.

Interest group strategies

Once a group has organized and determined its goals, the next step is to decide how to lobby. There are two types of possible tactics: **inside strategies**, which are actions taken in Washington, D.C., and **outside strategies**, which are actions taken outside of Washington, D.C.[14] (See How It Works: Lobbying the Federal Government.)

Inside strategies

Inside strategies involve contact with elected officials or bureaucrats. Thus, inside strategies require a group to establish an office in Washington or hire a lobbying firm to act on its behalf.

Direct Lobbying When interest group staff meet with officeholders or bureaucrats, they plead their case through **direct lobbying**, asking government officials to change policy in line with the group's goals.[15] Direct lobbying is generally aimed at officials and bureaucrats who are sympathetic to the group's goals.[16] In these efforts, interest groups and their representatives help like-minded legislators to secure policy changes that they both want. The interest groups' help can range from sharing information about the proposed changes, to providing lists of legislators who might be persuaded to support the group's goals, to drafting legislative proposals or regulations.

Interest groups also contact legislators who disagree with their goals, as well as fence-sitters (legislators who are not supporters or opponents), with the goal of converting them to supporters. These efforts are less extensive than the lobbying of supporters, because opponents are unlikely to change their minds unless a group can provide new information that causes them to rethink their position.

As these descriptions indicate, interest groups place a high priority on maintaining access to their lobbying targets and being able to present their arguments, regardless of whether they expect to get what they want. Of course, interest groups want to achieve their policy goals, but access is the first step that makes persuasion possible. Therefore, many interest groups try to keep their efforts low-key, providing information to friends and opponents alike, avoiding threats or harsh words, in the hope that they will leave a favorable impression and be able to gain access the next time they want to lobby these opponents. After all, people who oppose a group's current priorities one day may agree with them on some future issue.

In their efforts at direct lobbying, interest groups contact elected officials, members of the president's staff, and bureaucrats in the executive branch. They seek this wide range of contacts because different officials play distinct roles in the policy-making process and thus have various types of influence. Members of Congress shape legislation and budgets, members of the president's staff influence the formation of new policies and obtain presidential consent for new laws, and executive branch bureaucrats change the ways regulations are written and policies are implemented.

Drafting Legislation and Regulations Interest groups sometimes draft legislative proposals and regulations, which they deliver to legislators and bureaucrats as part of their lobbying efforts.[17] In the case of direct student loans, for example, the antireform forces developed a plan that would cut fees and lower interest rates for student loans but preserve the existing system.

Interest groups do not give proposals to just anyone. As with direct lobbying, they seek out legislators who already support their cause and who have significant influence within Congress. For example, a lobbying effort aimed at cutting interest rates on student loans would target supporters of this change who are also members of the congressional committee with jurisdiction over student loan programs—preferably someone who chairs the committee or one of its subcommittees.[18] Interest groups also lobby bureaucrats to influence the details of new regulations.[19] If the type of regulations involved can go into effect without congressional approval, then lobbying can give groups what they want directly. If new regulations require approval by Congress or White House staff, then interest groups can increase their chances of success by getting involved in the initial drafting.

Research Interest groups often prepare research reports on topics of interest to the group. For example, Public Citizen featured on its website a series of research reports on topics such as medical malpractice, the house-building industry, toy safety, and international trade.[20] Such reports may sway public opinion or help persuade elected officials or bureaucrats. They also help interest group staff claim expertise on some aspect of public policy. Members of Congress are more likely to accept a group's legislative proposal if they think that the group's staff has solid research to back up their claims. Journalists are also more likely to respond to an interest group's requests for publicity if they think that the group's staff has viable evidence supporting their claims.

Hearings and Litigation Interest group staff often testify before congressional committees. In part, this activity seeks to inform members of Congress about issues that matter to the group. For example, the NRA's website shows that its staff have testified in favor of "right-to-carry" laws as well as laws that would grant immunity to gun manufacturers for harm committed with weapons they produced.[21]

Another inside strategy involves taking the government to court. In bringing their case, groups can argue that the government's actions are not consistent with the Constitution or that the government has misinterpreted the existing law.[22] Groups can also

Lobbying the Federal Government: Inside and Outside Strategies

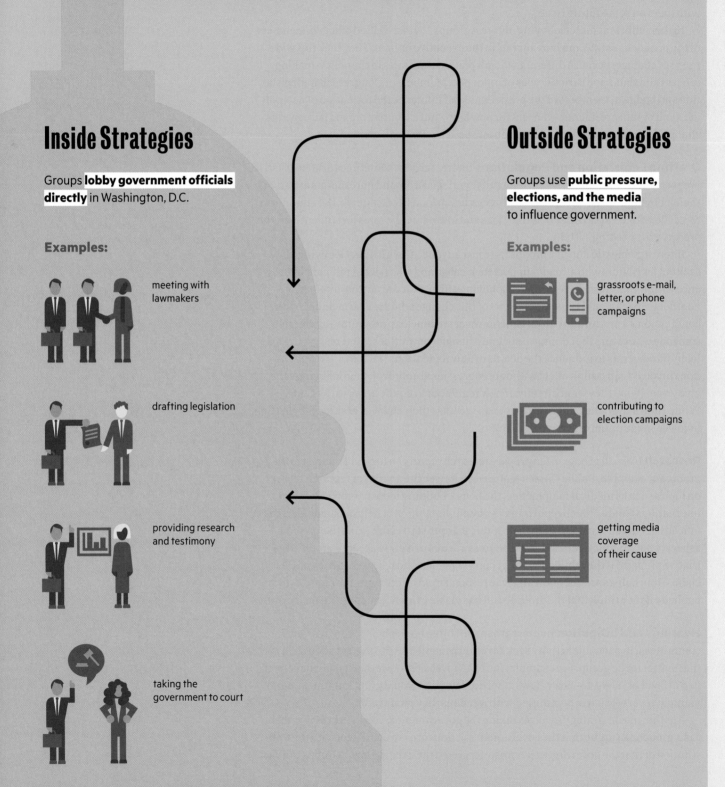

Inside Strategies

Groups **lobby government officials directly** in Washington, D.C.

Examples:

meeting with lawmakers

drafting legislation

providing research and testimony

taking the government to court

Outside Strategies

Groups use **public pressure, elections, and the media** to influence government.

Examples:

grassroots e-mail, letter, or phone campaigns

contributing to election campaigns

getting media coverage of their cause

AIPAC and the Iran Nuclear Deal

Throughout negotiations between Iran and the United States and its allies over limiting Iran's nuclear research program, and especially during congressional consideration of this agreement, the American Israel Public Affairs Committee (AIPAC)—an influential pro-Israel interest group—strongly opposed the deal. Using their connections throughout the country and in Washington, as well as their high level of funding, AIPAC engaged in a diverse set of lobbying activities with the goal of persuading members of Congress to disapprove the deal before a crucial deadline passed and the deal was enacted.

● Inside strategies

● Outside strategies

Do we have a deal?

July 14, 2015
The United States and its negotiation partners announce details of their **nuclear agreement with Iran.**

And they're off!

July 15, 2015
AIPAC announces its opposition to the Iran deal and **forms a new advocacy group to lobby** against the agreement.

Gathering forces.

July 2015
AIPAC organizes a series of **speeches** and **town hall meetings** in congressional districts and states of undecided legislators.

Making introductions.

July 28–29, 2015
AIPAC arranges a "Washington fly-in"—a series of **meetings between lawmakers and hundreds of constituents** who are opposed to the deal.

Running ads.

August 2015
AIPAC spends over **20 million dollars** running **television ads** opposing the deal in 23 states.

Funding trips.

August 2015
AIPAC organizes a **trip to Israel for 58 members of Congress** to meet with Israeli citizens and officials.

Going right to the source.

August 2015
AIPAC representatives **lobby undecided senators** to oppose the agreement.

We still have a deal!

September 2, 2015
Deadline for Congress to disapprove the deal passes without action.

While AIPAC's efforts were **ultimately unsuccessful**, they illustrate the many ways interest groups can work to influence the policy process.

?

Critical Thinking

1. **Despite its lobbying efforts, AIPAC's** side did not prevail in this situation. If you were advising them, what lobbying strategy would you suggest they spend more time on, if any? Why?

2. **Suppose you are the head of AIPAC.** How could you use the Iran agreement to illustrate AIPAC's power and influence in Washington, despite the fact that the group's position did not prevail?

become involved in an existing case by filing amicus curiae ("friend of the court") briefs; these are documents that offer the group's rationale for how the judges should decide the case. The drawback of litigation is that it is costly and time-consuming; cases can take years to work through the federal courts system. In fact, most groups that use the litigation strategy combine it with direct lobbying or other strategies.

Working Together To increase their chances for success, interest groups can work together in their lobbying efforts, formulating a common strategy and future plans. Legislators are more likely to respond, or at least provide access, when many groups with large or diverse memberships are all asking for the same thing.[23] In general, these collaborations are short-term efforts focused on achieving a specific outcome, like supporting or opposing the confirmation of judicial and cabinet nominees.[24] The fight against direct student loans, for example, involved corporations such as Citibank and Sallie Mae, along with the U.S. Chamber of Commerce. Support for change came from the Student Aid Alliance, a group comprised of colleges, think tanks, and associations of law schools and other professional schools. This group had formed in 1999 to lobby for increases in student aid and then stayed together to lobby on other issues.

The American Civil Liberties Union is an interest group that often uses litigation strategies in its efforts to change government policy. Here, members of the ACLU chapter in Washington State announce their filing of an abortion rights lawsuit against several local hospitals. #ACLU

The problem with working together is that groups may agree on general goals but disagree on specifics. If differences cannot be bridged, groups may undertake separate and possibly conflicting lobbying efforts or decide against lobbying entirely. For example, while there are many groups pressing for climate change legislation, they have not developed a unified lobbying effort. The problem? The groups disagree on which policies should be implemented, who should pay for them, and whether the government should aid companies that would be forced to purchase new antipollution equipment.[25] Here, again, we see how conflict and compromise infuse another aspect of the American political process.

Outside strategies

Outside strategies involve actions that interest groups undertake across the country rather than in Washington. Again, these activities can be orchestrated by the group or can be organized by a firm that the group hires.

Mass protests, such as the 2014 People's Climate March in New York City, are intended to attract media attention and demonstrate the depth of public support for a group's goals.

Grassroots Lobbying Directly involving interest group members in lobbying efforts is called **grassroots lobbying**. Members may send letters, make telephone calls, participate in a protest, or express their demands in other ways. Mass protests, another form of grassroots lobbying, seek to capture the attention of government officials and also to draw media coverage, with the idea of publicizing the group's goals and perhaps gaining new members or financial support.

Grassroots strategies are useful because elected officials do not like to act against a large group of citizens who care enough about an issue to express their position.[26] Officials may not agree with the group's goals, but they will likely arrange a meeting with its staff so that they appear willing to learn about their constituents' demands.[27] However, these member-based strategies work only for interest groups with a large number of members, because legislators pay attention to a letter-writing campaign only when they receive several thousand pieces of mail. In addition, the letters or other efforts have to come from a Congress member's own constituents. The effectiveness of grassroots lobbying also depends on perceptions of how much a group has done to motivate participation. Suppose a representative gets 10,000 e-mails demanding an increase in student aid, but virtually all the messages contain the same appeal because they were generated and sent from a group's website. Congressional staff refer to these efforts as **Astroturf lobbying**.[28] Given the letters' similarity, the representative may discount the effort, believing that it says more about the group's ability to make campaign participation accessible than it does about the number of district residents who strongly support an increase in student aid. Even so, the fact that so many people participated, even with facilitation by an interest group, means that their demands should at least be considered.

Mobilizing Public Opinion One strategy related to grassroots lobbying involves trying to change what the public thinks about an issue. The goal is not to get citizens to do anything, but simply to influence public opinion in the hope that elected officials will notice this change and respond by enacting (or opposing) new laws or regulations in order to keep their constituents happy. Virtually all interest groups try to influence opinion. Most maintain a Web page that presents their message and write press releases to get media coverage. Any contact with citizens, whether to encourage them to join the group, contribute money, or engage in grassroots lobbying, also involves elements of persuasion—trying to transform citizens into supporters and supporters into true believers and even activists. In the case of gun control, for example, the NRA has an aggressive campaign to make it easier for members to contact their elected officials and to express their opinions.

grassroots lobbying
A lobbying strategy that relies on participation by group members, such as a protest or a letter-writing campaign.

Astroturf lobbying
Any lobbying method initiated by an interest group that is designed to look like the spontaneous, independent participation of many individuals.

A focused mobilization effort involves contacting large numbers of potential supporters through e-mail, phone calls, direct mail, television advertising, print media, social media, and websites. In order to get legislators to respond, a group has to persuade large numbers of people to become involved.

Electioneering Interest groups get involved in elections by making contributions to candidates, urging people to help in a campaign, endorsing candidates, funding campaign ads, or mobilizing a candidate's or party's supporters. All these efforts seek to influence who gets elected, with the expectation that changing who gets elected will affect what government does.

Federal laws limit groups' electioneering and lobbying efforts. (See Nuts & Bolts 9.2.) For example, most private organizations and associations in America are organized as 501(c)(3) organizations, a designation based on their IRS classification, which means that donations to the group are tax deductible. However, 501(c)(3) organizations must not engage in any political activities or lobbying (other than certain voter education programs or voter registration drives that are conducted in a nonpartisan manner—although some groups are always looking for loopholes in these restrictions). Groups that want to engage in lobbying or electioneering without looking for exceptions can incorporate under other IRS designations and operate as a **political action committee (PAC)**, a **527 organization**, or a 501(c)(4) organization. Although contributions to these organizations are not tax deductible, such organizations have fewer restrictions on the size of the contributions or how their money is spent—for example, 527 organizations have no contribution or spending limits.

Two new options for electioneering by interest groups emerged in recent elections: "Super PACs" and 501(c)(4) organizations. The former was a consequence of the *Citizens United* Supreme Court decision that authorized unlimited independent spending by

political action committee (PAC)
An interest group or a division of an interest group that can raise money to contribute to campaigns or to spend on ads in support of candidates. The amount a PAC can receive from each of its donors and the amount it can spend on federal campaigning are strictly limited.

527 organization
A tax-exempt group formed primarily to influence elections through voter mobilization efforts and issue ads that do not directly endorse or oppose a candidate. Unlike PACs, 527s are not subject to contribution limits and spending caps.

⬡

NUTS & BOLTS 9.2

Interest Groups and Electioneering: Types of Organizations

An interest group's ability to engage in electioneering depends on how it is organized—specifically, what section of the IRS code applies to the organization. The following table gives details on four common organizations: 501(c) organizations, 527 organizations, PACs, and so-called Super PACs. Therefore, many choose to contribute money to nonprofits organized as 501(c)(4) groups, which can lobby and engage in electioneering as long as their "primary activity" (at least half of their overall activity) is not political.

Type of Organization	Advantages	Disadvantages
501(c)(3)	Contributions tax deductible	Cannot engage in political activities or lobbying, only voter education and mobilization
527	Can spend unlimited amounts on issue advocacy and voter mobilization	Cannot make contributions to candidates or coordinate efforts with candidates or parties
501(c)(4)	Can spend unlimited amounts on electioneering; do not have to disclose contributors	At least half of their activities must be nonpolitical; cannot coordinate efforts with candidates or parties
PACs	Can contribute directly to candidates and parties	Strict limits on direct contributions
Super PACs	Can spend unlimited amounts on electioneering; can support or oppose specific candidates	Cannot make contributions to candidates or coordinate efforts with candidates or parties

corporations and labor unions in federal elections.[29] Many groups set up new PACs to take advantage of these latest rules—the "super" label reflects the fact that these groups take in and spend much more money than the typical PAC. All of the major 2016 presidential candidates had an independent Super PAC running ad campaigns on their behalf.

In 2016, federally focused 527 organizations spent more than $400 million on electioneering and PACs and Super PACs spent over $2 billion on electioneering and contributions to candidates and parties.[30] However, these large numbers mask some important details, as illustrated by Figure 9.3. To begin with, look at the right-hand side of the figure—some of the largest firms in America (Google, Boeing, and Exxon Mobil) have PACs that spend only a million or so on contributions. Another large firm, Apple, has no PAC. The AMA's PAC is also small, and the other influential interest groups mentioned earlier (such as the AARP and Family Research Council) spend even less or don't have a PAC or a 527. These numbers suggest that money doesn't buy elections or policy outcomes—if it did, these organizations would probably spend a lot more on campaign donations and television ads.

The other groups in Figure 9.3 were some of the largest spenders in the 2016 election cycle. But even then, spending totals can be deceptive. The National Association of Realtors, for example, made over $10 million in contributions—but spread out over 500 candidates, slightly more going to Republicans. The PAC for Emily's List collects over

Contributions by PACs and 527s in 2016: A Closer Look

FIGURE 9.3

Although estimates of total campaign spending suggest that donors have tremendous influence over candidates, the reality is more complicated. Contributions don't buy victories; a substantial amount of campaign cash goes to administrative costs or is distributed across many candidates, and some organizations spend surprisingly little on campaign contributions. How could you use this data to argue against claims that interest groups are all-powerful players in American elections?

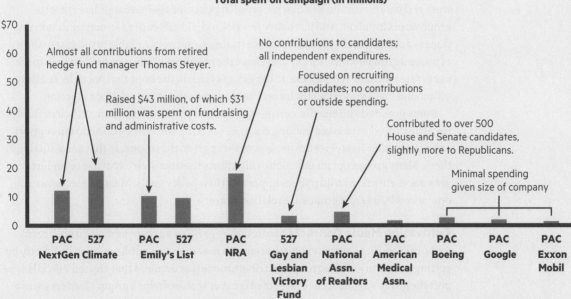

Sources: Data available at www.opensecrets.org and www.fec.gov (accessed 11/6/16).

Conservative Super PACs, such as the Conservative Political Action Conference (CPAC), hold conventions that give candidates a venue to present themselves to conservative activists and donors.
@CPAC

$40 million in contributions but spends most of this on the direct mail operation that generates funds, leaving only a fraction left for contributions. The Gay and Lesbian Victory Fund focuses on recruiting and endorsing candidates and makes no contributions at all. Finally, the largest spender in 2016, NextGen Climate Action, was funded largely by a single wealthy donor. Moreover, most of the candidates the organization supported in 2014 and 2016 lost their elections.

Finally, while the over $2 billion for overall spending by all of these groups seems large, the average each group spent is much smaller. Most PACs contribute to only a few candidates. And while there were over a thousand Super PACs active in the 2016 election and they spent over a billion dollars in total, most are small, with the average spending just over $500,000. These data highlight a sharp difference in electioneering strategies between the very few large, well-funded interest groups and everyone else. A few 527s, Super PACs, 501(c)(4)s, and PACs have the money to deploy massive advertising and mobilizing efforts for a candidate or issue they like or against those they don't like. There are also some very large associations that can persuade large numbers of members to work and vote for candidates that the group supports or against candidates that the group wants to defeat. And just a very few rich individuals can make outsized contributions to a candidate they favor. But these strategies are not available to the vast majority of interest groups, which simply don't have the resources. They give modest help to a few candidates who are sympathetic to the group's goals in the hope that once elected the officeholder will remember their contribution when the group asks for a meeting.

Some groups do no electioneering at all, possibly because they lack sufficient funds, because they want to avoid making enemies based on whom they do or do not support or because other strategies are more promising given the resources that are available to them. Many groups opt for quiet lobbying efforts that use their expertise or undertake grassroots efforts to build public support for their policy goals. Massive electioneering operations by interest groups are relatively rare.

Cultivating Media Contacts Media coverage helps a group publicize its concerns without spending any money. Such attention may mobilize public opinion indirectly by getting people to join the group, contribute money, or demand that elected officials support the group's agenda. Favorable media coverage also helps a group's leaders assure members that they are actively working on members' concerns.

Journalists listen when interest groups call if they feel that a group's story will catch their readers' attention or address their concerns. Smart interest group leaders make it easy for journalists to cover their cause, holding events that produce intriguing news stories. These stories may not change anyone's mind, but the media coverage provides free publicity for the groups' policy agendas.

At first glance, lobbying victories should go to the groups that can spend a lot on contributions to candidates or on direct lobbying. But there are many other ways to succeed in the battle to shape public policy, from organizing American citizens to preparing new proposals or doing background research. Policy influence isn't as much about the size of a group's budget as it is about factors such as the size of its membership or the perception of its expertise. Even poorly funded groups can find ways to win. If there's an issue that you believe in, find a group that supports it and get involved.

"Why Should I Care?"

How much power do interest groups have?

★

EVALUATE INTEREST GROUP INFLUENCE

One 2016 presidential candidate, Democrat Lawrence Lessig, built his entire campaign around a pledge to convince members of Congress to enact campaign finance reform. This, he argued, is the only way to break the influence of special interests over policy making in Washington. Once reform was enacted, Lessig promised to resign from office. While Lessig's campaign went nowhere, his pledge illustrates a widely held belief about how Washington works, that interest groups have too much power and something drastic must be done to end their domination over policy making in Washington. As we discuss in the What Do the Numbers Say? section, some studies of interest group influence support Lessig's claims—but others tell a very different story, one in which a group's chances of getting what it wants depend on whether there is organized opposition to its demand. In other words, as one analysis put it, "the solution to lobbying is more lobbying."[31]

What determines when interest groups succeed?

Three factors shape interest group influence. The first is what the group is trying to do—change a policy (including enacting a new policy) or prevent change. The second is the amount of public attention a group gets: How many Americans care about what a group is trying to do? The third is conflict: To what extent do other groups or the public oppose the policy change?

Change versus Preventing Change In general, groups are going to have an easier time preventing a change than working to implement one. As we discuss in Chapter 2, enacting a new policy requires the approval of both houses of Congress, the president's signature (or a veto override), and implementation from the appropriate bureaucratic agency. Each of these steps provides an opportunity for interest groups to lobby in favor

But this is the great danger America faces. That we will cease to be one nation and become instead a collection of interest groups: city against suburb, region against region, individual against individual. Each seeking to satisfy private wants.

—**Barbara Jordan,** civil rights leader and former member of Congress

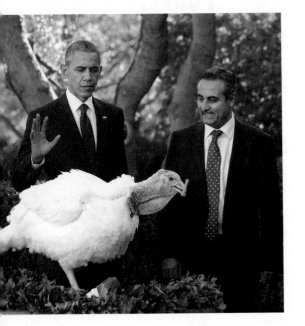

If you have ever heard of the National Turkey Federation, it's probably because of its participation in the annual presidential "pardoning" of a turkey before Thanksgiving. The federation's relative anonymity has been beneficial: its effort to increase the amount of turkey served in federally funded school lunches was aided by most Americans' lack of awareness of the proposal. @TurkeyGal

of doing nothing. And if groups are successful in the process, change will not occur. Studies show that groups are much more likely to be successful when their goals involve negative lobbying—blocking changes in policy.[32] Most of the NRA's legislative victories in recent years fit this description: they have successfully lobbied against a new ban on assault weapons, against reforms to the system of national background checks for handgun purchases, and against new limits on ownership of guns by mentally ill people.

While the success of the NRA's negative lobbying attracts considerable attention, its failures in lobbying for policy change do not. Consider the NRA's advocacy of concealed carry laws. As noted earlier, there is little doubt that the NRA's leaders and most of its members favor the passage of such laws nationwide, but efforts to lobby Congress in favor of such laws are unlikely to be successful given public opposition and well-funded interest groups that are against concealed carry. These groups could respond with negative lobbying against any effort the NRA might make. As a result, the NRA does not lobby for concealed carry—and the limits on its power over legislation are not evident.

Amount of Public Attention Interest groups are more likely to succeed when their request attracts little public attention.[33] When the average voter does not know or care about a group's request, legislators and bureaucrats do not have to worry about the political consequences of giving the group what it wants. The only question is whether the officials themselves favor the request or can be convinced that the group's desired change is worthwhile. In contrast, when the issue attracts a lot of public attention legislators' response to lobbying will hinge on their judgment of constituent opinion: Do voters favor what the group wants? After all, the average legislator has a strong interest in reelection and is unlikely to act against his or her constituents' wishes. As a result, lobbying may count for nothing in the face of public opposition or be superfluous when the group's position already has public support.[34]

The idea of interest group lobbying probably brings to mind titanic struggles on controversial issues (such as gun control, abortion rights, or judicial nominations) over which groups try to capture public attention as a way of pressuring the government. But not all interest group lobbying is so high profile. Remember the National Turkey Federation—the people who give the president a turkey every Thanksgiving? In the winter of 2014, the federation successfully lobbied federal bureaucrats to increase propane supplies to Midwest states facing record cold temperatures, including areas where the federation's members use propane to heat their barns. The policy change resulting from the federation's lobbying efforts attracted no publicity, which is precisely the point. When few people know or care about a policy change, interest groups are able to dominate the policy-making process.

Level of Conflict Interest group influence is much less apparent on highly conflictual issues—those over which public opinion is split and groups are active on all sides of the question. Consider gun control. The ongoing debate over gun control attracts many well-funded interest groups and coalitions, which support different versions of gun control or want no change at all. There is no consensus among members of Congress, interest groups, or the American public about which policy changes are needed. Under these conditions, access doesn't count for much; legislators have a keen sense of the political costs of accommodating a group's demands. As a result, stalemate is the likely result, which is exactly what has happened over the last few years. If policy change occurs at all, it is likely to reflect a complex process of bargaining and compromise, with no groups getting exactly what they want—which is what happened with gun control.

Interest Group Power

Conventional wisdom says that business interest groups have too much power over policy outcomes in Washington. But what do the numbers say?

To address this question, a group of political scientists tracked a series of issues through years of lobbying, congressional debate, legislative action and implementation by the bureaucracy. Their goal was to determine whether business groups were successful in getting what they want from Congress, particularly when their efforts were opposed by citizen groups or government officials. Here's what the researchers found:

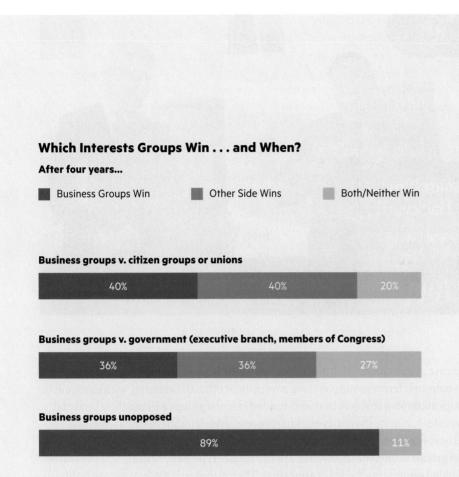

Which Interests Groups Win . . . and When?

After four years...

■ Business Groups Win   ■ Other Side Wins   ■ Both/Neither Win

Business groups v. citizen groups or unions

| 40% | 40% | 20% |

Business groups v. government (executive branch, members of Congress)

| 36% | 36% | 27% |

Business groups unopposed

| 89% | 11% |

Think about it

- Many people believe that business groups always succeed in their lobbying efforts. Does this chart confirm or deny these suspicions?
- After looking at these data, do you think business groups have too much power? How do these data help us understand the winners and losers in the student loan reform debate discussed at the beginning of this chapter?

Source: Marie Hojnacki, Kathleen Marchetti, Frank Baumgartner, Jeffrey M. Berry, David C. Kimball, and Beth L. Leech, "Assessing Business Advantage in Washington Lobbying," *Interest Groups and Advocacy* 4 (2015): 206–24.

While many observers credit lobbying by the pharmaceutical industry for policies such as the Medicare Prescription Drug Benefit (and its ban on importing medicines), favorable public opinion, the efforts of the AARP, and bureaucrats' independent judgments probably had greater influence on passing the Drug Benefit Act. @PHRMA @AARP

The case of gun control also illustrates that being large or well-funded does not always help an interest group convince government officials to comply with its requests. Although many people worry that well-funded interest groups will use their financial resources to dominate the policy-making process, even if public opinion is against them, these fears are largely unfounded. The conditions that are ripe for well-funded interest groups to become involved in a policy debate typically ensure that there will be well-funded groups on all sides of a question. Then no group is likely to get everything it wants and no group's lobbying efforts are likely to be decisive. Some groups may not get anything.

However, gun control is not a typical case. Most cases of interest group influence look a lot like the National Turkey Federation's request for more propane: a group asks for something, there is relatively little opposition, and Congress or the bureaucracy responds with appropriate policy changes. The situation might have been very different if another group had lobbied on the other side against the Turkey Federation. If so, satisfying one group would have required displeasing at least one other group. Faced with this no-win situation, bureaucrats or legislators would be less likely to give the group what it wanted. At a minimum, they would have had to measure the Turkey Federation's arguments against those made by the other groups.

"Why Should I Care?"

Suppose you want to change some federal government policy—you want more funding for a program, or an end to some regulation. Does having enough money guarantee a win? Generally speaking, the answer is no. What matters more is the salience of the policy or regulation you're trying to change and whether there is organized opposition on the other side. If your group is the only one lobbying, chances are good that you'll win. But if the issue is highly salient and you have opposition, your prospects aren't good, regardless of the size of your bankroll.

Conclusion

Many Americans think that interest groups are powerful manipulators of the American policy process and that they are able to get what they want regardless of the impact on everyone else. Federal direct student loans are seemingly a perfect example: a small number of well-funded lobbyists worked to defeat a policy change that would lower the cost of attending college for most students.

As you have seen, the truth is much more complex. Interest groups represent many different Americans, many of whom are unaware that lobbying occurs on their behalf. Moreover, for many groups, the challenge is to get organized in the first place or scrape together enough resources to start lobbying. These efforts don't always succeed. Interest groups are more likely to get what they want when their demands attract little public attention and no opposition from other groups. When a group asks for a large or controversial policy change, it stands little chance of success, even if the group has many members, a large lobbying budget, or an influential leader directing its operation.

The debate over direct student loans exemplifies all of these findings. Although the corporations that stood to lose from the direct loan proposal had significant lobbying operations, the proposal had relatively high salience and was controversial. Consequently, legislators' voting decisions were less likely to be affected by lobbying or other interest group strategies such as electioneering. These lobbying efforts may have helped to inform members of Congress about the details of the proposal or the impact that the change would have on employment in their districts, but there is no evidence that support for these proposals was shaped by lobbying. And although these lobbying efforts delayed the move to direct loans, they did not prevent it.

In sum, while individual lobbying efforts often reflect the efforts of small groups to achieve favored policy outcomes at the expense of the majority, when we look across the entire range of interest group activities a different picture emerges: in the main, interest groups reflect the conflictual nature of American politics and the resulting drive of individuals, groups, and corporations to shape American public policy in line with their policy goals. The average citizen benefits as well as loses from lobbying activities.

STUDY GUIDE

What are interest groups?

Define *interest groups* and describe the characteristics of different types of groups. (Pages 252–260)

Summary

Interest groups are organizations that seek to influence government policy by helping elect candidates who support their policy goals and by lobbying elected officials and bureaucrats. Although they are generally viewed with disdain, interest groups are ubiquitous—most organizations have lobbyists working on their behalf—and, under the theory of pluralism, are regarded as fundamental actors in American politics.

Key terms

interest group (p. 252)
lobbying (p. 252)
centralized groups (p. 253)
confederations (p. 253)
mass associations (p. 253)
peak associations (p. 254)

solidary benefits (p. 254)
purposive benefits (p. 254)
coercion (p. 254)
selective incentives (p. 254)
revolving door (p. 256)
trade association (p. 258)

Practice Quiz Questions

1. **In contrast to political parties, interest groups ____.**
   a. run candidates for office and coordinate activities
   b. coordinate the activities of elected officials
   c. guarantee that certain candidates appear on electoral ballots
   d. directly influence government activity
   e. indirectly influence government activity

2. **Why is the number of lobbyists increasing?**
   a. The federal government is growing in size and influence.
   b. Lobbying is not closely regulated.
   c. Citizens are now more supportive of special interests.
   d. Politicians can concurrently serve their terms and work as lobbyists.
   e. Interest groups have more money to spend.

3. **In contrast to a confederation, a centralized interest group ____.**
   a. maintains a number of independent chapters
   b. often has local chapters competing over resources
   c. deploys the group's resources more efficiently
   d. is able to find out what its members want
   e. has no weaknesses

4. **The practice of moving from government positions to working for interest groups is called ____.**
   a. interest-group capture
   b. the revolving door
   c. an iron triangle
   d. escalator politics
   e. the spoils system

5. **Purposive benefits come from ____, while solidary benefits come from ____.**
   a. working with like-minded people; working to achieve a desired policy goal
   b. receiving material goods; working with like-minded people
   c. receiving material goods; working to achieve a desired policy goal
   d. working to achieve a desired policy goal; receiving material goods
   e. working to achieve a desired policy goal; working with like-minded people

Interest group strategies

Explore the ways interest groups try to influence government policies. (Pages 260–269)

Summary

Interest groups have two types of tactics for lobbying elected officials. They can attempt to influence politics by taking action in Washington, or they can take action elsewhere. The decision to pursue an inside or outside strategy comes down to the interest group's resources and which strategy members think will be most effective.

Key terms

inside strategies (p. 260)
outside strategies (p. 260)
direct lobbying (p. 260)
grassroots lobbying (p. 265)

Astroturf lobbying (p. 265)
political action committee (PAC) (p. 266)
527 organization (p. 266)

Practice Quiz Questions

6. **Asking government officials to change policy in line with the group's goals is ____.**
   a. revolving door lobbying
   b. Astroturf lobbying
   c. direct lobbying

d. indirect lobbying

e. outside lobbying

7. Interest groups generally _____ draft legislation; they generally _____ provide testimony before committees.

a. do; do

b. do not; do

c. do; do not

d. do not; do not

8. Directly involving interest group members in lobbying efforts is called _____.

a. Astroturf lobbying

b. grassroots lobbying

c. democratic lobbying

d. lobbying through referendum

e. inside lobbying

9. For grassroots lobbying to be effective, _____.

a. only a few pieces of mail are necessary

b. mail must come from all over the country

c. all messages have to have exactly the same appeal

d. letters have to come from constituents

e. letters have to come from prominent officials

How much power do interest groups have?

Evaluate interest group influence. (Pages 269–272)

Summary

It is commonly argued that elected officials are letting interest groups define their agenda. However, the evidence on interest groups does not support these claims: there is no correlation between the amount of money spent on lobbying and a group's success, nor is there conclusive evidence that group lobbying influences policy. Groups are generally most influential when the issues attract little public attention and when an issue does not have organized opposition.

Practice Quiz Question

10. Interest groups are more likely to succeed when their request has _____ salience and when it has _____ conflict.

a. low; little

b. high; little

c. low; high

d. high; high

e. high; zero

Suggested Reading

Ainsworth, Scott. *Analyzing Interest Groups: Group Influence on People and Policies*. New York: W. W. Norton, 2002.

Baumgartner, Frank, Jeffrey M. Berry, Marie Hojnacki, David C. Kimball, and Beth L. Leech. *Lobbying and Policy Change: Who Wins, Who Loses, and Why*. Chicago: University of Chicago Press, 2009.

Carpenter, Daniel. *The Forging of Bureaucratic Autonomy: Reputations, Networks, and Policy Innovation in Executive Agencies, 1862-1928*. Princeton, NJ: Princeton University Press, 2002.

Gilens, Martin, and Benjamin Page. *Testing Theories of American Politics: Elites, Interest Groups, and Average Citizens*. Princeton, NJ: Princeton University Press, 2014.

Kollman, Kenneth. *Outside Lobbying: Public Opinion and Interest Group Strategies*. Princeton, NJ: Princeton University Press, 1998.

Olson, Mancur. *The Logic of Collective Action*, 2nd ed. Cambridge, MA: Harvard University Press, 1971.

Schattschneider, E. E. *The Semisovereign People*. New York: Harper and Row, 1959.

Schlozman, Kay Lehman, and John Tierney. *Organized Interests and American Democracy*. New York: HarperCollins, 1986.

Stigerwalt, Amy. *The Battle over the Bench: Senators, Interest Groups, and Lower Court Confirmations*. Charlottesville: University of Virginia Press, 2010.

Verba, Sidney, Kay Lehman Schlozman, and Henry Brady. *Voice and Equality: Civic Participation in America*. Cambridge, MA: Harvard University Press, 1995.

10
Congress

Who does Congress represent?

Early in March 2014, the casual observer reading the headline "Senate Approves McCaskill Sexual Assault Bill in 97–0 Vote" may have reasonably assumed that there was massive bipartisan agreement on this important issue.[1] However, digging past the headline would have revealed bruising partisan (and intraparty) conflict. Despite the unanimous support for the compromise bill in the Senate, the House declined to take up the bill, with then-Speaker John Boehner saying he wanted to see how previous reforms worked out: "I don't frankly see any reason at this point for any further action to be taken."

A 2013 Pentagon report showed that 26,000 troops had "unwanted sexual contact" in 2012, comprising 6.1 percent of active-duty women and 1.2 percent of active-duty men. This was a 37 percent increase in incidents of unwanted sexual contact compared with such incidents in 2010 and more than eight times the 3,374 sexual assaults reported in 2010.[2] The report led to an outcry in Congress, with two senators, Claire McCaskill (D-MO) and Kirsten Gillibrand (D-NY), providing alternative plans. Both bills provided much stronger protections for victims of sexual assaults by removing the "good soldier" defense (a defense that takes an accused soldier's good military record into account even if it is unrelated to the alleged crime) and strengthening prosecutors' role in advising commanders on whether to go to court martial. But Senator Gillibrand pushed for an even stronger overhaul that would have removed prosecutions for sexual assaults from the military chain of command, while Senator McCaskill did not. This difference led to a protracted battle that lasted nearly a year and isolated McCaskill as the only one of the 16 Democratic women senators to vote against Gillibrand's bill.[3] Nonetheless, as we noted earlier, McCaskill's version of the bill was the one that passed by a unanimous vote in the Senate. While supporters of the stronger reforms were disappointed, this case shows that even on a deeply conflictual issue such as how to address the problem of sexual assaults in the military it is possible to find common ground and a compromise that can win the support of a nearly unanimous majority in the Senate and perhaps at some point the House.

★

CHAPTER GOALS

Explain how members of Congress represent their constituents and how elections hold members accountable.
pages 278–291

Examine how parties, the committee system, and staffers enable Congress to function.
pages 291–300

Trace the steps in the legislative process.
pages 301–307

Describe how Congress ensures that the bureaucracy implements policies correctly.
pages 307–308

Kirsten Gillibrand (D-NY) greets panel members testifying at a Senate hearing on sexual assault in the military. Senator Gillibrand is trying to change how the Pentagon handles the increase in sexual assaults.Here, Gillibrand shakes hands with air force lieutenant general Richard Harding before greeting army lieutenant general Dana Chipman, who is next to him.

The essential nature of conflict and compromise in the legislative process is not very well understood by the general public. Americans often view the type of wheeling and dealing that is necessary to reach compromises as improper and wonder why there is so much conflict. A typical sentiment is, "Why does there have to be so much partisan bickering? Can't they just implement the best solutions to our problems?" Many don't even attempt to understand the legislative process and the nature of conflict and compromise because it seems hopelessly complex. Anyone who has watched congressional debates on C-SPAN knows that legislative maneuvers can make one's head spin, and the discussions can seem mind-numbing.

In this chapter, we show that the basic characteristics of Congress are straightforward and that the motivations that guide members' behavior and the way that Congress works are transparent. This chapter argues that members' behavior is driven by their desire to respond to constituent interests (and the closely related goal of reelection) and is constrained by the institutional structures within which they operate (such as the committee system, parties, and leadership). At the same time, members try to be responsible for the broader national interests, which are often at odds with their constituents' interests and, subsequently, the goal of reelection.

This tension between being responsible and responsive is a source of conflict and requires members of Congress to make tough decisions, often involving political trade-offs and compromises. Should a House member vote for dairy price supports for her local farmers even if it means higher milk prices for families around the nation? Should a senator vote to subsidize the production of tobacco, the biggest cash crop in his state, despite the tremendous health costs it imposes on millions of Americans? Should a member vote to close a military base, as requested by the Pentagon, even if it means the loss of thousands of jobs back home? These are difficult questions. On a complex issue such as how best to deal with sexual assaults in the military, there is no obvious "responsible" solution and fair-minded people can disagree. These disagreements take on a partisan edge, as most Republicans favor maintaining the chain of command while most Democrats do not, which obviously leads to conflict.

This chapter begins by examining the constitutional underpinnings of the representational tensions Congress must address. After exploring different ways of understanding representation, we describe Congress's image problem, the incumbency advantage, and Congress's central institutional features. We conclude by considering some potential reforms that might make Congress work better. How can members of Congress best serve the collective interests of the nation while also representing their local constituents? How do the institutions of Congress, such as committees and political parties, help members pursue their goals? What did the Founders envision as the proper role for Congress within our political system?

EXPLAIN HOW MEMBERS OF CONGRESS REPRESENT THEIR CONSTITUENTS AND HOW ELECTIONS HOLD MEMBERS ACCOUNTABLE

What Congress does

Congress and the Constitution

Congress was the "first branch" early in our nation's history. The Constitution specified for Congress a vast array of enumerated powers, including regulating commerce, coining money, raising and supporting armies, creating the courts, establishing post offices and roads, declaring war, and levying taxes (see Article I, Section 8, of the Constitution in the appendix). The president, in contrast, was given few explicit powers and played a much less prominent role early in our history. Furthermore, many of Congress's extensive powers came from its implicit powers, which were rooted in the elastic clause of Article I of the Constitution, which gives Congress the power "to make all Laws which shall be necessary and proper for carrying into Execution the foregoing Powers."

The compromises that gave rise to Congress's initial structure reflected an attempt to reconcile the competing interests of the day (large versus small states, northern versus southern interests, and proponents of strong national power versus state power). These compromises included establishing a system of **bicameralism**—that is, a bicameral (two-chambered) institution made up of a popularly elected House and a Senate chosen by state legislatures—allowing each slave to count as three-fifths of a person for purposes of apportionment for the House, and setting longer terms for senators (six years) than for House members (two years).

But these compromises also laid the foundation for the split loyalties that members of Congress have between their local constituencies and the nation's interests. Although the Founders hoped that Congress would pass legislation emphasizing the national good over local interests, they also recognized the importance of local constituencies. Thus, the two-year House term was intended to tie legislators to public sentiment. In general, the Founders viewed the Senate as the more likely institution to speak for the national interests; it was intended to check the more responsive and passionate House. Because senators were indirectly elected and served longer terms than House members, the Senate was more insulated from the people. A famous (although maybe fictional) story that points out the differences between the House and Senate involves an argument between George Washington and Thomas Jefferson. Jefferson did not think the Senate was necessary, while Washington supported having two chambers. During the argument, Jefferson poured some coffee he was drinking into his saucer. Washington asked him why he had done so. "To cool it," replied Jefferson. "Even so," said Washington, "we pour legislation into the senatorial saucer to cool it."

This idea of a more responsible Senate survived well into the twentieth century, even after the Seventeenth Amendment in 1913 allowed the direct, popular election of senators. Today the Senate is still more insulated than the House. Because of the six-year terms of senators, only one-third of the 100 Senate seats are contested in each election, while all 435 House members are elected every two years. However, differences between the House's and Senate's representational roles have become muted, as senators seem to campaign for reelection 365 days a year, every year, just like House members.[4] This "permanent campaign" means that senators are less insulated from electoral forces than previously.

The relationship between the president and Congress has also evolved significantly. Congress's roots in geographic constituencies made it well suited for the politics of the nineteenth century. Early in U.S. history, several great presidents left their mark on national politics (George Washington, Andrew Jackson, and Abraham Lincoln, among others), but Congress dominated much of the day-to-day politics, which revolved around issues such as the tariff (taxes on imported or exported goods), slavery, and internal improvements such as building roads and canals. Given the tendency to address these issues with patronage and the **pork barrel**—that is, jobs and policies targeted to benefit specific constituents—Congress was better suited for the task than the president was.

Beginning around the turn of the twentieth century and accelerating with the New Deal of the 1930s (which established modern social welfare and regulatory policies), the scope of national policy expanded and politics became more centered in Washington. With this nationalization of politics and the increasing importance of national security issues, the president assumed a more central policy-making role.

bicameralism
The system of having two chambers within one legislative body, like the House and Senate in the U.S. Congress.

A ROW IN CONGRESS.

The founders viewed the House as more passionate than the Senate, or as the "hot coffee" that needed to be cooled in the "saucer" of the Senate. This perception probably did not include coming to blows over differences in policy as Congressmen Albert G. Brown and John A. Wilcox did in 1851 about whether Mississippi should secede from the Union.

pork barrel
Legislative appropriations that benefit specific constituents, created with the aim of helping local representatives win reelection.

> **The American Republic will endure until the day Congress discovers that it can bribe the public with the public's money.**
>
> —**Alexis de Tocqueville**

However, the tensions between representing local versus national interests remain essential in understanding the legislative process and the relationship between members of Congress and their constituents.

Congress represents the people (or tries to)

Americans have a love–hate relationship with Congress—that is, we generally love our own member of Congress, but we hate the Congress as a whole. Well, "hate" is a strong word, but as we show later in this section, individual members of Congress routinely have approval ratings 30 to 40 points higher than the institution's. One poll found that members of Congress landed fifth from the bottom in a ranking of 26 professions in terms of perceived honesty and ethical standards.[5] A more whimsical poll by Public Policy Polling asked respondents questions such as "What do you have a higher opinion of, Congress or root canals?" Root canals won handily, 56 to 32 percent. Congress was also less popular than head lice, traffic jams, cockroaches, and Donald Trump, but narrowly beat out Lindsay Lohan and had a comfortable margin over the Ebola virus, the Kardashians, and meth labs.[6] Why is Congress so unpopular? How do members of Congress try to represent their constituents? And how do elections influence this important dynamic?

It may seem obvious why members of Congress are called representatives, but that role is more complex than you might imagine. Factors that influence this complexity include the different ways in which the members can represent the citizens who elected them to office and the different characteristics, desires, and needs of the district populations that each member represents.

Types of Representation Let's examine the two basic relationships between constituents and their member of Congress: descriptive representation and substantive representation. The former is rooted in the politician's side of the relationship: Does the member of Congress "look like" his or her constituents in demographic or socioeconomic terms—for example, African American, Latino, or white; male or female; Catholic, Protestant, or some other religion; middle-class or upper-class? Many people believe that such **descriptive representation** is a distinct value in itself. Having positive role models for various demographic groups helps create greater trust in the system. Moreover, there are benefits from being represented by someone who shares something as basic as skin color with constituents.

Descriptive representation is also related to the perceived responsiveness of a member of Congress. In general, constituents report higher levels of satisfaction with representatives who are of the same racial or ethnic background as the constituents themselves.[7] If you doubt that descriptive representation makes a difference, ask yourself whether it would be fair if all 435 House members and 100 senators were white, male Protestants. Although the demographics of Congress are considerably more diverse than this, the legislature does not come close to "looking like us" on a nationwide scale (see the What Do the Numbers Say? feature).

More important than a member's race, gender, or religion, many people argue, is the *substance* of what that person does. **Substantive representation** moves beyond appearances to specify how the member serves his or her constituents' interests. Two long-standing models of representation are (1) the **trustee**, who represents the constituents' interests from a distance, weighing numerous national, collective, local, and moral concerns; and (2) the **delegate**, who carries out the direct desires of the voters. In a sense, trustees are more concerned with being responsible and delegates are more interested in being responsive.

"
Suppose you were an idiot. And suppose you were a member of Congress. But I repeat myself.

—Mark Twain

DID YOU KNOW?

$1.1 million

was the average net worth of members of Congress in 2014. More than half of all members of Congress are millionaires (274 of 535).
Source: Center for Responsive Politics

descriptive representation
When a member of Congress shares the characteristics (such as gender, race, religion, or ethnicity) of his or her constituents.

substantive representation
When a member of Congress represents constituents' interests and policy concerns.

trustee
A member of Congress who represents constituents' interests while also taking into account national, collective, and moral concerns that sometimes cause the member to vote against the preference of a majority of constituents.

delegate
A member of Congress who loyally represents constituents' direct interests.

Descriptive Representation in Congress

Compared with a generation ago, the number of women and racial and ethnic minorities in Congress has increased. But on these dimensions, how representative of the people is Congress? How close does Congress come to "looking like us"? What do the numbers say?

Sources: U.S. Census; Congressional Research Service

Gender in Congress

	Female	Male
House	19	81
Senate	21	79
U.S. population	50.8	49.2

Racial and Ethnic Composition of Congress

White   Latino (any race)   African American
Asian American   Other

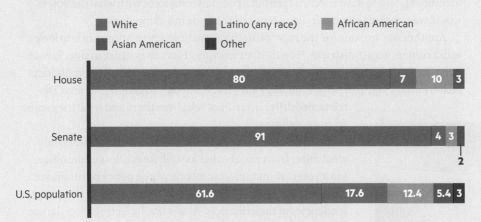

	White	Latino	African American	Asian American	Other
House	80	7	10	3	
Senate	91	4	3		2
U.S. population	61.6	17.6	12.4	5.4	3

Think about it

- Which comes closer to "looking like us," the House or the Senate?
- How could having more women or racial and ethnic minorities in Congress affect legislation and policy decisions?
- Latinos now make up the largest ethnic minority in the United States, yet they still lag behind African Americans in terms of representation in the House. Why do you think this is?

politico
A member of Congress who acts as a delegate on issues that constituents care about (such as immigration reform) and as a trustee on more-complex or less-salient issues (such as some foreign policy or regulatory matters).

Trustees, by definition, will do what they think is in the best long-term interests of their constituents and the nation, even though it may mean voting against their constituents' immediate wishes and risking defeat in the next election. Delegates, in contrast, do not have to worry about angering voters because they simply do what their constituents want. Truth be told, the trustee/delegate distinction is mostly important as a theoretical point of departure for talking about representation roles. Nearly all members of Congress act like trustees in some circumstances and like delegates in others. A third model of representation is the **politico**, who is more likely to act as a delegate on issues that are especially important to his or her constituency (such as immigration reform) but is more likely to act as a trustee on issues that constituents don't feel strongly about or on very complex issues (such as some foreign policies). Therefore, the crucial component of representation is the nature of the constituency and how the member of Congress attempts to balance and represent constituents' conflicting needs and desires.

The Role of the Constituency Most voters do not monitor their representatives' behavior closely. Can representation work if voters are not paying attention? Members of Congress behave as if voters were paying attention, even when constituents are inattentive. Incumbents know that at election time the challengers may raise issues that become important after the public thinks about them, so they try to deter challengers by anticipating what the constituents would want *if they were fully informed*.[8] For example, the public didn't know much about the FBI's inability to hack into locked phones, but it became an issue in the 2016 elections when the FBI tried to force Apple to allow them to access a phone used by a suspect in the San Bernardino shootings. Savvy incumbents would have tried to stake out a position consistent with what the voters would want *before* a strong challenger raised the issue in a campaign.

Another way to examine the representative–constituency relationship is to look at differences across districts. How do districts vary? First, they differ in size: Senate "districts" (that is, states) vary in terms of both area and population. House districts all have about 745,000 people, but they vary tremendously in geographic size. Districts also differ in terms of who lives there and what they want from government.

Because districts are so multifaceted, the legislators they elect differ from one another as well. Regardless of the office, most voters want to elect someone whose policy positions are close to theirs. As a result, legislators tend to reflect the central tendencies of their districts. At one level, electing a legislature that "thinks like America" sounds good: if legislators act and think like their districts, then the legislature will contain a good mixture of the interests representing the country or state. But finding an acceptable compromise is not easy. We elect legislators to get things done, but they may be unable to agree on anything because their disagreements are too fundamental to bridge. For example, the country is sharply divided on abortion rights, as are the House, the Senate, and most state legislatures. The fact that legislators have not come to a decision on this issue is no surprise: just as citizens disagree, so do their elected representatives.

Members of Congress spend a good deal of time in their districts, developing relationships with constituents. Here, Representative Jason Chaffetz (R-UT) meets constituents after a town hall meeting.
@jasoninthehouse

casework
Assistance provided by members of Congress to their constituents in solving problems with the federal bureaucracy or addressing other specific concerns.

Despite the vast differences among congressional constituencies, voters nationwide want many of the same things: a healthy economy, a safe country (in terms of national defense and local crime), good schools, and effective and affordable health care. As Figure 10.1 shows, citizens clearly want their elected officials to get them a fair share of the federal pie and to do **casework** for the district—that is, help their

**FIGURE
10.1**

What Do People Want from Congress?

Members of Congress are often criticized for being out of touch with their constituents. Based on a *USA Today* poll, Americans seem to want their congressional members to vote in line with their constituents' views, to work across party lines, and to spend more time in the district rather than Washington, D.C. But what happens if these goals conflict? What if the member represents a very partisan district where the majority does not want her to work with the other party? Also, is there no room for a trustee who follows her conscience and sticks to her principles?

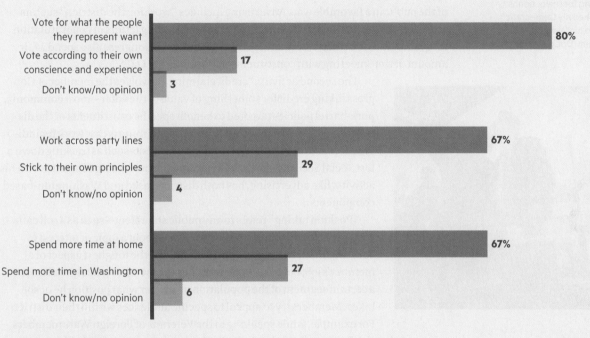

Vote for what the people they represent want	80%
Vote according to their own conscience and experience	17
Don't know/no opinion	3
Work across party lines	67%
Stick to their own principles	29
Don't know/no opinion	4
Spend more time at home	67%
Spend more time in Washington	27
Don't know/no opinion	6

Source: "Divided We Still Stand—And Getting Used To It," *USA Today*, www.usatoday.com (accessed 4/11/14).

constituents to solve bureaucratic problems or address specific concerns related to government. But survey respondents show little interest in having their representatives "spend more time in Washington" and would rather have them spend time at home. Thus, responsibilities for national interests may be more difficult for members of Congress to explain to their constituents.

Members of Congress want to keep their jobs

Members' relationship to their constituents also must be understood within the context of their desire to be reelected. Political scientist David R. Mayhew argues that reelection must come first.[9] Members of Congress certainly hold multiple goals, including making good policy; but if they cannot maintain their seats, then they cannot attain other goals while in office.

After assuming that reelection is central, Mayhew asks this question: "Members of Congress may be electorally motivated, but are they in a position to do anything about it?"[10] Although individual members of Congress cannot do much to alter national

electoral connection
The idea that congressional behavior is centrally motivated by members' desire for reelection.

Senator Mark Kirk (R-IL) is shown here campaigning for reelection. A Republican in a heavily Democratic state, Kirk lost to his Democratic challenger, Tammy Duckworth. @MarkKirk

economic or political forces, they can control their own activities in the House or Senate. The importance of the **electoral connection** in explaining members' behavior seems especially clear for marginal incumbents who are constantly trying to shore up their electoral base, but even incumbents in "safe" districts realize that their job security is not guaranteed.

Mayhew outlines three ways that members of Congress promote their chances for reelection: advertising, credit claiming, and position taking. Each approach shapes the way members relate to their constituents. "Advertising" in this context refers to appeals or appearances without issue content that get the member's name in front of the public in a favorable way. Advertising includes "working the district," such as attending town meetings, appearing in a parade, or sending letters of congratulation for graduations, birthdays, or anniversaries. Members of Congress also spend a fair amount of time meeting with constituents in Washington, D.C.

The second activity, "credit claiming," involves the member of Congress taking credit for something of value to the voter—most commonly, pork-barrel policies targeted to benefit specific constituents or the district as a whole. Another source of credit claiming is casework for individual constituents who request help with tasks such as tracking down a lost Social Security check or expediting the processing of a passport. This activity, like advertising, has both district-based and Washington-based components.

"Position taking" refers to any public statement—such as a roll call vote, speech, editorial, or position paper—about a topic of interest to constituents or interest groups. This may be the toughest aspect of a member's job, because on many issues the member is likely to alienate a certain segment of the population no matter what position he or she takes. Members try to appeal to specific audiences within their district. For example, while speaking to the Veterans of Foreign Wars members might emphasize their support for a particular new weapons program, but in meetings with college students they might highlight their opposition to the NSA's collection of millions of phone records.

The focus on reelection has some costs, two of which reflect widespread public opinion. First, the perception that Congress has granted itself too many special privileges aimed at securing reelection (such as funding for large staffs and the privilege of sending mail at no cost) leads to harsh criticism. Second, there is concern that members' time spent actively campaigning takes time away from the responsibilities of enacting laws and overseeing their implementation. Another cost is the possibility of passing contradictory policies in an effort to satisfy diverse interest groups.

incumbency advantage
The relative infrequency with which members of Congress are defeated in their attempts for reelection.

The Incumbency Advantage The desire to be reelected influences House members' and senators' behavior both in the district and in Congress. As we have mentioned, incumbents look for opportunities to shore up support for the next election, and their success at pleasing constituents produces large election rewards. As Figure 10.2 shows, few members are defeated in reelection races. This is known as the **incumbency advantage**. In the past two decades, incumbent reelection rates have been near record high levels, with 95 to 98 percent of House incumbents winning.[11] For example, in 2008, in an election that many called transformational, 95 percent of House incumbents were still reelected. Although the Democrats picked up some seats in the Senate, reelection remained the norm there as well. Even in the "tsunami" election of 2010, in which Republicans made the largest gains in the House since 1948, picking up 63 seats, 86 percent of incumbents were elected. Why are incumbents so successful? Scholars have offered several reasons for this incumbency advantage.

House and Senate Reelection Rates

FIGURE
10.2

The whole House is up for reelection every two years, so the line showing the reelection of House members in a given election year represents the percentage of the entire House. Since senators are up for reelection every six years, only one-third of the members are seeking reelection every two years. The line for the Senate represents the percentage of those who won who were up for reelection in that election year. Why do you think that House members have an easier time getting reelected than senators?

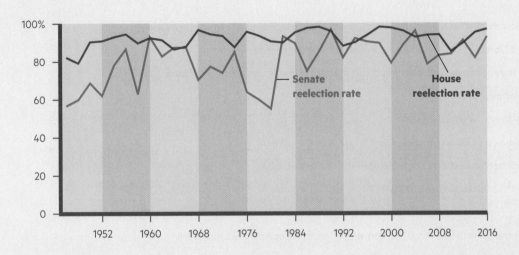

Sources: The 1946–2012 percentages were compiled from Norman J. Ornstein, Thomas E. Mann, Michael J. Malbin, and Andrew Rugg, "Vital Statistics on Congress," www.brookings.edu/vitalstats, pp. 49–50 (accessed 4/18/14); 2014 and 2016 percentages were calculated from election results.

In the District: Home Style One explanation for the increasing incumbency advantage is rooted in the diversity of congressional districts and states. Members of Congress typically respond to the diversity in their districts by developing an appropriate home style—a way of relating to the district.[12] A home style shapes the way members allocate resources, the way incumbents present themselves to their district, and the way they explain their policy positions.

Given the variation among districts, members' home styles vary as well. In some rural districts, it is important for representatives to have local roots and voters expect extensive contact with members. Urban districts expect a different kind of style. Because they have a more mobile population, voters there expect less direct contact and place more emphasis on how their elected members of Congress explain their policy positions.

Incumbency advantage may be explained in part by the skill with which members have cultivated their individual home styles in the last two decades. Members spend more time at home and less time in Washington than was true a generation ago. This familiarity with voters has helped them remain in office. Table 10.1 shows how one member, Senator Tammy Baldwin, spent her time in Washington and in her district as a House member.

Campaign Fund-Raising Raising money is also key to staying in office. Incumbents need money to pay for campaign staff, travel, and advertising. It takes at least $1 million to make a credible challenge to an incumbent in most districts, and in many areas with expensive media markets the minimum price tag is $2 million or more. Few challengers

TABLE
10.1

Typical Workdays for a Congressional Representative

Members of Congress are generally busy from morning until late at night, both in Washington, D.C., and in their districts, attending meetings and events. This is the actual schedule from Tammy Baldwin when she represented Wisconsin's 2nd congressional district in the House.

In Washington, D.C. (votes scheduled throughout the day)	
9:15–9:45	Office time
9:45–10:00	Caucus, Democratic members, Subcommittee on Energy and Environment on markup legislation
10:00–12:00	Markup H.R. 3276, H.R. 3258, H.R. 2868, Subcommittee on Energy and Environment
11:30–11:45	Step outside markup to meet with constituents on specifics of health care reform legislation
12:00–12:15	Travel to Department of Justice
12:15–1:15	Lunch with Attorney General Eric Holder
1:30–1:45	Meet with health care CEO on specifics of health care reform legislation
2:00–3:00	Meet with members who support single-payer health care amendment
3:00–4:30	Markup H.R. 3792, Subcommittee on Health
4:30–5:30	Office time
5:30–6:00	Caucus, Democratic members, Energy and Commerce Committee on financial services bill
6:00–6:30	Meet with legislative staff
6:30–7:00	Meet with chief of staff
7:00–7:50	Office time
8:00–10:00	Dinner with chief of staff and political adviser
In the District	
7:00 ET–8:00 CT	Fly from Washington, D.C., to Madison, WI
8:15–10:30	Free time at home
10:30–10:40	Phone interview with area radio station on constituent survey, health care reform, and upcoming listening session
12:15–12:25	Travel to office
12:25–1:00	Office time, edit/sign correspondence
1:00–1:20	Travel to Madison West High School
1:30–1:55	Remarks at school plaza dedication ceremony
2:00–2:30	Travel to Stoughton, WI
2:45–5:00	Listening session (originally scheduled for one hour but continued until all present could speak)
5:00–5:40	Travel home
5:15–5:20	Phone interview with University of Wisconsin student radio station
6:15–6:45	Travel to Middleton, WI
7:00–8:00	Attend and give brief remarks at NAACP annual banquet
8:05–8:25	Travel home

Note: The authors would like to thank then-Representative Tammy Baldwin and her press secretary, Jerilyn Goodman, for sharing this information. Ms. Goodman emphasized that there really isn't a "typical day" for a member but said that these two days illustrate the workload. Baldwin was elected to the U.S. Senate in 2012.

can raise that much money. The gap between incumbent and challenger spending has grown dramatically in the past decade, with incumbents now spending about three times as much as challengers. Incumbents have far greater potential to raise vast sums of money, in part because PACs are unwilling to risk alienating an incumbent by donating to challengers. (For more on campaign finance, see Chapters 8 and 9.)

Money also functions as a deterrent to potential challengers. A sizable reelection fund signals that an incumbent knows how to raise money and will run a strong campaign. The aim is to convince would-be challengers that they have a slim chance of beating the incumbent—and to convince contributors and party organizations that there's no point in trying to support a challenger. This point is crucial in explaining incumbency advantage because it is nearly impossible for a weak challenger to beat an incumbent. Consider that only 10 to 15 percent of challengers in a typical election year have any previous elective experience; when such a high proportion of challengers are amateurs, it is not surprising that so many incumbents win.

Constituency Service Another thing incumbents do to get reelected is "work their districts," taking every opportunity to meet with constituents, listen to their concerns, and perform casework (helping constituents interact with government programs or agencies). High levels of constituency service may help explain why some incumbents have become electorally secure.

Members of Congress love doing constituency service because it is an easy way to make voters happy. If a member can help a constituent solve a problem, that person will be more likely to support the member in the future.[13] Many voters might give the incumbent some credit simply for being willing to listen. Therefore, most members devote a significant portion of their staff to constituency service, publish newsletters that tout their good deeds on behalf of constituents, and solicit citizens' requests for help through their newsletters and websites.

This combination of factors gives incumbents substantial advantages over candidates who might run against them. By virtue of their position, they can help constituents who have problems with an agency or a program. They attract media attention because of their actions in office. And they use their official position as a platform for raising campaign cash. Finally, most incumbents represent states or districts whose

DID YOU KNOW?

On average, House incumbents spent
$1,504,038
on campaigns in 2016. The average Senate incumbent raised $12,283,715. This is compared with $211,371 and $1,479,910 for the average House and Senate challengers.
Source: Opensecrets.org

House Speaker Paul Ryan (R-WI) with his constituents at a "listening session" in Kenosha, Wisconsin.
@SpeakerRyan

partisan balance (the number of likely supporters of their party versus the number likely to prefer the other party) is skewed in their favor—if it weren't, they probably wouldn't have won the seat in the first place.

Redistricting Connects Representation and Elections The shape and makeup of congressional districts are critical to understanding representation in Congress and the electoral connection. District boundaries determine who is eligible to vote in any given congressional race, and these boundaries are re-drawn every 10 years, after each national census. **Redistricting** is the task of state legislatures. Its official purpose is to ensure that districts are roughly equal in population, which in turn ensures that every vote counts equally in determining the composition of the legislature.

District populations vary over time as people move from state to state or from one part of a state to another. At the national level, states gain or lose legislative seats after each census through a process called **apportionment**, which is the process of dividing the fixed number of House seats (435) among the states based on increases and decreases in state populations. Thus, states growing the fastest gain seats and states that are not growing as fast lose seats (for example, after the 2010 census Texas gained four seats in Congress while Ohio lost two). The one legislature in America that is not redistricted is the U.S. Senate, which has two legislators elected per state, thus giving voters in small states proportionally more influence than those in large states when it comes to the Senate.

In theory, redistricting proceeds from a set of principles that define what districts should look like. One criterion is that districts should be roughly equal in population based on the principles of "one-person, one-vote" established by the Supreme Court in the 1960s.[14] They should also reflect "communities of interest" by grouping like-minded voters in the same district. There are also technical criteria, including compactness (districts should not have extremely bizarre shapes) and contiguity (one part of a district cannot be completely separated from the rest of the district). Mapmakers also try to respect traditional natural boundaries, avoid splitting municipalities, preserve existing districts, and avoid diluting the voting power of racial minorities.

Partisan Redistricting Although the principles listed here are important, they are not the driving force in the redistricting process. In most states, the state legislature draws district boundaries and the majority party tries to draw districts that will give the greatest advantage to candidates from their party. Suppose a Democrat holds a state assembly seat from an urban district populated mainly by citizens with strong Democratic Party ties. After a census, the Republican-dominated state legislature develops a new plan that extends the representative's district into the suburbs, claiming that the change counteracts population declines within the city by adding suburban voters. However, these suburban voters will likely be Republicans, thus increasing the chance that the Democrat will face strong opposition in future elections and maybe lose his or her seat. Such changes have an important impact on voters as well. Voters who are "shifted" to a new district by a change in boundaries may be unable to vote for the incumbent they have supported for years and may instead get a representative who doesn't share their views.

In congressional redistricting, a reduction in the number of seats allocated to a state can lead to districting plans that put two incumbents in the same district, forcing them to run against each other. Incumbents from one party use these opportunities to defeat incumbents from the other party. Both parties use this technique and other tools of creative cartography to gain partisan advantage.

Attempts to use the redistricting process for political advantage are called **gerrymandering**. The term is named after Elbridge Gerry, an early Massachusetts House member and governor, vice president under James Madison, and author of one of the

redistricting
Re-drawing the geographic boundaries of legislative districts. This happens every 10 years to ensure that districts remain roughly equal in population.

apportionment
The process of assigning the 435 seats in the House to the states based on increases or decreases in state population.

gerrymandering
Attempting to use the process of re-drawing district boundaries to benefit a political party, protect incumbents, or change the proportion of minority voters in a district.

Types of Gerrymanders

We have learned that the redistricting process is a powerful tool politicians can use to help their party, or individual members, win and maintain seats in Congress. Let's look at two key types of gerrymandering.

Partisan gerrymanders

Elected officials from one party draw district lines that benefit candidates from their party and hurt candidates from other parties. This usually occurs when one party has majorities in both houses of the state legislature and occupies the governorship and can therefore enact redistricting legislation without input from the minority party.

Redistricting
- The new 9th district

Previous Districts
- 10th—Dennis Kucinich
- 13th—Betty Sutton
- 9th—Marcy Kaptur

After the 2010 census, Ohio lost two seats in Congress (see our discussion of apportionment on page 288). Republicans controlled the redistricting process and wanted the loss of seats to come from the Democrats. So the Republicans drew a new 9th congressional district that cut across the districts of three existing Democratic members of Congress. Obviously only one could win the Democratic primary—that happened to be Marcy Kaptur. Democrats Kucinich and Sutton had to leave Congress.

Racial gerrymanders

Redistricting is used to help or hurt the chances of minority legislative candidates. The Voting Rights Act (VRA) of 1965 mandated that districting plans for many parts of the South be approved by the U.S. Department of Justice or a Washington, D.C., district court. Subsequent interpretations of the 1982 VRA amendments and Supreme Court decisions led to the creation of districts in which racial minorities are in the majority. The aim of these majority-minority districts was to raise the percentage of African-American and Latino elected officials.

- The new 4th congressional district

Illinois's 4th congressional district is a clear example of racial gerrymandering. The district has a very odd shape, but it incorporates two heavily Latino areas. (The northern part has a high Puerto Rican population and the southern part is largely Mexican; both areas are heavily Democratic.) This district is a stronghold of Democrat Luis Gutierrez, who is of Puerto Rican descent, and is seen as a safe district for Democrats.

original partisan redistricting plans (including a district with a thin, winding shape resembling a salamander). In addition to the partisan gerrymanders discussed earlier, Nuts & Bolts 10.1 gives examples of redistricting strategies.

Racial Redistricting Redistricting may yield boundaries that look highly unusual, especially when such efforts address population groups based on race. During the 1992 redistricting in North Carolina, the Justice Department told state legislators that they needed to create two districts with majority populations of minority voters (called majority-minority districts). Figure 10.3 shows the plan they enacted, in which the district boundaries look like a pattern of spiderwebs and ink blots. Moreover, one of the districts had parts that ended up being only as wide as I-85, following the highway off an exit ramp, over a bridge, and down the entrance ramp on the other side. This move prevented the I-85 district from bisecting the district it was traveling through, which would have violated the state law requiring contiguous districts.

The North Carolina example shows how convoluted redistricting plans can become. Part of the complexity is due to the availability of census databases that enable line drawers to divide voters as closely as they want, moving neighborhood by neighborhood, even house by house. Why bother with this level of detail? Because redistricting influences who gets elected; it is active politicking in its most fundamental form. The North Carolina plan was ultimately declared unconstitutional by the Supreme Court—a ruling that opened the door for dozens of lawsuits about racial redistricting. (See the discussion in Chapter 5 of the Voting Rights Act of 1965 and the more recent Supreme Court rulings on racial redistricting, especially the 2013 case in which the Court struck down the part of the law that had identified states that needed to have their redistricting plans preapproved by the Justice Department.)[15] The current legal standard is that race cannot be the *predominant* factor in drawing congressional district lines, but it can be one of the factors.

The Responsibility–Responsiveness Dilemma As mentioned earlier, polls show that despite generally approving of their own member of Congress, people hold Congress itself in very low esteem. This is rooted in the conflicts that arise from Congress's

FIGURE 10.3

North Carolina Redistricting, 1992

This set of House districts was the subject of the landmark Supreme Court ruling *Shaw v. Reno* (1993), in which the Court said that "appearances matter" when drawing district lines. Do you agree? Should other factors such as race, party, and competitiveness play a greater role than district shape?

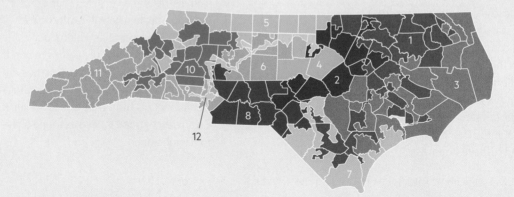

Source: North Carolina General Assembly, 1992 Congressional Base Plan No. 10, http://ncga.state.nc.us (accessed 10/26/12).

dual roles: responsibility for national policy making and responsiveness to local constituencies.[16] Part of the national frustration with Congress arises because we want our representatives to be both responsible *and* responsive; we want them to be great national leaders *and* take care of our local and, at times, personal concerns.

Rather than understanding these issues as inherent in the legislative process, we often accuse members of **gridlock** and partisan bickering when our conflicting demands are not met. For example, public-opinion polls routinely show that the public wants lower taxes; more spending in education, the environment, and health care; and balanced budgets—but those three things cannot happen simultaneously. We often expect the impossible from Congress and then are frustrated when it doesn't happen.

The responsibility–responsiveness dilemma brings us back to the puzzle we posed at the beginning of this section: Why is there a persistent 30 to 40 percent gap between approval ratings for individual members and for the institution? The answer may simply be that members of Congress tend to respond more to their constituents' demands than take on the responsibility of solving national problems. And when Congress becomes embroiled in debates about constituencies' conflicting demands, the institution may appear ineffectual. But as long as members keep the "folks back home" happy, their individual popularity will remain high. In the next section, we describe how members structure the institutions of Congress to help them get reelected.

gridlock
An inability to enact legislation because of partisan conflict within Congress or between Congress and the president.

How would you like your member of Congress to represent you? Should members represent the interests of just their district or the broader nation? Should they be responsive or responsible? Constituents have an interest in holding their members accountable, yet most congressional elections are not very competitive. So if you don't like how your member is representing you, what can you do about it? Understanding the nature of representation and the incumbency advantage can help answer these important questions.

"Why Should I Care?"

The structure of Congress

As we have seen, the goal of getting reelected greatly influences the behavior of members of Congress. The reelection goal also has a strong influence on the way that Congress is structured, both formally (staff, the committee system, parties, and the leadership) and informally (norms). Despite the importance of the electoral connection, the goal of being reelected cannot explain everything about members' behavior and the congressional structure. This section examines some other explanations for the way Congress is set up: the policy motivations of members, the partisan basis for congressional institutions, and the importance of the committee system.

★
EXAMINE HOW PARTIES, THE COMMITTEE SYSTEM, AND STAFFERS ENABLE CONGRESS TO FUNCTION

Informal structures

Various norms provide an informal structure for the way that Congress works. *Universalism* is a norm stating that when benefits are divided they should be awarded to as many districts and states as possible. Thus, for example, when it comes to handing out

The Politics of Pork

What is pork? Pork traditionally took the form of earmarked funding for a specific project that is not subject to standard, neutral spending formulas or a competitive process. However, since 2011 the House and Senate have banned formal earmarks, so members have created new ways to make sure that the benefits continue to flow to their constituents. Some broader definitions of pork include any benefit targeted to a particular political constituency (typically an important business in a member's district), even if the benefit is part of a stand-alone bill. Examples of this type of targeted federal largesse include the bill that provided federal support to the airlines after the September 11 attacks, which sailed through Congress without much debate, and the lucrative contracts to rebuild Iraq that were awarded to politically well-connected businesses.

Pork is simply wasteful spending.
Pork has plenty of critics. Citizens Against Government Waste, one of the most outspoken groups to tackle pork-barrel spending, compiles each year's federal pork-barrel projects into their annual *Congressional Pig Book* to draw attention to pork. The ban on earmarks has helped a great deal, but committee and informal earmarks are still pervasive. The arguments against pork are especially urgent during a time of massive budget deficits. According to this view, the national interest in a balanced budget should take priority over localized projects.

One common tactic previously used by legislators to win approval for pork was to insert earmarks into emergency spending bills that were expected to pass, such as disaster relief for flood and hurricane victims, spending for national security after the September 11 attacks, or funding for the wars in Iraq and Afghanistan. For example, the $636.3 billion defense appropriations bill in 2010 included $128.3 billion for the wars in Iraq and Afghanistan and was also stuffed with 1,719 earmarks worth $7.6 billion.[a] Even without specific earmarks, House members and senators were still claiming credit for plenty of pork in the 2016 omnibus spending bill: $120 million to upgrade the M1 Abrams tank, which is opposed by the Pentagon; $15 million for the Pacific Coastal Salmon Recovery Fund; and $4 million for an aquatic plant control program.[b] As one reporter explained, "[T]he truth is that earmarks haven't really vanished; they've merely changed shape.... Call it the era of vegan pork."[c] Members may simply be taking credit for something that was going to pass anyway or they may secure the project through "letter-marking"—writing a letter to the relevant agency to ask for the funding to be directed to their district. This type

📷 President Obama signs the omnibus spending bill in Washington, D.C., in January 2014. This bill funded a broad range of military and discretionary programs.

of "asking nicely" for pork (sometimes referred to as "stealth pork") can be effective because agencies know that their funding depends on keeping members of Congress happy.

Pork has its good side.
Nonetheless, some argue that pork is the "glue of legislating," because these small side payments secure the passage of larger bills. If it takes a little pork for the home district or state in order to get important legislation through Congress, so be it. The motives of budget reform groups that call for greater fiscal discipline in Congress may also be questioned, since many of these groups oppose government spending in general—not just on pork. In some cases, policies they identify as pork have significant national implications: military readiness, road improvements to support economic infrastructure, or the development of new agricultural and food products. National interests can be served, in other words, by allowing local interests to take a dip into the pork barrel. Put another way, "pork is in the eye of the beholder," or one person's pork is another person's essential spending. Finally, defenders of pork point out that even according to the critics' own definition, pork spending constitutes about one-half of 1 percent of the total federal budget.

take a stand

1. If you were a member of Congress, would you work hard to deliver pork to your district or work to eliminate as much pork as you could from the budget?

2. Why is it so difficult to eliminate pork even in the face of massive budget deficits?

federal highway dollars or expenditures for the Pentagon's weapons programs the benefits are broadly distributed across the entire country. (This means, however, that votes on such bills tend to be lopsided, as some areas of the country need the federal funds more urgently than others.)

Another norm, **logrolling**, reinforces universalism with the idea that "if you scratch my back, I'll scratch yours." This norm leads members of Congress to support bills—that they otherwise might oppose—in exchange for another member's vote on a bill that is very important to them. For example, House members from a dairy state might vote for tobacco price supports even if their state had no tobacco farmers and in return they would expect a member from the tobacco state to vote for the dairy price support bill. This norm can produce wasteful pork-barrel spending. In the 2011 budget, a $1.1 trillion omnibus appropriations bill contained more than 6,488 **earmarks** worth $8.3 billion, so nearly everyone gained something by passing it. The 2016 omnibus appropriations bill did not include any traditional earmarks, following the ban on formal earmarks in both the House and the Senate in 2011, but there were still billions of dollars in targeted spending as members of Congress found ways to secure funding for their district or state. Senator John McCain (R-AZ), Senate Armed Services Committee chairman, called it a last-minute mess full of "wasteful, unnecessary, and inappropriate pork-barrel projects."[17] The Take a Stand feature describes some of the fierce debates in Congress and among political commentators about the merit of this type of spending.[18]

The norm of *specialization* is also important, both for the efficient operation of Congress and for members' reelection. By specializing and becoming an expert on a given issue, members provide valuable information to the institution as a whole and also create a basis for credit claiming. This norm is stronger in the House, where members often develop a few areas of expertise, whereas senators tend to be policy generalists.

The **seniority** norm also serves individual and institutional purposes. This norm holds that the member with the longest service on a committee will chair the committee. Although there have been numerous violations of the norm, whereby the most senior member has been passed over for someone whom the party leaders favor instead, the norm benefits the institution by ensuring orderly succession in committee leadership.[19] The norm also benefits members by providing a tangible reason why voters should return them to Congress year after year.

Formal structures

Formal structures also shape members' behavior in Congress. Political parties, party leadership, the committee system, and staff provide the context within which members of Congress make policy and represent their constituents (see Nuts & Bolts 10.2).

Parties and Party Leaders Political parties are important for allocating power in Congress. Party leaders are always elected on straight party-line votes, and the majority party determines committee leadership, the division of seats on committees, and the allocation of committee resources. Without parties, the legislative process would be much more fractured because members would be autonomous agents in battle with one another. Parties provide a team framework that allows members to work together for broadly beneficial goals. Just think how difficult it would be for a member of Congress to get a bill passed if he or she had to build a coalition from scratch every time. Instead, parties provide a solid base from which coalition building may begin. As discussed in Chapter 7, political parties provide brand name recognition for members.

The top party leader in the House—and the only House leader mentioned in the Constitution—is the **Speaker of the House**. This individual is the head of the majority

logrolling
A form of reciprocity in which members of Congress support bills that they otherwise might not vote for in exchange for other members' votes on bills that are very important to them.

earmarks
Federally funded local projects attached to bills passed through Congress.

seniority
The informal congressional norm of choosing the member who has served the longest on a particular committee to be the committee chair.

Speaker of the House
The elected leader of the House of Representatives.

Majority-Party Structure in the House of Representatives and the Senate

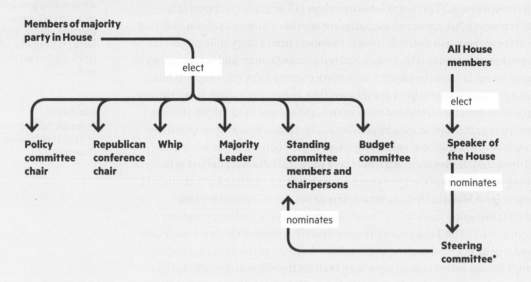

Members of majority party in House — elect

- Policy committee chair
- Republican conference chair
- Whip
- Majority Leader
- Standing committee members and chairpersons
- Budget committee

All House members — elect

- Speaker of the House — nominates → Steering committee*

Steering committee* — nominates → Standing committee members and chairpersons

* Steering committee includes the Speaker, majority leader, and whip, and some members who are appointed by the Speaker and some who are elected by the Conference.

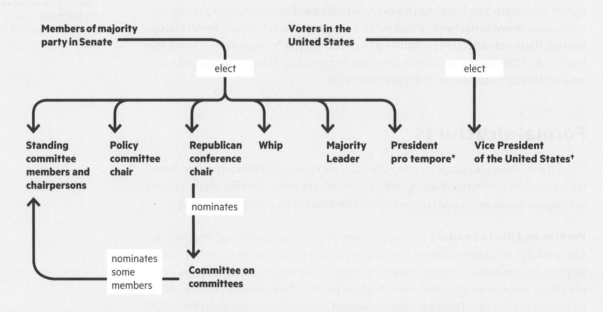

Members of majority party in Senate — elect

- Standing committee members and chairpersons
- Policy committee chair
- Republican conference chair
- Whip
- Majority Leader
- President pro tempore*

Voters in the United States — elect

- Vice President of the United States†

Republican conference chair — nominates → Committee on committees

Committee on committees — nominates some members → Standing committee members and chairpersons

* The President pro tempore is elected by the majority party members, but by custom is the most senior member of the majority party.
† The vice president of the United States is the president of the Senate, but rarely presides over the floor. The vice president's most important role is to break tie votes.

party, and he or she influences the legislative agenda, committee assignments, scheduling, and overall party strategy. The Speaker is aided by the **Majority Leader**, the Majority Whip, and the caucus chair (in addition to many other lower-level party positions). The Majority Leader not only is a key national spokesperson for the party but also helps with the day-to-day operation of the legislative process.

The Majority Whip oversees the extensive **whip system**, which has three functions: information gathering, information dissemination, and coalition building. The whips meet regularly to discuss legislative strategy and scheduling. The whips then pass along this information to colleagues in their respective parties and indicate the party's position on a given bill. Whips also take a head count of party members in the House on specific votes and communicate this information to the party leaders. If a vote looks close, whips try to persuade members to support the party's positions. The conference chair for the Republicans (or caucus chair for the Democrats) runs the party meetings to elect floor leaders, make committee assignments, and set legislative agendas. The minority party in the House has a parallel structure: its leader is the **Minority Leader**, and the second in command is the Minority Whip. ("Whip" comes from English fox hunting, referring to the person who keeps the hounds from wandering too far from the pack—the "whipper-in.")

The Senate leadership does not have as much power as that of the House, mostly because individual senators have more power than individual House members on account of the Senate's rule of unlimited debate. The Majority Leader and Minority Leader are the leaders of their respective parties; second in command are the Assistant Majority and Minority Leaders. The Senate also has a whip system, but it is not as extensive as the House system. Republicans have a separate position for the conference chair, while the Democratic leader also serves as the caucus chair. Officially, the country's vice president is also the president of the Senate, but he or she appears in the chamber only when needed to cast a tie-breaking vote. The Constitution also mentions the **president pro tempore** of the Senate, whose formal duties involve presiding over the Senate when the vice president is not present. This is typically the most senior member of the majority party, although the position does not have any real power. (In fact, the actual president pro tempore rarely presides over the Senate and the task is typically given to a more junior senator.)

Majority Leader
The elected head of the party holding the majority of seats in the House or Senate.

whip system
An organization of House leaders who work to disseminate information and promote party unity in voting on legislation.

Minority Leader
The elected head of the party holding the minority of seats in the House or Senate.

president pro tempore
A largely symbolic position usually held by the most senior member of the majority party in the Senate.

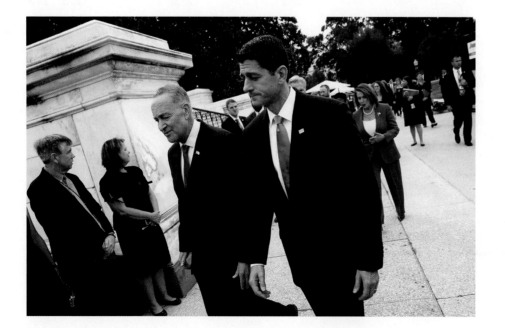

Party leadership is central in the legislative process. Senate Minority Leader Chuck Schumer (D-NY, left), Speaker of the House Paul Ryan (R-WI, right), and House Minority Leader Nancy Pelosi (D-CA, behind) must work together and with other members of Congress to pass legislation.

roll call vote
A recorded vote on legislation; members may vote yes, no, abstain, or present.

party vote
A vote in which the majority of one party opposes the position of the majority of the other party.

The Role of Parties Political parties in Congress reflect the individualism of the institution. In the U.S. Congress, the parties do not impose a party line or penalize members who vote against the party. Indeed, they have virtually no ability to impose electoral restrictions (such as denying the party's nomination) on renegade members.

Parties in Congress have greatly strengthened since the 1960s (see Figure 10.4). Partisanship—evident when party members stick together in opposition to the other party—reached its highest levels of the post–World War II era in the mid-1990s. About 70 percent of all **roll call votes** were **party votes**, in which a majority of one party opposed a majority of the other party. The proportion of party votes fell to between 50 and 60 percent over the next 15 years but recently hit new highs. The *Congressional Quarterly* created the measure in 1953, and since that time the highest proportions were

FIGURE 10.4

Party Votes and Unity in Congress, 1962–2015

(A) Party votes are said to occur when a majority of one party opposes a majority of the other party, and **(B)** party unity refers to the percentage of the party members who vote together on party votes. These two graphs make two important points. First, partisanship has increased in the last two decades, in terms of both the proportion of party votes and the level of party unity. Second, despite these increased levels of partisanship, only about two-thirds of all votes in the House and Senate divide the two parties. Given these potentially conflicting observations, how would you assess the argument that partisanship in Congress is far too intense?

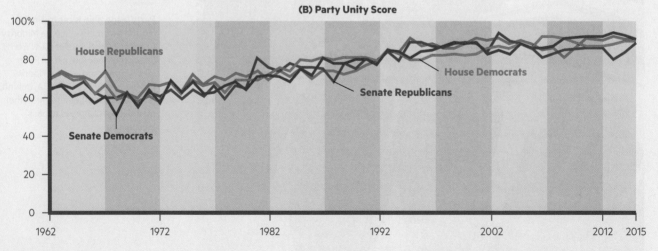

Source: CQ Roll Call, http://cqrollcall.com/cq/ (accessed 7/28/16).

72 percent in the Senate in 2009 and 75.8 percent in the House in 2011; the numbers were down a bit in the next two years but remained around 70 percent. **Party unity**, the percentage of party members voting together on party votes, soared during this period as well, especially in the House.

This greater cohesiveness within parties and separation across parties means that strong party leadership is possible in Congress, but only with the consent of party members.[20] That consent is more likely if there are strong differences between the parties but unity within the parties. Both of these conditions hold in recent years with high party unity, as shown in the previous paragraph, and greater distance between the parties as they have become more polarized (see Figure 10.5). Leaders' chief responsibility is to get their party's legislative agenda through Congress, but they primarily have to rely on persuasion and control over the timing of when bills come up for a vote rather than telling members what to do. Leaders' success largely depends on their personal skills, communicative abilities, and trustworthiness. Some of the most successful leaders, such as Lyndon Johnson (D-TX), Majority Leader of the Senate from 1955 to 1961, and Sam Rayburn (D-TX), Speaker of the House for more than 17 years, kept in touch with key members on a daily basis. Another important tool of the leadership is agenda control: both positive (getting bills to the floor that are favored by the party) and negative (preventing votes on bills that would divide the majority party).

Leaders also must have the ability to bargain and compromise. One observer noted, "To Senator Johnson, public policy evidently was an inexhaustibly bargainable product."[21] Such leaders find solutions where none appear possible. Leaders also do favors for members to engender a feeling of personal obligation to the leadership when it

party unity
The extent to which members of Congress in the same party vote together on party votes.

Ideological Polarization in Congress, 1879–2015

FIGURE 10.5

Although party polarization in Congress has been high in the past, it lessened in the early twentieth century. Polarization has increased steadily in the last 70 years, and today's Congress is more polarized than ever. What do you think causes this extreme polarization?

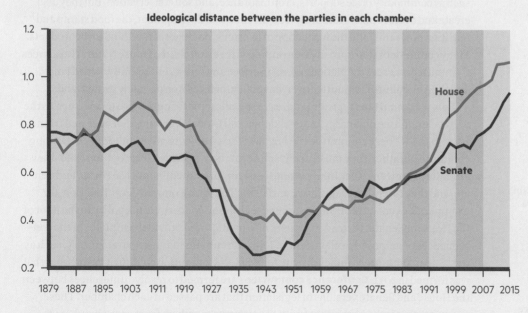

Ideological distance between the parties in each chamber

Source: "More on Polarization through the 114th," Voteview blog, January 30, 2016, https://voteviewblog.wordpress.com (accessed 5/16/16).

"

If you want to get along, go along.

—**Sam Rayburn,** former Speaker of the House

📷

A sitting president can be a powerful ally in a campaign. In 2016, President Obama campaigned with Senate candidate Catherine Cortez Masto (D-NV), who ultimately won her race.

standing committees
Committees that are a permanent part of the House or Senate structure, holding more importance and authority than other committees.

select committees
Committees in the House or Senate created to address a specific issue for one or two terms.

joint committees
Committees that contain members of both the House and Senate but have limited authority.

conference committees
Temporary committees created to negotiate differences between the House and Senate versions of a piece of legislation that has passed through both chambers.

needs a key vote. Such favors include making campaign appearances, helping with fund-raising, contributing to campaigns, helping members get desired committee assignments, and guiding pet projects through the legislative process.

The party's most powerful positive incentives are in the area of campaign finance. In recent years, the congressional campaign committees of both parties and the national party organizations have been supplying candidates with money and other resources in an attempt to gain more influence in the electoral process. Party leaders may also help arrange a campaign stop or a fund-raiser for a candidate with party leaders or the president. For example, President Barack Obama held dozens of fund-raisers for Democrats in 2014, earning him the label "Fundraiser-in-Chief" from CNN.[22] Such events typically raise $500,000 to more than $1 million.

Despite these positive reinforcements, members' desire for reelection always comes before party concerns and leadership rarely tries to force a member to vote against his or her constituents' interests. For example, Democrats from rural areas, where most constituents support gun ownership and many are hunters, would not be expected to vote the party line favoring a gun control bill. But if a member of Congress did something much more extreme that crossed the party's leadership—for example, supporting the opposing party's candidate for Speaker or passing strategic information to the opposition—he or she could expect to be disciplined by the party's leaders. In such cases, disciplinary measures might involve stripping the member of all committee assignments or even expelling the member from his or her seat. Despite occasional strong-arm tactics, party leaders have moved toward a service-oriented leadership, recognizing that their power is only as strong as the leeway granted by the rank-and-file membership.

The Committee System The committee system in the House and Senate is another crucial part of the legislative structure. There are four types of committees: standing, select, joint, and conference. **Standing committees**, which have ongoing membership and jurisdictions, are where most of the work of Congress gets done. These committees draft legislation and oversee the implementation of the laws they pass. For example, the Agriculture Committees in the House and Senate have jurisdiction over farm programs such as commodity price supports, crop insurance, and soil conservation. But they also create and oversee policy for rural electrification and development, the food stamp and nutrition programs, and the inspection of livestock, poultry, seafood, and meat products. Many committees share jurisdiction on policy: for example, the House Natural Resources Committee oversees the National Forest Service and forests on federally owned lands, and the Agriculture Committee oversees policy for forests on privately owned lands.

Select committees typically address a specific topic for one or two terms, such as the Select Committee on Energy Independence and Global Warming that operated from 2007 to 2010. These committees do not have the same legislative authority as standing committees; rather, they mostly collect information, provide policy options, and draw attention to a given issue. **Joint committees** comprise members of the House and Senate, and they rarely have legislative authority. The Joint Committee on Taxation, for example, does not have authority to send legislation concerning tax policy to the floor of the House or Senate. Instead, it gathers information and provides estimates of the consequences of proposed tax legislation. Joint committees may also be temporary, such as the "Supercommittee" (officially, the Joint Select Committee on Deficit Reduction) that was formed in 2011. **Conference committees** are formed to resolve differences between the House and Senate versions of legislation that are passed in each chamber. These committees mostly comprise standing committee members from each chamber who worked on the bill. Table 10.2 shows the policy areas covered by each type of committee.

The committee system creates a division of labor that helps members get reelected by supporting their specialization and credit claiming. For example, a chair of the Agriculture Committee or of a key agricultural subcommittee may reasonably take credit for passing an important bill for the farmers back home, such as the Cottonseed Payment Program that provides assistance to cottonseed farmers who have lost crops due to hurricanes. The number of members who could make these credible claims expanded dramatically in the 1970s with the proliferation of subcommittees (there are 100 in the House and 67 in the Senate). Speaking about the House, one observer said, with some exaggeration, that if you ever forget a member's name you can simply refer to him or her as "Mr. or Ms. Chairman" and you will be right about half the time.

This view of congressional committees is based on the *distributive theory*, which is rooted in the norm of reciprocity and the incentive to provide benefits for the district. The theory holds that members will seek committee assignments to best serve their

TABLE
10.2

Congressional Committees

There are equivalent committees in the House and Senate (and some joint committees) that work on similar problems and craft similar bills whose differences must be reconciled before a final bill becomes law. Equivalent or similar committees in both chambers are listed across from each other.

House Committees	Senate Committees	Joint Committees
Agriculture	Agriculture, Nutrition, and Forestry	Joint Economic Committee
Appropriations	Appropriations	Joint Committee on the Library
Armed Services	Armed Services	Joint Committee on Printing
Budget	Budget	Joint Committee on Taxation
Education and Workforce	Health, Education, Labor, and Pensions	
Energy and Commerce	Commerce, Science, and Transportation	
Ethics	Select Committee on Ethics	
Financial Services	Banking, Housing, and Urban Affairs	
Foreign Affairs	Foreign Relations	
Homeland Security	Homeland Security and Governmental Affairs	
House Administration	Rules and Administration	
Judiciary	Judiciary	
Natural Resources	Energy and Natural Resources	
Select Committee on Intelligence	Select Committee on Intelligence	
Small Business	Small Business and Entrepreneurship	
Transportation and Infrastructure	Environment and Public Works	
Veterans Affairs	Veterans Affairs	
Ways and Means	Finance	

Committees specific to the House	Committees specific to the Senate
Oversight and Government Reform	Special Committee on Aging
Rules	Indian Affairs
Science, Space, and Technology	

district's interests, the leadership will accommodate those requests, and the floor will respect the views of the committees (that is, committee members will support one another's legislation). This means that members tend to have an interest in and to support the policies produced by the committees they serve on. For example, members from farm states would want to serve on the Agriculture Committee and members with a lot of military bases or defense contractors in their districts would want to be on the Armed Services Committee.

Nonetheless, the committee system does not exist simply to further members' electoral goals. It also provides collective benefits to the rest of the members through committee members' expertise on policy, which helps reduce uncertainty about policy outcomes.[23] By deferring to expert committees, members are able to achieve beneficial outcomes while using their own time more efficiently.

Committees also serve the policy needs of the majority party, largely because it controls a majority of seats on every committee. The party ratios on each committee generally reflect the partisan distribution in the overall chamber, but the majority party gives itself somewhat larger majorities on the important committees such as Ways and Means (which controls tax policy), Appropriations, and Rules. The Rules Committee is important to the majority party because it structures the nature of debate in the House by setting the length of debate and the type and number of amendments to a bill that will be allowed. These decisions must be approved by a majority of the House members. The Rules Committee has become an arm of the majority-party leadership, and in many instances it provides rules that support the party's policy agenda or protect its members from having to take controversial positions. For example, the Rules Committee prevented many amendments on the 2010 health care reform bill; if the amendments had come to a vote, they would have divided the Democratic Party. Majority members are expected to support their party on votes concerning rules, even if they end up voting against the related legislation.

Congressional Staff The final component of the formal structure of Congress is congressional staff. The size of personal and committee staff exploded in the 1970s and 1980s and has since leveled off. Today the total number of congressional staff is more than four times as large as it was 50 years ago. Part of the motivation for this growth was to reduce the gap between the policy-making capability of Congress and the president, especially with regard to fiscal policy. The larger committee staffs gave members of Congress independent sources of information and expertise with which to challenge the president. The other primary motivation was electoral. By increasing the size of their personal staff, members were able to open multiple district offices and expand opportunities for helping constituents.

"Why Should I Care?"

The Constitution says very little about the internal structure of Congress, so the institution is largely the one the members want. The norms of the institution and its formal structure facilitate members' electoral and policy goals, so if they don't like the way something works they can change it. This may sound very self-serving, but members of Congress also serve broader collective and policy goals or they would be booted out of office. Understanding this fundamental point provides great insight into why Congress is structured the way that it is.

How a bill becomes a law

Every introductory textbook on American politics presents a diagram that describes how a bill becomes a law. This book is no exception. However, we provide an important truth-in-advertising disclosure: many important laws do not follow this orderly path.[24] After presenting the standard view, we describe the most important deviations from that path.

The conventional process

The details of the legislative process can be incredibly complex, but its basic aspects are fairly simple (see How It Works: Passing Legislation). The most important thing to understand about the process is that before a piece of legislation can become a law it must be passed *in identical form* by both the House and the Senate and signed by the president. If the president vetoes the bill, it can still be passed with a two-thirds vote in each chamber. The basic steps of the process are:

1. A member of Congress introduces the bill.
2. A subcommittee and committee craft the bill.
3. Floor action on the bill takes place in the first chamber (House or Senate).
4. Committee and floor action takes place in the second chamber.
5. The conference committee works out any differences between the House and Senate versions of the bill. (If the two chambers pass the same version, steps 5 and 6 are not necessary.)
6. The floor of each chamber passes the final conference committee version.
7. The president either signs or vetoes the final version.
8. If the bill is vetoed, both chambers can attempt to override the veto with a two-thirds vote in both chambers.

Early Steps The first part of the process, unchanged from the earliest Congresses, is the introduction of the bill. Only members of Congress can introduce a bill, either by

---

⬡

Types of Legislation

- **Bill:** A legislative proposal that becomes law if it is passed by both the House and the Senate in identical form and approved by the president. Each is assigned a bill number, with "H.R." indicating bills that originated in the House and "S.R." denoting bills that originated in the Senate. Private bills are concerned with a specific individual or organization and often address immigration or naturalization issues. Public bills affect the general public if enacted into law.
- **Simple resolution:** Legislation used to express the sense of the House or Senate, designated by "H.Res." or "S.Res." Simple resolutions affect only the chamber passing the resolution, are not signed by the president, and cannot become public law. Resolutions are often used for symbolic legislation, such as congratulating sports teams or naming a post office after a famous person.

- **Concurrent resolution:** Legislation used to express the position of both chambers on a nonlegislative matter to set the annual budget or to fix adjournment dates, designated by "H.Con.Res." or "S.Con.Res." Concurrent resolutions are not signed by the president and therefore do not carry the weight of law.
- **Joint resolution:** Legislation that has few practical differences from a bill (passes both chambers in identical form, signed by the president) unless it proposes a constitutional amendment. In that case, a two-thirds majority of those present and voting in both the House and the Senate, and ratification by three-fourths of the states, are required for the amendment to be adopted and it does not require the president's signature.

How it works:
Passing Legislation

Speaker of House Receives Bill

President of Senate Receives Bill

Committee*†

Committee*†

Subcommittee*†

Subcommittee*†

Bill Reported Out by Full Committee

Bill Reported Out by Full Committee

Rules Committee*†

Amends or Approves Bill from Committee

Amends or Approves Bill from Committee

Majority Leader

House Floor*†

House Bill

Senate Bill

Senate Floor*†

House Amends Senate Bill*†

Senate Amends House Bill*†

House Floor†

Senate Floor†

Conference Committee*†

House Modifies Senate Bill

Senate Modifies House Bill

Conference Report*†

House Approves Senate Bill†

Adoption by Both Houses†

Senate Approves House Bill†

White House†

Veto

Approve

House and Senate Floor†

Law

Veto Override

*Points at which a bill can be amended.
†Points at which a bill can die.

Passing the Affordable Care Act

The 2010 Affordable Care Act (ACA) provides an example of how passing legislation often deviates from the conventional method.

In the House...

3 committees crafted the bill.

↓

She added things.

Speaker Nancy Pelosi assumed a critical role in shaping the final bill, **adding things that weren't in the committee version.**

↓

House passes its version.

In the Senate...

5 committees worked on the Senate version.

↓

He added things.

After a deadlock between two committees, Majority Leader Harry Reid pushed through a merged version of the bill, **adding things that weren't in the committee version.**

↓

Senate passes its version.

Meanwhile...

President Obama was intensely involved. **The White House held daily meetings** with the committees.

No conference committee. Instead, committee leaders, White House staff, and party leadership negotiated the details of the bills.

So then...

?!

The Senate version of the **bill was passed by the House.**

But...

!

The House added things.

The House also passed a separate reconciliation bill that included many amendments to the Senate version.

Amended!

That reconciliation bill was then **amended by the Senate.**

Passed!

The amended reconciliation bill was then **passed by the House.**

Signed into law.

President Obama **signed the two acts into law,** both of which comprise the ACA.

? Critical Thinking

1. **What are the most significant ways in which** the process to pass the ACA deviated from the conventional method?

2. **Do you think the ACA could have been** passed without this unconventional process? Why or why not?

DID YOU KNOW?

10,000

to 14,000 bills are introduced in every Congress, but only 2 to 4 percent become law and another 6 to 10 percent are resolutions that are enacted. Most bills die in committee.
Source: Govtrack.us

markup
One of the steps through which a bill becomes a law, in which the final wording of the bill is determined.

cloture
A procedure through which the Senate can limit the amount of time spent debating a bill (cutting off a filibuster) if a supermajority of 60 senators agree.

filibuster
A tactic used by senators to block a bill by continuing to hold the floor and speak—under the Senate rule of unlimited debate—until the bill's supporters back down.

dropping it into the "hopper," a wooden box at the front of the chamber in the House, or by presenting it to one of the clerks at the presiding officer's desk in the Senate. Even the president would need to have a House member or senator introduce his bill. Each bill has one or more sponsors and often many co-sponsors. (See Nuts & Bolts 10.3 for a description of the different types of legislation.)

The next step is to send the bill to the relevant committee. House and Senate rules specify committee jurisdictions (there are more than 200 categories), and the bill is matched with the committee that best fits its subject matter. In the House, major legislation may be sent to more than one committee in a practice known as multiple referral, but one of the committees is designated the primary committee and the bill is reviewed by other committees sequentially or in parts. The practice is less common in the Senate, partly because senators have more opportunities to amend legislation on the floor.

Once the bill goes to a committee, the chair refers it to the relevant subcommittee, where much of the legislative work occurs. One important point: 80 to 90 percent of bills die at this stage of the process; they never make it out of the subcommittee or committee. For bills that see some action, the subcommittee holds hearings, calls witnesses, and gathers the information necessary to rewrite, amend, and edit the bill. The final language of the bill is determined in a collaborative process known as the **markup**. During this meeting, members debate aspects of the issue and offer amendments to change the language or content of the bill. After all amendments have been considered, a final vote is taken on whether to send the bill to the full committee. The full committee then considers whether to pass it along to the floor. They, too, have the option of amending the bill, passing it as-is, or tabling it (which kills the bill). Every bill sent to the floor by a committee is accompanied by a report and full documentation of all the hearings. These documents constitute the bill's legislative history, which the courts, executive departments, and the public use to determine the purpose and meaning of the law.

Debating the Bill When the bill makes it to the floor, it is placed on one of the various legislative calendars. Bills are removed from the calendar to be considered by the floor under a broad range of possible rules. When the bill reaches the floor, the majority party and minority party each designate a bill manager, who is responsible for guiding the debate on the floor. Debate in the House proceeds according to tight time limits and rules governing the nature of amendments. Senate debate is much more open and unlimited in most circumstances (unless all the senators agree to a limit).

Unless restricted by a unanimous consent agreement, senators can speak as long as they want and offer any amendment to a bill, even if it isn't germane (that is, directly related to the underlying bill). Debate may be cut off only if a supermajority of 60 senators agree in a process known as invoking **cloture**. Therefore, one senator can stop any bill by threatening to talk the bill to death if 40 of his or her colleagues agree. This practice, which is known as a **filibuster**, strengthens the hand of the minority party in the Senate, giving it veto power over legislation unless the majority party has 60 senators who unanimously support a bill.

When debate is completed and all amendments have been considered, the presiding officer calls for a voice vote, with those in favor saying "aye" and those opposed "no." If it is unclear which side has won, any member may call for a "division vote," which requires members on each side to stand and be counted. At that point, any member may call for a recorded vote (there is no way of recording members' positions on voice votes and division votes). If at least 25 members agree that a recorded vote is desired, buzzers go off in the office buildings and committee rooms, calling members to the floor for the vote. Once they reach the floor, members vote by an electronic system in which they insert ATM-like cards into slots and each vote is recorded on a big board at the front of the chamber.

Resolving Discrepancies If the bill passes the House and the Senate in different forms, the discrepancies have to be resolved. On many minor bills, one chamber may simply accept the other chamber's version to solve the problem. On other minor bills and some major bills, differences are resolved through a process known as amendments between the chambers. In this case, one chamber modifies a bill passed by the other chamber and sends it back. These modifications can go back and forth several times before both chambers agree on an identical bill. A complicated version of this approach was used to pass health care reform in 2010.

The most common way to resolve differences on major legislation is through a conference committee made up of key players in the House and the Senate. A majority of major bills go to a conference committee, but minor bills rarely do.[25] Sometimes the conferees split the difference between the House and Senate versions, but at other times the House and Senate approaches are so different that one must be chosen—an especially tricky prospect when different parties control the two chambers. Sometimes the conference committee cannot resolve differences and the bill dies. If the committee can agree on changes, each chamber must pass the final version—the conference report—by a majority vote and neither chamber is allowed to amend it.

One final point on how a bill becomes a law is important: any bill that appropriates money must pass through the two-step process of authorization and appropriation. In the authorization process, members debate the merits of the bill, determine its language, and limit the amount that can be spent on the bill. The appropriations process involves the Budget Committees in both the House and the Senate, which set the overall guidelines for the national budget, and the Appropriations Committees in the two chambers, which determine the actual amounts of money that will be spent (see How It Works in Chapter 14). In recent years, Congress has been unable to pass appropriations bills in time for the start of the new fiscal year, so it ends up passing "continuing resolutions" that spend money at the previous year's levels in order to keep the government open. Congress passed three continuing resolutions for the 2016 fiscal year. That may sound like a lot, but the record is 21 for the 2001 fiscal year.[26]

Presidential Approval or Veto The bill is then sent to the president. If the president approves and signs the measure within 10 days (not counting Sundays), it becomes law. If the president objects to the bill, he or she may **veto** it within 10 days by sending it back to the chamber where it originated, along with a statement of objections. Unless both the House and the Senate vote to override the veto by a two-thirds majority, the bill dies. If the president does not act within 10 days and Congress is in session, the bill becomes law without the president's approval. If Congress is not in session, the measure dies through a **pocket veto**.

Deviations from the conventional process

There are many ways in which legislation may not follow the typical path. First, in some Congresses up to 20 percent of *major* bills bypass the committee system. This may be done by a discharge petition, in which a majority of the members force a bill out of its assigned committee, or by a special rule in the House. In some cases, a bill may go to the relevant committee, but then party leadership may impose its version of the bill later in

Senator Ted Cruz (R-TX) held forth on the Senate floor for more than 21 hours expressing his opposition to the ACA in September 2013. @TedCruz

veto
The president's rejection of a bill that has been passed by Congress. A veto can be overridden by a two-thirds vote in both the House and Senate.

pocket veto
The automatic death of a bill passed by the House and Senate when the president fails to sign the bill in the last 10 days of a legislative session.

the process. Consider the USA PATRIOT Act, which Congress passed in the wake of the terrorist attacks of September 11 to give the government stronger surveillance powers. It was unanimously reported by the Judiciary Committee after five days of hard bipartisan work; but a few days later, according to committee member Representative Jerrold Nadler (D-NY), "Then the bill just disappeared. And we had a new several hundred page bill revealed from the Rules Committee" that had to be voted on the next day. Most members of Congress did not have a chance to read it.[27] The Affordable Care Act passed in 2010 also deviated from the standard path (see How It Works, earlier in this chapter).

Second, about one-third of major bills are adjusted post-committee and before the legislation reaches the floor by supporters of the bill to increase the chances of passage. Sometimes the bill goes back to the committee after these changes, and sometimes it does not. Thus, although most of the legislative work is accomplished in committees, a significant amount of legislation bypasses committee review.

Third, summit meetings between the president and congressional leaders may bypass or jump-start the normal legislative process. For example, rather than going through the Budget Committees to set budgetary targets, the president may meet with top leaders from both parties and hammer out a compromise that is presented to Congress as a done deal.

Fourth, **omnibus legislation**—massive bills that run hundreds of pages long and cover many different subjects and programs—often requires creative approaches by the leadership to guide the bill through the legislative maze. Leadership task forces may be used in place of committees, and alternatives to the conference committee may be devised to resolve differences between the two chambers. In addition, the massive legislation often carries riders—extraneous legislation attached to the "must pass" bill to secure approval for pet projects that would otherwise fail. This form of pork-barrel legislation is another mechanism used in the quest for reelection.

Key differences between House and Senate legislative processes

There are three central differences between the legislative processes of the House and the Senate: the continuity of the membership and the impact that has on the rules; the way in which bills get to the floor; and the structure of the floor process, including debate and amendments. First, because the Senate is a continuing body, with two-thirds of its members returning every session without facing reelection, there has been greater stability in the rules of the Senate than the House. However, Senate rules can be changed at the start of a session if necessary to accommodate new members' needs.

The floor process itself is simpler and less structured in the Senate than in the House. This is partly due to the relative size of the two chambers: the House, with 435 members, needs more rules than the Senate, with its 100 members. Moreover, the Senate is a more individualistic body, with unlimited debate and a very open amendment process. As mentioned earlier, unless restricted by a unanimous consent agreement, senators can speak as long as they want and offer any type of amendment to a bill. In contrast, the House is a more complex institution. The Rules Committee governs the nature of debate on a bill there: closed rules do not allow any amendments, open rules allow related amendments, and modified rules allow some amendments but not others. Floor managers control general debate under a five-minute rule, although that restriction is frequently circumvented through an elaborate process that allows more time.

Ironically, although the Senate is formally committed to unlimited debate, senators often voluntarily place limits on themselves, which makes them operate more like the

omnibus legislation
Large bills that often cover several topics and may contain extraneous, or pork-barrel, projects.

House. Similarly, although the House has strict rules concerning debate and amendments, there are ways of bending those rules to make that chamber operate more like the potentially freewheeling Senate.

"Why Should I Care?"

Otto von Bismarck, the Prussian statesman of the late nineteenth century, famously said, "Laws are like sausages; it is better not to see them being made." Indeed, the legislative process may be messy, but knowledge of how laws are made is important both for being an effective legislator and for being a good democratic citizen. Understanding how a bill becomes a law, seeing the various stages of the process, and recognizing the various veto points at which a bill may die all help put into context the simplistic complaints about gridlock and conflict. Now that you have a better understanding of the legislative process, you should have a stronger basis for evaluating what Congress is doing.

Oversight

★

DESCRIBE HOW CONGRESS ENSURES THAT THE BUREAUCRACY IMPLEMENTS POLICIES CORRECTLY

Once a bill becomes a law, Congress plays another crucial role by overseeing the implementation of the law to make sure the bureaucracy interprets it as Congress intended. Other motivations driving the oversight process are the desire to gain publicity that may help in the reelection quest or to embarrass the president if he or she is of the opposite party. For example, in 2015, Republicans used their oversight powers to call attention to Hillary Clinton's use of private servers for her work-related e-mail as secretary of state and the way that she handled the attack on the U.S. embassy in Benghazi. While these hearings were, at least in part, politically motivated (Clinton was no longer secretary of state), the most important motivation for oversight is to ensure that laws are implemented properly.[28]

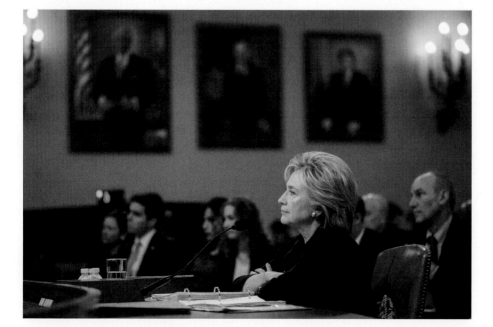

Former secretary of state and Democratic presidential candidate Hillary Clinton testifies before the House Select Committee on Benghazi in October 2015. Clinton faced tough questioning over her response to the attack on the U.S. diplomatic compound in Benghazi and her use of a private e-mail server while serving as secretary of state. #Benghazi @HillaryClinton

"

I have seen in the Halls of
Congress more idealism, more
humanness, more compassion,
more profiles of courage than in
any other institution that I have
ever known.

—**Hubert Humphrey,** former
senator and vice president

Congress may use several mechanisms to accomplish this goal (see Chapter 12). First, the bluntest instrument is the power of the purse. If members of Congress think an agency is not properly implementing their programs, they can simply cut off the funds. However, this approach is rarely used because budget cuts often eliminate good aspects of the agency along with the bad.

Second, Congress can hold hearings and investigations. By summoning administration officials and agency heads to a public hearing, Congress can use the media spotlight to focus attention on problems within the bureaucracy or on issues that have been overlooked. For example, House Republicans called former Health and Human Services secretary Kathleen Sebelius to testify several times in 2013 and 2014 about the rocky rollout of the healthcare.gov website for Obamacare. This type of oversight is known as "fire alarm oversight"—that is, members wait until there is a crisis before they spring to action.[29] It is in contrast to "police patrol" oversight, which involves constant vigilance in overseeing the bureaucracy. For example, the House Veterans' Affairs Committee recently investigated poor service and a cover-up of records at VA hospitals, which eventually led to General Eric Shinseki's resignation as the secretary of Veterans Affairs.[30] Of the two, fire alarm oversight is more common because Congress does not have the resources to constantly monitor the entire bureaucracy.

Last, the Senate exercises specific control over other executive functions through its constitutional responsibilities to provide "advice and consent" on presidential appointments and approval of treaties. The Senate typically defers to the president on these matters, but it may assert its power, especially when constituent interests are involved. One current example would be the Senate's increasing skepticism about free-trade agreements negotiated by the president's trade representatives and its holds on presidential nominations.

The ultimate in congressional oversight is the process of removing the president, vice president, other civil officers, or federal judges through impeachment. The House and Senate share this power. The House issues articles of impeachment, which outline the charges against the official, and the Senate conducts the trial of the impeached officials. Two presidents have been impeached: Andrew Johnson in the controversy over Reconstruction after the Civil War, and Bill Clinton over the scandal involving White House intern Monica Lewinsky. However, neither president was convicted and removed by the Senate.

Conclusion

Although the details of the legislative process and the institutions of Congress can be complicated, the basic explanations for member behavior are straightforward when viewed in terms of the trade-off between responsiveness and responsibility. Members of Congress want to be reelected, so they are generally quite responsive to constituents' interests. They spend considerable time on casework, meeting with people in the district, and delivering benefits for the district. At the same time, members are motivated to be responsible—to rise above local interests and attend to the nation's best interests.

The conflict between these two impulses can create contradictory policies that contribute to Congress's image problem. For example, we subsidize tobacco farming at the same time that we spend billions of dollars to treat the health problems that tobacco use creates. We have laws on water rights that encourage farmers to irrigate the desert at the same time that we pay farmers to leave parts of their land unplanted

Members of Congress want to be reelected, and this goal explains much of their behavior. In 2016, House Majority Leader Kevin McCarthy (R-CA) won reelection. Given his leadership position within the party, McCarthy must be especially careful to balance local interests with the good of the nation as a whole.
@KevinOMcCarthy

in areas of the country that are well suited for agriculture. These policies, and others, reflect both the desire to serve local interests and the norms of reciprocity and universalism.

Considering members' motivations is crucial to understanding how Congress functions, but their behavior is also constrained by the institutions in which they operate. The committee system is an important source of expertise and information, and it provides a platform from which members can take positions and claim credit. Parties in Congress provide coherence to the legislative agenda and help structure voting patterns on bills. Rules and norms constrain the nature of debate and the legislative process. Although these institutions shape members' behavior, members can also change those rules and institutions. Therefore, Congress has the ability to evolve with changing national conditions and demands from voters, groups, and the president.

In this context, much of what Congress does can be understood in terms of the conflicts inherent in politics. How can members act responsibly without sacrificing responsiveness? Can Congress be structured in a way that allows members to be responsive (and therefore have a better chance of getting reelected) without losing the ability to make unpopular decisions when needed? The example discussed in this chapter's introduction concerning sexual assaults in the military demonstrates that, even on issues that nearly everyone would agree are problems (nobody is in favor of sexual assaults), there are important differences of opinion about what actions should be taken. The compromise position that passed with nearly universal support in the Senate was not ideal for those who wanted stronger reforms, but compromise means that many people will not be completely satisfied with the final version. Congress does not always live up to the expectations of being the "first branch" of government, but it often does an admirable job of balancing the conflicting pressures it faces.

STUDY GUIDE

What Congress does

Explain how members of Congress represent their constituents and how elections hold members accountable. (Pages 278–291)

Summary

The Constitution gave Congress vast enumerated powers, making it the "first branch" of government. While Congress has long dominated day-to-day politics, the president has become considerably more powerful over time. Despite the low approval ratings for Congress itself, most voters like their members of Congress. Members of Congress work hard to strike a balance between responding to what constituents want, and what is in the constituency's best interest. In the balance, however, they prioritize district interests over national policy.

Key terms

bicameralism (p. 279)
pork barrel (p. 279)
descriptive representation (p. 280)
substantive representation (p. 280)
trustee (p. 280)
delegate (p. 280)
politico (p. 282)

casework (p. 282)
electoral connection (p. 284)
incumbency advantage (p. 284)
redistricting (p. 288)
apportionment (p. 288)
gerrymandering (p. 288)
gridlock (p. 291)

Practice Quiz Questions

1. **What did the Seventeenth Amendment do?**
   a. repeal Prohibition
   b. grant women's suffrage
   c. give senators six-year terms
   d. allow for direct election of senators
   e. lower the voting age to 18

2. **Why do senators have longer terms than members of the House of Representatives?**
   a. to reduce the number of candidates in each election
   b. to make sure senators are tied to public sentiment
   c. to provide more opportunities for pork-barrel legislation
   d. to make elections easier to administer
   e. to make sure that senators are somewhat insulated from the people

3. **What is the most common style of representation in Congress?**
   a. trustee
   b. politico
   c. delegate
   d. consulate
   e. adviser

4. **Members of Congress generally hold multiple goals. Which goal comes first?**
   a. getting reelected
   b. passing good policy
   c. serving their political party
   d. blocking the opposing party
   e. serving special interests

5. **What is apportionment?**
   a. determining presidential primary winners
   b. determining whether the state legislature or courts will re-draw district lines
   c. determining which states gain/lose seats in the Senate
   d. determining which states gain/lose seats in the House
   e. determining how many seats a party has in Congress

6. **On average, incumbents spend _____ times as much as challengers on campaigning.**
   a. one and one-half
   b. three
   c. five
   d. ten
   e. twenty

The structure of Congress

Examine how parties, the committee system, and staffers enable Congress to function. (Pages 291–300)

Summary

Many aspects of Congress are set up to meet the needs of its members. The norms of universalism and reciprocity still dominate, meaning that members of Congress share resources more broadly than partisan politics would dictate.

Key terms

logrolling (p. 293)
earmarks (p. 293)
seniority (p. 293)
Speaker of the House (p. 293)
Majority Leader (p. 295)
whip system (p. 295)
Minority Leader (p. 295)
president pro tempore (p. 295)

roll call vote (p. 296)
party vote (p. 296)
party unity (p. 297)
standing committees (p. 298)
select committees (p. 298)
joint committees (p. 298)
conference committees (p. 298)

Practice Quiz Questions

7. Under the norm of _____, federal highway dollars are likely to be divided up so that many districts benefit.

a. reciprocity

b. seniority

c. party unity

d. universalism

e. specialization

8. Committee leadership, division of seats on committee, and allocation of committee resources are determined by _____.

a. the majority party

b. the size of the election margin

c. unanimous consent

d. seniority

e. the president pro tempore

9. The Senate leadership is _____ the House leadership.

a. more powerful than

b. as powerful as

c. less powerful than

10. Party leaders have the power to _____.

a. force members of Congress to vote a particular way

b. keep a member of Congress off the ballot in the next election

c. force their members to share campaign money

d. exclude a member from a roll call vote

e. help their members get favorable committee assignments

How a bill becomes a law

Trace the steps in the legislative process. (Pages 301–307)

Summary

Most bills become law in a conventional manner, but major legislation generally deviates considerably from this path. The legislative process differs for the House and Senate, sometimes making it difficult to reconcile differences between bills.

Key terms

markup (p. 304)

cloture (p. 304)

filibuster (p. 304)

veto (p. 305)

pocket veto (p. 305)

omnibus legislation (p. 306)

Practice Quiz Question

11. Compared with the Senate, the floor process in the House is very _____ and _____.

a. unstructured; majoritarian

b. structured; majoritarian

c. unstructured; individualistic

d. structured; individualistic

e. individualistic; majoritarian

Oversight

Describe how Congress ensures that the bureaucracy implements policies correctly. (Pages 307–309)

Summary

After passing bills into law, Congress oversees the bureaucracy in its implementation of the law, making sure it fits Congress's intentions. Although controlling funding is the most powerful mechanism for this, Congress has a number of other mechanisms for achieving bureaucratic fidelity. Generally, Congress does not actively patrol the bureaucracy but waits until a crisis emerges to act.

Practice Quiz Question

12. Waiting for a crisis to emerge before taking action is called _____.

a. police patrol oversight

b. fire alarm oversight

c. emergency room oversight

d. reactionary oversight

e. bureaucratic oversight

Suggested Reading

Adler, Scott E., and John D. Wilkerson. *Congress and the Politics of Problem Solving*. New York: Cambridge University Press, 2013.

Bianco, William T. *Trust: Representatives and Constituents*. Ann Arbor: University of Michigan Press, 1994.

Canon, David T. *Race, Redistricting and Representation: The Unintended Consequences of Black Majority Districts*. Chicago: University of Chicago Press, 1999.

Fenno, Richard F. *Congressmen in Committees*. Boston: Little, Brown, 1973.

Hall, Richard L. *Participation in Congress*. New Haven, CT: Yale University Press, 1996.

Jacobson, Gary C. *The Politics of Congressional Elections*, 8th ed. New York: Pearson, 2012.

Lapinski, John S. *The Substance of Representation: Congress, American Political Development, and Lawmaking*. Princeton, NJ: Princeton University Press, 2013.

Mayhew, David R. *Congress: The Electoral Connection*, 2nd ed. New Haven, CT: Yale University Press, 2004.

Theriault, Sean. *Party Polarization in Congress*. New York: Cambridge University Press, 2008.

The Presidency

Why can't the president get more done?

Presidential campaigns often make it sound like the winner is going to be the most powerful person in the world. Candidates routinely promise to revitalize the economy, end poverty and injustice, defeat America's enemies, and whip the government into shape. It certainly matters who wins the election. Presidents can order military and covert forces into action. They lead the federal bureaucracy's implementation of congressional mandates. They serve as America's head of state. America looks different today because Barack Obama defeated John McCain in 2008 and Mitt Romney in 2012. And four years from now America will look different because Donald Trump won the 2016 election rather than his opponent, Hillary Clinton.

At the same time, descriptions of the president as some all-powerful force are clearly an exaggeration. Presidents have limited power to affect the economy. Their control over America's military is constrained by public opinion, congressional authority, and the reality that the use of force is often counterproductive. Bureaucrats have many ways to evade presidential directives. Members of Congress, even those from the president's party, are often in open revolt against presidential proposals. Given these problems, the question is not how Donald Trump will transform the government. Rather, the question is why he will be able to do anything at all.

This chapter examines the extent, and the limits, of presidential power. America's presidents have considerable power over U.S. foreign and domestic policy, and they have used this power to do things that have a massive effect on the lives of ordinary Americans. Even so, presidents are often driven to compromise or are forced to abandon deeply held policy goals in the face of opposition from Congress, bureaucrats, judges, or the American public. Why are presidents all-powerful in some cases and seemingly powerless in others?

This chapter shows that while U.S. presidents can sometimes change policy unilaterally, most times they require cooperation or consent from others. As a result, presidential success is not automatic. Presidents may face obstacles

📷

The transfer of presidential power pushes us
to ask fundamental questions about the tone
and policy direction of the country. What will
Trump do with the power of the presidency?
Will he work with Congress, or act more
unilaterally? What policies from the past will
he keep? What will he abandon? Will President
Trump be able to accomplish all he promised?

in their efforts to achieve their own policy goals, yet at the same time they must attempt to satisfy the demands of supporters and opponents—while trying to avoid alienating people who disagree with presidential decisions. To put it another way, although presidents are powerful, they are not kings or dictators. Presidents must also cultivate public opinion in order to get reelected or to help members of their party to be elected or reelected to office. Moreover, presidents and their staff must monitor the bureaucracy to make sure that presidential decisions are faithfully implemented. And sometimes presidents must decide whether to scale back on a proposal to make it more likely to pass Congress or to risk complete failure by holding firm to the original goal.

With these considerations in mind, we ask these fundamental questions in this chapter: What are the sources and limits of presidential power? When are presidents able to prevail in the face of conflict in the country, in Congress, or in the bureaucracy? Has presidential power grown over time? How does conflict affect the decisions that presidents make and the ways they try to implement their policy goals? How does the presidency really work?

★

TRACE THE EVOLUTION
OF PRESIDENTIAL
POWER

The development of presidential power

As we consider the history of America's 44 presidents and look ahead to the forty-fifth, four facts stand out. First, presidents matter. Their actions have had profound consequences for the nation, in both domestic and foreign policy. Second, presidents get their power from a variety of sources, from provisions of the Constitution to their management of and the actions taken by the executive branch of government. Third, presidential power has increased over time, not because of changes in the Constitution but because of America's growth as a nation, its emergence as a dominant actor in international politics, the expansion of the federal government, and acts of legislation that have given new authority to the president. Fourth, there are sharp limits to presidential power. Presidents are often forced to compromise or abandon their plans in the face of public, congressional, or foreign opposition.

Early years through World War I

Since the early years of the Republic, presidents' actions have had profound consequences for the nation. Presidents George Washington, John Adams, and Thomas Jefferson forged compromises on issues such as choosing a permanent location for the nation's capital, establishing the federal courts, and financing the government. Presidents Andrew Jackson and Martin Van Buren were instrumental in forming the Democratic Party and its local party organizations.[1]

Early presidents also made important foreign policy decisions. For example, the Monroe Doctrine, issued by President James Monroe in 1823, stated that America would remain neutral in wars involving European nations and that these nations must cease attempts to colonize or occupy areas in North and South America.[2] Presidents John Tyler and James Polk oversaw the admission of the huge territory of

Texas into the Union following the Mexican-American War as well as the acquisition of land that later became Oregon, Washington, Idaho, and parts of Montana and Wyoming.[3]

Presidents also played key roles in the conflict over slavery in America. President Millard Fillmore's support helped to enact the Compromise of 1850, which limited slavery in California, and Franklin Pierce supported the Kansas-Nebraska Act, which regulated slavery in those territories. And of course, Abraham Lincoln, who helped form the Republican Party in the 1850s, played a transformative role in setting policy as president during the Civil War. His orders raised the huge Union army, and as commander in chief he directed the conduct of the bloody war that ultimately brought the southern states back into the Union. Moreover, he issued the Emancipation Proclamation, which freed the slaves in the South.[4]

During the late 1800s and early 1900s, presidents were instrumental in federal responses to the nation's rapid expansion and industrialization.[5] The country's growing size and economy generated conflict over which services the federal government should provide to citizens and the extent to which the government should regulate individual and corporate behavior.[6] Various acts of legislation created new federal agencies and, in doing so, also created new presidential powers and responsibilities. For example, Republican president Theodore Roosevelt used the Sherman Antitrust Act to break up the Northern Securities Company, a mammoth nationwide railroad trust. Roosevelt also increased the power of the Interstate Commerce Commission to regulate businesses and expanded federal conservation programs. At the same time, the foreign policy initiatives of President Woodrow Wilson illustrate the limits of presidential power. Although he campaigned in the 1916 election on a promise to keep America out of World War I, he ultimately ordered American troops to fight on the side of the Allies. After the war, Wilson offered a peace plan that proposed (1) reshaping the borders of European countries in order to prevent future conflicts; (2) creating an international organization, the League of Nations, to prevent future conflicts; and (3) taking other measures to encourage free trade and democracy.[7] However, America's allies rejected most of Wilson's proposals and the Senate refused to allow American participation in the League of Nations.

George Washington remains, for many Americans, the presidential ideal—a leader whose crucial domestic and foreign policy decisions shaped the growth of America's democracy.

The Great Depression through the present

Presidential actions defined the government's response to the Great Depression—the worldwide economic collapse in the late 1920s and 1930s marked by high unemployment, huge stock market declines, and many bank failures.[7] After winning the 1932 election, Democrat Franklin Roosevelt and his staff began reshaping American government. Roosevelt's New Deal reforms created numerous federal agencies that helped individual Americans and imposed many new corporate regulations.[8] This expansion continued under Roosevelt's successors. Even Republican Dwight Eisenhower, whose party had initially opposed many New Deal reforms, presided over the creation of new agencies and the building of the interstate highway system.[9]

Presidents were instrumental in the civil rights reforms and expansion of the federal government in the 1960s. With congressional approval, President Lyndon Johnson's administration created a wide range of domestic programs, such as the Department of Housing and Urban Development, Medicare, Medicaid, and federal funding for schools. The job of enacting voting rights and civil rights legislation also took place during LBJ's presidency.

President Franklin Delano Roosevelt called on the public to support his New Deal programs and other policies. Here, he delivers one of his "fireside chat" radio broadcasts, designed to communicate his arguments to the American people and to win their support.

Both Johnson and his successor, Richard Nixon, directed America's involvement in the Vietnam War, with the goal of forcing the North Vietnamese to abandon their plans to unify North and South Vietnam. But presidential efforts in Vietnam did not meet with success. Despite enormous deployments of American forces and more than 58,000 American soldiers killed, Nixon eventually signed an agreement that allowed American troops to leave but did not end the conflict, which concluded only after a North Vietnamese victory in 1975.

The two presidents immediately after Nixon, Republican Gerald Ford and Democrat Jimmy Carter, faced the worst economic conditions since the Great Depression, largely due to increased energy prices. Both presidents offered plans to reduce unemployment and inflation, restore economic growth, and enhance domestic energy sources. But their efforts were largely unsuccessful, which became a critical factor in their failed reelection bids.

In the last generation, the political and policy importance of presidential actions has continued to increase. This trend continued during the presidency of Republican Ronald Reagan despite his platform of tax cuts, fewer regulations, and smaller government. Reagan and his staff also negotiated important arms control agreements with the Soviet Union. Reagan's successor, George H. W. Bush, led American and international participation in the Persian Gulf War during 1990 and 1991, which succeeded in removing Iraqi forces from Kuwait with minimal American casualties.

Democrat Bill Clinton's presidency was marked by passage of the North American Free Trade Agreement, welfare reform, arms control agreements, and successful peacekeeping efforts by U.S. troops in Haiti and the Balkans. His presidency also was distinguished by having one of the longest periods of economic growth in U.S. history and the first balanced budgets since the 1960s. President George W. Bush won congressional approval of his tax cuts and education reforms, but he is best remembered for managing America's response to the September 11 attacks, including the wars in Iraq and Afghanistan.

President Obama secured several notable changes in foreign and domestic policy, including the enactment of health care reform, economic stimulus legislation, new financial regulations, and appointment of two Supreme Court justices. However, he had to compromise in enacting many of the new policies, and in areas such as immigration reform and gun control he has been largely unsuccessful in achieving his policy goals.

"Why Should I Care?"

Presidents' performance is often evaluated as though their powers and foresight were unlimited. However, the history of presidential successes and failures highlights how presidents are often constrained by circumstances. Many of the problems they faced were totally unanticipated, or had no good solutions. Other times, attempts to address national needs failed because of congressional or bureaucratic intransigence. Thus, before we make judgments about presidential performance we need to understand their job and the resources they have to accomplish it.

The president's job description

This section describes the president's **constitutional authority** (powers derived from the provisions of the Constitution), **statutory authority** (powers that come from laws), and the additional capabilities that presidents derive from their position as the head of the executive branch of government. Constitutional and statutory powers are summarized in Nuts & Bolts 11.1. As the box indicates, some presidential powers arise from one source, such as the Constitution, and others derive from a combination of constitutional and statutory authority. Our aim is to show how these provisions operate in modern-day American politics: what kinds of opportunities and constraints they create for the current president and future holders of the office.

Head of the executive branch

A president's responsibilities and the source of presidential power begin with the constitutional responsibilities of the office. As stated in the Constitution's **vesting clause**, "The executive Power shall be vested in a President of the United States of America," thereby making the president the **head of government**, which grants him or her authority over the executive branch, as well as the **head of state**, who serves as the symbolic and political representative of the country. The Constitution also places the president in charge of the implementation of laws, saying "he shall take Care that the Laws be faithfully executed." Sometimes the implementation of a law is nearly automatic and all the president needs to do is ensure that bureaucrats use proper, lawful procedures to accomplish the implementation.

More commonly, the president's authority to implement the law requires using judgment to translate legislative goals into programs, budgets, and regulations. For example, the Affordable Care Act (ACA) of 2010 gave the president and the Department of Health and Human Services the authority to modify provisions of the new program, including the deadlines for people to purchase health insurance through the new federal and state exchanges. Although critics charged that congressional consent was required, the ACA was typical of major legislation in that it gave the administration significant leeway as it implemented the policy changes mandated by the law's passage.[10]

Finally, the president's control of the executive branch enables him or her to issue orders to government agencies that make significant policy changes. For example, in 2015 President Obama granted quasi-legal status and work permits to nearly a million illegal immigrants who entered the country as children. While many Republicans and some Democrats criticized the President's action, they were unable to take the steps needed to overturn it—write appropriate legislation, shepherd it through the House and Senate, and override a veto. Ultimately, Obama's order was struck down by a federal appeals court with this decision upheld by a tied Supreme Court. And of course, the order could have been removed by President Trump on his first day in office.

Appointments The president appoints ambassadors, senior bureaucrats, and members of the federal judiciary, including Supreme Court justices.[11] As head of the executive branch, the president controls about 8,000 positions, ranging from high-profile jobs such as secretary of state, to routine administrative and secretarial positions. About 1,200 of these appointments—generally high-level positions such as cabinet secretaries—require Senate confirmation. Because federal judgeships are lifetime

constitutional authority (presidential)
Powers derived from the provisions of the Constitution that outline the president's role in government.

statutory authority (presidential)
Powers derived from laws enacted by Congress that add to the powers given to the president in the Constitution.

vesting clause
Article II, Section 1, of the Constitution, which states: "The executive Power shall be vested in a President of the United States of America," making the president both the head of government and the head of state.

head of government
One role of the president, through which he or she has authority over the executive branch.

head of state
One role of the president, through which he or she represents the country symbolically and politically.

Presidential Powers

Power	Source of Power
Head of Government, Head of State (Vesting Clause)	Constitutional authority
Implementation of Laws ("Faithful Execution")	Constitutional and statutory authority
Executive Orders and Similar Directives (Rare)	Constitutional and statutory authority
Administration of Executive Branch	Constitutional authority
Nominations and Appointments to Executive Branch and Judiciary	Constitutional and statutory authority
Commander in Chief of Armed Forces	Constitutional authority
Negotiation of Treaties and Executive Agreements	Constitutional and statutory authority
Veto of Congressional Actions	Constitutional authority
Presidential Pardons	Constitutional authority
Other Ceremonial Powers	Constitutional authority
Executive Privilege	Other
Recommendation of Spending Levels and Other Legislative Initiatives	Other

appointments, they enable the president to put people into positions of power who will remain after the president leaves office. For example, President Obama's two Supreme Court appointments, Sonia Sotomayor and Elena Kagan, emerged as influential voices on such issues as health care and the rights of criminal defendants.

The need for Senate confirmation of the president's appointments is one of the fundamental limits on presidential power. Historically, the Senate has approved virtually all nominees without much debate or controversy, although in recent years senators (particularly Republicans during Obama's presidency) have blocked votes on many judicial and agency nominees. For example, Republican senators refused to hold hearings or a vote on Merrick Garland, Obama's 2016 Supreme Court nominee, which left the seat vacant for an entire year. If the Senate is in recess (adjourned for more than three days), the president can make a **recess appointment**, whereby an appointee is temporarily given a position without a Senate vote and holds the office until the beginning of the next congressional session. All presidents make recess appointments, but typically for relatively minor offices and for noncontroversial nominees—it would have been highly unusual (and highly controversial) for President Obama to appoint Garland to the Supreme Court via a recess appointment, and the constitutionality of this act is questionable. In any case, the Senate can eliminate the possibility of recess appointments by holding brief working sessions as often as needed to ensure that no recess lasts more than three days.

recess appointment
Selection by the president of a person to be an ambassador or the head of a department while the Senate is not in session, thereby bypassing Senate approval. Unless approved by a subsequent Senate vote, recess appointees serve only to the end of the congressional term.

executive orders
Proclamations made by the president that change government policy without congressional approval.

Executive Orders Presidents have the power to issue **executive orders**—that is, proclamations that unilaterally change government policy without subsequent congressional consent[12]—as well as other kinds of orders that change policy, such as National Security Presidential Directives and Presidential Findings (see the How It Works feature in this chapter). Responding to the December 2012 mass shooting of schoolchildren at Sandy Hook Elementary School in Newtown, Connecticut, in January 2013, President Obama signed 23 executive orders relating to gun control.[13] Many of these orders were relatively modest, such as releasing an analysis of how many lost or stolen guns are used in subsequent crimes. Other orders had more significant effects, such as ordering the Consumer Product Safety Commission (CPSC) to develop new requirements for gun locks. More significant policy changes proposed by Obama, such as banning the possession of armor-piercing bullets, limiting the size of handgun ammunition magazines, and increasing federal funding for local police officers, were part of a gun control package sent to Congress at the same time that the executive orders were signed. None of these proposals were enacted. As the What Do the Numbers Say? feature shows, all presidents issue many executive orders. Most are not consequential, like the annual order that gives federal employees an early dismissal on the last working day before Christmas. But some executive orders implement large changes in federal policy. Lincoln's Emancipation Proclamation was issued as an executive order.

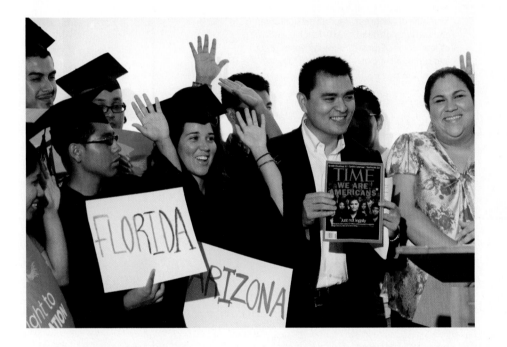

After Congress failed to pass the DREAM (Development, Relief, and Education for Alien Minors) Act, President Obama issued an executive order to stop the deportation of some young illegal immigrants in 2012. Although the scope of the order was subsequently constrained by a tied Supreme Court, Obama's action stands as an example of how presidential power derives from control over how laws are implemented. #DREAMAct

Executive orders may appear to give the president authority to do whatever he or she wants, even when facing strong opposition from Congress. However, as the gun control example illustrates, a president's power to issue executive orders generally involves purely administrative matters (such as releasing the study of lost and stolen guns). Or the president may be able to issue an executive order on a specific question because Congress has passed a law giving him or her some specific authority in this case (such as the ability to direct the CPSC to develop new gun lock regulations). Moreover, regardless of the authority used to issue an order, if members of Congress had objected to the policy changes or new regulations they could have passed a law overturning the orders. In light of congressional opposition to Obama's gun control legislation, if the president had tried to implement these changes through executive orders he would surely have faced either legislative or judicial action to overturn the orders.

Commander in Chief The Constitution makes the president the commander in chief of America's military forces but gives Congress the power to declare war. These provisions are potentially contradictory, and the Constitution leaves open the broader

How Presidents Make Policy outside the Legislative Process

The Constitution describes the president's influence over new policy initiatives in terms of the power to sign or veto acts of Congress. But what can the president do when Congress fails to act how he or she wants?

President + White House staff develop proposals—they talk to the public, members of Congress, interest groups, union and corporation heads, party leaders, and others. Some of these groups initiate contact and submit their own ideas or even fully drafted plans.

President + Congress sometimes find compromise proposals—but other times negotiations reveal that the president's plans will not receive majority support in the House and Senate.

President + White House staff investigate whether some or all of the president's goals can be achieved through executive order or other means.

President issues appropriate orders and directives.

Congress decides whether to enact legislation reversing the president's actions. They need a two-thirds majority in both houses to override an expected presidential veto.

Presidential appointees, assuming congressional attempts to reverse the new policies are unsuccessful, administer implementation of the new policies.

Obama Reestablishes Relations with Cuba

The reopening of diplomatic ties with Cuba illustrates how the president can bypass Congress and initiate meaningful policy change. Obama announced a series of policy changes in December 2014 after a long series of negotiations with the Cuban government, including an agreement to swap spies held by each government.

President + staff:

We're open to it.

2008: During the 2008 presidential campaign, Obama **said he was willing to meet with Cuban leaders.**

Here's a start.

After the election, Obama **eased restrictions** on Cuban Americans sending money to relatives in Cuba.

President + staff + Congress

Let's talk.

2014: Secret negotiations began with the Cuban regime.

...but just us.

Obama and his staff **decided against consulting members of Congress.**

Because...

They believed that Republicans and others who opposed a deal with Cuba would respond **by doing everything they could to end the talks.**

Welcome!

December 2014: Obama announces the **restoration of diplomatic relations with Cuba.**

Let's rebuild.

Florida

Cuba

Easing of restrictions on travel to Cuba, removal of Cuba from the list of state sponsors of terrorism, and other moves to rebuild ties between the two nations.

Welcome home!

The spy exchange takes place soon thereafter. Some Republicans in Congress criticized the spy swap.

President + presidential appointees + Congress

One more (big) thing.

Post-April 2015: Obama and his appointees lobbied Congress to **lift the trade embargo with Cuba.**

Just one catch.

Since the embargo was created by an act of legislation, **Congress must enact a new law to reverse it.** Moreover, all of the Obama administration's changes can be revoked by President Trump.

? Critical Thinking

1. **In addition to concerns about congressional opposition,** why else would the Obama administration decide to keep initial negotiations with Cuba a secret?

2. **Based on what you've read in this chapter,** what would Congress need to do to reverse Obama's actions?

The public sees presidents as speechmakers, but it's mostly butt-in-seat work, a continuous cycle of meetings, decisions, and preparation for meetings and decisions. Governing is a lot harder than tweeting.

—Michael Grunwald,
Politico reporter

question of who controls the military.[14] In practice, however, the president controls day-to-day military operations through the Department of Defense and has the power to order troops into action without explicit congressional approval. For example, in the summer of 2014 the Obama administration joined over a dozen other nations to aid rebel forces in the Syrian civil war. This included conducting air strikes against Syrian government forces and the ISIL terrorist organization. Members of Congress did not approve this action: an authorization resolution was proposed but never voted on in the Senate, and the House took no action at all. Similarly, the 2011 attack on Osama bin Laden's compound was carried out without prior congressional approval, although some congressional leaders were notified in advance.

In fact, even though the United States has been involved in hundreds of military conflicts, there have been only five declarations of war: the War of 1812, the Mexican-American War (1846), the Spanish-American War (1898), World War I (1917), and World War II (1941).

As a way of restraining presidential war-making power, Congress enacted the War Powers Resolution of 1973 (see Nuts & Bolts 11.2). However, between 1975 and 2003, despite dozens of U.S. military actions—ranging from embassy evacuations to large-scale operations, including the 1991 Persian Gulf War and the invasions of Iraq and Afghanistan—the War Powers Resolution has been invoked only once.[15] Moreover, despite being in effect for nearly 40 years, it has never faced Supreme Court review. Some scholars have argued that the resolution actually expands presidential power because it gives the president essentially unlimited control for the first 90 days of a military operation—and in some cases, such as the killing of bin Laden and the many drone attacks authorized in the last decade, 90 days is more than enough time to complete military action without getting Congress involved.[16]

Despite its limitations, the War Powers Resolution has forced presidents to gain congressional approval, in the form of congressional resolutions or at least consultation with congressional leaders, for large-scale military actions such as the invasion of Iraq, as well as for lesser operations such as anti-terrorist operations. Members of Congress can also curb a president's war-making powers through budget restrictions, legislative prohibitions, and, ultimately, impeachment.[17]

Treaty Making and Foreign Policy Treaty-making power is shared between Congress and the president: presidents and their staff negotiate treaties; these are then sent to the Senate for approval, with the support of a two-thirds majority. Congress considers treaties only after negotiations have ended; there is no way for members of Congress to force the president to negotiate a treaty or limit its scope. However, the

NUTS & BOLTS 11.2

The War Powers Resolution of 1973

1. The president is required to report to Congress any introduction of U.S. forces into hostilities or imminent hostilities.
2. The use of force must be terminated within 60 days unless Congress approves of the deployment. The time limit can be extended to 90 days if the president certifies that additional time is needed to safely withdraw American forces.
3. The president is required whenever possible to consult with Congress before introducing American forces into hostilities or imminent hostilities.
4. Any congressional resolution authorizing the continued deployment of American forces will be considered under expedited procedures.

Source: Richard F. Grimmett, "The War Powers Resolution: After Thirty Years," Congressional Research Service Report RL32267, March 11, 2004.

President Obama's Executive Orders

Many critics argued that President Obama issued an unprecedented number of executive orders. They said this was his strategy to bypass a Republican Congress that was unsympathetic to his policy proposals. What do the numbers say?

Executive Orders Issued by Recent Presidents

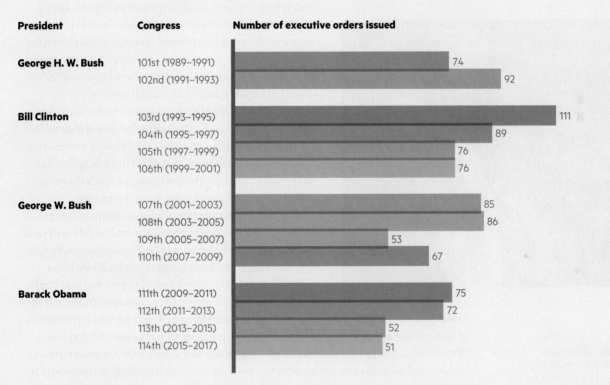

- ■ Divided government (president from one party and at least one branch of Congress from the other)
- ■ Unified government (president and both branches of Congress from the same party)

President	Congress	Number of executive orders issued
George H. W. Bush	101st (1989–1991)	74
	102nd (1991–1993)	92
Bill Clinton	103rd (1993–1995)	111
	104th (1995–1997)	89
	105th (1997–1999)	76
	106th (1999–2001)	76
George W. Bush	107th (2001–2003)	85
	108th (2003–2005)	86
	109th (2005–2007)	53
	110th (2007–2009)	67
Barack Obama	111th (2009–2011)	75
	112th (2011–2013)	72
	113th (2013–2015)	52
	114th (2015–2017)	51

Think about it

- Is there any evidence that Obama issued more executive orders than his predecessors?
- In light of past patterns, how many executive orders would you expect from incoming president Donald Trump?

Source: "Executive Orders Disposition Tables Index," *Federal Register*, www.archives.gov (accessed 11/6/16).

need for congressional approval often leads presidents to consider senators' preferences when negotiating treaties, leading again to significant compromise between the two branches.

Presidents have two strategies for avoiding a congressional treaty vote. One is to announce that the United States will voluntarily abide by a treaty without ratifying it. In the case of the 2015 Paris Climate Accord, one of the reasons why the United States supported voluntary targets for reductions in greenhouse gases was that such an agreement did not require Senate approval. It is also possible to structure a deal as an **executive agreement** between the executive branch and a foreign government, which does not require Senate approval. Relative to a ratified treaty, which remains in force after the president who negotiated it leaves office, both voluntary compliance and executive agreements have the disadvantage that a subsequent president can simply undo the action.

The president also serves as the principal representative of the United States in foreign affairs other than treaty negotiations. Presidential duties include communicating with foreign leaders, nongovernmental organizations, and even ordinary citizens to persuade them to act in ways that the president believes are in the best interest of the United States. For example, in March 2016 President Barack Obama traveled to Cuba, where he toured Cuba's capital, Havana, watched a baseball game between American and Cuban teams, met with Cuban dissidents, and gave a speech on Cuban television that criticized the regime for human rights violations. While speeches and baseball games have no direct effect on policy, they can raise public awareness of their government's shortcomings and perhaps increase pressures for change.

The amount of time the administration devotes to foreign policy is subject to domestic and world events and therefore not entirely under presidential control. Barack Obama campaigned on a pledge to reduce American military operations abroad and, six years into his time in office, America no longer had combat operations in Iraq and Afghanistan. But Obama expanded drone and Special Forces attacks on members of terrorist organizations, promoted American participation in Libya and Syria, and sent American forces to eastern Europe in response to Russia's annexation of Crimea. Obama and his aides also spent considerable time coordinating the global response to the financial crisis of 2008–2009, as well as natural disasters such as the 2010 earthquake in Haiti.

executive agreement
An agreement between the executive branch and a foreign government, which acts as a treaty but does not require Senate approval.

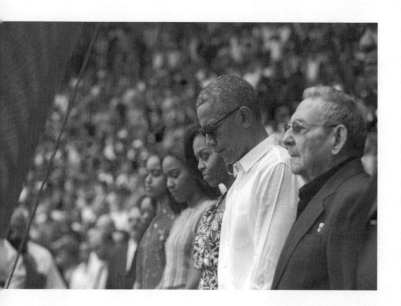

The president often meets with foreign leaders in both formal and informal settings—for example, he watched a baseball game in Havana, Cuba, with Cuban leader Raul Castro in March 2016. Such meetings provide a venue for the president to present American views and mediate disagreements, but also to act as a visible symbol of America's position as a world superpower.

State of the Union
An annual speech in which the president addresses Congress to report on the condition of the country and to recommend policies.

Legislative Power The Constitution establishes lawmaking as a shared power between the president and Congress, and compromise between the two branches is fundamental to passing laws that satisfy both the president and Congress.[18] The president can recommend policies to Congress, notably in the annual **State of the Union** address. The president and his or her staff also work with members of Congress to develop legislative proposals, and although the president cannot formally introduce legislation, it is typically easy to find a member of Congress willing to sponsor a presidential proposal.[19] Presidents and their legislative staff also spend time lobbying members of Congress to support their proposals and negotiating with legislative leaders over policy details.

The president's legislative power also stems from the ability to veto legislation. Once both chambers of Congress have passed a bill by simple majority, the president must decide within two weeks whether to sign it or issue a veto. Signed bills become law, but vetoed bills return to the House and Senate for a vote to override the veto. If both chambers enact the bill again with at least two-thirds majorities, the bill becomes law; otherwise, it is defeated. If Congress adjourns before the president has made a decision, the president can **pocket veto** the proposal by not responding to it. Pocket vetoes cannot be overridden, but congressional leaders can avoid them by keeping Congress in session for two weeks after a bill is enacted.

Figure 11.1 shows the number of vetoes issued by recent presidents—and the number overridden by Congress. In general, vetoes are most likely to occur under divided government, when a president from one party faces a House and Senate controlled by the other party (in the case of Obama, the relatively small number of vetoes reflects a sharp reduction in the number of laws enacted by Congress).[20] Vetoes are much less likely under unified government, when one party controls both Congress and the presidency, because the chances are much higher that the president and legislators from his or her party hold similar policy priorities.

A president's threats to veto legislation provide an additional source of power: they allow the president to specify what kinds of proposals he or she is willing or unwilling to accept from Congress. Legislators then know that they need to write a proposal that attracts two-thirds support in both houses or else accede to the president's demands. For example, during the 2012–2013 debate over raising the federal debt limit President Obama said he would veto any legislation that included repeal of his health care legislation, even if a veto led to a government shutdown. Whether Obama was willing to follow through with his threat is unclear, but the threat worked. In this sense, the veto power can facilitate compromise between presidents and members of Congress—compromises that favor the president's point of view.

Other Duties and Powers The Constitution gives the president several additional powers, including the authority to pardon people convicted of federal crimes or commute (reduce) their sentences. The only limit on this power is that a president cannot pardon anyone who has been impeached and convicted by Congress. (Thus, if a president is removed from office via impeachment he or she can neither pardon him- or herself nor be pardoned when the vice president assumes the presidency.)

Although most presidential pardons attract little attention, some have been extremely controversial. Presidents have pardoned their own appointees for crimes committed while serving in their administrations, and have also pardoned campaign contributors and personal friends. For example, in July 2007 President Bush commuted a 30-month jail term given to Lewis "Scooter" Libby, Vice President Dick Cheney's former aide. Libby had been convicted of lying to a grand jury about his role in leaking the name of a covert CIA agent to several journalists. Yet, in the main, most pardons attract little attention.

Executive Privilege Finally, although this power is not formally set out in the Constitution or a statute, all presidents have claimed to hold the power of **executive privilege**. This refers to the ability to shield themselves and their subordinates from revealing White House discussions, decisions, or documents (including e-mails) to members of the legislative or judicial branches of government.[21]

Although claims of executive privilege have been made since the ratification of the Constitution in 1789, it is still not clear exactly what falls under the privilege and what does not (see the Take a Stand feature). In the 1974 case *United States v. Nixon*, a special prosecutor appointed by the Justice Department to investigate the Watergate scandal challenged President Richard Nixon's claims of executive privilege to force him to hand over tapes of potentially incriminating Oval Office conversations involving

pocket veto
A president's ability to veto a piece of legislation by taking no action on it (possible only when Congress is not in session).

DID YOU KNOW?

Through November 8, 2016, President Obama pardoned or commuted the sentences of

844

individuals convicted of federal crimes.
Source: U.S. Department of Justice

executive privilege
The right of the president to keep executive branch conversations and correspondence confidential from the legislative and judicial branches.

**FIGURE
11.1**

Presidential Vetoes from Bush to Obama

The figure shows the number of vetoes issued by recent presidents in each congressional term they held office, along with whether the term involved unified or divided government. Do the data support the argument that vetoes are less likely given unified government? Compared with other presidents, has Barack Obama issued an inordinately high or low number of vetoes?

■ Regular and Pocket Vetoes　■ Veto Overrides

President	Congress	Presidential vetoes
George H. W. Bush	101st (1989–1991) Divided	19
	102nd (1991–1993) Divided	25 / 1
Bill Clinton	103rd (1993–1995) Unified	No vetoes
	104th (1995–1997) Divided	17 / 1
	105th (1997–1999) Divided	8 / 1
	106th (1999–2001) Divided	12
George W. Bush	107th (2001–2003) Divided	No vetoes
	108th (2003–2005) Unified	No vetoes
	109th (2005–2007) Unified	1
	110th (2007–2009) Divided	11 / 4
Barack Obama	111th (2009–2011) Unified	2
	112th (2011–2013) Divided	No vetoes
	113th (2013–2015) Divided	No vetoes
	114th (2015–2017) Divided	10 / 1

Source: Data aggregated by the authors.

📷

The president is the unofficial head of his party and works with fellow party members in government. Here, President Obama meets with Vice President Joe Biden and Democratic House leaders, clockwise from the bottom left, Steve Israel (D-NY), Chris Van Hollen (D-MD), Steny Hoyer (D-MD), House Minority Leader Nancy Pelosi (D-CA), James Clyburn (D-SC), Xavier Becerra (D-CA), and Joseph Crowley (D-NY).

Nixon and his senior aides. The Supreme Court ruled unanimously that executive privilege does exist, but that the privilege is not absolute. The Court's decision required Nixon to release the tapes, which proved his involvement with attempts to cover up the scandal, but the ruling did not clearly state the conditions under which a future president could withhold such information.[22]

Claims of executive privilege present a dilemma. On the one hand, members of Congress need to know what is happening in the executive branch. In the case of President Nixon and the Watergate scandal, claims of executive privilege allowed the Watergate cover-up to continue for more than a year and would have kept this information secret permanently if the Supreme Court had ruled in Nixon's favor.[23] Exercising executive privilege can also weaken accountability to the public, as restricting information may leave the average voter unaware of what an administration is doing. On the other hand, the president and his or her staff need to be able to communicate freely, discussing alternative strategies and hypothetical situations or national security secrets without fearing that they will be forced to reveal conversations that could become politically embarrassing or costly.

"Why Should I Care?"

Criticisms of presidents often center on cases of inaction or failure, where they do nothing to address a national problem, or where they try to change policy but are unsuccessful. The underlying expectation is that presidents are powerful and can do anything. The reality is that presidents are more powerful in some areas than in others—for example, when they negotiate with foreign leaders versus when they propose changes in spending, which requires congressional approval. Thus, when we judge presidents' performance we must consider what they were trying to do and whether they required the assistance of others to make their proposals a reality.

The Limits of Executive Privilege

Deciding what information a president can be compelled to release to the public or to other branches of government and what information can be kept confidential requires confronting fundamentally political questions. There are no right answers, and the limits of executive privilege remain unclear. On the one hand, members of Congress need facts, predictions, and estimates from the executive branch to make good public policy. On the other hand, the president and his or her staff have a right to keep their deliberations confidential, as well as a practical need to keep some things secret.

Consider the controversy over the Obama administration's policy of targeting terrorists using attacks by uncrewed drone aircraft. Compared with deployments of other military forces, on the one hand drone attacks have the advantages of surprise (drones are small and fly high enough to be invisible), low cost (drones are cheaper than fighters or bombers), and lower risk (the drones can be controlled from anywhere, so there is no risk of American casualties in an attack). On the other hand, drone attacks carry the risk of collateral damage—an attack may also hurt or kill innocent civilians. Moreover, because drone attacks are conducted in secret, there is little to no congressional oversight of who gets targeted by drone strikes or the potential for collateral damage. Should drone attacks fall under executive privilege?

Keep the attacks secret.
Clearly, revealing the targets of drone strikes in advance of the actual attacks would destroy the secrecy that makes these strikes so effective—terrorists could stop using cell phones, stay indoors as much as possible, travel only at night, and take other actions to make themselves hard to spot from the air. But there would be danger even in forcing an administration to release information after an attack, as such documents would reveal the criteria used to decide which terrorists to target, the limits of the drone technology, and what factors made it easier to carry out a successful attack. All of this information would help terror targets to evade future drone attacks and perhaps require a return to using Special Forces to attack terror targets, which would place American lives at risk.

📷 The president's role as commander in chief of America's armed forces gives him or her a tremendous amount of power—power that often can be exercised secretly. What should be the limits on presidential secrecy?

Reveal the information.
The problem with imposing a high level of secrecy on drone attacks is that it is an exception to the rule of keeping Congress informed about the use of military force. In the end, a drone is simply a different way of attacking terrorists or their organization. While the need for secrecy in advance of an attack makes sense, it is not obvious why it should continue after an attack has been carried out. In general, presidents are required to give Congress (in the case of secret operations, the chairs and ranking members of the Intelligence Committees) "prompt notification" of all secret operations. This rule was intended to govern reporting of all covert operations. Should drone attacks be given a higher level of secrecy, or should presidents be forced to keep members of Congress informed? Take a stand.

take a stand

1. One argument for using drones to attack terrorist targets highlights their greater effectiveness and lower costs than other options. But drone attacks also involve lower political risks to the president. Explain why this is so.

2. Under current law, the president only has to inform a few members of Congress about covert operations and can wait until an operation is in progress before releasing information. Why would members of Congress want to expand notification requirements, such as informing more members or requiring disclosure during the planning of an operation?

The presidency as an institution

★

EXPLAIN HOW THE EXECUTIVE OFFICE OF THE PRESIDENT, THE VICE PRESIDENT, THE FIRST SPOUSE, AND THE CABINET HELP THE PRESIDENT

As head of the executive branch, the president runs a huge, complex organization with hundreds of thousands of employees. This section describes the organizations and staff who help the president exercise these vast responsibilities, from managing disaster-response efforts to implementing policy changes.[24] Among these employees are appointees who hold senior positions in the government. These individuals serve as the president's eyes and ears in the bureaucracy, making sure that bureaucrats are following presidential directives.

The Executive Office of the President

The executive branch's organizational chart begins with the **Executive Office of the President (EOP)**, which has employed about 1,800 people in recent administrations. About one-third of these employees are concentrated in two offices, the Office of Management and Budget, which develops the president's budget proposals and monitors spending by government agencies, and the Office of the United States Trade Representative, which negotiates trade agreements with other nations. Nuts & Bolts 11.3 lists the organizations that make up the EOP.

One of the most important duties of EOP staff is helping presidents achieve their policy goals and get reelected. For example, two of President Obama's key political operatives, David Plouffe and David Axelrod, served in the EOP as senior advisers during Obama's first term. Their job was to link the administration and the reelection campaign—as one article put it, "making sure that the actions of one did not threaten the success of the other."[25] Similarly, Donald Trump named two key campaign advisers, Reince Priebus and Steve Bannon, as chief of staff and senior counselor, respectively.

Executive Office of the President (EOP)
The group of policy-related offices that serve as support staff to the president.

The Executive Office of the President

NUTS & BOLTS 11.3

Council of Economic Advisers	Office of National Drug Control Policy
Council on Environmental Quality	Office of Science and Technology Policy
Domestic Policy Council	Office of the First Lady
Homeland Security Council	Office of the United States Trade Representative
National Economic Council	President's Foreign Intelligence Advisory Board
National Security Council	Privacy and Civil Liberties Oversight Board
Office of Administration	USA Freedom Corps
Office of Faith-Based and Community Initiatives	White House Fellows Office
Office of Management and Budget	White House Military Office
Office of National AIDS Policy	White House Office

"

You don't need to know who's playing on the White House tennis court to be a good president.

—**James Baker,** former White House Chief of Staff

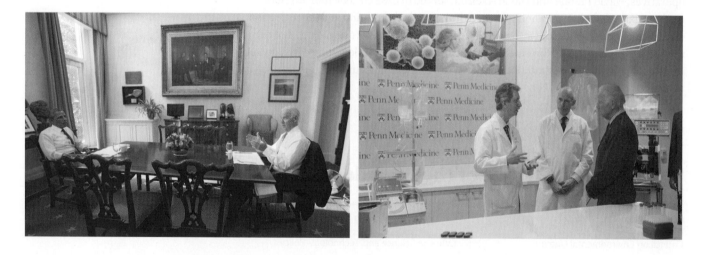

While many people perceive the vice president's position to be ceremonial and relatively powerless, recently the vice president's role has expanded significantly. President Obama's vice president Joe Biden served as a trusted policy adviser and directed several initiatives such as the Cancer Moonshot 2020. @JoeBiden #CancerMoonshot

The most influential EOP staff occupy the offices in the West Wing of the White House. The West Wing contains the president's office, known as the Oval Office, and space for the president's chief aide and personal secretary, as well as senior aides such as the vice president, the president's press secretary, and the chief of staff, who manages all aspects of White House operations—including, as former Reagan chief of staff James Baker put it, who gets to play tennis on the White House courts. Many recent chiefs of staff have been central in the development of policy proposals and negotiations with members of Congress. However, the chief of staff serves as the agent of the president—what matters is what the president wants, not a chief of staff's policy preferences.

Most EOP staff members are presidential appointees who retain their positions only as long as the president who appointed them remains in office, although some EOP offices—such as the Office of Management and Budget, the Office of the United States Trade Representative, and the National Security Council (NSC)—also have a significant number of permanent staff analysts and experts.[26] When the president appoints people to EOP positions, the primary expectation of them is loyalty rather than a concern for the general public or policy expertise.[27] The president needs staff who understand what he or she wants the government to do and who will dedicate themselves to implementing the president's vision.[28] However, the emphasis on loyalty in presidential appointments has obvious drawbacks: appointees may not know much about the jobs they are given and may not be very effective at managing the agencies they are supposed to control. For example, Ron Klain, Obama's choice to lead the government's efforts to stem the spread of the Ebola virus, was criticized for his lack of experience in medicine and public health.

The vice president

As set out in the Constitution, the vice president's job is to preside over Senate proceedings. This largely ceremonial job is usually delegated to the president pro tempore of the Senate, who in turn typically gives the duty to a more junior member. The vice president also has the power to cast tie-breaking votes in the Senate. As mentioned earlier, the vice president's other formal responsibility is to become president if the current president dies, becomes incapacitated, resigns, or is impeached. Of the 45 people who have become president, 9 were vice presidents who became president in midterm.

These rather limited official duties of the vice president pale in comparison with the influential role played by recent vice presidents. Vice President Dick Cheney, who served with President George W. Bush, exerted a significant influence over many policy decisions, including the rights of terror suspects, tax and spending policy, environmental decisions, and the writing of new government regulations.[29]

Although Cheney's level of influence was unique, other recent vice presidents have also had real power. For example, Vice President Al Gore was an important adviser to President Bill Clinton. And Barack Obama's vice president, Joe Biden, played an important role, attending all significant meetings and serving as the last person the president consulted before making a decision. Donald Trump's vice president, Mike Pence, will likely play a similar role in his administration.

The first spouse

Presidential spouses have also played a key but largely informal role in presidential administrations, typically as one of a president's most important advisers. There are examples where they have been an informal conduit for expressing the president's opinions to political appointees, members of Congress, or the media. They also represent America at a wide range of international events, from funerals to conferences. And of course, presidential spouses are a highly visible symbol of the nation, performing a role similar to the president's role as head of state.

Attempts by first spouses to have an official policy-making role in a president's administration are generally limited. For one thing, a first spouse's staff is not set up to assess policy problems or solutions. The commitments of first spouses often keep them out of Washington for substantial periods. Finally, insofar as the first spouse's work is controversial at all, opponents can always argue that the first spouse should not be involved in policy making, as he or she was not elected to do so. Thus, during Bill Clinton's presidency, then–first spouse Hillary Clinton was criticized for her leadership role in health care reform efforts.

In light of these constraints, most first spouses pick a largely noncontroversial policy area to focus their official efforts. For example, George W. Bush's spouse, Laura Bush, made numerous public appearances to support education and literacy programs as well as international HIV/AIDS treatment and prevention efforts. Michelle Obama worked to support exercise and healthy eating programs (including changes to federal student lunch guidelines). Similarly, after the failure of health care reform in the Clinton presidency Hillary Clinton changed her focus to less visible, less controversial initiatives, such as efforts to expand human rights and women's rights throughout the world. Donald Trump's spouse, Melania Trump, has suggested that she will focus her efforts on steps to deter cyberbullying.

The president's Cabinet

The president's **Cabinet** is composed of the heads of the 15 executive departments in the federal government, along with other appointees given cabinet rank by the president. Nuts & Bolts 11.4 lists the Cabinet and cabinet-level positions. The cabinet members' principal job is to be the frontline implementers of the president's agenda in their executive departments. As we discuss in Chapter 12, these appointees monitor the actions of the lower-level bureaucrats who retain their jobs regardless of who is president and who are not necessarily sympathetic to the president's priorities.

Cabinet
The group of 15 executive department heads who implement the president's agenda in their respective positions.

Cabinet and Cabinet-Level Positions

The president's Cabinet is composed of the heads of the 15 executive departments along with other appointees given cabinet rank by the president.

Secretary of Agriculture	Secretary of Transportation
Secretary of Commerce	Secretary of the Treasury
Secretary of Defense	Secretary of Veterans Affairs
Secretary of Education	Vice president
Secretary of Energy	White House chief of staff
Secretary of Health and Human Services	Attorney general
Secretary of Homeland Security	Head of the Environmental Protection Agency
Secretary of Housing and Urban Development	Head of the Office of Management and Budget
Secretary of the Interior	Head of the Office of National Drug Control Policy
Secretary of Labor	United States Trade Representative
Secretary of State	

Like other presidential appointees, cabinet members are chosen for a combination of loyalty to the president and expertise. Although he served under a Democratic president, President Obama's first secretary of defense Chuck Hagel was a former Republican senator and a Vietnam veteran. And Obama's secretary of Energy Ernest Moniz was a nuclear physicist who served on Obama's Science and Technology Advisory Council prior to his appointment.

"Why Should I Care?"

Having read the job description for America's president, you might reasonably ask, how does any one person handle all of these responsibilities? The answer is that presidents have help, trusted advisers and people chosen for policy knowledge, political skills, and loyalty. Put another way, if you want to know whether someone will make a good president, don't look at his or her experience or campaign promises—look at the people he or she picks to help run the government.

★

EXPLAIN HOW MODERN PRESIDENTS HAVE BECOME EVEN MORE POWERFUL

Presidential power today

Throughout American history, presidents have accomplished major achievements. They have expanded the territorial boundaries of the United States, fought wars, and enacted large government programs. Yet the Constitution grants the president only limited powers. Presidents have also gained powers from new statutory authority (laws passed by Congress). Even so, assessing presidential power requires expanding our notions of where this power comes from. Saying that the presidents became more powerful because of the expansion of the United States or the increased size of the federal budget or bureaucracy tells only part of the story. What about these circumstances made presidents more powerful?

One important clue about where presidential power comes from is that after more than two centuries, many of the limits to these powers—including which executive actions require congressional approval and which ones can be reversed by Congress—are not well defined.

In addition to these ambiguities, presidents also gain real power from other, more informal aspects of their office. Presidents can offer small inducements like visits to the Oval Office and campaign assistance, and they can draw on the natural respect that most people (including members of Congress) feel for the presidency regardless of who holds the office, thereby achieving compromises that enable the president to reach his or her policy goals.[30]

The very ambiguity of the Constitution also creates opportunities for the exercise of presidential power. As we have seen, the Constitution makes the president military commander in chief but gives Congress the power to declare war and to raise and support armies, without specifying which branch of government is in charge of the military. Thus, at least part of presidential authority must be derived or assumed from what the Constitution and statutes *do not say*—that is, the ways in which they fail to define or delineate presidential power—and how presidents use this ambiguity to pursue their goals.

Unilateral actions and signing statements

Constitutional and statutory ambiguities in some cases enable presidents to take **unilateral action**—that is, changing policy on their own without consulting Congress or anyone else.[31] The 2011 debate over U.S. military action in Syria provides a good example of how constitutional ambiguities create opportunities for unilateral action. The Obama administration argued that because the operation only involved air strikes and very limited deployment of advisers, it did not trigger the provisions of the "hostilities or imminent hostilities" provisions of the War Powers Act. While some in Congress disagreed and wanted to vote on whether to authorize the operation, no such vote was ever taken.

This example is far from the first time that a president has argued that military operations were not subject to congressional review. During the Iraq War, some Democrats in Congress wanted to cut off war funding to force the withdrawal of American forces, but supporters of the Bush administration maintained that the Constitution's description of the president as commander in chief meant that even if Congress refused to appropriate funds for the war, the president could (1) order American forces to stay in Iraq and (2) order the Treasury Department to spend any funds necessary to continue operations. Ultimately, members of Congress approved a funding resolution.

Even when a president takes a unilateral action, it may not lead to policy change. Presidents and their staffs still have to monitor subsequent actions by bureaucrats to make sure they are implementing the president's decision. Most presidents have tried to control the implementation of laws by issuing a **signing statement** when signing a bill into law. These documents, which explain the president's interpretation of the new law, are issued most often when the president disagrees with the interpretation of members of Congress who supported the legislation but still wants to approve the bill. Presidents issue signing statements so that if the courts have to resolve uncertainties about the bill's intent judges can take into account not only the views expressed during congressional debates about the bill but also the president's interpretation of it.[32]

unilateral action (presidential) Any policy decision made and acted upon by the president and presidential staff without the explicit approval or consent of Congress.

signing statement A document issued by the president when signing a bill into law explaining his or her interpretation of the law, which often differs from the interpretation of Congress, in an attempt to influence how the law will be implemented.

Congressional responses to unilateral action

In theory, members of Congress can undo a president's unilateral action by enacting a law to overturn it, but this is harder than it may sound.[33] Some members of Congress may approve of what the president has done or be indifferent to it, or they may give a higher priority to other policies. Still, reversals do happen: after President Obama announced plans to close the Guantánamo Bay detention center for terrorist suspects, the House and Senate added an amendment to a spending bill stating that the prison could not be closed until the administration released plans explaining where the prisoners would be sent. The facility remains open to this day.

Members of Congress can also write laws in a way that limits the president's authority over their implementation.[34] The problem with this approach is that members of Congress delegate authority to the president or the executive branch bureaucracy for good reasons—either because it is difficult for legislators to predict how a policy should be implemented or because they cannot agree among themselves on an implementation plan.[35] Members of Congress from the president's party may also want to grant presidential authority because they hold policy goals similar to the president's and would therefore benefit from the exercise of unilateral power.

In sum, ambiguities in the Constitution create opportunities for unilateral presidential action. These actions are subject to reversal through legislation, court decisions, and impeachment, but members of Congress face significant costs if they undertake any of these options. As long as the president is careful to limit the exercise of unilateral power to actions that do not generate intense opposition in Congress, he or she can implement a wide range of policy goals without official congressional consent—provided that bureaucrats go along with the president's wishes (see Chapter 12). Thus, presidential power has important consequences for government policy—but it is not unlimited.

Congress has the power to block most types of presidential action, if it chooses. For example, in 2009 President Obama ordered the closure of the detention center for terror suspects at Guantánamo Bay, Cuba, but Congress passed legislation preventing the closure until the Obama administration developed detailed plans for relocating the prisoners.

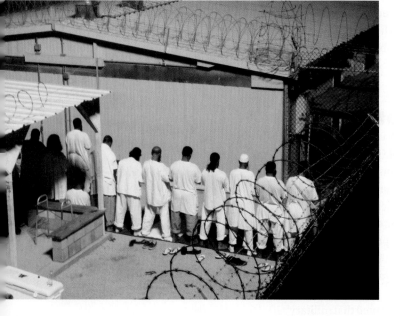

The president as politician

As we have discussed, statutory and constitutional authority give the president considerable influence over policy. However, the reality of presidential power is closer to President Harry Truman's description of what incoming president (and former army general) Dwight Eisenhower would find when he entered the White House: much of what presidents do (or want to do) requires support from others, including legislators, bureaucrats, and citizens. As a result, the presidency is an inherently political office—something that all presidents learn is true, regardless of their expectations when they took office.[36] The president has to take into account the political consequences of his or her decisions—for their effect on his or her political support, reelection prospects, and party. A president must also contend with the fact that achieving policy goals often requires bargaining and compromising with others, both inside and outside government.

In part, presidents must keep their eye on the political implications of their actions in office because they want to be reelected to a second term. One important indicator of

> He'll sit here, and he'll say, "Do this! Do that!" And nothing will happen. Poor Ike—it won't be a bit like the Army. He'll find it very frustrating.
>
> —President Harry Truman,
> describing incoming president Dwight Eisenhower

presidential performance is a president's **approval rating**, the percentage of the public who think the president is doing a good job in office. Figure 11.2, which shows approval ratings for the last six presidents who ran for reelection, reveals that first-term presidents with less than 50 percent approval are in real trouble. No recent president has been reelected with less than a 50 percent approval rating.

Of course, it would be wrong to say that presidents are single-mindedly focused on keeping their approval rating as high as possible. For one thing, presidential approval is shaped by factors that they have only limited control over, such as the state of the economy. And every president has taken actions that were politically costly because they believed that the policies were worthwhile—for example, President Obama ordered U.S. armed forces to intervene in the Syrian civil war despite polls showing that a majority of Americans opposed this strategy. Even so, presidents and their advisers are keenly aware of the political consequences of their actions and there is no doubt that these consequences shape both their decisions and how they explain these actions to American citizens.

The president as party leader

The president is the unofficial head of his or her political party and generally picks the party's day-to-day leadership, or at least has considerable influence over the selection. This process begins when a presidential candidate captures the party's nomination. For example, in 2008, soon after Barack Obama became the presumptive Democratic Party nominee, some of his senior aides and advisers took on leadership positions in the

presidential approval rating
The percentage of Americans who think that the president is doing a good job in office.

FIGURE 11.2

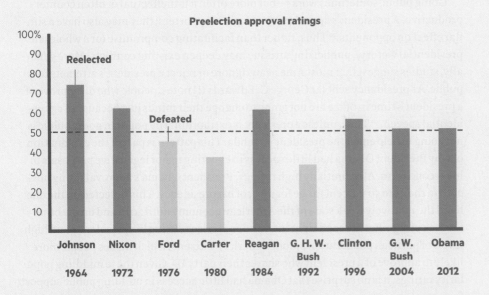

Presidential Popularity and Reelection

This figure shows the preelection year average approval ratings for recent presidents who ran for reelection. It shows that a president's chances of winning reelection are related to his popularity. At what level of approval would you say that an incumbent president is likely to be reelected?

Preelection approval ratings

Source: Approval data from the Roper Center for Public Opinion Research, University of Connecticut, "Data Access: Presidential Approval," http://webapps.ropercenter.uconn.edu (accessed 10/26/12).

Democratic Party organization.[37] During the 2012 campaign, some of these individuals returned to help Obama get reelected, such as Deputy Campaign Manager Jennifer O'Malley Dillon, who had served as the executive director of the Democratic National Committee.

The president's connection to the party reflects their intertwined interests. The president needs support from members of his or her party in Congress to enact legislation, and the party and its candidates need the president to compile a record of policy achievements that reflect well on the organization and to help raise the funds needed for the next election. Therefore, party leaders generally defer to a presidential candidate's (or a president's) staffing requests and most presidents and presidential candidates take time to meet with national party leaders and the congressional leadership from their party to plan legislative strategies, make joint campaign appearances, and raise funds for the party's candidates.

The president's value to the party also depends on his or her popularity. When presidential approval ratings drop to low levels, most members of Congress see no political advantage in campaigning with the president or supporting White House proposals and they may become increasingly reluctant to comply with the president's requests. On the one hand, in the 2010 and (to a lesser extent) 2014 midterm elections some Democratic candidates believed that campaigning with Obama would reduce their chances of reelection, as it would remind voters of unpopular proposals championed by Obama, such as health care reform. On the other hand, Obama's increasing popularity in the final year of his term made him a valuable campaign asset for some Democratic candidates in the 2016 election, although his efforts were not enough to secure victory for Hillary Clinton.

Going Public Presidents are in an excellent position to communicate with the American people because of their prominent role and the extensive media coverage devoted to anything the president says to the nation. Broadcast and cable networks even give the president prime-time slots for the State of the Union speech and other major addresses. The media attention that comes with the presidency provides the president with a unique strategy for shaping government policy: **going public**, or appealing directly to American citizens, in the hopes of getting the electorate to pressure members of the House and Senate to do what the president wants.[38]

Going public sometimes works—but more often it is ineffectual or often counterproductive. A president's appeals may energize supporters; they may also have a similar effect on opponents.[39] Thus, rather than facilitating compromise (or a wholesale presidential victory), publicizing an issue may deepen existing conflicts. More generally, studies suggest that most Americans ignore or reject a president's attempts to go public. As presidency scholar George C. Edwards III notes, people who disapprove of a president's time in office are not going to change their minds just because of a presidential speech.[40] Thus, unless a president is extraordinarily popular, going public is not going to help enact the president's agenda. This pattern is part of the explanation of why President Obama had little success in enacting major legislative proposals in his second term. After initially high ratings, President Obama's approval rating hovered in the 45 to 50 percent range for most of his presidency. This reflected on the one hand the relatively weak state of the American economy until 2016 and on the other the lack of significant scandals or international crises during his presidency and high levels of partisan polarization among American citizens, which makes people more likely to approve of a president who shares their party ID. Given these middling popularity ratings, it is no surprise that Obama had little success in building public support for proposals such as increased controls on gun ownership or immigration reform.

going public
A president's use of speeches and other public communications to appeal directly to citizens about issues the president would like the House and Senate to act on.

DID YOU KNOW?

President Obama made

18

major speeches (often televised) calling for new regulations on handgun purchases and ownership.

The Constitution makes the president commander in chief but limits that power by giving Congress the power to raise and support armies. Thus, while President Obama could order American forces to conduct air strikes on the ISIL terrorist organization in Syria, members of Congress would have several legislative options to limit or even stop these operations.

Conclusion

President Donald Trump occupies an office whose power is derived from constitutional authority, statutory authority, and ambiguities that enable unilateral action. Even so, presidential power is limited. The president shares many powers with Congress. Moreover, presidents are politicians who need public support, both to win reelection and to persuade members of Congress to approve their policy initiatives. Public evaluation is based on how the president handles those issues that are considered a priority by many Americans, such as the economy, health care, and national security.

Taken together, these factors help to explain why presidents appear powerful in some policy areas but not others. Military actions, such as the bin Laden raid or drone attacks on terrorist organizations, do not require congressional assent, at least not in the short term. The same is true of many other foreign policy actions. However, major changes in policy (particularly domestic policy) or spending are unlikely unless the president's party controls both houses of Congress. A president can also change policy by controlling the implementation of existing legislation, or by acting unilaterally, but this process requires a compliant bureaucracy and is subject to being overturned by congressional action.

All this considered, Donald Trump's presidency may be less transformational than his supporters believe. Some of Trump's proposals can be implemented through unilateral executive action. Others will require the cooperation of members of Congress, bureaucrats, or even the leaders of other nations. Given these constraints, it is almost surely true that Trump will fall short of achieving a fundamental renovation of American government. However, this outcome—if it occurs—does not reflect any limitations that Trump might have as a politician. Rather, it is a consequence of how the rules and institutions of American politics both empower and constrain presidential actions.

STUDY GUIDE

Key terms

constitutional authority
(presidential) (p. 317)

statutory authority
(presidential) (p. 317)

vesting clause (p. 317)

head of government (p. 317)

head of state (p. 317)

recess appointment (p. 318)

executive orders (p. 318)

executive agreement (p. 324)

State of the Union (p. 324)

pocket veto (p. 325)

executive privilege (p. 325)

The development of presidential power

Trace the evolution of presidential power. (Pages 314–316)

Summary

Presidents get their powers from a variety of sources: some powers are from the Constitution; others have more informal origins. Although the president's constitutional powers have not changed, presidential power has grown substantially over time. Nonetheless, even presidents' power is still limited in a number of contexts.

Practice Quiz Questions

1. **The government's response to the Great Depression was defined by _____.**
   a. presidential actions
   b. presidential inaction
   c. congressional action
   d. popular protest
   e. international pressure

2. **Since the Great Depression, presidential power has _____.**
   a. increased
   b. decreased
   c. stayed the same

The president's job description

Describe the constitutional and statutory powers of the president today. (Pages 317–328)

Summary

The president's formal powers arise from a combination of constitutional provisions and additional laws that give him or her increased responsibilities. The president has many duties, but the primary responsibilities of the office are to oversee the executive branch and implement laws passed by Congress. Although some presidents might prefer to focus on either domestic or foreign policy, most find that their priorities are determined by domestic and world events.

Practice Quiz Questions

3. **Presidents use recess appointments when they are trying to _____.**
   a. fill a judicial vacancy outside the scheduled period
   b. fill a vacant seat in Congress
   c. temporarily dodge the need for Senate approval
   d. temporarily dodge the need for House approval
   e. fill vacancies with a permanent replacement

4. **A presidential proclamation that unilaterally changes government policy without congressional consent is called _____.**
   a. an executive privilege
   b. a fast-track authority
   c. an executive agreement
   d. an executive order
   e. statutory authority

5. **Some scholars argue that the War Powers Resolution has effectively expanded the power of _____.**
   a. the president
   b. Congress
   c. the Supreme Court
   d. the Department of Defense
   e. the State Department

The presidency as an institution

Explain how the Executive Office of the President, the vice president, the first spouse, and the Cabinet help the president. (Pages 329–332)

Summary

The executive branch is a huge, complex organization that helps the president exercise vast responsibilities. Appointees to the branch serve as the president's eyes and ears on the bureaucracy. Almost all appointees are replaced when a new administration begins.

Key terms

Executive Office of the
President (EOP) (p. 329)

Cabinet (p. 331)

Practice Quiz Questions

6. In most appointments to EOP positions, presidents generally emphasize _____.

   a. experience

   b. loyalty

   c. effectiveness

   d. public opinion

   e. expertise

7. Recent vice presidents have had _____ official duties and/but _____ been influential in their role.

   a. no; have not

   b. limited; have

   c. limited; have not

   d. extensive; have

   e. extensive; have not

Presidential power today

Explain how modern presidents have become even more powerful. (Pages 332–336)

Summary

While presidents have gained power over time, the Constitution grants the president rather limited powers. The growth of presidential power is closely related to the fact that most limits on it are not well defined and presidents have succeeded in taking advantage of these ambiguities.

Key terms

unilateral action (presidential) (p. 333)

signing statement (p. 333)

presidential approval rating (p. 335)

going public (p. 336)

Practice Quiz Questions

8. Most presidents use the _____ to control the interpretation and implementation of laws.

   a. line-item veto

   b. recess appointment

   c. executive order

   d. signing statement

   e. pocket veto

9. Congressional challenges to presidential unilateral action are _____ used and are generally _____ at constraining presidential power.

   a. rarely; successful

   b. rarely; unsuccessful

   c. commonly; successful

   d. commonly; unsuccessful

10. Presidential approval is generally based on _____.

   a. economic conditions

   b. policy positions

   c. presidential actions

   d. presidential appointments

   e. an absence of scandals

11. What is the best explanation for the ability of presidents to act unilaterally in the face of congressional opposition?

   a. Americans' dislike of Congress

   b. the perception that presidents only act in the interests of the entire nation

   c. the doctrine of executive privilege

   d. the difficulty of enacting a law to reverse the president's actions

   e. the theory of the unitary executive

12. For most presidents, the problem with going public is that _____.

   a. the public is more focused on Congress

   b. the president's speeches are not very persuasive

   c. they energize their opponents

   d. they generally address unimportant issues

   e. they do not reach their target audience

Suggested Reading

Alter, Jonathan. *The Promise: President Obama, Year One*. New York: Simon and Schuster, 2010.

Canes-Wrone, Brandice. *Who Leads Whom? Presidents, Policy, and the Public*. Chicago: University of Chicago Press, 2006.

Edwards, George C., III. *Predicting the Presidency: The Potential of Persuasive Leadership*. Princeton, NJ: Princeton University Press, 2015.

Hallett, Brian. *Declaring War: Congress, the President, and What the Constitution Does Not Say*. New York: Cambridge University Press, 2012.

Howell, William G. *Power without Persuasion: The Politics of Direct Presidential Action*. Princeton, NJ: Princeton University Press, 2003.

Katznelson, Ira. *Fear Itself: The New Deal and the Origins of Our Time*. New York: W. W. Norton, 2013.

Lewis, David E. *Presidents and the Politics of Agency Design: Political Insulation in the United States Government Bureaucracy, 1946–1997*. Palo Alto, CA: Stanford University Press, 2003.

Mayer, Kenneth. *With the Stroke of a Pen: Executive Orders and Presidential Power*. Princeton, NJ: Princeton University Press, 2001.

Neustadt, Richard E. *Presidential Power and the Modern Presidents: The Politics of Leadership from Roosevelt to Reagan*. New York: Free Press, 1990.

Rudalevige, Andrew. *Managing the President's Program: Presidential Leadership and Legislative Policy Formation*. Princeton, NJ: Princeton University Press, 2002.

Skowronek, Stephen. *Presidential Leadership in Political Time: Reprise and Reappraisal*. Lawrence: University of Kansas Press, 2008.

12

The Bureaucracy

What's with all this red tape?

Millions of Americans work in the federal bureaucracy, doing everything from processing paperwork to driving scientific rovers on Mars. In some cases, these individuals find themselves as poster children for epic government failures. Consider the case of Flint, Michigan, where residents discovered in 2016 that their drinking water was contaminated by dangerously high levels of lead. Most of the blame falls on state officials, who allowed the local water authority to stop using chemicals to prevent lead pipes from contaminating the water supply. However, while scientists in the U.S. Environmental Protection Agency (EPA) were aware of the risks created by this decision, agency officials spent months debating whether it had the authority to order the state to change its policy even as many Flint children began to show symptoms of lead poisoning. In the end, the EPA did a poor job of safeguarding the health of the people of Flint even though this task is a fundamental part of its mission statement.

In other cases, though, civil servants produce near miracles. NASA's *Opportunity* rover, for example, was built to last only 90 days on Mars—but NASA's scientists have managed to keep it operating for more than 12 years after it landed. *Opportunity* and its sister rover, *Spirit* (which lasted 9 years before getting trapped in a Martian sand dune), have made many important discoveries about Martian geology, including clues about the presence of water on the surface of Mars and the prospects for life on the planet.

These two examples illustrate only a tiny part of the federal bureaucracy. Americans encounter the bureaucracy every day: when they sort through mail delivered by the Postal Service, drive on highways funded by the Department of Transportation, or purchase food inspected by the Food and Drug Administration (FDA). The prices Americans pay to surf the Web, watch television, or use a cell phone are influenced by regulations issued by the Federal Communications Commision (FCC). When they go on vacation, their bags are inspected by the Transportation Security Administration (TSA), the aircraft and pilots are scrutinized by the Federal Aviation Administration (FAA), and many beaches may be maintained by the Army Corps of Engineers.

Although many federal bureaucrats work diligently to serve the American public, the comparison of the EPA's inaction on Flint's water supply with the

★

CHAPTER GOALS

Define *bureaucracy* and explain its major functions.
pages 342–348

Trace the expansion of the federal bureaucracy over time.
pages 349–351

Describe the size and structure of the executive branch today.
pages 352–356

Describe who bureaucrats are and the regulations that govern their employment.
pages 357–359

Explain how Congress and the president oversee the executive branch.
pages 360–365

📷

It's not hard to understand why Americans have such a strong negative view of American bureaucracy when government agencies fail at basic tasks—as in the case of Flint, Michigan, where national, state, and local authorities failed to prevent lead contamination of the city's water supply. Flint residents like LeeAnne Walters, pictured here, confronted city and state officials with samples of contaminated water taken from their homes. Is this negative view accurate? How can we trust government to act in our interests given such failures?

long-lasting Mars rovers illustrates a fundamental fact: the same federal bureaucracy that accomplishes so many big tasks also does things that are inefficient, wasteful, and downright dumb. Do these shortcomings result from inevitable accidents—or are they the consequence of deliberate actions? And if so, why were agencies designed to fail or to do things that look a lot like failure? How does conflict over what government should do translate into bureaucratic successes and failures?

DEFINE *BUREAUCRACY* AND EXPLAIN ITS MAJOR FUNCTIONS

bureaucracy
The system of civil servants and political appointees who implement congressional or presidential decisions; also known as the *administrative state*.

civil servants
Employees of bureaucratic agencies within the government.

political appointees
People selected by an elected leader, such as the president, to hold a government position.

What is the federal bureaucracy?

The federal **bureaucracy** that makes up the government's executive branch comprises millions of **civil servants**, who work for the government in permanent positions, and thousands of **political appointees**, who hold short-term, usually senior positions and are appointed by an elected leader, such as the president. Another name for the bureaucracy is the administrative state, or the state.

What do bureaucrats do?

The task of the bureaucracy is to implement policies established by congressional acts or presidential decisions. Sometimes the tasks are very specific. For example, in the appropriations bill for fiscal year 2016, Congress mandated that the navy purchase an additional five F-35 attack jets from defense contractor Lockheed Martin. This provision required no discretion on the part of the bureaucrats who were tasked to implement it—all they needed to do was sign the contract and make sure that the jets were delivered and Lockheed Martin was paid.

More commonly, however, legislation determines only the general guidelines for meeting governmental goals, allowing bureaucrats to develop specific policies and programs. In these cases, bureaucrats' actions constitute the essence of government action, determining "who gets what, when, and how."[1] For example, the 1938 Federal Food, Drug, and Cosmetic Act gave the FDA the job of determining which drugs are safe and effective, but it allowed FDA bureaucrats to develop their own procedures for making these determinations.[2]

In general, the job of the federal bureaucracy includes a wide range of tasks, from regulating the behavior of individuals and corporations to buying everything from pencils to jet fighters. These activities are inherently political and often conflictual: ordinary citizens, elected officials, and bureaucrats themselves often disagree about aspects of these activities, and they work to influence bureaucratic actions to suit their policy goals.

regulation
A rule that allows the government to exercise control over individuals and corporations by restricting certain behaviors.

Regulations A **regulation** is a rule that allows the government to exercise control over individuals and corporations by restricting their behavior. It does so by either allowing or prohibiting behavior, setting out the conditions under which certain behaviors can occur, or assessing costs or granting benefits based on behavior. Bureaucrats gain the authority to write regulations by the statute that establishes their agency or by a subsequent act of Congress. Consider the EPA's Clean Power Plan, which imposes limits on the amount of carbon dioxide that can be emitted from electrical power plants. These

Although the term "bureaucracy" may suggest workers sitting behind desks in offices, the agencies of the federal bureaucracy perform a wide range of tasks. Following the explosion of BP's *Deepwater Horizon* oil rig in 2010, the Coast Guard—a government agency—responded to try to put out the fire. #DeepwaterHorizon #BPoilspill #USCG

new regulations, as well as limits on other power plant emissions, follow from authority given to the EPA by the Clean Air Act, legislation that was enacted in the 1970s (for more details, see How It Works: Bureaucracy and Legislation).

Regulations are developed according to the **notice-and-comment procedure**.[3] Before a new regulation can take effect, it must be published in the *Federal Register*, an official publication that includes rules, proposed rules, and other types of government documents. Individuals and companies that the regulation will affect can then respond to the agency that proposed it, either supporting or opposing it, and offering different versions for consideration. Those potentially affected can also appeal to members of Congress or to the president's staff for help in getting the proposed rule revised. The agency then issues a final regulation, incorporating changes based on the comments. This final regulation is also published in the *Federal Register* and then put into effect. The process is time-consuming. The FAA's release in 2015 of regulations on the use of drone aircraft—including a provision requiring all but the smallest drones to be registered with the agency—began with a congressional mandate issued in 2012. Many regulations can take even longer to craft from beginning to end.

The process of devising or modifying regulations is often political. Members of Congress and the president usually have strong opinions about how new regulations should look—and even when they don't, they may still get involved on behalf of a constituent or an interest group. Bureaucrats take account of these pressures for two reasons. First, the bureaucrats' policy-making power may derive from a statute that members of Congress could overturn. Second, bureaucrats need congressional support to get larger budgets and to expand their agency's mission. Thus, despite bureaucrats' power to implement policies, their agencies' budgets, appointed leaders, and overall missions are subject to elected officials' oversight.

Federal regulations affect most aspects of everyday life. They influence the gas mileage of cars sold in the United States, the materials used to build roads, and the price of gasoline. They determine the amounts that doctors can charge senior citizens for medical procedures; the hours that medical residents can work; the criteria used to determine who gets a heart, lung, or kidney transplant; and the allowable emissions from power plants. Regulations set the eligibility criteria for student loans, limit how the military can recruit on college campuses, determine who can get a home mortgage and what their interest rate will be, and describe what constitutes equal funding for

notice-and-comment procedure
A step in the rule-making process in which proposed rules are published in the *Federal Register* and made available for debate by the general public.

Bureaucracy and Legislation

After Congress passes legislation and the president signs it, the transition from legislation to regulation begins. Input from local government officials, interest groups, and others helps to refine the regulations as they are developed, and has a strong influence on how regulations will affect people "on the ground."

Congress passes legislation.

↓

The president signs the bill into law.

↓

Bureaucrats interpret the law and design appropriate regulations.

↓

Courts respond to challenges to the law, and they can provide guidelines for implementation.

Other bureaucrats disseminate regulations to state and local governments, corporations, and individuals, and they monitor compliance.

Citizens and interest groups provide information and proposals to bureaucrats, and they lobby for their preferred implementation of the legislation.

↓

Regulations can be revised in light of changing circumstances, different political climates, or unanticipated consequences.

Regulating Greenhouse Gas Emissions

In August 2015, the Environmental Protection Agency (EPA) announced its Clean Power Plan, which imposes new state-by-state limits on emissions of CO_2 (carbon dioxide) from fossil fuel power plants. This regulatory change was the product of a decade-long process of judicial decisions and actions by EPA bureaucrats.

New Acts!

Congressional Action: Congress enacts two Clean Air Acts in 1963 and 1970, with amendments in 1977 and 1990, authorizing the government to monitor and limit emissions of harmful chemicals into the atmosphere.

Although... maybe not?

Bureaucratic Action (2003): The EPA announces that the **Clean Air Act does not give it the authority to regulate CO_2** and other greenhouse gases.

Actually...yes.

Judicial Action (2007): In response to a case brought by 12 states, the Supreme Court rules that **greenhouse gases are covered by the Clean Air Act.**

Second try.

March 2012: The EPA **issues a draft of a new regulation** that would limit CO_2 emissions from new power plants.

Obama weighs in.

Presidential Directive, June 2013: President Obama **directs the EPA to develop additional regulations** for limiting CO_2 emission from new and existing power plants.

Results?

September 2013: The EPA modifies its draft regulations to place **CO_2 standards** on new power plants and issues a revised proposal.

June 2014: The EPA proposes an additional rule that aims to **cut CO_2 emissions from existing power plants.**

Feedback.

September 2013– March 2014: Supporters and opponents of the new rules submit over **6 million comments.**

Third try!

New Regulations Finalized (August 2015): The EPA **announces its Clean Power Plan,** which will regulate CO_2 emissions from both new and existing power plants.

Please stand by.

February 2016: The Supreme Court puts implementation of the Clean Power Plan for existing plants on hold, pending litigation. Moreover, these regulations are subject to change by the Trump administration.

?

Critical Thinking

1. **Critics of the regulatory process complain that unelected** bureaucrats make most of the decisions while elected officials sit on the sidelines. Is this complaint supported by the case of the Clean Power Plan?

2. **The Clean Power Plan illustrates how acts of legislation are often** reinterpreted years after their passage. Why don't members of Congress write legislation in ways that prevent this from happening?

Federal regulations influence many aspects of everyday life that would not seem likely to be affected by government action. The increase in the number of women's intercollegiate athletic teams is partly due to regulations that require equal funding for men's and women's teams. Pictured here is the University of Connecticut's 2016 NCAA women's basketball championship team. @UConnWBB #TitleIX

DID YOU KNOW?

In 2015, the federal government completed work on

2,353

new regulations or rules, 81 of which were "major" (with annual costs exceeding $100 million).

state capacity
The knowledge, personnel, and institutions that the government requires to effectively implement policies.

men's and women's college sports teams. Regulations also shape contribution limits and spending decisions in political campaigns.

Regulations are often controversial because they involve trade-offs between incompatible goals as well as decisions made under uncertain circumstances. For example, the FDA drug-approval process prioritizes the goal of preventing harmful drugs from coming to market.[4] As a result, patients sometimes cannot get access to experimental treatments because FDA approval has not been granted, even when those treatments are the patients' only remaining option.[5] Advocates for patients have argued that people with dire prognoses should be allowed to use an experimental treatment as a potentially lifesaving last resort.[6] However, FDA regulations prevent them from doing so except under very special circumstances, arguing that unapproved treatments may do more harm than good and that allowing wider access to these drugs may tempt manufacturers to market new drugs without adequate testing.

Research, Development, and New Policies Government scientists work in areas from medicine to astronomy to agriculture. Sometimes they do basic research, such as working for the National Institutes of Health (NIH) to discover mechanisms that govern cell reproduction and death. Government scientists also do applied research, from developing new cancer drugs to improving crop-management techniques. Federal funds support university and corporate research in many universities and corporations that examine similar issues.

Bureaucrats are also an important source of changes in government policies. For example, Congress and the president give civilian and military personnel in the Department of Defense the job of revising military doctrines—broad directives on how our armed forces should go about accomplishing specific tasks such as fighting the ISIL terrorist organization in Syria, building civil society in Afghanistan, or running military training operations in Africa. While military doctrines reflect input from members of Congress, the State Department and the president's appointees, and groups outside government (including lobbyists, think tanks, and defense contractors), they also reflect the preferences of the bureaucrats assigned to the task. Thus, as in the case of regulations, bureaucrats are not just implementers; they have a significant influence on what government does and does not do.

Bureaucratic expertise and its consequences

Bureaucrats are experts. Even compared with most members of Congress or presidential appointees, the average bureaucrat is a specialist in a certain policy area (often holding an advanced degree), with a better grasp of his or her agency's mission. For example, people who hold scientific or management positions in the FDA usually know more about the benefits and risks of new drugs than people outside the agency do. A bureaucracy of experts is an important part of **state capacity**—the knowledge, personnel, and institutions needed to effectively implement policies that benefit society.[7]

Red Tape and Standard Operating Procedures Despite bureaucrats' policy expertise, their decisions often appear to take too much time, rely on arbitrary judgments of what is important, and have unintended consequences—to the point that actions designed to solve one problem may create worse ones. Many critics cite the abundance of **red tape**, which refers to excessive or unnecessarily complex regulations, or **standard operating procedures**, which are the rules that lower-level bureaucrats must follow when implementing policies regardless of whether those rules are applicable.

Cases of bureaucratic ineptitude and failed reform efforts raise a critical question: How can an organization full of experts develop such dysfunctional ways of doing business? Bureaucrats are neither clueless nor malevolent. What, then, explains red tape and counterproductive standard operating procedures? The answer is the very strength of the American bureaucracy: its expertise.

Because bureaucrats know things that elected officials do not and because bureaucrats have their own policy goals, it is hard for elected officials to evaluate what bureaucrats are doing. For example, building the *Opportunity* and *Spirit* Mars rovers cost considerably more than planned. But did NASA bureaucrats mislead Congress about the difficulty of building the rovers, or was the overrun an honest mistake, resulting from factors that could not be anticipated? Of course, given that *Spirit* and *Opportunity* have far outlasted their expected lifetimes, the program is seen as a success and a bargain. But if things had turned out differently (if one or both of the rovers had crash-landed on Mars or had stopped working shortly after landing), members of Congress might easily have thought that NASA had presented the best-case scenario in order to secure funding.

Of course, sometimes bureaucrats simply make mistakes. For example, the FDA has delayed helpful drugs from reaching the market and has approved drugs that were later found to have harmful side effects. However, these decisions may have been justified based on the information available to bureaucrats at the time. Here again, it is hard to say whether bureaucrats are at fault for such decisions.

The Problem of Control The difficulty that elected officials and their staff face when trying to interpret or influence bureaucratic actions is the **problem of control**.[8] A classic example is the **principal–agent game**, which describes an interaction where an individual or a group (an "agent") acts on behalf of another (the "principal"). In the federal government, for example, the president and Congress are principals and bureaucrats are agents. An agent may prefer outcomes that the principal does not like. Moreover, because the agent is an expert at the task he or she has been given, the agent has additional knowledge and experiences that are inaccessible to the principal. The conundrum for the principal, then, is this: giving the agent very specific orders prevents the agent from acting based on his or her expertise, but if the principal gives the agent the freedom to make decisions based on expertise the principal has less control over the agent's actions.

Suppose Congress and the president directed the FDA to shorten its drug-approval process. FDA officials might have mandated a lengthy process based on their expert assessment of the best way to screen out harmful drugs. By giving orders that superseded the FDA officials' screening process, elected officials would be sacrificing the valuable bureaucratic expertise behind the policy and risking the hasty approval of unsafe drugs. But if Congress and the president allowed FDA bureaucrats to devise their own procedures and regulations, there would be a chance that the FDA could use this freedom to pursue goals that have nothing to do with drug safety. For example, critics of the FDA's procedures have asserted that a drawn-out approval process favors large companies that already have drugs on the market over smaller companies trying to get approval for drugs that would compete with existing products.

The principal–agent game can also be framed in terms of citizens. Figure 12.1 shows that a majority of survey respondents agreed that the federal government is typically inefficient and wasteful—although the percentage agreeing with this assessment declined from its peak in 1992 until more recent years, when it again increased. Such opinions give citizens a strong motivation to demand that elected officials control

red tape
Excessive or unnecessarily complex regulations imposed by the bureaucracy.

standard operating procedures
Rules that lower-level bureaucrats must follow when implementing policies.

problem of control
A difficulty faced by elected officials in ensuring that when bureaucrats implement policies they follow these officials' intentions but still have enough discretion to use their expertise.

principal–agent game
The interaction between a principal (such as the president or Congress), who needs something done, and an agent (such as a bureaucrat), who is responsible for carrying out the principal's orders.

Despite their policy expertise, bureaucrats still make mistakes. When the Medicare program implemented the Prescription Drug Benefit in 2006, information about the coverage was available on an easy-to-read website, but the agency soon learned that many seniors who needed the information did not know how to use a Web browser.

FIGURE 12.1

How Americans View the Federal Bureaucracy

Many Americans believe the bureaucracy is wasteful and inefficient. Note, however, that the magnitude of negative feelings varies over time. Consider the time frame represented on the graph. What happened during these years that might explain the changes in citizens' opinions about the government?

Source: Pew Research Center, "Beyond Distrust: How Americans View Their Government," November 23, 2015, www.people-press.org (accessed 5/6/16).

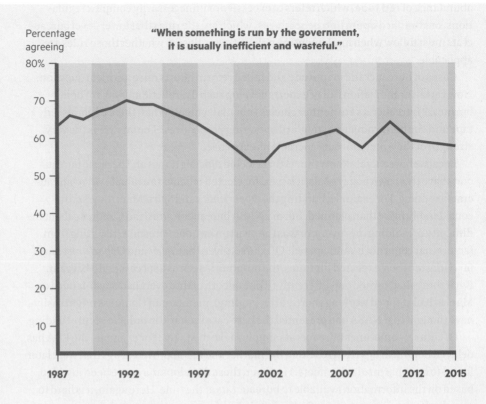

Percentage agreeing

"When something is run by the government, it is usually inefficient and wasteful."

The nine most terrifying words in the English language are: I'm from the government, and I'm here to help.

—President Ronald Reagan

the bureaucracy—to reduce the waste and inefficiency or, as the quote from Ronald Reagan suggests, to prevent bureaucrats from overly intruding into American society.

The problem of control has existed throughout the history of the federal government. It affects both the kinds of policies that bureaucrats implement and the structure of the federal bureaucracy, including the number of agencies and their missions, staff, and tasks. Moreover, elected officials use a variety of methods to solve the problem of control, including making it easier for people outside government to learn about agency actions before they take effect. However, all these tactics are at best partial solutions to the problem of control. The trade-off between expertise and control remains.

"Why Should I Care?"

Bureaucrats aren't mindless paper pushers. Rather, they are experts who have considerable power to shape what government does. The way many elected officials talk, it's easy to think that once they pass a piece of legislation or issue an executive order government policy automatically changes. In most cases, however, these directives are only the first step. To bring these changes to life, bureaucrats must step in to translate often-vague goals into concrete regulations, budgets, and actions. In other words, while you might think that bureaucrats are useless, they can have a profound effect on your daily life.

How has the American bureaucracy grown?

The evolution of America's federal bureaucracy was not steady or smooth. Most of its important developments occurred during three short periods: the late 1890s and early 1900s, the 1930s, and the 1960s.[9] In all three periods, the driving force was a combination of demands from citizens for enhanced government services and the desire of people in government to either respond to these demands or increase the size and scope of the federal government to be more in line with their own policy goals.

The beginning of America's bureaucracy

From the Founding of the United States until the election of Andrew Jackson in 1828, the staff of the entire federal bureaucracy numbered at most in the low thousands. There were only three executive departments (State, Treasury, and War), along with a postmaster general.[10] The early federal government also performed a narrow range of tasks. It collected taxes on imports and exports and delivered the mail. The national army consisted of a small Corps of Engineers and a few frontier patrols. The attorney general was a private attorney who had the federal government as one of his clients. Members of Congress outnumbered civil servants in Washington, and the president had very little staff at all.[11] The small size of the federal government during those years reflected Americans' deep suspicion of government, especially unelected officials.[12]

The election of Andrew Jackson brought the first large-scale use of the spoils system, in which people who had worked in Jackson's campaign were rewarded with new positions in the federal government (usually as local postmasters).[13] The spoils system was extremely useful to party organizations, as it gave them a powerful incentive with which to convince people to work for the party—a particularly important tool for Jackson, as his campaign organization was at that time the largest ever organized.

The challenge facing the spoils system was ensuring that these government employees, who often lacked experience in their new fields, could actually carry out their jobs. The solution was to develop procedures so that these employees knew exactly what to do even if they had no experience or training.[14] These instructions became one of the earliest uses of standard operating procedures. They ensured that the government could function even if many employees had been hired in reward for political work rather than because of their qualifications.[15]

As America expanded, so did the federal government, which saw an almost eightfold increase in the bureaucracy between 1816 and the beginning of the Civil War in 1861. This growth did not reflect a fundamental change in what the government did; in fact, much of the increase came in areas such as the Post Office, which needed to serve a geographically larger nation—and, of course, to provide "spoils" for party workers in the form of government jobs.[16] Even by the end of the Civil War, the federal government still had very little involvement in the lives of ordinary Americans. State and local governments provided services such as education, public works, and welfare benefits, if they were provided at all. The federal government's role in daily life was limited to mail delivery, collecting import and export taxes, and a few other areas.

This cartoon of a monument to President Andrew Jackson riding a pig decries his involvement in the spoils system, which allowed politicians to dole out government service jobs in return for political support.

Building a new American state: the Progressive Era

Changes in the second half of the nineteenth century transformed America's bureaucracy.[17] This transformation began after the Civil War, but the most significant changes occurred during the Progressive Era, from 1890 to 1920. Many laws and executive actions increased the government's regulatory power during this period, including the Sherman Antitrust Act of 1890, the Pure Food and Drug Act of 1906, the Federal Meat Inspection Act of 1906, expansion of the Interstate Commerce Commission, and various conservation measures.[18] Now the federal government had an indirect impact on several aspects of everyday life: when Americans bought food or other products, went to work, or traveled, the choices available to them were shaped by the actions of federal bureaucrats.

These developments were matched by a fundamental change in the federal bureaucracy following passage of the 1883 Pendleton Civil Service Act. This measure created the **federal civil service**, in which the merit system (qualifications, not political connections) became the basis for hiring and promoting bureaucrats.[19] In other words, when a new president took office he or she could not replace government workers with his or her own campaign workers. Initially, only about 13,000 federal jobs acquired civil service protections, but subsequently many additional positions were incorporated into the civil service, to the point that today virtually all full-time, permanent government employees have civil service protection. These reforms created a bureaucracy in which people could build a career in government without having to fear being fired when a new president or Congress took office.[20]

federal civil service
A system created by the 1883 Pendleton Civil Service Act in which bureaucrats are hired on the basis of merit rather than political connections.

The New Deal, the Great Society, and the Reagan Revolution

Dramatic expansion of the federal bureaucracy occurred during the New Deal period in the 1930s and during the mid-1960s Great Society era. In both cases, the changes were driven by a combination of citizen demands and the preferences of elected officials who favored an increased role of government in society. This expansion was only marginally curtailed during the Reagan Revolution of the 1980s.

The New Deal The New Deal comprised government programs implemented during Franklin Roosevelt's first term as president in the 1930s. These programs were partly a response to the Great Depression and the inability of local governments and private charities to provide adequate support to Americans during this economic crisis. Many advocates of the New Deal also favored an expanded role for government in American society, regardless of the immediate need for intervention.[21] Roosevelt's programs included reforms to the financial industry as well as efforts to help people directly, including stimulating employment, economic growth, and the formation of labor unions. The Social Security Act, the first federally funded pension program for all Americans, was also passed as part of the New Deal.[22]

These reforms represented a vast increase in the size and responsibilities of the bureaucracy, as well as a large transfer of power to bureaucrats and to the president.[23] Before the New Deal, the federal government influenced citizens' choices through activities such as regulating industries and workplace conditions. Afterward, it took on the role of delivering a wide range of benefits and services directly to individuals, from jobs to electricity. It also increased the regulation of many industries, including those in the banking and financial sectors.

Franklin Roosevelt's New Deal programs greatly expanded the power of the federal government and the bureaucracy. As this cartoon shows, these changes were controversial, with some seeing them as moving too much power from Congress to the president and bureaucracy.

Expansion of the federal government and the subsequent delegation of power to bureaucrats and to the president were controversial changes.[24] Many Republicans opposed New Deal reforms because they believed that the federal government could not deliver services efficiently and that an expanded federal bureaucracy would create a modern spoils system. Many southerners worried that the federal government's increased involvement in everyday life would endanger the system of racial segregation in southern states.[25] Even so, Democratic supporters of the New Deal, aided by public support, carried the day.

The Great Society The Great Society was a further expansion in the size and activities of the bureaucracy that occurred during Lyndon Johnson's presidency (1963–1969). Johnson proposed and Congress enacted programs that funded bilingual education, loans and grants for college students, special education, preschools, construction of elementary and secondary schools, mass-transit programs in many cities, health care for seniors and poor people, job training and urban renewal, enhanced voting rights and civil rights for minorities, environmental protection, funding for the arts and cultural activities, and space exploration.[26]

The Great Society programs had mixed success. Voting rights and civil rights reforms ended the "separate but equal" system of social order in southern states and dramatically increased political participation by African Americans.[27] At the same time, many antipoverty programs were dismal failures. Poverty rates among most groups remained relatively constant, and other indicators, such as the rate of teen pregnancy, actually increased.[28] In retrospect, the people who designed and implemented these programs did not realize the complexities of the problems they were trying to address.[29] Despite these shortcomings, the expansion of the federal government during the New Deal and Great Society has remained in place well into the twenty-first century.

The Reagan Revolution and Afterward The election of Ronald Reagan to the presidency in 1980, along with a Republican takeover of the Senate and Republican gains in the House of Representatives, created an opportunity for conservatives to roll back the size and scope of the federal government. However, 30 years after Reagan's presidency, despite the election of two subsequent Republican presidents and many years with unified Republican control of Congress, the growth of the federal government has not slowed. Members of Congress and presidents from both parties have fought for large expansions in government policy. For example, while Democrat Barack Obama's administration issued many new environmental regulations and profoundly changed the American health care system, these changes are not too different in magnitude from the reforms championed by Republican George W. Bush, including education policies that increased federal control over local school districts, new drug financing benefits for seniors, and changes to financial regulations that increased financial reporting requirements for corporations. Over the next four years, the Trump administration will have a similar impact on the bureaucracy and its policies.

Under President George W. Bush the federal bureaucracy continued to expand. Programs like No Child Left Behind increased the role of government in society. #NCLB

Though sometimes their rhetoric seems otherwise, the difference between Republicans and Democrats is not over the size of the federal government, but over what government should do. While Republicans often argue for making government smaller and Democrats respond by highlighting the consequences of even a small cut in services, the fact is that most people on both sides accept the fact that a large federal government is here to stay. Knowing how the federal bureaucracy has grown and evaluating whether this growth has caused problems or created benefits is central to building your own ideas about what government should do.

"Why Should I Care?"

The modern federal bureaucracy

The size and scope of the modern federal bureaucracy reflect the expansion of the federal government over the last half century and its increased role in citizens' lives. The bureaucracy's structure also reflects ongoing attempts by presidents, members of Congress, and others to control bureaucratic actions in line with their policy goals.

The structure of the federal government

Nuts & Bolts 12.1 shows the structure of the executive branch of the federal government. As discussed in Chapter 11, the Executive Office of the President (EOP) contains organizations that support the president and implement presidential policy initiatives; individuals working in these organizations are part of the administrative presidency that seeks to ensure that bureaucrats implement the president's policy priorities, bringing the actions of bureaucrats (agents) in line with the president's (principal's) preferences.[30] Among its many offices, the EOP contains the **Office of Management and Budget**, which prepares the president's annual budget proposal to Congress and monitors government spending as well as the development of new regulations. Below the EOP are the 15 executive departments, from the Department of Agriculture to the Department of Veterans Affairs. The heads of these 15 organizations make up the president's cabinet. Each executive department contains many smaller organizations. For example, Nuts & Bolts 12.2 shows the organizational chart for the Department of Agriculture.

Below the executive departments, but not subordinate to them, are agencies, commissions, and government corporations that are called **independent agencies**, or independent establishments, to highlight that they are not part of an executive department. Most of these carry out specialized functions, such as NASA and the EPA, but also manage the Federal Reserve System (which manages the money supply, banking system, and interest rates) and the Federal Deposit Insurance Corporation (which regulates the banking industry). Nuts & Bolts 12.1 only includes some noteworthy agencies; there are many more.

There are two important lessons to draw from these charts. First, the federal government handles an enormous range of functions. Second, the division of activities among executive departments and independent agencies does not always have an obvious logic. Why, for example, does the Department of Agriculture administer rural utilities programs and food stamps? Similarly, it is not always clear why certain tasks are handled by an independent agency while others fall within the scope of an executive department.[31] Why is the Federal Reserve an independent agency rather than part of the Department of the Treasury?

Part of the difference between independent agencies and the organizations contained within executive departments has to do with the president's ability to control these organizations' activities. Organizations that fall within an executive department, such as the FAA or the Federal Highway Administration (FHA) (both within the Department of Transportation) or the Internal Revenue Service, can be subject to presidential control (to some extent) through his or her appointees.[32] In contrast, independent agencies have more freedom from oversight and control by the president and Congress. For example, the president nominates governors of the Federal Reserve, who (if the Senate confirms them) can serve for 14 years. Outside the nomination and confirmation process, the president and Congress have very little control over the Federal

Office of Management and Budget
An office within the EOP that is responsible for creating the president's annual budget proposal to Congress, reviewing proposed rules, and performing other budget-related tasks.

independent agencies
Government offices or organizations that provide government services and are not part of an executive department.

The Executive Branch of the Federal Government

The executive branch includes the 15 cabinet offices, as well as several independent agencies, commissions, and government corporations.

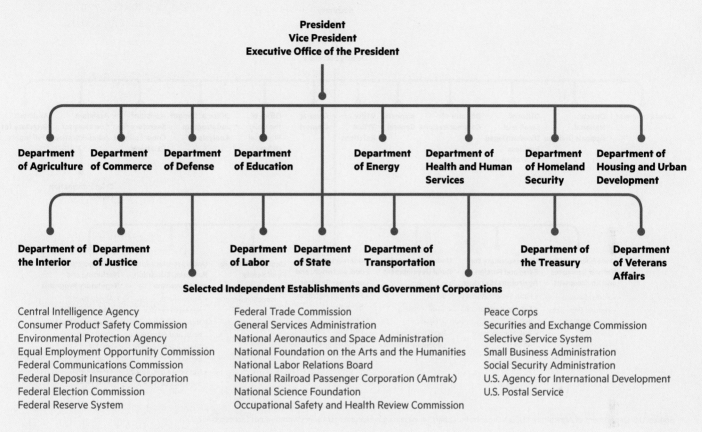

President
Vice President
Executive Office of the President

Department of Agriculture | **Department of Commerce** | **Department of Defense** | **Department of Education** | **Department of Energy** | **Department of Health and Human Services** | **Department of Homeland Security** | **Department of Housing and Urban Development**

Department of the Interior | **Department of Justice** | **Department of Labor** | **Department of State** | **Department of Transportation** | **Department of the Treasury** | **Department of Veterans Affairs**

Selected Independent Establishments and Government Corporations

Central Intelligence Agency
Consumer Product Safety Commission
Environmental Protection Agency
Equal Employment Opportunity Commission
Federal Communications Commission
Federal Deposit Insurance Corporation
Federal Election Commission
Federal Reserve System

Federal Trade Commission
General Services Administration
National Aeronautics and Space Administration
National Foundation on the Arts and the Humanities
National Labor Relations Board
National Railroad Passenger Corporation (Amtrak)
National Science Foundation
Occupational Safety and Health Review Commission

Peace Corps
Securities and Exchange Commission
Selective Service System
Small Business Administration
Social Security Administration
U.S. Agency for International Development
U.S. Postal Service

Source: Based on *GPO Access: Guide to the U.S. Government*, http://bensguide.gpo.gov/files/gov_chart.pdf (accessed 9/22/12).

Reserve's policies; the organization is self-financing, and its governors can be removed from office only if Congress impeaches them. These kinds of details about the hiring and firing of bureaucrats and the location of agencies in the structure of the federal government matter because they determine the amount of political control that other parts of the government can exercise over an agency, as well as who gets to exercise this power.[33]

The size of the federal government

The federal government employs millions of people. Table 12.1 shows the number of employees in each executive department. Millions of additional people work for the government as members of the armed forces, as employees of the Postal Service, for civilian companies that contract with the government, or as recipients of federal grant money.

The Structure of the Department of Agriculture

The Department of Agriculture is headed by the secretary of Agriculture and the deputy secretary of Agriculture and includes various assistant secretaries and undersecretaries for specific areas such as natural resources and the environment, farm services, rural development, and food safety.

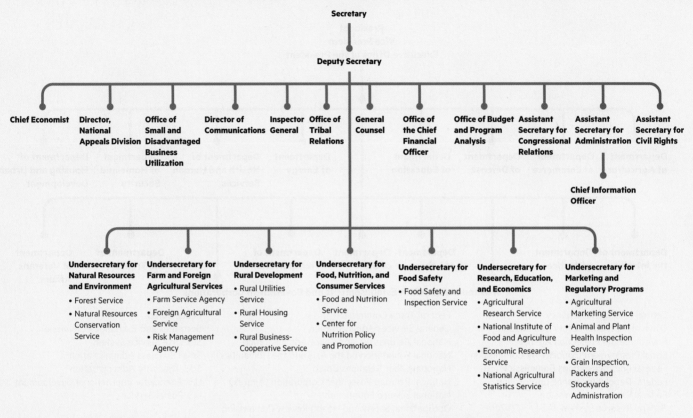

Source: U.S. Department of Agriculture, "USDA Organization Chart," www.usda.gov/documents/AgencyWorkflow.pdf (accessed 4/23/10).

DID YOU KNOW?

Since 1992, the federal civilian workforce has shrunk by

18%

Source: Office of Management and Budget

The What Do the Numbers Say? feature in this chapter shows the size of the federal budget since 2012. Clearly, the budget has steadily increased, to the point that recent annual spending is nearly $4 trillion per year. The best explanation for the size of the federal government is the size of America itself—more than 320 million people spread out over an area more than twice the size of the EU—coupled with America's position as the most powerful nation in the world with the largest military.

However, some observers argue that the real explanation has to do with bureaucrats themselves—that bureaucrats never pass up a chance to increase their own funding, regardless of whether the new spending is worthwhile.[34] This argument misses some important points. First, the increase in total federal spending masks the fact that many agencies see their budgets shrink.[35] Particularly in recent administrations, one of the principal missions of presidential appointees, both in agencies and in the EOP, has been to scrutinize budget requests with an eye to cutting spending as much as possible.[36] And every year, some government agencies are eliminated (in fact, most of the executive department head counts in Table 12.1 have grown smaller in recent editions of this text).[37]

TABLE
12.1

Employment in Selected Cabinet Departments

Organization	Total employees
Defense (civilian only)	732,000
Veterans Affairs	366,500
Homeland Security	188,100
Justice	119,800
Treasury	103,000
Agriculture	90,500
Health and Human Services	74,400
Interior	66,700
Transportation	56,200
Commerce	45,600
State	34,500
Labor	17,700
Energy	16,100
Housing and Urban Development	8,400
Education	4,500

Source: "Budget of the United States Government Fiscal Year 2017: Analytical Perspectives, Chapter 11—Improving the Federal Workforce," www.whitehouse.gov/sites/default/files/omb/budget/fy2017/assets/ap_8_strengthening.pdf (accessed 5/6/16).

Moreover, public-opinion data demonstrate the American public's demand for services.[38] Despite complaints about the federal bureaucracy, polls find little evidence of demands for less government. When the Pew Research Center asked people in 2013 to decide which two programs should have their spending cut as a way of reducing the budget deficit, a majority favored cutting relatively small programs: 34 percent picked the State Department and 48 percent picked foreign economic aid. Far fewer people favored cuts in the programs that account for most federal spending: defense (42 percent), health care (22 percent), and Social Security (12 percent).[39] In other words, while in the abstract Americans might want a smaller government that is less involved in everyday life, they do not support the large-scale budget cuts that would be necessary to achieve this goal. The public's desire for more government services is often encouraged by elected officials, who create new government programs (and expand existing ones) as a way of building support and improving their chances of reelection.

"Why Should I Care?"

You might think that the government spends too much and that the bureaucracy is too large. The questions you have to ask yourself are: What am I willing to sacrifice to make government smaller? Am I OK with a smaller military, fewer regulations on banks and credit card companies, less oversight of food and drug safety? And how much would these changes save? We have a large, costly federal government because in the end, most people want it that way.

Is the Federal Bureaucracy Too Big?

One of the most intense conflicts in American political life is over the size of the federal government. Generally, Republicans say that the size of federal bureaucracy should be reduced, while Democrats tend to favor increasing the size of government programs. However, the size of government has increased steadily over time. Has the size of the bureaucracy gotten out of control? What do the numbers say?

■ Democratic administrations   ■ Republican administrations

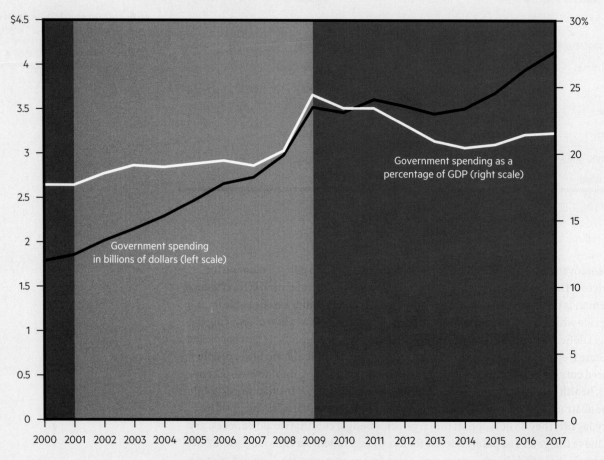

Government spending as a percentage of GDP (right scale)

Government spending in billions of dollars (left scale)

Think about it

- **Some people worry that the level of government spending is growing too fast. Does this graph support or refute this argument?**
- **The debate between Republicans and Democrats is often framed as an argument over increased government spending (Democrats favor increases; Republicans don't). Does this graph support or refute this argument?**

Source: Office of Management and Budget, "The President's Budget for Fiscal Year 2017," www.whitehouse.gov/omb/budget (accessed 5/6/16).

The human face of the bureaucracy

★

DESCRIBE WHO BUREAUCRATS ARE AND THE REGULATIONS THAT GOVERN THEIR EMPLOYMENT

The term "bureaucrat" applies to an array of people with different qualifications and job descriptions (see Figure 12.2). The federal government includes so many different kinds of jobs because of the vast array of services it provides. Although complaints about federal bureaucrats' efficiency or motivations are common, surveys show that many employees in these positions have a strong interest in public service or implementing good public policy. In fact, these motivations are often strong enough that scholars such as James L. Perry have argued against attempts to motivate federal workers with monetary incentives—bureaucrats who work hard because they feel it is the right thing to do may resent incentive schemes that presume they are lazy or only interested in money.[40]

Civil service regulations

Most jobs in the federal bureaucracy are subject to the civil service regulations mentioned earlier.[41] The current civil service system sets out job descriptions and pay ranges for all federal jobs.[42] The civil service system also establishes tests that determine who is hired for low-level clerical and secretarial positions; people with less than a college degree are generally eligible for clerical and low-level technical jobs. As in the private sector, a college degree or an advanced degree and work experience qualify an individual for higher-level positions. Federal salaries are supposed to be comparable to what people earn in similar, private-sector positions, and salaries are increased somewhat for federal employees who work in areas with a high cost of living.

Types of Federal Workers

FIGURE 12.2

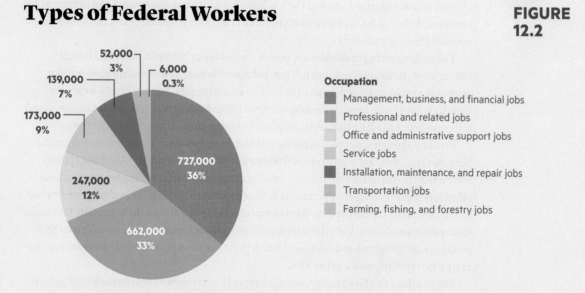

Occupation
- Management, business, and financial jobs
- Professional and related jobs
- Office and administrative support jobs
- Service jobs
- Installation, maintenance, and repair jobs
- Transportation jobs
- Farming, fishing, and forestry jobs

52,000 — 3%
6,000 — 0.3%
139,000 — 7%
173,000 — 9%
247,000 — 12%
727,000 — 36%
662,000 — 33%

Source: Based on the U.S. Bureau of Labor Statistics, "Occupational Employment Statistics NAICS 999100–Federal Executive Branch," www.bls.gov (accessed 5/6/2016).

Civil service regulations provide job security. After three years of satisfactory performance, employees cannot be fired except "for cause," meaning that the firing agency must cite a reason. Civil service regulations set out a multistep procedure for firing someone, beginning with low performance evaluations, then warning letters given to the employee, followed by a lengthy appeals process before a firing takes place.[43] A subpar performer may be assigned other duties, transferred to another office, or even given nothing to do in the hope that the person will leave voluntarily out of boredom.

Civil service regulations are extraordinarily cumbersome.[44] The hiring criteria remove a manager's discretion to hire someone who would do an excellent job but lacks the education or work experience that the regulations specify as necessary for the position. The firing requirements make it difficult to remove poor performers. The salary and promotion restrictions create problems with rewarding excellent performance or promoting the best employees rather than those with the most seniority.

Why do civil service requirements exist? Recall that the aim of these regulations was to separate politics from policy. The mechanism for achieving this goal was a set of rules that made it hard for elected officials to control the hiring and firing of government employees to further their own political goals. In effect, even though civil service regulations have drawbacks, they also provide this very important benefit. For example, without civil service protections employees in the Office of Personnel Management might be pressured by members of Congress who wanted to increase pensions for retiring federal workers who were their constituents. Although loyalty to the president is a widely accepted criterion for hiring agency heads and other presidential appointees, professionals with permanent civil service positions are supposed to be hired on the basis of their qualifications, not their political beliefs.

Political appointees and the Senior Executive Service

Not every federal employee is a member of the civil service. The president appoints over 7,000 individuals to senior positions in the executive branch who are not subject to civil service regulations, such as the leaders of executive departments and independent agencies such as NASA, as well as members of the EOP. (In some cases, the Senate must confirm these nominees.)

The majority of a president's appointees act as his or her eyes, ears, and hands throughout the executive branch. They hold positions of power within government agencies, serving as secretaries of executive departments, agency heads, or senior deputies. Their jobs involve finding out what the president wants from their agency and ordering or persuading their subordinates to implement presidential directives.

In many agencies, people in the top positions are members of the Senior Executive Service (SES), who are also exempt from civil service restrictions.[45] As of 2014, there were a few thousand SES members—mostly career government employees who held relatively high-level agency positions before moving to the SES. This change of employment status costs them their civil service protections but allows them to apply for senior leadership positions in the bureaucracy. Some political appointees are also given SES positions, although most do not have the experience or expertise held by career bureaucrats who typically move to the SES.

The president's ability to appoint bureaucrats in many different agencies helps him or her control the bureaucracy. By selecting people who are loyal or like-minded, the

💡

DID YOU KNOW?

28%

of federal bureaucrats have an advanced degree (post-bachelor). The corresponding percentage for large private businesses is about 11 percent.
Source: Office of Management and Budget

president can attempt to control the actions of lower-level bureaucrats and implement his or her policy agenda. The SES also provides civil servants an incentive to do their jobs well, as good performance in an agency position can help build a career that might allow them to transfer to the SES.

Federal employees must be careful that their comments to the media comply with Hatch Act restrictions. President Obama's secretary of Housing and Urban Development, Julian Castro, shown here at the Common Sense Media awards in 2016, violated the Hatch Act when he spoke about the 2016 presidential campaign during an interview with journalist Katie Couric.

Limits on political activity

Federal employees are limited in their political activities. The Hatch Act, enacted in 1939 and amended in 1940, prohibited federal employees from engaging in organized political activities[46]: employees could vote and contribute to candidates but could not work for candidates or for political parties. These restrictions were modified under the 1993 Federal Employees Political Activities Act, allowing federal employees to undertake a wider range of political activities, including fund-raising and serving as an officer of a political party. Senior members of the president's White House staff and political appointees are exempt from most of these restrictions, although they cannot use government resources for political activities.

The problem of control shapes the kinds of people who are hired as bureaucrats as well as their job protections. Political appointees and members of the SES are supposed to ride herd on the rest of the bureaucracy. Civil service protections exist to ensure that bureaucrats' decisions reflect expertise rather than political considerations.

Controlling the bureaucracy

As the expert implementers of legislation and presidential directives, bureaucrats hold significant power to influence government policy. This situation creates the problem of political control illustrated by the principal–agent game: elected officials must figure out how to reap the benefits of bureaucratic expertise without simply giving bureaucrats free rein to do whatever they want.

One strategy is to take away discretion and give bureaucrats simple, direct orders. For example, from 1996 to 2015 a law passed by Congress forbade the U.S. Centers for Disease Control from conducting research that would "advocate or promote gun control"—which was interpreted by the CDC as limiting all gun-related research by agency scientists or by outside researchers who received agency funds.[47] (The ban was repealed after a series of mass shootings in 2013, although to this day the CDC conducts very little gun-related research.)

The problem with eliminating bureaucrats' discretion in this way is that it limits the positive influence of their expertise. Particularly when new policies are being developed, taking away bureaucratic discretion is costly for legislators or presidential appointees, as it forces them to work out the policy details themselves—and it may produce less effective policies than those constructed by bureaucrats with specialized knowledge.[48] Moreover, preventing bureaucrats from using their judgment makes it impossible for them to craft policies that take into account new developments or unforeseen circumstances.[49] For all these reasons, elected officials must find other ways to reduce or eliminate **bureaucratic drift** (that is, bureaucrats pursuing their own goals rather than their assignments from officeholders or appointees) while still reaping the benefits of bureaucratic expertise. This section describes two common strategies: changing the way agencies are organized and staffed and using standardized procedures for monitoring agency actions (see the Take a Stand feature).

bureaucratic drift
Bureaucrats' tendency to implement policies in a way that favors their own political objectives rather than following the original intentions of the legislation.

The Senate's power over the confirmation of senior agency officials is often used as a tool to shape agency policy and operations. Richard Cordray, the first head of the Consumer Financial Protection Agency, was nominated after some senators objected to President Obama's first nominee, Elizabeth Warren, who was a Harvard Law professor at the time.

Agency organization

Political scientists have shown how agencies can be organized to minimize bureaucratic drift.[50] Specifically, when an agency is set up or given new responsibilities the officials who initiated the change don't simply tell the agency what to do. To ensure that they get the policies they want, they also determine where the agency is located within the federal government structure and who runs it. These efforts may occur solely within Congress, or involve both Congress and the president, or be arranged by presidential actions.[51]

For example, one of the Obama administration's responses to the 2008–2009 financial crisis was to form a new agency, the Consumer Financial Protection Bureau, which would help to enforce new bank regulations and investigate consumer complaints about financial firms. In 2011, it was expected that Elizabeth Warren, a Harvard law professor who had helped to set up the agency, would become the first head of the agency. However, many Republican and some Democratic senators and financial-industry lobbyists opposed Warren's appointment, believing she would encourage

Is Political Control of the Bureaucracy Beneficial?

When working with bureaucrats, elected officials (the president or members of Congress) face the problem of political control: Should they allow bureaucrats to exercise judgment when implementing policies or give them specific, narrow directives? Compounding this problem is the fact that most bureaucrats are civil service employees, meaning they cannot be fired except under very extreme circumstances. As a result, even when elected officials give very specific directives to an agency they may find that bureaucrats essentially ignore the directives and that very little can be done to force compliance (after all, regardless of what bureaucrats do or don't do, they will still have a job). Civil service protections also mean that members of Congress or a new presidential administration cannot clean house in an agency, replacing untrustworthy bureaucrats with individuals who will do what they are told. Should civil service protections be abolished?

Get rid of civil service protections.

The civil service system began in an era when few government jobs required specialized knowledge, expertise, or an advanced degree. Under these conditions, a new administration might be tempted to implement mass firings, rewarding political supporters with jobs in the federal bureaucracy, as the new workers would be just as effective as the people they replaced. At the same time, there would be little cost to getting rid of a bureaucrat who refused an order, as most positions could be filled by anyone.

The modern federal bureaucracy is exactly the opposite: most jobs, particularly those that involve real policy-making power, require expertise to be done effectively. Under these conditions, civil service protections are to some extent unnecessary, as bureaucrats have considerable job security because of their expertise and experience. Getting rid of recalcitrant bureaucrats involves significant costs: by removing their knowledge of the policies being decided and the procedures by which decisions are made, it may become impossible for an agency to function at all. Moreover, a bureaucrat's reluctance to behave as ordered may be a sign that something is wrong—that the directive makes no sense or that there are easier ways of accomplishing the task.

Civil service protections are still needed.

The fact that firing bureaucrats costs the government the benefit of their experience and expertise does not mean that elected officials will never threaten to do so, or even carry out

The State Department's backlog of passport applications is a good example of how bureaucrats' actions (or inactions) can affect the lives and plans of ordinary Americans.

their threats. A new president might simply decide that he or she wants a loyal bureaucracy; even if this outcome requires getting rid of everyone who has any experience with agency operations. A congressional majority might want a new policy enough to enact a bill that freezes the salaries of any bureaucrats who do not behave as ordered. In both cases, removing civil service protections—making bureaucrats vulnerable to threats about their future employment—could easily lead to bad policy outcomes.

The deeper problem with removing civil service protections is that it would likely change the kinds of people who undertake careers in government service. Civil service protections enable policy experts to work for the government without fearing that they will be fired for simply voicing their concerns or because a new administration places a high value on loyalty. Without the protections afforded by civil service regulations, these individuals might choose a different career, depriving the federal government (and the American people) of the benefits of their knowledge and training.

take a stand

1. In general, contemporary Democratic politicians tend to favor civil service protections, while Republicans want to weaken them. Does this preference make sense in light of what we know about the differences between the parties in their beliefs about the size and scope of government?

2. Not all jobs in the federal bureaucracy require specialized knowledge and expertise. Would it make sense to abandon civil service protections for low-level jobs such as clerical positions? Would such a change help elected officials manage the problem of control? Why or why not?

her subordinates to be excessively pro-consumer in their investigations. As a result, Obama appointed the former attorney general of Ohio, Richard Cordray, who was more acceptable to more senators, while Warren was elected as a U.S. Senator from Massachusetts in 2012.

Monitoring

One of the most important ways elected officials prevent bureaucratic drift is to know what bureaucrats are doing or planning to do. Information gathering by members of Congress about bureaucratic actions is termed **oversight**. Congressional committees often hold hearings to question agency heads, secretaries of executive departments, or senior agency staff. Similarly, one responsibility of presidential appointees is to monitor how bureaucrats are responding to presidential directives. However, presidential appointees may be unable to fulfill this role. Because they are chosen for their loyalty to the president, they may lack the experience needed to fully understand what bureaucrats in their agency are doing. Moreover, given that appointees typically hold their position for only a year or two, they have little time to learn the details of agency operations.

Advance Warning Members of Congress, the president, and his or her staff gain advance knowledge of bureaucratic actions through the notice-and-comment procedure described earlier, which requires bureaucrats to disclose proposed changes before they take effect.[52] This delay gives opponents the opportunity to register complaints with their congressional representatives, and it allows these legislators time either to pressure the agency to revise the regulation or even to enact another law undoing or modifying the agency action. Members of Congress also pressure bureaucrats to release memos, working drafts, and other documents as a way of keeping track of what bureaucrats are doing—for example, in 2015 Republicans on the House Science and Technology Committee demanded the release of e-mails sent by scientists analyzing climate change for the National Oceanographic and Atmospheric Administration.[53] (Some of the scientists later testified before the committee, but the e-mail request was rejected.)

Investigations: Police Patrols and Fire Alarms Investigations involve Congress, legislative staff, or presidential appointees scrutinizing some government program or office, its expenditures, and its activities. There are two types of oversight: police patrols and fire alarms. Ideally, every agency would be investigated as often as possible, with agencies that have large budgets or carry out important functions being investigated more frequently. These investigations may involve fact-finding trips to local offices, interviews with senior personnel, audits of agency accounts, and calls to the agency to see how it responds to citizens' requests. This method of investigation is called **police patrol oversight**.[54] Think of a police officer walking his or her beat, rattling doors to see if they are locked, checking out broken windows, and looking down alleys for suspicious behavior.

The disadvantage of police patrol oversight is that it is costly in terms of money and staff time. Moreover, these investigations often find that agencies are doing what they should. Because of these problems, Congress and the president also look outside government for information on what bureaucrats are doing. Rather than initiating

oversight
Congressional efforts to make sure that laws are implemented correctly by the bureaucracy after they have been passed.

police patrol oversight
A method of oversight in which members of Congress constantly monitor the bureaucracy to make sure that laws are implemented correctly.

After news of an $800,000 General Services Administration (GSA) conference at a Las Vegas resort came to light in 2012, Congress held hearings on the agency's practices. Here, former Representative John Mica (R-FL) criticizes the apparent misuse of taxpayer money.

investigations, they wait until they receive a complaint about bureaucratic actions and then focus investigative efforts on those cases, a practice labeled **fire alarm oversight**.[55]

The so-called fire alarm can take many different forms. Representatives and their staff meet frequently with constituents, who may let them know of a problem with the bureaucracy. Similarly, lobbyists, corporate executives, and ordinary citizens often contact the president and his or her staff with complaints about bureaucratic actions. Newspaper reporters and Internet bloggers, too, provide information about what bureaucrats are doing. Some agencies have advisory committees that not only help make agency decisions but also keep Congress and the president informed about them.[56] Such fire alarm communications tell Congress and the president where to focus their efforts to monitor the bureaucracy, rather than trying to oversee the entire government at once.

Correcting violations

When members of Congress or the president find a case of bureaucratic drift, they can choose from many tactics to bring a wayward agency into line. Legislation or an executive order can send a clear directive to an agency or remove its discretion, tasks and programs can be moved to an agency more closely aligned with elected officials' goals, political appointees at an agency can be replaced, and agencies can be reorganized.

A significant difficulty in dealing with bureaucratic drift is disagreement between members of Congress and the president about whether an agency is doing the right thing—regardless of whether it is following its original orders. Most of the tactics listed require joint action by the president and congressional majorities. Without presidential support, members of Congress need a two-thirds majority to impose corrections. Without congressional support, the president can only threaten to cut an agency's proposed budget, change its home within the federal bureaucracy, or establish a new agency to do what the errant agency refuses to do; actually carrying out these threats requires congressional approval. As a result, disagreements between the president and Congress can give an agency significant freedom, as long as it retains the support of at least one branch of government.

An agency may also be able to fend off elected officials' attempts to take political control if it has a reputation for expertise. For example, one reason that attempts to pass legislation forcing the FDA to alter its drug-approval process have had little success is that the FDA's process is thought to have worked mostly as intended, approving new drugs that are safe and effective and keeping ineffective or unsafe drugs off the market. At the same time, the FDA has responded to pressure from Congress and the president to revise some rules on its own.[57]

Finally, agencies can sometimes combat attempts to control their behavior by appealing to groups that benefit from agency actions.[58] For example, since the 1980s the Occupational Safety and Health Administration (OSHA) has resisted attempts by Republican presidents and Republican members of Congress to eliminate the agency or limit its operations.[59] One element of its strategy has been to build strong ties to labor unions; as a result, OSHA is much more likely to receive complaints about workplace safety from companies with strong unions. The strategy has also involved building cooperative arrangements with large companies to prevent workplace accidents, an approach that not only protects workers but also can save companies a lot of money

fire alarm oversight
A method of oversight in which members of Congress respond to complaints about the bureaucracy or problems of implementation only as they arise rather than exercising constant vigilance.

The Environmental Protection Agency created the Flint Water Advisory Task Force to coordinate federal, state, and local efforts to fix the contamination of Flint's water supply. Besides changing the implementation of existing regulations, the task force will also investigate the need for new regulations to prevent similar problems from developing in other cities. #FlintWaterCrisis @EPAwater

over the long term. Moreover, when OSHA levies fines against companies that violate safety regulations the fines are generally much less than would be allowed by law. As a result, when proposals to limit or eliminate OSHA are debated in Congress members hear from unions as well as many large corporations in support of keeping the agency in place. Over time, this strategy has generated support for the agency from congressional Democrats and Republicans.

The consequences of control

This discussion of attempts to control what bureaucrats do while at the same time tapping their expertise explains many of the seemingly dysfunctional aspects of the bureaucracy. Part of the problem is the nature of the tasks given to bureaucrats: even when members of Congress and the president agree on which problems deserve attention, bureaucrats face the much harder task of translating these goals into concrete policies. Given the magnitude of this job, it is no surprise that even the best efforts of government agencies do not always succeed.

Most important, the use of standard operating procedures is rooted partly in the complexity of bureaucrats' tasks—but also in the desire of agency heads and elected officials to control the actions of lower-level staff. Some of the EPA's delays in responding to the crisis in Flint were the product of preset plans and procedures that did not anticipate the need for fast action to protect a community from an unsafe water supply. Moreover, giving laptops to government employees so they can work while out of the office sounds like a good idea, but it also puts sensitive data at risk because laptops are easily lost or stolen. And while the FDA's drug-approval process succeeds for the most part in preventing harmful drugs from coming to market, the delays imposed by the process do prevent some patients from receiving lifesaving treatments. However, in all these cases the decisions do not reflect incompetence or malice. Rules and procedures are needed in any organization to ensure that decisions are fair and reflect the goals of the organization. Yet it is impossible to find procedures that will work well in all cases, particularly for the kinds of policy decisions bureaucrats must make.

Cases of bureaucratic failure (poorly conceived policies or regulations, inaction, red tape) are often cited to "prove" that bureaucrats are incompetent, lazy, or dumb. The real story is that bureaucrats are often given nearly impossible tasks or political mandates that limit their authority. In this sense, complaints about bureaucrats have more to do with what we want them to do rather than their unwillingness or inability to execute these missions.

"Why Should I Care?"

Conclusion

Bureaucrats implement government policy—often in situations in which the problems and potential solutions are vast and poorly understood and in the face of sharp disagreements about what government should do. On the government's behalf, bureaucrats spend money on everything from paper clips to Mars rovers. They formulate regulations that determine what can be created, produced, transported, bought, sold, consumed, and disposed of in America. Elected officials want to control what bureaucrats do while also tapping into their expertise on policy matters. In this way, conflict

Many government regulations work as intended. An increase in regulatory attention to environmental protection and cleanup of polluted sites has dramatically improved water quality nationwide, including that of the Hudson River in New York, shown here.

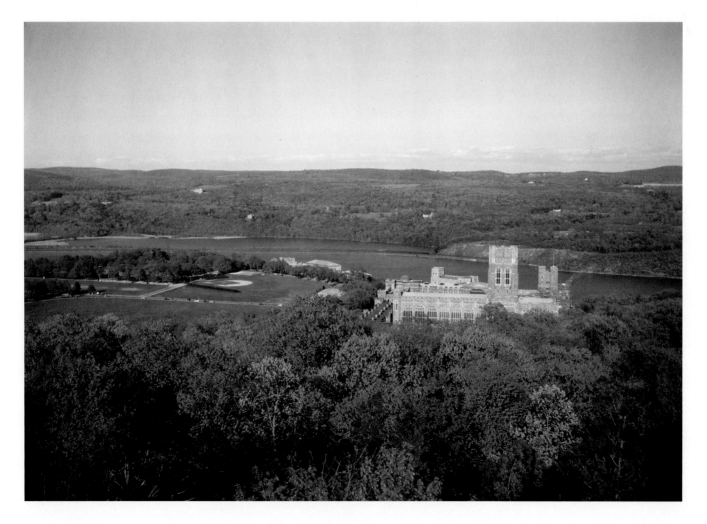

over public policy often translates into conflicting ideas about what bureaucrats should do, resulting in complex, often-contradictory mandates and directions imposed on those workers. For example, EPA inaction on the Flint water crisis was driven by disagreements within the agency on whether they had the authority to force state and local officials to address the problem.

These characteristics of the bureaucracy and the fundamentally political nature of bureaucrats' jobs explain many cases of ineptitude and red tape. Sometimes bureaucrats simply make mistakes, choosing the wrong policy because they lack full information about the tasks they were given. Bureaucrats may drag their feet when they oppose their tasks on policy grounds. Policies may reflect direct or implicit orders given by elected officials or political appointees. For example, the EPA's reluctance to act in the case of Flint may reflect a lack of easy solutions or the desire not to get involved in a purely local problem. Attempts at political control also shape the structure of the bureaucracy, from influencing which agencies function independently and which ones fall within executive departments to determining the qualifications for commissioners and agency heads and the rules they must follow when making decisions.

STUDY GUIDE

What is the federal bureaucracy?

Define *bureaucracy* and explain its major functions. (Pages 342–348)

Summary

The bureaucracy is composed of both civil servants and political appointees and is in charge of interpreting and implementing a wide range of government policies. While bureaucrats are policy experts, most members of Congress are not. Nonetheless, Congress tries to control how the bureaucracy operates, which can result in inefficiencies.

Key terms

bureaucracy (p. 342)

civil servants (p. 342)

political appointees (p. 342)

regulation (p. 342)

notice-and-comment procedure (p. 343)

state capacity (p. 346)

red tape (p. 347)

standard operating procedures (p. 347)

problem of control (p. 347)

principal–agent game (p. 347)

Practice Quiz Questions

1. **A government rule that affects the choices that individuals or corporations make is called _____.**
   a. an initiative
   b. a referendum
   c. a regulation
   d. a procurement
   e. an appropriation

2. **One of the reasons bureaucrats respond to pressure from elected officials is because _____.**
   a. they need congressional support to get larger budgets
   b. elected officials are experts
   c. they are all appointed by members of Congress
   d. their offices are housed in the Congress
   e. they are required by law to do so

3. **In the problem of control, the _____ is the principal and the _____ is the agent.**
   a. bureaucracy; president
   b. bureaucracy; Congress
   c. president; Congress
   d. president; bureaucracy
   e. Congress; president

How has the American bureaucracy grown?

Trace the expansion of the federal bureaucracy over time. (Pages 349–351)

Summary

The bureaucracy has grown substantially since the turn of the twentieth century, largely in response to citizen demands that the government do more for the people. The federal government had a very limited role in daily life for much of the nineteenth century, but it expanded during the Progressive Era, when regulatory activity increased and the spoils system was replaced by the federal civil service. The bureaucracy expanded again with the New Deal and Great Society programs, which increased the number of services the government provided.

Key term

federal civil service (p. 350)

Practice Quiz Questions

4. **How did the bureaucracy change during the Progressive Era?**
   a. It expanded the delivery of government services directly to individuals.
   b. The spoils system was first established.
   c. It created a number of antipoverty and educational programs.
   d. It reduced the government's regulatory activity.
   e. It increased the government's regulatory activity.

5. **The civil service reforms of the Progressive Era _____ the spoils system and _____ the power of party organizations.**
   a. ended; increased
   b. ended; decreased
   c. instituted; increased
   d. instituted; decreased
   e. expanded; increased

6. **What effect did the Reagan Revolution have on bureaucracy?**
   a. The government stopped passing regulatory policies.
   b. The size of the federal government shrank.
   c. The size of the federal government increased.
   d. The civil service reforms were weakened.
   e. The civil service reforms were strengthened.

The modern federal bureaucracy

Describe the size and structure of the executive branch today. (Pages 352–356)

Summary

The modern bureaucracy serves a wide range of functions, but the division of labor within the bureaucracy does not always have an obvious logic. Overlapping or confusing jurisdictions can be the result of elected officials attempting to shape agency behavior by assigning a task to an executive department rather than an independent agency. The overall size of the bureaucracy reflects the demands of constituents but also fits the needs of elected officials to improve their chances of reelection.

Key terms

Office of Management and Budget (p. 352)   **independent agencies** (p. 352)

Practice Quiz Questions

7. **What is the job of the Office of Management and Budget?**
   a. to prepare the president's annual budget proposal for the Congress
   b. to prepare a response to the budget passed by Congress
   c. to prepare annual budget proposals for the states
   d. to monitor government spending for the Supreme Court
   e. to monitor government spending for Congress

8. **Independent agencies have _____ freedom from oversight than executive departments do and _____ be controlled by the president through his or her appointees.**
   a. more; cannot
   b. more; can
   c. less; cannot
   d. less; can

9. **The federal budget is growing in size because _____.**
   a. bureaucrats are budget maximizers
   b. politicians do not scrutinize budget requests
   c. government agencies are never eliminated
   d. the public does not support large-scale budget cuts
   e. a growing percentage of Americans are going into civil service

The human face of the bureaucracy

Describe who bureaucrats are and the regulations that govern their employment. (Pages 357–359)

Summary

The regulations within the civil service system were established to separate politics from policy. Rather than getting and retaining a job for political reasons, individuals are hired based on merit and are quite difficult to fire. However, the president makes senior-level appointments that are not protected by civil service regulations and are more political in nature. These appointments are instrumental in helping the president control the bureaucracy.

Practice Quiz Questions

10. **Compared with employees in private business, government employees are motivated _____ by salary and benefits than/as by the chance to make a difference.**
    a. more
    b. just as much
    c. less

11. **The civil service regulations _____ the flexibility that managers have in their hiring decisions and _____ the influence of elected officials.**
    a. decrease; decrease
    b. increase; increase
    c. increase; decrease
    d. decrease; increase
    e. increase; have no effect on

Controlling the bureaucracy

Explain how Congress and the president oversee the executive branch. (Pages 360–365)

Summary

With their expertise, bureaucrats have the power to significantly influence government policy. This creates a dilemma for elected officials, who want to enjoy the benefits of the expertise while retaining control of the bureaucracy. Lawmakers can generally organize agencies and monitor their behavior to reduce, but not eliminate, bureaucratic drift.

Key terms

bureaucratic drift (p. 360)   **police patrol oversight** (p. 362)
oversight (p. 362)   **fire alarm oversight** (p. 363)

Practice Quiz Questions

12. **When bureaucrats pursue their own goals rather than their assignments from officeholders, this is called _____.**
    a. an iron triangle
    b. regulatory capture
    c. problem of control
    d. turkey farming
    e. bureaucratic drift

13. **Giving direct orders to bureaucrats _____ the influence of their policy expertise and _____ the potential to respond to unforeseen circumstances.**

    a. limits; reduces

    b. increases; reduces

    c. limits; increases

    d. increases; increases

    e. limits; has no effect on

14. **While police patrol oversight has the advantage of being _____, it has the drawback of being _____.**

    a. affordable; unresponsive

    b. responsive; costly

    c. affordable; generally unnecessary

    d. responsive; unpopular

    e. affordable; ineffective

Suggested Reading

Brehm, John, and Scott Gates. *Teaching, Managing Tasks, and Brokering Trust: Functions of the Public Executive*. New York: Russell Sage Foundation, 2008.

Carpenter, Daniel P. *The Forging of Bureaucratic Autonomy: Reputations, Networks, and Policy Innovation in Executive Agencies, 1862–1928*. Princeton, NJ: Princeton University Press, 2001.

Huber, John D., and Charles R. Shipan. *Deliberate Discretion? The Institutional Foundations of Bureaucratic Autonomy*. New York: Cambridge University Press, 2002.

Lewis, David E. *The Politics of Presidential Appointments: Political Control and Bureaucratic Performance*. Princeton, NJ: Princeton University Press, 2010.

Light, Paul. *A Government Well-Executed: Public Service and Public Performance*. Washington, DC: Brookings Institution Press, 2003.

McCubbins, Mathew D., Roger G. Noll, and Barry R. Weingast. "Structure and Process as Solutions to the Politician's Principal–Agency Problem," *Virginia Law Review* 74 (1989): 431–82.

Miller, Gary. *Managerial Dilemmas: The Political Economy of Hierarchy*. New York: Cambridge University Press, 1987.

Moe, Terry M. "Political Control and the Power of the Agent." *Journal of Law, Economics, and Organization* 22 (2006): 1–29.

Nelson, Michael. "A Short, Ironic History of American National Bureaucracy." *Journal of Politics* 44 (1982): 747–78.

Skowronek, Stephen. *Building a New American State: The Expansion of National Administrative Capacities, 1877–1920*. New York: Cambridge University Press, 1982.

Workman, Samuel. *The Dynamics of Bureaucracy in the U.S. Government*. New York: Cambridge University Press, 2015.

13

The Courts

What is the role of courts in our political system?

On February 13, 2016, Justice Antonin Scalia died in his sleep while visiting a West Texas ranch. Scalia was an intellectual force on the Court known for his sharp wit, tough (and frequent) questions during oral arguments, and scathing dissents. His death had momentous political implications: with the Court now divided 4–4 between liberals and conservatives, President Obama could tip the balance in favor of the liberals for the first time in a generation. However, within an hour of the confirmation of Scalia's death Senate Majority Leader Mitch McConnell announced that there would be no hearing and no vote on any nomination by President Obama. The next president would get to decide the future balance of the Court.[1]

About a month later, President Obama nominated Merrick Garland to fill the vacancy. A respected judicial moderate, Garland served for nearly two decades on the Washington, D.C., appeals court, the second most important court in the nation. Despite a nomination that was intended to appeal to moderate Republican senators, Senate leadership held firm to their vow to let the vacancy be filled by the next president.

The immediate implication of the deadlock was that five cases were split 4–4, meaning that no new precedents were established and the lower courts' decisions would stand. Several of these cases, including a California case on public sector unions and a Texas case concerning immigration policy, were significant cases that will likely be addressed by a future Court.[2] Some cases appeared to be unanimous, but masked a 4–4 split. For example, the Court punted on the question of whether a religious organization could be required to provide coverage of contraceptives in a parallel insurance plan (they cannot be forced to provide coverage directly). Rather than deciding whether this was an infringement of the group's religious freedom, the Court sent the case back to the lower court in a unanimous 8–0 decision, which meant the case would

Explain how the power of judicial review was established.
pages 373–376

Outline the structure of the court system.
pages 376–385

Describe how cases reach the Supreme Court.
pages 386–389

Describe the Supreme Court's procedures for hearing a case.
pages 389–392

Analyze the factors that influence Supreme Court decisions.
pages 393–397

People outside the Supreme Court in April 2016 urge the Senate to "do [their] job" and hold hearings on the nomination of Merrick Garland. The vacancy in 2016 was one of the longest for the Court in U.S. history. #DoYourJob ultimately be decided by a future court. The Court also responded by deciding to hear far fewer cases in their fall term (8 compared to 13 at this time the previous year).

Supreme Court politics also spilled over to the 2016 elections. Democrats urged Republican senators to "do [their] job," pointing out that every Supreme Court nominee since 1875 had received a hearing or vote and since 1900 six justices were confirmed during a presidential election year.[3] It became a central issue in the presidential campaign, with exit polls showing that 21 percent of voters said the Supreme Court vacancy was the most important factor in determining their vote. Another 48 percent said it was "an important factor." Of those saying it was "most important," 56 percent voted for Trump and 41 percent for Clinton (while those saying it was important split evenly).

Why all the fuss? If justices are simply interpreting the Constitution and neutrally applying it to law, why should it matter so much which president gets to fill a vacancy? The simple answer is that justices are more than baseball umpires calling the balls and strikes, as Chief Justice John G. Roberts Jr. famously said. As they interpret the Constitution, they also play one of two roles in our political system: either asserting their own policy-making authority or deferring to the decisions of others (Congress, the president, or the people). The Court's decision about which path to take in a given case is often political, involving conflict, trade-offs, and compromise, much like decision making in Congress.

That the Supreme Court is a policy-making and political institution may seem inappropriate. After all, the guiding principles of the "rule of law" in the American political system—embodied in the words carved above the entrance to the Supreme Court ("equal justice under the law") and the statue of Justice represented as a blindfolded woman holding a set of scales—seem to contradict the view of a political Supreme Court. We normally think of the Court as objectively applying the law and interpreting the Constitution for each case. Indeed, there is often consensus among the justices on how to rule in a given case. In the 2015–2016 term, nearly half of the decisions were unanimous (38 of 82) and 12 more only had one dissenting vote. But, the recent immigration case illustrates that politics is an inherent part of the judiciary and a single set of objective standards is not always available for a given case. The 4–4 split upheld the lower court's injunction blocking Obama's deferred deportation program for illegal immigrants. The one-sentence decision offered no clues about the Court's reasoning, but the oral arguments made it clear that four justices saw Obama's actions as executive overreach and four viewed them as proper bureaucratic discretion.[4] On the other hand, the Court also issued a 4–3 decision upholding the University of Texas's affirmative action policy. This type of deference to state policy is an example of judicial restraint.[5]

For those who resist the view that the courts are a policy-making institution, the theme "political process matters" may not seem to apply in this chapter. However, the courts often *do* make policy, and the way they make decisions has an impact on outcomes. To see how political process matters for the courts, it is important to answer the following questions: What are the different roles of the courts? What is the structure of the judicial system? How do court decisions shape policy? In a nutshell, what is the nature of judicial decision making? This chapter also examines the questions suggested by the immigration and affirmative action cases. What is the proper place of the courts within our political system? How do the courts work? How much power should unelected judges have? Are the courts a necessary check on the other branches of government or a source of unaccountable power that contradicts core principles of democracy? Before addressing these questions, we discuss how the Founders viewed the judicial system.

The development of an independent and powerful federal judiciary

The Constitution did not definitively establish the role of the courts in American politics and the Supreme Court's authority as the ultimate interpreter of the Constitution. The powers of the Supreme Court evolved over time, and debates about its proper role continue to this day.

The Founders' views of the courts: the weakest branch?

The Federalists and Antifederalists did not see eye to eye on much, and the judiciary was no exception. Alexander Hamilton, writing in *Federalist 78*, said that the Supreme Court would be "beyond comparison the weakest of the three departments of power." In contrast, an author of the *Antifederalist Papers* wrote: "The supreme court under this constitution would be exalted above all other power in the government and subject to no control."[6] Hmmm, which is it—weakest or strongest? While the framers could not agree on the likely relative power of the Court, there was surprisingly little debate at the Constitutional Convention about the judiciary. Article III of the Constitution, which concerns the judicial branch of government (see Nuts & Bolts 13.1), created one Supreme Court and gave the courts independence by providing federal judges with lifetime terms (assuming "good behavior").

⬡

NUTS & BOLTS 13.1

Jurisdiction of the Federal Courts as Defined in Article III of the Constitution

Jurisdiction of Lower Federal Courts

- Cases involving the U.S. Constitution, federal laws, and treaties.
- Controversies between two or more states. (Congress passed a law giving the Supreme Court exclusive jurisdiction over these cases.)
- Controversies between citizens of different states.
- Controversies between a state and citizens of another state. (The Eleventh Amendment removed federal jurisdiction in these cases.)
- Controversies between a state or its citizens and any foreign states, citizens, or subjects.
- Cases affecting ambassadors, public ministers, and consuls.
- Cases of admiralty and maritime jurisdictions.
- Controversies between citizens of the same state claiming lands under grants of different states.

Jurisdiction of the Supreme Court
Original Jurisdiction*

- Cases involving ambassadors, public ministers, and consuls.
- Cases to which a state is a party.

Appellate Jurisdiction

- Cases falling under the jurisdiction of the lower federal courts, "with such exceptions, and under such Regulations as the Congress shall make."

---

*This does not imply exclusive jurisdiction. For example, the Supreme Court may refer to a district court for a case involving an ambassador (the more likely outcome).

Source: Lee Epstein and Thomas G. Walker, *Constitutional Law for a Changing America: Institutional Powers and Constraints*, 5th ed. (Washington, DC: CQ Press, 2004), p. 65.

The main disagreements about the judiciary had to do with how independent the courts should be *vis-à-vis* the other branches of government and how much power to give the courts. Some of the framers feared a tyrannical Congress and wanted to create judicial and executive branches that could check this power. Others argued for making the executive and judicial branches more closely related so that they would be better able to balance Congress. A central debate was whether to give the judiciary some "revisionary power" over Congress, similar to the president's veto power. This idea of judicial review would have given the Supreme Court the power to strike down laws passed by Congress that violated the Constitution. The framers could not agree on judicial review, so the Constitution remained silent on the matter. As the power of judicial review has evolved, it has become a central part of the system of checks and balances (see Chapter 2).

Many details about the Supreme Court were left up to Congress, including its size, the time and place it would meet, and its internal organization. These details, as well as the system of lower federal courts, were outlined in the **Judiciary Act of 1789**. This law set the number of justices at six (one chief justice and five associates). The number of justices gradually increased to ten by the end of the Civil War and was then restricted to seven under Reconstruction policies. The number was set at nine in 1869, where it has remained since.[7]

The 1789 act also created a system of federal courts, which included thirteen **district courts** and three circuit courts—the intermediate-level courts with **appellate jurisdiction** (cases heard on appeal from lower courts). The district courts each had one judge; the circuits comprised two Supreme Court justices and one district judge. Today separate judges are appointed to fill the circuit courts (what we call appeals courts). The Supreme Court had a rough start. Indeed, it seemed determined to prove Alexander Hamilton right, that it was the weakest branch. Of the six original justices appointed by George Washington, one declined to serve and another never showed up for a formal session. The Court's first sessions lasted only a few days because it did not have much business. In fact, the Court did not decide a single case in 1791 or 1792. When Justice Rutledge resigned in 1791 to take a state court position, two potential appointees turned down the job in order to keep their positions in their state legislatures! Such career decisions would be unimaginable today, when serving on the Supreme Court is considered the pinnacle of a legal career.[8]

Judicial review and *Marbury v. Madison*

The Court started to gain more power when John Marshall was appointed chief justice in 1801. Marshall single-handedly transformed the Court into an equal partner in the system of checks and balances. The most important step was the decision *Marbury v. Madison* (1803), which gave the Supreme Court the power of **judicial review**. As noted, the framers were split on the wisdom of giving the Court the power to strike down laws passed by Congress and the Constitution does not explicitly address the issue. However, historians have established that a majority of the framers, including the most influential ones, favored judicial review. Given that the Constitution did not address the issue of judicial review, Marshall simply asserted that the Supreme Court had the power to determine when a law was unconstitutional.

Although the idea was not original to Marshall (the framers debated the issue and Hamilton endorsed it in some detail in *Federalist 78*), the Court had never exercised its authority to rule on the constitutionality of a federal law. The facts of the *Marbury* case involved a partisan dispute over last-minute appointments to a lower court by the outgoing Adams administration. The new Jefferson administration did not honor those appointments, and one of the people who didn't get his position, Mr. Marbury, brought the case to the Supreme Court. Marshall said that Marbury was due his commission,

Judiciary Act of 1789
The law in which Congress laid out the organization of the federal judiciary. The law refined and clarified federal court jurisdiction and set the original number of justices at six. It also created the Office of the Attorney General and established the lower federal courts.

district courts
Lower-level trial courts of the federal judicial system that handle most U.S. federal cases.

appellate jurisdiction
The authority of a court to hear appeals from lower courts and change or uphold the decision.

judicial review
The Supreme Court's power to strike down a law or an executive branch action that it finds unconstitutional.

but the Court did not have the power to give him his job because the part of the Judiciary Act of 1789 that gave it that power was unconstitutional! The core issue was Section 13 of the Act, which gave the Court the power to issue orders (writs of mandamus) to anyone holding federal office. This section expanded the **original jurisdiction** of the Supreme Court, and that was where Congress overstepped its bounds, according to Marshall. The original jurisdiction of the Court is clearly specified in the Constitution, so any attempt by Congress to change that jurisdiction through legislation would be unconstitutional; the only way to change original jurisdiction would be through a constitutional amendment.[9] Marshall wrote: "It is emphatically the province and duty of the judicial department to say what the law is. . . . If two laws conflict with each other, the courts must decide on the operation of each. So if a law be in opposition to the Constitution . . . the courts must determine which of these conflicting rules governs the case. This is of the very essence of judicial duty."[10]

By asserting its power to review the constitutionality of laws passed by Congress, the Court became an equal partner in the institutional balance of power. Although more than 50 years would pass before the Court would use judicial review again to strike down a law passed by Congress (in the unfortunate 1857 *Dred Scott* case concerning slavery that effectively led to the Civil War), the reasoning behind *Marbury* has never been challenged by subsequent presidents or Congresses.[11]

Interpreting federal laws may seem a logical responsibility for the Supreme Court, but what about state laws? Should the Supreme Court have final say over them as well? The Constitution does not answer this question. However, the supremacy clause requires that the Constitution and national laws take precedence over state constitutions and state laws when they conflict. And the Judiciary Act of 1789 made it clear that the Supreme Court would rule on these matters.

It didn't take long for the Court to assert its power in this area. In 1796, the Court heard a case concerning a British creditor who was trying to collect a debt from the state of Virginia. The state had passed a law canceling all debts owed by Virginians (or the state) to British subjects. However, the Treaty of Paris, which ended the Revolutionary War and recognized American independence, ensured the collection of such debts. This conflict was resolved when the Court struck down the state law and upheld Americans' commitments under the treaty.[12] Advocates of states' rights were not happy with this ruling, but it was crucial for the national government that the Constitution be applied uniformly rather than be subject to different interpretations by every state.

Judicial review in practice

The contours of the relationship between the national government and the states were largely defined by how active the Supreme Court was in asserting judicial review and how willing it was to intervene in matters of state law. For much of the nineteenth century, the Court embraced dual federalism, in which the national government and the states operated on two separate levels (see Chapter 3). Later the Court involved itself more in state law as it moved toward an increasingly active role for the national government in regulating interstate commerce and using the Fourteenth Amendment to selectively incorporate the amendments that constitute the Bill of Rights (see Chapter 4).

All in all, the Court has struck down more than 180 acts of Congress (and about 1,400 state laws). This sounds like a lot, but Congress passed more than 60,000 laws in its first 225 years. Over time, the Court has ruled on state laws in many important areas, including civil liberties, desegregation and civil rights, abortion, privacy, redistricting, labor laws, employment and discrimination, and business and environmental regulation.

original jurisdiction
The authority of a court to handle a case first, as in the Supreme Court's authority to initially hear disputes between two states. However, original jurisdiction for the Supreme Court is not exclusive; it may assign such a case to a lower court.

Chief Justice John Marshall favored the idea of judicial review and claimed this power for the Court in the *Marbury v. Madison* decision.

constitutional interpretation
The process of determining whether a piece of legislation or governmental action is supported by the Constitution.

statutory interpretation
The various methods and tests used by the courts for determining the meaning of a law and applying it to specific situations. Congress may overturn the courts' interpretation by writing a new law; thus, it also engages in statutory interpretation.

When the Supreme Court strikes down a congressional or state law, it engages in **constitutional interpretation**—that is, it determines that the law is unconstitutional. But the Supreme Court also engages in **statutory interpretation**—that is, it applies national and state laws to particular cases (statutes are laws that are passed by legislatures). Often the language of a statute may be unclear and the Court must interpret how to apply the law. For example, should the protection of endangered species prevent economic development that destroys the species' habitat? How does one determine whether an employer is responsible for sexual harassment in the workplace? How should the voting rights of minorities be protected? In cases such as these, the Court must interpret the relevant statutes to determine what Congress or the state legislatures really meant when issuing them.

Although politicians and other political actors accept judicial review as a central part of the political system, critics are concerned about its antidemocratic nature. Why, for example, do we give nine unelected justices such awesome power over our elected representatives? Debates about the proper role for the Court will continue as long as it is involved in controversial decisions. We will take up this question later in this chapter, when we address the concepts of judicial activism and judicial restraint.

"Why Should I Care?"

Judicial review may seem like "inside baseball" that doesn't really matter for most Americans. However, the power to strike down laws and government actions means that the Court may act against political majorities to strike down unconstitutional actions such as segregating schools by race and discriminating against same-sex marriage. Judicial review may also be used, however, to frustrate popular majorities during times of political change, such as during the New Deal of the 1930s. In either case, this is an awesome political power that puts the Supreme Court on an equal institutional footing with Congress and the president.

★

OUTLINE THE STRUCTURE OF THE COURT SYSTEM

The American legal and judicial system

Two sets of considerations shed light on the overall nature of our judicial system: the fundamentals of the legal system that apply to all courts in the United States, and the structure of the court system within our system of federalism.

Court fundamentals

plaintiff
The person or party who brings a case to court.

defendant
The person or party against whom a case is brought.

plea bargain
An agreement between a plaintiff and a defendant to settle a case before it goes to trial or the verdict is decided. In a civil case, this usually involves an admission of guilt and an agreement on monetary damages; in a criminal case, this often involves an admission of guilt in return for a reduced charge or sentence.

The general characteristics of the court system begin with the people who are in the courtroom. The **plaintiff** brings the case, and the **defendant** is the party who is being sued or charged with a crime. If the case is appealed, the petitioner is the person bringing the appeal and the respondent is on the other side of the case. In a civil case, the plaintiff sues to determine who is right or wrong and to gain something of value, such as monetary damages, the right to vote, or admission to a university. In a criminal case, the plaintiff is the government and the prosecutor attempts to prove the guilt of the defendant (the person accused of the crime).

Many, but not all, civil and criminal cases are heard before a jury that decides the outcome in the case, which is called the verdict. Often cases get settled before they go to trial (or even in the middle of the trial) in a process known as **plea bargaining**. In a civil case, this would mean that the plaintiff and the defendant agree on a monetary settlement and admission of guilt (or not; in some cases, the defendant may agree to pay a fine or damages but not to admit guilt). In a criminal case, the defendant may agree to plead guilty in exchange for being charged with a lesser crime or for receiving a shorter sentence than might be imposed in a jury trial. Plea bargaining is an excellent example of how legal conflict between two parties can be resolved through compromise.

One type of civil suit is the **class-action lawsuit**, a case brought by a group of individuals on behalf of themselves and others in similar circumstances. The target may be a corporation that produced hazardous or defective products or that engaged in illegal behavior that harmed a particular group. For example, 1.5 million current and former female Walmart employees sued the retailing giant for sex discrimination in 2011, claiming that the store had paid women less than men for the same work and had promoted fewer women than men.[13] Class-action suits are often filed on behalf of shareholders of companies that have lost value because of fraud committed by corporate leaders. Cases like these are an important mechanism for providing accountability and justice in our economic system.

Common Law and Precedent Forty-nine of the 50 states and the federal courts operate under a system of **common law**, which means that legal decisions build from precedent established in previous cases and apply commonly throughout the jurisdiction of the court. The alternative, which is practiced only in Louisiana, is the civil law tradition that is based on a detailed codification of the law that is applied to each specific case.

The notion of **precedent** (or stare decisis—"let the decision stand") deserves special attention. Precedent is a previously decided case or set of decisions that serves as a guide for future cases on the same topic. Lower courts are bound by Supreme Court decisions when there is a clear precedent that is relevant for a given case. In many cases, following precedent is not clear-cut because several precedents may seem relevant. The lower courts have considerable discretion in sorting out which precedents are the most important. The Supreme Court tries to follow its own precedents, but in the past 50 years justices have been willing to deviate from earlier decisions when they think that the precedent is flawed. Precedent is not a rule the Court must follow but a norm that constrains its behavior.

Standing Another factor must be considered before a case is filed: the person bringing the case must have **standing** to sue in a civil case, which means that there is a legitimate basis for bringing the case. This usually means that the individual has suffered some direct and personal harm from the action addressed in the court case. Standing is easy to establish for private parties—for example, if your neighbor destroys your fence you have been harmed. However, it gets more interesting when the government is a party. For example, when an environmental group challenged the Interior Department's interpretation of the Endangered Species Act the Supreme Court ruled that the group did not have standing because it did not demonstrate that the government's policy would cause "imminent" injury to the group.[14] Later, in the section discussing how cases get to the Supreme Court, we will see that justices have some leeway in defining standing.

Jurisdiction The final general characteristic of the legal system is the **jurisdiction** of the court: when bringing a case before the court, you must choose a court that actually has the power to hear your case. For example, if you wanted to contest a speeding ticket you would not file your case in the state supreme court or in the federal district court; you would file it in your local traffic court. What if you believed you were the victim of discrimination in the workplace? Would you sue in state or federal court? You probably could do either, but the decision would be based on which set of laws would provide you with more protection from discrimination. This varies by state, so the proper jurisdiction for a given case is often a judgment call based on specific legal questions.

class-action lawsuit
A case brought by a group of individuals on behalf of themselves and others in the general public who are in similar circumstances.

O. J. Simpson dons a pair of gloves during testimony in his double-murder trial in Los Angeles in June 1995. The jury was not convinced of his guilt "beyond a reasonable doubt" and thus acquitted Simpson in this criminal trial. However, a subsequent civil trial found that a "preponderance of evidence" was against him.

common law
Law based on the precedent of previous court rulings rather than on legislation. It is used in all federal courts and 49 of the 50 state courts.

precedent
A legal norm established in court cases that is then applied to future cases dealing with the same legal questions.

standing
Legitimate justification for bringing a civil case to court.

jurisdiction
The sphere of a court's legal authority to hear and decide cases.

Structure of the court system and federalism

The structure of the court system is like that of the rest of the political system: it is divided within and across levels of government. Across the levels of government, the court system operates on two parallel tracks within the state and local courts and the federal courts. Within each level of government, both tracks include courts of original jurisdiction, appeals courts, and courts of special jurisdiction. As How It Works: The Court System shows, the state courts are entirely separate from the federal courts, with the exception of the small proportion of cases that are appealed from a state supreme court to the U.S. Supreme Court. There is much variation in the structure of state courts in terms of their names and the number of levels of courts. However, they all follow the same general pattern of trial courts with limited and general original jurisdiction and appeals courts (either one or two levels, depending on the state).

District Courts Workhorses of the federal system, the district courts handle more than a quarter of a million filings a year. There are 89 districts in the 50 states, with at least one district court for each state. There are also district courts in Puerto Rico, the Virgin Islands, the District of Columbia, Guam, and the Northern Mariana Islands; this brings the total to 94 districts with 677 judges.[15] There are two limited-jurisdiction district courts: the Court of International Trade, which addresses cases involving international trade and customs issues, and the U.S. Court of Federal Claims, which handles most claims for money damages against the United States, disputes over federal contracts, unlawful "takings" of private property by the federal government, and other claims against the United States.

Appeals Courts The appeals courts (called circuit courts until 1948) are the intermediate courts of appeals, but in practice they are the final court for most federal cases that are appealed from the lower courts. The losing side in a federal case can appeal to the Supreme Court, but the highest court in the land hears so few cases that the appeals courts usually get the final word. Appeals courts did not always have this much power; in fact, through much of the nineteenth century they had very limited appellate jurisdiction and did not hear many significant cases.

The number of appeals courts in the nation slowly expanded as the workload of these courts grew, to the current 12 regional courts and the court of appeals for the Federal Circuit, which handles specialized cases from all over the country. Today the only appeals of district court cases that go directly to the Supreme Court and bypass the appeals court are cases that concern legislative reapportionment and redistricting, voting rights, and some issues related to the 1964 Civil Rights Act.

The Supreme Court The Supreme Court sits at the top of the federal court system. The Supreme Court is the "court of last resort" for cases coming from both the state and the federal courts. One important function of the Court is to resolve conflicts between lower courts, or between a state law and federal law, or between laws in different states, to ensure that the application and interpretation of the Constitution are consistent nationwide. A district court or appeals court ruling is applicable only for the specific region of that court, whereas Supreme Court rulings apply to the entire country. Although the Supreme Court is the most important interpreter of the Constitution, the president and Congress also interpret the Constitution on a regular basis. This means that the Supreme Court does not always have the final say. For example, if the Court strikes down a federal law for being overly vague Congress can rewrite the law to clarify the offending passage. When this happens, Congress may have the final word. For example, Congress overturned *Ledbetter v. Goodyear Tire & Rubber Co.* (2007) when it passed the Lilly Ledbetter Fair Pay Act in 2009. The law said that the Supreme Court

appeals courts
The intermediate level of federal courts that hear appeals from district courts. More generally, an appeals court is any court with appellate jurisdiction.

Presidents can influence the direction of the federal courts by selecting judges who share their views. President Obama is shown with Judge Merrick B. Garland, who he nominated to the U.S. Supreme Court to fill the vacancy created by the death of Justice Antonin Scalia.

had misinterpreted the 1964 Civil Rights Act when the Court ruled in 2007 that Ledbetter would have had to file her pay discrimination suit within 180 days of being hired.[16]

Even on matters of constitutional interpretation rather than statutory interpretation, Congress can fight back by passing a constitutional amendment. However, this is a difficult and time-consuming process (see Chapter 2). Nevertheless, that option is available as a way of overturning an unpopular Court decision.

How judges are selected

There are many mechanisms for placing judges in courts. At the national level, the president makes the appointments with the advice and consent of the Senate. This process may be extremely contentious, as discussed in the chapter opener about filling Justice Scalia's vacancy. At the state level, various methods are in use.

State-Level Judges At the state level, there are 147 trial courts (some states have multiple levels), 94 appeals courts, and 52 supreme courts. At the state level, judges can be selected for trial courts in five different ways: appointment by the governor (6 courts), appointment by the state legislature (5 courts), partisan elections (39 courts), nonpartisan elections (34 courts), and the system called the Missouri Plan in which the governor makes appointments from a list compiled by a nonpartisan screening committee (46 courts). Seventeen courts use some combination of these methods.[17] With this last method, the appointed judge usually has to run in a retention election within several years of the appointment, making this system a hybrid of the political nomination and popular election routes to the court.

There is some controversy over the wisdom of electing judges, as doing so may undermine the courts' role as the protector of unpopular minority rights. Even in states where judicial elections are officially nonpartisan, it is clear who the liberal and conservative candidates are, so judicial elections can be very partisan. Electing judges also raises the potential for conflicts of interest if campaign contributors have cases before the court.[18] However, elected judges will be more responsive to public opinion, especially on salient issues such as the death penalty[19] and abortion.[20] Furthermore, the alternative to elections—appointing judges—has been criticized as elitist. These critics

The Court System

If federal question →

State Supreme Courts or Courts of Last Resort

52 courts (Texas and Oklahoma each have two courts of last resort)

346 judges; about 85,000 cases per year

Final Appeals Courts

U.S. Supreme Court

Received 7,033 filings in the 2014–2015 term; 75 cases were argued; 75 were disposed of in 66 signed opinions.

Courts of Appeals

94 courts in 41 states

939 judges; about 300,000 cases per year

Intermediate Appeals Courts

U.S. Courts of Appeals

12 regional courts and the U.S. Court of Appeals for the Federal Circuit

52,698 filings in the 2014–2015 term

Trial Courts of Limited and Special Jurisdiction

16,920 judges
About 48 million cases per year

Examples: juvenile court, traffic court, small claims court, justice of the peace, family court

Trial Courts of General and Original Jurisdiction

10,650 judges
About 75 million cases per year

Examples: district courts, county courts, municipal courts

Trial Courts

Trial Courts of General and Original Jurisdiction

94 district courts
279,039 civil cases and 80,069 criminal cases filed in the 2014–2015 term

Trial Courts of Limited and Special Jurisdiction

Examples: federal claims court, tax court, Court of International Trade, Court of Veterans Appeals

State and Local Courts

Federal Courts

Sources: Data on federal courts are from the U.S. Supreme Court, "2015 Year-End Report on the Federal Judiciary," www.supremecourt.gov/publicinfo/year-end/2015year-endreport.pdf (accessed 3/11/16). Data on state courts are from National Center for State Courts, www.ncsc.org (accessed 10/26/16); Ballotpedia.org, "Intermediate Appellate Courts," https://ballotpedia.org/Intermediate_appellate_courts (accessed 3/18/16) and Ron Malega and Thomas H. Cohen, "State Court Organization, 2011," U.S. Department of Justice, Bureau of Justice Statistics, www.bjs.gov/content/pub/pdf/sco11.pdf (accessed 3/18/16).

Same–Sex Marriage through the Court System

Same-sex marriage has been addressed in dozens of state and federal court cases in the past decade. A landmark case decided in June 2015 illustrates how cases make their way through the court system and how the Supreme Court resolves conflicts between the lower courts.

Okay, let's resolve this.

Supreme Court:
The Supreme Court resolved this conflict in a landmark 5–4 decision, *Obergefell v. Hodges* (2015), holding that the fundamental **right to marry is guaranteed to same-sex couples** by both the due process clause and the equal protection clause of the Fourteenth Amendment to the U.S. Constitution.

The conflict between the circuit courts meant that same-sex marriage was legal in some states, but not in others. At the end of June 2015, same-sex couples could marry in 29 states and the District of Columbia, but not in 21 states.

It's constitutional.

Federal Court of Appeals:
Appeals court rulings from the Fourth, Seventh, Ninth, and Tenth Circuits, representing 23 states, **struck down state-level bans on same-sex marriage** as unconstitutional.

It's unconstitutional.

Federal Court of Appeals:
Six federal district court cases from Michigan, Ohio, Kentucky, and Tennessee were appealed to the Sixth Circuit Court, which **upheld the bans on same-sex marriage in these four states.**

Yeah, but...

Eleven federal district court decisions were appealed by states attempting to uphold their bans.

Rights awarded!

State and Federal Trial Courts:
Following the Supreme Court's landmark ruling in 2013 striking down the Defense of Marriage Act, more than **two dozen state courts and federal district courts struck down bans on same-sex marriage.**

? Critical Thinking

1. **What are the advantages and disadvantages** of having such a complex court system?

2. **When does a case that goes through the state courts** end up in the U.S. Supreme Court? Can you think of an issue other than same-sex marriage where this is likely to occur?

also say that there's not much evidence that the process of appointing judges is more "merit based" than judicial elections.[21]

Federal Judges The Constitution does not specify requirements for serving on the federal courts, unlike the detailed stipulations for members of Congress and the president. Federal judges don't even have to have a law degree! (This is probably due to the limited number of law schools at the time of the Founding; when the Constitution was written, someone who wanted to be a lawyer generally would serve as an apprentice in a law office to learn the trade.) The president appoints federal judges with the "advice and consent" of the Senate (the Senate must approve the nominees with a majority vote).

Nomination battles for federal judges can be intense, because the stakes are high. As the discussion of judicial review made clear, the Supreme Court plays a central role in the policy process, and because a justice has life tenure a justice's impact can outlive the president and Senate who put him or her on the Court. Judges often serve for decades, much longer than the people who appoint them.

The Role of the President Given the Constitution's silence on the qualification of federal judges, presidents have broad discretion over whom to nominate. Presidents have always tried to influence the direction of the federal courts and especially the Supreme Court by picking people who share their views. Because the Senate often has different ideas about the proper direction for the court, nomination disputes end up being a combination of debates over the merit of a nominee and of partisan battles about the ideological composition of the courts.

Although presidents would *like* to influence the direction of the courts, it is not always possible to predict how judges will behave once they are on the federal bench. However, the president can make a good guess about how a justice is likely to vote based on the nominee's party affiliation and the nature of his or her legal writings and decisions (if the nominee has prior judicial experience). Not surprisingly, 102 of 112 justices who have served on the Supreme Court have shared the nominating president's party (91 percent). Overall, more than 90 percent of the lower-court judges appointed by presidents in the twentieth century also belonged to the same party as the president.

The most partisan move to influence the Court was President Franklin Delano Roosevelt's infamous plan to pack the Court. FDR was frustrated because the Court had struck down several pieces of important New Deal legislation, so to get a more sympathetic Court he proposed nominating a new justice for every justice who was more than 70 years old. Six justices were over 70, so this would have increased the size of the Court to 15 justices. The plan to pack the Court ran into opposition, but in the switch in time that saved nine, as it was called, the Court started ruling in favor of the New Deal legislation, so the plan was dropped.

In addition to ideological considerations about whom to nominate, the president also considers the individual's reputation as a legal scholar and his or her personal relationship to the candidate. Further considerations are the candidate's ethical standards, gender, and race (see Figure 13.1 for data on the latter two points). Donald Trump thrust judges' demographic backgrounds into the limelight when he said that federal district judge Gonzalo P. Curie could not be objective in the lawsuit concerning Trump University because Curie was a Mexican (the judge was born in Indiana and his parents are from Mexico).

The Role of the Senate The Senate is the other half of the equation to determine the composition of the federal courts. It has shifted from having a very active role in providing "advice and consent" on court appointments, to playing a passive role, and then back to an active

DID YOU KNOW?

46

of the 112 people to serve on the Supreme Court have had law degrees. However, all since 1942 have had law degrees and all of the current Court justices attended either Harvard or Yale law school.
Source: SupremeCourt.gov

Senate hearings on Supreme Court nominations have been more conflictual since the 1960s. Although President Obama's nomination of Sonia Sotomayor was confirmed by a 68–31 vote in 2009, Senate Republicans challenged her to explain and defend her views on several issues.

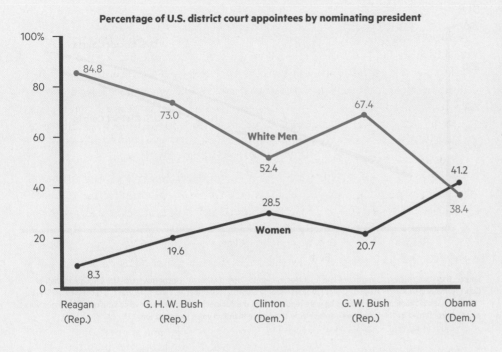

Percentage of U.S. district court appointees by nominating president

100%

84.8

80

73.0

White Men

67.4

60

52.4

41.2

40

28.5

38.4

20.7

20

19.6

Women

8.3

0

| Reagan (Rep.) | G. H. W. Bush (Rep.) | Clinton (Dem.) | G. W. Bush (Rep.) | Obama (Dem.) |

■■l

FIGURE 13.1

Race and Gender on the Federal District Courts

Since the 1980s, the proportion of women on the federal bench has gone up by fivefold while the percentage of white men has plummeted by more than half. Do you think that descriptive representation in the judicial branch is important?

Source: Max Ehrenfreund, "The Number of White Dudes Becoming Judges Has Plummeted under Obama," *Washington Post*, February 18, 2016, www.washingtonpost.com (accessed 6/8/16).

role. One constant is that the Senate rarely rejects nominees because of their qualifications; rather, it tends to reject them for political reasons. Of 28 Supreme Court nominees rejected by the Senate in the history of the United States, only 2 were turned down because they were seen as unqualified. The other 26 nominees were rejected for political reasons. Most commonly, when a president makes a nomination close to an election and the Senate is controlled by the opposing party the Senate will kill the nomination, hoping that its party will win the presidency and nominate a justice more to its liking.

However, not all recent Supreme Court nominations have been controversial. President Bill Clinton's two Supreme Court picks were judicial moderates who were overwhelmingly confirmed—Ruth Bader Ginsburg by a 96–3 vote and Stephen Breyer by an 87–9 vote. George W. Bush's nominees, John Roberts and Samuel Alito Jr., were confirmed by comfortable margins. President Obama appointed the first Hispanic to serve on the Supreme Court, Sonia Sotomayor, who was confirmed by a 68–31 vote. Elena Kagan's confirmation by a 63–37 vote in 2010 meant that three women were serving on the Court for the first time. As noted in the opener, the Senate denied President Obama the opportunity to fill the vacancy created by Justice Scalia's death. President Trump will decide on a new nominee early in 2017.

Battles over Lower-Court Judges Contentious battles do occur, however, between the president and the Senate over nominees to the federal bench and the Supreme Court, and these have recently expanded to include nominees to the district and appeals courts. For much of the nation's history, the president did not play a very active role in the nomination process for district courts; instead, he deferred to the home-state senators of his own party to suggest candidates—a norm called **senatorial courtesy**. If neither senator from the state was from the president's party, he would consult House members from his party and other high-ranking party members from

senatorial courtesy
A norm in the nomination of district court judges in which the president consults with his or her party's senators from the relevant state in choosing the nominee.

FIGURE
13.2

Average Confirmation Delay for Uncontroversial Federal Court Nominations, 1981–2012

Since the 1980s, the length of time needed to confirm federal court nominations has increased dramatically. Why do you think this happened? Why does it matter?

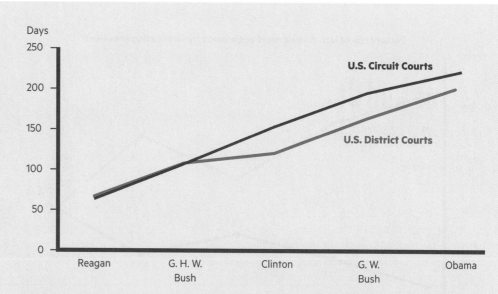

Source: Barry J. McMillion, "Length of Time from Nomination to Confirmation for 'Uncontroversial' U.S. Circuit and District Court Nominees: Detailed Analysis," Congressional Research Service, September 18, 2012, http://fas.org (accessed 6/25/14). "Uncontroversial" nominees are those who were reported from the Judiciary Committee by a voice vote or a unanimous vote and were confirmed by the Senate with a voice vote or no more than five votes in opposition.

the state for district court nominees. The president typically has shown more interest in appeals court nominations. The Justice Department plays a key role in screening candidates, but the local senators of the president's party remain active.

Recently the process has become much more contentious. While the confirmation rate for federal judges has been relatively stable in the past 35 years (between 80 and 90 percent), the average time to confirm nominees has increased dramatically. The average length of delay from nomination to confirmation has also increased (see Figure 13.2). The situation has intensified since then. Democrats blocked 39 of President George W. Bush's nominees between 2001 and 2009,[22] and Republicans have since been returning the favor, blocking dozens of President Obama's nominees, which included employing a record number of filibusters of lower-court nominees. After the Senate blocked three nominees to the D.C. Court of Appeals, the second most important court in the nation, Democrats responded in November 2013 by eliminating the filibuster on lower-court and executive branch nominations but not Supreme Court nominations (see the Take a Stand feature).[23]

"Why Should I Care?"

It is safe to assume that most Americans do not follow the details of battles over court nominations. However, these battles are every bit as important as the elections that *do* capture much attention. Unelected judges often serve for 20 or 30 years, much longer than the average member of Congress, and then have the power to strike down laws that Congress passes. These confirmation battles also support our argument that politics is conflictual and that we should expect it to be that way. The Founders certainly did not expect that the process would be free of politics or that the Senate would be an essentially passive and subordinate player in a nominally joint enterprise. Even George Washington had two of his nominations turned down by the Senate for political reasons. Therefore, politics will continue to play an important role in deciding who serves on the federal bench.

Advice and Consent: Detonating the Nuclear Option

The use of the filibuster to stop presidential nominations to the federal courts has been the source of intense partisan battles in the past 20 years (until recently, 41 senators could stop action on any nomination through a filibuster). However, the positions in those battles are determined by which party controls the Senate and the presidency. Democrats who railed against Republican obstruction when Clinton was president used the same tactics when they were the minority party and George W. Bush was president. The tables were turned again as Republicans filibustered many of Obama's court nominees.

For nearly 10 years, there have been serious discussions about limiting the use of the filibuster for court nominations. When the Democrats blocked many of President George W. Bush's lower-court nominees, the Republican leadership in the Senate considered implementing the "nuclear option," which would have prevented filibusters on judicial nominations. (This plan gets its name because Democrats threatened to essentially shut down the Senate if they lost the use of the filibuster.) This crisis was defused when the "Gang of 14"—seven moderate Republicans and seven moderate Democrats—agreed to a compromise that preserved the Democrats' right to filibuster a nominee, but only in the most extreme cases.

The compromise was honored for a while, but then Republicans obstructed many of President Obama's nominees. Between 1967 and 2013, there were 77 attempts to invoke cloture (to stop a filibuster) on a court nomination. More than half of those (41) came during Obama's presidency.[a] The compromise dissolved in 2013 when Republicans refused to act on *any* nominee to the D.C. Court of Appeals, the second-most important court in the nation, in an effort to preserve the even partisan balance on that court. When Democrats were unable to stop filibusters on three nominees to that court, they detonated the nuclear option, so a simple majority of the Senate could stop a filibuster for lower-court nominations (but the filibuster was preserved for Supreme Court nominations). Republicans responded by forcing Democrats to invoke cloture on every judicial nomination and generally slowing down the process.

Abolish the filibuster for Supreme Court nominations.

For purposes of this exercise, we are going to do a thought experiment to try to strip partisanship from this issue and

When they have been the minority party in the Senate, both Democrats and Republicans have been willing to use the filibuster to block judicial nominees.

figure out if you support the principle of filibustering judicial nominations for the Supreme Court. President Donald Trump has nominated a strong conservative for the open seat on the Court, but Senate Democrats are filibustering the nomination in hopes of getting a more moderate nominee. There are 52 votes in favor of the nomination, but not the 60 needed to cut off the filibuster. Supporters of the nomination are urging Senate leadership to abolish the filibuster for Supreme Court nominations, arguing that the voters have spoken by electing President Trump and that he should be able to nominate who he wants to serve on the Supreme Court. The filibuster is overturning the will of the people.

Preserve the filibuster.

Supporters of the filibuster argue that the Constitution gives the Senate the power to "advise and consent" on presidential nominations and that senators should be able to have significant influence on who serves on the Supreme Court. Most senators who are opposing President Trump's nominee say that they would support a more moderate nominee (a conservative version of Merrick Garland). They argue that this is consistent with the Gang of 14 compromise.

Would you support the filibuster? Take a stand.

take a stand

1. What would you do in the situation just described? Why?

2. Now to complete the thought experiment, assume that Hillary Clinton had been elected and she has nominated a judicial liberal to fill the vacancy on the Court and Republicans are filibustering the nomination. Is your position still the same?

Access to the Supreme Court

It is extremely difficult to have a case heard by the Supreme Court. Currently the Court hears about 1 percent of the cases submitted (76 of 7,509 cases in the most recent completed term). This section explains how the Court decides which cases to hear. When a case is submitted, the clerk of the Court assigns it a number and places it on the docket, which is the schedule of cases.

The Court's workload

Statistics on the Supreme Court's workload initially suggest that the size of the docket has increased dramatically since the 1970s (see Figure 13.3). However, a majority of cases are frivolous and are dismissed after limited review.

Although the increase in workload is not as significant as it appears due to the high number of frivolous cases, another change is more important: the number of opinions issued by the Court has fallen by more than half in the past 20 years. The Court heard about 150 cases each year through the 1980s, but this number has fallen to only 75 to 85 in recent years (see again Figure 13.3).[24] There is no good explanation for why the Court issues half as many opinions as it used to, other than that the chief justices have decided that the Court shouldn't issue so many opinions.[25] The 2016–2017 term is almost certain to show an additional drop in the number of cases heard because of the vacancy created by Justice Scalia's death. Because of the potential 4–4 deadlock, justices were unwilling to take on some cases until they were back to full strength.

Rules of access

With the smaller number of cases being heard, it is even more important to understand how the Court decides which ones to consider. There are four paths that a case may take to get to the Supreme Court.

First, Article III of the Constitution specifies that the Court has original jurisdiction in cases involving foreign ambassadors or foreign countries and cases in which a state is a party. As a practical matter, the Court shares jurisdiction with the lower courts on these issues. In recent years, the Court has invoked original jurisdiction only in cases involving disputes between two or more states over territorial or natural resource issues. For example, New Jersey and New York disagreed over which state should control about 24 acres of filled land that the federal government had added around Ellis Island and Kansas and Colorado disagreed over which state should have access to water from the Arkansas River (recent disputes often concern water rights).[26] In the history of our nation, only about 175 cases have made it to the Court through this path, and typically these cases do not have any broader significance beyond the interest of the parties involved.[27]

The other three routes to the Court are all on appeal: as a matter of right (usually called on appeal), through certification, or through a **writ of *certiorari*** (from the Latin "to be informed"). Cases on appeal are those that Congress has determined to be so important that the Supreme Court must hear them. Lately, Congress has given the Court much more discretion on these cases; the only ones that the Court is still compelled to take on appeal are some voting rights and redistricting cases.

writ of *certiorari*
The most common way for a case to reach the Supreme Court, in which at least four of the nine justices agree to hear a case that has reached them via an appeal from the losing party in a lower court's ruling.

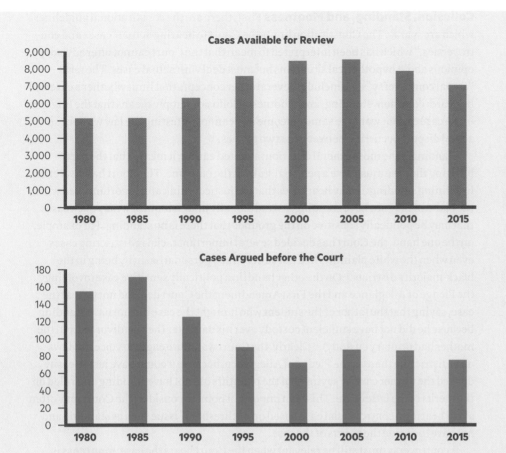

FIGURE 13.3

The Court Sees More Opportunities ... but Hears Fewer Cases

The Supreme Court's workload appears to be headed in two directions: the Court is receiving more cases but hearing fewer of them. What are the implications of having the Supreme Court hear fewer cases? Should something be done to try to get the Court to hear more cases?

Source: Data compiled from "Chief Justice's Year-End Reports on the Federal Judiciary," www.supremecourt.gov (accessed 5/24/16).

A writ of certification occurs when an appeals court asks the Court to clarify a new point of federal law in a specific case. The Court can agree to hear the case, but given that appeals court judges and state supreme court judges are the only people who can make these requests, this path to the Court is very rare. (In fact, since 1982 the Court has not taken up a certified question from one of the appeals courts and has certified only five cases from state supreme courts.)[28]

The third path is the most common: at least 95 percent of the cases in most sessions arrive through a writ of *certiorari*. In these cases, a litigant who lost in lower court can file a petition to the Supreme Court explaining why it should hear the case. If four justices agree, the case will get a full hearing (this is called the Rule of Four). This process may sound simple, but sifting through the 7,500 or so cases that the Court receives every year and deciding which 75 of them will be heard is daunting. In fact, former justice William O. Douglas said that this winnowing process is "in many respects the most important and interesting of all our functions."[29]

The Court's criteria

How does the Court decide which cases to hear? Several factors come into play, including the specific characteristics of the case and the broader politics surrounding it. Although several criteria generally must be met before the Court will hear the case, justices still have leeway in defining the boundaries of these conditions.

Collusion, Standing, and Mootness First, there are the constitutional guidelines, which are sparse. The Constitution limits the Court to hearing actual "cases and controversies," which has been interpreted to mean that the Court cannot offer advisory opinions about hypothetical situations but must deal with actual cases. The term "actual controversy" also includes several other concepts that limit whether a case will be heard: collusion, standing, and mootness. Collusion simply means that the litigants in the case cannot want the same outcome and cannot be testing the law without an actual dispute occurring between the two parties.[30]

Standing is the most general criterion; as noted earlier, it means that the party bringing the case must have a personal stake in the outcome. The Court has discretion in defining standing: it may hear cases that the justices think are important even when the plaintiff may not have standing, as traditionally understood, or it may duck cases that may be politically sensitive on the grounds that there is no standing. For example, on the one hand, the Court has decided several important racial redistricting cases even when the white plaintiffs had not suffered any personal harm by being in the black-majority districts.[31] On the other hand, in a politically sensitive case involving the Pledge of Allegiance and the First Amendment the Court decided not to hear the case, saying that the father of the student who brought the case did not have standing because he did not have sufficient custody over his daughter (he was divorced and the mother had primary custody).[32] Clearly, the Court was more eager to voice its views on redistricting than on the Pledge of Allegiance, because it could have just as easily ducked the former case by saying that the plaintiffs did not have standing and ruled on the merits of the latter case. This is an important point to consider: the Court may often avoid hearing a controversial case based on a "threshold" issue such as standing and not have to decide the merits of the case.

A controversy must still be relevant when the Court hears the case; **mootness** is when a case is irrelevant by the time it is brought before a federal court. Nonetheless, there have to be exceptions to this principle because some types of cases would always be moot by the time they reach the Supreme Court. For example, exceptions have been made for abortion cases because a pregnancy lasts only nine months and the time that it takes to get a case from district court to the appeals court to the Supreme Court always takes longer than that. Thousands of cases every year meet the basic criteria. One very simple guideline eliminates the largest number of cases: if a case does not involve a "substantial federal question," it will not be heard. This essentially means that the Court does not have to hear a case if the justices do not think the case is important enough. Of course, the "federal" part of this standard is also important: if a case is governed by state law rather than by federal law, the Court would decline to hear the case unless there are constitutional implications.

Internal Politics Since the late 1970s, most justices have used a **cert pool**, whereby their law clerks take a first cut at the cases. (Law clerks to the justices are top graduates of elite law schools who help the justices with background research at several stages of the process.) Clerks write joint memos about groups of cases, providing their recommendations about which cases should be heard. The ultimate decisions are up to the justices, but clerks have significant power to help shape the agenda.

The chief justice has an important agenda-setting power: he or she decides the "discuss list" for a given day. Any justice can add a case to the list, but there is no systematic evidence on how often this happens. Only 20 to 30 percent of the cases are discussed in conference, which means that about three-quarters of the cases that are submitted to the Supreme Court are never even discussed by the Court. In most cases, this is justified because of the high proportion of frivolous suits submitted to the Court.[33]

mootness
The irrelevance of a case by the time it is received by a federal court, causing the Court to decline to hear the case.

cert pool
A system initiated in the Supreme Court in the 1970s in which law clerks screen cases that come to the Supreme Court and recommend to the justices which cases should be heard.

Many factors outside the legal requirements or internal processes of the Court influence access to the Court and which cases will be heard. Cases that have generated a lot of activity from interest groups or other governmental parties, such as the solicitor general, are more likely to be heard. The **solicitor general** is a presidential appointee who works in the Justice Department and supervises the litigation of the executive branch. In cases in which the federal government is a party, the solicitor general or someone else from that office will represent the government in court. The Court accepts about 70 to 80 percent of cases in which the U.S. government is a party, compared to about 1 percent overall.[34]

Even with these influences, the Court has a great deal of discretion on which cases it hears. Well-established practices such as standing and mootness may be ignored (or modified) if the Court wants to hear a specific case. However, one final point is important: although the justices may pick and choose their cases, they cannot set their own agenda. They can select only from the cases that come to them.

Hearing cases before the Supreme Court

A surprisingly small proportion of the Court's time is actually spent hearing cases—only about 37 days per term. The Court is in session from the first Monday in October through the end of June. It hears cases on Mondays through Wednesdays in alternating two-week cycles in which it is in session from 10 A.M. to 3 P.M. with a one-hour break for lunch. In the other two weeks of the cycle when it is not in session, justices review briefs, write opinions, and sift through the next batch of petitions. On most Fridays when the Court is in session, the justices meet in conference to discuss cases that have been argued and decide which cases they will hear. Opinions are released throughout the term, but the bulk of them come in May and June.[35]

The Court is in recess from July through September. The justices may take some vacation, but they mostly use the time for studying, reading, writing, and preparing for the next term. During the summer, the Court also considers emergency petitions (such as stays of execution) and occasionally hears exceptionally important cases—as it did in 2009, for example, when the Court heard a challenge to the Bipartisan Campaign Reform Act, more commonly known as the McCain–Feingold Act after its two principal sponsors. Congress urged the Court to give the law a speedy review given its importance for the upcoming 2010 elections. In the blockbuster case *Citizens United v. Federal Election Commission*, the Supreme Court decided that independent spending in campaigns by corporations and labor unions is protected by the First Amendment.

Briefs

During the regular sessions, the Court follows rigidly set routines. The justices prepare for a case by reading the briefs that both parties submit. Because the Supreme Court hears only appeals, it does not call witnesses or gather new evidence. Instead, in structured briefs of no more than 50 pages the parties present their arguments about why they either support the lower-court decision or believe the case was improperly decided. Interest groups often submit **amicus curiae** ("friend of the court") briefs that

solicitor general
A presidential appointee in the Justice Department who conducts all litigation on behalf of the federal government before the Supreme Court and supervises litigation in the federal appellate courts.

★
DESCRIBE THE SUPREME COURT'S PROCEDURES FOR HEARING A CASE

amicus curiae
Latin for "friend of the court," referring to an interested group or person who shares relevant information about a case to help the Court reach a decision.

convey their opinions to the Court; in fact, 85 percent of cases before the Supreme Court have at least one amicus brief.[36] The federal government also files amicus briefs on important issues such as school busing, school prayer, abortion, reapportionment of legislative districts, job discrimination against women and minorities, and affirmative action in higher education.

It is difficult to determine the impact of amicus briefs on the outcome of a case, but those that are filed early in the process increase the chances that the case will be heard.[37] Given the limited information that the justices have about any given case, interest group involvement can be a strong signal about the importance of a case.

Oral argument

oral arguments
Spoken presentations made in person by the lawyers of each party to a judge or an appellate court outlining the legal reasons their side should prevail.

Once the briefs are filed and have been reviewed by the justices, cases are scheduled for **oral arguments**. Except in unusual circumstances, each case gets one hour, which is divided evenly between the two parties. In especially important cases, extra time may be granted (for example, the Obamacare case had six hours of oral argument, which was the most since a VRA case in 1966). Usually there is only one lawyer for each side who presents the case, but parties that have filed amicus briefs may participate if their arguments "would provide assistance to the Court not otherwise available." Given the tight time pressures, the Court generally does not extend the allotted time to allow "friends of the court" to testify.

Some lawyers may not use all of their time because their train of thought is interrupted by aggressive questioning. Transcripts reveal that justices jump in with questions almost immediately and some attorneys never regain their footing. The frequency and pointedness of the questions vary by justice, with Justices Breyer, Roberts, and Sotomayor being the most aggressive on the current Court, while Justice Clarence Thomas went more than 10 years without asking a single question. Justice Thomas broke his streak in 2016, perhaps feeling the need to fill the void created by the death

Cameras are not allowed in the Supreme Court, so artists' sketches are the only images of oral arguments. Depicted here is the oral argument in the 2016 case concerning the affirmative action policy at the University of Texas, Austin.

of Justice Scalia.[38] Cameras are not allowed in the courtroom, so most Americans have never seen the Court in action—although a small live audience is admitted every morning the Court is in session. If you are curious about oral arguments, audio recordings of every case since 1995 are available at www.oyez.org.

Conference

After oral arguments, the justices meet in conference to discuss and then vote on the cases. As with the initial conferences, these meetings are conducted in secret. We know, based on notes in the personal papers of retired justices, that the conferences are orderly and structured but can become quite heated. The justices take turns discussing the cases and outlining the reasons for their positions. This is the kind of internal debate that the justices have argued should remain confidential. They have expressed concern that premature disclosure of their private debates and doubts may undermine the Court's credibility and inhibit their exchange of ideas.

Opinion writing

After the justices indicate how they are likely to vote on a case, if the chief justice is in the majority (which is most of the time) the chief justice decides who will write the majority opinion. Otherwise, the most senior justice in the majority assigns the opinion. Many considerations determine how a case will be assigned. First, the chief justice will try to ensure the smooth operation of the Court, including considerations such as which justices may be able to take on the work of writing a given opinion. A second factor is the justices' individual areas of expertise. For example, Justice Sandra Day O'Connor developed expertise in racial redistricting cases and authored most of those decisions in the 1990s.

Strategy on the Court Another factor in how opinions are assigned is more strategic: it includes the Court's external relations, internal relations, and the personal policy goals of the opinion assigner. The Court must be sensitive to how others might respond to its decisions because it must rely on the other branches of government to enforce its decisions. One famous example of this consideration in an opinion assignment came in a case from the 1940s that struck down a practice that had prevented African Americans from voting in Democratic primaries.[39] Originally, the opinion was assigned to Justice Felix Frankfurter, but Justice Robert Jackson wrote a memo suggesting that it might be unwise to have a liberal, politically independent Jew from the Northeast write an opinion that was sure to be controversial in the South. Chief Justice Harlan Fiske Stone agreed and reassigned the opinion to Justice Stanley Reed, a Protestant and Democrat from Kentucky.[40] It may not seem that the Court is sensitive to public opinion, but these kinds of considerations happen fairly frequently in important cases. Internal considerations occasionally cause a justice to vote strategically—that is, differently from his or her sincere preference—in order to be in the majority so that the justice can assign the opinion (often to himself or herself) as the most senior justice in the majority.

After the opinions are assigned, the justices work on writing a draft opinion. Law clerks typically help with this process. The drafts are circulated to the other justices for comment and reactions. Some bargaining may occur, in which a justice says he or

DID YOU KNOW?

The late Justice Scalia was the funniest justice. According to one study, he prompted

77

rounds of laughter in the term, which made him 19 times funnier than his friend Justice Ginsburg.
Source: thedailybeast.com

If he or she is in the majority, the chief justice decides who will write the majority opinion. Otherwise, the most senior justice in the majority makes the assignment. Since being named chief justice in 2005, John Roberts has spread opinion-writing duties fairly evenly among the justices.

Types of Supreme Court Decisions

- **Majority opinion:** The core decision of the Court that must be agreed upon by at least five justices. The majority opinion presents the legal reasoning for the Court's decision.

- **Concurring opinion:** Written by a justice who agrees with the outcome of the case but not with part of the legal reasoning. Concurring opinions may be joined by other justices. A justice may sign on to the majority opinion and write a separate concurring opinion.

- **Plurality opinion:** Occurs when a majority cannot agree on the legal reasoning in a case. The plurality opinion is the one that has the most agreement (usually three or four justices). Because of the fractured nature of these opinions, they typically are not viewed as having as much clout as majority opinions.

- **Dissent:** Submitted by a justice who disagrees with the outcome of the case. Other justices can sign on to a dissent or write their own, so there can be as many as four dissents. Justices can also sign on to part of a dissent but not the entire opinion.

- **Per curiam (Latin for "by the court") opinion:** An unsigned opinion of the Court or a decision written by the entire Court. However, this is not the same as a unanimous decision that is signed by the entire Court. Per curiam opinions are usually very short opinions on noncontroversial issues, but not always. For example, *Bush v. Gore*, which decided the outcome of the 2000 presidential election, was a per curiam opinion. Per curiam decisions may also have dissents.

> **So that's the dissenter's hope: that they are writing not for today but for tomorrow.**
>
> —Justice Ruth Bader Ginsburg

she will withdraw support unless a provision is changed. Justices may join the majority opinion, may write a separate concurring opinion, or may dissent (see Nuts & Bolts 13.2 for details on the types of opinions).

Dissents Two final points about the process of writing and issuing opinions are important. First, until the 1940s a premium was placed on unanimous decisions. This changed dramatically in the 1940s, when most cases had at least one dissent.[41] Lately, about two-thirds of cases have had a dissent. However, in the 2013–2014 term two-thirds of the cases were unanimous, the highest proportion since at least 1946. That proportion fell to 46 percent in the 2015–2016 term.[42] Second, dissents serve an important purpose: not only do they allow the minority view to be expressed, but they also often provide the basis for subsequently reversing a poorly reasoned case. Moreover, when justices strongly oppose the majority decision they may take the unusual step of reading a portion of their dissent from the bench.

"Why Should I Care?"

The process of hearing cases before the Court, including the written briefs, oral arguments, discussions in conference, and opinion assignment, is a very political one. As discussed in the chapter opener, it may be disturbing to think of the Court as a political institution that bargains and considers external forces like public opinion. Despite not having to answer to voters, justices are still sensitive to a broad range of considerations in hearing cases.

Supreme Court decision making

Judicial decision making is influenced by many different factors, but the two main categories are *legal* and *political*. Legal factors include the precedents of earlier cases and norms that justices must follow the language of the Constitution. Political influences include the justices' preferences or ideologies, their stances on whether the Court should take a restrained or activist role with respect to the elected branches, and external factors such as public opinion and interest group involvement.

Legal factors

The most basic legal factor is precedent, which we discussed earlier. Precedent does not determine the outcome of any given case, because every case has a range of precedent that can serve to justify a justice's decision. The "easy" cases, in which settled law makes the outcome obvious, are less likely to be heard by the Court because of the justices' desire to focus on the more controversial areas of unsettled law or when there is conflict between lower courts' decisions. However, in some areas of the law—such as free speech, the death penalty, and search and seizure—precedent is an important explanation for how the justices decide a case.

The various perspectives that emphasize the language of the Constitution all fall under the heading of **strict construction**. The most basic of these is the literalist view of the Constitution. Literalists argue that justices need to look no further than the actual words of the Constitution. However, critics of strict construction point out that the Constitution is silent on many important points (such as a right to privacy) and could not have anticipated the changes in technology in the twentieth and twenty-first centuries that have many legal implications, such as eavesdropping devices, cloning, and the Internet. Also, although the language of the First Amendment is relatively clear when it comes to political speech, other equally important words of the Constitution such as "necessary and proper," "executive power," "equal protection," and "due process" are open-ended and vague.

Critics of the strict constructionist view are often described as supporting a **living Constitution** perspective on the document (see Chapter 2). They argue that strict construction can "make a nation the prisoner of its past, and reject any constitutional development save constitutional amendment."[43] If the justices are bound to follow the literal words of the Constitution, *with the meaning they had when the document was written*, we certainly could be legally frozen in time. Amending the Constitution is a long and difficult process, so that option is not always a viable way for the Constitution to reflect changing norms and values.

Political factors

The living Constitution perspective points to the second set of influences on Supreme Court decision making: political factors. Indeed, many people are uncomfortable thinking about the Court in political terms and prefer to think of the image of "blind justice," in which constitutional principles are fairly applied. However, political influences are clearly evident in the Court—maybe less than in Congress or the presidency,

strict construction
A way of interpreting the Constitution based on its language alone.

living Constitution
A way of interpreting the Constitution that takes into account evolving national attitudes and circumstances rather than the text alone.

99

**The words of the Constitution ... are so unrestricted by their intrinsic meaning or by their history or by tradition or by prior decisions that they leave the individual Justice free, if indeed they do not compel him, to gather meaning not from reading the Constitution but from reading life.
—Justice Felix Frankfurter**

but they are certainly present. This means that the courts respond to and shape politics in ways that often involve compromise, both within the courts themselves and in the broader political system.

Political Ideology and Attitudes The most important political factor is the justices' ideology or attitudes about various issues. Liberal judges are strong defenders of individual civil liberties (including defendants' rights), tend to be pro-choice on abortion, support regulatory policy to protect the environment and workers, support national intervention in the states, and favor race-conscious policies such as affirmative action. Conservative judges favor state regulation of private conduct (especially on moral issues), support prosecutors over defendants, tend to be pro-life on abortion, and support the free market and property rights over the environment and workers, states' rights over national intervention, and a color-blind policy on race. These are, of course, just general tendencies. However, they do provide a strong basis for explaining patterns of decisions, especially on some types of cases.

In a survey taken about the judicial branch, most respondents were unable to name any Supreme Court justices. Just so you are not in danger of falling into that category, as of the fall of 2016 the justices were (front row, left to right) Clarence Thomas, a blank space representing the justice who will replace Antonin Scalia, John G. Roberts Jr. (chief justice), Anthony M. Kennedy, Ruth Bader Ginsburg, (standing, left to right) Sonia Sotomayor, Stephen Breyer, Samuel Alito Jr., and Elena Kagan.

The Strategic Model A strategic approach to understanding Supreme Court decision making focuses on justices' calculations about the preferences of the other justices, the president, and Congress, the choices that other justices are likely to make, and the institutional context within which they operate. After all, justices do not operate alone: at a minimum, they need the votes of four of their colleagues if they want their position to prevail. Therefore, it makes sense to focus on the strategic interactions that take place to build coalitions.

The median voter on the Court—the one in the middle when the justices are arrayed from the most liberal to the most conservative—has an especially influential role in the strategic model. For many years, the median justice was Sandra Day O'Connor; when Samuel Alito replaced her, Anthony M. Kennedy became the new median justice. The four conservatives to his right and the four liberals to his left all wanted to attract his vote. When Justice Sotomayor replaced Justice David Souter and when Justice Kagan replaced Justice John Paul Stevens, Kennedy remained the median voter on the Court. Research shows that at least one justice switches his or her vote at some stage in the

The Shifting Ideological Balance of the Court

After Justice Antonin Scalia died in early 2016, the open seat on the Supreme Court became a major issue in the presidential election. Why? As this figure shows, when justices are replaced the ideological shifts can be quite large (as when Clarence Thomas replaced Thurgood Marshall) or nonexistent (as when Sonia Sotomayor replaced David Souter). Many people said that replacing Scalia would drastically alter the ideological makeup of the Court, given the 4–4 split on the Court between liberal and conservative justices. What do the numbers say?

WHAT DO THE NUMBERS SAY?

Arrows represent a shift in ideology when a vacancy is filled on the Court, either to a more conservative or more liberal justice.

Each dot represents the ideology of the incoming and outgoing justice.

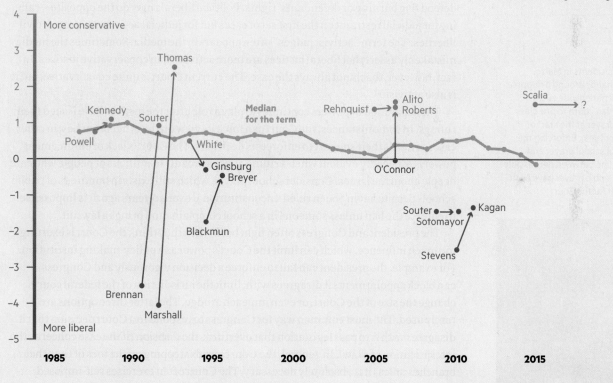

Think about it

- Look at where Scalia is on the ideological scale. If Hillary Clinton had been elected, where would Scalia's dot have likely moved?
- President Trump is expected to nominate a conservative, similar to Scalia. What will happen to the median justice in that case?
- Will the ideological shift of the Court's median be large, small, or stay the same? Why?

Source: The Upshot, "A Supreme Court with Merrick Garland Would Be the Most Liberal in Decades," www.nytimes.com (accessed 8/26/16).

process (from the initial conference to oral arguments to the final vote) on at least half of the cases, so strategic bargaining appears to be fairly common.[44] Our earlier discussion of opinion assignment and writing opinions to attract the support of a specific justice is more evidence in support of the strategic model.

Separation of Powers Another political influence on justices' decision making is their view of the place of the Court with respect to the democratically elected institutions (Congress and the president). Specifically, do they favor an activist or a restrained role for the Court? Advocates of **judicial restraint** argue that judges should defer to the elected branches and not strike down their laws or other actions. In contrast, advocates of **judicial activism** argue that the Court must play an active role in interpreting the Constitution to protect minority rights even if this means overturning the actions of the elected branches. Yet another approach says that these normative arguments about how restraint or activism ought to work don't really matter because the Court usually follows public opinion and rarely plays a lead role in promoting policy change.

Judicial Activism Often assessments of the Court's role vary with the views of a specific line of cases. A political conservative may favor "activist" decisions striking down environmental laws or workplace regulations but oppose activist decisions that defend flag burning or defendants' rights. Political liberals may do the opposite—calling for judicial restraint on the first set of cases but for judicial activism to protect civil liberties. The term "activist judges" often appears in the media. Sometimes the media mistakenly assert that liberal justices are more activist than conservative justices. In fact, however, that is not always the case. The current Court is quite conservative, but it is also activist.[45]

The separation of powers continues to play a role after the justices have issued their rulings. In some instances, the Court can force its view on the other branches; in other cases, it needs their support to enforce its decisions. The Court's lack of enforcement power is especially evident when a ruling applies broadly to millions of people who care deeply about the issues. Consider school prayer, which still exists in hundreds of public schools despite having been ruled unconstitutional over 40 years ago. It is impossible to enforce the ban unless someone in a school complains and brings a lawsuit.

The president and Congress often fight back when they think the Court is exerting too much influence, which can limit the Court's power as a policy-making institution. For example, the president can fail to enforce a decision vigorously and Congress can block appointments it disagrees with, limit the jurisdiction of the federal courts, change the size of the Court, or even impeach a judge. The latter three options are rarely used. The most common way for Congress to respond to a Court decision that it disagrees with is to pass legislation that overturns the decision (if the case concerns the interpretation of a law). In general, the Court avoids stepping on the toes of the other branches unless it is absolutely necessary. The Court often exercises self-imposed restraint and refuses to act on "political questions"—issues that are outside the judicial domain and should be decided by elected officials.

Outside Influences: Interest Groups and Public Opinion Finally, there are external influences on the Court, such as public opinion and interest groups. We have already talked about the role of interest groups in filing amicus briefs. When it comes to the Court, this is the only avenue of influence open to interest groups; other tactics such as lobbying and fund-raising are either inappropriate or irrelevant (because justices are not elected). The role of public opinion is more complex. Obviously, justices do not consult public-opinion polls the way elected officials do. However, there are several indirect ways that the Court expresses the public's preferences.

judicial restraint
The idea that the Supreme Court should defer to the democratically elected executive and legislative branches of government rather than contradicting existing laws.

judicial activism
The idea that the Supreme Court should assert its interpretation of the law even if it overrules the elected executive and legislative branches of government.

High school students in Maize, Kansas, join hands around a flagpole at the annual nationwide event calling Christian youth to pre-class schoolyard prayer at the start of the new school year. Enforcing the prohibition of school prayer and drawing the line between permissible and impermissible prayer have both been difficult for the Court.

The first indirect way involves the fact that the public elects the president and the Senate, who nominate and confirm the justices. Therefore, sooner or later the Court should reflect the views of the public. Work by political scientists has confirmed this to be largely the case,[46] especially in recent years when Supreme Court nominations have become more political and more important to the public.[47]

The second mechanism through which public opinion may influence the Court is somewhat more direct: when the public has a clear position on an issue that is before the Court, the Court tends to agree with the public.[48] Several high-profile examples support the idea that the Court is sensitive to public opinion: the Court's switch during the New Deal in the 1930s to support Roosevelt's policy agenda after standing in the way for four years, giving in to wartime opinion to support the internment of Japanese Americans during World War II, limiting an accused child molester's right to confront his or her accuser in a courtroom, and declaring that laws limiting sex between consenting gay adults were unconstitutional. In each of these cases, the justices reflected the current public opinion of the nation rather than a strict reading of the Constitution or the Founders' intent.

Another way that the Court may consider the public mood is to shift the timing of a decision. The best example here is the landmark school desegregation case *Brown v. Board of Education* (1954), which the Court sat on for more than two years—until after the 1952 presidential election—because it didn't think the public was ready for its bombshell ruling.[49] Others have argued that the Court rarely *changes* its views to reflect public opinion, but at a minimum the evidence supports the notion that the Court is usually in step with the public.

> The Supreme Court, of course, has the responsibility of ensuring that our government never oversteps its proper bounds or violates the rights of individuals. But the Court must also recognize the limits on itself and respect the choices made by the American people.
>
> —Justice Elena Kagan

"Why Should I Care?"

Shouldn't the Court be neutrally applying the words of the Constitution to the cases it hears? While a normatively appealing view, this textualist view ignores many of the realities of how the Court actually operates. Justices often let their own political views shape their decisions, but more neutral forces such as precedent and deferring to the elected branches also play important roles. Having a realistic understanding of the various factors that go into a justice's decision explains why the Court strikes down some laws and upholds others.

Conclusion

The judicial branch as a whole contains a paradox: it may simultaneously be seen as the least democratic and the most democratic branch of government.[50] The least democratic aspect is obvious: federal judges and many state and local judges are unelected and are not accountable to voters (except indirectly through the leaders who appoint them). But the courts can also be seen as the most democratic branch. Cases that are brought to the courts come from the people, and as long as the legal criteria for bringing a case are met the courts must hear those cases. Although only a small fraction of the cases brought to the Supreme Court are heard, the court system as a whole may be seen as providing an important outlet for participation in our political system.

The courts also demonstrate that politics is conflictual. And many conflicts demonstrate that the courts are political. Although plenty of unanimous Supreme Court

The Court has been an important protector of minority rights, including in the civil rights era. This picture from 1953 shows people waiting in line at the Supreme Court to hear oral arguments in *Brown v. Board of Education*. But at other times, the Court has supported the will of the majority.

decisions do not involve much conflict among the justices, many landmark cases deeply divide the Court on constitutional interpretation and how to balance those competing interpretations against other values and interests. These conflicts in the Court often reveal deeper fault lines in the broader political system.

It shouldn't be surprising that political process matters in the courts. The rules of courtroom procedures, including how evidence is gathered and presented, can have an important impact on outcomes. If lawyers do not follow these procedural rules, a case that otherwise could have been won might be thrown out by a judge. Political process is also important for selecting judges and determining which cases the Supreme Court hears.

Politics is indeed everywhere, even in the courts, where you would least expect to see it. Politics affects everything from the selection of judges to the decisions they make. Some characteristics of the federal courts (most important of which is judges' lifetime tenure) insulate the system from politics. However, courts are subject to influence by judges' ideologies, interest groups, and the president and Senate, who try to shape the courts' composition through the nomination process.

The chapter-opening example demonstrates the important role that the courts play in the political system. Recall that the Supreme Court deferred to the elected branches of Texas in upholding their affirmative action policy for college admissions. But that same week, the Court struck down President Obama's deportation deferral program, throwing 4.3 million immigrants into legal limbo. Thus, the federal courts can serve as a referee between the other branches of government, and between the national and state governments, by defining the boundaries of permissible conduct.

STUDY GUIDE

The development of an independent and powerful federal judiciary

Explain how the power of judicial review was established. (Pages 373–376)

Summary

In contrast to other branches of government, the Constitution offers few specifics on the organization of the judiciary. In fact, most of the details on the arrangement of the judiciary do not come from the Constitution at all, but from congressional action. In addition, the Supreme Court's strongest power—judicial review—is not even mentioned in the Constitution but was established in the *Marbury v. Madison* decision.

Key terms

Judiciary Act of 1789 (p. 374)   **original jurisdiction** (p. 375)
district courts (p. 374)   **constitutional interpretation** (p. 376)
appellate jurisdiction (p. 374)
judicial review (p. 374)   **statutory interpretation** (p. 376)

Practice Quiz Questions

1. **Most of the details about the Supreme Court were established in ____.**
   a. the Judiciary Act of 1789
   b. Article I of the Constitution
   c. Article II of the Constitution
   d. the *Federalist Papers*
   e. *Marbury v. Madison*

2. **_Marbury v. Madison_ is significant because it ____.**
   a. established the Supreme Court
   b. introduced the process of selective incorporation
   c. changed the manner of judicial selection
   d. established judicial review
   e. gave Supreme Court justices lifetime appointments

3. **Judicial review enables the Supreme Court to ____.**
   a. submit legislation to Congress
   b. strike down laws passed by Congress
   c. revise laws passed by Congress
   d. oversee presidential appointments to the bureaucracy
   e. approve judicial appointments to lower courts

The American legal and judicial system

Outline the structure of the court system. (Pages 376–385)

Summary

All courts within the United States have a similar set of fundamental attributes, such as the distinction between civil and criminal cases and the reliance on legal precedent. The judicial system is divided between state and federal courts, and within each level of government there are courts of original jurisdiction and appeals courts.

Key terms

plaintiff (p. 376)   **precedent** (p. 377)
defendant (p. 376)   **standing** (p. 377)
plea bargain (p. 376)   **jurisdiction** (p. 377)
class-action lawsuit (p. 377)   **appeals courts** (p. 378)
common law (p. 377)   **senatorial courtesy** (p. 383)

Practice Quiz Questions

4. **A system of ____ relies on legal decisions that are built from precedent established in previous cases.**
   a. common law
   b. civil law
   c. statutory law
   d. stare decisis
   e. plea bargaining

5. **When one has suffered direct and personal harm from the action addressed in a case, it is called ____.**
   a. precedent
   b. appellant
   c. plea bargaining
   d. jurisdiction
   e. standing

6. **The president appoints federal judges with the "advice and consent" of the ____.**
   a. House of Representatives
   b. Senate
   c. Supreme Court
   d. attorney general
   e. vice president

Access to the Supreme Court

Describe how cases reach the Supreme Court.
(Pages 386–389)

Summary

The Supreme Court hears only about 1 percent of the cases that are brought to it. To help decide which cases to hear, the Court generally uses three factors: collusion, standing, and mootness. Ultimately, the justices have a great deal of discretion in deciding to hear a case, but they can only hear cases that come to them.

Key terms

writ of *certiorari* (p. 386)   cert pool (p. 388)

mootness (p. 388)   solicitor general (p. 389)

Practice Quiz Questions

7. **When a litigant who lost in a lower court files a petition, the case reaches the Supreme Court _____.**

    a. as a matter of right

    b. through a writ of certification

    c. through a writ of *certiorari*

    d. as a matter of original jurisdiction

    e. through senatorial courtesy

8. **_____ means that the controversy is not relevant when the Court hears the case.**

    a. Mootness

    b. Amicus

    c. Collusion

    d. Standing

    e. Precedent

9. **Most justices _____ in initially deciding which cases should be heard.**

    a. personally review all cases

    b. personally review a random sample of cases

    c. follow the recommendations of the chief justice

    d. use a random selection process

    e. use a cert pool

Hearing cases before the Supreme Court

Describe the Supreme Court's procedures for hearing a case. (Pages 389–392)

Summary

When hearing a case, the justices prepare by reading briefs before they hear the oral arguments. After oral arguments, the justices meet in conference to discuss and vote on the cases. The majority opinion explains the rationale for how a decision is reached, although justices can also write dissenting and concurring opinions if they agree with the outcome of the case but not the legal reasoning.

Key terms

amicus curiae (p. 389)   oral arguments (p. 390)

Practice Quiz Questions

10. **The most important impact of a case having a large number of amicus curiae briefs is _____.**

    a. the decision is more likely to be unanimous

    b. the case is more likely to be heard

    c. the decision is more likely to go against the government

    d. the case is less likely to be heard

    e. the decision is more likely to have a liberal outcome

11. **Oral arguments generally last _____, and justices _____ wait until the end of the arguments to ask questions.**

    a. one hour; will

    b. one hour; do not

    c. one day; will

    d. one week; will

    e. one week; do not

12. **Generally, the chief justice or the _____ justice decides who writes the majority opinion; justices' individual areas of expertise _____ a factor in making this assignment.**

    a. most junior; are not

    b. most junior; are

    c. most senior; are not

    d. most senior; are

    e. dissenting; does not

Supreme Court decision making

Analyze the factors that influence Supreme Court decisions. (Pages 393–397)

Summary

The Court makes decisions based on legal factors such as legal precedent and informal legal norms, and political factors, such as the justices' own ideologies and positions on the role that the Court plays in government. Although the Court does not consider public opinion the way elected officials do, most decisions generally stay in step with the views of the public.

Practice Quiz Questions

13. Advocates of _____ argue that the Court must defer to the elected branches and not strike down their laws.

- **a.** judicial restraint
- **b.** judicial activism
- **c.** judicial limitation
- **d.** legal maximization
- **e.** the strategic model

14. In general, the Court _____ challenges with the elected branches and often _____ to act on "political questions."

- **a.** avoids; agrees
- **b.** avoids; refuses
- **c.** pursues; agrees
- **d.** pursues; refuses

Suggested Reading

Baum, Lawrence. *Judges and Their Audiences: A Perspective on Judicial Behavior.* Princeton, NJ: Princeton University Press, 2006.

Black, Ryan C., and Ryan J. Owens, *The Solicitor General and the United States Supreme Court: Executive Influence and Judicial Decisions.* New York: Cambridge University Press, 2012.

Cornell University Law School, Supreme Court Collection, www.law.cornell.edu/supremecourt/text/home.

Eisgruber, Christopher L. *Constitutional Self-Government.* Cambridge, MA: Harvard University Press, 2001.

Hansford, Thomas G., and James F. Spriggs II. *The Politics of Precedent on the U.S. Supreme Court.* Princeton, NJ: Princeton University Press, 2006.

Northwestern University, Oyez: Supreme Court Multimedia, www.oyez.org.

O'Brien, David M. *Storm Center: The Supreme Court in American Politics,* 9th ed. New York: W. W. Norton, 2011.

Rosen, Jeffrey. *The Most Democratic Branch: How the Courts Serve America.* New York: Oxford University Press, 2006.

Sunstein, Cass R., David Schkade, Lisa M. Ellman, and Andres Sawicki. *Are Judges Political? An Empirical Analysis of the Federal Judiciary.* Washington, DC: Brookings Institution Press, 2006.

Tushnet, Mark. *A Court Divided: The Rehnquist Court and the Future of Constitutional Law.* New York: W. W. Norton, 2006.

U.S. Supreme Court website, www.supremecourt.gov.

14

Economic and Social Policy

What should the government do to promote a strong economy and provide a social safety net?

The 2016 presidential campaign was the most conflictual in recent memory. While the range of disagreements between Hillary Clinton and Donald Trump was vast, many of their differences centered on economic policy and the core question of this chapter: What should the government do to promote a strong economy and provide a social safety net? Clinton's plan for economic growth and creating jobs was based on a more active role for the government and higher taxes on the wealthy, while Trump called for lower taxes and less government regulation.

One area of fundamental disagreement between the candidates concerned the proper level of taxation. Tax policies are inherently conflictual, due to their redistributive nature: when the government takes money from one group and gives it to another, there will be conflict over those decisions. For example, if tax policy is used to help the poor, the wealthy will necessarily pay a larger percentage of their income in taxes than the poor. But even taxes that do not seem obviously redistributive hit some people harder than others. A 5 percent sales tax is more of a burden for the poor than for the nonpoor because poorer people spend a higher proportion of their income. The home mortgage interest deduction on income tax benefits homeowners over renters. The 15 percent tax rate on dividends favors people who invest in stocks over bonds (because interest on bonds is taxed as regular income, usually at a much higher rate than 15 percent). In short, tax policies aimed at helping one segment of the economy come at the expense of another part, which creates political conflict.

The tax with the greatest redistributive potential is the estate tax—taxes paid by heirs on the net worth of people who have died (opponents call it a

★ CHAPTER GOALS

Trace the steps through which problems are addressed by government policies.
pages 405–413

Explain the main purposes of government involvement in the economy and how fiscal, monetary, and regulatory policies influence the economy.
pages 414–428

Explain what we mean by social policy, discuss how the national government's role in social policy has evolved, and analyze the current major areas of social policy.
pages 428–440

📷

Economic policies have generated intense conflict in recent years. Both candidates in the 2016 presidential race claimed that they had a better plan than their opponent to help spur economic growth and job creation. Here, Hillary Clinton greets an assembly worker at a furniture factory during a campaign stop designed to draw awareness to her positions on trade policy and the economy.

Supporters of a $15-an-hour minimum wage push for a change in the law in California. The state became the first to adopt the $15 wage; it will be fully implemented by 2022. #FightFor15

"death tax"). Currently, the estate tax is applied to only the wealthiest households (estates with a net worth of at least $5.45 million for an individual and $10.9 million for a couple). That said, 99.8 percent of households do not pay any estate tax. Clinton proposed both changing the requirements so more people pay the tax and increasing the tax rate from 40 percent to 45 percent. Trump wanted to eliminate the tax entirely.[1] The Clinton proposal on estate taxes would raise $161 billion in revenue over ten years, while Trump's plan would cost $275 billion. Analysts also pointed out that eliminating the estate tax would amount to $4 to 7 billion in tax savings for Trump's heirs. Trump's personal taxes became a prominent issue in the presidential campaign when the *New York Times* revealed that he reported a $916 million tax loss in 1995, which means he may not have paid federal income tax for 18 years. Trump admitted this in the second presidential debate; when asked if he used the loss to avoid paying taxes he said, "Of course I do."[2]

Clinton and Trump also differed greatly in their proposals for individual and corporate taxes. Trump proposed to cut the top personal tax rate somewhat and cut the corporate rate by more than half. The conservative-leaning Tax Foundation estimated that the plan would reduce federal tax revenue by $4.4 to $5.9 trillion over 10 years (about 11 percent) with the biggest benefits going to the top 1 percent of households.[3] Clinton proposed to impose a 4 percent tax surcharge for income over $5 million and make those with income over $1 million pay at least 30 percent in taxes. Overall, Clinton's tax policies would raise $1.1 trillion over 10 years.[4] Clinton also supported a $12 national minimum wage, and $15 per hour where it is economically feasible, while Trump supported a $10 minimum wage, but said "the states should call the shots."

Conflict over economic policy goes beyond tax policy. Many of America's political debates concern economic policy: Should we run deficits or have balanced budgets? Should we have a largely unregulated, free market—or regulations for things like pollution and health care? Should we spend more money to create "green jobs" and promote alternative energy, or subsidize more offshore drilling and build pipelines to maximize the extraction of oil and natural gas? Democrats tend to favor a more activist government that supports a broader range of redistributive programs and regulates the economy to ensure a range of public goods, such as rebuilding the infrastructure. Republicans tend to favor a more-limited approach to government that promotes lower taxes and less regulation and allows the free market to determine more social and economic decisions, such as allowing greater development of domestic energy sources.

In most areas there were clear differences between Clinton and Trump, with Clinton calling for a more active role for the government and Trump a smaller role. The one exception was rebuilding infrastructure: both candidates called for spending hundreds of billion of dollars over the next 10 years to rebuild highways, bridges, airports, water and sewage systems, and public transportation.

As our political leaders debate how best to support a growing economy it becomes increasingly important to understand the economic policy-making process. What are the goals of economic policy, and how can political institutions meet those goals? What is the proper role of the government in a free market economy? How do political players deal with the conflict that is inherent in economic policy making?

As our political leaders debate how best to support a growing economy and resolve trade-offs between social policy and other government priorities, it becomes increasingly important to understand the economic and social policy-making process. What are the goals of economic and social policy, and how can political institutions meet those goals? What is the proper role of the government in a free market economy? How do political players deal with the conflict that is inherent in social and economic policy making?

Making public policy

Public policy is a course of action pursued by government to address a specific problem. For example, various social policies, such as Medicare or Social Security, are aimed at addressing the medical and economic needs of retired American citizens. In this section, we outline the policy-making process and discuss the key players in shaping economic and social policy.

The policy-making process

How are policies shaped and implemented? All policies go through similar stages in this process. The first stage involves defining a problem as an issue that requires the federal government's attention. Of the thousands of possible issues, Congress acts on only a relatively small number. Consider food stamps: poor and hungry people have been part of American society since the arrival of the first settlers, but this was not seen as a problem requiring government intervention until the twentieth century. What causes a society to change its assumptions about whether and how government should address social problems?

Sometimes there is a triggering event: the assassination of President John F. Kennedy led to the passage of gun control legislation, the energy crisis of the early 1970s led to the first comprehensive discussions of energy policy, and Hurricane Katrina in 2005 led to a reexamination of our readiness for emergencies and our social safety net. Sometimes redefining an issue can move the policy to the next step of the process. For example, the estate tax has been part of our tax system since 1917, but when Republican leaders in Congress redefined it as the "death tax" in the late 1990s it transformed the politics of the debate and made it a problem that needed a solution. After all, who could support a tax on dead people? (Of course, dead people don't pay taxes—the estate's heirs do—but that nuance was lost in the redefinition of the problem.)

★

TRACE THE STEPS THROUGH WHICH PROBLEMS ARE ADDRESSED BY GOVERNMENT POLICIES

public policy
A law, rule, statute, or edict that expresses the government's goals and provides for rewards and punishments to promote their attainment.

policy agenda
The set of desired policies that
political leaders view as their top
priorities.

Recognizing and defining a problem is just the first step; it still needs to come to the attention of political leaders and get on the **policy agenda**. When conditions are right, with the appropriate national political mood and participation from key interest groups and government actors, an issue can reach the agenda.

Once the issue is on the active agenda, alternatives are proposed and debated and the final version of the policy is formulated in Congress (if it is a bill) or the executive branch (if it is an administrative action). Enactment involves either (1) a roll call vote in the House and the Senate and then a signature by the president, (2) a regulatory decision or administrative action by the bureaucracy, or (3) unilateral action by the president (such as an executive order or agreement).

Many factors determine whether the policy is implemented successfully. First, the problem has to be solvable and the policy must be clear and consistent in its objectives. It wouldn't make sense for Congress to pass a law telling the Department of Health and Human Services to "make sure everyone has health care," because such a law could not indicate how to accomplish that broad goal. Second, the policy must be funded adequately and administered by competent bureaucrats who have the required expertise. Finally, external support from the public and relevant interest groups may be critical to the policy's success. For example, AARP's support is absolutely essential for the success of any social policy that affects older Americans. Its support helped pass the Prescription Drug Benefit that was added to Medicare in 2003 and comprehensive health care reform in 2010.[5]

Implementation of a policy is an ongoing process. To ensure that the desires of Congress and the president are being followed, policy evaluation is a critical stage of the process. (See Chapter 12 for a discussion of Congress's and the president's attempts to control the bureaucracy.) Although policy evaluation has become increasingly visible since passage of the Government Performance and Results Act of 1993, which requires agencies to publish strategic plans and performance measures, it is incredibly difficult to assess whether a government program is achieving its aims.

Political scientist James Q. Wilson explains the difference in measuring success in the private sector and the public sector—specifically, he compares McDonald's with the Department of Motor Vehicles (DMV).[6] It is relatively easy to know whether

Though few issues have been as contentious as health care reform, social policies can be complicated, conflictual, and personal. The political process used to tackle these conflicts is often tedious, complex, and time-consuming. #ACA #Obamacare

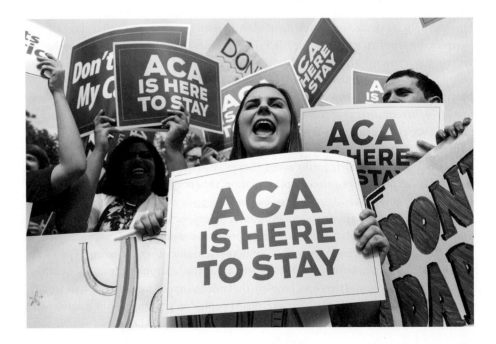

McDonald's is doing a good job: simply compare the profits being generated with those of the previous period. If profits are going up at a reasonable pace, the burger flippers and fry cooks are doing their jobs. The DMV's performance is much more difficult to assess because there is no simple measure, such as profit, to look at. Maybe you could review the number of people served per hour or the average time that people have to wait to get their driver's license. But that would ignore many other considerations, such as how well the DMV serves disadvantaged populations or people for whom English is a second language. In a DMV office where 50 percent of the applicants don't speak English, we wouldn't expect the workers to be as efficient as in one where all applicants speak English.

Evaluating a public agency such as the State Department is even more difficult. How do we know if diplomacy is being conducted in a manner consistent with congressional and presidential preferences? Would success be defined as staying out of war? Increasing economic activity or cultural exchanges between countries? Strengthening democratic institutions in emerging democracies? Getting cooperation in the war on terrorism? Measuring the achievement of objectives like these is very difficult even if those goals can be clearly defined.

Despite these limitations, extensive efforts to evaluate policy do provide decision makers with some basis for deciding whether to modify, expand, or terminate a policy. Programs are notoriously difficult to cut or eliminate.

The key players in economic and social policy making

Congress, the president, and the bureaucracy all play important roles in making economic and social policy. Congress, through the "power of the purse," has the constitutional authority to determine the nation's fiscal policy, but the president also can shape taxing and spending policy for the nation. The Federal Reserve and the Treasury implement the nation's monetary policy, while other bureaucratic agencies implement social policy. Additional significant players include the courts, state governments, and interest groups.

Congress The Constitution places Congress at the center of economic policy making by giving legislators the "power of the purse"—that is, power over the nation's fiscal policy of taxing and spending. In a way, everything Congress does has an impact on the economy, whether it is providing money for an interstate highway or a student loan, regulating the level of air pollutants, or funding the Social Security system. Some committees are more directly related to economic policy: budget, appropriations, and tax committees (Ways and Means in the House and Finance in the Senate; see Chapter 10) direct Congress's **fiscal policy**—taxing and spending—whereas the banking committees have a hand in overseeing aspects of the nation's **monetary policy**, controlling the money supply and interest rates. (However, as we discuss later in this chapter, monetary policy is primarily the domain of the Federal Reserve System, or "the Fed.") The commerce committees, especially in the House, also influence a range of economic policies. The budget process is the most important of Congress's economic policy-making responsibilities.

Budget making in Congress was decentralized through much of the nation's history, with various committees and subcommittees serving as the centers of the legislative process and no real way to coordinate activity among them. The appropriations committees tried to be the "guardians of the Treasury," but it was difficult to keep the spending requests from other committees in line with overall budgetary expectations

fiscal policy
Government decisions about how to influence the economy by taxing and spending.

monetary policy
Government decisions about how to influence the economy using control of the money supply and interest rates.

budget making
The processes carried out in Congress to determine how government money will be spent and revenue will be raised.

How it works: in theory
The Budget Process

First Monday in February:
The president submits budget request to Congress.

February 15:
Congressional Budget Office (CBO) issues budget and economic outlook report.

Within six weeks of president's submission:
Other committees with budgetary responsibilities submit "views and estimates" to budget committees.

Early April:
House Budget Committee creates its budget resolution and the House votes on it.

Early April:
Senate Budget Committee creates its budget resolution and the Senate votes on it.

Early April:
Budget Conference Committee reconciles the House and Senate versions of the budget resolution.

By April 15:
House votes on conference version. Senate votes on conference version.

Appropriations:
After both houses approve the budget resolution, appropriations committees draft legislation authorizing expenditures to the relevant agencies. Each appropriations bill must be passed by both houses and signed into law by the president. If this process is not completed by October 1, and no temporary measure (a "continuing resolution") is in place, the government will shut down.

October 1:
Start of the fiscal year.

The 2016 Budget Process

While there is a "textbook" path that politicians try to follow when passing a budget, they almost always deviate wildly from it. For example, it has been 20 years since Congress passed all 12 appropriations bills using the regular process. In 2016, they resorted to continuing resolutions and an omnibus bill that combined the 12 appropriations bills. Conflict over the 2016 budget also led to the resignation of the House Speaker, but avoided a government shutdown.

Let's get started.

March 4: President Obama **submits his budget for the 2016 fiscal year** and signs the last appropriations bill from the previous year.

We're on track.

March 25: House passes budget resolution.

March 27: Senate passes budget resolution.

So far, so good.

April 30: House passes a conference report that **works out the differences** between the House and Senate budget resolutions.

May 5: Senate passes conference report (this is the **first time in 6 years** that a budget resolution is passed).

Twist!

July 28: Rep. Mark Meadows (R-NC) introduces a measure to **remove Republican John Boehner as Speaker of the House** amid tensions between the Tea Party wing of the Republican Party and establishment conservatives.

Pressure builds.

August: Pressure on Boehner builds throughout the summer, and a floor vote on his status as Speaker becomes more likely.

Shut it down.

September 18: House Republicans vote to defund Planned Parenthood, with some Freedom Caucus members **threatening to shut down the government** on September 25 if their demands are not met.

See ya!

September 25: Boehner says **he will step down** as Speaker because of the split within his party over the budget.

Close call.

September 30 and October 1: Congress passes a continuing resolution with a few hours to spare **to keep the government open.**

Making promises.

October 29: New Speaker Paul Ryan elected; vows not to shut down the government.

We're getting somewhere.

October 31: Congress passes a budget agreement, raising the debt ceiling and agreeing to spending targets.

Whew!

December 11 and December 16: Congress passes continuing resolutions **to keep the government open.**

Passed.

December 18, 2015: Congress passes omnibus spending bill authorizing $1.1 trillion in spending and $650 billion in tax cuts.

?

Critical Thinking

1. **How might the type of "brinkmanship" budgeting** described here—that is, each side threatening the other and predicting dire consequences if the other side does not bend—affect the economy?

2. **If you were a businessperson trying to decide** whether or not to expand, do you think the uncertainty created by a threatened shutdown might affect your decision?

because of Congress's two-step process to approve spending: the authorizing committee writes the law that authorizes the spending, and then the appropriations committee approves the level of spending.[7] As a result, budgetary power shifted from Congress to the president, starting with the Budget and Accounting Act of 1921. Since then, presidents have played a central role in the budget process by submitting their budgets to Congress. The president's budget often serves as the starting point for the congressional budget (see How It Works: The Budget Process).

Today, as evidence that politics is conflictual, increased partisan polarization is occurring in Congress over budget making. Differences between Democrats' and Republicans' views of taxing and spending policy make it difficult to pass a budget on time. Recently Congress has relied on "continuing resolutions," which keep spending at the level of the previous year's budget, when they cannot agree on a new budget. Even traditionally noncontroversial aspects of fiscal policy, such as increasing the debt ceiling to authorize government borrowing, have become opportunities for partisan politics.

Congress also plays a central role in shaping social policy. Many important social policies such as Social Security, Medicare, Medicaid, and food stamps started out as presidential initiatives. But Congress writes the laws and then reforms and expands them over the years.

The President Presidents know that the public expects them to promote a healthy economy. Indeed, the state of the economy influences the public's assessment of presidential performance and also influences election outcomes. President Obama focused on the economy in his first months in office, pushing through a massive stimulus bill; later, facing high levels of unemployment, Obama also signed legislation aimed at creating more jobs.

As mentioned in Chapter 11, the president cannot accomplish much single-handedly on the economic front: Congress, the Fed, and broader domestic and international economic forces all have an impact on the health of the economy. However, the president has a large advising structure to help formulate economic policy. The Office of Management and Budget (OMB), the Council of Economic Advisers (CEA), the Office of the **United States Trade Representative (USTR)**, and the **National Economic Council (NEC)** all provide important economic advice to the president.

The OMB solicits spending requests from all federal agencies, suggests additional cuts, and then coordinates these requests with presidential priorities. It ultimately puts together the president's budget, which is then submitted to Congress. The OMB also oversees government reorganization plans and recommends improvements in departmental operations.

The CEA primarily provides the president with objective data on the state of the economy and expert advice on economic policy. The agency is responsible for creating the *Annual Economic Report of the President*, which has a wealth of data on the economy and an overview of the president's policies. Although presidents have varied in how closely they work with the CEA or other parts of their economic team, some prominent CEA members have significantly influenced the administration's tax policy and jobs program.

Interactions between Congress and the president are central to understanding economic and social policy. If the president's party controls Congress, then the president's budget becomes the starting point for congressional negotiations over the budget. If the opposing party controls Congress, then the president's budget is usually considered "dead on arrival" and Congress creates its own document. Of course, the president can use the veto threat to try to move Congress closer to his or her position, but when the

United States Trade Representative (USTR)
An agency founded in 1962 to negotiate with foreign governments to create trade agreements, resolve disputes, and participate in global trade-policy organizations. Treaties negotiated by the USTR must be ratified by the Senate.

National Economic Council (NEC)
A group of economic advisers created in 1993 to work with the president to coordinate economic policy.

budget is contained in one large package that must be signed or vetoed in its entirety it is difficult to carry out such threats.[8]

Similarly, in some instances the president may take the lead in formulating social policy, as Franklin Delano Roosevelt did with the New Deal and Lyndon Johnson with the Great Society. In other instances, Congress plays a central role, as with health care reform in 2009–2010. In all cases, the president and Congress must find some common ground.

The Bureaucracy You might assume that the bureaucracy makes little difference in social policy and simply implements the policies determined by Congress and the president. For some policies, that is somewhat true—such as Social Security, whose benefit levels are determined by law. Implementing this policy largely involves determining that the proper amount of money is going to the right people and making sure that they receive their payments. However, as discussed in Chapter 12, with many social policies the "on-the-ground" public employees have a great deal of discretion. One study found that welfare agencies that distributed **Aid to Families with Dependent Children (AFDC)** benefits had a more "hostile and punitive" attitude toward their clients than those that administered the disability program under Social Security. Welfare offices in general tend not to be very welcoming places. People often have to wait for hours, and office workers are sometimes rude. Some potential welfare recipients are so alienated by the process that they give up.[9] (This is not true of all welfare offices, but there are general differences in how recipients are treated in different types of social welfare programs.) Sometimes problems of bureaucratic implementation may be at the top, as when problems concerning Veterans Affairs (VA) hospitals came to light in 2014. Thousands of veterans had long waits for services that were covered up by VA hospital administrators. Veterans Affairs Secretary Eric Shinseki was forced to resign for his failure to address the problem.[10]

Bureaucratic discretion may also serve more positive ends, however. In fact, many bureaucratic agencies in the late nineteenth and early twentieth centuries developed political autonomy and strong reputations that enabled them to analyze and solve problems, create new programs, and plan and administer programs efficiently.[11] Many of the same insights apply to agencies that deliver social policies today, such as the Social Security Administration, which has a very strong base of popular and political support.

In terms of economic policy, two bureaucratic agencies are key in creating monetary policy: the **Federal Reserve System** (an independent agency) and the **Treasury Department** (a cabinet-level department). The Treasury Department's mission "is to promote the conditions for prosperity and stability in the United States and encourage prosperity and stability in the rest of the world."[12] Some of these responsibilities overlap with the Fed's, especially supervising banks and managing the public debt. In most instances, the responsibilities are complementary rather than competing, such as the management of currency and coins: the Treasury produces currency and coins, and the Fed distributes them to member banks.[13] Financing federal debt is another matter. The Treasury prefers lower interest rates to keep down the cost of financing the debt and to promote economic growth, while the Fed is also concerned about keeping rates high enough to avoid inflation. Therefore, the Fed and the Treasury must coordinate their policies to avoid working at cross-purposes.

Other Important Players By providing a necessary legal foundation, *the courts* ensure fair application of economic and social policy laws and regulations. For example, contract law, patent law, banking and finance law, and property rights are all elements of a legal system that provides the foundation for economic development. Courts issue rulings on the regulation of telecommunications, banking, and energy industries

Aid to Families with Dependent Children (AFDC)
The federal welfare program in place from 1935 until 1995, when it was replaced by TANF under President Clinton.

Federal Reserve System
An independent agency that serves as the central bank of the United States to bring stability to the nation's banking system.

Treasury Department
A cabinet-level agency that is responsible for managing the federal government's revenue. It prints currency, collects taxes, and sells government bonds.

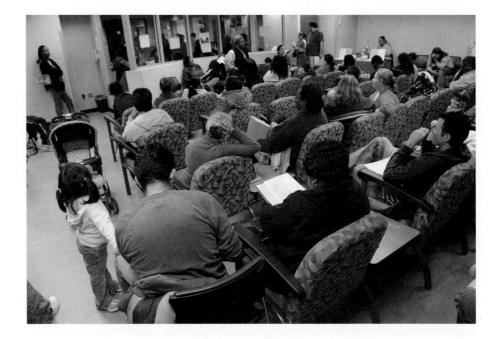

Welfare offices can be alienating places in which it is very difficult to navigate through the bureaucracy. Here, dozens of people wait to speak to counselors in this Lawrenceville, Georgia, welfare office.

and decisions on environmental law and eminent domain that affect property rights. All these policies have an impact on economic policy. Courts are also important in helping to shape economic and social policy by deciding when laws passed by Congress may be unconstitutional.

State governments have a central role in areas such as education and welfare. Welfare has always been administered at the state and local level, with varying degrees of national control. Medicaid is administered at the state level (with federal assistance), and education is almost completely controlled by local and state governments. One sticking point with health care reform in 2009–2010 was the extent to which policy would be centered in the states or have a stronger national component. (The stronger national approach failed, but the new law signaled a definite shift to a more national role in health care.)

Education policy, too, is seeing more involvement by the national government. But even with the national accountability mechanisms and testing requirements established by President George W. Bush's No Child Left Behind Act and the incentives provided by President Barack Obama's "Race to the Top" program, education policy remains largely a state and local affair.

In contrast, economic policy making is more of a national responsibility. States are severely constrained in making fiscal policy because they must have balanced budgets every year (unlike the national government, which may run deficits to stimulate the economy). Monetary policy is entirely the domain of the national government.

Interest groups constitute another important player in shaping policy, although those advocating for social policy are not as influential as groups focusing on business, labor, the environment, or gun ownership. A major exception is AARP, a highly powerful lobby that addresses policy issues affecting the elderly (see Chapter 9). AARP has had an especially strong voice on behalf of Social Security and Medicare. Many other interest groups and think tanks work on behalf of the poor, the homeless, and other disadvantaged people, but Washington is generally less responsive to their concerns because these groups are not politically powerful.

Lately, interest groups and social movements have gotten involved in economic policy. The Tea Party advocates less government spending and more focus on the debt, while the Occupy movement directs attention to income inequality and the need for more regulation of Wall Street. More long-standing groups, such as the Concord Coalition, have organized to influence fiscal policy in Washington.

Alternative perspectives on the policy-making process

The "stages model" of policy making described earlier is a pretty basic description of the process. Several elaborations and extensions provide a more nuanced understanding of the process.[14] For example, the first two steps, problem recognition and agenda setting, were conceptualized by John Kingdon as multiple streams of problems, policies, and politics. These three streams are independent and may or may not intersect. Objective conditions may or may not turn into problems. For example, the abuse of opioid painkillers has been evident for many years. But the death of the musician Prince called attention to this condition and turned it into a problem that policy makers felt more pressure to address. There are typically various policy options available to address any given problem, but whether or not they are acted on depends on either a policy entrepreneur who pushes for change or, more broadly, political change that creates a "policy window," or opportunity to implement the policy. Political change comes about with a change in the national mood, interest-group politics, or an administrative or legislative change in control.[15] So agenda setting and eventually passing a law is not as linear and static as implied by the basic stages model.

Frank R. Baumgartner and Bryan D. Jones provide additional insight into *how* policy change happens with their "punctuated equilibrium" model. They argue that the policy process features long periods of incremental change punctuated by brief periods of major policy change. Change comes about when an alternative "policy image" can expand an issue beyond the control of the policy specialists who resist change. For example, the ACA overcame decades of resistance to major change in health insurance by emphasizing a policy image that focused on the millions of Americans who did not have insurance.[16]

The last part of the process also has been elaborated by scholars of policy diffusion. They explain why some policies quickly spread across the country and others are adopted in only a few states. The idea that states are "laboratories of democracy" is an invitation to explore that variation. One comprehensive study took up the challenge and examined 130 policy innovations, explaining the relative rates of diffusion by the type of policy and the level of government attention.[17] Another analysis of anti-smoking policy found that learning from early adopters, economic competition between proximate cities, imitation of larger cities, and coercion from state governments all explained whether or not a city adopted an anti-smoking policy.[18]

Understanding the policy-making process and the key actors in that process is important for seeing why policies are adopted. Why do some policies, such as a 21-year-old drinking age or anti-smoking policies, spread quickly across the country while others, such as legalizing marijuana or some environmental regulations, are adopted in a few states and spread more slowly? If Congress gets involved, as with health care reform, or the Supreme Court decides an issue, like with same-sex marriage, then policy change can happen in big, non-incremental steps.

"Why Should I Care?"

EXPLAIN THE MAIN
PURPOSES OF
GOVERNMENT
INVOLVEMENT IN THE
ECONOMY AND HOW
FISCAL, MONETARY,
AND REGULATORY
POLICIES INFLUENCE
THE ECONOMY

Economic policy

Here we take a closer look at the goals and theories that influence specific economic policies passed by the government. We also examine the trade-offs among various goals.

Goals of economic policy

Policy makers have specific goals in mind when they try to influence the economy. Many seem obvious, such as full employment (it's better to have more people working than not working), but others may be less clear. Also, it is difficult to pursue all the goals simultaneously because there are trade-offs among some of them.

Full Employment Employment seems like a good starting point for a healthy economy. If people have jobs, they pay taxes and do not directly depend on the government for support. Despite this, full employment was not an explicit goal of economic policy until 1946, when Congress passed the Employment Act. Leaders were concerned that with millions of returning World War II veterans and the wartime economy gearing down, the nation might slide back into the economic depression that had created so much hardship in the 1930s. Although the act was largely symbolic (there was no guaranteed right to employment), it did create the Council of Economic Advisers (CEA), which provides the president with economic information and advice. A more concrete effort to ensure that returning veterans could find jobs was the Servicemen's Readjustment Act (the GI Bill). Enacted in 1944, it provided higher education assistance and low-interest home mortgages for millions of veterans. Today the government seeks to support the creation of as many jobs as possible through a strong economy.

Stable Prices The importance of price stability is not as obvious as the need for jobs. Why are rising prices—inflation—a problem? This is a common question during periods of low inflation. Especially for workers who have automatic raises (cost of living adjustments, or COLAs) as part of their basic pay package, moderate inflation isn't much of a problem. For example, if your rent goes up by 4 percent, the price of groceries goes up by 3 percent, and you get a 4 percent raise you will probably manage to be at least as well off as you were in the previous year (see Figure 14.1).

However, high inflation can have serious effects on the economy. First, some people experience an erosion of their purchasing power. So if your rent goes up by 10 percent and groceries are up by 15 percent, but your pay goes up by only 4 percent, you will be substantially worse off. Second, high inflation penalizes savers and benefits debtors as savings interest rates may be outstripped by inflation (so savings are worth *less* over time), but people who go into debt can repay those debts with dollars that are worth less in the future. Finally, long-term economic planning by businesses becomes more difficult when inflation is high, because investors demand high interest rates to compensate for the added risk of future inflation.

As counterintuitive as it may sound, *falling* prices or deflation may be as equally devastating for an economy as prices that are rising too quickly. In the Great Depression, prices fell by 10 percent a year from 1930 to 1933, which exacerbated the depression as businesses made less money, wages fell (for those who were still working), production fell, and real debt increased. American policy makers were concerned about possible deflation after the Great Recession of 2008-2009, but those fears subsided as inflation remained at a low level.[19]

full employment
The theoretical point at which all citizens who want to be employed have a job.

economic depression
A deep, widespread downturn in the economy, like the Great Depression of the 1930s.

Council of Economic Advisers (CEA)
A group of economic advisers, created by the Employment Act of 1946, that provides objective data on the state of the economy and makes economic-policy recommendations to the president.

inflation
The increase in the price of consumer goods over time.

deflation
A decrease in the general prices of goods and services.

**FIGURE
14.1**

Inflation and Unemployment, 1960–2016

The Misery Index is the sum of the unemployment rate and the inflation rate. Which periods have had the highest misery rate since 1960? Were there any external explanations for the high misery rate? How did the government respond to the high levels of unemployment and inflation?

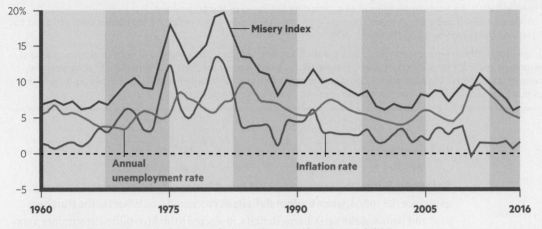

Source: Data from the U.S. Department of Labor, Bureau of Labor Statistics, www.bls.gov (accessed 7/7/16).

Typically, unemployment and inflation are not high at the same time, so there can be a trade-off in focusing on one or the other in economic policy. There tend to be basic partisan differences on the goals of full employment and stable prices, with Democrats being more concerned about employment and Republicans more concerned about inflation. This is no surprise, given the Democratic Party's base of support within labor unions and blue-collar workers and the Republican Party's stronger support on Wall Street and with investors whose income is likely to be eroded by high inflation.

Promoting the Free Market and Growth The American economy is a capitalist system, which means that most economic decisions are voluntarily made between individuals and firms for their mutual benefit. The government generally stays out of most economic activity, except to regulate the market when it produces too much of something that is not in the public's interest, such as pollution or unsafe products. Economists tout the advantage of the free market as promoting the most efficient use of resources. Economic growth, traditionally defined in terms of **gross domestic product (GDP)**, is also a central goal, for a growing economy provides a better standard of living for each generation.

The government does not get directly involved in most economic transactions, but it can provide the foundation for a strong free market and economic growth. The government protects property rights so that businesses that invest in the growth of their company know that another firm or the government cannot take away their property. The foundation for the free market is also provided by secure and transparent capital markets through the oversight of the Securities and Exchange Commission, and through a secure banking system as ensured by the Federal Deposit Insurance Corporation and the Federal Reserve System.

As we will see later in this chapter, the economic meltdown of 2008–2009 raised basic questions about the efficiency of economic markets and the need for more regulation of the financial sector.

gross domestic product (GDP)
The value of a country's economic output taken as a whole.

Deficits and Debt

Budget deficits and the federal debt are related concepts that are easily confused.

- A **budget deficit** occurs when tax revenue is not sufficient to cover government spending in a given year. If tax revenue is higher than spending, then there is a budget surplus.
- The **federal debt** is the total accumulation of all outstanding borrowing by the government.
- The concepts of deficit and debt are related because when the government runs a deficit it must borrow money to cover the gap. This borrowing then builds up the federal debt.

You can think of this in terms of your own spending habits. Any time you spend more money in a given month than you earn, you are running a deficit. You must borrow money to make up that deficit from a bank, from your parents, or by running up the balance on your credit card. The accumulated sum of your monthly deficits is the total debt that you owe. However, there is one obvious point that should be made: you cannot print your own money, unlike the government!

balanced budget
A spending plan in which the government's expenditures are equal to its revenue.

budget deficits
The amount by which a government's spending in a given fiscal year exceeds its revenue.

Balanced Budgets Maintaining a **balanced budget** has been a central economic goal since the 1980s, when **budget deficits** skyrocketed (see What Do the Numbers Say? and Nuts & Bolts 14.1). Large deficits, projected to be $550 billion in 2017, are a concern for several reasons. First, they take a big bite out of current spending. About $306 billion, or 7.5 percent, of the 2017 fiscal year budget is for financing the federal debt. These dollars went to people and financial institutions that earn interest on the money that they loaned to the federal government; this money did not pay for a single uniform for a soldier, highway exit ramp, or student loan. Second, the total federal debt is a burden on future generations. Each man, woman, and child in the United States in effect carries more than $55,559 of federal debt. (Total debt has grown steadily; see What Do the Numbers Say?)

Trade-Offs among Economic-Policy Goals One challenge facing economic policy makers is that it is difficult to "have it all." Throughout most of the 1990s, the United States enjoyed economic growth, low unemployment, and low inflation with falling budget deficits. This was relatively unusual. Typically, at least part of the economy is not performing well and some goals are not being met, so policy makers must tread carefully when addressing economic problems to ensure that they do not make some other problem worse.

Tools and theories of economic policy

Now that we know the key players in economic policy and their goals, it is time to examine the tools those policy makers use to accomplish those goals. Policy makers cannot pull levers and push buttons to achieve desired outcomes, nor are they immune from external forces that can sink the economy despite their best efforts. However, leaders can do certain things to move the massive U.S. economy in the right direction.

Keynesian economics
The theory that governments should use economic policy, like taxing and spending, to maintain stability in the economy.

Fiscal Policy Fiscal policy is the use of the government's taxing and spending power to influence the direction of the economy. Developed by economist John Maynard Keynes in the 1930s, **Keynesian economics** argues that policy makers can soften the effects of a recession by stimulating the economy when overall demand is low—during a recession, when people aren't spending much—through tax cuts or increased government spending. Tax cuts put more money in people's pockets, enabling them to spend

Are Deficits and the National Debt Out of Control?

Many politicians say that government spending has gotten out of control and that the federal budget deficit (the amount by which the government's spending exceeds its revenue in a given year) and the federal debt (the accumulation of these annual deficits) are too high. Is this true? What do the numbers say? Let's look at each in two different ways.

Budget Deficits

Note: Deficits include the Social Security Trust Fund.

Public Debt

Note: This figure shows publicly held debt, excluding intragovernmental holdings.

Source: Congressional Budget Office, Budget Projections, various documents from www.cbo.gov/topics/budget (accessed 6/8/16).

Think about it

- What is the biggest difference between the figures on the left and right of each chart?
- Which data, the left or the right, do you think are a better indication of the size of our budget deficit and debt? Why? Do both sets of numbers reveal something useful?
- Economists argue that debt becomes a potentially serious problem when it is as big as the overall economy. Did we ever hit that level since 1940?
- After examining these data, do you think the United States' budget deficits and national debt are out of control? Why or why not?

more than they otherwise would, whereas government spending stimulates the economy through the purchase of various goods, such as highways or military equipment, or direct payments to individuals, such as unemployment compensation. From this perspective, it is acceptable to run budget deficits in order to increase employment and national income to give a short-term boost to the economy. Keynes also pointed out that if overall demand is too high, which might result in inflation, policy makers should cool off the economy by cutting spending or raising taxes.[20]

A more recent version of fiscal policy was the basis for Ronald Reagan's tax cuts in 1981 and has been the centerpiece of economic policy for many Republicans since then. **Supply-side economics** focuses on the ways that tax policy and regulations affect the labor supply rather than on these policies' impact on overall demand. The primary focus is on the way tax rates affect how much people work rather than how they spend. The idea is that if tax rates are too high people will work less because a large percentage of their income goes to the government.

However, when taxes were cut under Reagan, with the top marginal rate (the income tax rate paid on the top slice of earned income) going from 70 to 50 percent, revenue fell and the budget deficits exploded. Supporters of the supply-side theory argue that the problem was on the spending side of the equation rather than with tax revenue. That is, deficits went up because the Democratic Congress spent too much, not because of Reagan's tax cuts. However, taxes and spending as a share of the overall economy both fell during the Reagan presidency, which suggests that spending was not the source of the budget deficits in the 1980s.[21] A similar relationship between cutting tax rates and falling revenue could be observed with the Bush tax cuts in 2001.

Economists continue to debate the extent to which fiscal policy can influence the economy. Two factors have limited the effectiveness of fiscal policy. First, fiscal policies often cannot be implemented quickly enough to have the intended impact on the **business cycle**—the normal expansion and contraction of the economy. This is especially true when one party controls Congress and the other controls the presidency, but it happens even during unified government. The $787 billion American Recovery and Reinvestment Act of 2009, designed to stimulate the economy and create jobs, encountered problems along these lines. Although the legislation had some immediate impact on the economy, it is impossible to spend that much money (or implement tax cuts) without some time lag. Republicans criticized Democrats for spending too much money and not enacting policies that would have had a more immediate effect (such as payroll tax cuts), and other critics argued that the stimulus wasn't big enough.

Second, on the other side of the Keynesian coin, increasing taxes or cutting spending during good economic times is much more difficult to implement than the more politically popular tax cuts or spending increases. After all, politicians do not like to raise taxes or cut spending. Furthermore, even if politicians *wanted* to cut spending this aspect of fiscal policy is becoming increasingly difficult to use because a growing portion of the federal budget is devoted to **mandatory spending**—that is, entitlements such as Social Security, which must be spent by law, and interest on the federal debt, which must be paid (if the United States defaulted on its debt, there would be an international economic meltdown). So reducing the federal deficit by cutting spending is increasingly difficult. With the 2017 deficit at $550 billion, Congress would have to eliminate nearly all **discretionary spending**—spending that can be cut from the budget without changing the underlying law—including defense spending and everything else the government does, to balance the budget.[22] (See Figure 14.2.)

Fiscal policy may have a relatively modest impact on the economy, but it determines how the tax burden is distributed and which parts of the economy and policy areas benefit from federal spending. In other words, fiscal policy has *redistributive* implications. There are two ways of thinking about the characteristics of federal taxes:

supply-side economics
The theory that lower tax rates will stimulate the economy by encouraging people to save, invest, and produce more goods and services.

"

No nation has ever taxed itself into prosperity.

—Rush Limbaugh

business cycle
The normal pattern of expansion and contraction of the economy.

mandatory spending
Expenditures that are required by law, such as the funding for Social Security.

discretionary spending
Expenditures that can be cut from the budget without changing the underlying law.

**FIGURE
14.2**

Mandatory and Discretionary Spending, 1962–2017

The percentage of the budget allocated for discretionary spending has been shrinking since the 1960s. What implications does this have for members of Congress and the president as they try to reduce the federal deficits?

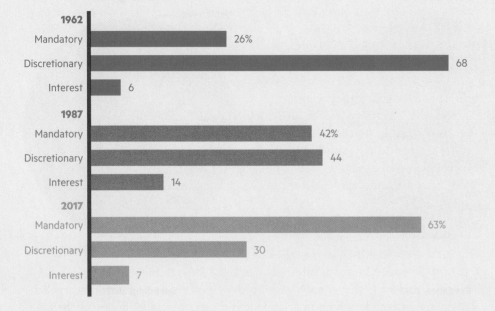

Source: Congressional Budget Office, *Updated Budget Projections, 2016–2026*, Table 1, p. 15, www.cbo.gov (accessed 6/3/16).

(1) the different types of taxes and (2) their redistributive nature—that is, whether a specific tax is regressive, neutral, or progressive. There are four major types of federal taxes: personal income taxes, corporate taxes, payroll taxes (for Social Security and Medicare), and excise taxes (such as taxes on cigarettes, alcohol, gasoline, air travel, and telephone lines). Figure 14.3 shows how the distribution of tax revenue changed between 1962 and 2017. The proportion of personal income taxes held fairly steady, but excise taxes and corporate taxes fell and payroll taxes more than doubled.

The increasing share of revenue that comes from payroll taxes has important implications for the redistributive nature of taxes. Payroll taxes are **regressive** because everyone who works pays the same rate of 6.2 percent up to a certain income level ($118,500 in 2016; also, all workers pay an additional 1.45 percent on all income to support Medicare). Thus, someone who earns $118,500 pays the same *amount* of Social Security tax ($7,347) as a wealthy individual such as Bill Gates does, but the tax represents a much larger share of the lesser-paid person's income than it does for Gates's. Income taxes, in contrast, are **progressive**: upper-income people pay a larger portion of their income in taxes than low-income people do.

One criticism of Donald Trump's tax plan in the 2016 campaign was that a disproportionate share of the proposed cuts would go to the wealthiest people in the country, making taxes less progressive. This may make sense from one perspective, given that the bottom 45 percent of taxpayers do not pay any personal income tax. However, poor and lower-middle-income people do pay a large share of the total payroll tax. Thus,

regressive
Taxes that take a larger share of poor people's income than wealthy people's income, such as sales taxes and payroll taxes.

progressive
Taxes that require upper-income people to pay a higher tax rate than lower-income people, such as income taxes.

FIGURE 14.3

Federal Revenues and Spending, 1962 and 2017

A much larger share of tax revenue comes from payroll taxes than was true in the 1960s. What implications does this have for the redistributive nature of federal taxes? What have been the biggest changes since the 1960s in the way the federal tax dollar is spent? Are these trends likely to reverse or continue in the next 30 years?

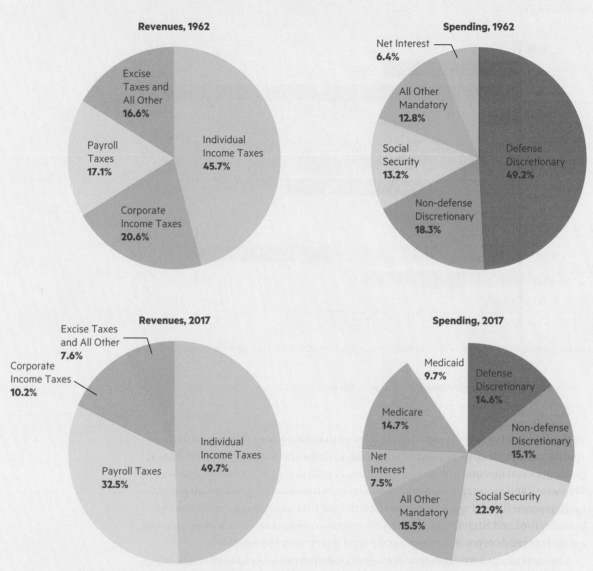

Revenues, 1962

Excise Taxes and All Other **16.6%**
Payroll Taxes **17.1%**
Corporate Income Taxes **20.6%**
Individual Income Taxes **45.7%**

Spending, 1962

Net Interest **6.4%**
All Other Mandatory **12.8%**
Social Security **13.2%**
Non-defense Discretionary **18.3%**
Defense Discretionary **49.2%**

Revenues, 2017

Excise Taxes and All Other **7.6%**
Corporate Income Taxes **10.2%**
Payroll Taxes **32.5%**
Individual Income Taxes **49.7%**

Spending, 2017

Medicaid **9.7%**
Medicare **14.7%**
Net Interest **7.5%**
All Other Mandatory **15.5%**
Defense Discretionary **14.6%**
Non-defense Discretionary **15.1%**
Social Security **22.9%**

Source: Congressional Budget Office, *Updated Budget Projections, 2016–2026*, Table 1, p. 15, and Table 4, pp. 21–22, www.cbo.gov/sites/default/files/114th-congress-2015-2016/reports/51384-MarchBaseline_OneCol.pdf (accessed 6/3/16).

DID YOU KNOW?

45%

of Americans pay no income tax.
Source: Tax Policy Center

the top fifth of the income distribution paid more than 85 percent of all income taxes but only 45.5 percent of payroll taxes.[23] So income tax cuts will help wealthier people because they pay most of the income tax, whereas payroll tax cuts would help poor and middle-income people more. At the same time, the top marginal tax rate is close to the lowest it has been since the 1920s (Figure 14.4). As a result, the overall personal income tax rate for the top fifth of the income distribution dropped from 17.5 percent in 2000 to 15 percent in 2013. This lower overall tax rate for the wealthy is also explained by the lower 15 percent rate for capital gains and dividends mentioned in the chapter opener.[24]

Top Marginal Tax Rates, 1913–2016

FIGURE 14.4

The top marginal tax rate, which is the tax rate paid by the richest Americans on their income above some threshold ($415,051 in 2016 for a single taxpayer), has plummeted in the past 50 years from more than 90 percent to 35 percent in 2012 and then back up to 39.6 percent in 2013 (and has held steady at that rate since). What are the arguments for and against increasing the top marginal tax rate?

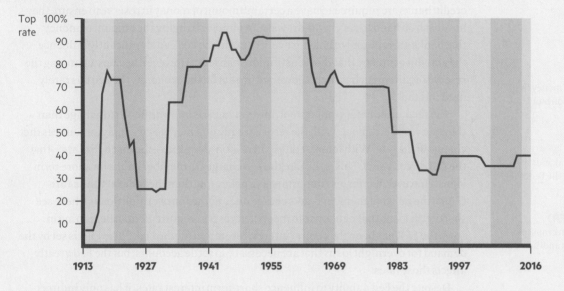

Sources: Data from the Internal Revenue Service, "Internal Revenue Bulletin: 2007-45," November 5, 2007, Rev. Proc. 2007-66 and 2008–2016 rates from www.irs.gov (accessed 6/3/16).

Monetary Policy and the Federal Reserve System Monetary policy includes influencing interest rates and the money supply and regulating the lending activity of banks. The Federal Reserve Act of 1913 established the Federal Reserve System to bring stability and continuity to the nation's banking system. The chair and six other governors serve on the board of governors of the Federal Reserve System. The board is responsible for establishing monetary policy for the nation. There are 12 regional Federal Reserve banks and more than 3,000 member banks out of the more than 8,000 banks in the nation.[25] The Fed monitors levels of bank lending, the money supply, and interest rates. Bank lending is important for economic growth because businesses borrow money to expand and as they grow they add jobs. If credit is tight and businesses cannot borrow money, economic growth will suffer, as became painfully evident in late 2008 and 2009.

The second target of monetary policy, the money supply, is also central to economic growth and directly related to levels of lending activity. The Fed can influence the amount of money in the system by making it easier or harder for banks to lend money. According to the **monetarist theory**, the amount of money in circulation is the most important determinant of economic activity and inflation. If too much money is chasing too few goods, there could be inflationary pressure on the economy and prices might rise too quickly.[26] In contrast, if there isn't enough money available, a recession could occur.

Perhaps the most obvious targets of monetary policy are interest rates. Changing interest rates affects the economy by making borrowing money either less or more expensive. Businesses and consumers are more likely to borrow if the interest rate is 6 percent than 12 percent. Consumer purchases of big-ticket items, those things that are financed by borrowing rather than being purchased with cash, also increase when

monetarist theory
The idea that the amount of money in circulation (the money supply) is the primary influence on economic activity and inflation.

"

> It is well enough that people of
> the nation do not understand our
> banking and monetary system,
> for if they did, I believe there
> would be a revolution before
> tomorrow morning.
>
> —Henry Ford

reserve requirement
The minimum amount of money that
a bank is required to have on hand to
back up its assets.

discount rate
The interest rate that a bank must pay
on a short-term loan from the Federal
Reserve Bank.

federal funds rate (FFR)
The interest rate that a bank must pay
on an overnight loan from another
bank.

open market operations
The process by which the Federal
Reserve System buys and sells
securities to influence the money
supply.

interest rates are low. These purchases dry up when interest rates are high. That is why so many appliance stores and car dealers advertise: "Zero dollars down, and zero percent interest until next January!" Entire sectors of the economy, such as housing, construction, consumer durables, and cars, are very sensitive to interest rates.

What can the Fed do to meet its targets on credit availability, the money supply, and interest rates? There are three central tools of monetary policy. First, the **reserve requirement** is the most potentially powerful tool for affecting the availability of credit: banks are required to have a certain amount of money in reserve to ensure they have cash on hand to cover withdrawals. By simply changing the amount of money that banks are required to hold for every deposit, the Fed can significantly influence the amount of money that those institutions can lend. However, because changing the reserve requirement has such a powerful impact on the economy, the Fed has rarely used this tool.[27]

The second monetary-policy tool, interest rates, is more difficult to manage than the reserve requirement. With the reserve requirement, the Fed simply announces the change in the rate. With interest rates, there is only one rate—the **discount rate**—that the Fed directly sets. This is the rate the Fed charges to member banks for short-term loans. However, it is far less important as a policy tool than the **federal funds rate (FFR)**, the rate that member banks charge one another on overnight loans (these are short-term loans that banks use to meet their reserve requirements). Beginning in 1995, the FFR has been the central interest rate target for the Fed.[28] The FFR is set by the demand for overnight loans that are necessary to settle accounts, but the Fed greatly affects those rates.

Despite the Fed's ability to influence short-term interest rates, it has only indirect impact on long-term interest rates, including consumer rates such as those for mortgages and student loans. Long-term rates are set by the market. If an investor thinks that inflation will increase from 3 percent to 6 percent over the next five years, he or she will demand a higher interest rate for lending money to the government or a corporation than if the investor thinks inflation will hold steady at about 3 percent.

The last tool the Fed uses to meet its monetary targets is **open market operations**—the buying and selling of securities. This is the most important tool because it influences the FFR and the level of bank reserves—and thus the money supply. If the Fed wants to increase the money supply and put downward pressure on the FFR, it will purchase securities such as government bonds from a bank. The bank gives the Fed its bonds, and the Fed deposits the appropriate amount of money into the bank's account at the Fed. The bank can use this money to support new loans. Open market operations may also serve to contract the money supply or raise interest rates; if this is the desired outcome, the Fed will sell government securities. The member bank will give the Fed money to cover the cost of the bond and therefore take money out of circulation.

One example of when new money was desperately needed in the economy was the "credit crunch" that emerged with the meltdown of the subprime mortgage market and related problems in the bond markets in 2008. Fed chair Ben Bernanke responded by "flooding the street with money," as the famous banker Benjamin Strong had advocated as the appropriate response to the Great Depression.[29] The Fed increased its assets from $927 billion on September 10, 2008, to an eye-popping $2.26 trillion by November 11, 2008. About $1.6 trillion of the money injected into the economy came through efforts to stabilize short-term lending, money market funds, and the bailout of American International Group (AIG), one of the world's largest insurance corporations (among other things). By October 2012, those loans had been almost entirely repaid as credit markets stabilized. However, overall Fed assets remained at $2.26 trillion, as the securities held by the Fed climbed from $514 billion to $2 trillion from February 2009 to September 2010 (including $1.1 trillion in mortgage-backed securities that the Fed

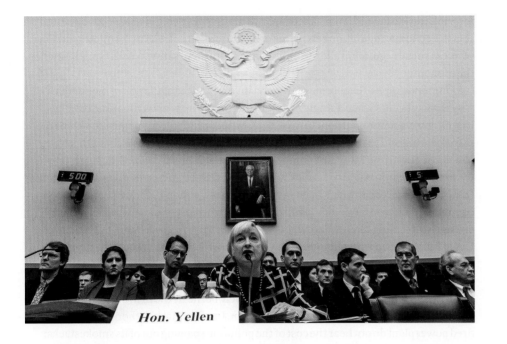

U.S. Federal Reserve chair Janet Yellen gives her first testimony to Congress during a House Financial Services Committee hearing on February 11, 2014, a week after she became the first woman to lead the Fed.
@FederalReserve

purchased from stressed financial institutions).[30] Early in 2013, the Fed continued to expand its injection of money into the economy by purchasing an additional $1.3 trillion in securities; as of late 2015, the Fed had $4.5 trillion in assets (about $2.4 trillion in government securities and $1.7 trillion in mortgage-backed securities), and the Fed's assets have held steady at that level since then.[31] This unprecedented intervention in the financial sector prevented a serious crisis, but critics argue that the Fed has become a too powerful, unaccountable player in economic policy making.

One crucial characteristic of the Fed is its political independence: its decisions are not subject to presidential or congressional review. A strong indication of the Fed's independence is that presidents typically reappoint chairs who were initially appointed by presidents of the other party.[32] Most recently, Ben Bernanke was nominated by Bush and renominated by Obama. But the Fed is not immune to political influence. In fact, one line of research argues that the Fed tries to help presidents during reelection years by encouraging a pro-growth economy.[33] Evidence on this point is mixed, but at a minimum, presidents do have the ability to make it clear when they disagree with the Fed's policies. Presidents also have the opportunity to appoint the chair and vice chair of the Fed, but presidents rarely fire them because they do not want to upset the financial markets. Other research has shown that the Fed is at least somewhat sensitive to the preferences of the president and Congress.[34]

The Fed's ultimate accountability is to Congress, because if things really get out of hand—for example, if the Fed were to increase interest rates to 20 percent without good reason—Congress could amend the Federal Reserve Act and remove the Fed's responsibility or autonomy in specific areas. The Fed must report to Congress annually on its activities and to the banking committees of Congress twice a year on its plans for monetary policy. The Fed's annual report is subject to an outside audit. Fed officials also frequently testify before Congress on a range of issues. And Congress and the president may publicly criticize the Fed when they disagree with the Fed's policies.

Regulatory Policy Government regulation has a huge impact on the economy. For example, the federal government regulates the quality of food and water, the safety of workplaces and airspaces, and the integrity of the banking and finance system. In general, regulations address market failures such as monopolies and imperfect

DID YOU KNOW?

The Fed owns

$2.46 trillion

in U.S. Treasury securities, which is slightly more than the U.S. debt that is owned by China and Japan combined.
Source: FederalReserve.gov

information (discussed later). There are two main types of regulation: economic and social. Economic regulation sets prices or conditions on entry of firms into an industry, whereas social regulation addresses issues of quality and safety.[35] Both types influence the economy.

A common type of economic regulation involves price regulation of monopolies. A monopoly occurs when a single firm controls the entire market for a product; thus, it is not subject to competition. In this event, the firm with the monopoly could charge extremely high prices if the government did not regulate it. Concern about this type of behavior led to the Interstate Commerce Act (1887), which created the Interstate Commerce Commission to regulate railroad rates, and the Sherman Antitrust Act (1890), which served to break up Standard Oil in 1910, among other monopolies. More common than a true monopoly are firms that control most of a market rather than all of it and start acting like a monopoly. For example, Microsoft was sued by the Justice Department and 19 states in 1998 for trying to quash its competition in the rapidly growing area of Internet browsers.

The most common market failures that lead to social regulation occur in situations when the costs of a firm's behavior are not entirely borne by the firm but are passed on to other people. The classic example is pollution. In a free market, the owners of a coal-fired power plant do not bear the cost of the pollution spewing out of its smokestacks; instead, the people who live downwind from the plant bear the cost. Therefore, the power plant owners have little incentive to curb pollution unless the government regulates it. Other examples of agencies that set social regulations are those that promote safety, such as the National Highway Traffic Safety Administration, the Consumer Product Safety Commission, and OSHA. Carbon emissions are another good example of a product (carbon) that will be overproduced by the market if there are no regulations.

Regulatory policy also involves interbranch politics between Congress and the bureaucracy. Even when members of Congress agree on a general policy goal—for example, limiting air pollution—they often cannot agree on the precise mechanisms for achieving that goal, so they delegate authority to a regulatory agency. As discussed in Chapter 12, this produces a "principal–agent problem" in which Congress (the principal) cannot be sure that the bureaucracy (the agent) will implement policy according to their legislative goals. Another area in which regulatory policy has generated political heat concerns the debate about the trade-off between regulation and economic growth. Regulations impose costs on the free market, which may limit job growth. However, in recent years new approaches in environmental regulation have attempted to address that concern. Environmentalists have learned that using market principles can work to their advantage, as the example of grazing rights in the West shows (see the Take a Stand feature).

Government regulation affects many aspects of our lives. Regulations may be aimed at producing a cleaner environment (left) or preventing monopolies (Microsoft founder Bill Gates testifies about possible antitrust violations, right).

Grazing Rights and Free Market Environmentalism

📷 Rancher Dell LeFevre and two of his children.

Grazing rights, environmental policy, and control of western lands have been controversial for decades. The issue received attention in the 2016 presidential campaign when Senator Marco Rubio said "the federal government controls far too much land in the western parts of the United States," indicating that he favors transferring some federal lands to the states.[a] The federal government owns more than 600 million acres, including 47 percent of the land in western states, and there are intense disagreements between environmentalists and ranchers, loggers, and miners about how those lands should be used.

There are three basic positions on this issue: pro-business and antiregulation (ranchers, loggers), the pro-environment regulatory approach (conservationists and recreational users), and a middle ground called free market environmentalism that attempts to find free market solutions to protect the environment.

The scenario that you have to consider here is an actual case publicized in a *New York Times* op-ed piece.[b] The case involves a fifth-generation rancher in southern Utah named Dell LeFevre. He is no friend of environmentalism, saying, "We've got easterners who don't know the land telling us what to do with it. I am a bitter old cowboy." His bitterness was deepened back in 1991 when he found two dozen of his cows shot to death. He thinks the deed was done by an environmentalist who was trying to get ranchers to leave a scenic part of the Escalante River canyon. So LeFevre seems to be an unlikely candidate to have sat down with an environmentalist named Bill Hedden to accomplish that very goal of ending ranching in the area. Hedden works for a group called the Grand Canyon Trust (GCT) that, as the *New York Times* article explained, "doesn't use lobbyists or lawsuits (or guns) to drive out ranchers. These environmentalists get land the old-fashioned way. They buy it." The GCT spent about $100,000 to buy and retire the grazing rights from LeFevre for this scenic canyon area. The environmentalists are happy because the vegetation is coming back, and LeFevre is happy because he doesn't have to battle the environmentalists anymore and was able to buy grazing rights in a different area that is better for his cattle. Supporters of "free market environmentalism" say this is a perfect example of allowing the market to determine the best use of the land.

The pro-business approach.
If the story ended here, there would be no controversy. But local groups, such as the Canyon Country Rural Alliance, which opposed all limitations on ranchers' grazing rights, lobbied Congress and the Interior Department to disallow such arrangements that remove grazing rights from some public lands. Bowing to pressure, the Interior Department decided that "only Congress may permanently exclude lands from grazing use," so the GCT had no guarantee that the Bureau of Land Management would not change its mind and allow grazing. The process of resolving this conflict bounced around the Interior Department and the federal courts for nearly 10 years.

The free market environmental compromise.
The GCT went to plan B: they decided to become ranchers. If the Interior Department wouldn't grant permanent conservation use permits on land designated for grazing, they would buy some cattle. The GCT is now one of the largest ranchers on the Colorado Plateau, with 1,000 acres of private land and grazing permits that cover 860,000 acres of federal and state lands, including a large part of the Kaibab National Forest adjacent to the North Rim of the Grand Canyon. They are managing the land in an eco-friendly manner with only 800 head of cattle. Though it may seem odd that an environmental group had to take up ranching to get the policy outcome they wanted, it was a compromise that made all sides of the dispute relatively happy. As one opponent of the GCT put it, "We turned them from environmentalists into cowboys. I guess what they can do is get their cows and start losing money like the rest of us."[c]

take a stand

1. Do you favor the regulatory approach of permanently removing grazing rights from land that an environmental group would buy, the business approach of not having any permanent limits on grazing rights, or the free market environmental approach of allowing the environmental groups to buy land and grazing rights and become ranchers to protect the land?

2. Does the compromise position of the GCT taking up ranching strike you as a reasonable middle ground? Why or why not?

Thus, while political debates over regulatory policy can still be intense, common ground may be found in pursuing market solutions to regulatory problems. In general, the public interest is often served by regulations that protect the environment, ensure the safety of the food supply, and regulate the dumping of hazardous chemicals, whether it is through traditional economic regulations or more recent market approaches. In each instance, *politics* defines how the public interest is served through regulation.

Case study: the 2008–2009 economic crisis

The economic meltdown of 2008–2009 is an excellent example of how policy makers respond to a crisis and how they can influence the direction of the economy.

Background Problems in the subprime, or high-risk, mortgage market, the collapse of housing prices, and the tightening of credit markets had been putting pressure on the economy through the spring and summer of 2008. The first sign of serious trouble came in March, when the New York Federal Reserve loaned $30 billion to JP Morgan Chase to facilitate the buyout of Bear Stearns, the investment bank that was going bankrupt because of its exposure to mortgage-backed securities. Concerns deepened in September, when the federal government took over the Federal National Mortgage Association and the Federal Home Mortgage Corporation because they were about to go under. These two government-sponsored enterprises, nicknamed "Fannie Mae" and "Freddie Mac," fund most of the home loans in the nation. This federal acquisition, involving a commitment of $200 billion to back up Fannie's and Freddie's assets, was "one of the most sweeping government interventions in private financial markets in decades."[36] The takeover calmed the credit markets for a few days, until it became evident that two Wall Street giants, the investment banks Lehman Brothers and Merrill Lynch, were also going under. Lehman Brothers went bankrupt, Merrill Lynch was bought by Bank of America, and the markets panicked.

The next day brought more bad news: the world's largest insurance company, AIG, was also deep in the subprime mess and teetering on the edge of bankruptcy, so the Fed stepped in with an $85 billion loan to save it. Despite these dramatic moves, credit markets seized up and investors started pulling money out of anything remotely related to the financial crisis. A few days later, Washington Mutual, the nation's sixth-largest bank, failed.

Crafting a Financial Rescue Throughout the crisis, which was the worst since the Great Depression, Fed chair Ben Bernanke, Treasury Secretary Henry Paulson, and congressional leaders worked together to restore confidence in financial institutions.[37] After initially rejecting the plan in a stunning rebuke to party leaders and President Bush, Congress passed a $700 billion Troubled Asset Relief Program (TARP) and increased the amount of savings insured by the federal government from $100,000 to $250,000 per account to help restore confidence in regular savings accounts. President Bush signed the Emergency Economic Stabilization Act into law on October 3, 2008.

Despite this significant rescue plan, the crisis spiraled out of control in the following weeks. Stock markets plunged worldwide, with the U.S. stock market shedding 35 percent of its value in the two months after the crisis began. Credit markets remained frozen, and it became clear that an alternative approach was needed. The government's purchase of "toxic debt" posed many technical obstacles, and financial markets had no confidence that the plan would work. The Treasury decided to abandon its plan to buy toxic debt and use all the funds to directly invest in banks. By mid-November, the economic panic had eased, but the situation remained fragile.

📷

During the financial crisis of 2008–2009, the government had to take unprecedented action to avoid an even deeper crisis. Here, then–Senate Majority Leader Harry Reid (D-NV) speaks to reporters. He was joined by other congressional leaders and Ben Bernanke (far right), who was Federal Reserve chairman at the time.

When President Obama took office in 2009, things were still very grim. Stocks finally bottomed in March 2009 (down 56 percent from their October 2007 high), shortly after Treasury Secretary Timothy Geithner announced the administration's Financial Stability Plan. The plan focused on four problems: frozen credit markets, weakened bank capital, a backlog of troubled mortgage assets on bank balance sheets, and falling home prices. Working with the Fed to stabilize the financial markets, the Treasury had largely resolved three of those four problems one year later. Credit markets were operating, and banks were in much better shape, having raised more than $140 billion in capital and $60 billion in unsecured debt. Banks used these funds to repay the Treasury, which as of June 2014 had shown an 18 percent profit to the government. The Treasury expects to eventually recover all of the TARP expenditures (with 99.4 percent recovered to date).[38] The housing market, although not fully recovered, has also stabilized, with sales up and prices steady in most markets. Troubled mortgage assets remained on the balance sheets of many banks, but with their stronger base of capital and the strengthened housing market, these securities were in much better shape.[39]

Despite the broad success of the financial rescue, it remained a political liability. The rescue was widely perceived as a bailout of Wall Street. Many citizens were outraged over corporate salaries and bonuses, the bailout of the auto industry, and the perception that not enough was being done to help average Americans. The economy lost 8.4 million jobs in 2008-2009, millions of Americans were losing their homes, and unemployment remained stuck around 8 percent through 2012. Discontent with the bailout contributed to the crushing defeat for Democrats in the 2010 midterm elections, despite the fact that it was a bipartisan plan passed at the end of the Bush administration. While the financial rescue remains unpopular, it is clear that things would have been much worse without the swift action by Congress, the Treasury, and the Fed. Still, the financial

📷

Protesters at a rally against government bailouts for Wall Street called for the resignation of the chief executive of Goldman Sachs and cancellation of bonuses for all Goldman employees. Huge profits and bonuses on Wall Street in 2009–2010 were very controversial, as the national unemployment rate held at nearly 10 percent.

rescue and the regulation of Wall Street remained pertinent issues in the 2016 elections, as both Bernie Sanders and Donald Trump criticized Hillary Clinton for earning hundreds of thousands of dollars making speeches to Wall Street firms while not releasing the transcripts of those talks. Despite those ties to Wall Street, Clinton vowed much tougher regulation of the financial sector than Trump, while Trump wanted to repeal recent financial reform legislation.

"Why Should I Care?"

Tax and spending policy, monetary policy, regulatory policy, and trade have more effect on your everyday life than anything else the government does. From the taxes you pay, to the interest rate on your student loan, to the quality of the air you breathe and the water you drink, to the cheap consumer goods that you are able to buy, decisions by policy makers, the president, Congress, and the Fed have a tremendous effect on your economic world.

★

EXPLAIN WHAT WE MEAN BY SOCIAL POLICY, DISCUSS HOW THE NATIONAL GOVERNMENT'S ROLE IN SOCIAL POLICY HAS EVOLVED, AND ANALYZE THE CURRENT MAJOR AREAS OF SOCIAL POLICY

social policy
An area of public policy related to maintaining or enhancing the well-being of individuals.

welfare
Financial or other assistance provided to individuals by the government, usually based on need.

99

The test of our progress is not whether we add more to the abundance of those who have much; it is whether we provide enough for those who have too little.

—President Franklin D. Roosevelt

Social policy

Social policy is generally defined in terms of the "social safety net," or **welfare**, which the *American Heritage Dictionary* defines as "receiving regular assistance from the government or a private agency because of need." A broader conception includes government programs aimed at achieving a general social goal, such as support for public education, the income tax deduction for interest paid on home mortgages (to encourage home ownership), or job creation and growth. This section addresses both conceptions of social policies and also discusses how some traditional social welfare programs such as Social Security are not based on need.

History and context of social policy

This section outlines the evolution of social policy in the United States and describes the various types of social policy. It is also important to understand the need for social policy by examining the nature of poverty in the United States.

Historical Overview Early in our nation's history, the federal government took little responsibility for social welfare. Private charities, churches, and families largely took responsibility for the poor and disadvantaged. The first significant social policy appeared in the nineteenth century in the form of federal financial support for Civil War veterans and their families. Between 1880 and 1910, the national government spent more than a quarter of its budget on Civil War pensions and support for veterans' widows.[40] During the recession of the mid-1890s, populist and progressive reformers sought a national system of unemployment compensation, but the desire for such extensive policies was several decades ahead of its time (see Nuts & Bolts 14.2).

Not until the 1930s and Franklin Delano Roosevelt's presidency did the government undertake broad-scale social policies. The stock market crash in 1929 and the ensuing Great Depression created a desperate economic situation for millions of Americans. An immediate concern was to alleviate the suffering caused by unemployment, but FDR

Types of Social Policy

NUTS
& BOLTS
14.2

1. **Contributory** (or social insurance) programs include Social Security, Medicare, disability insurance, and unemployment compensation.
   - similar to insurance programs in that people pay a specified amount of money to cover some future benefit (either expected, as with the programs related to retirement, or unexpected, as with disability and unemployment)
   - not means-tested; that is, all people may participate in the program regardless of their income
2. **Noncontributory** (or public-assistance) programs include Medicaid, food stamps, housing assistance, welfare, and school lunches
   - recipients are not expected to pay for the programs, which are means-tested, meaning that they are aimed at helping poor people

The ACA ("Obamacare") has elements of both contributory and noncontributory programs. People who are required to buy health insurance are "contributing" to their own insurance. However, those who cannot afford to pay for their insurance receive government subsidies (and thus are participating in a noncontributory program).

also wanted to implement a broader "preventative social policy."[41] Thus, his **New Deal** policies, enacted between 1933 and 1935, included:

- the Agricultural Adjustment Administration, which provided farmers with much-needed assistance;
- the National Recovery Administration and Public Works Administration, which reinvigorated the business sector;
- the Federal Emergency Relief Administration, which provided $500 million in emergency aid for the poor (about $7 billion in today's dollars);
- jobs programs such as the Civil Works Administration and Civilian Conservation Corps, which put more than 2 million people to work, and later the Works Progress Administration, a broader program that employed at least one-third of the nation's unemployed;
- Social Security, which included the familiar retirement policy and supported the states for spending on unemployment compensation, disability programs, and support for dependent children of single mothers—the precursor of the central welfare program;
- the National Labor Relations Act, which guaranteed the right to organize a union and set regulations for collective bargaining between management and labor.[42]

With these policies, the role of the federal government in social policy was forever changed. Although some aspects of the New Deal, such as the jobs programs, were never repeated on a similarly broad scale, most of its other programs became the cornerstone of social policy for subsequent generations.

The next major expansion of social policy occurred during the **Great Society** of President Lyndon Johnson in the mid-1960s. We discussed part of this social agenda in Chapter 5: the civil rights movement, which culminated with the passage of the Civil Rights Act in 1964 and the VRA in 1965. The other important aspect of Johnson's Great Society included the War on Poverty and programs concerning health, education, and housing. Perhaps most significant was the creation of Medicare, the national program that funds medical care for the elderly, and Medicaid, which funds health care for the poor.[43] By the late 1960s, the mounting costs of the Vietnam War created a trade-off:

Before the New Deal programs in the 1930s, poverty relief was provided mainly by private charities. Here, future first lady Eleanor Roosevelt serves meals to unemployed women and their children in a New York restaurant.

New Deal
The set of policies proposed by President Franklin Roosevelt and enacted by Congress between 1933 and 1935 to promote economic recovery and social welfare during the Great Depression.

Great Society
The wide-ranging social agenda promoted by President Lyndon Johnson in the mid-1960s that aimed to improve Americans' quality of life through governmental social programs.

ownership society
The term used to describe the social-policy vision of President George W. Bush, in which citizens take responsibility for their own social welfare and the free market plays a greater role in social policy.

> Working for a just distribution of the fruits of the earth and human labor is not mere philanthropy. It is a moral obligation. For Christians, the responsibility is even greater: it is a commandment.
>
> —Pope Francis

> There's class warfare, all right, but it's my class, the rich class, that's making war, and we're winning.
>
> —Warren Buffett, America's third wealthiest person

it wasn't possible to continue funding ambitious social programs and the war without causing inflation. Over the following decades, conservative backlash against the "welfare state," especially during the Reagan years (1981–1989), led to cuts in spending on social programs.

President George W. Bush continued this general direction for social policy, maintaining most programs with some cuts and one major expansion—the addition of a prescription benefit to Medicare. As a "compassionate conservative," Bush attempted to place his stamp on American social policy with the idea of an **ownership society**, in which people take more responsibility for their own social welfare. He proposed privatizing part of Social Security and creating private savings accounts to cover more out-of-pocket medical expenses, in combination with more free market forces and a bigger role for private and religious charity. President Obama favored an approach that emphasized the market and community, while preserving an important role for government.

Poverty and Income Inequality Today The persistence of poverty remains the primary motivator for most social policy today. In 2015, the poverty line for a family of four was an annual income of $24,257; for a single person it was $12,082.[44] In 2015, official estimates determined that 43.1 million Americans were living in poverty—13.5 percent of the population. Even the social programs that do not directly help the poor and disadvantaged, such as Social Security and Medicare, impact poverty. The percentage of the elderly population living in poverty plummeted from more than 35 percent in 1959 to 7.5 percent in 2015.[45]

Another source of concern is the growing income and wealth inequality in the United States. In the economic recovery from 2009 to 2014, 58 percent of the net income gains went to the top 1 percent of the income distribution, and from 1993 to 2014, 55 percent of the gains went to the top 1 percent. These trends have produced a growing concentration of income at the top. In 2014, the top 10 percent of households—those earning more than $121,400 a year—earned half of the income, which is the highest proportion since 1917; and in 2012, the top 1 percent, those earning more than $423,000, earned 22 percent of the nation's income.[46] The wealth gap is even greater: the median (half are above this level and half are below) net worth of U.S. households in 2013 was $177,900, but the median wealth for the top 10 percent was $1.87 million and this group held 75.3 percent of the nation's wealth.

Despite these patterns of inequality, people who earn more than $100,000 receive more benefits from the federal government ($5,690 on average) than people who earn less than $10,000 ($5,560). How can that be? Consider, for example, that 82 percent of the tax savings from deducting mortgage interest goes to people who make more than $100,000 a year.[47] Other government policies that help the wealthy include patent and copyright law, bankruptcy law, bailouts of the financial sector, immigration policy, enforcement of tax law, and monetary policy.[48] Government programs that help the wealthy also benefit corporations. These policies, often called corporate welfare, include programs such as crop subsidies to large corporate farmers and tax deductions for oil companies to encourage exploration and drilling.[49] Clearly, there is much more to welfare policies than programs for the poor.

Politicians' differing reactions to the types of statistics presented here remind us that politics is conflictual. Republicans argue that the best way to address poverty is to create jobs and have a healthy economy through supply-side tax cuts that promote the creation of capital, investment, and jobs. Democrats argue that making the wealthy pay a larger share of their income in taxes could fund programs to help the poor directly rather than waiting for the trickle-down effect of tax cuts for the wealthy. From this perspective, a trade-off exists between inequality and reducing poverty, and progressive taxes are needed to help the poor.

Social policy today

In the 2017 fiscal year, Social Security, Medicare, and Medicaid constitute nearly half of all federal spending ($1.9 trillion out of $4.1 trillion). With an aging population and health care costs that are rising as a percentage of the economy, these policies will continue to take an even greater share of the budget. Here we explain the nature of these important programs and discuss recent efforts to reform them.

Social Security Social Security is the most popular social program in the United States. Consequently, it has developed a reputation as the third rail of politics (like the dangerous, power-conducting rail on electrified train tracks) because a politician who dares to touch Social Security risks political death. Despite serious problems concerning its long-term solvency, Social Security has proven remarkably immune to any steps that could be taken to shore up its financial health, such as cutting benefits or raising the Social Security tax.

One reason that Social Security is so popular is its universal quality—that is, nearly every working American participates in the program, from Donald Trump to the teenager flipping burgers at McDonald's. Once people reach a certain age, they are all entitled to Social Security checks without regard to how much income they have from other sources, such as dividends, interest, or other pensions. Thus, Social Security does not pit citizens from different classes or ethnic groups against one another. The program is also popular because it works. Fewer than 10 percent of the nation's elderly are in poverty today. Census data show that nearly half of the elderly (44 percent) would be in poverty today without their Social Security payments.[50] (See Nuts & Bolts 14.3.)

Despite its successes and overall popularity, Social Security faces long-term problems. The source of the problem is that there are basic changes in the nation's demographic profile. The **baby-boom generation** (people born between 1946 and 1964) is just starting to retire, and between 2000 and 2030 the number of Americans over age 65 will more than double, while the number under 65 will grow by only 18 percent.[51] When this happens, there will be fewer workers to support the retirees.[52] (See Figure 14.5 for evidence of the aging population.) "Wait a minute," you may be saying. "Why

baby-boom generation
Americans born between 1946 and 1964, who will be retiring in large numbers over the next 20 years.

NUTS
& BOLTS
14.3

Social Security

Number of Recipients for Old-Age, Survivors, and Disability Insurance

Old-Age Insurance (the basic retirement program)	43,658,000
Survivors Insurance (retirement program for widows, widowers, and the children of deceased primary wage earners)	6,084,000
Disability Insurance (payments for people and their families who cannot work because of a disability and are not yet retired)	10,780,000

Monthly Retirement Benefits

Individual	Average: $1,336	Maximum: $2,663
Couple	Average: $2,233	Maximum: $4,660 (if one spouse does not work and the other earns the maximum)

Source: Figures on the number of recipients are from the U.S. Social Security Administration Office of Policy, "Monthly Statistical Snapshot, May, 2016," available at www.ssa.gov; figures on monthly benefits are from www.ssa.gov (accessed 7/19/16).

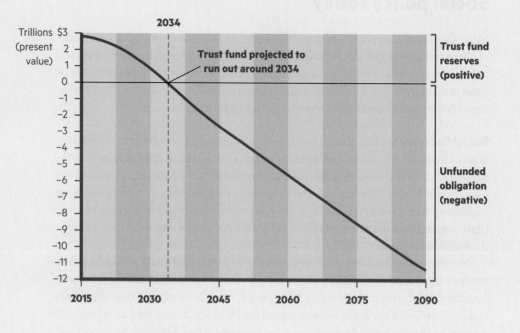

FIGURE 14.5

Social Security Trust Fund

As of 2015, the cost of the Social Security program exceeds Social Security payroll taxes, so taxes will need to be raised to cover the trust fund's obligations and the program's ongoing expenses. What do you think are the best solutions to address the long-term future of Social Security? What are the politically viable solutions?

Source: Social Security Administration, *2016 OASDI Trustees Report*, Figure II D6, p. 8 www.ssa.gov (accessed 7/18/16).

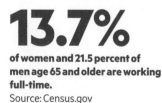

DID YOU KNOW?

13.7%

of women and 21.5 percent of men age 65 and older are working full-time.
Source: Census.gov

does it matter how many workers there are for each retiree? I thought that Social Security was a pension program that you pay into while you're working and then get the benefits when you retire." Not exactly. Social Security is a "pay as you go" system under which today's workers support today's retirees through the payroll tax discussed earlier. Therefore, the huge increase in the number of retirees will strain the system because each worker will have to pay higher taxes to maintain the same level of Social Security benefits for retirees.

Before we examine the various proposals to change Social Security, it is important to explain how the program works. Social Security is funded by a payroll tax of 6.2 percent on income up to $118,500 (in 2016) with an equal 6.2 percent that is paid by employers. Faced with its first real crisis in the early 1980s, as benefits had increased faster than payroll taxes throughout the 1970s, several changes were made to Social Security in 1983 to strengthen its long-term finances. One significant change was a gradual increase in the retirement age from 65 to 67. People born in 1937 or earlier could retire in 2002 at age 65 and receive full benefits. Between 2003 and 2027 the retirement age increases gradually to 67 for full benefits. Early retirement at 62 is an option, if the retiree is willing to accept a permanently reduced benefit level. Delaying retirement until age 70 permanently increases the retiree's Social Security benefits.

In addition to increasing the retirement age, the 1983 reforms increased payroll taxes to generate a surplus for a trust fund to take care of the additional burden of the boomers' retirement.

The trust fund is a source of great confusion and controversy. The idea behind the trust fund was sound: build up a surplus while the boomers are working, and use that money to pay for their retirement. The problem is that the money wasn't really saved but went for general government spending (for example, the war in Afghanistan, food stamps, school loans, and funding the FBI) and in turn the government gave the Social Security trust fund an IOU in the form of "special public-debt obligation." This means that the government will pay off these IOUs, but the only way it can do so is by increasing taxes, cutting spending in other areas, or borrowing even more. The trust fund is expected to run out in 2034, at which point the Social Security system will be able to fund only about 75 percent of its obligations.[53]

So what is to be done? Dozens of plans have been suggested. There is a surprising amount of agreement that saving Social Security requires a mixture of benefit cuts and tax increases. The calculations get very complicated in terms of the projected fiscal impact of various reforms, but a mixture of these options would take care of the long-term fiscal problems of Social Security[54]:

- Raise payroll taxes by 1 percent and increase the income ceiling that is taxable.
- Lower benefits for nonworking spouses. Currently, nonworking spouses receive 50 percent of the benefit of their working spouse. Some proposals would cut that benefit to 33 percent.
- Index current and future benefits to inflation instead of wages. Currently benefit increases are linked to national average wage increases. Because inflation does not increase as fast as wages, linking benefit increases to inflation would generate significant savings.
- Gradually raise the retirement age to 70 (by 2030). Changing the retirement age to 70 would save $620 billion by 2040.

More controversial proposals include these:

- Lower benefits for wealthier recipients. The strongest argument in favor of this approach is that wealthy people don't need the measly couple of thousand dollars they will receive each month from Social Security. The main argument against this proposal is that it would end the universal nature of Social Security and possibly turn it into another welfare program.
- Partial or full **privatization** of Social Security. This is the main issue that divides Democrats and Republicans: Democrats favor maintaining the basic structure of Social Security's public social insurance system, and Republicans favor moving part or all of the "pay-as-you-go" system to private accounts. The central argument in favor of private accounts is that over the long term investing in the stock market has historically provided higher returns than the expected returns from Social Security. Advocates argue that if everyone were able to take their 6.2 percent payroll tax and put that in a retirement account they would have a modest nest egg by the time they retired that would almost certainly provide a stream of benefits larger than the Social Security check they would receive under the current system. Democrats point out the problems with this approach—most important, the transition costs. Because the current system is "pay-as-you-go," if we stopped taking payroll taxes and allowed people to put the money into private accounts there wouldn't be any money to pay for today's retirees. These transition costs—having to cover the retirement of all current retirees and everyone else who has paid into the system for a substantial number of years—are estimated to be $7 to 8 *trillion*! A second criticism of these plans is that investing in the stock market is fine as a supplement to Social Security, but everyone needs that dependable check and investing in the stock market is too risky (as the collapse of the stock market in 2008–2009 reminded us).

These issues are not likely to be resolved anytime soon, which illustrates that politics is conflictual. Social Security reform can pit one generation against another or wealthy people against poor people. The stakes in Social Security are extremely high because it is the most popular and visible social program, which makes it all the more difficult to handle.

privatization
The process of transferring the management of a government program (like Social Security) from the public sector to the private sector.

Health Care Health care policy has seemed as difficult to reform as Social Security. Every president since Theodore Roosevelt who attempted comprehensive reform failed until President Obama's success in 2010 with the ACA. In order to understand the law, we have to understand how health care is provided in the United States and what factors it addresses: the nation's aging population, health care costs that are rising faster than inflation, and the more than 28.8 million Americans who have no health insurance.[55] Americans spend more on health care than citizens of any other nation in the world—$3.0 trillion, or 17.5 percent of GDP, compared with 8.9 percent on average for citizens of other developed countries.[56]

The current system combines government spending (Medicare and Medicaid), private insurance, charity (donated care), and out-of-pocket payments. **Medicare**, the federal health care program for retired people, covers most health care costs and about 75 percent of the cost of prescription drugs.

The other government health care program is **Medicaid**, which serves poor people who otherwise would have no health care. Medicaid is administered through the states with substantial funding from the federal government. Although Medicaid is an **entitlement**, states have considerable discretion over the program. Each state (1) establishes its own eligibility standards; (2) determines the type, amount, duration, and scope of services; (3) sets the rate of payment for services; and (4) administers its own program.[57] (See Nuts & Bolts 14.4.)

The variation in state Medicaid coverage means that some states cover virtually all poor people and others cover as few as one-third of those in need. Overall, nearly 68.9 million Americans receive health care through Medicaid at a projected cost of $528 billion.[58] The federal government reimburses the states for 63 percent of the costs ($331 billion in 2015), but this percentage varies by the relative total personal income in the states (that is, poorer states get more of their costs reimbursed than wealthier states).[59] Like Medicare, Medicaid faces growing budgetary pressures in the coming years. An increasing share of Medicaid's costs goes toward long-term nursing home care for the indigent elderly, which continues to grow as the population ages.

Medicare
The federal health care plan created in 1965 that provides coverage for retired Americans for hospital care (Part A), medical care (Part B), and prescription drugs (Part D).

Medicaid
An entitlement program funded by the federal and state governments that provides health care coverage for low-income Americans who would otherwise be unable to afford health care.

entitlement
Any federal government program that provides benefits to Americans who meet requirements specified by law.

NUTS & BOLTS 14.4

Medicare Coverage

Medicare Premiums for 2016

- **Part A (hospital insurance):** Most people do not pay Part A premiums because they or a spouse has 40 or more quarters of Medicare-covered employment.
- **Part B (medical insurance):** $104.90 per month.
- **Part D (prescription drugs):** Varies by plan, $41 average per month in 2016, plus an additional $13 to $73 a month, depending on income level (95 percent will pay $13 or $33).

Medicare Deductible and Co-insurance Amounts for 2016

- **Part A:** Medicare pays all covered costs except a deductible of $1,260 during the first 60 days and co-insurance amounts of up to $315 per day for days 61 through 90 of a hospital stay and $630 per day for up to 60 "lifetime reserve days" that can be used at any time during one's lifetime. No costs beyond 150 days are covered.
- **Part B:** $147 per year and then a 20 percent co-pay after meeting the $147 deductible.
- **Part D:** A maximum of $360 per year and then a 25 percent co-pay for the first $3,310 of drugs. The beneficiary then pays 45 to 58 percent of the next $1,540 of drug costs. After a $4,850 out-of-pocket annual limit is reached, Medicare pays 95 percent of the costs of drugs.

Note: Part C, known as Medicare Advantage, is not included here because it is not used nearly as widely as Part A or Part B and its provisions get quite complicated.

Source: Medicare.gov, "Medicare Costs at a Glance," available at www.medicare.gov (accessed 6/10/16).

The long-term fiscal problems of Medicare and Medicaid are severe. In fact, they dwarf Social Security's problems. The *2016 Medicare Trustees Report* estimates that Social Security's unfunded liabilities through 2090, or the amount of additional money (beyond the current payroll tax) required to fund all the program's commitments, are $14.2 trillion, while Medicare has unfunded liabilities of $32.4 trillion.[60] Even though such projections depend on assumptions about future economic performance, demographic trends, and other uncertain variables, the *relative* difference between the two programs is significant. Medicare's troubles are more than twice as serious as those of Social Security!

Another study estimates that by 2046 federal spending on health care, Social Security, and interest on the debt would reach about 21 percent of GDP. That is, if the size of the federal government stays around its historic average of 20 percent of GDP the two major social-policy programs would constitute nearly all of federal spending that is not interest on the debt by 2046. The choices are clear: either everything else must be cut from the budget (defense, education, transportation), health care costs and Social Security must be reined in, or the size of government will grow. Clearly, the current trends are not sustainable (see Figure 14.6 for a breakdown of spending on health care).

Although comprehensive health care reform had been shot down repeatedly before the passage of the ACA in 2010, several incremental reforms added up to substantial change. In 1996, Congress passed the Health Insurance Portability and Accountability Act, which guaranteed that people could not be denied health care coverage when they switched jobs. Medicaid was expanded in 1997 to provide health care for children in families that make too much to qualify for Medicaid but not enough to buy private insurance for their children (incomes that are no more than double the poverty level). By 2015, more than 8.4 million children were enrolled in the program (and 36.8 million additional children are covered by Medicaid).[61] Under the Bush administration, Congress passed limited tax-free health savings accounts that may be used for paying routine out-of-pocket health care expenses or saving for more substantial, unexpected health care costs. Also, Medicare's prescription drug plan went into effect in 2006. Despite these reforms, however, discontent with the system continued.

President Obama's primary focus when he took office in 2009 was to get the economy going; however, he also campaigned on reforming our health care system—controlling costs, providing as close to universal coverage as possible, and paying for the program without adding to the deficit. His goal of comprehensive coverage was essential. If insurance companies were forced to cover people with preexisting conditions without a mandate that everyone have insurance, people would wait until they were seriously ill to get coverage. Healthy people had to be pooled with sick people to spread the costs of expensive care. This was achieved by requiring businesses with more than 50 employees to provide coverage and individuals not covered by employers to purchase insurance through state-regulated private health insurance exchanges (which were implemented in 2014). Businesses and individuals that did not comply with the mandate would face fines. However, individuals who could not afford insurance would receive federal subsidies on a sliding scale (a formula that provides the biggest subsidies to the poorest people and some support all the way up to four times the federal poverty rate). Other features of the law include incentives to computerize medical records, seen as a way to improve the quality of care by reducing medical mistakes and facilitating medical evaluations and resultant care.

Another goal was that health care had to pay for itself. With a price tag of just under $1 trillion over the first 10 years, paying for the bill was a challenge. However, a combination of higher Medicare taxes, a new investment tax on the wealthy, an excise tax on insurers for expensive health care plans, new fees for drug companies and health

The unfunded liabilities for Medicare are estimated to be about six times as large as the Social Security shortfall. Yet Congress has a very difficult time acting because any solution involves the politically unpopular combination of tax increases and benefit cuts.

FIGURE 14.6

The Health Care Dollar: Where It Came from and Where It Went

Funding for our current health care system comes from a variety of sources and is spent on many types of care. In an effort to slow the increases in health care costs, which areas should receive the most attention?

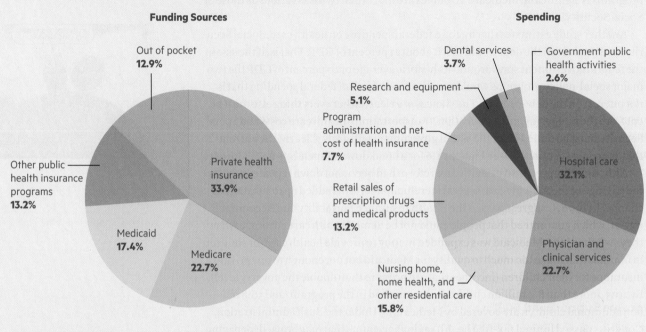

Funding Sources

- Out of pocket 12.9%
- Private health insurance 33.9%
- Other public health insurance programs 13.2%
- Medicaid 17.4%
- Medicare 22.7%

Spending

- Dental services 3.7%
- Government public health activities 2.6%
- Research and equipment 5.1%
- Program administration and net cost of health insurance 7.7%
- Retail sales of prescription drugs and medical products 13.2%
- Hospital care 32.1%
- Physician and clinical services 22.7%
- Nursing home, home health, and other residential care 15.8%

Note: Percentages shown may not add up to 100 percent because of rounding.

Source: Centers for Medicare and Medicaid Services, National Health Expenditures data; spending data from Table 2; funding sources from Table 6, www.cms.gov (accessed 7/19/16).

insurers, and cuts in Medicare reimbursement meant that the law would actually reduce the federal deficit by $143 billion over the first decade.[62]

Yet the battle over health care reform was not over when Obama signed the bill into law. House Republicans repeatedly attempted to repeal the law. While these efforts were not successful—because Democrats still controlled the Senate until 2015 and President Obama would have vetoed any bill of that kind that reached his desk—the rollout of the law was very rocky. The national health care insurance exchange, Healthcare.gov, was supposed to be operational on October 1, 2013, but the system repeatedly crashed during the first several months of operation, leading to substantial delays and great frustration for those Americans attempting to enroll. Millions of poor Americans were not able to get coverage when the states they lived in declined the option to expand Medicaid to cover everyone whose income was 138 percent of the poverty line. Because of the bumpy start, President Obama granted about a dozen extensions of various deadlines, including enrollment deadlines for the individual mandate, the employer mandate to cover all employees for businesses with between 50 and 100 employees (which was extended until 2016), the high-risk pool (which was intended to be temporary), and requiring people who had previously been covered by a substandard insurance policy to get insurance on the exchange (this, too, was extended until the end of 2016).[63] An additional problem is that not as many young healthy people have signed up on the exchanges as predicted. So some insurance companies, such as Aetna and United Health, lost significant amounts of money and are pulling out of many states. This means less competition and rising rates.

President Trump and the Republican leadership in Congress have vowed to "repeal and replace" Obamacare. However, they will face many challenges. More than 22 million more Americans had health insurance early in 2016 because of the law: 13.9 million Americans who previously did not have health insurance have successfully used the exchanges to sign up for insurance, and 6.1 million young adults have been able to remain on their parents' health insurance.[64] Also, 8.8 million new enrollees are covered through the expansion of Medicaid.[65]

But keeping the popular parts and getting rid of the unpopular parts (such as the individual mandate) will be tricky. If the insurance companies must provide coverage for people with preexisting conditions, but people are not required to buy insurance, then people will wait until they have some serious condition before they sign up for insurance, while healthy people will opt out. This means that rates will go up for everyone, making it even more difficult to get coverage. While Republicans agree on repealing Obamacare, no single Republican alternative has universal support within the party. Most Republicans have argued for market-based reforms that would introduce more competition into the system to help keep costs down and health savings accounts that would be tax deductible. But the basic problem has not been resolved of how to maintain coverage for the 22 million people who currently have insurance under Obamacare. Critics say that Medicare is more efficient than private insurance, so such reforms will only drive up the overall cost of health care. However, Medicare is currently not on a sustainable path, so some change is necessary.

Income Support and Welfare Welfare is usually thought of as cash support for people who cannot support themselves. However, **income support** can take many forms, including food stamps, unemployment insurance, Supplemental Security Income (SSI), and the Earned Income Tax Credit (EITC). Moreover, a significant reform of welfare occurred in 1996.

The Supplemental Nutrition Assistance Program (SNAP) provides food stamps, which today are government-issued debit cards that may be used as cash to buy groceries. Anyone whose income is less than 130 percent of the poverty level and whose resources do not exceed specific levels may qualify for food stamps. In 2016, the maximum monthly gross income for a family of four to qualify for food stamps was $2,628. As the effects of the recent economic crisis lingered through 2013, the number of people using food stamps peaked at a record of nearly 47.8 million in June 2013, with an average monthly benefit of $133 per person. As the economy improved, by early 2016 the numbers had dropped to 44.4 million and $126 per person.[66]

The Federal-State Unemployment Compensation Program was established in 1935 as part of the Social Security Act. The U.S. Department of Labor oversees the program, but it is administered by the states. The program provides temporary and partial wage replacement for people who have been laid off and helps to stabilize the economy during recessions. States set a broad range in benefit levels, minimum amount of income earned, and hours worked during the period leading up to unemployment. Also, laid-off workers have to make themselves "available for work." About 97 percent of all workers are covered by unemployment insurance, but only about half of the eligible unemployed make use of the benefit. The regular state programs provide up to 26 weeks of income support, and the Federal-State Extended Benefits Program temporarily provides up to 20 additional weeks in states with relatively high unemployment rates. In the first quarter of 2016, 3.7 million Americans filed claims (with 14.2 million

DID YOU KNOW?

60% of uninsured Americans can get health care coverage for

$100

or less per month, and 87% of those with a marketplace account got some assistance.
Source: ObamacareFacts.com

income support
Government programs that provide support to low-income Americans, such as welfare, food stamps, unemployment compensation, and the EITC.

in the previous 12 months) and the average weekly benefit check was $345, which replaced 33.6 percent of the average worker's previous salary.[67]

The EITC is one of the most successful programs for providing income support for the working poor. Established in 1975, the program aims to help poor people move from welfare to work: it provides tax credits to those who do not earn enough to pay income taxes and are relatively poor. It is intended to offset the burden of Social Security taxes, which all workers pay as part of payroll taxes. In 2016, an individual could qualify for an EITC if she or he had two children and earned less than $44,648, one child and earned less than $39,296, or no children and earned less than $14,880; the figures are about $5,500 higher if the individuals are married and filing jointly.[68] The federal government provided $66.7 billion in EITCs in 2015 to more than 27.5 million recipients, with an average monthly benefit of $200 per recipient.[69]

Welfare is straight cash assistance for people who are not working and do not qualify for unemployment compensation. The primary welfare program for the latter half of the twentieth century was AFDC. This program became increasingly unpopular through the 1980s, and in 1992 Bill Clinton was the first Democratic presidential nominee to campaign against welfare, promising to "end welfare as we know it."[70] President Clinton did not make this the top priority of his first year in office and instead focused on health care reform and balancing the budget. He began addressing welfare reform in 1993 by appointing a task force on the issue. When the Republicans took over Congress in 1994, the momentum for reform grew. Clinton and Congress haggled over the specifics for two years but then agreed on a major reform called **Temporary Assistance for Needy Families (TANF)**.

Temporary Assistance for Needy Families (TANF)
The welfare program that replaced AFDC in 1996, eliminating the entitlement status of welfare, shifting implementation of the policy to the states, and introducing several new restrictions on receiving aid. These changes led to a significant decrease in the number of welfare recipients.

The new law set a five-year lifetime limit on welfare benefits, required single mothers with children above age 5 to find work after two years of receiving benefits, required unmarried mothers who were under age 18 to live with an adult and attend school to get full benefits, denied benefits to drug users who were convicted of a felony, and limited people who were not raising children and were between the ages of 18 and 50 to three months of food stamps in any three-year period in which they were not working. Perhaps most important, welfare lost its status as an entitlement and would be administered by the states with the assistance of federal block grants. In 2006, Congress reauthorized TANF and required that half the recipients in a state's caseload participate in work activities for at least 30 hours per week. (Congress has not reauthorized TANF since 2010 but has extended the program through annual block grants to states.)

Welfare reform significantly reduced the number of people on welfare, as Figure 14.7 shows, but it has been criticized for being too hard on the people who need government assistance the most. When the policy was enacted in 1996, two-thirds of all families in poverty received TANF assistance; in 2014 it was less than one-quarter (23 percent). Critics also point out that TANF block grants have not been adjusted for inflation in most states since they were first created and were worth 20 percent less in 2014 than in 1996.[71]

Education policy

Education policy is largely the domain of state and local governments. For the first century of our nation's history, the national government played virtually no role in education. One important exception was the Morrill Act in 1862, also known as the Land Grant College Act, which gave land to eligible states to establish colleges focusing on practical professions such as agriculture and mechanical arts. More than 75 colleges and universities today are land grant institutions. The next major forays by the federal government into education policy came with the GI Bill of Rights in 1944, which

Participation in Means-Tested Programs

**FIGURE
14.7**

The social-policy "safety net" is supposed to protect poor Americans during periods of economic recession. A deep recession happened in the early 1980s, and the other recession during the time frame depicted here was in the early 1990s. To what extent did the safety net accomplish that for which it was intended?

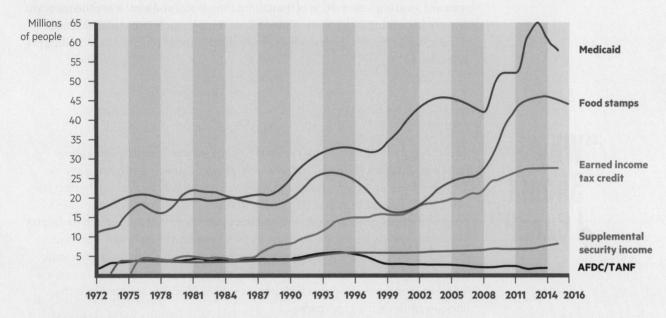

Sources: Data for 1972–2013 from Congressional Research Service, "Temporary Assistance for Needy Families (TANF): Size and Characteristics of the Cash Assistance Caseload," January 29, 2016, p. 7, available at www.fas.org, and from Congressional Budget Office, "Changes in Participation in Means-Tested Programs," February 2013, available at www.cbo.gov (accessed 11/15/16). Most recent data collected by the author from various sources.

provided access to higher education for returning World War II veterans, and the Elementary and Secondary Education Act of 1965, which was part of President Johnson's War on Poverty. The Department of Education was created in 1980, signaling the government's interest in playing an important role in education policy.

A recent debate concerning the national government's role in education policy has focused on standards-based education reform: Should the national government establish standards and impose accountability as a way to improve public schools? The No Child Left Behind Act of 2001 required yearly statewide standardized testing in math and reading. If the test results show that a school is not meeting annual academic benchmarks, it loses some federal funding and its students may transfer to another public school. Critics argue that standardized test results are a poor measurement of progress, as schools "teach to the test" and manipulate other aspects of the evaluation system. Responding to these concerns that one size does not fit all, Congress enacted the Every Student Succeeds Act in 2015. The new law maintains annual testing, but gives states more control over setting student performance targets and school ratings.

President Obama's Race to the Top grant program used a "carrot" rather than a "stick" approach to educational innovation, dedicating $4.35 billion to competitive grants from 2010 to 2013 to encourage schools to adopt more challenging standards and better tools of assessment, promote better leadership and methods for assessing and rewarding excellent teaching, create better data systems for tracking students' progress, and obtain stronger commitments for improving the worst-performing schools.

These grants were aimed at strengthening the quality of public education while improving accountability.[72] The emphasis on accountability was criticized by both the Left and the Right. There was more bipartisan support behind Obama's effort to expand programs to improve access to higher education, such as increasing the number of Pell Grant recipients to 9.3 million and in 2016 launching a new online "college scorecard" to provide objective information about college costs and quality.

Even with these efforts at imposing a national approach, there can be variations in state and local implementation of the national law. States and local school districts are also experimenting with policies aimed at introducing more competition for public schools, including public school choice and publicly funded vouchers for attending private schools.

"Why Should I Care?"

Social Security and Medicare may seem like things you don't have to worry about for at least 40 years. However, 7.65 percent of every dollar you earn goes to pay for those programs and, given changes that will almost certainly be made in the next few years, it is important to understand what is at stake. The income inequalities these programs are designed to address have also become a central issue in the past decade. This was especially true in the 2016 presidential campaign as Bernie Sanders thrust the issue onto the national stage and many college students were "feeling the Bern." While Democrats and Republicans alike agree that steps need to be taken to address inequality and the looming shortfalls related to Social Security and Medicare, they obviously differ in their approaches.

Conclusion

The experiences with social-policy reform illustrate the themes of this book. First, health care reform and repeated efforts to repeal the ACA in the House illustrate the conflictual nature of politics.

Similarly, conflict is natural in many economic-policy decisions, and politics is a part of this process. Any economic policy has winners and losers, and elected leaders must be involved in this process if representative democracy is to have any meaning. This is especially true of the budget process because the redistributive implications of taxing and spending are so clear, but even monetary policy is not insulated from politics. This role for politics is guaranteed by our system of checks and balances: Congress, the president, and to some extent the courts all have a hand in shaping economic policy.

It shouldn't be surprising when politics enters the economic-policy debate. Elected leaders should be responsive to what their constituents think about the central questions concerning the direction of the economy. The struggles over economic and social policies—especially in Congress—demonstrate that political process matters. Politicians' decisions have a key impact on policy outcomes, and the timing and politics of the policy-making process drive the results. Finally, politics is everywhere: social and economic policies touch every American, and the struggles over reforming these policies are at the core of contemporary American politics.

STUDY GUIDE

Making public policy

Trace the steps through which problems are addressed by government policies. (Pages 405–413)

Summary

Once an issue is recognized and defined as a problem and when the conditions are right, the issue reaches the congressional agenda. Once a policy is in place, its effectiveness and implementation are evaluated in an ongoing process, although very few programs are ultimately terminated.

Key terms

public policy (p. 405)
policy agenda (p. 406)
fiscal policy (p. 407)
monetary policy (p. 407)
budget making (p. 407)
United States Trade Representative (USTR) (p. 410)
National Economic Council (NEC) (p. 410)

Aid to Families with Dependent Children (AFDC) (p. 411)
Federal Reserve System (p. 411)
Treasury Department (p. 411)

Practice Quiz Questions

1. **What is the policy agenda?**
   a. the set of desired policies political leaders view as priorities
   b. the set of issues political leaders view as priorities
   c. the set of issues that issue groups view as priorities
   d. the set of desired policies that issue groups view as priorities
   e. the set of desired policies that issue groups and political leaders view as priorities

2. **Relative to the private sector, public-sector programs are _____ to evaluate.**
   a. easier
   b. equally easy
   c. harder
   d. equally as hard
   e. not important

3. **States influence policies on _____, but not _____.**
   a. Social Security; education
   b. education; Medicaid
   c. Medicaid; education
   d. Medicaid; Social Security
   e. Medicare; Medicaid

4. **The difference between fiscal policy and monetary policy is that fiscal policy is concerned with _____, while monetary policy is concerned with _____.**
   a. taxing and spending; controlling the money supply and interest rates
   b. controlling the money supply and interest rates; taxing and spending
   c. controlling the money supply and spending; taxing and interest rates
   d. taxing and controlling the money supply; spending and interest rates
   e. taxing and interest rates; spending and controlling the money supply

5. **The Treasury generally prefers _____ interest rates; the Federal Reserve Board generally prefers _____.**
   a. higher; lower
   b. higher; higher
   c. lower; lower
   d. lower; higher
   e. stable; lower

Economic policy

Explain the main purposes of government involvement in the economy and how fiscal, monetary, and regulatory policies influence the economy. (Pages 414–428)

Summary

Policy makers' pursuit of economic goals—such as full employment, stable prices, or growth—is a complex process. Policy makers have a variety of tools at their disposal to help push the economy in their desired direction. The government utilizes fiscal policy, monetary policy, and regulation to influence the country's economic performance, but the pursuit of one goal often comes at the expense of other economic goals.

Key terms

full employment (p. 414)

economic depression (p. 414)

Council of Economic Advisers (CEA) (p. 414)

inflation (p. 414)

deflation (p. 414)

gross domestic product (GDP) (p. 415)

balanced budget (p. 416)

budget deficits (p. 416)

Keynesian economics (p. 416)

supply-side economics (p. 418)

business cycle (p. 418)

mandatory spending (p. 418)

discretionary spending (p. 418)

regressive (p. 419)

progressive (p. 419)

monetarist theory (p. 421)

reserve requirement (p. 422)

discount rate (p. 422)

federal funds rate (FFR) (p. 422)

open market operations (p. 422)

Practice Quiz Questions

6. The CEA was established ____.

   a. by the Employment Act of 1946

   b. by the Balanced Budget Amendment

   c. in Article I of the Constitution

   d. in Article III of the Constitution

   e. by the Federal Reserve Board

7. Keynesian economics argues that the effects of an economic recession can be reduced by ____.

   a. decreasing government spending

   b. increasing government spending

   c. increasing income taxes

   d. reducing the budget deficit

   e. discouraging consumer spending

8. Reducing the federal deficit by cutting spending is difficult because ____.

   a. the interest rates are too high

   b. the majority of the budget is mandatory spending

   c. the majority of the budget is discretionary spending

   d. members of Congress put too much pork in budgetary bills

   e. large deficits benefit the economy in the long run

9. Regressive taxes, like the payroll tax, mean that compared with the wealthy, poor people spend ____ of their income on taxes.

   a. slightly less

   b. an equal amount

   c. more

   d. considerably less

   e. none

10. The "reserve requirement" refers to ____.

   a. the interest rates the Fed charges to member banks

   b. the rate member banks charge one another on overnight loans

   c. the minimum activity level of the Fed's open market operations

   d. the lowest price for government bonds

   e. the minimum level of money banks must always have on hand

Social policy

Explain what we mean by social policy, discuss how the national government's role in social policy has evolved, and analyze the current major areas of social policy. (Pages 428–440)

Summary

"Social policy" is the catchall term for government programs that are designed to achieve a general social goal. While the early federal government took little responsibility for social welfare, it currently plays a significant role in ensuring the welfare of its people. The most important social programs currently center on the issues of poverty, an aging population, and health care. Unfortunately, the political realities of the system make reforms difficult.

Key terms

social policy (p. 428)

welfare (p. 428)

New Deal (p. 429)

Great Society (p. 429)

ownership society (p. 430)

baby-boom generation (p. 431)

privatization (p. 433)

Medicare (p. 434)

Medicaid (p. 434)

entitlement (p. 434)

income support (p. 437)

Temporary Assistance for Needy Families (TANF) (p. 438)

Practice Quiz Questions

11. Social Security was established under the ____ program; Medicare was established under the ____ program.

   a. New Deal; Great Society

   b. New Deal; New Deal

   c. Great Society; Great Society

   d. Great Society; New Deal

12. The principle of the "ownership society" is that ____.

   a. the government has responsibility for the people's social welfare

   b. the government has responsibility for the poor's social welfare

   c. the government has responsibility for health care but not education

   d. the rich have responsibility for the poor's social welfare

   e. people have responsibility for their own welfare

13. **The primary motivator for social policy is _____.**
    a. inter-generational equality
    b. poverty
    c. the deficit
    d. care for the elderly
    e. gender inequality

14. **The primary reason Social Security will be financially strained in the coming years is because _____.**
    a. it is a pay-as-you-go program
    b. its stipends are indexed to inflation
    c. it is transitioning to privately held accounts
    d. compensation to nonworking spouses is equal to benefits for the working spouses
    e. most Americans don't approve of Social Security

15. **In President Obama's health care plan, why was it essential to guarantee comprehensive coverage?**
    a. to make sure enough people were paying into the system
    b. to pool risk between sick and healthy people
    c. to reduce the risks of fraud
    d. to prevent individuals from having only one price to pay
    e. to win broad political support

Suggested Reading

Altman, Nancy J. *The Battle for Social Security: From FDR's Vision to Bush's Gamble*. New York: Wiley, 2005.

Bartels, Larry M. *Unequal Democracy: The Political Economy of the New Gilded Age*. Princeton, NJ: Princeton University Press, 2008.

Friedman, Milton. *Capitalism and Freedom*, 40th anniversary ed. Chicago: University of Chicago Press, 2002.

Friedman, Thomas L. *The World Is Flat: A Brief History of the Twenty-First Century*. New York: Farrar, Straus and Giroux, 2005.

Keynes, John Maynard. *The General Theory of Employment, Interest and Money*. 1936. Reprint, New York: Macmillan, 2007.

King, Ronald F. *Budgeting Entitlements: The Politics of Food Stamps*. Washington, DC: Georgetown University Press, 2000.

Krugman, Paul. *The Great Unraveling: Losing Our Way in the New Century*. New York: W. W. Norton, 2003.

Lewis, Michael. *The Big Short: Inside the Doomsday Machine*. New York: W. W. Norton, 2010.

Oberlander, Jonathan. *The Political Life of Medicare*. Chicago: University of Chicago Press, 2003.

Phillips, Kevin. *Bad Money: Reckless Finance, Failed Politics, and the Global Crisis of American Capitalism*. New York: Viking, 2008.

Piketty, Thomas. *Capital in the Twenty-First Century*. Cambridge, MA: Belknap Press, 2014.

Skocpol, Theda. *Social Policy in the United States: Future Possibilities in Historical Perspective*. Princeton, NJ: Princeton University Press, 1995.

Soros, George. *The New Paradigm for Financial Markets: The Credit Crash of 2008 and What It Means*. New York: PublicAffairs Books, 2008.

Soss, Joe. *Unwanted Claims: The Politics of Participation in the U.S. Welfare System*. Ann Arbor: University of Michigan Press, 2000.

Stiglitz, Joseph E. *Globalization and Its Discontents*. New York: W. W. Norton, 2003.

Weaver, R. Kent. *Ending Welfare as We Know It*. Washington, DC: Brookings Institution Press, 2000.

15
Foreign Policy
What is America's role in the world?

Many Americans expect foreign policy to be an area of consensus—that we all hold similar ideas of what our country should be doing outside our borders. As a result many Americans agree with Senator Arthur Vandenberg, who said in 1945, "Politics stops at the water's edge." Americans tend to see disagreement over foreign policy as somehow unpatriotic. One of the central goals of this chapter is to demonstrate that simple answers are rare in foreign policy and that conflict over the means and ends of American foreign policy reflects sincere differences of opinion among elected officials and the public.

The debate over what to do about the terrorist group ISIL (Islamic State of Iraq and the Levant) is a good example. ISIL, an offshoot of the Al Qaeda group that attacked the United States on September 11, 2001, is fighting a bloody conflict with the Syrian, Iraqi, and Libyan governments, with the goal of establishing an Islamic state throughout the Middle East. They have attacked civilians, destroyed civilian neighborhoods and infrastructure, established Sharia law in the areas they control, beheaded Western journalists and aid workers—and released videos of the executions. Millions of refugees have fled the conflict, creating a huge problem for many European nations. Many Western states, along with America's allies in the Middle East, worry that ISIL might launch terrorist attacks throughout the world and move to overthrow other Middle Eastern states, including oil-rich Saudi Arabia and America's ally Israel.

To some elected officials in Washington, D.C., these factors add up to a compelling case for U.S. intervention—that America must take steps by itself or with allies to destroy ISIL, using air strikes or even putting "boots on the ground." During the 2016 presidential campaign, for example, Donald Trump promised a more aggressive military effort against ISIL, combined with increased cooperation with Russia and the Syrian dictator Bashar al-Assad. Although polls show some support for intervention (particularly if ground forces are not involved), some opponents argue that the United States has no responsibility to bear the cost of dealing with these conflicts, while others question whether intervention would have much chance of succeeding. Just as ISIL emerged after Al Qaeda was devastated by a series of U.S.-led attacks, another group might form after ISIL's destruction. And there is no assurance

★

CHAPTER GOALS

Describe the major approaches to understanding foreign policy and trace how America's role in the world has evolved.
pages 446–453

Explain how the various branches of government shape foreign policy.
pages 454–461

Examine the ways American foreign policy is implemented.
pages 462–466

Analyze several major areas of foreign policy and why they are often controversial.
pages 466–472

📷

Foreign policy is full of controversial questions. For example, should America provide air strikes against militant groups such as ISIL (pictured here)? Should America's ground forces be deployed against these groups? Debate over these issues intensified during the 2016 election as Republican Donald Trump's campaign emphasized criticisms of the Obama administration's foreign policy.

that intervention in the Syrian civil war (whether in concert with Russia or not) would lead to a peaceful, democratic Syria.

This example demonstrates that we should expect disagreement over America's foreign policy. And we should not be surprised when these disagreements occur in government, even between civilians and military personnel. Though we will return to the case of ISIL and the Syrian civil war throughout the chapter, we could just as easily focus on the debate over how to deal with the Zika virus to illustrate the causes and consequences of these conflicts.

This chapter will show how other areas of foreign policy are beset with conflict—and how making and executing policy often require actors to compromise on their differences. Our discussion will also highlight how America's foreign and domestic policies are increasingly intertwined. Consider the state of America's economy. Over the last generation, American politicians have approved numerous treaties that reduced tariffs on imports and exports, thereby generating enormous profits for some American companies. However, trade liberalization has hurt companies that could not respond to increased foreign competition, such as the financially troubled American auto producers that have required substantial federal aid just to stay in business. Many of their workers have been laid off or have taken buyouts to quit their jobs or retire early rather than face an uncertain future of layoffs and wage cuts.

Examples of national unity in foreign policy are actually quite rare. Even after the September 11 attacks, the initial surge of unity and common purpose dissolved into debate over the specifics of America's response—from the initial decisions to invade Afghanistan and Iraq to contemporary debates over how best to fight the ongoing threat of terrorist attacks. This conflict is nothing new. Throughout American history, there have been many disagreements over foreign policy issues, from whether and how to use military force or form alliances to questions about foreign trade agreements and human rights policies. Although these debates often have political consequences, with positions sometimes taken for political gain, in the main they reflect sincere differences of opinion; in this sense, foreign policy closely resembles domestic policy.

So, who gets to decide America's foreign policy? How is foreign policy made?

★

DESCRIBE THE MAJOR APPROACHES TO UNDERSTANDING FOREIGN POLICY AND TRACE HOW AMERICA'S ROLE IN THE WORLD HAS EVOLVED

foreign policy
Government actions that affect countries, corporations, groups, or individuals outside America's borders.

What is foreign policy?

Foreign policy encompasses government actions involving countries, corporations, groups, and individuals that lie outside America's borders. Foreign policy includes military operations, economic interactions, human rights policies, environmental agreements, foreign aid, democracy assistance, interventions in civil wars and other conflicts, and international efforts to limit weapons of mass destruction (WMDs), including nuclear weapons.

Foreign policy principles and perspectives

Foreign policy actions are often rooted in general principles or rules that guide people in their decision making. These principles and rules capture the decision to act,

Theories of Foreign Policy

Realism	Foreign policy is driven by a state's national interest, as defined by its leaders.
Idealism	Foreign policy reflects the ideals held by a state's leaders, such as protection of human rights.
Internationalism	States should, whenever possible, pursue their foreign policy goals by working together with other nations.
Isolationism	States should, whenever possible, work alone to define and implement their foreign policy, working with other nations only when absolutely necessary.
Constructivism	Foreign policy is not determined by objective factors such as national interest, by ideologies such as idealism, or by admonitions about working alone or with other nations, but by how a state's leaders define these factors.

whether America acts alone or with other nations, and the motivations for actions. (See Nuts & Bolts 15.1 for a summary of these guiding principles.)

Should We Act Alone? Unilateral action occurs when one country does something on its own, without coordinating with other countries. For example, some U.S. antiterrorism operations under both President George W. Bush and President Barack Obama, particularly in Pakistan, have been undertaken without any consultation with or notice to U.S. allies—not even the Pakistanis.[1] This trend will no doubt contnue under President Trump. However, American foreign policy more commonly involves multilateral action by the United States alongside other countries or international organizations such as the UN. For example, after civil strife broke out in Syria in 2011 the United States, in cooperation with the UN and several other nations, has sought to force the Syrian government to negotiate with rebel forces and end the civil war there peacefully. Similarly, the United States and the EU worked together to coordinate aid to African nations to successfully contain the Ebola virus.

Should We Intervene? A second important distinction in foreign policy is between isolationism and internationalism. Isolationists believe that the United States should avoid making alliances and agreements with other nations, concentrate on defending our own borders, and let the people in other countries work out their problems for themselves. In the case of the humanitarian crisis in Syria, an isolationist might argue that U.S. intervention would be futile or potentially counterproductive, too costly, or simply inappropriate—that it is not America's problem to solve.[2] An internationalist, however, would likely argue that the United States should establish many agreements with other nations and intervene in international crises whenever it may be able to help, both because of possible economic and security gains and because intervening in civil wars and helping to solve humanitarian crises is morally right. In the case of ISIL, internationalists would at a minimum support U.S. efforts to help and protect the local population, either in concert with other nations or alone if other nations are unwilling to intervene.[3]

Are We Only Out for Ourselves? The third major distinction in foreign policy making is between realism and idealism.[4] Realists believe that countries pursue their own interests, seeking to increase their economic and military power and their international influence. In approaching a policy decision, a realist would choose the policy that

unilateral action (national)
Independent acts of foreign policy undertaken by a nation without the assistance or coordination of other nations.

multilateral action
Foreign policy carried out by a nation in coordination with other nations or international organizations.

isolationism
The idea that a country should refrain from involvement in international affairs.

internationalism
The idea that a country should be involved in the affairs of other nations, out of both self-interest and moral obligation.

realism
The idea that a country's foreign policy decisions are motivated by self-interest and the goal of gaining more power.

idealism
The idea that a country's foreign policy decisions are based on factors beyond self-interest, including upholding important principles or values.

maximizes U.S. military and economic power relative to that of other states. Idealists, in contrast, believe that states' concerns extend beyond increasing their power, including the promotion of principles such as freedom, liberty, or democracy. For an idealist, upholding these principles should be a primary goal of U.S. foreign policy—for example, idealists generally believe in helping nondemocratic nations transform themselves into democracies with strong court systems (also called **nation building**). **Constructivism** offers an alternative to both positions, arguing that state actions are shaped by how leaders interpret events for their citizens.

These terms are used often in foreign policy debates because they offer convenient ways to summarize the motivations behind policy decisions. That is how we use the terms in this chapter, but in reality none of them provides a fully accurate definition of what motivates nations or individuals. As the quote below from President Barack Obama illustrates, no one is a realist or an idealist all the time. For example, Obama's support for intervention in the Libyan civil war was squarely idealist in its motivation—done with the hope that dissident elements in Libya could unite to build a stable democracy. Conversely, Obama's reluctance to undertake a large-scale operation in Syria is a classic example of realism: while the situation was a human rights catastrophe, it put no fundamental American interests at stake.

nation building
The use of a country's resources, including the military, to help create democratic institutions abroad and prevent violence in other countries.

constructivism
The idea that foreign policy is shaped by how a state's leaders define the national interest, ideology, and other factors.

When the United States acts multilaterally in foreign policy, it often works through organizations such as the UN. Here, President Barack Obama addresses a session of the UN General Assembly. @UN #UnitedNations

You take the victories where you can. You make things a little bit better rather than a little bit worse. And that's in no way a concession to this idea that America is withdrawing or there's not much we can do. It's just a realistic assessment of how the world works.

—President Barack Obama

History of American foreign policy

In this section, we review the evolution of American foreign policy. Our aim is to illustrate the types of choices American politicians face, how these policy options have changed over time, and the lack of agreement among American politicians about how to resolve these issues.

The Founding to World War I Until America's entry into World War I in 1917, American foreign policy was largely isolationist. Isolationism made sense during this period for several reasons: America's distance from Europe reduced the potential for international economic interactions, lowered the level of military threat, and gave early America room to expand without conflicting with European nations.[5] The

Monroe Doctrine, established by President James Monroe in 1823, stated that America would remain neutral in wars involving European nations and that the United States expected these nations to stop trying to colonize or occupy areas in North and South America.[6] During this time, America expanded by purchasing land from other countries (it added much of the Midwest through the Louisiana Purchase) and by annexing land after military conflicts (it acquired a large section of the Southwest from Mexico following the Mexican-American War).

America's foreign policy was never completely isolationist, however, even in the early years. The navy was deployed on many occasions to protect U.S. ships and citizens, and America had colonies far beyond its borders. America also built the Panama Canal, leasing land from Panama in the process, and sent troops into conflicts in Nicaragua and other Central American countries. Moreover, America maintained significant trading relationships with nations in Europe and elsewhere.

Still, America's involvement in World War I (1914–1918) marked a sharp departure in foreign policy, both in the nation's participation in an international alliance and in the president's willingness to continue these activities after the conflict.[7] With the war almost over, President Woodrow Wilson offered a peace plan, the Fourteen Points, which proposed (1) reshaping the borders of European countries in order to mitigate future conflict, (2) taking measures to encourage free trade and democracy, and (3) establishing an international organization that would prevent future conflicts.[8] American diplomats participated in the negotiations that culminated in the Treaty of Versailles, which officially ended the war.[9] The treaty created the League of Nations, an organization similar to the modern UN, but the U.S. Senate rejected the treaty, with the result that the United States never joined the League of Nations.[10]

The Rise of Internationalism A great transition in American foreign policy occurred during World War II (1939–1945). The United States did not become directly involved in the conflict until December 8, 1941, declaring war on Japan the day after Japanese air attacks on Pearl Harbor in Hawaii and American bases in the Philippines. Germany subsequently declared war on the United States on December 11. However, prior to the United States' official involvement, the U.S. military had been supplying Great Britain and its allies with arms, ships, and other supplies in return for payments and long-term leases on British military bases throughout the world. (All these actions had narrowly escaped a congressional veto—yet another illustration that making foreign policy is conflictual.)

During World War II, the Allied Powers—the United States, Great Britain, the Soviet Union, and other countries—fought as a formal alliance, making joint plans and sharing military hardware and intelligence. After World War II, however, American politicians and scholars felt that the United States should be a central actor in world affairs. This new policy was justified on the basis of realist arguments, such as the need to deter future conflicts and the desire for economic benefits through trade with other nations.[11] Yet idealists argued for the same policies on the grounds that America had a moral obligation to preserve world peace.[12] However, the nation's shift toward internationalism only increased the amount of conflict in American foreign policy, as actors disagreed on where the United States should get involved; what the goals should be; whether intervention should involve military force, foreign aid, diplomacy, or some other policy tool; and whether the United States should act alone or in concert with other nations.

The Cold War Soon after World War II ended, the **Cold War** (1945–1991) began as the victorious Allies disagreed over the reconstruction of Germany and the reformation of Eastern European countries that Germany had occupied during the war. In a 1946 speech, former British prime minister Winston Churchill referred to an "iron curtain"

Monroe Doctrine
The American policy, initiated under President James Monroe in 1823, stating that the United States would remain neutral in conflicts between European nations and that these nations should stop colonizing or occupying areas of North and South America.

Cold War
The period of tension and arms competition between the United States and the Soviet Union that lasted from 1945 until 1991.

The Marshall Plan, which helped European nations rebuild their economies after World War II, was part of America's strategy to build alliances against the Soviet Union.

containment
An important feature of American Cold War policy in which the United States used diplomatic, economic, and military strategies in an effort to prevent the Soviet Union from expanding its influence.

mutually assured destruction
The idea that two nations that possess large stores of nuclear weapons—like the United States and the Soviet Union during the Cold War—would both be annihilated in any nuclear exchange, thus making it unlikely that either country would launch a first attack.

that had split Eastern and Western Europe, leaving the East under Soviet domination with few political freedoms.[13] The American diplomat George F. Kennan argued for **containment**—that America should use diplomatic, economic, and military means to prevent the Soviet Union from expanding the set of countries that it controlled or was allied with.[14] This idea served as a guiding principle for American foreign policy over the next generation.[15]

During this period, the United States implemented several measures to build and strengthen alliances against the Soviet threat. The first was the Marshall Plan, a series of aid and development programs enacted in the late 1940s to restore the economies of Western European countries that had been devastated during World War II.[16] In addition, the United States was instrumental in the formation of the World Bank and the IMF, as well as other international trade agreements.

The United States also formed alliances with other countries, including NATO in 1949. The goal of these alliances and organizations was collective security, based on the principle that "an attack against one is an attack against all."[17] The aim was to deter Soviet attacks throughout the world by formalizing America's commitment to defend its allies. Of course, the Soviets formed their own alliances, most notably the Warsaw Pact with nations in Eastern Europe.[18]

On another front the United States was behind the 1945 creation of the UN, an international organization with the goal of preventing wars by facilitating negotiations between combatants and, if necessary, by sending military forces from member states to stop conflicts. Other aspects of the UN's role have included administering relief efforts for refugees, undertaking development efforts, codifying international law, and publicizing and condemning human rights violations.

Clearly, the goal of containment influenced every aspect of American foreign policy after World War II.[19] America maintained large military forces, beginning its first peacetime draft in the 1950s and building up a large store of nuclear weapons. These weapons were intended to deter war with the Soviet Union through the threat of **mutually assured destruction**—the idea that even if the Soviet Union unleashed an all-out nuclear assault on the United States enough American weapons would remain intact to deliver a similarly devastating counterattack. As part of this effort, throughout much of the mid-twentieth century the United States stationed hundreds of thousands of troops in Western Europe and elsewhere to deter the Soviet threat. Yet in 1962, war nearly broke out during the Cuban missile crisis, when the Soviets tried to site nuclear missiles in Cuba—within striking range of the United States. However, the issue was defused by a Soviet withdrawal in the face of an American naval blockade of Cuba and a secret American promise to withdraw similar missiles from Turkey in return.

In the early 1960s, America also became involved in the conflict in Vietnam, believing that North Vietnam's drive to take over South Vietnam was part of the Soviet Union's plan for world domination.[20] A popular theory at the time held that if the United States did not prevent the fall of South Vietnam the next step would be a Soviet-backed conflict in the Philippines, in Australia, or in the territory of some other American ally. However, the conflict between North and South Vietnam was a civil war rather than an international event.[21] Although the North Vietnamese accepted Soviet support, they did not take orders from the Soviets.

Beginning in the early 1970s, President Richard Nixon and his National Security Advisor, Henry Kissinger, began a process of **détente** with the Soviet Union. This involved a series of negotiations and cultural exchanges designed to reduce tensions and promote cooperation.[22] These efforts culminated in the 1972 Strategic Arms Limitation Treaty (SALT I), which limited the growth of U.S. and Soviet missile forces.[23]

At the same time, the Arab nations' embargo prohibiting oil shipments to Western nations after the 1973 Arab-Israeli war was a reminder that containment of the Soviet Union could not be America's only foreign policy priority. Tensions over oil increased again when the Organization of the Petroleum Exporting Countries (OPEC) raised prices in 1979. Both events contributed to a recession in America and the electoral defeats of two incumbent presidents: Gerald Ford in 1976 and Jimmy Carter in 1980.

After the Cold War: Human Rights, Trade, Terrorism, and Other Concerns

In 1991, the Soviet Union splintered into 15 countries, effectively ending the Cold War. The end of this conflict, along with the growing number of democracies worldwide and the development of democratic peace theories (which argue that democracies will not fight other democracies), suggested to some observers that military conflicts would become much rarer, so that other concerns would more strongly influence America's foreign policy.[24] Events early in the post–Cold War era seemed to support this thesis. For example, human rights became a more important foreign policy topic[25] and the United States became involved in humanitarian relief and nation-building efforts in Somalia, Bosnia, and Kosovo. Moreover, a series of agreements, including the North American Free Trade Agreement (NAFTA) in 1994 and the formation of the World Trade Organization (WTO) in 1995, lowered tariffs throughout the world. These developments are consistent with the idea of soft power, that America can have influence over other nations through increased economic interactions and cultural ties rather than the use of military force.[26]

However, new security threats emerged in the form of terrorist groups, most notably Al Qaeda, led by Osama bin Laden. Al Qaeda organized several attacks on Americans, including the bombing of U.S. embassies in Tanzania and Kenya in 1998 and an attack on an American warship in 2000. Then came the attacks of September 11, 2001. Some analysts and politicians, including President George W. Bush, described these attacks as part of a worldwide "clash of civilizations" or a global war on terrorism, pitting the secular, open West against radical Islam.[27] After the attacks, President George W. Bush announced a new U.S. policy, the **Bush Doctrine**, or the doctrine of preemption, whereby the United States would not wait until after an attack to respond but, instead, would use military force to eliminate potential threats before they could be put in motion. This policy change was intended to prevent another September 11 attack, as the quote from Bush's National Security Advisor and Secretary of State Condoleezza Rice illustrates.

In several respects, Barack Obama's presidency represented a sharp reversal of many Bush-era policies. Obama has emphasized improving foreign perceptions of

détente
An approach to foreign policy in which cultural exchanges and negotiations are used to reduce tensions between rival nations, such as between the United States and the Soviet Union during the 1970s.

"

We don't want the smoking gun to be a mushroom cloud.

—Secretary of State Condoleezza Rice

Bush Doctrine
The foreign policy of President George W. Bush, under which the United States would use military force preemptively against threats to its national security.

العربية

خاص بالجزيرة

مسجل

أسامة بن لادن
زعيم تنظيم القاعدة

خبر عاجل

📷

The Al Qaeda terrorist organization headed by Osama bin Laden was the driving force behind many terrorist attacks on Americans, including the 2001 attacks on the World Trade Center and the Pentagon. In 2011 American forces killed bin Laden, but the group, along with newer organizations such as ISIL, remains a significant threat.

America and Americans and avoiding unilateral action in favor of multilateral coalitions. The U.S.-led intervention against ISIL is typical of this new approach. However, many of Obama's policies in regard to the War on Terror, such as his emphasis on drone attacks (see the Take a Stand feature in this chapter), were quite similar to those established by the Bush administration. And in the case of more recent events, such as the Syrian civil war, the ISIL conflict, or Russia's conflict with Ukraine, there are no clear differences between the Obama administration's response and policies that would have been chosen by the Bush administration. Donald Trump promised significant changes in U.S. foreign policy, but the constraints and costs discussed throughout this chapter are likely to limit the changes that actually occur.

"Why Should I Care?"

Maybe you don't care about foreign policy—although as we discuss throughout this chapter, you probably should, as America's security and its economic well-being hinge on its foreign policy choices. Making sense of America's foreign policy (or deciding where you stand on foreign policy questions) requires you to know some history and some basic terminology. History helps you to understand America's place in the world and how different issues came about. Knowing the basic terminology used in foreign affairs helps you to understand what politicians and pundits are talking about when they discuss foreign policy issues.

Should America Carry Out Drone Attacks against Terrorists?

One of the elements of President Barack Obama's strategy to fight terrorist groups was the increased use of drones—small, pilotless aircraft that fly into foreign airspace, monitor the activities of terror suspects on the ground, and launch missiles against these targets. Over the last several years, drone attacks in countries such as Afghanistan, Yemen, and Pakistan have decimated the leadership and infrastructure of terrorist groups and inflicted significant casualties on lower-level fighters. Drones also played a key role in identifying the safe house in Pakistan where Al Qaeda leader Osama bin Laden was located, making possible the attack that resulted in bin Laden's death in 2011. However, the use of drones by American forces continues to be highly controversial inside the United States and throughout the world.

Drones are an effective tool.
Drone attacks allow the United States to combat terrorists throughout the world without putting American troops at risk. Drone attacks are also less expensive than conventional forces. For example, rather than sending a special operations unit across the world to attack a target in the Middle East, American crews working at a base in Nevada can remotely control drones launched from a secure base in Saudi Arabia. Because drones have no crew, they can be small and quiet and stay in the air for long periods of time, making a surprise attack more feasible. Even if an attack is not being planned, drones allow the United States to monitor suspected terrorists and deter future operations.

Describing drones as a tool also highlights their similarity to other examples of military force. How different is it if a terrorist camp is attacked by a drone rather than U.S. ground troops? Any argument against drones (the danger of civilian casualties or that terrorists can publicize the attack as a way of galvanizing public opposition to the U.S. strategy) can be applied just as well to other ways the United States might attack terrorists.

Drones bring risks, and negatively affect decision making.
Some people foresee that the very advantages ascribed to drones—that they are relatively inexpensive and require no human pilots—could likely lead decision makers to use drones more quickly than they might conventional weapons.

The use of drones is controversial. Here, a protester in Yemen holds a sign denouncing the practice.

In a similar vein, there are those who believe that drones remove the personal element from warfare, making it easier to disregard the moral implications of an attack.

Moreover, at least up to now, drone strikes have occurred with little congressional oversight or approval. As we discussed in Chapter 11, Congress has the power to limit military operations—but doing so in the case of drones would be difficult because most of these operations are carried out in secret. How could members stop an operation they didn't know about until after it occurred?

While mistakes are possible in any military operation, drone attacks involve special risks. Because drone operators view their targets through long-range cameras mounted on the drones, the chances of civilian casualties or other collateral damage are probably higher than with Special Forces units who carry out their attacks at short range.

The problem for decision makers is this: prohibiting drone attacks on suspected terrorists does not mean that these individuals and organizations will go scot-free; most of these operations will instead be carried out by American armed forces, with the risk that some of these troops will be wounded, killed, or taken hostage. Should decision makers use drones or send in the troops?

take a stand

1. If you were writing a letter to your member of Congress about the use of drones, what position would you take? What arguments would you use to support your position?

2. If you favor the use of drones, are there situations where we shouldn't use them? If you oppose them, are there situations where drones have advantages over traditional troops?

Foreign policy makers

We begin with the president and the executive branch, and then we consider Congress, the courts, and, finally, other groups and individuals outside the government. Nuts & Bolts 15.2 summarizes the foreign policy powers of the two most important actors, the president and Congress.

The president and the executive branch

The president is the dominant actor in American foreign policy.[28] Working with staff, the president can negotiate treaties or executive agreements with other nations, change policy through executive orders or findings, mobilize public opinion to prompt action by Congress, and shape foreign policy by appointing people to agencies and departments that administer these policies (see Chapter 11). The president also serves as commander in chief of America's armed forces.

Within the Executive Office of the President, the principal foreign policy agency is the **National Security Council (NSC)**, which develops foreign policy options and presents them to the president. The EOP also includes the Office of the United States Trade Representative, which focuses on tariffs and trade disputes; the president's Foreign Intelligence Advisory Board, a group of academics, politicians, and former government officials who advise the president; and the Office of Management and Budget, which prepares the president's annual budget proposals for federal agencies and departments, including those with foreign policy responsibilities.

National Security Council (NSC)
Within the EOP, an agency that advises the president on matters of foreign policy.

The Department of State The principal foreign policy department in the executive branch is the Department of State. Its head, the secretary of state, acts as the official spokesperson for the United States in foreign relations and is an important adviser to the president. Aside from senior staff such as the secretary of state, who is nominated by the president and confirmed by the Senate, State Department personnel are generally career civil servants who remain in their positions even after a new president takes office.

State Department officials operate U.S. embassies abroad and interact extensively with the leaders of other countries; they also offer expertise on the politics, economics, and cultures of other nations. There are many different offices and working groups in the State Department, from people who deal with treaties to coordinators of international aid, arms control, or assistance for refugees.

NUTS & BOLTS 15.2

Foreign Policy Powers of the President and Congress

President	Congress
Commander in chief of armed forces	Can declare war
Nominates and appoints senior officials in Department of Defense	Senate must approve Defense nominees
Negotiates treaties and executive agreements with other nations	Treaties take effect only if approved by Senate
Changes policy with executive orders and findings	Can overturn orders and findings with legislation
Attempts to mobilize public opinion behind foreign policy goals	Makes policy using "power of the purse" (annual budget)

The Department of Defense The Department of Defense carries out military actions as ordered by civilian authorities, ranging from full-scale wars such as those in Iraq and Afghanistan to smaller operations such as the ongoing drone attacks against Al Qaeda and ISIL forces throughout the Middle East or sending ships and aircraft to monitor a North Korean attempt to launch a satellite into orbit.

The military's role in foreign policy is not limited to uses of force. Military personnel also deliver humanitarian aid and help American citizens evacuate from areas of conflict. For example, U.S. Navy ships and helicopters delivered relief aid to Haiti after the 2010 earthquake and wounded Haitians were airlifted to military ships and facilities in the United States for medical treatment. Moreover, the American military advises and trains armed forces in other countries, including hot spots such as Syria, Somalia, and Yemen, and senior military personnel sometimes serve as consultants during foreign policy debates.

The overriding principle of America's military is the concept of **civilian control**—the idea that military personnel do not formulate policy but, rather, implement directives from their civilian leaders in the executive branch (the president and senior leaders in the Defense Department) and Congress. In general, the norm is that disagreements between the civilians and the military are accepted as long as (1) they are kept private and (2) military leaders carry out without hesitation the orders they are ultimately given.

DID YOU KNOW?

In 2015, American military personnel acted as advisers or trainers in

162

countries.
Source: State Department report

civilian control
The idea that military leaders do not formulate military policy but rather implement directives from civilian leaders.

Diplomacy often involves protracted negotiations and many participants. The nuclear deal with Iran was negotiated by the government of Iran and representatives from China, Russia, the European Union, and the United States. @TheIranDeal #IranDeal

The Department of Homeland Security The Department of Homeland Security was formed after the September 11 attacks by combining the Coast Guard, the Transportation Security Administration, the Border Patrol, and several other agencies. The department's responsibilities are to secure America's borders, prevent future terrorist attacks, and coordinate intelligence gathering. On the one hand, Homeland Security's record is exemplary: there has not been a major terrorist attack on American soil since September 11, 2001. On the other, there is concern that many Homeland Security policies (such as requiring extensive screening for all airline passengers) impose large societal costs while having a marginal impact on safety.[29]

Intelligence Agencies Agencies such as the CIA and NSA are primarily responsible for government intelligence gathering. Most of their work consists of gathering information from public or semipublic sources, such as data on industrial outputs. However, these agencies also undertake covert operations to acquire intelligence, use satellites and other technology to monitor communications, or even attack individuals, other nations, or organizations. The Director of National Intelligence in the EOP leads and coordinates the activities of the various intelligence agencies.

Congress

Although the president dominates foreign policy, several groups within Congress participate in making foreign policy and Congress can reverse or thwart any presidential initiatives. The Committee on Foreign Affairs in the House and the Foreign Relations Committee in the Senate are responsible for writing legislation that deals with foreign policy, including setting the annual budget for agencies that carry out those policies. These committees also hold hearings in which they pose questions to foreign policy experts from inside and outside the government.

There is an Intelligence Committee in both the House and the Senate; these committees oversee covert operations and the actions of the CIA, the NSA, and similar agencies. Current law requires the president to give Congress "timely notification" of covert intelligence operations.[30] These arrangements ensure that someone outside the executive branch knows about secret operations and can organize congressional opposition if these actions are deemed illegal, immoral, or unwise.

Congress holds three types of influence over foreign policy. The first is the power of the purse. Since members of Congress write annual budgets for every government department and agency, one way for members to shape foreign policy is to forbid expenditures on activities that members want to prevent.

Second, the Senate has the power to approve treaties and confirm the appointments of senior members of the president's foreign policy team—including the secretaries of state and defense, the Director of National Intelligence, and America's ambassador to the UN. Although it is rare for senators to reject a treaty or a nominee, sometimes they issue preemptive warnings about what kinds of treaties they will accept or, more commonly, never put to a vote any treaties that might be voted down.

Third, the Constitution grants Congress the power to declare war on other nations. However, as we saw in Chapter 10, the Constitution does not say that this declaration must occur before hostilities can begin or whether the declaration is necessary at all. In an attempt to codify war-making powers, in 1973 Congress adopted the War Powers Resolution, although the question of which branch of the government ultimately controls America's armed forces remains controversial.

Of course, members of Congress always have the power to block a president's foreign policy initiatives, but doing so requires enacting a law with enough votes to override a presidential veto (often an impossible task). In the debate over funding for the Iraq War, in 2007 the House and Senate passed a funding resolution that included a withdrawal time line for U.S. troops, but it was approved by a margin of only a few votes in each chamber. After President George W. Bush vetoed the resolution, the two houses passed a new funding resolution without these restrictions. The How It Works graphic illustrates the basic powers of Congress and the president when it comes to military conflict.

The federal courts

The federal courts, including the Supreme Court, weigh in on foreign policy questions through judicial review. This involves determining whether laws, regulations, and presidential actions are consistent with the Constitution. For example, a series of lower-court and Supreme Court decisions forced the Bush administration to revise its policies of holding terror suspects indefinitely without charges; the rulings required that the suspects be charged with crimes and tried on those charges. Although the courts can reverse presidential actions, it is worth noting that these trials occurred only after several cases spent years proceeding through the judicial system. During that time, the administration's policy remained in place.[31] Even at the end of 2016, dozens of suspects remained imprisoned in a federal facility in Guantánamo, Cuba, years after they were initially detained, with no trial date in sight.

Groups outside the federal government

A variety of individuals, groups, and forces outside of government influence foreign policy. These may be interest groups; the media; public opinion; as well as intergovernmental, nongovernmental, and international organizations.

Interest Groups Interest groups are organizations that work to convince elected officials and bureaucrats to implement policy changes in line with the group's goals. A diverse set of groups and organizations lobby government over foreign policy.[32] For example, during the congressional debate in the summer of 2015 over the agreement with Iran regarding its nuclear weapons program, the American-Israel Public Affairs Committee (AIPAC), one of the most powerful interest groups in Washington, led opposition to the deal. President Obama and a coalition of smaller groups (including J Street, another pro-Israel lobbying organization that often opposes AIPAC on issues related to Israel, as well as groups of scientists and the left-leaning organization Moveon.org) lobbied in favor of approval.

Lobbying efforts can even involve foreign governments. In these cases, lobbying efforts center on economic and military aid, trade deals, and more general efforts to improve a country's image among members of Congress and the bureaucracy. In the case of the Iran deal, Israel's ambassador to the United States called many members of Congress to try to persuade them to oppose the deal.

Sometimes interest group lobbying pits business interests against other concerns such as national security. For example, the Chinese government and one of its major technology firms, Huawei, have complained that the U.S. government has prevented Huawei from expanding into U.S. markets, even though its prices are lower than those charged by their U.S. rivals such as Cisco Systems.[33] Cisco and other firms argue that Huawei should be kept out of the United States because they sell equipment to the Chinese military that is used for spying and cyberattacks. While these charges might be true (the evidence is classified, and Huawei might not know what their equipment is used for), it is also the case that U.S. technology firms have lost market share to Huawei in recent years. Raising national security concerns may just be a way to force the federal government to keep Huawei out of the lucrative American market.

Other groups focus on publicizing international events in the hope of prompting citizens to demand government action. For example, in 2015 and 2016 religious groups met with elected officials and worked to gain press coverage of the plight of refugees fleeing the civil war in Syria. At the same time, major American media outlets published photos of squalid refugee camps and refugee children who drowned after the boat they were traveling on sank in the Mediterranean.

As mentioned in Chapter 9, the impact of lobbying efforts like these is hard to determine. For example, although AIPAC is a powerful interest group, they were unsuccessful in their efforts to defeat the agreement with Iran. And while America's foreign

DID YOU KNOW?

87

foreign governments lobbied the legislative or executive branch of the federal government in 2013.
Source: Sunlight Foundation

U.S. politicians and government officials regularly speak at AIPAC events; presidential candidate Hillary Clinton is shown here addressing AIPAC's annual convention. However, it would be a mistake to conclude that the attention paid to this or other interest groups automatically translates into U.S. government support for the groups' policy proposals. @AIPAC

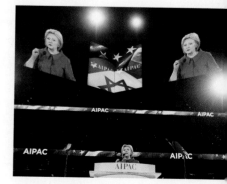

War Powers: Who Controls the Armed Forces?

The President

Has the power to deploy troops as commander in chief

Under the War Powers Resolution, has to notify Congress, and the use of force must be terminated within 60 days if Congress does not approve. However, Congress has never voted to terminate military action, and most presidents have argued that the act is unconstitutional.

Armed Forces

Has the power to declare war
Congress has not used this power since World War II.

Has the power of the purse
Congress can provide or withhold funding for military action.

Congress

America's Role in Libya's Civil War

America's 2011 intervention in the Libyan civil war illustrates how the constitutional allocation of war powers plays out in practice. Although President Obama had the authority to order American armed forces to participate in the operation, his decision came only after United Nations (UN) action and was subject to congressional control through the power of the purse.

No-fly zone?

March 1: Senate passes nonbinding resolution calling for a no-fly zone over Libya. **American and NATO naval forces move into position off Libyan coast.**

No-fly zone!

March 7–14: International leaders and organizations **call for no-fly zone.**

No-fly zone.

March 17: UN Security Council **passes resolution calling for no-fly zone.**

Let's meet.

March 18: President Obama **meets with senior members of Congress.**

Meanwhile...

March 19: U.S. and NATO forces begin to carry out **air strikes on Libyan ground targets,** enforce no-fly zone, and **send military supplies to Libyan rebels.**

Congress should know.

March 21: President Obama sends letter to Congressional leaders **formally notifying Congress** of American involvement in Libyan conflict.

America should know.

March 28: President Obama **gives speech to nation** on Libyan operation.

So what do you think?

May 11: President Obama **calls on Congress to approve American involvement** in Libyan operations.

Well...

June 15: House Speaker Boehner sends President Obama a letter **warning that he would be in violation of War Powers Act** unless Congress voted to approve Libyan operations.

Nope.

June 24: Approval resolution disapproved in House. However, attempts to cut off funds for operations were also rejected.

And we're out.

June–November: Libyan air strikes, no-fly zone, and shipments continue until the **Libyan operation ends on November 1,** although planning continues for possible drone strikes or special forces attacks.

❓ Critical Thinking

1. **As you see in this example, while the president** is commander in chief, military action generally follows an extended process of consultation and negotiation with members of Congress and representatives from other nations. What are the benefits and costs of this deliberative process?

2. **Earlier in the chapter, we noted that some Americans** believe that "politics stops at the water's edge." On balance, does U.S. and NATO intervention in the Libyan civil war confirm or contradict this statement?

policy is strongly pro-Israel (Israel is the largest recipient of foreign aid), it is likely that America's foreign policy would largely favor Israel regardless of AIPAC's actions.[34] Interest groups' influence over foreign policy depends mainly on the same two factors as their influence over domestic policy: groups hold the most sway when few citizens care about the matter and when the issue is noncontroversial.

President Obama's trip to Vietnam in 2016 illustrates that one type of important foreign policy decision involves deciding which countries the president should visit and whom he or she should shake hands with while there.

The Media Television, radio, print media, and the Internet all inform the public about events in America and elsewhere. However, it is not clear that evaluations of America's foreign policy are driven solely by the news media's decisions about what to cover and how to report it. In the case of ISIL, there is no doubt that one highlight of media coverage during 2016 was on the costs and risks involved with military intervention, and the dismal prospects for building a stable democracy in the region. This perspective reflected the facts on the ground during that time: a divided insurgency with some extreme elements, and deep tribal and cultural divisions within the population.

Public Opinion Foreign policy decisions are also sensitive to public opinion. In the case of Syrian refugees, American public opinion has consistently been opposed to allowing them to live in the United States. (This finding is not exceptional—in many other cases, Americans have opposed admission of refugees from political crises.[35]) While these opinions did not deter the Obama administration from proposing to admit several thousand Syrian refugees, they likely deterred the administration from pursuing a larger resettlement effort. Moreover, public opposition to admitting refugees gave members of Congress a strong incentive to oppose Obama's plan.

When citizens are relatively less interested in foreign policy and uninformed about it, elected officials can place a low priority on responding to public opinion and can instead pursue their own foreign policy goals. For example, President Obama ordered American forces to intervene in the Syrian civil war with air strikes, arms shipments, and military assistance despite the fact that a strong majority of the American public favored different policies (some Americans wanted a more aggressive effort, while others favored disengagement).

Intergovernmental Organizations, Nongovernmental Organizations, and International Organizations America's relationship with the rest of the world is not just about government action; it also reflects actions on the part of several types of organizations. For example, members of **intergovernmental organizations (IGOs)** and **nongovernmental organizations (NGOs)** provide information and humanitarian assistance and carry out other activities that the U.S. government is unable or unwilling to undertake. IGOs are associations of sovereign states, while NGOs are private organizations. Thousands of IGOs and NGOs operate throughout the world.[36]

A primary goal of NGOs and IGOs is to promote global economic development and growth. Thus, one of the largest IGOs, the **World Bank**, funds economic development projects worldwide. Another IGO, the **International Monetary Fund (IMF)**, helps countries manage budget deficits and control the value of their currencies. Many NGOs, such as the Asia Foundation, focus on development in a particular region or on certain activities.

A second goal of NGOs is to provide humanitarian relief. In the wake of a disaster such as an earthquake or a flood, or during a famine or a war, organizations such as Oxfam International supply populations in crisis with basic necessities. Other groups such as Doctors without Borders provide medical care to populations threatened by violence, epidemics, or natural disasters. These groups played a key role in the response to Ebola in Africa. Some NGOs also promote human rights. For example, Amnesty International spotlights international cases of people jailed for their political beliefs or held without trial and the use of cruel punishments such as stoning. Amnesty's campaigns, as well as those of other NGOs, are not always supportive of U.S. policy. In recent years, for example, Amnesty has criticized the rendition of terror suspects by the United States.[37]

Finally, NGOs help build democracies. The Open Society Institute funds efforts to increase mass political participation, strengthen political organizations, and verify the fairness of elections in new democracies throughout the world. The National Democratic Institute and the International Republican Institute conduct similar activities. Both organizations, for example, are working with groups in countries such as Burma, Ukraine, and Pakistan to increase the transparency of electoral institutions, recruit candidates, and help citizens build political organizations.

The United States is also a member of many international organizations. Best known is the **United Nations (UN)**, an assembly of ambassadors representing almost all of the world's nations that addresses issues of worldwide concern. The UN is involved in economic development, environmental protection, humanitarian relief, and peacekeeping efforts. Inside the UN, the Security Council—a group of 15 nations (permanent members Britain, China, France, Russia, and the United States, plus 10 rotating nations)—makes the most important decisions, particularly those involving UN military missions. The UN General Assembly, in which each nation has one vote, debates and votes on other concerns.

intergovernmental organizations (IGOs)
Organizations that seek to coordinate policy across member nations.

nongovernmental organizations (NGOs)
Groups operated by private institutions (rather than governments) to promote growth, economic development, and other agendas throughout the world.

World Bank
A nongovernmental organization established in 1944 that provides financial support for economic development projects in developing nations.

International Monetary Fund (IMF)
A nongovernmental organization established in 1944 to help stabilize the international monetary system, improve economic growth, and aid developing nations.

United Nations (UN)
An international organization made up of representatives from nearly every nation, with a mission to promote peace and cooperation, uphold international law, and provide humanitarian aid.

It may look to you like foreign policy is all about what the president wants. However, for the most part, the same kinds of people (in many cases, the same people) who influence domestic policy choices also shape America's foreign policy—including elected officials, interest groups, and the public at large. The president is a key player in making foreign policy choices, but he or she is far from being the only voice that matters.

"Why Should I Care?"

The tools of foreign policy

Now that we know the key players in foreign policy making, what are the tools and methods these players use to implement policy?

Diplomacy

The process of diplomacy involves using personal contact and negotiations with national leaders and representatives to work out international agreements or persuade other nations to change their behavior. Sometimes these efforts involve the threat of military action or economic sanctions, or incentives such as economic assistance or other forms of aid. The United States may participate directly in such efforts or mediate between parties in a dispute. Diplomacy has often been a limited but useful foreign policy tool. For example, the efforts of American and Russian diplomats were instrumental in establishing a limited cease-fire in Syria in 2016 and in getting both sides to allow convoys carrying relief supplies to enter besieged areas of the country.

Trade and economic policies

Foreign policy is also aimed at sustaining economic growth in the United States and elsewhere, as well as creating foreign markets for the goods produced by America's domestic industries. Figure 15.1 shows total American trade (imports and exports) with other countries over the last 30 years, expressed as a percentage of U.S. GDP (a measure of the size of the U.S. economy). In recent years, imports and exports have constituted almost 30 percent of GDP.

The main tools of trade policy are tariffs and trade agreements. A **tariff** is a tax on the import or export of certain commodities, and a trade agreement sets tariff levels or limits the quantities of particular items that can be imported or exported. The United States International Trade Commission maintains a list of all tariffs in effect.[38] By adjusting tariff rates, the government can help or hurt domestic industries: high tariffs on imports help American producers charge lower prices than foreign competitors can, and low tariffs on exports help American producers sell to overseas markets.

Over the last two generations, the United States and most other nations have been lowering tariffs and establishing free-trade zones, which reflect agreements to eliminate tariffs on all imports and exports among specific nations. Examples include NAFTA, a multilateral agreement involving the United States, Canada, and Mexico; and the Central America Free Trade Agreement (CAFTA) among the United States, five Central American nations, and the Dominican Republic. Other organizations, such as the **World Trade Organization (WTO)**, facilitate negotiations over tariffs and provide a mechanism for adjudicating cases in which one nation believes that another is using tariffs unfairly. Finally, the United States has granted many other countries **most-favored-nation status**: tariffs on imports to the United States from these nations are set at the lowest rate placed on any other nation.

Trade deals are inherently controversial because they almost always involve winners and losers. Even if a deal increases overall economic growth in the United States, some people will be made worse off. For example, if a deal makes it possible for an

tariff
A tax levied on imported and exported goods.

World Trade Organization (WTO)
An international organization created in 1995 to oversee trade agreements between nations by facilitating negotiations and handling disputes.

most-favored-nation status
A standing awarded to countries with which the United States has good trade relations, providing the lowest possible tariff rate. WTO members must give one another this preferred status.

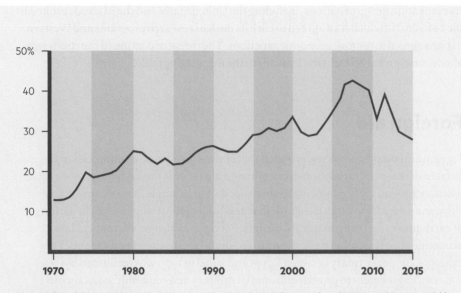

**FIGURE
15.1**

U.S. Imports and Exports as a Percentage of GDP

This figure illustrates the importance of trade to the U.S. economy. In recent years imports and exports have accounted for almost 40 percent of U.S. economic activity, and the percentage is increasing over time. Based on these data, what arguments would you make for lowering or increasing barriers to trade?

Source: Office of the United States Trade Representative, *2016 Trade Policy Agenda and 2015 Annual Report*, available at www.ustr.gov (accessed 9/6/16).

entrepreneur in a developing nation to sell goods in the United States at a lower price than domestic suppliers, Americans who buy the goods are better off (they pay less for the same product), but the people who work for the U.S. suppliers are in trouble (their employer may go out of business if they cannot find another market for their products). As a result, trade agreements generally split both Democratic and Republican party coalitions, with supporters and opponents on both sides. Trade deals also play a pivotal role in U.S. elections. One reason for Donald Trump's victory in 2016 was high support from rural communities (particularly in the Midwest "Rust Belt") that have lost manufacturing jobs as companies responded to lower tariffs by moving factories overseas.

Trade is an important part of foreign policy. The United States can use free-trade agreements and tariffs to bargain with countries for concessions in noneconomic policy areas or to cement international alliances. One of the reasons why America played a central role in crafting the TPP was the goal of strengthening America's political and economic ties with Asian nations, as a counter to the increased regional economic and military power of China. Even if the TPP is never ratified, these other foreign policy issues will need to be addressed.

Economic policies are also used to threaten or sanction countries as a way of inducing them to change their behavior. For example, in 2007 the UN Security Council authorized **economic sanctions** against Iran aimed at forcing the nation to stop enriching uranium, a first step in the production of nuclear weapons.[39] These sanctions included freezing bank accounts held by members of Iran's nuclear team and banning arms sales to the country. Additional sanctions imposed in 2012 made it difficult for Iranian citizens and corporations to do business outside their nation's borders. If Iran agreed to stop its program, it would receive incentives such as civilian nuclear reactor technology and direct talks with the United States over various issues. At the same time, the United States also discouraged Israel from attacking Iranian nuclear facilities. This combination of carrots and sticks led to ongoing negotiations between the

economic sanctions
Penalties applied by one country or group of countries on another, usually in the form of tariffs or other trade barriers.

One of the most conflictual issues involving international trade is the enforcement of copyrights on movies, music, and computer software. The Chinese government's refusal to enforce American copyrights has been a source of tension between the two nations. @CopyrightOffice

DID YOU KNOW?

The United States spends

<1%

of its annual budget on foreign aid. According to one poll, Americans on average think the country spends 28 percent.
Source: Kaiser Family Foundation Poll

Iranians and a group of nations, including the United States and the EU, and resulted in the 2016 deal in which Iran agreed to curb its nuclear research programs and Western nations agreed to remove economic sanctions. The threat of continued sanctions was almost surely what brought the Iranians to the negotiating table.

Foreign aid

Foreign aid comprises money, products, or services given to other countries or the citizens of these countries. Sometimes foreign aid reflects the desire to provide basic assistance to satisfy fundamental human needs. For example, American military ships and aircraft are often used to deliver food and medical supplies to the victims of earthquakes and other natural disasters. Foreign aid also serves to stimulate economic growth in other nations and to facilitate international agreements. For example, the peace treaty between Egypt and Israel in 1979 was facilitated by America's agreement to provide substantial military and economic assistance to both countries.[40]

Figure 15.2 shows the level of American nonmilitary foreign aid in 2015, measured as a percentage of gross national income (GNI, which includes GDP plus income earned by citizens of a country who live abroad, minus income earned in the domestic economy by nonresidents) compared with some other nations. Considering the amount of U.S. foreign aid as a percentage of GNI suggests that the United States gives relatively little to other countries. Part of the reason for this perception lies in the size of the U.S. economy: America's foreign aid contributions are the largest of any country when measured in total dollars, but it also has the largest GNI of any country.

Alliances and treaties

A treaty is an agreement between nations to work together on economic or security issues. An alliance is an agreement that commits nations to security guarantees, which are assurances that one country will help another if it is attacked. America is a member of many international alliances, most notably NATO. This alliance was formed by the North Atlantic Treaty after World War II to provide collective security against the Soviet Union and Warsaw Pact countries, but after the Cold War the organization's mission shifted to coordinating military force toward common goals. NATO's 2011 intervention in the Libyan civil war was the first instance of operations outside Europe. Historically, the United States has paid a disproportionate share of the cost of NATO operations. This policy drew criticism from Donald Trump during the 2016 campaign. Trump argued that the United States should stop subsidizing NATO, as its allies had strong economies and could therefore afford to increase their military expenditures.

The United States is a party to treaties with many countries.[41] Treaties and alliances enable the United States to commit itself to a course of action or signal its intentions to other nations.[42] By joining NATO and stationing troops in Europe, for example, the United States guaranteed that if Warsaw Pact troops invaded the West, U.S. forces would be directly involved in the defense of Western Europe. More recently, when Russian forces threatened to invade Ukraine in recent years, America and its NATO partners sent aircraft, troops, and ships to countries adjacent to Ukraine to signal their opposition to Russia's plans and their support for the Ukrainian government.

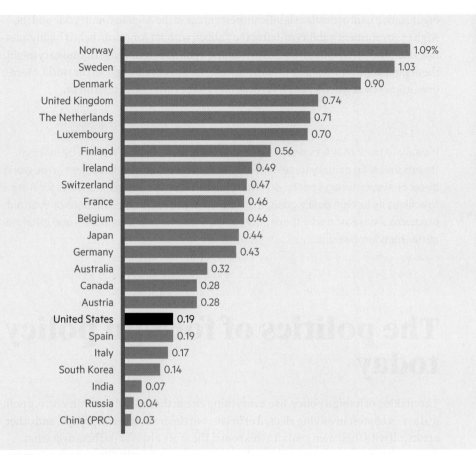

Country	Value
Norway	1.09%
Sweden	1.03
Denmark	0.90
United Kingdom	0.74
The Netherlands	0.71
Luxembourg	0.70
Finland	0.56
Ireland	0.49
Switzerland	0.47
France	0.46
Belgium	0.46
Japan	0.44
Germany	0.43
Australia	0.32
Canada	0.28
Austria	0.28
United States	0.19
Spain	0.19
Italy	0.17
South Korea	0.14
India	0.07
Russia	0.04
China (PRC)	0.03

FIGURE 15.2

U.S. Foreign Aid in Comparative Perspective

This figure shows foreign aid contributions expressed as a percentage of gross national income (GNI). Do these data imply that America is less generous than other nations in its willingness to donate aid?

Source: Organization for Economic Cooperation and Development, "Development Cooperation Report 2015," available at www.oecd.org (accessed 5/16/16).

Military force

Military force is a fundamental tool of foreign policy. America's military forces serve throughout the world as a deterrent to conflict, and military exercises by U.S. troops, aircraft, and ships serve to remind potential adversaries of America's military power. For example, in early 2016, in response to Chinese claims of sovereignty over the South China Sea, U.S. military aircraft and ships began to regularly transit the region to underscore the U.S. position that the sea was international waters and to demonstrate that America was ready to keep the sea open by using force if necessary.

The United States has also fought wars and lesser conflicts to further its foreign policy goals. Some were all-out military operations, such as the invasion of Iraq. More commonly, these deployments are short-lived operations ranging from the evacuation of American civilians from areas of unrest to the delivery of humanitarian assistance or the use of ship-launched cruise missiles to attack terrorist camps and similar targets.[43] In the case of fighting ISIL, America has sent military advisers and training personnel to several nations, carried out numerous attacks by Special Forces and drones, and, in the case of Syria and Iraq, conducted many air strikes against ISIL forces and infrastructure.

The size and power of America's military provide numerous options for policymakers. For example, after the September 11 attacks, in an attempt to prevent future terror attacks by Al Qaeda, U.S. forces invaded Afghanistan, which had been used as a base of operations for the organization.[44] It is highly unlikely that any other country could carry out such a large-scale operation so far from home. Nonetheless, military force is not all-powerful. For example, despite over a decade of combat operations in Afghanistan and large amounts of economic and military aid to the Afghan government, the Taliban (a religious–political organization) still controls a significant percentage of the Afghan countryside and the Afghan government's ability to defeat the Taliban without American help is highly questionable. Similarly, while air strikes in Iraq and Syria have reduced ISIL's military might, the organization remains able to plan future terror attacks throughout the world. Moreover, it is not clear whether any level of military force can remove this threat.

"Why Should I Care?"

It's easy to think that America can get what it wants from other nations by making threats involving military force—after all, America's military is the largest in the world by far. However, foreign policy isn't that simple. There are many other ways for America to achieve its foreign policy goals, from diplomacy to economic sanctions or even aid programs. The reason why these strategies are used is that they work—and often work better than force would.

ANALYZE SEVERAL MAJOR AREAS OF FOREIGN POLICY AND WHY THEY ARE OFTEN CONTROVERSIAL

The politics of foreign policy today

The making of foreign policy, like everything else in the federal government, is a political act—a contest involving elected officials, bureaucrats, interest groups, and other actors, all with their own goals. In this sense, there are always conflicts over what America's foreign policy should look like and compromise will always be fundamental to the making of foreign policy.

Conflict over foreign policy has several sources. One is the realist–idealist distinction discussed earlier. Self-interest is another powerful factor. For example, several studies have found that as National Guard units were mobilized for service in Iraq, support for the war declined in the communities where these units were based.[45] Disagreements over foreign policy may also reflect citizens' exposure to different information or their disparate ways of understanding the world. Indeed, there are sharp disagreements among citizens over the existence of climate change and its cause—natural phenomena or human activity.[46]

Disagreements may also originate in differing expectations about whether policies will work as intended, as well as the basic facts of a situation. For example, during the debate over whether the United States and its allies should support rebel groups in the Syrian civil war that began in 2011 some members of Congress and Obama administration officials argued that Syria's central geographic and political position in the Middle East made intervention essential—while others cited the same factors to argue against getting involved.[47]

In sum, disagreements about foreign policy are unavoidable, both in government and among the general public. These conflicts will surely continue. For a variety of reasons, citizens and elected officials will disagree on what America's foreign policy should look like and they will work in elections and in the government to influence those choices.

Foreign policy issues facing America today

This section discusses three of the major foreign policy issues facing America in the contemporary era: trade, terrorism, and nuclear proliferation—and how all of these issues raise human rights concerns. In each case, we will focus on one country: China, Afghanistan, and North Korea. These issues demonstrate the complexity of America's foreign policy choices, and how these decisions are shaped both by conflicts and by political processes.

Managing International Trade: China For the United States, trade is a necessity. America imports a wide range of resources and manufactured goods from other countries. Increased trade or outsourcing of manufacturing and service delivery can also enhance economic growth and thereby create new jobs for Americans.

These practices are examples of **globalization**, reflecting the trend toward increasing interaction and connections among individuals, corporations, and nations. New technologies have leveled the global playing field, allowing suppliers of goods and services to sell their products throughout the world. At the same time, there have been many new international agreements to reduce or eliminate tariffs among nations and adjudicate disputes.[48]

America's relations with China are a prime example of these developments. Many American companies have factories in China to serve American markets. China is a major producer of rare earth metals that are used to build computer chips. American corporations are also opening stores in China—the coffee chain Starbucks, for example, opened over 500 stores in China in 2016. In recent years, China has been one of America's largest trading partners, with more than $562 billion in trade during 2013. Notably, Chinese citizens purchased over $59 billion worth of iPhones, iPads, and other Apple products.

Although these moves generate significant benefits, the changes do not make everyone better off. American jobs have been lost as factories that could not compete with cheaper foreign suppliers have closed.[49] Support from individuals hurt by these changes was one reason for Donald Trump's victory in 2016. Moreover, there have been numerous complaints that Chinese companies have stolen trade secrets from American corporations or violated American copyright laws—in some cases, with the apparent support of the Chinese government.

In 1989, the fall of the Berlin Wall, which separated West Berlin from communist East Berlin, provided a powerful symbol of the end of the Cold War. With just one superpower—the United States—left, many predicted that democracy would spread and peace would prevail. However, new foreign policy challenges quickly emerged.

globalization
The increase over the last generation in trade, travel, and the flow of ideas and beliefs between nations.

"

What I'm saying is this: I'm saying that we do it, but if they [China] don't start treating us fairly and stop devaluing and let their currency rise so that our companies can compete and we don't lose all of these millions of jobs that we're losing, I would certainly start taxing goods that come in from China. Who the hell has to lose $505 billion a year?

—**Donald Trump,** Republican debate, January 13, 2016

These developments raise questions for American citizens and elected officials. First, how should America respond to nations that close off their markets, especially given that the same economic and employment pressures exist in America? For example, in recent years the Chinese government has done many things to restrict imports and expand exports. While Donald Trump has promised to respond aggressively to countries that abuse trade agreements, the fact that the United States exports a large amount to China means that shutting down American markets to Chinese exports could hurt American workers and companies.

The second question concerns how to help Americans who are hurt by globalization. While there are some federal programs to retrain workers whose jobs are eliminated because of new trade agreements, these programs reach only a fraction of displaced workers.

Finally, globalization raises new human rights questions. For example, do U.S. companies such as Apple, which has outsourced the production of iPhones to factories in China, have a responsibility to monitor conditions in these factories and ensure that workers are paid a fair wage? More generally, should the United States increase its trade with a country such as China that restricts the freedoms of its citizens in ways that most Americans would find objectionable? Or should it increase trade, on the grounds that exposure to American commerce and culture will encourage the other country's citizens to press their government for reforms?

One way to respond to these complications is to take a stand along the lines of the quote from Republican Donald Trump—that the United States should renegotiate trade agreements to protect American workers and increase American exports, with the threat that American will impose high import tariffs on countries that refuse to

One of the most visible examples of globalization is the number of American companies that have opened stores or facilities in other countries. KFC, for example, has more than 4,600 stores in China. Another aspect of globalization is that factories are located wherever production costs are lowest. On the right, Chinese workers assemble electronic components for the global market.

comply with these demands. This attitude illustrates a central truth: decisions to encourage trade and globalization are real choices, choices that are sure to generate high levels of conflict in American politics. While U.S. policy can encourage or discourage trade, outsourcing, and other interactions that cross national borders, all of these choices will make some people better off and some worse off. As in so many other areas of American politics, because of the wide range of interests that Americans bring to the table there is no one trade policy that is clearly better than all of the others.

Fighting Terrorism: ISIL There have been no major terrorist attacks on the United States since September 11, 2001, and the worldwide Al Qaeda organization that planned the September 11 attacks has been decimated by a decade-long series of U.S. counterattacks. Nevertheless, the potential for terrorism remains, and groups such as ISIL have continued to carry out small-scale attacks, such as the attack in Paris, France, on November 13, 2015. ISIL has also encouraged individuals to plan and execute their own attacks, such as the attacks in San Bernardino by an American citizen and a permanent resident in December 2015 and the attacks by an American citizen in a Miami nightclub in June 2016.

The fight against global terror is different from a conventional war. In a conventional war, there are clear victory criteria: the losing nation's government capitulates. In the War on Terror, eliminating one individual or group may not reduce future attacks, because these victories do not address the factors that drive terrorism, including poverty and a deep-set anger that some individuals have against Western interests.

For example, consider one of the most visible of America's antiterrorism efforts, the fight against Al Qaeda. Over the last 14 years, the United States has invaded Afghanistan (where the organization was based at the time of the attacks), removed the Afghani Taliban government that supported Al Qaeda, destroyed many camps and other centers in Afghanistan and elsewhere, and captured or killed many operatives and leaders of the organization, including its founder, Osama bin Laden, during an attack in Pakistan in August 2011.

However, while Al Qaeda is far weaker than it was in 2001, the possibility of an attack on Americans in the United States or abroad by the remnants of Al Qaeda remains very real (although as we discuss in the What Do the Numbers Say? feature, many Americans overestimate the threat of terrorist attacks). Moreover, even after over a decade of military action and efforts to build a stable democracy and a growing economy, Afghanistan remains a dangerous, unstable place. Should the United States be responsible for creating a stable, prosperous Afghan nation? What will happen if America withdraws its support? Would the Taliban and Al Qaeda return, or would another equally bad group emerge?

Similar questions can be asked about the Syrian civil war and one of the principal protagonists, ISIL. While ISIL is weaker than it was before American and international air strikes, the Paris attacks are evidence that the organization is still capable of striking civilians throughout the world. Moreover, it is not clear how ISIL can be destroyed— even if America and its allies were willing to deploy troops to invade and occupy areas that ISIL currently controls (which they are not), there is no assurance that such an effort would eliminate the threat.

Human rights concerns also shape antiterrorism efforts. American attacks against terror groups have the potential to cause civilian casualties—especially in places such as Afghanistan, where these groups have tried to hide among civilians to discourage such attacks. Moreover, investigating terror groups may involve increased surveillance of Americans and their communications. American decision makers must also decide whether they will overlook problems in other countries to pursue terror suspects. For example, the government of Pakistan is routinely cited for human rights abuses, but Pakistani officials have aided in the capture of Taliban fighters in Afghanistan and have allowed the United States to use Pakistani airspace to send drones into Iraq and Iran.

In sum, regardless of what happens in Syria, Afghanistan, and other areas where ISIL and other terrorist organizations operate, the fight against global terrorism will continue for the foreseeable future. It is easy to work backward from this conclusion to a critique of past policies—to conclude, for example, that things would be better if the United States had sent more troops or economic aid to Afghanistan, did not invade Iraq, or refused to intervene in the Libyan civil war. However, because terror attacks can come from many sources, because the fight against these organizations touches on human rights concerns, and because it is not clear how to eliminate the threat, there is no clearly best strategy in the War on Terror. As a result, the threat from terrorism, and the debate over how to respond, will persist.

One of the United States' strategies to increase stability in Afghanistan is to train the Afghan National Army and police in order to provide the Afghan government a greater level of control over the region.

weapons of mass destruction (WMDs)
Weapons that have the potential to cause large-scale loss of life, such as nuclear bombs and chemical or biological weapons.

Preventing the Spread of WMDs: North Korea The term "**weapons of mass destruction (WMDs)**" refers to nuclear bombs, chemical weapons such as nerve gas, and biological weapons such as anthrax. Given the potential for these weapons to inflict mass casualties, the United States has placed a high priority on (1) limiting the number of nations that have these weapons and (2) preventing terrorist organizations from obtaining or developing them.

Until recently, very few countries possessed WMDs. Only five countries admitted to having nuclear weapons: the United States, Russia, China, Great Britain, and France—although a sixth nation, Israel, was generally thought to have them as well. Over the last two generations, many countries—including Sweden, Brazil, Libya, and South Africa—have voluntarily ended weapon-development programs and signed nonproliferation treaties. However, new efforts to develop nuclear weapons have kept WMDs on the foreign policy agenda. Neither Pakistan nor India signed the nonproliferation treaty; then both countries developed and tested nuclear weapons in the 1990s. North Korea withdrew from the treaty in 2003, banned International Atomic Energy Agency (IAEA) inspectors, began reprocessing nuclear reactor fuel into bomb-grade material, detonated several nuclear devices, and, more recently, has tested a missile with the range to reach the United States and other countries. It has also resisted pressure to abandon its nuclear arsenal.

The problem for the United States is to determine how to respond to North Korea's nuclear capabilities. Military operations are problematic, as North Korea's weapons and the factories that manufacture them are buried deep underground and may not be destroyed even by a massive attack. An unsuccessful attack might goad the North Korean government to launch its remaining weapons against U.S., Korean, or Japanese targets. Moreover, how should America respond to a WMD attack against its citizens or its allies, particularly if it is unclear which nation or group is responsible?

In other cases of nuclear proliferation—Libya and Iran, for example—the United States and other nations have used economic and military sanctions to pressure nations that continue to develop weapons, while offers of economic aid and even civilian nuclear reactors serve to persuade nations to give up their weapons programs.[50] Of course, because these agreements are voluntary, nations giving up their nuclear weapons programs get something in return. In the case of the deal with Iran, the United States and its allies made crucial concessions—the lifting of economic sanctions and the return of Iranian assets held after the Iranian Revolution of 1979. These concessions were hugely valuable to the Iranian regime because of their import in the Iranian economy.

The Threat of Terrorism

As the Gallup poll here indicates, a substantial percentage of Americans worry that they or members of their family will be the victims of a terrorist attack—in fact, these concerns even predate the September 11 attacks. Are these fears justified? How great is the risk? What do the numbers say?

How Worried Are You That You or Someone in Your Family Will Become a Victim of Terrorism?

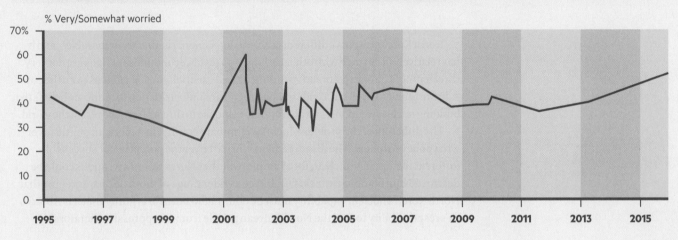

% Very/Somewhat worried

Hazard	Annual Fatality Risk
Traffic accidents	1 in 8,200
Homicide	1 in 22,000
Industrial accidents	1 in 53,000
Natural disasters	1 in 480,000
Drowning in bathtub	1 in 950,000
Home appliances	1 in 1,500,000
Deer accidents	1 in 2,000,000
Commercial aviation	1 in 2,300,000
Peanut allergies	1 in 6,000,000
Lightning	1 in 7,000,000
Terrorist attack	1 in 110,000,000

Sources: Gallup Poll, "Terrorism in the United States," www.gallup.com (accessed 5/16/16); John Mueller and Mark G. Stewart, *Chasing Ghosts: The Policing of Terrorism* (New York: Oxford University Press, 2015).

Think about it

- Is the public's concern over the dangers of terrorist attacks justified by the fatality data?
- Suppose you were a bureaucrat from the Department of Homeland Security who was testifying before Congress on the need to increase funding for antiterrorism programs. One of the members of Congress at the hearing argued such funding was unnecessary because the likelihood of dying from a terrorist incident was so low. How would you respond?

North Korea has one of the world's least predictable and most isolated political regimes. Their nuclear capabilities and large military make North Korea a threat to the stability of the region. However, because of the poor state of the country's economy, economic sanctions are unlikely to foster changes toward democracy and openness.

North Korea presents a different problem. Its economy is already in shambles, and it has relatively little trade with other nations. As a result, economic sanctions are not very threatening. The North Korean government has essentially cut off citizens from the outside world and carried out a widespread program of indoctrination to reinforce beliefs that building nuclear weapons is an appropriate response to threats from the rest of the world.

The difficulty of the problem does not eliminate conflict in American politics over what policy to follow. The disagreement is in part over the potential for success of different tactics. It is unclear, for example, whether North Korea's weapons could be destroyed by a bombing attack. Others see a wider range of motivations, agreeing that North Korea's nuclear capability must be eliminated but also arguing that it is America's responsibility to free the North Korean people from an oppressive dictatorship.

Conclusion

Foreign policy definitely matters. Consider the following four statements: (1) National security is a top priority for many Americans. (2) The state of the American economy, from home prices to the unemployment rate, is affected by economic conditions elsewhere. (3) Trade agreements with other nations determine how much American companies are allowed to export and what taxes and fees they must pay to import raw materials and other goods. (4) Solutions to pressing environmental problems such as climate change are inherently international. As these statements show, it is hard to find a domestic issue that does not have a foreign policy component. And some questions, like the fight against ISIL, raise concerns about America's responsibility to protect human rights, even when victims are not American citizens.

Foreign policy is also conflictual. Disagreements among elected officials over what to do about ISIL, or over trade agreements or any other question of foreign policy, are not just attempts to attract political support or gain media attention. These differences of opinion reflect real dilemmas over what government should do and how it should do it.

In all these respects, all of the issues discussed in this chapter, including the fight against global terrorism, the Middle East, the Zika virus, conflicts with China over trade policy, and persuading Iran to curb its nuclear ambitions, are not exceptions to the rule. Rather, these events epitomize just how close to home foreign policy is. Foreign policy is not something that happens "out there," in isolation from the American public; from the state of the economy to public safety, ordinary Americans are finding their lives increasingly affected by actions taken by individuals, organizations, and countries outside America's borders—a trend that is likely to continue over the next generation.

STUDY GUIDE

What is foreign policy?

Describe the major approaches to understanding foreign policy and trace how America's role in the world has evolved. (Pages 446–453)

Summary

Foreign policy is any government action toward a group outside of America's borders. Foreign policy goals are complex, and debates on what America's goals should be are traditionally framed in terms of general principles. The goals of American foreign policy have changed over time and have become increasingly internationalist.

Key terms

foreign policy (p. 446)
unilateral action (national) (p. 447)
multilateral action (p. 447)
isolationism (p. 447)
internationalism (p. 447)
realism (p. 447)
idealism (p. 447)
nation building (p. 448)

constructivism (p. 448)
Monroe Doctrine (p. 449)
Cold War (p. 449)
containment (p. 450)
mutually assured destruction (p. 450)
détente (p. 451)
Bush Doctrine (p. 451)

Practice Quiz Questions

1. **When one country does something on its own without coordinating with other countries, it is _____.**
   a. isolationist
   b. internationalist
   c. acting unilaterally
   d. acting multilaterally
   e. nation building

2. **_____ believe that countries pursue their own interests.**
   a. Realists
   b. Idealists
   c. Constructivists
   d. Internationalists

3. **The Monroe Doctrine stated that in European wars America would _____.**
   a. support Britain
   b. support the attacking country
   c. support the attacked country
   d. provide arms but not troops
   e. remain neutral

4. **American foreign policy became increasingly internationalist following _____.**
   a. the Civil War
   b. World War I
   c. World War II
   d. the Vietnam War
   e. the Cold War

5. **The goal of containment influenced the _____ and _____.**
   a. war in Iraq; the war in Afghanistan
   b. Korean War; the war in Iraq
   c. Vietnam War; the war in Iraq
   d. Korean War; the Cuban missile crisis
   e. Vietnam War; World War II

Foreign policy makers

Explain how the various branches of government shape foreign policy. (Pages 454–461)

Summary

The major actors in foreign policy are the president and Congress, although the Supreme Court, interest groups, and public opinion all influence foreign policy decisions to a degree. The president's advantage over Congress lies in the ambiguity in the Constitution and the unilateral presidential power.

Key terms

National Security Council (NSC) (p. 454)
civilian control (p. 455)
intergovernmental organizations (IGOs) (p. 461)

nongovernmental organizations (NGOs) (p. 461)
World Bank (p. 461)
International Monetary Fund (IMF) (p. 461)
United Nations (UN) (p. 461)

Practice Quiz Questions

6. **The principal foreign policy department in the executive branch is _____.**
   a. the Department of Defense
   b. the Council on Foreign Relations
   c. the Department of International Relations
   d. the Department of State
   e. the Foreign Intelligence Advisory Board

7. **The idea that military personnel do not formulate policy but rather implement directives from civilians is _____.**
   a. military deference
   b. civilian control
   c. the Geneva system
   d. civilian–military alliance
   e. the Bush Doctrine

8. **Congress holds the _____ and the _____, which both influence foreign policy.**
   a. power to deploy troops; power of the purse
   b. power to approve treaties; power to deploy troops
   c. power to declare war; power of the purse
   d. power to deploy troops; power to declare war
   e. power to approve appointments; power to deploy troops

9. **The War Powers Resolution was designed to _____.**
   a. limit the president's war-making powers
   b. limit the Congress's war-making powers
   c. limit the Department of Defense's war-making powers
   d. limit the Pentagon's war-making powers
   e. limit the State Department's war-making powers

The tools of foreign policy

Examine the ways American foreign policy is implemented. (Pages 462–466)

Summary

American foreign policy is implemented using a variety of tools—beyond the use of military force, other tools include the provision of foreign aid or changes to trade policy. Though all tools can be used in pursuit of desired policy outcomes, the specific tool is selected based on careful consideration of context.

Key terms
tariff (p. 462)
World Trade Organization (WTO) (p. 462)
most-favored-nation status (p. 462)
economic sanctions (p. 463)

Practice Quiz Questions

10. **The process of _____ involves using personal contact and negotiations with leaders to work out international agreements.**
    a. nation building
    b. diplomacy
    c. unilateralism
    d. the Bush Doctrine
    e. the use of force

11. **When a country is given "most-favored-nation" status, it means that the United States _____ any other nation.**
    a. gives the country higher levels of foreign aid than
    b. gives the country higher levels of military aid than
    c. sets tariffs on imports to the United States to the lowest rate given to
    d. sets tariffs on exports from the United States to the lowest rate given to
    e. sends that country more troops than

12. **NAFTA is an example of _____**
    a. a bilateral agreement
    b. an alliance
    c. a tariff
    d. a multilateral agreement
    e. a sanction

The politics of foreign policy today

Analyze several major areas of foreign policy and why they are often controversial. (Pages 466–472)

Summary

Focusing on three contemporary foreign policy issues—trade, terrorism, and WMDs—reveals a variety of conflicts among citizens and elected officials alike over how America's foreign policy should look. Notwithstanding this conflict, it is clear that America's policy choices on these issues will have enormous consequences both for American citizens and for people throughout the world.

Key terms
globalization (p. 467)
weapons of mass destruction (WMDs) (p. 470)

Practice Quiz Questions

13. **What factor limits the American response to potential terrorist threats?**
    a. American public opinion opposes attacks on terrorist organizations.
    b. The War Powers Resolution limits military actions to those approved by Congress.
    c. Other nations would impose economic sanctions on American corporations.
    d. It is difficult to identify terrorists or determine their plans.
    e. Addressing terrorism requires a multilateral effort, which is difficult to coordinate.

14. **The American government hesitates to pressure Pakistan on human rights violations most likely because _____ .**

    a. doing so would threaten economic ties with Pakistan

    b. attempts to protect human rights may make it harder for the United States to achieve goals in Afghanistan

    c. evidence of human rights violations in Pakistan is unreliable

    d. there is little international condemnation for the Pakistani violations of human rights

    e. Pakistan enforces a Bill of Rights

15. **Efforts to eliminate the threat of North Korean WMDs are limited by all of these factors except _____ .**

    a. Russian support for the North Korean regime

    b. the limited impact of economic sanctions

    c. the possibility that North Korea would respond militarily to an attack

    d. the isolation of North Korea's population

    e. the fact that North Korean WMDs are stored in well-protected facilities

Suggested Reading

Auerswald, David P., and Stephen Saideman. *NATO in Afghanistan: Fighting Together, Fighting Alone*. Princeton, NJ: Princeton University Press, 2014.

Bueno de Mesquita, Bruce. *Principles of International Politics*. Washington, DC: CQ Press, 2005.

Fisher, Louis. *Presidential War Power*. Lawrence: University Press of Kansas, 2004.

Huntington, Samuel P. *The Clash of Civilizations and the Remaking of World Order*. New York: Free Press, 2002.

Keohane, Robert O. *After Hegemony: Cooperation and Discord in the International System*. Princeton, NJ: Princeton University Press, 2005 (originally published 1984).

Mearsheimer, John J. *The Tragedy of Great Power Politics*. New York: W. W. Norton, 2001.

Mueller, John, and Mark G. Stewart. *Chasing Ghosts: The Policing of Terrorism*. New York: Oxford University Press, 2015.

Nye, Joseph. *Soft Power: The Means to Success in World Politics*. New York: Hachette Book Group.

Ricks, Thomas. *The Gamble: General David Petraeus and the American Military Adventure in Iraq, 2006–2008*. New York: Penguin Press, 2009.

Sen, Amartya. *Identity and Violence: The Illusion of Destiny*. New York: W. W. Norton, 2007.

Simmons, Beth, Frank Dobbin, and Geoffrey Garrett. *The Global Diffusion of Markets and Democracy*. New York: Cambridge University Press, 2008.

Stiglitz, Joseph E. *Making Globalization Work*. New York: W. W. Norton, 2007.

APPENDIX

The Declaration of Independence

In Congress, July 4, 1776

The unanimous Declaration of the thirteen united States of America,

When in the Course of human events, it becomes necessary for one people to dissolve the political bands which have connected them with another, and to assume among the powers of the earth, the separate and equal station to which the Laws of Nature and of Nature's God entitle them, a decent respect to the opinions of mankind requires that they should declare the causes which impel them to the separation.

We hold these truths to be self-evident, that all men are created equal, that they are endowed by their Creator with certain unalienable Rights, that among these are Life, Liberty and the pursuit of Happiness.—That to secure these rights, Governments are instituted among Men, deriving their just powers from the consent of the governed.—That whenever any Form of Government becomes destructive of these ends, it is the Right of the People to alter or to abolish it, and to institute new Government, laying its foundation on such principles and organizing its powers in such form, as to them shall seem most likely to effect their Safety and Happiness. Prudence, indeed, will dictate that Governments long established should not be changed for light and transient causes; and accordingly all experience hath shewn, that mankind are more disposed to suffer, while evils are sufferable, than to right themselves by abolishing the forms to which they are accustomed. But when a long train of abuses and usurpations, pursuing invariably the same Object evinces a design to reduce them under absolute Despotism, it is their right, it is their duty, to throw off such Government, and to provide new Guards for their future security.—Such has been the patient sufferance of these Colonies; and such is now the necessity which constrains them to alter their former Systems of Government. The history of the present King of Great Britain is a history of repeated injuries and usurpations, all having in direct object the establishment of an absolute Tyranny over these States. To prove this, let Facts be submitted to a candid world.

He has refused his Assent to Laws, the most wholesome and necessary for the public good.

He has forbidden his Governors to pass Laws of immediate and pressing importance, unless suspended in their operation till his Assent should be obtained; and when so suspended, he has utterly neglected to attend to them.

He has refused to pass other Laws for the accommodation of large districts of people, unless those people would relinquish the right of Representation in the Legislature, a right inestimable to them and formidable to tyrants only.

He has called together legislative bodies at places unusual, uncomfortable, and distant from the depository of their public Records, for the sole purpose of fatiguing them into compliance with his measures.

He has dissolved Representative Houses repeatedly, for opposing with manly firmness his invasions on the rights of the people.

He has refused for a long time, after such dissolutions, to cause others to be elected; whereby the Legislative powers, incapable of Annihilation, have returned to the People at large for their exercise; the State remaining in the mean time exposed to all the dangers of invasion from without, and convulsions within.

He has endeavoured to prevent the population of these States; for that purpose obstructing the Laws for Naturalization of Foreigners; refusing to pass others to encourage their migrations hither, and raising the conditions of new Appropriations of Lands.

He has obstructed the Administration of Justice, by refusing his Assent to Laws for establishing Judiciary powers.

He has made Judges dependent on his Will alone, for the tenure of their offices, and the amount and payment of their salaries.

He has erected a multitude of New Offices, and sent hither swarms of Officers to harrass our people, and eat out their substance.

He has kept among us, in times of peace, Standing Armies without the Consent of our legislatures.

He has affected to render the Military independent of and superior to the Civil power.

He has combined with others to subject us to a jurisdiction foreign to our constitution, and unacknowledged by our laws; giving his Assent to their Acts of pretended Legislation:

For Quartering large bodies of armed troops among us:

For protecting them, by a mock Trial, from punishment for any Murders which they should commit on the Inhabitants of these States:

For cutting off our Trade with all parts of the world:

For imposing Taxes on us without our Consent:

For depriving us in many cases, of the benefits of Trial by Jury:

For transporting us beyond Seas to be tried for pretended offences:

For abolishing the free System of English Laws in a neighboring Province, establishing therein an Arbitrary government, and enlarging its Boundaries so as to render it at once an example and fit instrument for introducing the same absolute rule into these Colonies:

For taking away our Charters, abolishing our most valuable Laws, and altering fundamentally the Forms of our Governments:

For suspending our own Legislatures, and declaring themselves invested with power to legislate for us in all cases whatsoever.

He has abdicated Government here, by declaring us out of his Protection and waging War against us.

He has plundered our seas, ravaged our Coasts, burnt our towns, and destroyed the lives of our people.

He is at this time transporting large Armies of foreign Mercenaries to compleat the works of death, desolation and tyranny, already begun with circumstances of Cruelty & perfidy scarcely paralleled in the most barbarous ages, and totally unworthy the Head of a civilized nation.

He has constrained our fellow Citizens taken Captive on the high Seas to bear Arms against their Country, to become the executioners of their friends and Brethren, or to fall themselves by their Hands.

He has excited domestic insurrections amongst us, and has endeavoured to bring on the inhabitants of our frontiers, the merciless Indian Savages, whose known rule of warfare, is an undistinguished destruction of all ages, sexes and conditions.

In every stage of these Oppressions We have Petitioned for Redress in the most humble terms: Our repeated Petitions have been answered only by repeated injury. A Prince whose character is thus marked by every act which may define a Tyrant, is unfit to be the ruler of a free people.

Nor have We been wanting in attentions to our Brittish brethren. We have warned them from time to time of attempts by their legislature to extend an unwarrantable jurisdiction over us. We have reminded them of the circumstances of our emigration and settlement here. We have appealed to their native justice and magnanimity, and we have conjured them by the ties of our common kindred to disavow these usurpations, which, would inevitably interrupt our connections and correspondence. They too have been deaf to the voice of justice and of consanguinity. We must, therefore, acquiesce in the necessity, which denounces our Separation, and hold them, as we hold the rest of mankind, Enemies in War, in Peace Friends.

We, Therefore, the Representatives of the United States of America, in General Congress, Assembled, appealing to the Supreme Judge of the world for the rectitude of our intentions, do, in the Name, and by Authority of the good People of these Colonies, solemnly publish and declare, That these United Colonies are, and of Right ought to be Free and Independent States; that they are Absolved from all Allegiance to the British Crown, and that all political connection between them and the State of Great Britain, is and ought to be totally dissolved; and that as Free and Independent States, they have full Power to levy War, conclude Peace, contract Alliances, establish Commerce, and to do all other Acts and Things which Independent States may of right do. And for the support of this Declaration, with a firm reliance on the protection of divine Providence, we mutually pledge to each other our Lives, our Fortunes and our sacred Honor.

The foregoing Declaration was, by order of Congress, engrossed, and signed by the following members:

John Hancock

New Hampshire
Josiah Bartlett
William Whipple
Matthew Thornton

Massachusetts Bay
Samuel Adams
John Adams
Robert Treat Paine
Elbridge Gerry

Rhode Island
Stephen Hopkins
William Ellery

Connecticut
Roger Sherman
Samuel Huntington
William Williams
Oliver Wolcott

New York
William Floyd
Philip Livingston
Francis Lewis
Lewis Morris

New Jersey
Richard Stockton
John Witherspoon
Francis Hopkinson
John Hart
Abraham Clark

Pennsylvania
Robert Morris
Benjamin Rush
Benjamin Franklin
John Morton
George Clymer
James Smith
George Taylor
James Wilson
George Ross

Delaware
Caesar Rodney
George Read
Thomas M'Kean

Maryland
Samuel Chase
William Paca
Thomas Stone
Charles Carroll, of Carrollton

Virginia
George Wythe
Richard Henry Lee
Thomas Jefferson
Benjamin Harrison
Thomas Nelson, Jr.
Francis Lightfoot Lee
Carter Braxton

North Carolina
William Hooper
Joseph Hewes
John Penn

South Carolina
Edward Rutledge
Thomas Heyward, Jr.
Thomas Lynch, Jr.
Arthur Middleton

Georgia
Button Gwinnett
Lyman Hall
George Walton

Resolved, That copies of the Declaration be sent to the several assemblies, conventions, and committees, or councils of safety, and to the several commanding officers of the continental troops; that it be proclaimed in each of the United States, at the head of the army.

The Articles of Confederation

Agreed to by Congress November 15, 1777;
ratified and in force March 1, 1781

To all whom these Presents shall come, we the undersigned Delegates of the States affixed to our Names, send greeting. Whereas the Delegates of the United States of America, in Congress assembled, did, on the fifteenth day of November, in the Year of Our Lord One thousand Seven Hundred and Seventy seven, and in the Second Year of the Independence of America, agree to certain articles of Confederation and perpetual Union between the States of Newhampshire, Massachusetts-bay, Rhodeisland and Providence Plantations, Connecticut, New-York, New-Jersey, Pennsylvania, Delaware, Maryland, Virginia, North-Carolina, South-Carolina and Georgia in the words following, viz. "Articles of Confederation and perpetual Union between the states of Newhampshire, Massachusettsbay, Rhodeisland and Providence Plantations, Connecticut, New-York, New-Jersey, Pennsylvania, Delaware, Maryland, Virginia, North-Carolina, South-Carolina and Georgia.

Art. I. The Stile of this confederacy shall be "The United States of America."

Art. II. Each state retains its sovereignty, freedom and independence, and every Power, Jurisdiction and right, which is not by this confederation expressly delegated to the United States, in Congress assembled.

Art. III. The said states hereby severally enter into a firm league of friendship with each other, for their common defence, the security of their Liberties, and their mutual and general welfare, binding themselves to assist each other, against all force offered to, or attacks made upon them, or any of them, on account of religion, sovereignty, trade, or any other pretence whatever.

Art. IV. The better to secure and perpetuate mutual friendship and intercourse among the people of the different states in this union, the free inhabitants of each of these states, paupers, vagabonds and fugitives from Justice excepted, shall be entitled to all privileges and immunities of free citizens in the several states; and the people of each state shall have free ingress and regress to and from any other state, and shall enjoy therein all the privileges of trade and commerce, subject to the same duties, impositions and restrictions as the inhabitants thereof respectively, provided that such restriction shall not extend so far as to prevent the removal of property imported into any state, to any other state, of which the Owner is an inhabitant; provided also that no imposition, duties or restriction shall be laid by any state, on the property of the united states, or either of them.

If any Person guilty of, or charged with treason, felony, or other high misdemeanor in any state, shall flee from Justice, and be found in any of the united states, he shall, upon demand of the Governor or executive power, of the state from which he fled, be delivered up and removed to the state having jurisdiction of his offence.

Full faith and credit shall be given in each of these states to the records, acts and judicial proceedings of the courts and magistrates of every other state.

Art. V. For the more convenient management of the general interests of the united states, delegates shall be annually appointed in such manner as the legislature of each state shall direct, to meet in Congress on the first Monday in November, in every year, with a power reserved to each state, to recall its delegates, or any of them, at any time within the year, and to send others in their stead, for the remainder of the Year.

No state shall be represented in Congress by less than two, nor by more than seven Members; and no person shall be capable of being a delegate for more than three years in any term of six years; nor shall any person, being a delegate, be capable of holding any office under the united states, for which he, or another for his benefit receives any salary, fees or emolument of any kind.

Each state shall maintain its own delegates in a meeting of the states, and while they act as members of the committee of the states.

In determining questions in the united states, in Congress assembled, each state shall have one vote.

Freedom of speech and debate in Congress shall not be impeached or questioned in any Court, or place out of Congress, and the members of congress shall be protected in their persons from arrests and imprisonments, during the time of their going to and from, and attendance on congress, except for treason, felony, or breach of the peace.

Art. VI. No state without the Consent of the united states in congress assembled, shall send any embassy to, or receive any embassy from, or enter into any conference, agreement, or alliance or treaty with any King, prince or state; nor shall any person holding any office or profit or trust under the united states, or any of them, accept of any present, emolument, office or title of any kind whatever from any king, prince or foreign state; nor shall the united states in congress assembled, or any of them, grant any title of nobility.

No two or more states shall enter into any treaty, confederation or alliance whatever between them, without the consent of the united states in congress assembled, specifying accurately the purposes for which the same is to be entered into, and how long it shall continue.

No state shall lay any imposts or duties, which may interfere with any stipulations in treaties, entered into by the united states in congress assembled, with any king, prince or state, in pursuance of any treaties already proposed by congress, to the courts of France and Spain.

No vessels of war shall be kept up in time of peace by any state, except such number only, as shall be deemed necessary by the united states in congress assembled, for the defence of such state, or its trade; nor shall any body of forces be kept up by any state, in time of peace, except such number only, as in the judgment of the united states, in congress assembled, shall be deemed requisite to garrison the forts necessary for the defence of such state; but every state shall always keep up a well regulated and disciplined militia, sufficiently armed and accoutred, and shall provide and constantly have ready for use, in public stores, a due number of field pieces and tents, and a proper quantity of arms, ammunition and camp equipage.

No state shall engage in any war without the consent of the united states in congress assembled, unless such state be actually invaded by enemies, or shall have received certain advice of a resolution being formed by some nation of Indians to invade such state, and the danger is so imminent as not to admit of a delay, till the united states in congress asssembled can be consulted; nor shall any state grant commissions to any ships or vessels of war, nor letters of marque or reprisal, except it be after a declaration of war by the united states in congress assembled, and then only against the kingdom or state and the subjects thereof, against which war has been so declared, and under such regulations as shall be established by the united states in congress assembled, unless such state be infested by pirates; in which case vessels of war may be fitted out for that occasion, and kept so long as the danger shall continue, or until the united states in congress assembled shall determine otherwise.

Art. VII. When land-forces are raised by any state for the common defence, all officers of or under the rank of colonel, shall be appointed by the legislature of each state respectively, by whom such forces shall be raised, or in such manner as such state shall direct, and all vacancies shall be filled up by the state which first made the appointment.

Art. VIII. All charges of war, and all other expences that shall be incurred for the common defence or general welfare, and allowed by the united states in congress assembled, shall be defrayed out of a common treasury, which shall be supplied by the several states in proportion to the value of all land within each state, granted to or surveyed for any Person, as such land and the buildings and improvements thereon shall be estimated according to such mode as the united states in congress assembled, shall from time to time direct and appoint.

The taxes for paying that proportion shall be laid and levied by the authority and direction of the legislatures of the several states within the time agreed upon by the united states in congress assembled.

Art. IX. The united states in congress assembled, shall have the sole and exclusive right and power of determining on peace and war, except in the cases mentioned in the sixth article—of sending and receiving ambassadors—entering into treaties and alliances, provided that no treaty of commerce shall be made whereby the legislative power of the respective states shall be restrained from imposing such imposts and duties on foreigners, as their own people are subjected to, or from prohibiting the exportation of any species of goods or commodities whatsoever—of establishing rules for deciding in all cases, what captures on land or water shall be legal, and in what manner prizes taken by land or naval forces in the service of the united states shall be divided or appropriated—of granting letters of marque and reprisal in times of peace—appointing courts for the trial of piracies and felonies committed on the high seas and establishing courts for receiving and determining finally appeals in all cases of captures, provided that no member of congress shall be appointed a judge of any of the said courts.

The united states in congress assembled shall also be the last resort on appeal in all disputes and differences now subsisting or that hereafter may arise between two or more states concerning boundary, jurisdiction or any other cause whatever; which authority shall always be exercised in the manner following. Whenever the legislative or executive authority or lawful agent of any state in controversy with another shall present a petition to congress stating the matter in question and praying for a hearing, notice thereof shall be given by order of congress to the legislative or executive authority of the other state in controversy, and a day assigned for the appearance of the parties by their lawful agents, who shall then be directed to appoint by joint consent, commissioners or judges to constitute a court for hearing and determining the matter in question: but if they cannot agree, congress shall name three persons out of each of the united states, and from the list of such persons each party shall alternately strike out one, the petitioners beginning, until the number shall be reduced to thirteen; and from that number not less than seven, nor more than nine names as congress shall direct, shall in the presence of congress be drawn out by lot, and the persons whose names shall be so drawn or any five of them, shall be commissioners or judges, to hear and finally determine the controversy, so always as a major part of the judges who shall hear the cause shall agree in the determination: and if either party shall neglect to attend at the day appointed, without shewing reasons, which congress shall judge sufficient, or being present shall refuse to strike, the congress shall proceed to nominate three persons out of each state, and the secretary of congress shall strike in behalf of such party absent or refusing; and the judgment and sentence of the court to be appointed, in the manner before prescribed, shall be final and conclusive; and if any of the parties shall refuse to submit to the authority of such court, or to appear to defend their claim or cause, the court shall nevertheless proceed to pronounce sentence, or judgment, which shall in like manner be final and decisive, the judgment or sentence and other proceedings being in either case transmitted to congress, and lodged among the acts of congress for the security of the parties concerned: provided that every commissioner, before he sits in judgment, shall take an oath to be administered by one of the judges of the supreme or superior court of the state, where the cause shall be tried, "well and truly to hear and determine the matter in question, according to the best of his judgment, without favour, affection or hope of reward:" provided also, that no state shall be deprived of territory for the benefit of the united states.

All controversies concerning the private right of soil claimed under different grants of two or more states, whose jurisdictions as they may respect such lands, and the states which passed such grants are adjusted, the said grants or either of them being at the same time claimed to have originated antecedent to such settlement of jurisdiction, shall on the petition of either party to the congress of the united states, be finally determined as near as may be in the same manner as is before prescribed for deciding disputes respecting territorial jurisdiction between different states.

The united states in congress assembled shall also have the sole and exclusive right and power of regulating the alloy and value of coin struck by their own authority, or by that of the respective states—fixing the standard of weights and measures throughout the united states—regulating the trade and managing all affairs with the Indians, not members of any of the states, provided that the legislative right of any state within its own limits be not infringed or violated—establishing and regulating post-offices from one state to another, throughout all the united states, and exacting such postage on the papers passing thro' the same as may be requisite to defray the expences of the said office—appointing all officers of the land forces, in the service of the united states, excepting regimental officers—appointing all the officers of the naval forces, and commissioning all officers whatever in the service of the united states—making rules for the government and regulation of the said land and naval forces, and directing their operations.

The united states in congress assembled shall have authority to appoint a committee, to sit in the recess of congress, to be denominated "A Committee of the States," and to consist of one delegate from each state; and to appoint such other committees and civil officers as may be necessary for managing the general affairs of the united states under their direction—to appoint one of their number to preside, provided that no person be allowed to serve in the office of president more than one year in any term of three years; to ascertain the necessary sums of Money to be raised for the service of the united states, and to appropriate and apply the same for defraying the public expenses—to borrow money, or emit bills on the credit of the united states, transmitting every half year to the respective states an account of the sums of money so borrowed or emitted,—to build and equip a navy—to agree upon the number of land forces, and to make requisitions from each state for its quota, in proportion to the number of white inhabitants in such state; which requisition shall be binding, and thereupon the legislature of each state shall appoint the regimental officers, raise the men and cloath, arm and equip them in a soldier like manner, at the expense of the united states; and the officers and men so cloathed, armed and equipped shall march to the place appointed, and within the time agreed on by the united states in congress assembled: But if the united states in congress assembled shall, on consideration of circumstances judge proper that any state should not raise men, or should raise a smaller number than its quota, and that any other state should raise a greater number of men than the quota thereof, such extra number shall be raised, officered, cloathed, armed and equipped in the same manner as the quota of such state, unless the legislature of such state shall judge that such extra number cannot be safely spared out of the same, in which case they shall raise officer, cloath, arm and equip as many of such extra number as they judge can be safely spared. And the officers and men so cloathed, armed and equipped, shall march to the place appointed, and within the time agreed on by the united states in congress assembled.

The united states in congress assembled shall never engage in a war, nor grant letters of marque and reprisal in time of peace, nor enter into any treaties or alliances, nor coin money, nor regulate the value thereof, nor ascertain the sums and expenses necessary for the defence and welfare of the united states, or any of them, nor emit bills, nor borrow money on the credit of the united states, nor appropriate money, nor agree upon the number of vessels of war, to be built or purchased, or the number of land or sea forces to be raised, nor appoint a commander in chief of the army or navy, unless nine states assent to the same: nor shall a question on any other point, except for adjourning from day to day be determined, unless by the votes of a majority of the united states in congress assembled.

The congress of the united states shall have power to adjourn to any time within the year, and to any place within the united states, so that no period of adjournment be for a longer duration than the space of six Months, and shall publish the Journal of their proceedings monthly, except such parts thereof relating to treaties, alliances or military operations, as in their judgment require secrecy; and the yeas and nays of the delegates of each state on any question shall be entered on the Journal, when it is desired by any delegate; and the delegates of a state, or any of them, at his or their request shall be furnished with a transcript of the said Journal, except such parts as are above excepted, to lay before the legislatures of the several states.

Art. X. The committee of the states, or any nine of them, shall be authorised to execute, in the recess of congress, such of the powers of congress as the united states in congress assembled, by the consent of nine states, shall from time to time think expedient to vest them with; provided that no power be delegated to the said committee, for the exercise of which, by the articles of confederation, the voice of nine states in the congress of the united states assembled is requisite.

Art. XI. Canada acceding to this confederation, and joining in the measures of the united states, shall be admitted into, and entitled to all the advantages of this union: but no other colony shall be admitted into the same, unless such admission be agreed to by nine states.

Art. XII. All bills of credit emitted, monies borrowed and debts contracted by, or under the authority of congress, before the assembling of the united states, in pursuance of the present confederation, shall be deemed and considered as a charge against the united states, for payment and satisfaction whereof the said united states and the public faith are hereby solemnly pledged.

Art. XIII. Every state shall abide by the determinations of the united states in congress assembled, on all questions which by this confederation are submitted to them. And the Articles of this confederation shall be inviolably observed by every state, and the union shall be perpetual; nor shall any alteration at any time hereafter be made in any of them; unless such alteration be agreed to in a congress of the united states, and be afterwards confirmed by the legislatures of every state.

And Whereas it hath pleased the Great Governor of the World to incline the hearts of the legislatures we respectively represent in congress, to approve of, and to authorize us to ratify the said articles of confederation and perpetual union. Know Ye that we the undersigned delegates, by virtue of the power and authority to us given for that purpose, do by these presents, in the name and in behalf of our respective constituents, fully and entirely ratify and confirm each and every of the said articles of confederation and perpetual union, and all and singular the matters and things therein contained: And we do further solemnly plight and engage the faith of our respective constituents, that they shall abide by the determinations of the united states in congress assembled, on all questions, which by the said confederation are submitted to them. And that the articles thereof shall be inviolably observed by the states we respectively represent, and that the union shall be perpetual. In Witness whereof we have hereunto set our hands in Congress. Done at Philadelphia in the state of Pennsylvania the ninth day of July, in the Year of our Lord one Thousand seven Hundred and Seventy-eight, and in the third year of the independence of America.

The Constitution of the United States of America

[PREAMBLE]

We the People of the United States, in Order to form a more perfect Union, establish Justice, insure domestic Tranquility, provide for the common defence, promote the general Welfare, and secure the Blessings of Liberty to ourselves and our Posterity, do ordain and establish this Constitution for the United States of America.

Article I

SECTION 1

[LEGISLATIVE POWERS]

All legislative Powers herein granted shall be vested in a Congress of the United States, which shall consist of a Senate and House of Representatives.

SECTION 2

[HOUSE OF REPRESENTATIVES, HOW CONSTITUTED, POWER OF IMPEACHMENT]

The House of Representatives shall be composed of Members chosen every second Year by the People of the several States, and the Electors in each State shall have the Qualifications requisite for Electors of the most numerous Branch of the State Legislature.

No Person shall be a Representative who shall not have attained to the Age of twenty five Years, and been seven Years a Citizen of the United States, and who shall not, when elected, be an Inhabitant of that State in which he shall be chosen.

Representatives and *direct Taxes*[1] shall be apportioned among the several States which may be included within this Union, according to their respective Numbers, *which shall be determined by adding to the whole Number of free Persons, including those bound to Service for a Term of Years, and excluding Indians not taxed, three fifths of all other Persons.*[2] The actual Enumeration shall be made within three Years after the first Meeting of the Congress of the United States, and within every subsequent Term of ten Years, in such Manner as they shall by Law direct. The Number of Representatives shall not exceed one for every thirty Thousand, but each State shall have at Least one Representative; *and until such enumeration shall be made, the State of New Hampshire shall be entitled to chuse three, Massachusetts eight, Rhode-Island and Providence Plantations one, Connecticut five, New-York six, New Jersey four, Pennsylvania eight, Delaware one, Maryland six, Virginia ten, North Carolina five, South Carolina five, and Georgia three.*[3]

When vacancies happen in the Representation from any State, the Executive Authority thereof shall issue Writs of Election to fill such Vacancies.

The House of Representatives shall chuse their Speaker and other Officers; and shall have the sole Power of Impeachment.

SECTION 3

[THE SENATE, HOW CONSTITUTED, IMPEACHMENT TRIALS]

The Senate of the United States shall be composed of two Senators from each State, *chosen by the Legislature thereof,*[4] for six Years; and each Senator shall have one Vote.

Immediately after they shall be assembled in Consequence of the first Election, they shall be divided as equally as may be into three Classes. The Seats of the Senators of the first Class shall be vacated at the Expiration of the second Year, of the second Class at the Expiration of the fourth Year, and of the third Class at the Expiration of the sixth Year, so that one third may be chosen every second Year; *and if Vacancies happen by Resignation, or otherwise, during the Recess of the Legislature of any State, the Executive thereof may make temporary Appointments until the next Meeting of the Legislature, which shall then fill such Vacancies.*[5]

No Person shall be a Senator who shall not have attained to the Age of thirty Years, and been nine Years a Citizen of the United States, and who shall not, when elected, be an Inhabitant of that State for which he shall be chosen.

The Vice President of the United States shall be President of the Senate, but shall have no Vote, unless they be equally divided.

The Senate shall chuse their other Officers, and also a President pro tempore, in the Absence of the Vice President, or when he shall exercise the Office of President of the United States.

The Senate shall have the sole Power to try all Impeachments. When sitting for that Purpose, they shall be on Oath or Affirmation. When the President of the United States is tried, the Chief Justice shall preside: And no Person shall be convicted without the Concurrence of two thirds of the Members present.

Judgment in Cases of Impeachment shall not extend further than to removal from Office, and disqualification to hold and enjoy any Office of honor, Trust or Profit under the United States: but the Party convicted shall nevertheless be liable and subject to Indictment, Trial, Judgment and Punishment, according to Law.

SECTION 4

[ELECTION OF SENATORS AND REPRESENTATIVES]

The Times, Places and Manner of holding Elections for Senators and Representatives, shall be prescribed in each State by the Legislature thereof; but the Congress may at any time by Law make or alter such Regulations, except as to the Places of chusing Senators.

The Congress shall assemble at least once in every Year, and such Meeting shall be on the first Monday in December, unless they shall by Law appoint a different Day.[6]

SECTION 5

[QUORUM, JOURNALS, MEETINGS, ADJOURNMENTS]

Each House shall be the Judge of the Elections, Returns and Qualifications of its own Members, and a Majority of each shall constitute a Quorum to do Business; but a smaller Number may adjourn from day to day, and may be authorized to compel the

---

[1] Modified by Sixteenth Amendment.
[2] Modified by Fourteenth Amendment.
[3] Temporary provision.
[4] Modified by Seventeenth Amendment.
[5] Modified by Seventeenth Amendment.
[6] Modified by Twentieth Amendment.

Attendance of absent Members, in such Manner, and under such Penalties as each House may provide.

Each House may determine the Rules of its Proceedings, punish its Members for disorderly Behaviour, and, with the Concurrence of two thirds, expel a Member.

Each House shall keep a Journal of its Proceedings, and from time to time publish the same, excepting such Parts as may in their Judgment require Secrecy; and the Yeas and Nays of the Members of either House on any questions shall, at the Desire of one fifth of those Present, be entered on the Journal.

Neither House, during the Session of Congress, shall, without the Consent of the other, adjourn for more than three days, nor to any other Place than that in which the two Houses shall be sitting.

SECTION 6
[COMPENSATION, PRIVILEGES, DISABILITIES]

The Senators and Representatives shall receive a Compensation for their Services, to be ascertained by Law, and paid out of the Treasury of the United States. They shall in all Cases, except Treason, Felony and Breach of the Peace, be privileged from Arrest during their Attendance at the Session of their respective Houses, and in going to and returning from the same; and for any Speech or Debate in either House, they shall not be questioned in any other Place.

No Senator or Representative shall, during the Time for which he was elected, be appointed to any civil Office under the Authority of the United States, which shall have been created, or the Emoluments whereof shall have been encreased during such time; and no Person holding any Office under the United States, shall be a Member of either House during his Continuance in Office.

SECTION 7
[PROCEDURE IN PASSING BILLS AND RESOLUTIONS]

All Bills for raising Revenue shall originate in the House of Representatives; but the Senate may propose or concur with Amendments as on other Bills.

Every Bill which shall have passed the House of Representatives and the Senate, shall, before it become a Law, be presented to the President of the United States: If he approve he shall sign it, but if not he shall return it, with his Objections to that House in which it shall have originated, who shall enter the Objections at large on their Journal, and proceed to reconsider it. If after such Reconsideration two thirds of that House shall agree to pass the Bill, it shall be sent, together with the Objections, to the other House, by which it shall likewise be reconsidered, and if approved by two thirds of that House, it shall become a Law. But in all such Cases the Votes of both Houses shall be determined by yeas and Nays, and the Names of the Persons voting for and against the Bill shall be entered on the Journal of each House respectively. If any Bill shall not be returned by the President within ten Days (Sundays excepted) after it shall have been presented to him, the Same shall be a Law, in like Manner as if he had signed it, unless the Congress by their Adjournment prevent its Return, in which Case it shall not be a Law.

Every Order, Resolution, or Vote to which the Concurrence of the Senate and House of Representatives may be necessary (except on a question of Adjournment) shall be presented to the President of the United States; and before the Same shall take Effect, shall be approved by him, or being disapproved by him, shall be repassed by two thirds of the Senate and House of Representatives, according to the Rules and Limitations prescribed in the Case of a Bill.

SECTION 8
[POWERS OF CONGRESS]

The Congress shall have Power

To lay and collect Taxes, Duties, Imposts and Excises, to pay the Debts and provide for the common Defence and general Welfare of the United States; but all Duties, Imposts and Excises shall be uniform throughout the United States;

To borrow Money on the credit of the United States;

To regulate Commerce with foreign Nations, and among the several States, and with the Indian Tribes;

To establish an uniform Rule of Naturalization, and uniform Laws on the subject of Bankruptcies throughout the United States;

To coin Money, regulate the Value thereof, and of foreign Coin, and fix the Standard of Weights and Measures;

To provide for the Punishment of counterfeiting the Securities and current Coin of the United States;

To establish Post Offices and post Roads;

To promote the Progress of Science and useful Arts, by securing for limited Times to Authors and Inventors the exclusive Right to their respective Writings and Discoveries;

To constitute Tribunals inferior to the supreme Court;

To define and punish Piracies and Felonies committed on the high Seas, and Offences against the Law of Nations;

To declare War, grant Letters of Marque and Reprisal, and make Rules concerning Captures on Land and Water;

To raise and support Armies, but no Appropriation of Money to that Use shall be for a longer Term than two Years;

To provide and maintain a Navy;

To make Rules for the Government and Regulation of the land and naval Forces;

To provide for calling forth the Militia to execute the Laws of the Union, suppress Insurrections and repel Invasions;

To provide for organizing, arming, and disciplining, the Militia, and for governing such Part of them as may be employed in the Service of the United States, reserving to the States respectively, the Appointment of the Officers, and the Authority of training the Militia according to the discipline prescribed by Congress;

To exercise exclusive Legislation in all Cases whatsoever, over such District (not exceeding ten Miles square) as may, by Cession of particular States, and the Acceptance of Congress, become the Seat of the Government of the United States, and to exercise like Authority over all Places purchased by the Consent of the Legislature of the State in which the Same shall be, for the Erection of Forts, Magazines, Arsenals, dock-Yards, and other needful Buildings;—And

To make all Laws which shall be necessary and proper for carrying into Execution the foregoing Powers, and all other Powers vested by this Constitution in the Government of the United States, or in any Department or Officer thereof.

SECTION 9
[SOME RESTRICTIONS ON FEDERAL POWER]

The Migration or Importation of such Persons as any of the States now existing shall think proper to admit, shall not be prohibited by the Congress prior to the Year one thousand eight hundred and eight, but a Tax or duty may be imposed on such Importation, not exceeding ten dollars for each Person.[7]

---

[7] Temporary provision.

The Privilege of the Writ of Habeas Corpus shall not be suspended, unless when in Cases of Rebellion or Invasion the public Safety may require it.

No Bill of Attainder or ex post facto Law shall be passed.

No Capitation, or other direct, Tax shall be laid, unless in Proportion to the Census or Enumeration herein before directed to be taken.[8]

No Tax or Duty shall be laid on Articles exported from any State.

No Preference shall be given by any Regulation of Commerce or Revenue to the Ports of one State over those of another; nor shall Vessels bound to, or from, one State, be obliged to enter, clear, or pay Duties in another.

No Money shall be drawn from the Treasury, but in Consequence of Appropriations made by Law; and a regular Statement and Account of the Receipts and Expenditures of all public Money shall be published from time to time.

No Title of Nobility shall be granted by the United States: And no Person holding any Office of Profit or Trust under them, shall, without the Consent of the Congress, accept of any present, Emolument, Office, or Title, of any kind whatever, from any King, Prince, or foreign State.

SECTION 10
[RESTRICTIONS UPON POWERS OF STATES]

No State shall enter into any Treaty, Alliance, or Confederation; grant Letters of Marque and Reprisal; coin Money; emit Bills of Credit; make any Thing but gold and silver Coin a Tender in Payment of Debts; pass any Bill of Attainder, ex post facto Law, or Law impairing the Obligation of Contracts, or grant any Title of Nobility.

No State shall, without the Consent of the Congress, lay any Imposts or Duties on Imports or Exports, except what may be absolutely necessary for executing its inspection Laws: and the net Produce of all Duties and Imposts, laid by any State on Imports or Exports, shall be for the Use of the Treasury of the United States; and all such Laws shall be subject to the Revision and Control of the Congress.

No State shall, without the Consent of Congress, lay any Duty of Tonnage, keep Troops, or Ships of War in time of Peace, enter into any Agreement or Compact with another State, or with a foreign Power, or engage in War, unless actually invaded, or in such imminent Danger as will not admit of delay.

Article II

SECTION 1
[EXECUTIVE POWER, ELECTION, QUALIFICATIONS OF THE PRESIDENT]

The executive Power shall be vested in a President of the United States of America. *He shall hold his Office during the Term of four Years, and, together with the Vice President, chosen for the same Term, be elected, as follows*[9]

Each State shall appoint, in such Manner as the Legislature thereof may direct, a Number of Electors, equal to the whole Number of Senators and Representatives to which the State may be entitled in the Congress: but no Senator or Representative, or Person holding an Office of Trust or Profit under the United States, shall be appointed an Elector.

The electors shall meet in their respective States, and vote by ballot for two Persons, of whom one at least shall not be an Inhabitant of the same State with themselves. And they shall make a List of all the Persons voted for, and of the Number of Votes for each; which List they shall sign and certify, and transmit sealed to the Seat of the Government of the United States, directed to the President of the Senate. The President of the Senate shall, in the Presence of the Senate and House of Representatives, open all the Certificates, and the Votes shall then be counted. The Person having the greatest Number of Votes shall be the President, if such Number be a Majority of the whole Number of Electors appointed; and if there be more than one who have such Majority, and have an equal Number of Votes, then the House of Representatives shall immediately chuse by Ballot one of them for President; and if no Person have a Majority, then from the five highest on the List the said House shall in like Manner chuse the President. But in chusing the President, the Votes shall be taken by States, the Representation from each State having one Vote; A quorum for this Purpose shall consist of a Member or Members from two thirds of the States, and a Majority of all the States shall be necessary to a Choice. In every Case, after the Choice of the President, the person having the greatest Number of Votes of the Electors shall be the Vice President. But if there should remain two or more who have equal Votes, the Senate shall chuse from them by Ballot the Vice President.[10]

The Congress may determine the Time of chusing the Electors, and the Day on which they shall give their Votes; which Day shall be the same throughout the United States.

No Person except a natural born Citizen, or a Citizen of the United States, at the time of the Adoption of this Constitution, shall be eligible to the Office of President; neither shall any Person be eligible to that Office who shall not have attained to the Age of thirty five Years, and been fourteen Years a Resident within the United States.

In Case of the Removal of the President from Office, or his Death, Resignation, or Inability to discharge the Powers and Duties of the said Office, the Same shall devolve on the Vice President, and the Congress may by Law provide for the Case of Removal, Death, Resignation or Inability, both of the President and Vice President, declaring what Officer shall then act as President, and such Officer shall act accordingly, until the Disability be removed, or a President shall be elected.

The President shall, at stated Times, receive for his Services, a Compensation, which shall neither be increased nor diminished during the Period for which he shall have been elected, and he shall not receive within that Period any other Emolument from the United States, or any of them.

Before he enter on the Execution of his Office, he shall take the following Oath or Affirmation:—"I do solemnly swear (or affirm) that I will faithfully execute the Office of President of the United States, and will to the best of my Ability, preserve, protect and defend the Constitution of the United States."

SECTION 2
[POWERS OF THE PRESIDENT]

The President shall be Commander in Chief of the Army and Navy of the United States, and of the Militia of the several States, when called into the actual Service of the United States; he may require the Opinion, in writing, of the principal Officer in each of the executive Departments, upon any Subject relating to the Duties of their respective Offices, and he shall have Power to grant Reprieves and Pardons for Offences against the United States, except in Cases of Impeachment.

He shall have Power, by and with the Advice and Consent of the Senate, to make Treaties, provided two thirds of the Senators present concur; and he shall nominate, and by and with the Advice

---

[8] Modified by Sixteenth Amendment.
[9] Number of terms limited to two by Twenty-second Amendment.
[10] Modified by the Twelfth and Twentieth Amendments.

and Consent of the Senate, shall appoint Ambassadors, other public Ministers and Consuls, Judges of the supreme Court, and all other Officers of the United States, whose Appointments are not herein otherwise provided for, and which shall be established by Law: but the Congress may by Law vest the Appointment of such inferior Officers, as they think proper, in the President alone, in the Courts of Law, or in the Heads of Departments.

The President shall have Power to fill up all Vacancies that may happen during the Recess of the Senate, by granting Commissions which shall expire at the End of their next Session.

SECTION 3
[POWERS AND DUTIES OF THE PRESIDENT]

He shall from time to time give to the Congress Information of the State of the Union, and recommend to their Consideration such Measures as he shall judge necessary and expedient; he may, on extraordinary Occasions, convene both Houses, or either of them, and in Case of Disagreement between them, with Respect to the Time of Adjournment, he may adjourn them to such Time as he shall think proper; he shall receive Ambassadors and other public Ministers; he shall take Care that the Laws be faithfully executed, and shall Commission all the Officers of the United States.

SECTION 4
[IMPEACHMENT]

The President, Vice President and all civil Officers of the United States, shall be removed from Office on Impeachment for, and Conviction of, Treason, Bribery, or other high Crimes and Misdemeanors.

Article III

SECTION 1
[JUDICIAL POWER, TENURE OF OFFICE]

The judicial Power of the United States, shall be vested in one supreme Court, and in such inferior Courts as the Congress may from time to time ordain and establish. The Judges, both of the supreme and inferior Courts, shall hold their Offices during good Behaviour, and shall, at stated Times, receive for their Services, a Compensation, which shall not be diminished during their Continuance in Office.

SECTION 2
[JURISDICTION]

The judicial Power shall extend to all Cases, in Law and Equity, arising under this Constitution, the Laws of the United States, and Treaties made, or which shall be made, under their Authority;—to all Cases affecting Ambassadors, other public Ministers and Consuls;—to all Cases of admiralty and maritime Jurisdiction;—to Controversies to which the United States shall be a Party;—to Controversies between two or more States;—*between a State and Citizens of another State;*—between Citizens of different States,—between Citizens of the same State claiming Lands under Grants of different States, *and between a State,* or the Citizens thereof, *and foreign States, Citizens or Subjects.*[11]

In all Cases affecting Ambassadors, other public Ministers and Consuls, and those in which a State shall be Party, the supreme Court shall have original Jurisdiction. In all the other Cases before mentioned, the supreme Court shall have appellate Jurisdiction, both as to Law and Fact, with such Exceptions, and under such Regulations as the Congress shall make.

The Trial of all Crimes, except in Cases of Impeachment, shall be by Jury; and such Trial shall be held in the State where the said Crimes shall have been committed; but when not committed within any State, the Trial shall be at such Place or Places as the Congress may by Law have directed.

SECTION 3
[TREASON, PROOF, AND PUNISHMENT]

Treason against the United States, shall consist only in levying War against them, or in adhering to their Enemies, giving them Aid and Comfort. No Person shall be convicted of Treason unless on the Testimony of two Witnesses to the same overt Act, or on Confession in open Court.

The Congress shall have Power to declare the Punishment of Treason, but no Attainder of Treason shall work Corruption of Blood, or Forfeiture except during the Life of the Person attainted.

Article IV

SECTION 1
[FAITH AND CREDIT AMONG STATES]

Full Faith and Credit shall be given in each State to the public Acts, Records, and judicial Proceedings of every other State. And the Congress may by general Laws prescribe the Manner in which such Acts, Records and Proceedings shall be proved, and the Effect thereof.

SECTION 2
[PRIVILEGES AND IMMUNITIES, FUGITIVES]

The Citizens of each State shall be entitled to all Privileges and Immunities of Citizens in the several States.

A Person charged in any State with Treason, Felony or other Crime, who shall flee from Justice, and be found in another State, shall on Demand of the executive Authority of the State from which he fled, be delivered up, to be removed to the State having Jurisdiction of the Crime.

No person held to Service or Labour in one State, under the Laws thereof, escaping into another, shall, in Consequence of any Law or Regulation therein, be discharged from such Service or Labour, but shall be delivered up on Claim of the Party to whom such Service or Labour may be due.[12]

SECTION 3
[ADMISSION OF NEW STATES]

New States may be admitted by the Congress into this Union; but no new State shall be formed or erected within the Jurisdiction of any other State; nor any State be formed by the Junction of two or more States, or Parts of States, without the Consent of the Legislatures of the States concerned as well as of the Congress.

The Congress shall have Power to dispose of and make all needful Rules and Regulations respecting the Territory or other Property belonging to the United States; and nothing in this Constitution shall be so construed as to Prejudice any Claims of the United States, or of any particular State.

---

[11] Modified by the Eleventh Amendment.

[12] Repealed by the Thirteenth Amendment.

SECTION 4
[GUARANTEE OF REPUBLICAN GOVERNMENT]

The United States shall guarantee to every State in this Union a Republican Form of Government, and shall protect each of them against Invasion; and on Application of the Legislature, or of the Executive (when the Legislature cannot be convened), against domestic Violence.

Article V
[AMENDMENT OF THE CONSTITUTION]

The Congress, whenever two thirds of both Houses shall deem it necessary, shall propose Amendments to this Constitution, or, on the Application of the Legislatures of two thirds of the several States, shall call a Convention for proposing Amendments, which, in either Case, shall be valid to all Intents and Purposes, as Part of this Constitution, when ratified by the Legislatures of three fourths of the several States, or by Conventions in three fourths thereof, as the one or the other Mode of Ratification may be proposed by the Congress; *Provided that no Amendment which may be made prior to the Year One thousand eight hundred and eight shall in any Manner affect the first and fourth Clauses in the Ninth Section of the first Article;* and that no State, without its Consent, shall be deprived of its equal Suffrage in the Senate.

Article VI
[DEBTS, SUPREMACY, OATH]

All Debts contracted and Engagements entered into, before the Adoption of this Constitution, shall be as valid against the United States under this Constitution, as under the Confederation.

This Constitution, and the Laws of the United States which shall be made in Pursuance thereof; and all Treaties made, or which shall be made, under the Authority of the United States, shall be the supreme Law of the Land; and the Judges in every State shall be bound thereby, any Thing in the Constitution or Laws of any State to the Contrary notwithstanding.

The Senators and Representatives before mentioned, and the Members of the several State Legislatures, and all executive and judicial Officers, both of the United States and of the several States, shall be bound by Oath or Affirmation, to support this Constitution; but no religious Test shall be required as a Qualification to any Office or public Trust under the United States.

Article VII
[RATIFICATION AND ESTABLISHMENT]

The Ratification of the Conventions of nine States, shall be sufficient for the Establishment of this Constitution between the States so ratifying the Same.

Done in Convention by the Unanimous Consent of the States present the Seventeenth Day of September in the Year of our Lord one thousand seven hundred and Eighty seven and of the Independence of the United States of America the Twelfth. *In Witness* whereof We have hereunto subscribed our Names,

G:° WASHINGTON—
Presidt. and deputy from Virginia

New Hampshire
John Langdon
Nicholas Gilman

Massachusetts
Nathaniel Gorham
Rufus King

Connecticut
Wm. Saml. Johnson
Roger Sherman

New York
Alexander Hamilton

New Jersey
Wil: Livingston
David Brearley
Wm. Paterson
Jona: Dayton

Pennsylvania
B Franklin
Thomas Mifflin
Robt. Morris
Geo. Clymer
Thos. FitzSimons
Jared Ingersoll
James Wilson
Gouv Morris

Delaware
Geo: Read
Gunning Bedford jun
John Dickinson
Richard Bassett
Jaco: Broom

Maryland
James McHenry
Dan of St Thos. Jenifer
Danl. Carroll

Virginia
John Blair—
James Madison Jr.

North Carolina
Wm. Blount
Richd. Dobbs Spaight
Hu Williamson

South Carolina
J. Rutledge
Charles Cotesworth
Pinckney
Charles Pinckney
Pierce Butler

Georgia
William Few
Abr Baldwin

Amendments to the Constitution

Proposed by Congress and Ratified by the Legislatures of the
Several States, Pursuant to Article V of the Original Constitution.

Amendments I–X, known as the Bill of Rights, were proposed by Congress on September 25, 1789, and ratified on December 15, 1791.

Amendment I
[FREEDOM OF RELIGION, OF SPEECH, AND OF THE PRESS]

Congress shall make no law respecting an establishment of religion, or prohibiting the free exercise thereof; or abridging the freedom of speech, or of the press; or the right of the people peaceably to assemble, and to petition the Government for a redress of grievances.

Amendment II
[RIGHT TO KEEP AND BEAR ARMS]

A well regulated Militia, being necessary to the security of a free State, the right of the people to keep and bear Arms, shall not be infringed.

Amendment III
[QUARTERING OF SOLDIERS]

No Soldier shall, in time of peace be quartered in any house, without the consent of the Owner, nor in time of war, but in a manner to be prescribed by law.

Amendment IV
[SECURITY FROM UNWARRANTABLE SEARCH AND SEIZURE]

The right of the people to be secure in their persons, houses, papers, and effects, against unreasonable searches and seizures, shall not be violated, and no Warrants shall issue, but upon probable cause, supported by Oath or affirmation, and particularly describing the place to be searched, and the persons or things to be seized.

Amendment V
[RIGHTS OF ACCUSED PERSONS IN CRIMINAL PROCEEDINGS]

No person shall be held to answer for a capital, or otherwise infamous crime, unless on a presentment or indictment of a Grand Jury, except in cases arising in the land or naval forces, or in the Militia, when in actual service in time of War or in public danger; nor shall any person be subject for the same offence to be twice put in jeopardy of life or limb; nor shall be compelled in any criminal case to be a witness against himself, nor be deprived of life, liberty, or property, without due process of law; nor shall private property be taken for public use, without just compensation.

Amendment VI
[RIGHT TO SPEEDY TRIAL, WITNESSES, ETC.]

In all criminal prosecutions, the accused shall enjoy the right to a speedy and public trial, by an impartial jury of the State and district wherein the crime shall have been committed, which district shall have been previously ascertained by law, and to be informed of the nature and cause of the accusation; to be confronted with the witnesses against him; to have compulsory process for obtaining witnesses in his favor, and to have the Assistance of Counsel for his defence.

Amendment VII
[TRIAL BY JURY IN CIVIL CASES]

In suits at common law, where the value in controversy shall exceed twenty dollars, the right of trial by jury shall be preserved, and no fact tried by a jury, shall be otherwise reexamined in any Court of the United States, than according to the rules of the common law.

Amendment VIII
[BAILS, FINES, PUNISHMENTS]

Excessive bail shall not be required, nor excessive fines imposed, nor cruel and unusual punishments inflicted.

Amendment IX
[RESERVATION OF RIGHTS OF PEOPLE]

The enumeration in the Constitution, of certain rights, shall not be construed to deny or disparage others retained by the people.

Amendment X
[POWERS RESERVED TO STATES OR PEOPLE]

The powers not delegated to the United States by the Constitution, nor prohibited by it to the States, are reserved to the States respectively, or to the people.

Amendment XI
[*Proposed by Congress on March 4, 1794; declared ratified on January 8, 1798.*]
[RESTRICTION OF JUDICIAL POWER]

The Judicial power of the United States shall not be construed to extend to any suit in law or equity, commenced or prosecuted against one of the United States by Citizens of another State, or by Citizens or Subjects of any Foreign State.

Amendment XII
[*Proposed by Congress on December 9, 1803; declared ratified on September 25, 1804.*]
[ELECTION OF PRESIDENT AND VICE PRESIDENT]

The Electors shall meet in their respective states and vote by ballot for President and Vice-President, one of whom, at least, shall not be an inhabitant of the same state with themselves; they shall name in their ballots the person voted for as President, and in distinct ballots the person voted for as Vice-President, and they shall make distinct lists of all persons voted for as President, and of all persons voted for as Vice-President, and of the number of votes for each, which lists they shall sign and certify, and transmit sealed to the seat of the government of the United States, directed to the President of the Senate;—the President of the Senate shall, in presence of the Senate and House of Representatives, open all the certificates and the votes shall then be counted;—The person having the greatest number of votes for President, shall be the President, if such number be a majority of the whole number of Electors appointed; and if no person have such majority, then from the persons having the highest numbers not exceeding three on the list of those voted for as President, the House of Representatives shall choose immediately, by ballot, the President. But in choosing the President, the votes shall be taken by states, the representation from each state having one vote; a quorum for this purpose shall consist of a member or members from two-thirds of the states, and a majority of all the states shall be necessary to a choice. And if the House of Representatives shall not choose a President whenever the right of choice shall devolve upon them, before the fourth day of March next following, then the Vice-President shall act as President, as in the case of the death or other constitutional disability of the President.—The person having the greatest number of votes as Vice-President, shall be the Vice-President, if such number be a majority of the whole number of Electors appointed, and if no person have a majority, then from the two highest numbers on the list, the Senate shall choose the Vice-President; a quorum for the purpose shall consist of two-thirds of the whole number of Senators, and a majority of the whole number shall be necessary to a choice. But no person constitutionally ineligible to the office of President shall be eligible to that of Vice-President of the United States.

Amendment XIII
[*Proposed by Congress on January 31, 1865; declared ratified on December 18, 1865.*]

SECTION 1
[ABOLITION OF SLAVERY]

Neither slavery nor involuntary servitude, except as a punishment for crime whereof the party shall have been duly convicted, shall exist within the United States, or any place subject to their jurisdiction.

SECTION 2
[POWER TO ENFORCE THIS ARTICLE]

Congress shall have power to enforce this article by appropriate legislation.

Amendment XIV
[*Proposed by Congress on June 13, 1866; declared ratified on July 28, 1868.*]

SECTION 1
[CITIZENSHIP RIGHTS NOT TO BE ABRIDGED BY STATES]

All persons born or naturalized in the United States, and subject to the jurisdiction thereof, are citizens of the United States and of the State wherein they reside. No State shall make or enforce any law which shall abridge the privileges or immunities of citizens of the United States; nor shall any State deprive any person of life, liberty, or property, without due process of law; nor deny to any person within its jurisdiction the equal protection of the laws.

SECTION 2
[APPORTIONMENT OF REPRESENTATIVES IN CONGRESS]

Representatives shall be apportioned among the several States according to their respective numbers, counting the whole number of persons in each State, excluding Indians not taxed. But when the right to vote at any election for the choice of electors for President and Vice-President of the United States, Representatives in Congress, the Executive and Judicial officers of a State, or the members of the Legislature thereof, is denied to any of the male inhabitants of such State, being twenty-one years of age, and citizens of the United States, or in any way abridged, except for participation in rebellion, or other crime, the basis of representation therein shall be reduced in the proportion which the number of such male citizens shall bear to the whole number of male citizens twenty-one years of age in such State.

SECTION 3
[PERSONS DISQUALIFIED FROM HOLDING OFFICE]

No person shall be a Senator or Representative in Congress, or elector of President and Vice-President, or hold any office, civil or military, under the United States, or under any State, who, having previously taken an oath, as a member of Congress, or as an officer of the United States, or as a member of any State legislature, or as an executive or judicial officer of any State, to support the Constitution of the United States, shall have engaged in insurrection or rebellion against the same, or given aid or comfort to the enemies thereof. But Congress may by a vote of two-thirds of each House, remove such disability.

SECTION 4
[WHAT PUBLIC DEBTS ARE VALID]

The validity of the public debt of the United States, authorized by law, including debts incurred for payment of pensions and bounties for services in suppressing insurrection or rebellion, shall not be questioned. But neither the United States nor any State shall assume or pay any debt or obligation incurred in aid of insurrection or rebellion against the United States, or any claim for the loss or emancipation of any slave; but all such debts, obligations and claims shall be held illegal and void.

SECTION 5
[POWER TO ENFORCE THIS ARTICLE]

The Congress shall have power to enforce, by appropriate legislation, the provisions of this article.

Amendment XV
[*Proposed by Congress on February 26, 1869; declared ratified on March 30, 1870.*]

SECTION 1
[NEGRO SUFFRAGE]

The right of citizens of the United States to vote shall not be denied or abridged by the United States or by any State on account of race, color, or previous condition of servitude.

SECTION 2
[POWER TO ENFORCE THIS ARTICLE]

The Congress shall have power to enforce this article by appropriate legislation.

Amendment XVI

[*Proposed by Congress on July 2, 1909;
declared ratified on February 25, 1913.*]
[AUTHORIZING INCOME TAXES]

The Congress shall have power to lay and collect taxes on incomes, from whatever source derived, without apportionment among the several States, and without regard to any census or enumeration.

Amendment XVII

[*Proposed by Congress on May 13, 1912;
declared ratified on May 31, 1913.*]
[POPULAR ELECTION OF SENATORS]

The Senate of the United States shall be composed of two Senators from each State, elected by the people thereof, for six years; and each Senator shall have one vote. The electors in each State shall have the qualifications requisite for electors of the most numerous branch of the State legislatures.

When vacancies happen in the representation of any State in the Senate, the executive authority of such State shall issue writs of election to fill such vacancies: *Provided,* That the legislature of any State may empower the executive thereof to make temporary appointments until the people fill the vacancies by election as the legislature may direct.

This amendment shall not be so construed as to affect the election or term of any Senator chosen before it becomes valid as part of the Constitution.

Amendment XVIII

[*Proposed by Congress December 18, 1917; declared ratified on January 29, 1919.*]

SECTION 1
[NATIONAL LIQUOR PROHIBITION]

After one year from the ratification of this article the manufacture, sale, or transportation of intoxicating liquors within, the importation thereof into, or the exportation thereof from the United States and all territory subject to the jurisdiction thereof for beverage purposes is hereby prohibited.

SECTION 2
[POWER TO ENFORCE THIS ARTICLE]

The Congress and the several States shall have concurrent power to enforce this article by appropriate legislation.

SECTION 3
[RATIFICATION WITHIN SEVEN YEARS]

This article shall be inoperative unless it shall have been ratified as an amendment to the Constitution by the legislatures of the several States, as provided in the Constitution, within seven years from the date of the submission hereof to the States by the Congress.[1]

Amendment XIX

[*Proposed by Congress on June 4, 1919;
declared ratified on August 26, 1920.*]

---

[1] Repealed by the Twenty-first Amendment.

[WOMAN SUFFRAGE]

The right of citizens of the United States to vote shall not be denied or abridged by the United States or by any State on account of sex.

Congress shall have power to enforce this article by appropriate legislation.

Amendment XX

[*Proposed by Congress on March 2, 1932; declared ratified on February 6, 1933.*]

SECTION 1
[TERMS OF OFFICE]

The terms of the President and Vice President shall end at noon on the 20th day of January, and the terms of Senators and Representatives at noon on the 3d day of January, of the years in which such terms would have ended if this article had not been ratified; and the terms of their successors shall then begin.

SECTION 2
[TIME OF CONVENING CONGRESS]

The Congress shall assemble at least once in every year, and such meeting shall begin at noon on the 3d day of January, unless they shall by law appoint a different day.

SECTION 3
[DEATH OF PRESIDENT-ELECT]

If, at the time fixed for the beginning of the term of the President, the President elect shall have died, the Vice President elect shall become President. If a President shall not have been chosen before the time fixed for the beginning of his term, or if the President elect shall have failed to qualify, then the Vice President elect shall act as President until a President shall have qualified; and the Congress may by law provide for the case wherein neither a President elect nor a Vice President elect shall have qualified, declaring who shall then act as President, or the manner in which one who is to act shall be selected, and such person shall act accordingly until a President or Vice President shall have qualified.

SECTION 4
[ELECTION OF THE PRESIDENT]

The Congress may by law provide for the case of the death of any of the persons from whom the House of Representatives may choose a President whenever the right of choice shall have devolved upon them, and for the case of the death of any of the persons from whom the Senate may choose a Vice President whenever the right of choice shall have devolved upon them.

SECTION 5
[AMENDMENT TAKES EFFECT]

Sections 1 and 2 shall take effect on the 15th day of October following the ratification of this article.

SECTION 6
[RATIFICATION WITHIN SEVEN YEARS]

This article shall be inoperative unless it shall have been ratified as an amendment to the Constitution by the legislatures of three-fourths of the several States within seven years from the date of its submission.

Amendment XXI

[*Proposed by Congress on February 20, 1933; declared ratified on December 5, 1933.*]

SECTION 1
[NATIONAL LIQUOR PROHIBITION REPEALED]

The eighteenth article of amendment to the Constitution of the United States is hereby repealed.

SECTION 2
[TRANSPORTATION OF LIQUOR INTO "DRY" STATES]

The transportation or importation into any State, Territory, or Possession of the United States for delivery or use therein of intoxicating liquors, in violation of the laws thereof, is hereby prohibited.

SECTION 3
[RATIFICATION WITHIN SEVEN YEARS]

This article shall be inoperative unless it shall have been ratified as an amendment to the Constitution by conventions in the several States, as provided in the Constitution, within seven years from the date of the submission hereof to the States by the Congress.

Amendment XXII

[*Proposed by Congress on March 21, 1947; declared ratified on February 27, 1951.*]

SECTION 1
[TENURE OF PRESIDENT LIMITED]

No person shall be elected to the office of President more than twice, and no person who has held the office of President or acted as President, for more than two years of a term to which some other person was elected President shall be elected to the office of the President more than once. But this Article shall not apply to any person holding the office of President when this Article was proposed by the Congress, and shall not prevent any person who may be holding the office of President, or acting as President, during the term within which this Article becomes operative from holding the office of President or acting as President during the remainder of such term.

SECTION 2
[RATIFICATION WITHIN SEVEN YEARS]

This article shall be inoperative unless it shall have been ratified as an amendment to the Constitution by the legislatures of three-fourths of the several States within seven years from the date of its submission to the States by the Congress.

Amendment XXIII

[*Proposed by Congress on June 16, 1960; declared ratified on March 29, 1961.*]

SECTION 1
[ELECTORAL COLLEGE VOTES FOR THE DISTRICT OF COLUMBIA]

The District constituting the seat of Government of the United States shall appoint in such manner as the Congress may direct:

A number of electors of President and Vice President equal to the whole number of Senators and Representatives in Congress to which the District would be entitled if it were a State, but in no event more than the least populous State; they shall be in addition to those appointed by the States, but they shall be considered, for the purposes of the election of President and Vice President, to be electors appointed by a State; and they shall meet in the District and perform such duties as provided by the twelfth article of amendment.

SECTION 2
[POWER TO ENFORCE THIS ARTICLE]

The Congress shall have power to enforce this article by appropriate legislation.

Amendment XXIV

[*Proposed by Congress on August 27, 1962; declared ratified on January 23, 1964.*]

SECTION 1
[ANTI-POLL TAX]

The right of citizens of the United States to vote in any primary or other election for President or Vice President, for electors for President or Vice President, or for Senator or Representative of Congress, shall not be denied or abridged by the United States or any State by reason of failure to pay any poll tax or other tax.

SECTION 2
[POWER TO ENFORCE THIS ARTICLE]

The Congress shall have power to enforce this article by appropriate legislation.

Amendment XXV

[*Proposed by Congress on July 6, 1965; declared ratified on February 10, 1967.*]

SECTION 1
[VICE PRESIDENT TO BECOME PRESIDENT]

In case of the removal of the President from office or his death or resignation, the Vice President shall become President.

SECTION 2
[CHOICE OF A NEW VICE PRESIDENT]

Whenever there is a vacancy in the office of the Vice President, the President shall nominate a Vice President who shall take the office upon confirmation by a majority vote of both houses of Congress.

SECTION 3
[PRESIDENT MAY DECLARE OWN DISABILITY]

Whenever the President transmits to the President pro tempore of the Senate and the Speaker of the House of Representatives his written declaration that he is unable to discharge the powers and duties of his office, and until he transmits to them a written declaration to the contrary, such powers and duties shall be discharged by the Vice President as Acting President.

SECTION 4
[ALTERNATE PROCEDURES TO DECLARE AND TO END PRESIDENTIAL DISABILITY]

Whenever the Vice President and a majority of either the principal officers of the executive departments, or of such other body as Congress may by law provide, transmit to the President pro tempore of the Senate and the Speaker of the House of Representatives their written declaration that the President is unable to discharge the powers and duties of his office, the Vice President shall immediately assume the powers and duties of the office as Acting President.

Thereafter, when the President transmits to the President pro tempore of the Senate and the Speaker of the House of Representatives his written declaration that no inability exists, he shall resume the powers and duties of his office unless the Vice President and a majority of either the principal officers of the executive department, or of such other body as Congress may by law provide, transmit within four days to the President pro tempore of the Senate and the Speaker of the House of Representatives their written declaration that the President is unable to discharge the powers and duties of his office. Thereupon Congress shall decide the issue, assembling within forty eight hours for that purpose if not in session. If the Congress, within twenty one days after receipt of the latter written declaration, or, if Congress is not in session, within twenty one days after Congress is required to assemble, determines by two-thirds vote of both Houses that the President is unable to discharge the powers and duties of his office, the Vice President shall continue to discharge the same as Acting President; otherwise, the President shall resume the powers and duties of his office.

Amendment XXVI

[*Proposed by Congress on March 23, 1971; declared ratified on July 1, 1971.*]

SECTION 1
[EIGHTEEN-YEAR-OLD VOTE]

The right of citizens of the United States, who are eighteen years of age or older, to vote shall not be denied or abridged by the United States or by any State on account of age.

SECTION 2
[POWER TO ENFORCE THIS ARTICLE]

The Congress shall have power to enforce this article by appropriate legislation.

Amendment XXVII

[*Proposed by Congress on September 25, 1789; declared ratified on May 8, 1992.*]
[CONGRESS CANNOT RAISE ITS OWN PAY]

No law varying the compensation for the services of the Senators and Representatives, shall take effect, until an election of representatives shall have intervened.

The Federalist Papers

No. 10: Madison

Among the numerous advantages promised by a well constructed Union, none deserves to be more accurately developed than its tendency to break and control the violence of faction. The friend of popular governments never finds himself so much alarmed for their character and fate, as when he contemplates their propensity to this dangerous vice. He will not fail therefore to set a due value on any plan which, without violating the principles to which he is attached, provides a proper cure for it. The instability, injustice, and confusion introduced into the public councils have, in truth, been the mortal diseases under which popular governments have everywhere perished, as they continue to be the favorite and fruitful topics from which the adversaries to liberty derive their most specious declamations. The valuable improvements made by the American constitutions on the popular models, both ancient and modern, cannot certainly be too much admired; but it would be an unwarrantable partiality to contend that they have as effectually obviated the danger on this side, as was wished and expected. Complaints are everywhere heard from our most considerate and virtuous citizens, equally the friends of public and private faith and of public and personal liberty, that our governments are too unstable, that the public good is disregarded in the conflicts of rival parties, and that measures are too often decided, not according to the rules of justice and the rights of the minor party, but by the superior force of an interested and overbearing majority. However anxiously we may wish that these complaints had no foundation, the evidence of known facts will not permit us to deny that they are in some degree true. It will be found, indeed, on a candid review of our situation, that some of the distresses under which we labor have been erroneously charged on the operation of our governments; but it will be found, at the same time, that other causes will not alone account for many of our heaviest misfortunes; and, particularly, for that prevailing and increasing distrust of public engagements and alarm for private rights which are echoed from one end of the continent to the other. These must be chiefly, if not wholly, effects of the unsteadiness and injustice with which a factious spirit has tainted our public administration.

By a faction I understand a number of citizens, whether amounting to a majority or minority of the whole, who are united and actuated by some common impulse of passion, or of interest, adverse to the rights of other citizens, or to the permanent and aggregate interests of the community.

There are two methods of curing the mischiefs of faction: the one, by removing its causes; the other, by controlling its effects.

There are again two methods of removing the causes of faction: the one, by destroying the liberty which is essential to its existence; the other, by giving to every citizen the same opinions, the same passions, and the same interests.

It could never be more truly said than of the first remedy, that it is worse than the disease. Liberty is to faction what air is to fire, an aliment without which it instantly expires. But it could not be a less folly to abolish liberty, which is essential to political life, because it nourishes faction, than it would be to wish the annihilation of air, which is essential to animal life, because it imparts to fire its destructive agency.

The second expedient is as impracticable, as the first would be unwise. As long as the reason of man continues fallible, and he is at liberty to exercise it, different opinions will be formed. As long as the connection subsists between his reason and his self-love, his opinions and his passions will have a reciprocal influence on each other; and the former will be objects to which the latter will attach themselves. The diversity in the faculties of men, from which the rights of property originate, is not less an insuperable obstacle to a uniformity of interests. The protection of these faculties is the first object of Government. From the protection of different and unequal faculties of acquiring property, the possession of different degrees and kinds of property immediately results; and from the influence of these on the sentiments and views of the respective proprietors, ensues a division of the society into different interests and parties.

The latent causes of faction are thus sown in the nature of man; and we see them everywhere brought into different degrees of activity, according to the different circumstances of civil society. A zeal for different opinions concerning religion, concerning Government, and many other points, as well of speculation as of practice; an attachment to different leaders ambitiously contending for pre-eminence and power; or to persons of other descriptions whose fortunes have been interesting to the human passions, have in turn divided mankind into parties, inflamed them with mutual animosity, and rendered them much more disposed to vex and oppress each other, than to co-operate for their common good. So strong is this propensity of mankind to fall into mutual animosities, that where no substantial occasion presents itself, the most frivolous and fanciful distinctions have been sufficient to kindle their unfriendly passions, and excite their most violent conflicts. But the most common and durable source of factions has been the various and unequal distribution of property. Those who hold and those who are without property have ever formed distinct interests in society. Those who are creditors, and those who are debtors, fall under a like discrimination. A landed interest, a manufacturing interest, a mercantile interest, a moneyed interest, with many lesser interests, grow up of necessity in civilized nations, and divide them into different classes, actuated by different sentiments and views. The regulation of these various and interfering interests forms the principal task of modern Legislation, and involves the spirit of party and faction in the necessary and ordinary operations of Government.

No man is allowed to be judge in his own cause, because his interest would certainly bias his judgment and, not improbably, corrupt his integrity. With equal, nay with greater reason, a body of men are unfit to be both judges and parties at the same time; yet what are many of the most important acts of legislation but so many judicial determinations, not indeed concerning the rights of single persons, but concerning the rights of large bodies of citizens; and what are the different classes of legislators but advocates and parties to the causes which they determine? Is a law proposed concerning private debts? It is a question to which the creditors are parties on one side and the debtors on the other. Justice ought to hold the balance between them. Yet the parties are, and must be, themselves the judges; and the most numerous party, or in other words, the most powerful faction must be expected to prevail. Shall domestic manufacturers be encouraged, and in what degree, by restrictions on foreign manufacturers? are questions which would be differently decided by the landed and the manufacturing classes, and probably by neither with a sole regard to justice and the public good. The apportionment of taxes on the various descriptions of property is an act which seems to require the most exact impartiality; yet there is, perhaps, no legislative act in which greater opportunity and temptation are given to a predominant party to trample on the rules of justice. Every shilling with which they overburden the inferior number is a shilling saved to their own pockets.

It is in vain to say that enlightened statesmen will be able to adjust these clashing interests and render them all subservient to the public good. Enlightened statesmen will not always be at the helm. Nor, in many cases, can such an adjustment be made at all without taking into view indirect and remote considerations, which will rarely prevail over the immediate interest which one party may find in disregarding the rights of another or the good of the whole.

The inference to which we are brought is that the *causes* of faction cannot be removed and that relief is only to be sought in the means of controlling its *effects*.

If a faction consists of less than a majority, relief is supplied by the republican principle, which enables the majority to defeat its sinister views by regular vote. It may clog the administration, it may convulse the society; but it will be unable to execute and mask its violence under the forms of the Constitution. When a majority is included in a faction, the form of popular government, on the other hand, enables it to sacrifice to its ruling passion or interest both the public good and the rights of other citizens. To secure the public good and private rights against the danger of such a faction, and at the same time to preserve the spirit and the form of popular government, is then the great object to which our enquiries are directed. Let me add that it is the great desideratum by which alone this form of government can be rescued from the opprobrium under which it has so long labored and be recommended to the esteem and adoption of mankind.

By what means is this object attainable? Evidently by one of two only. Either the existence of the same passion or interest in a majority at the same time must be prevented, or the majority, having such co-existent passion or interest, must be rendered, by their number and local situation, unable to concert and carry into effect schemes of oppression. If the impulse and the opportunity be suffered to coincide, we well know that neither moral nor religious motives can be relied on as an adequate control. They are not found to be such on the injustice and violence of individuals, and lose their efficacy in proportion to the number combined together, that is, in proportion as their efficacy becomes needful.

From this view of the subject it may be concluded that a pure Democracy, by which I mean a Society consisting of a small number of citizens, who assemble and administer the Government in person, can admit of no cure for the mischiefs of faction. A common passion or interest will, in almost every case, be felt by a majority of the whole; a communication and concert results from the form of Government itself; and there is nothing to check the inducements to sacrifice the weaker party or an obnoxious individual. Hence it is that such Democracies have ever been spectacles of turbulence and contention; have ever been found incompatible with personal security or the rights of property; and have in general been as short in their lives as they have been violent in their deaths. Theoretic politicians, who have patronized this species of Government, have erroneously supposed that by reducing mankind to a perfect equality in their political rights, they would at the same time be perfectly equalized and assimilated in their possessions, their opinions, and their passions.

A Republic, by which I mean a Government in which the scheme of representation takes place, opens a different prospect and promises the cure for which we are seeking. Let us examine the points in which it varies from pure Democracy, and we shall comprehend both the nature of the cure and the efficacy which it must derive from the Union.

The two great points of difference between a Democracy and a Republic are: first, the delegation of the Government, in the latter, to a small number of citizens elected by the rest; secondly, the greater number of citizens and greater sphere of country over which the latter may be extended.

The effect of the first difference is, on the one hand, to refine and enlarge the public views by passing them through the medium of a chosen body of citizens, whose wisdom may best discern the true interest of their country and whose patriotism and love of justice will be least likely to sacrifice it to temporary or partial considerations. Under such a regulation it may well happen that the public voice, pronounced by the representatives of the people, will be more consonant to the public good than if pronounced by the people themselves, convened for the purpose. On the other hand, the effect may be inverted. Men of factious tempers, of local prejudices, or of sinister designs, may, by intrigue, by corruption, or by other means, first obtain the suffrages, and then betray the interests of the people. The question resulting is, whether small or extensive Republics are most favorable to the election of proper guardians of the public weal; and it is clearly decided in favor of the latter by two obvious considerations.

In the first place it is to be remarked that however small the Republic may be, the Representatives must be raised to a certain number in order to guard against the cabals of a few; and that however large it may be they must be limited to a certain number in order to guard against the confusion of a multitude. Hence, the number of Representatives in the two cases not being in proportion to that of the Constituents, and being proportionally greatest in the small Republic, it follows that if the proportion of fit characters be not less in the large than in the small Republic, the former will present a greater option, and consequently a greater probability of a fit choice.

In the next place, as each Representative will be chosen by a greater number of citizens in the large than in the small Republic, it will be more difficult for unworthy candidates to practise with success the vicious arts by which elections are too often carried; and the suffrages of the people being more free, will be more likely to centre on men who possess the most attractive merit and the most diffusive and established characters.

It must be confessed that in this, as in most other cases, there is a mean, on both sides of which inconveniencies will be found to lie. By enlarging too much the number of electors, you render the representative too little acquainted with all their local circumstances and lesser interests; as by reducing it too much, you render him unduly attached to these, and too little fit to comprehend and pursue great and national objects. The Federal Constitution forms a happy combination in this respect; the great and aggregate interests being referred to the national, the local and particular to the State legislatures.

The other point of difference is the greater number of citizens and extent of territory which may be brought within the compass of Republican than of Democratic Government; and it is this circumstance principally which renders factious combinations less to be dreaded in the former than in the latter. The smaller the society, the fewer probably will be the distinct parties and interests composing it; the fewer the distinct parties and interests, the more frequently will a majority be found of the same party; and the smaller the number of individuals composing a majority, and the smaller the compass within which they are placed, the more easily will they concert and execute their plans of oppression. Extend the sphere and you take in a greater variety of parties and interests; you make it less probable that a majority of the whole will have a common motive to invade the rights of other citizens; or if such a common motive exists, it will be more difficult for all who feel it to discover their own strength and to act in unison with each other. Besides other impediments, it may be remarked, that where there is a consciousness of unjust or dishonorable purposes, communication is always checked by distrust in proportion to the number whose concurrence is necessary.

Hence, it clearly appears that the same advantage which a Republic has over a Democracy in controlling the effects of faction is enjoyed by a large over a small republic—is enjoyed by the Union over the States composing it. Does this advantage consist in the substitution of representatives whose enlightened views and virtuous sentiments render them superior to local prejudices and to schemes of injustice? It will not be denied that the representation of the Union will be most likely to possess these requisite endowments. Does it consist in the greater security afforded by a greater variety of parties, against the event of any one party being able to outnumber and oppress the rest? In an equal degree does the increased variety of parties comprised within the Union increase this security? Does it, in fine, consist in the greater obstacles opposed to the concert and accomplishment of the secret wishes of an unjust and interested majority? Here again the extent of the Union gives it the most palpable advantage.

The influence of factious leaders may kindle a flame within their particular States but will be unable to spread a general conflagration through the other States: a religious sect may degenerate into a political faction in a part of the Confederacy; but the variety of sects dispersed over the entire face of it must secure the national Councils against any danger from that source: a rage for paper money, for an abolition of debts, for an equal division of property, or for any other improper or wicked project, will be less apt to pervade the whole body of the Union than a particular member of it; in the same proportion as such a malady is more likely to taint a particular county or district than an entire State.

In the extent and proper structure of the Union, therefore, we behold a republican remedy for the diseases most incident to Republican Government. And according to the degree of pleasure and pride we feel in being republicans ought to be our zeal in cherishing the spirit and supporting the character of federalist.

PUBLIUS

No. 51: Madison

To what expedient, then, shall we finally resort, for maintaining in practice the necessary partition of power among the several departments as laid down in the constitution? The only answer that can be given is that as all these exterior provisions are found to be inadequate the defect must be supplied, by so contriving the interior structure of the government as that its several constituent parts may, by their mutual relations, be the means of keeping each other in their proper places. Without presuming to undertake a full development of this important idea I will hazard a few general observations which may perhaps place it in a clearer light, and enable us to form a more correct judgment of the principles and structure of the government planned by the convention.

In order to lay a due foundation for that separate and distinct exercise of the different powers of government, which to a certain extent is admitted on all hands to be essential to the preservation of liberty, it is evident that each department should have a will of its own; and consequently should be so constituted that the members of each should have as little agency as possible in the appointment of the members of the others. Were this principle rigorously adhered to, it would require that all the appointments for the supreme executive, legislative, and judiciary magistracies should be drawn from the same fountain of authority, the people, through channels having no communication whatever with one another. Perhaps such a plan of constructing the several departments would be less difficult in practice than it may in contemplation appear. Some difficulties, however, and some additional expense would attend

the execution of it. Some deviations, therefore, from the principle must be admitted. In the constitution of the judiciary department in particular, it might be inexpedient to insist rigorously on the principle: first, because peculiar qualifications being essential in the members, the primary consideration ought to be to select that mode of choice which best secures these qualifications; second, because the permanent tenure by which the appointments are held in that department must soon destroy all sense of dependence on the authority conferring them.

It is equally evident that the members of each department should be as little dependent as possible on those of the others for the emoluments annexed to their offices. Were the executive magistrate, or the judges, not independent of the legislature in this particular, their independence in every other would be merely nominal.

But the great security against a gradual concentration of the several powers in the same department consists in giving to those who administer each department the necessary constitutional means and personal motives to resist encroachments of the others. The provision for defence must in this, as in all other cases, be made commensurate to the danger of attack. Ambition must be made to counteract ambition. The interest of the man must be connected with the constitutional rights of the place. It may be a reflection on human nature that such devices should be necessary to control the abuses of government. But what is government itself but the greatest of all reflections on human nature? If men were angels, no government would be necessary. If angels were to govern men, neither external nor internal controls on government would be necessary. In framing a government which is to be administered by men over men, the great difficulty lies in this: You must first enable the government to control the governed; and in the next place oblige it to control itself. A dependence on the people is, no doubt, the primary control on the government; but experience has taught mankind the necessity of auxiliary precautions.

This policy of supplying, by opposite and rival interests, the defect of better motives, might be traced through the whole system of human affairs, private as well as public. We see it particularly displayed in all the subordinate distributions of power, where the constant aim is to divide and arrange the several offices in such a manner as that each may be a check on the other; that the private interest of every individual may be a sentinel over the public rights. These inventions of prudence cannot be less requisite in the distribution of the supreme powers of the State.

But it is not possible to give to each department an equal power of self-defense. In republican government, the legislative authority necessarily predominates. The remedy for this inconveniency is to divide the legislature into different branches; and to render them, by different modes of election and different principles of action, as little connected with each other as the nature of their common functions and their common dependence on the society will admit. It may even be necessary to guard against dangerous encroachments by still further precautions. As the weight of the legislative authority requires that it should be thus divided, the weakness of the executive may require, on the other hand, that it should be fortified. An absolute negative on the legislature appears, at first view, to be the natural defense with which the executive magistrate should be armed. But perhaps it would be neither altogether safe nor alone sufficient. On ordinary occasions it might not be exerted with the requisite firmness, and on extraordinary occasions it might be perfidiously abused. May not this defect of an absolute negative be supplied by some qualified connection between this weaker branch of the stronger department, by which the latter may be led to support the constitutional rights of the former, without being too much detached from the rights of its own department?

If the principles on which these observations are founded be just, as I persuade myself they are, and they be applied as a criterion to the several State constitutions, and to the federal Constitution, it will be found that if the latter does not perfectly correspond with them, the former are infinitely less able to bear such a test.

There are, moreover, two considerations particularly applicable to the federal system of America, which place that system in a very interesting point of view.

First. In a single republic, all the power surrendered by the people is submitted to the administration of a single government; and usurpations are guarded against by a division of the government into distinct and separate departments. In the compound republic of America, the power surrendered by the people is first divided between two distinct governments, and then the portion allotted to each subdivided among distinct and separate departments. Hence a double security arises to the rights of the people. The different governments will control each other, at the same time that each will be controlled by itself.

Second. It is of great importance in a republic not only to guard the society against the oppression of its rulers, but to guard one part of the society against the injustice of the other part. Different interests necessarily exist in different classes of citizens. If a majority be united by a common interest, the rights of the minority will be insecure. There are but two methods of providing against this evil: The one by creating a will in the community independent of the majority—that is, of the society itself; the other, by comprehending in the society so many separate descriptions of citizens as will render an unjust combination of a majority of the whole very improbable, if not impracticable. The first method prevails in all governments possessing an hereditary or self-appointed authority. This, at best, is but a precarious security; because a power independent of the society may as well espouse the unjust views of the major as the rightful interests of the minor party, and may possibly be turned against both parties. The second method will be exemplified in the federal republic of the United States. Whilst all authority in it will be derived from and dependent on the society, the society itself will be broken into so many parts, interests and classes of citizens, that the rights of individuals, or of the minority, will be in little danger from interested combinations of the majority. In a free government the security for civil rights must be the same as that for religious rights. It consists in the one case in the multiplicity of interests, and in the other in the multiplicity of sects. The degree of security in both cases will depend on the number of interests and sects; and this may be presumed to depend on the extent of country and number of people comprehended under the same government. This view of the subject must particularly recommend a proper federal system to all the sincere and considerate friends of republican government: Since it shows that in exact proportion as the territory of the Union may be formed into more circumscribed Confederacies, or States, oppressive combinations of a majority will be facilitated; the best security, under the republican form, for the rights of every class of citizens, will be diminished; and consequently the stability and independence of some member of the government, the only other security, must be proportionally increased. Justice is the end of government. It is the end of civil society. It ever has been and ever will be pursued until it be obtained, or until liberty be lost in the pursuit. In a society under the forms of which the stronger faction can readily unite and oppress the weaker, anarchy may as truly be said to reign as in a state of nature, where the weaker individual is not secured against the violence of the stronger: And as, in the latter state, even the stronger individuals are prompted, by the uncertainty of their condition, to submit to a government which may protect the weak as well as themselves: So, in the former state, will the more powerful factions or parties be gradually induced, by a like motive, to wish for a government which will protect all parties, the weaker as well as the more powerful. It can be little doubted that if the State of Rhode Island was separated from the Confederacy and left to itself, the insecurity of rights under the popular form of government within such narrow limits would be displayed by such reiterated

oppressions of factious majorities that some power altogether independent of the people would soon be called for by the voice of the very factions whose misrule had proved the necessity of it. In the extended republic of the United States, and among the great variety of interests, parties, and sects which it embraces, a coalition of a majority of the whole society could seldom take place on any other principles than those of justice and the general good; and there being thus less danger to a minor from the will of the major party, there must be less pretext, also, to provide for the security of the former, by introducing into the government a will not dependent on the latter, or, in other words, a will independent of the society itself. It is no less certain than it is important, notwithstanding the contrary opinions which have been entertained, that the larger the society, provided it lie within a practicable sphere, the more duly capable it will be of self-government. And happily for the *republican cause,* practicable sphere may be carried to a very great extent by a judicious modification and mixture of the *federal principle.*

PUBLIUS

No. 78: Hamilton

To the People of the State of New York:

we proceed now to an examination of the judiciary department of the proposed government.

In unfolding the defects of the existing Confederation, the utility and necessity of a federal judicature have been clearly pointed out. It is the less necessary to recapitulate the considerations there urged, as the propriety of the institution in the abstract is not disputed; the only questions which have been raised being relative to the manner of constituting it, and to its extent. To these points, therefore, our observations shall be confined.

The manner of constituting it seems to embrace these several objects: 1st. The mode of appointing the judges. 2d. The tenure by which they are to hold their places. 3d. The partition of the judiciary authority between different courts, and their relations to each other.

First. As to the mode of appointing the judges; this is the same with that of appointing the officers of the Union in general, and has been so fully discussed in the two last numbers, that nothing can be said here which would not be useless repetition.

Second. As to the tenure by which the judges are to hold their places; this chiefly concerns their duration in office; the provisions for their support; the precautions for their responsibility.

According to the plan of the convention, all judges who may be appointed by the United States are to hold their offices DURING GOOD BEHAVIOR; which is conformable to the most approved of the State constitutions and among the rest, to that of this State. Its propriety having been drawn into question by the adversaries of that plan, is no light symptom of the rage for objection, which disorders their imaginations and judgments. The standard of good behavior for the continuance in office of the judicial magistracy, is certainly one of the most valuable of the modern improvements in the practice of government. In a monarchy it is an excellent barrier to the despotism of the prince; in a republic it is a no less excellent barrier to the encroachments and oppressions of the representative body. And it is the best expedient which can be devised in any government, to secure a steady, upright, and impartial administration of the laws.

Whoever attentively considers the different departments of power must perceive, that, in a government in which they are separated from each other, the judiciary, from the nature of its functions, will always be the least dangerous to the political rights of the Constitution; because it will be least in a capacity to annoy or injure them. The Executive not only dispenses the honors, but holds the sword of the community. The legislature not only commands the purse, but prescribes the rules by which the duties and rights of every citizen are to be regulated. The judiciary, on the contrary, has no influence over either the sword or the purse; no direction either of the strength or of the wealth of the society; and can take no active resolution whatever. It may truly be said to have neither FORCE nor WILL, but merely judgment; and must ultimately depend upon the aid of the executive arm even for the efficacy of its judgments.

This simple view of the matter suggests several important consequences. It proves incontestably, that the judiciary is beyond comparison the weakest of the three departments of power; that it can never attack with success either of the other two; and that all possible care is requisite to enable it to defend itself against their attacks. It equally proves, that though individual oppression may now and then proceed from the courts of justice, the general liberty of the people can never be endangered from that quarter; I mean so long as the judiciary remains truly distinct from both the legislature and the Executive. For I agree, that "there is no liberty, if the power of judging be not separated from the legislative and executive powers." And it proves, in the last place, that as liberty can have nothing to fear from the judiciary alone, but would have every thing to fear from its union with either of the other departments; that as all the effects of such a union must ensue from a dependence of the former on the latter, notwithstanding a nominal and apparent separation; that as, from the natural feebleness of the judiciary, it is in continual jeopardy of being overpowered, awed, or influenced by its co-ordinate branches; and that as nothing can contribute so much to its firmness and independence as permanency in office, this quality may therefore be justly regarded as an indispensable ingredient in its constitution, and, in a great measure, as the citadel of the public justice and the public security.

The complete independence of the courts of justice is peculiarly essential in a limited Constitution. By a limited Constitution, I understand one which contains certain specified exceptions to the legislative authority; such, for instance, as that it shall pass no bills of attainder, no ex-post-facto laws, and the like. Limitations of this kind can be preserved in practice no other way than through the medium of courts of justice, whose duty it must be to declare all acts contrary to the manifest tenor of the Constitution void. Without this, all the reservations of particular rights or privileges would amount to nothing.

Some perplexity respecting the rights of the courts to pronounce legislative acts void, because contrary to the Constitution, has arisen from an imagination that the doctrine would imply a superiority of the judiciary to the legislative power. It is urged that the authority which can declare the acts of another void, must necessarily be superior to the one whose acts may be declared void. As this doctrine is of great importance in all the American constitutions, a brief discussion of the ground on which it rests cannot be unacceptable.

There is no position which depends on clearer principles, than that every act of a delegated authority, contrary to the tenor of the commission under which it is exercised, is void. No legislative act, therefore, contrary to the Constitution, can be valid. To deny this, would be to affirm, that the deputy is greater than his principal; that the servant is above his master; that the representatives of the people are superior to the people themselves; that men acting by virtue of powers, may do not only what their powers do not authorize, but what they forbid.

If it be said that the legislative body are themselves the constitutional judges of their own powers, and that the construction they put upon them is conclusive upon the other departments, it may be answered, that this cannot be the natural presumption, where it is not to be collected from any particular provisions in the Constitution. It is not otherwise to be supposed, that the Constitution could intend to enable the representatives of the people to substitute their will to that of their constituents. It is far more rational to suppose, that the courts were designed to be an intermediate body between the people and the legislature, in order, among other things, to keep the latter within the limits assigned to their authority. The interpretation of the laws is the proper and peculiar province of the courts. A constitution is, in fact, and must be regarded by the judges, as a fundamental law. It therefore belongs to them to ascertain its meaning, as well as the meaning of any particular act proceeding from the legislative body. If there should happen to be an irreconcilable variance between the two, that which has the superior obligation and validity ought, of course, to be preferred; or, in other words, the Constitution ought to be preferred to the statute, the intention of the people to the intention of their agents.

Nor does this conclusion by any means suppose a superiority of the judicial to the legislative power. It only supposes that the power of the people is superior to both; and that where the will of the legislature, declared in its statutes, stands in opposition to that of the people, declared in the Constitution, the judges ought to be governed by the latter rather than the former. They ought to regulate their decisions by the fundamental laws, rather than by those which are not fundamental.

This exercise of judicial discretion, in determining between two contradictory laws, is exemplified in a familiar instance. It not uncommonly happens, that there are two statutes existing at one time, clashing in whole or in part with each other, and neither of them containing any repealing clause or expression. In such a case, it is the province of the courts to liquidate and fix their meaning and operation. So far as they can, by any fair construction, be reconciled to each other, reason and law conspire to dictate that this should be done; where this is impracticable, it becomes a matter of necessity to give effect to one, in exclusion of the other. The rule which has obtained in the courts for determining their relative validity is, that the last in order of time shall be preferred to the first. But this is a mere rule of construction, not derived from any positive law, but from the nature and reason of the thing. It is a rule not enjoined upon the courts by legislative provision, but adopted by themselves, as consonant to truth and propriety, for the direction of their conduct as interpreters of the law. They thought it reasonable, that between the interfering acts of an equal authority, that which was the last indication of its will should have the preference.

But in regard to the interfering acts of a superior and subordinate authority, of an original and derivative power, the nature and reason of the thing indicate the converse of that rule as proper to be followed. They teach us that the prior act of a superior ought to be preferred to the subsequent act of an inferior and subordinate authority; and that accordingly, whenever a particular statute contravenes the Constitution, it will be the duty of the judicial tribunals to adhere to the latter and disregard the former.

It can be of no weight to say that the courts, on the pretense of a repugnancy, may substitute their own pleasure to the constitutional intentions of the legislature. This might as well happen in the case of two contradictory statutes; or it might as well happen in every adjudication upon any single statute. The courts must declare the sense of the law; and if they should be disposed to exercise WILL instead of judgment, the consequence would equally be the substitution of their pleasure to that of the legislative body. The observation, if it prove any thing, would prove that there ought to be no judges distinct from that body.

If, then, the courts of justice are to be considered as the bulwarks of a limited Constitution against legislative encroachments, this consideration will afford a strong argument for the permanent tenure of judicial offices, since nothing will contribute so much as this to that independent spirit in the judges which must be essential to the faithful performance of so arduous a duty.

This independence of the judges is equally requisite to guard the Constitution and the rights of individuals from the effects of those ill humors, which the arts of designing men, or the influence of particular conjunctures, sometimes disseminate among the people themselves, and which, though they speedily give place to better information, and more deliberate reflection, have a tendency, in the meantime, to occasion dangerous innovations in the government, and serious oppressions of the minor party in the community. Though I trust the friends of the proposed Constitution will never concur with its enemies, in questioning that fundamental principle of republican government, which admits the right of the people to alter or abolish the established Constitution, whenever they find it inconsistent with their happiness, yet it is not to be inferred from this principle, that the representatives of the people, whenever a momentary inclination happens to lay hold of a majority of their constituents, incompatible with the provisions in the existing Constitution, would, on that account, be justifiable in a violation of those provisions; or that the courts would be under a greater obligation to connive at infractions in this shape, than when they had proceeded wholly from the cabals of the representative body. Until the people have, by some solemn and authoritative act, annulled or changed the established form, it is binding upon themselves collectively, as well as individually; and no presumption, or even knowledge, of their sentiments, can warrant their representatives in a departure from it, prior to such an act. But it is easy to see, that it would require an uncommon portion of fortitude in the judges to do their duty as faithful guardians of the Constitution, where legislative invasions of it had been instigated by the major voice of the community.

But it is not with a view to infractions of the Constitution only, that the independence of the judges may be an essential safeguard against the effects of occasional ill humors in the society. These sometimes extend no farther than to the injury of the private rights of particular classes of citizens, by unjust and partial laws. Here also the firmness of the judicial magistracy is of vast importance in mitigating the severity and confining the operation of such laws. It not only serves to moderate the immediate mischiefs of those which may have been passed, but it operates as a check upon the legislative body in passing them; who, perceiving that obstacles to the success of iniquitous intention are to be expected from the scruples of the courts, are in a manner compelled, by the very motives of the injustice they meditate, to qualify their attempts. This is a circumstance calculated to have more influence upon the character of our governments, than but few may be aware of. The benefits of the integrity and moderation of the judiciary have already been felt in more States than one; and though they may have displeased those whose sinister expectations they may have disappointed, they must have commanded the esteem and applause of all the virtuous and disinterested. Considerate men, of every description, ought to prize whatever will tend to beget or fortify that temper in the courts: as no man can be sure that he may not be to-morrow the victim of a spirit of injustice, by which he may be a gainer to-day. And every man must now feel, that the inevitable tendency of such a spirit is to sap the foundations of public and private confidence, and to introduce in its stead universal distrust and distress.

That inflexible and uniform adherence to the rights of the Constitution, and of individuals, which we perceive to be indispensable in the courts of justice, can certainly not be expected from judges who hold their offices by a temporary commission. Periodical appointments, however regulated, or by whomsoever made, would, in some way or other, be fatal to their necessary independence. If the power of making them was committed either to the Executive or legislature, there would be danger of an improper complaisance to the branch which possessed it; if to both, there would be an unwillingness to hazard the displeasure of either; if to the people, or to persons chosen by them for the special purpose, there would be too great a disposition to consult popularity, to justify a reliance that nothing would be consulted but the Constitution and the laws.

There is yet a further and a weightier reason for the permanency of the judicial offices, which is deducible from the nature of the qualifications they require. It has been frequently remarked, with great propriety, that a voluminous code of laws is one of the inconveniences necessarily connected with the advantages of a free government. To avoid an arbitrary discretion in the courts, it is indispensable that they should be bound down by strict rules and precedents, which serve to define and point out their duty in every particular case that comes before them; and it will readily be conceived from the variety of controversies which grow out of the folly and wickedness of mankind, that the records of those precedents must unavoidably swell to a very considerable bulk, and must demand long and laborious study to acquire a competent knowledge of them. Hence it is, that there can be but few men in the society who will have sufficient skill in the laws to qualify them for the stations of judges. And making the proper deductions for the ordinary depravity of human nature, the number must be still smaller of those who unite the requisite integrity with the requisite knowledge. These considerations apprise us, that the government can have no great option between fit character; and that a temporary duration in office, which would naturally discourage such characters from quitting a lucrative line of practice to accept a seat on the bench, would have a tendency to throw the administration of justice into hands less able, and less well qualified, to conduct it with utility and dignity. In the present circumstances of this country, and in those in which it is likely to be for a long time to come, the disadvantages on this score would be greater than they may at first sight appear; but it must be confessed, that they are far inferior to those which present themselves under the other aspects of the subject.

Upon the whole, there can be no room to doubt that the convention acted wisely in copying from the models of those constitutions which have established good behavior as the tenure of their judicial offices, in point of duration; and that so far from being blamable on this account, their plan would have been inexcusably defective, if it had wanted this important feature of good government. The experience of Great Britain affords an illustrious comment on the excellence of the institution.

PUBLIUS

Endnotes

Chapter 1

1. Thomas Hobbes, *Leviathan* (1651; repr., Indianapolis, IN: Bobbs, Merrill, 1958).

2. Alexander Hamilton, James Madison, and John Jay, *The Federalist Papers*, ed. Roy P. Fairfield, 2nd ed. (1788; repr., Baltimore, MD: Johns Hopkins University Press, 1981), p. 160.

3. Hamilton, Madison, and Jay, *The Federalist Papers*, p. 18.

4. Examples include E. E. Schattschneider, *The Semisovereign People: A Realist's View of Democracy in America* (New York: Holt, Rinehart, and Winston, 1960); Larry Bartels, *Unequal Democracy: The Politics of the New Gilded Age* (Princeton, NJ: Princeton University Press, 2008); and Jeffrey A. Segal and Howard Spaeth, *The Supreme Court and the Attitudinal Model Revisited* (New York: Cambridge University Press, 2002).

5. Morris Rosenberg, "Some Determinants of Political Apathy," *Public Opinion Quarterly* 18 (Winter 1954–55): 349–66; Jane Mansbridge, *Beyond Adversary Democracy* (New York: Basic Books, 1980); Nina Eliasoph, *Avoiding Politics: How Americans Produce Apathy in Everyday Life* (New York: Cambridge University Press, 1998); Melanie C. Green, Penny S. Visser, and Philip E. Tetlock, "Coping with Accountability Cross-Pressures: Low-Effort Evasive Tactics and High-Effort Quests for Complex Compromises," *Personality and Social Psychology Bulletin* 26:11 (2000): 1380–91.

6. John R. Hibbing and Elizabeth Theiss-Morse, *Stealth Democracy: Americans' Beliefs about How Government Should Work* (New York: Cambridge University Press, 2002), p. 147. See Diana E. Hess, *Controversy in the Classroom: The Democratic Power of Discussion* (New York: Routledge, 2009), for evidence that diverse viewpoints in the classroom have important effects on discussion.

7. Donald Green, Bradley Palmquist, and Eric Schickler, *Partisan Hearts and Minds* (New Haven, CT: Yale University Press, 2004); Christopher Achen, "Political Socialization and Rational Party Identification," *Political Behavior* 24:2 (2002): 151–70.

8. Robert S. Erikson, Michael B. MacKuen, and James A. Stimson, *The Macro Polity* (New York: Cambridge University Press, 2002).

9. Congressional Budget Office, "Current Budget Projections," www.cbo.gov/ftpdocs/108xx/doc10871/budgetprojections.pdf; The President's Budget for Fiscal Year 2016, "Historical Federal Workplace Tables," Office of Policy and Management, https://www.opm.gov/policy-data-oversight/data-analysis-documentation/federal-employment-reports/historical-tables/total-government-employment-since-1962; *Federal Register*, www.gpoaccess.gov/fr (all accessed 2/15/16).

10. For details, see Paul R. Abramson, John H. Aldrich, and David W. Rohde, *Change and Continuity in the 2012 and 2014 Elections* (Washington, DC: Congressional Quarterly Press, 2015).

11. Charles Taylor, *Multiculturalism: Examining the Politics of Recognition*, ed. Amy Gutmann, with commentary by K. Anthony Appiah, Jürgen Habermas, Steven C. Rockefeller, Michael Walzer, and Susan Wolf (Princeton, NJ: Princeton University Press, 1994); Will Kymlicka, *Multicultural Citizenship: A Liberal Theory of Minority Rights* (New York: Oxford University Press, 1995).

12. Morris P. Fiorina, with Samuel J. Abrams and Jeremy C. Pope, *Culture War: The Myth of a Polarized America*, 3rd ed. (New York: Pearson, Longman, 2010), pp. 46–7.

13. For more on political culture, see Herbert McClosky and John Zaller, *The American Ethos* (Cambridge, MA: Harvard University Press, 1984), and Pippa Norris, *Democratic Deficit: Critical Citizens Revisited* (New York: Cambridge University Press, 2011).

14. Frank M. Bryan, *Real Democracy: The New England Town Meeting and How It Works* (Chicago: University of Chicago Press, 2004).

Chapter 2

1. Jim DeMint, "Constitution of No," *National Review Online*, June 8, 2010, www.nationalreview.com/articles/229909/constitution-no/jim-demint?pg=2 (accessed 10/16/11).

2. Mark Trumbull, "On Constitution Day, Tea Party and Foes Duel over Our Founding Document," *Christian Science Monitor*, September 17, 2011, www.csmonitor.com/USA/Politics/2011/0917/On-Constitution-Day-tea-party-and-foes-duel-over-our-founding-document (accessed 10/16/11).

3. For a good overview of the political thought of the American Revolution, see Gordon S. Wood, *The Radicalism of the American Revolution* (New York: Vintage Books, 1993). For an excellent summary of the history, see Wood's *The American Revolution: A History* (New York: Modern Library, 2003).

4. J. W. Peltason, *Corwin and Peltason's Understanding the Constitution*, 7th ed. (Hinsdale, IL: Dryden Press, 1976), p. 12.

5. The pamphlet sold 120,000 copies within a few months of publication, a figure that would leave the Harry Potter books in the dust in terms of the proportion of the literate public that purchased the book.

6. Many delegates probably assumed that the electors would reflect the wishes of the voters in their states, but there is no clear indication of this in Madison's notes. (Hamilton makes this argument in the *Federalist Papers*.) Until the 1820s, many electors were directly chosen by state legislatures rather than by the people. In the first presidential election, George Washington won the unanimous support of the electors, but in only five states were the electors chosen by the people.

7. The actual language of the section avoids the term "slavery." Instead, it says: "The Migration or Importation of such Persons as any of the States now existing shall think proper to admit,

shall not be prohibited by Congress prior to the Year one thousand eight hundred and eight." The ban on the importation of slaves was implemented on the earliest possible date, January 1, 1808.

8. Cass R. Sunstein, "Making Amends," *New Republic*, March 3, 1997, p. 42.

9. *Furman v. Georgia*, 408 U.S. 238 (1972).

10. The case concerning minors was *Roper v. Simmons*, 543 U.S. 551 (2005), and the case concerning the mentally retarded was *Atkins v. Virginia*, 536 U.S. 304 (2002).

Take a Stand

a. Jocelyn Kiley, "Americans Divided on How the Supreme Court Should Interpret the Constitution," Pew Research Center, July 31, 2014, www.pewresearch.org/fact-tank/2014/07/31/americans-divided-on-how-the-supreme-court-should-interpret-the-constitution (accessed 10/30/15).

b. Clarence Thomas, "How to Read the Constitution," *Wall Street Journal*, October 20, 2008.

c. *State of Missouri v. Holland*, 252 U.S. 416 (1920), 252.

d. William Rehnquist, "The Notion of a Living Constitution," *Harvard Journal of Law and Public Policy* 29 (2006): 402.

e. Rehnquist, "The Notion," p. 405.

f. Thurgood Marshall at the Annual Seminar of the San Francisco Patent and Trademark Law Association, Maui, Hawaii, May 6, 1987, www.thurgoodmarshall.com/speeches/constitutional_speech.htm (accessed 12/20/13).

Chapter 3

1. The full title of the law is the Patient Protection and Affordable Care Act (PPACA).

2. *State of Florida, et al. v. U.S. Department of Health and Human Services, et al.*, Petition for Writ of Certiorari to the United States Court of Appeals for the Eleventh Circuit, September 27, 2011, www.azgovernor.gov/dms/upload/PR_092811_Petition.pdf (accessed 10/19/12).

3. Obamacare Medicaid expansion, http://obamacarefacts.com/obamacares-medicaid-expansion (accessed 10/14/16).

4. Robert Pear, "Missouri Citizens Face Obstacles to Coverage," *New York Times*, August 2, 2013, www.nytimes.com/2013/08/03/us/missouri-citizens-face-obstacles-to-coverage.html?_r=1& (accessed 3/5/14).

5. See www.cisstat.com/eng/cis.htm for more information about the CIS.

6. *United States v. Windsor*, 570 U.S. (2013).

7. *Obergefell v. Hodges*, 576 U.S. (2015).

8. "The Supreme Court: Excerpts from Court's Welfare Ruling and Rehnquist's Dissent," *New York Times*, May 18, 1999, p. A20.

9. John W. Wright, ed., *New York Times 2000 Almanac* (New York: Penguin Reference, 1999), p. 165. Estimates from various online sources are quite a bit higher, averaging about 620,000 deaths.

10. Slaughterhouse Cases, 83 U.S. 36 (1873). See Ronald M. Labbe and Jonathan Lurie, *The Slaughterhouse Cases: Regulation, Reconstruction, and the Fourteenth Amendment* (Lawrence: University Press of Kansas, 2003).

11. Civil Rights Cases, 109 U.S. 3 (1883).

12. *Hammer v. Dagenhart*, 247 U.S. 251 (1918).

13. *Lochner v. New York*, 198 U.S. 45 (1905).

14. Wendy J. Schiller and Charles Stewart, *Electing the Senate: Indirect Democracy before the Seventeenth Amendment* (Princeton, NJ: Princeton University Press, 2014).

15. Four key cases are *West Coast Hotel Company v. Parrish* (1937); *Wright v. Vinton Branch* (1937); *Virginia Railway Company v. System Federation* (1937); and *National Labor Relations Board v. Jones and Laughlin Steel Corporation* (1937).

16. Martin Grodzins, *The American System* (New York: Rand McNally, 1966).

17. John Shannon, "Middle Class Votes Bring a New Balance to Federalism," February 1, 1997, policy paper 10 from the Urban Institute series "The Future of the Public Sector," www.urban.org/url.cfm?ID=307051 (accessed 6/30/16).

18. *Brown v. Board of Education*, 347 U.S. 483 (1954); *Swann v. Charlotte-Mecklenburg Board of Education*, 402 U.S. 1 (1971).

19. *Miranda v. Arizona*, 384 U.S. 436 (1966); *Mapp v. Ohio*, 367 U.S. 643 (1961).

20. *Shelby County v. Holder*, 570 U.S. (2013).

21. Paul Posner, "The Politics of Coercive Federalism in the Bush Era," *Publius* 37:3 (May 2007): 390–412.

22. Gallup, "Trust in Government," September 9–13, 2015, www.gallup.com/poll/5392/trust-government.aspx (accessed 12/10/15).

23. Barry Rabe, "Environmental Policy and the Bush Era: The Collision between the Administrative Presidency and State Experimentation," *Publius* 37:3 (May 2007): 413–31.

24. Lois Beckett, "Nullification: How States Are Making It a Felony to Enforce Federal Gun Laws," *ProPublica*, May 2, 2013, www.propublica.org/article/nullification-how-states-are-making-it-a-felony-to-enforce-federal-gun-laws (accessed 3/5/14).

25. From a review of Michael S. Greve, *Real Federalism: Why It Matters, How It Could Happen* (Washington, DC: American Enterprise Institute Press, 1999), www.federalismproject.org/publications/books (accessed 10/10/07).

26. Cass Sunstein, *Designing Democracy: What Constitutions Do* (New York: Oxford University Press, 2001), p. 107.

27. J. W. Peltason, *Corwin and Peltason's Understanding the Constitution*, 7th ed. (Hinsdale, IL: Dryden Press, 1976), p. 177.

28. *Garcia v. San Antonio Metropolitan Transit Authority*, 469 U.S. 528 (1985).

29. *City of Boerne v. Flores*, 521 U.S. 507 (1997), 520.

30. *Alabama v. Garrett*, 531 U.S. 356 (2001).

31. *Shelby County v. Holder*, 570 U.S. (2013).

32. *United States v. Lopez*, 514 U.S. 549 (1995).

33. *United States v. Morrison*, 529 U.S. 598 (2000).

34. *Romer v. Evans*, 517 U.S. 620 (1996).

35. *Gonzales v. Raich*, 545 U.S. 1 (2005).

36. *National Federation of Independent Businesses et al. v. Sebelius*, 132 S. Ct. 2566 (2012).

37. *National Federation of Independent Businesses et al. v. Sebelius*, p. 51.

38. Jonathan Turley, "It's Not the Cannabis, It's the Constitution," *Los Angeles Times*, August 5, 2002, Metro section, part 2, p. 11.

39. Robert S. Erikson, Gerald C. Wright, and John P. McIver, *Statehouse Democracy: Public Opinion and Policy in the American States* (Cambridge: Cambridge University Press, 1993). For the policy specific evidence see Jeffrey R. Lax and Justin H. Phillips, "The Democratic Deficit in the States," *American Journal of Political Science* 56:1 (January 2012): 148–66. While Lax and Phillips show that states are responsive

to opinion in eight specific policy areas, they also show that there is a "democratic deficit" in that majority opinion is often ignored in state policy.

40. American Society of Civil Engineers, "Report Card for America's Infrastructure: 2009," www.infrastructurereportcard.org/ (accessed 11/14/11).

41. Martha Derthick, *Keeping the Compound Republic: Essays in American Federalism* (Washington, DC: Brookings Institution, 2001), pp. 9–32.

Take a Stand

a. Steven Nelson, "Spending Deal Protects Medical Pot, Blocks Legalization in D.C.," *U.S. News and World Reports*, December 9, 2014, www.usnews.com/news.com/news/articles/2014/12/09/spending-deal-protects-medical-pot-blocks-legalization-in-dc (accessed 12/11/15).

Chapter 4

1. Alan Blinder, "Kentucky Clerk in Gay Marriage Dispute, Kim Davis, Joining G.O.P.," *New York Times,* September 25, 2015, www.nytimes.com/2015/09/26/us/kentucky-clerk-in-gay-marriage-dispute-kim-davis-joining-gop.html?_r=0 (accessed 1/6/16).

2. Elizabeth Daley, "Gov. Matt Bevin Just Removed All Clerks' Names from Kentucky Marriage Licenses," *Advocate*, December 22, 2015, www.advocate.com/marriage-equality/2015/12/22/gov-matt-bevin-grant-kim-davis-christmas-wish-no-clerks-marriage (accessed 1/6/16).

3. Ariane De Vogue, "Hobby Lobby Wins Contraceptive Ruling in Supreme Court," ABC News, June 30, 2014, http://abcnews.go.com/Politics/hobby-lobby-wins-contraceptive-ruling-supreme-court/story?id=24364311 (accessed 1/6/16).

4. Maggie Fox, "Supreme Court on Birth Control: What Hobby Lobby Ruling Means," NBC News, June 30, 2014, www.nbcnews.com/health/health-care/supreme-court-birth-control-what-hobby-lobby-ruling-means-n144526 (accessed 1/6/16).

5. *Arar v. Ashcroft et al.*, 2006 WL 346439 (E.D.N.Y.). The case was also dismissed because Arar, a Canadian citizen, did not have standing to sue the U.S. government. Supporters of this decision (and the practice more generally) say that it is an essential part of the war on terrorism and that the enemy combatants who are arrested have no legal rights. Opponents say that the practice violates international law and our own standards of decency; furthermore, torture almost never produces useful information because people will say anything to get the torture to stop.

6. Max Farrand, ed., *The Records of the Federal Convention of 1787*, rev. ed. (New Haven, CT: Yale University Press, 1937), pp. 587–88, 617–18.

7. The two that were not ratified by the states were a complicated amendment on congressional apportionment and a pay raise amendment.

8. There is an intense scholarly debate on whether the authors of the Fourteenth Amendment intended for it to apply the Bill of Rights to the states. The strongest argument against this position is Raoul Berger, *The Fourteenth Amendment and the Bill of Rights* (Norman: University of Oklahoma Press, 1989), and a good book in support is Akhil Reed Amar, *The Bill of Rights* (New Haven, CT: Yale University Press, 1998).

9. The Slaughterhouse Cases, 83 U.S. 36 (1873).

10. *Gitlow v. New York*, 268 U.S. 652 (1925).

11. James Hutson, "A Wall of Separation," *Library of Congress Information Bulletin* 57, no. 6 (June 1998), www.loc.gov/loc/lcib/9806/danbury.html (accessed 3/3/08).

12. *Engel v. Vitale*, 370 U.S. 421 (1962).

13. *Wallace v. Jaffree*, 482 U.S. 38 (1985).

14. *Lee v. Weisman*, 505 U.S. 577 (1992); *Santa Fe Independent School District v. Doe*, 530 U.S. 290 (2000).

15. *Marsh v. Chambers*, 463 U.S. 783 (1983); *Jones v. Clear Creek Independent School*, 61 LW 3819 (1993).

16. *Town of Greece, New York v. Galloway*, 572 U.S. (2014).

17. *Lemon v. Kurtzman*, 403 U.S. 602 (1971).

18. *Lynch v. Donnelly*, 465 U.S. 668 (1984), 672–73.

19. Jeffrey Rosen, "Big Ten," *The New Republic*, March 14, 2004, p. 11.

20. *Arizona Christian School Tuition Organization v. Winn*, U.S. Supreme Court slip. op. 09-987 and 09-991 (2011).

21. *Mitchell v. Helms*, 530 U.S. 793 (2000).

22. *Zobrest v. Catalina Foothills School District*, 509 U.S. 1 (1993).

23. We will not cite all of the cases here. See Abraham and Perry, *Freedom and the Court*, Chapter 6, for a summary of cases on this topic, especially Tables 6.1 and 6.2.

24. *Employment Division, Department of Human Resources of Oregon v. Smith*, 494 U.S. 872 (1990), 878–80. This case is often erroneously reported as having banned the religious use of peyote. In fact, the Court said: "Although it is constitutionally permissible to exempt sacramental peyote use from the operation of drug laws, it is not constitutionally required."

25. *City of Boerne v. Flores*, 521 U.S. 527 (1997); *Cutter v. Wilkinson*, No. 03-9877 (2005); *Gonzales v. O Centro Espirita Beneficente Uniao do Vegetal (UDV) et al.*, 546 U.S. 418 (2006). The Sherbert test comes from *Sherbert v. Verner*, 374 U.S. 398 (1963).

26. *Burwell v. Hobby Lobby*, 573 U.S. (2014).

27. *Police Department of Chicago v. Mosley*, 408 U.S. 92 (1972).

28. *United States v. O'Brien*, 391 U.S. 367 (1968); *Ladue v. Gilleo*, 512 U.S. 43 (1994).

29. *Schenck v. United States*, 249 U.S. 47 (1919), 52.

30. Alan Dershowitz, *Shouting Fire: Civil Liberties in a Turbulent Age* (New York: Little, Brown, 2002).

31. *Brandenburg v. Ohio*, 395 U.S. 444 (1969).

32. *Snyder v. Phelps*, 131 S.Ct. 1207 (2011).

33. *Smith v. Goguen*, 415 U.S. 566 (1974).

34. *Tinker v. Des Moines School District*, 393 U.S. 503 (1969).

35. *Spence v. Washington*, 418 U.S. 405 (1974).

36. *Texas v. Johnson*, 491 U.S. 397 (1989).

37. *United States v. Eichman*, 496 U.S. 310 (1990).

38. *Buckley v. Valeo*, 424 U.S. 1 (1976).

39. *Davis v. Federal Election Commission*, 554 U.S. 724 (2008).

40. *Citizens United v. Federal Election Commission*, 558 U.S. 310 (2010).

41. *McCutcheon v. Federal Election Commission*, 572 U.S. ____ (2014).

42. *McConnell v. Federal Election Commission*, 540 U.S. 93 (2003).

43. Kermit L. Hall, "Free Speech on Public College Campuses: Overview," www.firstamendmentcenter.org/speech/pubcollege/overview.aspx (accessed 2/10/08).

44. Carolyn J. Palmer, Sophie W. Penney, Donald D. Gehring, and Jan A. Neiger, "Hate Speech and Hate Crimes: Campus Conduct Codes and Supreme Court Rulings," *National Association of Student Personnel Administrators Journal* 34,

no. 2 (1997), http://publications.naspa.org/naspajournal/
vol34/iss2/art4 (accessed 12/18/07).

45. Liam Stacknov, "Yale's Halloween Advice Stokes a Racially
Charged Debate," *New York Times,* November 8, 2015, www.
nytimes.com/2015/11/09/nyregion/yale-culturally-
insensitive-halloween-costumes-free-speech.html?_r=0
(accessed 12/30/15).

46. Michael D. Regan, "Yale Lecturer Resigns over Halloween
Costume Email Controversy," *Christian Science
Monitor,* December 8, 2015, www.csmonitor.com/USA/
Education/2015/1208/Yale-lecturer-resigns-over-Halloween-
costume-email-controversy (accessed 12/30/15).

47. Yanan Wang, "Obama to Campus Protesters: Don't 'Shut
Up' Opposing Viewpoints," *Washington Post,* December
22, 2015, www.washingtonpost.com/news/morning-mix/
wp/2015/12/22/obama-to-campus-protesters-dont-shut-up-
opposing-viewpoints (accessed 12/30/15).

48. *City of St. Paul v. RAV,* 505 U.S. 377 (1992).

49. *Virginia v. Black,* 538 U.S. 343 (2003).

50. The Editorial Board, "Hate Speech on Facebook," *New
York Times,* May 30, 2013, www.nytimes.com/2013/05/31/
opinion/misogynist-speech-on-facebook.html (accessed
1/28/14).

51. Facebook "community standards" on hate speech,
www.facebook.com/communitystandards (accessed
1/28/14).

52. Jeffrey Rosen, "Who Decides? Civility v. Hate Speech on the
Internet," *Insights on Law and Society* 13, no. 2 (Winter 2013):
32–36.

53. Pete Kasperowicz, "13 House Democrats Offer Bill Demanding
Government Study on Internet Hate Speech," *The Hill,*
January 16, 2014, www.thehill.com/blogs/floor-action/
technology/195647-dems-demand-government-study-on-
internet-hate-speech (accessed 1/29/14).

54. The Supreme Court declined to review the case in *Smith v.
Collin,* 439 U.S. 916 (1978), which meant that the lower-court
rulings stood: 447 F. Supp. 676 (1978), 578 F 2d 1197 (1978).
See Donald A. Downs, *Nazis in Skokie: Freedom, Community
and the First Amendment* (Notre Dame, IN: University of
Notre Dame Press, 1985), for an excellent analysis of this
important case.

55. *Frisby et al. v. Schultz et al.,* 487 U.S. 474 (1988).

56. *New York Times Co. v. United States,* 403 U.S. 713 (1971).

57. *Chaplinsky v. State of New Hampshire,* 315 U.S. 568 (1942).

58. *Chaplinsky v. State of New Hampshire.*

59. *New York Times v. Sullivan,* 376 U.S. 254 (1964), cited in Henry
J. Abraham and Barbara A. Perry, *Freedom and the Court: Civil
Rights and Liberties in the United States,* 8th ed. (Lawrence:
University Press of Kansas, 2003), p. 193.

60. Hustler *v. Falwell,* 485 U.S. 46 (1988).

61. *Virginia State Board of Pharmacy v. Virginia Citizens Consumer
Council, Inc.,* 425 U.S. 748 (1976); *City of Cincinnati v. Discovery
Network, Inc., et al.,* 507 U.S. 410 (1993).

62. *Central Hudson Gas & Electric v. Public Service Commission,* 447
U.S. 557 (1980).

63. *Lorillard Tobacco v. Reilly,* 533 U.S. 525 (2001).

64. In 1996, Congress passed the Child Pornography Prevention
Act. This law makes the possession, production, or
distribution of child pornography a criminal offense punishable
with up to 15 years in jail and a fine. However, two parts of the
law were struck down by the Court for being "overbroad and
unconstitutional." *Ashcroft v. Free Speech Coalition,* 353 U.S. 234
(2002).

65. *Jacobellis v. Ohio,* 378 U.S. 184, 197 (1964).

66. *Miller v. California,* 413 U.S. 15 (1973).

67. *Reno et al. v. American Civil Liberties Union et al.,* 521 U.S. 844
(1997).

68. *Ashcroft v. American Civil Liberties Union,* 535 U.S. 564 (2004).

69. Law Center to Prevent Gun Violence, New Gun Legislation:
Summary of Enacted Laws since Newtown, January 22, 2015,
http://smartgunlaws.org/category/gun-laws-policies/new-
gun-legislation (accessed 1/5/16).

70. *District of Columbia v. Heller,* 554 U.S. 290 (2008).

71. *McDonald v. Chicago,* 08-1521 (2010).

72. Juliet Eilperin and David Nakamura, "Obama Moves
to Further Regulate Gun Sales with Executive Actions
That Circumvent Congress, " *Washington Post,*
January 5, 2016, www.washingtonpost.com/politics/
obama-moves-on-guns-with-executive-actions-
that-circumvent-congress/2016/01/05/97f23336-
b3bc-11e5-a76a-0b5145e8679a_story.
html?hpid=hp_hp-top-table-main_obamaguns-
1215pm%3Ahomepage%2Fstory (accessed 1/5/16).

73. See Abraham and Perry, *Freedom and the Court,* Chapter 4, for a
discussion of these cases.

74. *Florence v. County of Burlington,* U.S. 10-945 (2012).

75. *Riley v. California,* 573 U.S. ____ (2014)

76. *United States v. Jones,* 565 U.S. ____ (2012).

77. *Mapp v. Ohio,* 367 U.S. 643 (1961).

78. *Herring v. United States,* 555 U.S. 135 (2009).

79. *Vernonia School District v. Acton,* 515 U.S. 646 (1995); *Board
of Education of Pottawatomie County v. Earls,* 536 U.S. 832
(2002).

80. *Chandler v. Miller,* 520 U.S. 305 (1997).

81. Leslie Cauley, "NSA Has Massive Database of Americans'
Phone Calls," *USA Today,* May 11, 2006, p. 1.

82. Lorraine Woellert and Dawn Kopecki, "The Snooping Goes
beyond Phone Calls," *Business Week,* May 29, 2006, p. 38; "Data
Mining: Federal Efforts Cover a Wide Range of Uses," GAO
Report 04-548, May 2004, www.gao.gov/assets/250/242241.
pdf (accessed 5/13/14).

83. *Miranda v. Arizona,* 384 U.S. 436 (1966).

84. *Dickerson v. United States,* 530 U.S. 428 (2000).

85. *Benton v. Maryland,* 395 U.S. 784 (1969).

86. *Lucas v. South Carolina Coastal Council,* 505 U.S. 1003 (1992).

87. *Kelo v. City of New London,* 505 U.S. 469 (2005).

88. National Conference of State Legislatures, "Eminent Domain
Overview," www.ncsl.org/research/environment-and-
natural-resources/eminent-doman-overview.aspx (accessed
1/31/14).

89. *Powell v. Alabama,* 287 U.S. 45 (1932).

90. *Gideon v. Wainwright,* 372 U.S. 335 (1963).

91. *Evitts v. Lucy,* 469 U.S. 387 (1985); *Wiggins v. Smith,* 539 U.S.
510 (2003). See Elizabeth Gable and Tyler Green, "*Wiggins v.
Smith:* The Ineffective Assistance of Counsel Standard Applied
Twenty Years after *Strickland,*" *Georgetown Journal of Legal
Ethics* (Summer 2004): 755-71, for a discussion of many of these
issues.

92. *Klopfer v. North Carolina,* 386 U.S. 213 (1967).

93. The law is 18 U.S.C. § 3161(c)(1), and the ruling is *Zedner v.
United States,* 05-5992 (2006).

94. The case concerning African Americans is *Batson v. Kentucky,*
106 S.Ct. 1712 (1986); the case about Latinos is *Hernandez v.*

New York, 500 U.S. 352 (1991); and the gender case is *J.E.B. v. Alabama ex rel. T.B.*, 511 U.S. 127 (1994). Two recent cases affirming that peremptory challenges could not be used in a racially discriminatory fashion were *Miller-El v. Dretke*, 545 U.S. 231 (2005), and *Snyder v. Louisiana*, 552 U.S. 472 (2008).

95. Death Penalty Information Center, "Number of Executions since 1976," www.deathpenaltyinfo.org/executions-year (accessed 1/5/16); *Hall v. Florida*, 572 U.S. ___ (2014).

96. Erik Eckholm, "One Execution Botched, Oklahoma Delays the *Next,*" *New York Times*, April 29, 2014, *www.nytimes. com/2014/04/30/us/oklahoma-executions.html (accessed 5/13/14).*

97. *Furman v. Georgia*, 408 U.S. 238 (1972); *Gregg v. Georgia*, 428 U.S. 513 (1976).

98. See Abraham and Perry, *Freedom and the Court*, pp. 72–73, for a discussion of the earlier cases, and Charles Lane, "5–4 Supreme Court Abolishes Juvenile Executions," *Washington Post*, March 2, 2005, p. A1, for a discussion of the 2002 and 2005 cases. The 2008 case was *Kennedy v. Louisiana*, 554 U.S. 407 (2008).

99. *Griswold v. Connecticut*, 381 U.S. 479 (1965), 482–86.

100. *Griswold v. Connecticut*, 381 U.S. 479 (1965), 512–13.

101. *Roe v. Wade*, 410 U.S. 113 (1973), 129.

102. *Planned Parenthood of Southeastern Pennsylvania v. Casey*, 505 U.S. 833 (1992).

103. Katharine Q. Seeyle, "Mississippi Voters Reject Anti-Abortion Measure," *New York Times*, November 8, 2011, www.nytimes.com/2011/11/09/us/politics/votes-across-the-nation-could-serve-as-a-political-barometer.html (accessed 12/5/11).

104. Erik Eckholm, "Access to Abortion Falling as States Pass Restrictions," *New York Times*, January 3, 2014, www.nytimes.com/2014/01/04/us/women-losing-access-to-abortion-as-opponents-gain-ground-in-state-legislatures.html (accessed 1/31/14).

105. *Whole Woman's Health v. Hellerstedt*, 579 U.S. ___ (2016).

106. *Lawrence v. Texas*, 539 U.S. 558 (2003).

Take a Stand

a. *Florida v. Jardines*, 569 U.S. ___ (2013), 6–7.

b. Oral arguments in *U.S. v. Jones* (2012), November 8, 2011, www.supremecourt.gov/oral_arguments/argument_transcripts/10-1259.pdf, p. 44 (accessed 8/20/12).

Chapter 5

1. Complaint in *United States v. Maricopa County, Arizona and Joseph M. Arpaio*, May 10, 2012, Federal District Court of Arizona, www.justice.gov/iso/opa/resources/512012510134311376158.pdf (accessed 4/6/14).

2. Mark Lacey, "U.S. Finds Pervasive Bias against Latinos by Arizona Sheriff," *New York Times*, December 16, 2011, www.nytimes.com/2011/12/16/us/arizona-sheriffs-office-unfairly-targeted-latinos-justice-department-says.html?ref=josephmarpaio (accessed 1/31/12).

3. "The Persistence of Racial and Ethnic Profiling in the United States," American Civil Liberties Union and the Rights Working Group, New York, August 2009, p. 42, www.aclu.org/files/pdfs/humanrights/cerd_finalreport.pdf (accessed 1/31/12).

4. Supplemental Permanent Injunction, *Manuel de Jesus Ortega Melendres v. Joseph M. Arpaio*, Federal District Court of Arizona, October 2, 2013, www.aclu.org/sites/default/files/assets/2013.10.02.606_supplemental_permanent_injunction_judgment_order.pdf (accessed 4/6/14).

5. Fernanda Santos, "Angry Judge Says Sheriff Defied Order on Latinos," *New York Times*, March 24, 2014, www.nytimes.com/2014/03/25/us/judge-says-arpaio-defied-order-on-profiling-latinos.html (accessed 4/6/14).

6. Jacques Billeaud, "Arizona Sheriff's Bid for Leniency Met with Skepticism," *Arizona Daily Sun*, July 22, 2016, http://azdailysun.com/news/state-and-regional/arizona-sheriff-s-bid-for-leniency-met-with-skepticism/article_aa3322a5-48f7-5be7-8629-d86198f01c4d.html (accessed 8/11/16).

7. Julia Preston and John H. Cushman Jr., "Obama to Permit Young Migrants to Remain in U.S.," *New York Times*, June 15, 2012, www.nytimes.com/2012/06/16/us/us-to-stop-deporting-some-illegal-immigrants.html?pagewanted=all (accessed 4/6/14).

8. The number of slaves who died in transit is hotly contested. The most common estimate is that one-sixth of slaves died in transit on the "Middle Passage" to the American colonies. Much higher mortality rates occurred in the slave trade to the Middle East and South America. See "Learning about the Transatlantic Slave Trade," www.antislavery.org/breakingthesilence (accessed 1/26/12).

9. Howard Dodson, "How Slavery Helped Build a World Economy," February 3, 2003, in Schomburg Center for Research in Black Culture of the New York City Public Library, *Jubilee: The Emergence of African-American Culture* (Washington, DC: National Geographic Press, 2003).

10. John W. Wright, ed., *New York Times 2000 Almanac* (New York: Penguin Reference, 1999), p. 165. Estimates from various online sources are quite a bit higher, averaging about 620,000 deaths.

11. Chandler Davidson, "The Voting Rights Act: A Brief History," in *Controversies in Minority Voting: The Voting Rights Act in Perspective*, ed. Bernard Grofman and Chandler Davidson (Washington, DC: Brookings Institution, 1992), p. 21.

12. "Indian Removal: 1814–1848," Public Broadcasting System, www.pbs.org/wgbh/aia/part4/4p2959.html (accessed 1/26/12).

13. *Cherokee Nation v. Georgia*, 30 U.S. 1 (1831).

14. *United States v. Wong Kim Ark*, 169 U.S. 649 (1898).

15. Bilal Qureshi, "From Wrong to Right: A U.S. Apology for Japanese Internment," August 9, 2013, National Public Radio, www.npr.org/sections/codeswitch/2013/08/09/210138278/japanese-internment-redress (accessed 1/29/16).

16. Institute for Advanced Technology in the Humanities, University of Virginia, Abigail Adams to John Adams, March 31, 1776, www.iath.virginia.edu/seminar/unit1/text/adams.htm (accessed 7/30/08).

17. Lucian K. Truscott IV, "The Real Mob at Stonewall," *New York Times*, June 25, 2009, p. A19.

18. ABC News/Washington Post poll on gay rights, February 27–March 2, 2014, and various other polls reported on www.pollingreport.com (accessed 4/7/14).

19. *Obergefell v. Hodges*, 576 U.S. ___ (2015).

20. Davidson, "The Voting Rights Act," p. 22. See U.S. Department of Justice, Civil Rights Division, "About Section 5 of the Voting Rights Act," www.justice.gov/crt/vot/sec_5/obj_activ.php?, for a complete list of cases in which the Justice Department has denied "preclearance" of a change in an electoral practice

under Section 5 of the Voting Rights Act. Note that in racially homogeneous single-member districts, minority candidates usually win. In at-large elections, in which representatives are elected citywide or countywide, the majority-white voters can out-vote the minority voters and elect an all-white city council or school board.

21. "New Voting Restrictions in Place for 2016 Presidential Election," Brennan Center for Justice, www.brennancenter. org/voting-restrictions-first-time-2016 (accessed 10/16/16).

22. Bernadette D. Proctor, Jessica L. Semega, and Melissa A. Kollar, "Income and Poverty in the United States: 2015," United States Census, Current Population Reports, September 2016, poverty rates from Table 3, p. 13, income from Table 1, p. 6, www.census. gov/content/dam/Census/library/publications/2016/demo/ p60-256.pdf (accessed 10/17/16).

23. Jesse Bricker et al., "Changes in U.S. Family Finances from 2010 to 2013: Evidence from the Survey of Consumer Finances," *Federal Reserve Bulletin* 100:4 (September 2014), Table 2, p. 12, www.federalreserve.gov/pubs/ bulletin/2014/pdf/scf14.pdf (accessed 9/30/14).

24. Life expectancy and infant mortality rates are from the Centers for Disease Control, www.cdc.gov/NCHS/data/nvsr/nvsr58/ nvsr58_19.pdf; maternity mortality rates are from the National Center for Health Statistics, http://mchb.hrsa.gov/mchirc/ chusa_04/pages/0409mm.htm (both accessed 3/21/08). Other health data are available from the Department of Health and Human Services, www.hhs.gov (accessed 4/17/14).

25. See the National Resources Defense Council's research on the Environmental Justice Movement, www.nrdc.org/ej/ history/hej.asp, and the Environmental Justice and Health Alliance for Chemical Policy reform's report, "Who's in Danger? Race, Poverty, and Chemical Disasters," May 2014, www.comingcleaninc.org/assets/media/images/Reports/ Who's%20in%20Danger%20Report%20and%20Table%20 FINAL.pdf (accessed 1/30/16).

26. Greg Botelho, Sarah Jorgensen, and Joseph Netto, "Water Crisis in Flint, Michigan, Draws Federal Investigation," CNN.com, January 9, 2016, www.cnn.com/2016/01/05/health/flint-michigan-water-investigation (accessed 1/30/16).

27. "The Counted," *The Guardian*, www.theguardian.com/ us-news/ng-interactive/2015/jun/01/the-counted-police-killings-us-database# (accessed 1/30/16).

28. "Trayvon Martin, George Zimmerman Case," *Orlando Sentinel*, www.orlandosentinel.com/news/local/trayvon-martin (accessed 4/6/14).

29. Hundreds of studies have examined these patterns, and, not surprisingly, there are divergent findings. However, most have found differences in sentencing based on race. A meta-analysis of 85 studies by Ojmarrh Mitchell and Doris L. MacKenzie funded by the U.S. Department of Justice found, "after taking into account defendant criminal history and current offense seriousness, African-Americans and Latinos were generally sentenced more harshly than whites." See Mitchell and MacKenzie, "The Relationship between Race, Ethnicity, and Sentencing Outcomes: A Meta-Analysis of Sentencing Research," December 2004, www.ncjrs.gov/pdffiles1/ nij/grants/208129.pdf. For government studies of racial profiling, see the Justice Department's "A Resource Guide on Racial Profiling Data Collection Systems," November 2000, www.ncjrs.gov/pdffiles1/bja/184768.pdf. For President Bush's statement on racial profiling, see Department of Justice, "Fact Sheet: Racial Profiling," June 17, 2003, www.usdoj.gov/ opa/pr/2003/June/racial_profiling_fact_sheet.pdf. For a Government Accountability Office study, see "Racial Profiling: Limited Data on Motorist Stops," March 2000, www.gao.gov/

new.items/gg00041.pdf. Government statistics on crime may be found on the FBI site at www.fbi.gov. (All documents accessed 3/21/08.)

30. "2014 Hate Crime Statistics," U.S. Department of Justice, www.fbi.gov/about-us/cjis/ucr/hate-crime/2014/tables/ table-1 (accessed 1/30/16).

31. Clayborne Carson, David J. Garrow, Gerald Gill, Vincent Harding, and Darlene Clark Hine, eds., *The Eyes on the Prize Civil Rights Reader* (New York: Penguin Books, 1997).

32. Nate Silver, "Tea Party Nonpartisan Attendance Estimates: Now 300,000," April 16, 2009, www.fivethirtyeight. com/2009/04/tea-party-nonpartisan-attendance.html (accessed 1/19/10).

33. *Missouri ex rel. Gaines v. Canada*, 305 U.S. 377 (1938).

34. *Sweatt v. Painter*, 339 U.S. 629 (1950).

35. *Brown v. Board of Education*, 347 U.S. 483 (1954).

36. *Brown v. Board of Education II*, 349 U.S. 294 (1955).

37. Paul Brest and Sanford Levinson, *Process of Constitutional Decision Making: Cases and Material* (Boston: Little, Brown, 1982), pp. 471–80.

38. *Swann v. Charlotte-Mecklenberg Board of Education*, 402 U.S. 1 (1971).

39. *Milliken v. Bradley*, 418 U.S. 717 (1974).

40. *Board of Education of Oklahoma City v. Dowell*, 498 U.S. 237 (1991).

41. *Missouri v. Jenkins*, 515 U.S. 70 (1995).

42. *Parents Involved in Community Schools Inc. v. Seattle School District*, 05-98 (2007); *Meredith v. Jefferson County (Ky.) Board of Education*, 551 U.S. 701 (2007).

43. *Griggs v. Duke Power*, 401 U.S. 424 (1971).

44. *Easley v. Cromartie*, 532 U.S. 234 (2001), rehearing denied, 532 U.S. 1076 (2001).

45. *Easley v. Cromartie*, 532 U.S. 1076 (2001).

46. *Shelby County v. Holder*, 570 U.S. ___ (2013).

47. *Reed v. Reed*, 404 U.S. 71 (1971).

48. *Frontiero v. Richardson*, 411 U.S. 677 (1973).

49. *Craig v. Boren*, 429 U.S. 190 (1976).

50. *United States v. Virginia*, 518 U.S. 515 (1996).

51. *Johnson v. Transportation Agency of Santa Clara*, 480 U.S. 616 (1987).

52. *Harris v. Forklift Systems*, 510 U.S. 17 (1993).

53. *Grove City College v. Bell*, 465 U.S. 555 (1984).

54. *Ledbetter v. Goodyear Tire & Rubber Co.*, 550 U.S. 618 (2007).

55. Julie Hirschfeld Davis, "Obama Moves to Expand Rules Aimed at Closing Gender Pay Gap," *New York Times*, January 29, 2016, www.nytimes.com/2016/01/29/us/politics/obama-moves-to-expand-rules-aimed-at-closing-gender-pay-gap.html (accessed 1/30/16).

56. *Bowers v. Hardwick*, 478 U.S. 186 (1986), rehearing denied, 478 U.S. 1039 (1986).

57. *Romer v. Evans*, 517 U.S. 620 (1996).

58. *Lawrence v. Texas*, 539 U.S. 558 (2003). Because the basis for the decision was the due process clause of the Fourteenth Amendment and not the equal protection clause, this ruling upheld a civil liberty rather than a civil right. As such, it applied to all laws regarding sodomy, not just those that applied to gays. However, the decision has been widely regarded as a landmark civil rights case because it provided equal rights for gays.

59. The three cases are *Hollingsworth v. Perry*, 570 U.S. ____ (2013), *United States v. Windsor*, 570 U.S. ____ (2013), and *Obergefell v. Hodges*, 576 U.S. ____ (2015).

60. Drew S. Days III, "Section 5 Enforcement and the Justice Department," in *Controversies in Minority Voting: The Voting Rights Act in Perspective*, ed. Bernard Grofman and Chandler Davidson (Washington, DC: Brookings Institution Press, 1992), p. 52; Frank R. Parker, *Black Votes Count* (Chapel Hill: University of North Carolina Press, 1990), p. 1.

61. "Fair Housing: It's Your Right," U.S. Department of Housing and Urban Development, http://portal.hud.gov/hudportal/HUD?src=/program_offices/fair_housing_equal_opp/FHLaws/yourrights (accessed 2/2/12).

62. *United States v. Morrison*, 529 U.S. 598 (2000).

63. *Board of Trustees of the University of Alabama v. Garrett*, 531 U.S. 356 (2001). However, in *State of Tennessee v. George Lane and Beverly Jones*, 541 U.S. 509 (2004), the Court ruled that the disabled must have access to courthouses.

64. The White House, "Remarks by the President at Reception Commemorating the Enactment of the Matthew Shepard and James Byrd Jr. Hate Crimes Prevention Act," October 28, 2009, www.whitehouse.gov/the-press-office/remarks-president-reception-commemorating-enactment-matthew-shepard-and-james-byrd (accessed 1/21/10).

65. Tim Mak, "Post 'Don't Ask,' Gay Navy Lt. Marries," *Politico*, September 20, 2011, www.politico.com/news/stories/0911/63909.html (accessed 1/12/12).

66. *New York Times*/CBS poll, December 6–9, 1997. Fifty-nine percent of whites and 82 percent of blacks favored the education programs, while 57 percent of whites but only 23 percent of blacks opposed preferences in hiring and promotion "to make up for past discrimination."

67. A training program case was *United Steel Workers of America v. Weber*, 443 U.S. 193 (1979); a labor union case was *Sheet Metal Workers v. EEOC*, 478 U.S. 421 (1986); and a case involving Alabama state police was *U.S. v. Paradise*, 480 U.S. 149 (1987).

68. *Richmond v. J. A. Croson Co.*, 488 U.S. 469 (1989).

69. *Adarand Constructors, Inc. v. Pena*, 515 U.S. 200 (1995).

70. *Ricci v. DeStefano*, 557 U.S. ____ (2009).

71. *Regents of the University of California v. Bakke*, 438 U.S. 265 (1978).

72. *Grutter v. Bollinger*, 123, 539 U.S. 306 (2003), was the law school case and *Gratz v. Bollinger*, 539 U.S. 244 (2003), was the undergraduate admissions case.

73. In *Bakke*, Justice Lewis Powell was the only member of the Court who held this position, even if it became the basis for all affirmative action programs over the next 25 years. Four justices in the *Bakke* decision wanted to get rid of race as a factor in admissions, and another four thought that the "strict scrutiny" standard should not even be applied in this instance.

74. *Schuette v. Coalition to Defend Affirmative Action*, 572 U.S. (2014).

75. *Fisher v. University of Texas, Austin*, 579 U.S. ____ (2016).

76. *Alexander v. Sandoval*, 532 U.S. 275 (2001).

77. *Arizona v. United States*, 567 U.S. ____ (2012).

78. Fernanda Santos, "Arizona Immigration Law Survives Ruling," *New York Times*, September 6, 2012, www.nytimes.com/2012/09/07/us/key-element-of-arizona-immigration-law-survives-ruling.html?_r=0 (accessed 10/5/12).

79. "An Act Providing for the Collection of Data Relative to Traffic Stops," Massachusetts state law, Chapter 228 of the Acts of 2000, www.mass.gov/legis/laws/seslaw00/sl000228.htm (accessed 7/22/08).

Chapter 6

1. For a review, see Arthur Lupia and Mathew D. McCubbins, *The Democratic Dilemma* (New York: Cambridge University Press, 1998).

2. Robert S. Erikson, Michael B. Mackuen, and James A. Stimson, *The Macro Polity* (New York: Cambridge University Press, 2002).

3. John Zaller, "Coming to Grips with V. O. Key's Concept of Latent Opinion" (unpublished paper, University of California, Los Angeles, 1998).

4. Morris Fiorina, *Retrospective Voting in American National Elections* (Cambridge, MA: Harvard University Press, 1981).

5. John Zaller, *The Nature and Origins of Mass Opinion* (New York: Cambridge University Press, 1992).

6. R. Michael Alvarez and John Brehm, *Hard Choices, Easy Answers* (Princeton, NJ: Princeton University Press, 2002).

7. John Zaller and Stanley Feldman, "A Theory of the Survey Response: Revealing Preferences versus Answering Questions," *American Journal of Political Science* 36 (1992): 579–616.

8. Janet M. Box-Steffensmeier and Susan DeBoef, "Macropartisanship and Macroideology in the Sophisticated Electorate," *Journal of Politics* 63:1 (2001): 232–48.

9. Jack Citrin, Donald P. Green, Christopher Muste, and Cara Wong, "Public Opinion toward Immigration Reform: The Role of Economic Motivations," *American Journal of Political Science* 59:3 (1997): 858–82.

10. William G. Jacoby, "Issue Framing and Public Opinion on Government Spending," *American Journal of Political Science* 44:4 (2000): 750–67; L. M. Bartels, "Beyond the Running Tally: Partisan Bias in Political Perceptions," *Political Behavior* 24:2 (2002): 117–50.

11. Donald R. Kinder, "Exploring the Racial Divide: Blacks, Whites, and Opinion on National Policy," *American Journal of Political Science* 45:2 (2001): 439–49; Paul M. Sniderman and Thomas Piazza, *The Scar of Race* (Cambridge, MA: Harvard University Press, 1993).

12. Robert Huckfeldt, Jeffery Levine, William Morgan, and John Sprague, "Accessibility and the Political Utility of Partisan and Ideological Orientations," *American Journal of Political Science* 43:3 (July 1999): 888–911.

13. George E. Marcus, John L. Sullivan, Elizabeth Theiss-Morse, and Sandra L. Wood, *With Malice toward Some: How People Make Civil Liberties Judgments* (New York: Cambridge University Press, 1995).

14. Stanley Feldman and Marco R. Steenbergen, "The Humanitarian Foundation of Public Support for Social Welfare," *American Journal of Political Science* 45:3 (2001): 658–77.

15. R. Michael Alvarez and John Brehm, "American Ambivalence towards Abortion Policy: Development of a Heteroskedastic Probit Model of Competing Values," *American Journal of Political Science* 39:4 (1995): 1055–82.

16. R. Michael Alvarez and John Brehm, "Are Americans Ambivalent towards Racial Policies?," *American Journal of Political Science* 41 (1997): 345–74.

17. Virginia Sapiro, "Not Your Parents' Political Socialization: Introduction for a New Generation," *Annual Review of Political Science* 7 (2004): 1–23.

18. M. Kent Jennings and Richard G. Niemi, *Generations and Politics: A Panel Study of Young Adults and Their Parents*

(Princeton, NJ: Princeton University Press, 1981).

19. Robert Putnam, *Bowling Alone: The Collapse and Revival of American Community* (New York: Simon and Schuster, 2000).

20. Richard G. Niemi and Mary Hepburn, "The Rebirth of Political Socialization," *Perspectives on Politics* 24 (1995): 7–16.

21. David Campbell, *Why We Vote: How Schools and Communities Shape Our Civic Life* (Princeton, NJ: Princeton University Press, 2006).

22. Sidney Verba, Kay Schlozman, and Henry Brady, *Voice and Equality: Civic Volunteerism in American Politics* (Cambridge, MA: Harvard University Press, 1995).

23. Paul Allen Beck and M. Kent Jennings, "Pathways to Participation," *American Political Science Review* 76 (1982): 94–108.

24. Fiorina, *Retrospective Voting*.

25. Pew Research Center, "In Gay Marriage Debate, Both Supporters and Opponents See Legal Recognition as 'Inevitable,'" June 6, 2013, www.people-press. org/2013/06/06/in-gay-marriage-debate-both-supporters-and-opponents-see-legal-recognition-as-inevitable (accessed 10/30/15).

26. Darren W. Davis and Brian D. Silver, "Civil Liberties vs. Security: Public Opinion in the Context of the Terrorist Attacks in America," *American Journal of Political Science* 48:1 (2004): 28–46; Leonie Huddy, Nadia Khatib, and Theresa Capelos, "The Polls: Trends," *Public Opinion Quarterly* 66 (2002): 418–50.

27. Eric Wemple, "*Fox & Friends* Fails on Obama–Muslim Museum Connection: No Surprise Here," *Washington Post*, October 7, 2013, www.washingtonpost.com/blogs/erik-wemple/ wp/2013/10/07/fox-friends-failson-obama-muslim-museum-connection-no-surprise-here (accessed 12/26/13).

28. Richard Nadwau et al., "Class, Party and South–Nonsouth Differences," *American Politics Research* 32 (2004): 52–67.

29. Donald P. Green, Bradley Palmquist, and Eric Schickler, *Partisan Hearts and Minds* (New Haven, CT: Yale University Press, 2002).

30. Pew Research Center, "Young Voters Supported Obama Less, but May Have Mattered More," November 26, 2012, www. people-press.org/2012/11/ 26/young-voters-supported-obama-less-but-may-have-mattered-more (accessed 3/17/14).

31. Jack Citrin and David O. Sears, *American Identity and the Politics of Multiculturalism* (New York: Cambridge University Press, 2014).

32. For elaboration on this point, see William T. Bianco, Richard G. Niemi, and Harold W. Stanley, "Partisanship and Group Support over Time: A Multivariate Analysis," *American Political Science Review* 80 (September 1986): 969–76.

33. Arthur Lupia and Mathew D. McCubbins, *The Democratic Dilemma* (New York: Cambridge University Press, 1998).

34. Lawrence R. Jacobs and Robert Y. Shapiro, *Politicians Don't Pander: Political Manipulation and the Loss of Democratic Responsiveness* (Chicago: University of Chicago Press, 2000).

35. Robert Y. Shapiro and Lawrence Jacobs, "Simulating Representation: Elite Mobilization and Political Power in Health Care Reform," *The Forum* 8:1 (2010): article 4.

36. Kaiser Family Foundation, Kaiser Health Tracking Poll: The Public's Views on the ACA, 2016, http://kff.org/interactive/ kaiser-health-tracking-poll-the-publics-views-on-the-aca/#?response=Favorable--Unfavorable&aRange=twoYear (accessed 11/1/15).

37. Christopher Wlezien and Robert S. Erikson, "The Horse Race: What Polls Reveal as the Election Campaign Unfolds," *International Journal of Public Opinion Research* 19:1 (2007): 74–88

38. Pollster.com, "IVR and Internet: How Reliable?," September 28, 2006, www.pollster.com/mystery_pollster/ivr_internet_ how_reliable.php (accessed 2/21/08).

39. For data on reported and actual turnout, see Chapter 7.

40. Anton J. Nederhof, "Methods of Coping with Social Desirability Bias: A Review," *European Journal of Social Psychology* 15:3 (2006): 263–80.

41. James H. Kuklinski et al., "Misinformation and the Currency of Democratic Citizenship," *Journal of Politics* 62:3 (2000): 790–816.

42. Sarah Kliff, "Obamacare Is 5 Years Old, and Americans Are Still Worried about Death Panels," Vox.com, May 23, 2015, www. vox.com/2015/3/23/8273007/obamacare-poll-death-panels (accessed 11/2/15).

43. George H. Bishop, *The Illusion of Public Opinion: Fact and Artifact in Public Opinion Polls* (Washington, DC: Rowman & Littlefield, 2004).

44. Michael X. Delli Carpini and Scott Keeter, *What Americans Know about Politics and Why It Matters* (New Haven, CT: Yale University Press, 1997).

45. Delli Carpini and Keeter, *What Americans Know about Politics*.

46. For a review of the literature on trust in government, see Karen Cook, Russell Hardin, and Margaret Levi, *Cooperation without Trust* (New York: Russell Sage Foundation, 2005); and Marc J. Hetherington, *Why Trust Matters: Declining Political Trust and the Demise of American Liberalism* (Princeton, NJ: Princeton University Press, 2004).

47. William T. Bianco, *Trust: Representatives and Constituents* (Ann Arbor: University of Michigan Press, 1994).

48. Sean M. Theriault, *The Power of the People: Congressional Competition, Public Attention, and Voter Retribution* (Columbus: Ohio State University Press, 2005).

49. Thomas Rudolph and Jillian Evans, "Political Trust, Ideology, and Public Support for Government Spending," *American Journal of Political Science* 49 (2005): 660–71.

50. Patricia Moy and Michael Pfau, *With Malice toward All? The Media and Public Confidence in Democratic Institutions* (Boulder, CO: Praeger, 2000).

51. Robert S. Erikson, Michael B. Mackuen, and James A. Stimson, *The Macro Polity* (New York: Cambridge University Press, 2002).

52. James A. Stimson, *Public Opinion in America: Moods, Swings, and Cycles* (Boulder, CO: Westview Press, 1999).

53. Robert S. Erikson, Michael B. Mackuen, and James A. Stimson, "American Politics: The Model" (unpublished manuscript, Columbia University, 2000).

54. Larry Bartels, "Constituency Opinion and Congressional Policy Making: The Reagan Defense Buildup," *American Political Science Review* 85 (June 1991): 457–74; Jonathan Kastellec, Jeffrey R. Lax, and Justin H. Phillips, "Public Opinion and Senate Confirmation of Supreme Court Nominees," *Journal of Politics* 72 (2010): 767–84.

55. Lawrence R. Jacobs and Robert Y. Shapiro, *Politicians Don't Pander: Political Manipulation and the Loss of Democratic Responsiveness* (Chicago: University of Chicago Press, 2000).

56. See www.nationalreview.com.

57. SCOTUSblog, www.scotusblog.com (accessed 9/17/12).

58. See www.themonkeycage.org (accessed 9/17/12).

59. See, for example, James J. Cramer, "Newspapers Still Stumble Online," RealMoney.com, May 2, 2005, www.thestreet.com/p/_rms/rmoney/jamesjcramer/10221101.html (accessed 2/26/08).

60. This discussion draws on the summary "Merging Media: How Relaxing FCC Ownership Rules Has Affected the Media Business," www.pbs.org/newshour/media/conglomeration/fcc2.html (accessed 2/26/08).

61. The Project for Excellence in Journalism, "The State of the News Media, 2007: Ownership," 2007, www.stateof thenewsmedia.org/2007/narrative_overview_ownership .asp?cat=5&media=1 (accessed 2/26/08).

62. *Columbia Journalism Review* maintains a list of holdings for major media companies at Who Owns What, www.cjr.org/ tools/owners.

63. For a discussion of these concepts, see Paul M. Sniderman and Sean M. Theriault, "The Structure of Political Argument and the Logic of Issue Framing," in *Studies in Public Opinion*, ed. William E. Saris and Paul M. Sniderman (Princeton, NJ: Princeton University Press, 2004); and Shanto Iyengar and Donald Kinder, *News That Matters* (Chicago: University of Chicago Press, 1987). See also Maxwell McCombs and Donald L. Shaw, "The Agenda-Setting Functions of Mass Media," *Public Opinion Quarterly* 36 (1972): 176–87; and Amos Tversky and Daniel Kahnemann, "The Framing of Decisions and the Psychology of Choice," *Science* 211 (1981): 453–58.

64. Markus Prior, "Media and Political Polarization," *Annual Review of Political Science* 16 (2013): 101–27.

65. Kevin Arceneaux et al., "The Influence of News Media on Political Elites: Investigating Strategic Responsiveness in Congress," *American Journal of Political Science* 60:1 (2016): 5–29.

66. Matthew S. Levendusky, "Why Do Partisan Media Polarize Viewers?," *American Journal of Political Science* 57.3 (2013): 611–23.

67. Kevin Arceneaux, Martin Johnson, and Chad Murphy, "Polarized Political Communication, Oppositional Media Hostility, and Selective Exposure," *Journal of Politics* 74:01 (2012): 174–86.

68. Stefano DellaVigna and Ethan Kaplan, "The Fox News Effect: Media Bias and Voting," *Quarterly Journal of Economics* 122 (2007): 1187–1234.

Chapter 7

1. Marty Cohen et al., *The Party Decides: Presidential Nominations before and after Reform* (Chicago: University of Chicago Press, 2008).

2. Joseph Schlesinger, *Political Parties and the Winning of Office* (Ann Arbor: University of Michigan Press, 1994).

3. William Nesbit Chambers and Walter Dean Burnham, *The American Party Systems: Stages of Political Development* (Oxford, UK: Oxford University Press, 1966).

4. John Aldrich, *Why Parties?* (Chicago: University of Chicago Press, 2005).

5. James MacPherson, *Battle Cry of Freedom: The Civil War Era* (New York: Oxford University Press, 1988).

6. Michael F. Holt, *The Rise and Fall of the Whig Party: Jacksonian Politics and the Onset of the Civil War* (New York: Oxford University Press, 1999).

7. Harold W. Stanley, William T. Bianco, and Richard G. Niemi, "Partisanship and Group Support over Time: A Multivariate Analysis," *American Political Science Review* 80 (1986): 969–76.

8. Frank Baumgartner and Bryan D. Jones, *Agendas and Instability in American Politics* (Chicago: University of Chicago Press, 2009).

9. Hans Noel, *Political Ideologies and Political Parties in America* (New York: Cambridge University Press, 2014).

10. The full list of Democratic constituency groups is available at www.democrats.org/people. A list of Republican coalition groups is available at www.gop.com/coalition-support (accessed 10/18/12).

11. Jon F. Hale, "The Making of the New Democrats," *Political Science Quarterly* 110:2 (1995): 207–32.

12. Christopher S. Parker and Matt A. Barreto, *Change They Can't Believe In: The Tea Party and Reactionary Politics in America* (Princeton, NJ: Princeton University Press, 2015).

13. James Monroe, *The Political Party Matrix* (Albany: SUNY Press, 2001).

14. Gary Cox and Mathew McCubbins, *Legislative Leviathan* (Berkeley: University of California Press, 1993); James M. Snyder and Michael M. Ting, "An Informational Rationale for Political Parties," *American Journal of Political Science* 46 (2002): 90–110.

15. Jason Roberts and Steven Smith, "Procedural Contexts, Party Strategy, and Conditional Party Government," *American Journal of Political Science* 47:2 (2003): 205–317.

16. David Rohde, *Parties and Leaders in the Post-reform House* (Chicago: University of Chicago Press, 1991); Keith Poole, "An Update on Polarization through the 113th Congress," *Voteview*, September 8, 2013, http://voteview.com/blog/?p=887 (accessed 4/24/14).

17. Catherine Rampell, "Tax Pledge May Scuttle a Deal on Deficit," *New York Times*, November 18, 2011, p. B1.

18. Michael Meffert, Helmut Norpoth, and Anirudh V. S. Ruhil, "Realignment and Macropartisanship," *American Political Science Review* 95:4 (2001): 953–62.

19. Larry M. Bartels, "Partisanship and Voting Behavior, 1952–1996," *American Journal of Political Science* 44:1 (2000): 35–50.

20. Patrick Egan, *Partisan Priorities: How Issue Ownership Drives and Distorts American Politics* (New York: Cambridge University Press, 2013).

21. Daniel Schlotzman, *When Movements Anchor Parties: Electoral Alignments in American History* (Princeton, NJ: Princeton University Press, 2015).

22. Jill Lawrence, "Party Recruiters Lead Charge for '06 Vote; Choice of Candidates to Run in Fall May Decide Who Controls the House," *USA Today*, May 25, 2006, p. A5.

23. Compiled from information available at www.ballot-access.org (accessed 12/17/09).

24. Kyle Mattes and David Redlawsk, *The Positive Case for Negative Campaigning* (Chicago: University of Chicago Press, 2014).

25. Patricia Zapor, "Pro-life Democrats Describe Lonely Role, but See Improvements," Catholic News Service, July 28, 2004, www.catholicnews.com/data/stories/cns/0404122.htm (accessed 3/27/08).

26. See www.lp.org/our-history (accessed 6/5/12).

27. Pew Research & American Life Project surveys 2000–2009, www.pewinternet.org/static-pages/trend-data/online-activities-20002009.aspx (accessed 12/1/09).

28. See www.constitutionparty.com/party_platform.php (accessed 6/5/12).

Take a Stand

a. Nelson Polsby, *Consequences of Party Reform* (New York: Oxford University Press, 1983).

b. Daniel A. Smith and Caroline J. Tolbert, *Educated by Initiative: The Effects of Direct Democracy on Citizens and Political Organizations in the American States* (Ann Arbor: University of Michigan Press, 2004).

Chapter 8

1. Morris P. Fiorina, *Retrospective Voting in American National Elections* (New Haven, CT: Yale University Press, 1981); V. O. Key, *The Responsible Electorate* (New York: Vintage Books, 1966).

2. David Mayhew, *Congress: The Electoral Connection* (New Haven, CT: Yale University Press, 1973).

3. For details on early voting, see the Early Voting Information Center site, http://earlyvoting.net (accessed 10/19/12).

4. Michael Alvarez, Lonna Rae Atkeson, and Thad E. Hall, *Evaluating Elections: A Handbook of Standards and Methods* (New York: Cambridge University Press, 2013).

5. Minor-party candidates are typically selected during party conventions.

6. Barbara Norrander, "Presidential Nomination Politics in the Post-reform Era," *Political Research Quarterly* 49 (1996): 875–90.

7. Larry Bartels, *Presidential Primaries and the Dynamics of Public Choice* (Princeton, NJ: Princeton University Press, 1988).

8. FairVote, "Maine and Nebraska," www.fairvote.org/e_college/me_ne.htm (accessed 10/19/12).

9. James Q. Wilson, "Is the Electoral College Worth Saving?," *Slate*, November 3, 2000, www.slate.com/id/92663 (accessed 10/19/12).

10. Robert Erikson and Christopher Wlezien, *The Timeline of Presidential Elections* (Chicago: University of Chicago Press, 2013).

11. Larry M. Bartels and Christopher H. Achen, *Democracy for Realists: Why Elections Do Not Produce Responsive Government* (Princeton, NJ: Princeton University Press, 2016).

12. Steven Ansolabehere and Allan Gerber, "Incumbency Advantage and the Persistence of Legislative Majorities," *Legislative Studies Quarterly* 22 (1997): 161–80.

13. For a discussion of Johnson's decision, see Robert A. Caro, *The Path to Power* (New York: Knopf, 1983).

14. Thomas Mann and Norman Ornstein, *The Permanent Campaign and Its Future* (Washington, DC: American Enterprise Institute, 2000).

15. David Mayhew, *Congress: The Electoral Connection* (New Haven, CT: Yale University Press, 1973).

16. Jonathan Krasno and Donald P. Green, "The Dynamics of Campaign Fundraising in House Elections," *Journal of Politics* 56 (1991): 459–74.

17. Michael J. Goff, *The Money Primary: The New Politics of the Early Presidential Nomination Process* (New York: Rowman & Littlefield, 2007).

18. Chris Cillizza, "Consulting Firms Face Conflict in 2008," *Roll Call*, June 20, 2005, p. 1.

19. Matt Bai, "Turnout Wins Elections," *New York Times Magazine*, December 14, 2003, p. 100.

20. Christopher Drew, "New Telemarketing Ploy Steers Voters on Republican Path," *New York Times*, November 6, 2006.

21. Michael Babaro, "Candidates Stick to Script, If Not the Truth, in the 2016 Race," *New York Times*, November 7, 2015, p. A1.

22. For a history of presidential debates, see the Commission on Presidential Debates site, www.debates.org (accessed 10/19/12).

23. For a video library of presidential campaign ads, see Museum of the Moving Image, "The Living Room Candidate: Presidential Campaign Commercials 1952–2012," http://livingroomcandidate.org (accessed 10/19/12).

24. For examples of this argument, see Thomas Patterson, *The Vanishing Voter* (New York: Knopf, 2002); and Jules Witcover, *No Way to Pick a President: How Money and Hired Guns Have Debased American Politics* (London: Routledge, 2001).

25. Paul Freeman, Michael Franz, and Kenneth Goldstein, "Campaign Advertising and Democratic Citizenship," *American Journal of Political Science* 48 (2004): 723–41.

26. Constantine J. Spilotes and Lynn Vavreck, "Campaign Advertising: Partisan Convergence or Divergence?," *Journal of Politics* 64 (2002): 249–61.

27. Kathleen Hall Jameson, *Packaging the Presidency: A History and Criticism of Presidential Campaign Advertising* (New York: Oxford University Press, 1996).

28. For a review of the literature on issue voters, see Jon K. Dalager, "Voters, Issues, and Elections: Are Candidates' Messages Getting Through?," *Journal of Politics* 58 (1996): 486–515.

29. Brian Stelter, "The Price of 30 Seconds," *New York Times*, October 1, 2007, http://mediadecoder.blogs.nytimes.com/2007/10/01/the-price-of-30-seconds (accessed 10/19/12).

30. For a review of this literature, see Michael Malbin, *The Election after Reform: Money, Politics, and the Bipartisan Campaign Reform Act* (Washington, DC: Rowman & Littlefield, 2006).

31. David Karol, "If You Think Super PACS Have Changed Everything about Presidential Primaries, Think Again," September 21, 2015, www.washingtonpost.com/blogs/monkey-cage/wp/2015/09/21/if-you-think-super-pacs-have-changed-everything-about-the-presidential-primary-think-again (accessed 7/29/16).

32. For a discussion, see Patterson, *The Vanishing Voter*, especially Chapter 1, "The Incredible Shrinking Electorate," pp. 3–22.

33. William H. Riker and Peter Ordeshook, "A Theory of the Calculus of Voting," *American Political Science Review* 62 (1968): 25–39.

34. Michael McDonald, "The United States Elections Project," http://elections.gmu.edu (accessed 10/19/12).

35. Pew Research Center, "Regular Voters, Intermittent Voters, and Those Who Don't," October 18, 2006, www.people-press.org/files/legacy-pdf/292.pdf (accessed 7/29/16).

36. Richard P. Lau and David P. Redlawsk, *How Voters Decide: Information Processing during Electoral Campaigns* (New York: Cambridge University Press, 2006).

37. Samuel Popkin, *The Reasoning Voter* (Chicago: University of Chicago Press, 1991).

38. Richard R. Lau and David P. Redlawsk, "Advantages and Disadvantages of Cognitive Heuristics in Political Decision Making," *American Journal of Political Science* 45 (2001): 951–71.

39. For 2006 exit poll data, see Pew Research Center, "Public Cheers Democratic Victory," November 16, 2006, http://people-press.org/reports/display.php3?ReportID=296 (accessed 10/19/12).

Chapter 9

1. Robert H. Salisbury, John P. Heinz, Edward O. Laumann, and Robert L. Nelson, "Who Works with Whom? Interest Group Alliances and Opposition," *American Political Science Review* 81 (1987): 1217–34.

2. Business-Industry Political Action Committee, "About BIPAC," www.bipac.org/about/about.asp (accessed 4/8/08).

3. James Q. Wilson, *Political Organizations* (New York: Basic Books, 1974).

4. American Automobile Association, Foundation for Traffic Safety, www.aaafoundation.org/home (accessed 7/29/16).

5. Scott Ainsworth, *Analyzing Interest Groups: Group Influence on People and Policies* (New York: W. W. Norton, 2002).

6. Timothy Egan, "For Thirsty Farmers, Old Friends at Interior," *New York Times*, March 3, 2006, p. A1.

7. Data available at https://www.opensecrets.org/revolving/departing.php?cong=113.

8. Lobbying regulations are often changed; the discussion here is just a general guide. Regular reports on past, current, and proposed lobbying regulations can be found on the website of the Congressional Research Service at www.opencrs.com (accessed 9/19/12).

9. Frank Baumgartner and Beth Leech, *Basic Interests: The Importance of Interest Groups in Politics and in Political Science* (Princeton, NJ: Princeton University Press, 1999), p. 109.

10. Timothy M. LaPira and Nicholas A. Semanko, "Drawing Lobbyists to Washington: Government Activity and the Demand for Advocacy," *Political Research Quarterly* 58:1 (March 2005): 19–30.

11. Roxana Tiron, "Lockheed Martin Leads Expanded Lobbying by US Defense Industry," *Washington Post*, January 26, 2012, www.washingtonpost.com/business/economy/lockheed-martin-leads-expanded-lobbying-by-us-defense-industry/2012/01/26/gIQAlgQtaQ_story.html (accessed 2/4/14).

12. Tony LaPira, Lee Drutman, and Matthew Glassman, "The Interest Group Top Tier: More Groups, Concentrated Clout," paper presented at the 2014 American Political Science Association Annual Meeting.

13. For more on this argument, see Tim Harford, "There's Not Enough Money in Politics," *Slate*, April 1, 2006, www.slate.com/id/2138874 (accessed 7/29/16); and Stephen Ansolabehere, John M. de Figueiredo, and James M. Snyder, "Why Is There So Little Money in American Politics?," *Journal of Economic Perspectives* 17 (2003): 105–30.

14. Ken Kollman, *Outside Lobbying* (Princeton, NJ: Princeton University Press, 1998).

15. Jack Walker, *Mobilizing Interest Groups in America* (Ann Arbor: University of Michigan Press, 1991).

16. John P. Heinz, Edward O. Laumann, and Robert Salisbury, *The Hollow Core: Private Interests in National Policymaking* (Cambridge, MA: Harvard University Press, 1993).

17. Kay Lehman Schlozman and John Tierney, *Organized Interests and American Democracy* (New York: HarperCollins, 1986).

18. Christine A. DeGregorio, *Networks of Champions: Leadership, Access, and Advocacy in the U.S. House of Representatives* (Ann Arbor: University of Michigan Press, 1992).

19. Daniel Carpenter, *The Forging of Bureaucratic Autonomy: Reputations, Networks, and Policy Innovation in Executive Agencies, 1862–1928* (Princeton, NJ: Princeton University Press, 2002).

20. Public Citizen Publications, www.citizen.org/publications (accessed 7/29/16).

21. Derived from a search of the NRA Institute for Legislative Action site, www.nraila.org (accessed 9/19/12).

22. Kim Scheppele and Jack L. Walker, "The Litigation Strategies of Interest Groups," in *Mobilizing Interest Groups in America*, ed. Jack Walker (Ann Arbor: University of Michigan Press, 1991), pp. 157–84.

23. Kevin W. Hula, *Lobbying Together: Interest Group Coalitions in Legislative Politics* (Washington, DC: Georgetown University Press, 1999).

24. Lauren Cohen Bell, *Warring Factions: Interest Groups, Money, and the New Politics of Senate Confirmation* (Columbus: Ohio State University Press, 2002).

25. Jeanne Cummings, "Word Games Could Threaten Climate Bill," June 9, 2009, www.politico.com/news/stories/0609/24059.html (accessed 9/19/12).

26. Richard Fenno, *Home Style: U.S. House Members in Their Districts* (Boston: Little, Brown, 1978). See also Brandice Caines-Wrone, David W. Brady, and John F. Cogan, "Out of Step, Out of Office: Electoral Accountability and House Members' Voting," *American Political Science Review* 96 (2002): 127–40.

27. Emily Yoffe, "Am I the Next Jack Abramoff?," April 1, 2006, www.slate.com/id/2137886 (accessed 8/28/09).

28. Kollman, *Outside Lobbying*.

29. *Citizens United v. Federal Election Commission*, 558 U.S. 310 (2010).

30. Data from www.opensecrets.org and www.fec.gov (accessed 11/1/16).

31. Lee Drutman, "The Solution to Lobbying Is More Lobbying," *Washington Post*, April 29, 2015, www.washingtonpost.com/blogs/monkey-cage/wp/2015/04/29/the-solution-to-lobbying-is-more-lobbying (accessed 2/16/16).

32. Amy McKay, "Negative Lobbying and Policy Outcomes," *American Politics Review* 40 (2011): 116–46.

33. John M. Berry, *The Interest Group Society* (New York: HarperCollins, 1997); Raymond A. Bauer, Ithiel de Sola Pool, and Lewis Dexter, *American Business and Public Policy* (New York: Atherton Press, 1963).

34. Kollman, *Outside Lobbying*.

Take a Stand

a. Jacob Weisberg, "Three Cities, Three Scandals: What Jack Abramoff, Anthony Pellicano, and Jared Paul Stern Have in Common," *Slate*, April 9, 2006, www.slate.com/id/2140238 (accessed 10/25/12).

Chapter 10

1. Ramsey Cox and Jeremy Herb, "Senate Approves McCaskill Sexual Assault Bill in 97–0 Vote," *The Hill*, March 10, 2014, http://thehill.com/blogs/floor-action/senate/200393-senate-votes-97-0-for-military-sexual-assault-bill#ixzz2yaauKflt (accessed 4/9/14).

2. *Department of Defense Annual Report on Sexual Assault in the Military, Fiscal Year 2012*, vol. 1, May 3, 2013, www.sapr.mil/public/docs/reports/FY12_DoD_SAPRO_Annual_Report_on_Sexual_Assault-VOLUME_ONE.pdf (accessed 4/9/14).

3. Ed O'Keefe, "How Kirsten Gillibrand Won by Losing," *Washington Post*, March 6, 2014, www.washingtonpost.com/blogs/the-fix/wp/2014/03/06/how-kirsten-gillibrand-won-by-losing (accessed 4/9/14).

4. See Paul Gronke, *The Electorate, the Campaign, and the Office: A Unified Approach to Senate and House Elections* (Ann Arbor: University of Michigan Press, 2000), for research showing that House and Senate elections have many similar characteristics. See Richard F. Fenno, *Senators on the Campaign Trail: The Politics of Representation* (Norman: University of Oklahoma Press, 1996), for a good general discussion of Senate elections.

5. All poll data except the poll comparing Congress with other occupations is from PollingReport.com (www.pollingreport.com). The occupations poll was cited in Karlyn Bowman and Everett Carll Ladd, "Public Opinion toward Congress: A Historical Look," in *Congress, the Press, and the Public*, ed. Thomas E. Mann and Norman J. Ornstein (Washington, DC: Brookings Institution Press, 1994), p. 50.

6. "Congress Less Popular than Cockroaches, Traffic Jams," Public Policy Polling, January 8, 2013, www.publicpolicypolling.com/pdf/2011/PPP_Release_Natl_010813_.pdf (accessed 4/11/14).

7. Claudine Gay, "Spirals of Trust? The Effect of Descriptive Representation on the Relationship between Citizens and Their Government," *American Journal of Political Science* 46:4 (October 2002): 717–32; Katherine Tate, *Black Faces in the Mirror: African Americans and Their Representatives in the U.S. Congress* (Princeton, NJ: Princeton University Press, 2003), Chap. 7. However, Tate shows that African Americans who are represented by African Americans in Congress are not any more likely to vote, be involved in politics, or have higher overall approval rates of Congress than African Americans who are not descriptively represented.

8. R. Douglas Arnold, *The Logic of Congressional Action* (New Haven, CT: Yale University Press, 1990), pp. 60–71.

9. David R. Mayhew, *Congress: The Electoral Connection* (New Haven, CT: Yale University Press, 1974).

10. Mayhew, *Congress*, p. 17.

11. Gary C. Jacobson, *The Politics of Congressional Elections*, 5th ed. (New York: Longman, 2001), pp. 24–30.

12. Richard F. Fenno, *Home Style: House Members in Their Districts* (Boston: Little, Brown, 1978).

13. Morris Fiorina, *Congress: Keystone of the Washington Establishment*, rev. ed. (New Haven, CT: Yale University Press, 1989).

14. The language used by the Court in the 1960 was "one-man, one-vote." The Court ruled in *Baker v. Carr*, 369 U.S. 186 (1962), that state legislative districts that were unequal in population violated the equal protection clause of the Fourteenth Amendment. *Wesberry v. Sanders*, 376 U.S. 1 (1964), applied the same principle to U.S. House districts.

15. *Shelby County v. Holder*, 570 U.S. (2013).

16. See Kenneth R. Mayer and David T. Canon, *The Dysfunctional Congress: The Individual Roots of an Institutional Dilemma*, 2nd ed. (New York: Columbia University Press, 2011), for an extended discussion of this argument.

17. Leo Shane III, "2016 Defense Budget Deal Finally Nailed Down by Congress," *Military Times*, December 18, 2015, www.militarytimes.com/story/military/capitol-hill/2015/12/18/omnibus-passage-partisan-success/77569538 (accessed 3/19/16).

18. Jonathan Weisman and Jim VandeHei, "Road Bill Reflects the Power of Pork: White House Drops Effort to Rein In Hill," *Washington Post*, August 11, 2005, p. A1.

19. Republicans imposed an important qualification to the norm in 1995 when they set a six-year term limit for committee and subcommittee chairs.

20. David Rohde and John Aldrich, "The Transition to Republican Rule in the House: Implications for Theories of Congressional Politics," *Political Science Quarterly* 112: 4 (Winter 1997–98): 541–67.

21. Nelson W. Polsby, *Congress and the Presidency*, 4th ed. (Englewood Cliffs, NJ: Prentice Hall, 1986), p. 111.

22. Paul Steinhauser, "Obama 2014 Campaign Role: Fundraiser-in-Chief," *CNN Politics*, March 20, 2014, http://politicalticker.blogs.cnn.com/2014/03/20/obama-2014-campaign-role-fundraiser-in-chief (accessed 4/16/14).

23. Keith Krehbiel, *Information and Legislative Organization* (Ann Arbor: University of Michigan Press, 1992).

24. Barbara Sinclair, *Unorthodox Lawmaking* (Washington, DC: CQ Press, 2000), p. xiv.

25. Edward Epstein, "Dusting Off Deliberation," *CQ Weekly*, June 14, 2010, 1436–42.

26. Kenneth Chamberlain, "Government Shutdown Scares through the Years," *National Journal*, December 14, 2011, www.nationaljournal.com/congress/government-shutdown-scares-through-the-years-20111214 (accessed 12/19/11).

27. Daphne Eviatar, "Patriot Act Renewal Kicks Off over Party Lines," *Washington Independent*, September 23, 2009, http://washingtonindependent.com/60575/debate-over-patriot-act-renewal-kicks-off-over-party-lines (accessed 12/19/11).

28. Philip Rucker and Robert Costa, "McCarthy's Comments on Benghazi Probe May Be a Political Gift to Clinton," *Washington Post*, October 1, 2015, www.washingtonpost.com/politics/mccarthys-comments-on-benghazi-probe-may-be-a-political-gift-to-clinton/2015/10/01/6ceb6e88-6857-11e5-9223-70cb36460919_story.html (accessed 3/20/16). House Majority Leader Kevin McCarthy told Fox News host Sean Hannity: "Everybody thought Hillary Clinton was unbeatable, right? But we put together a Benghazi special committee, a select committee. What are her numbers today? Her numbers are dropping. Why? Because she's un-trustable. But no one would have known any of that had happened had we not fought."

29. Mathew McCubbins and Thomas Schwartz, "Congressional Oversight Overlooked: Police Patrol versus Fire Alarm," *American Journal of Political Science* 28:1 (February 1984): 165–77.

30. Richard Simon, Christi Parsons, and Michael A. Memoli, "VA Chief and White House Spokesman Resign, Fueling Unease," *Los Angeles Times*, May 30, 2014, www.latimes.com/nation/la-na-shinseki-20140531-story.html#page=1 (accessed 6/6/14).

Take a Stand

a. This figure comes from a report by the Citizens Against Government Waste, "Pork Alert: Defense Conference Report Loaded with Earmarks," www.cagw.org/newroom/releases/2009/pork-alert-defense.html (accessed 1/6/10). A lower figure of $4 billion in earmarks was reported in John D. McKinnon and Brody Mullins, "Defense Bill Earmarks Total $4 Billion," *Wall Street Journal*, December 23, 2009, p. A1.

b. Sean Kennedy and Curtis Kalin, *2015 Congressional Pig Book*, Citizens Against Government Waste, http://cagw.org/reporting/pig-book (accessed 3/19/16).

c. Alex Altman, "Congress Feasts on Vegan Pork despite Earmark Ban," *Time*, January 16, 2014, http://swampland.time.com/2014/01/16/congress-feasts-on-vegan-pork-despite-earmark-ban (accessed 4/16/14).

Chapter 11

1. John Aldrich, *Why Parties?* (Chicago: University of Chicago Press, 1995).

2. Ernest R. May, *The Making of the Monroe Doctrine* (Cambridge, MA: Harvard University Press, 1975).

3. Arthur M. Schlesinger Jr., *The Age of Jackson* (Boston: Little, Brown, 1945).

4. David Greenberg, "Lincoln's Crackdown," *Slate*, November 30, 2001, www.slate.com/id/2059132 (accessed 8/8/16).

5. Stephen Skowronek, *Building a New American State: The Expansion of National Administrative Capacities* (New York: Cambridge University Press, 1982).

6. Theda Skocpol, *Protecting Soldiers and Mothers: The Political Origins of Social Policy in the United States* (Cambridge, MA: Harvard University Press, 1995).

7. Thomas J. Knock, *To End All Wars: Woodrow Wilson and the Quest for a New World Order* (New York: Oxford University Press, 1992).

8. William E. Leuchtenburg, *FDR Years: On Roosevelt and His Legacy* (New York: Columbia University Press, 1995).

9. Chester Pach and Elmo Richardson, *The Presidency of Dwight D. Eisenhower* (Lawrence: University Press of Kansas, 1991).

10. Sarah Kliff, "The White House Keeps Changing Obamacare: Is That Legal?," *Washington Post*, August 7, 2013, www.washingtonpost.com/blogs/wonkblog/wp/2013/08/07/the-white-house-keeps-changing-obamacare-is-that-legal (accessed 4/28/14).

11. Thomas J. Weko, *The Politicizing Presidency: The White House Personnel Office, 1948-1994* (Lawrence: University Press of Kansas, 1995).

12. Kenneth Mayer, *With the Stroke of a Pen: Executive Orders and Presidential Power* (Princeton, NJ: Princeton University Press, 2001).

13. "What's in Obama's Gun Control Proposal?," *New York Times*, January 16, 2013, www.nytimes.com/interactive/2013/01/16/us/obama-gun-control-proposal.html (accessed 4/26/14).

14. David G. Adler, "The Constitution and Presidential Warmaking: An Enduring Debate," *Political Science Quarterly* 103 (1988): 1-36.

15. Richard F. Grimmett, "The War Powers Resolution: After Thirty Years," Congressional Research Service Report RL32267, March 11, 2004.

16. Lewis Fisher and David G. Adler, "The War Powers Resolution: Time to Say Goodbye," *Political Science Quarterly* 113:1 (1998): 1-20.

17. William G. Howell and Jon C. Pevehouse, *While Dangers Gather: Congressional Checks on Presidential War Powers* (Princeton, NJ: Princeton University Press, 2007).

18. Mark A. Peterson, *Legislating Together: The White House and Capitol Hill from Eisenhower to Reagan* (Cambridge, MA: Harvard University Press, 1990).

19. Andrew Rudalevige, *Managing the President's Program: Presidential Leadership and Legislative Policy Formation* (Princeton, NJ: Princeton University Press, 2002).

20. Charles Cameron and Nolan M. McCarty, "Models of Vetoes and Veto Bargaining," *Annual Review of Political Science* 7 (2004): 409-35.

21. Mark J. Rozell, "The Law: Executive Privilege: Definition and Standards of Application," *Presidential Studies Quarterly* 29:4 (1999): 918-30.

22. See Oyez, *United States v. Nixon*, 418 U.S. 683 (1974), www.oyez.org/cases/1970-1979/1974/1974_73_1766, for a summary of the case (accessed 11/1/12).

23. Mark J. Rozell, *Executive Privilege: The Dilemma of Secrecy and Democratic Accountability* (Baltimore, MD: Johns Hopkins University Press, 1994).

24. John Hart, *The Presidential Branch: From Washington to Clinton*, 2nd ed. (Chatham, NY: Chatham House, 1995).

25. Jackie Calmes, "As Plouffe Departs, a West Wing Job Is Redefined," *New York Times*, January 26, 2013, p. A17, www.nytimes.com/2013/01/27/us/politics/david-plouffe-senior-adviser-leaves-white-house.html?_r=0 (accessed 7/14/14).

26. David E. Lewis, "Staffing Alone: Unilateral Action and the Politicization of the Executive Office of the President, 1988-2004," *Presidential Studies Quarterly* 35 (2005): 496-514.

27. Charles E. Walcott and Karen M. Hult, "White House Staff Size: Explanations and Implications," *Presidential Studies Quarterly* 29 (1999): 638-56.

28. Karen M. Hult and Charles E. Walcott, *Empowering the White House: Governance under Nixon, Ford, and Carter* (Lawrence: University Press of Kansas, 2004).

29. For a series of articles detailing Cheney's role, see "Angler: The Cheney Vice Presidency," *Washington Post*, June 24-27, 2007, www.washingtonpost.com/cheney (accessed 4/29/08).

30. Richard E. Neustadt, *Presidential Power and the Modern Presidents: The Politics of Leadership from Roosevelt to Reagan* (New York: Simon and Schuster, 1991).

31. Terry M. Moe and William G. Howell, "The Presidential Power of Unilateral Action," *Journal of Law, Economics, and Organization* 15 (1999): 132-46.

32. Louis Fisher, *Presidential War Power*, 2nd ed. (Lawrence: University Press of Kansas, 2004); James M. Lindsay, "Deference and Defiance: The Shifting Rhythms of Executive-Legislative Relations in Foreign Policy," *Presidential Studies Quarterly* 33:3 (2003): 530-46; Lawrence Margolis, *Executive Agreements and Presidential Power in Foreign Policy* (New York: Praeger, 1985), 209-32.

33. Christopher Deering and Forrest Maltzman, "The Politics of Executive Orders: Legislative Constraints on Presidential Power," *Political Research Quarterly* 52:4 (1999): 767-83.

34. David E. Lewis, *Presidents and the Politics of Agency Design: Political Insulation in the United States Government Bureaucracy, 1946-1997* (Palo Alto, CA: Stanford University Press, 2003).

35. David Epstein and Sharyn O'Halloran, *Delegating Powers* (Cambridge, UK: Cambridge University Press, 1999).

36. William G. Howell, *Thinking about the Presidency: The Primacy of Power* (Princeton, NJ: Princeton University Press, 2015).

37. Ben Smith and David Paul Kuhn, "Obama Moves Quickly to Reshape DNC," *Politico*, June 13, 2008, www.politico.com/news/stories/0608/11045.html (accessed 8/8/16).

38. George C. Edwards III, *The Public Presidency* (New York: St. Martin's Press, 1983); George C. Edwards III, *On Deaf Ears* (New Haven, CT: Yale University Press, 2003).

39. For evidence, see Edwards, *On Deaf Ears*.

40. George C. Edwards III, *Predicting the Presidency: The Potential of Persuasive Leadership* (Princeton, NJ: Princeton University Press, 2015).

Chapter 12

1. The original quote is from Robert Dahl and was used in this context in David E. Lewis, *Presidents and the Politics of Agency Design: Political Insulation in the United States Government* (Palo Alto, CA: Stanford University Press, 2003).

2. For a history of the FDA, see John P. Swann, FDA History Office, "History of the FDA," www.fda.gov/oc/history/historyoffda/section2.html (accessed 7/15/08).

3. For details, see Cornelius Kerwin, *Rulemaking: How Government Agencies Write Law and Make Policy* (Washington, DC: CQ Press, 1999).

4. Andrew Pollack, "New Sense of Caution at FDA," *New York Times*, September 29, 2006, www.nytimes.com/2006/09/29/business/29caution.html?_r=0 (accessed 8/29/16).

5. There are two exceptions. A patient can enroll in a clinical trial for a new drug during the approval process, but there is a good chance that he or she will get a placebo or a previously approved treatment rather than the drug being tested. The FDA does allow companies to provide some experimental drugs to patients who cannot participate in a trial but only those drugs that have passed early screening trials.

6. Susan Okie, "Access before Approval—a Right to Take Experimental Drugs?," *New England Journal of Medicine* 355 (2004): 437-40.

7. Stephen Skowronek, *Building a New American State: The Expansion of National Administrative Capacities, 1877-1920* (New York: Cambridge University Press, 1982).

8. Terry Moe, "An Assessment of the Positive Theory of Congressional Dominance," *Legislative Studies Quarterly* 4 (1987): 475-98.

9. Karen Orren and Steven Skorownek, "Regimes and Regime Building in American Government: A Review of the Literature on the 1940s," *Political Science Quarterly* 113 (1998): 689-702.

10. Michael Nelson, "A Short, Ironic History of American National Bureaucracy," *Journal of Politics* 44 (1982): 747-78.

11. Nelson, "A Short, Ironic History of American National Bureaucracy."

12. Nelson, "A Short, Ironic History of American National Bureaucracy."

13. John Aldrich, *Why Parties?* (Chicago: University of Chicago Press, 1995).

14. Nelson, "A Short, Ironic History of American National Bureaucracy."

15. Matthew A. Crenson, *The Federal Machine: Beginnings of Bureaucracy in Jacksonian America* (Baltimore, MD: Johns Hopkins University Press, 1975).

16. James Q. Wilson, "The Rise of the Bureaucratic State," in *The American Commonwealth*, ed. Nathan Glazer and Irving Kristol (New York: Basic Books, 1976).

17. Skowronek, *Building a New American State.*

18. Robert Harrison, *Congress, Progressive Reform, and the New American State* (New York: Cambridge University Press, 2004).

19. The U.S. State Department has an excellent summary of the Pendleton Act at http://usinfo.state.gov/usa/infousa/facts/democrac/28.htm.

20. Lawrence C. Dodd and Richard L. Schott, *Congress and the Administrative State* (New York: Wiley, 1979).

21. Ira Katznelson and Bruce Pietrykowski, "Rebuilding the American State: Evidence from the 1940s," *Studies in American Political Development* 5:2 (1991): 301-39.

22. David Plotke, *Building a Democratic Political Order: Reshaping American Liberalism in the 1930s and 1940s* (New York: Cambridge University Press, 1996).

23. Theda Skocpol and Kenneth Finegold, "State Capacity and Economic Intervention in the Early New Deal," *Political Science Quarterly* 97 (1999): 255-70.

24. Michael Brown, "State Capacity and Political Choice: Interpreting the Failure of the Third New Deal," *Studies in American Political Development* 9 (1995): 187-212.

25. Ira Katznelson, Kim Geiger, and Daniel Kryder, "Limiting Liberalism: The Southern Veto in Congress, 1933-1950," *Political Science Quarterly* 108 (1993): 283-306.

26. Joseph Califano, "What Was Really Great about the Great Society," *Washington Monthly*, October 1999, www.washingtonmonthly.com/features/1999/9910.califano.html (accessed 7/16/08).

27. David T. Canon, *Race, Redistricting, and Representation: The Unintended Consequences of Black Majority Districts* (Chicago: University of Chicago Press, 1999).

28. Charles Murray, *Losing Ground: American Social Policy, 1950-1980* (New York: Basic Books, 1984)

29. Henry J. Aaron, *Politics and the Professors: The Great Society in Perspective* (Washington, DC: Brookings Institution Press, 1978).

30. Richard P. Nathan, *The Administrative Presidency* (New York: Wiley, 1983).

31. Andrew Rudalevige, "The Structure of Leadership: Presidents, Hierarchies, and Information Flow," *Presidential Studies Quarterly* 35 (2005): 333-60.

32. Lewis, *Presidents and the Policy of Agency Design.*

33. Moe, "An Assessment of the Positive Theory of Congressional Dominance," 475-98.

34. William A. Niskanen, *Bureaucracy and Public Economics* (Washington, DC: Edward Elgar, 1976); Robert Waples and Jac C. Heckelman, "Public Choice Economics: Where Is There Consensus?," *American Economist* 49 (2005): 66-79.

35. Alan Schick and Felix LoStracco, *The Federal Budget: Politics, Process, Policy* (Washington, DC: Brookings Institution Press, 2000).

36. Joel D. Aberbach, "The Political Significance of the George W. Bush Administration," *Social Policy and Administration* 39:2 (2005): 130-49.

37. David E. Lewis, "The Politics of Agency Termination: Confronting the Myth of Agency Immortality," *Journal of Politics* 64 (2002): 89-107.

38. Ronald A. Wirtz, "Put It on My . . . Er, His Tab: Opinion Polls Show a Big Gap between the Public's Desire for Services and Its Willingness to Pay for These Services," *Fedgazette*, January 2004, www.minneapolisfed.org/pubs/fedgaz/04-01/tab.cfm (accessed 7/16/08).

39. Harris Poll, "Cutting Government Spending May Be Popular but Majorities of the Public Oppose Cuts in Many Big Ticket Items in the Budget," March 1, 2012, www.harrisinteractive.com (accessed 7/19/12).

40. James L. Perry and Annie Hondeghem, *Motivation in Public Management: The Call of Public Service* (Oxford, UK: Oxford University Press, 2008).

41. Paul Light, *A Government Well-Executed: Public Service and Public Performance* (Washington, DC: Brookings Institution Press, 2003).

42. This discussion of the details of the civil service system is based on Bureau of Labor Statistics, "Career Guide to Industries," March 12, 2008, www.bls.gov/oco/cg/cgs041.htm (accessed 7/16/08).

43. Dennis Cauchon, "Some Federal Workers More Likely to Die Than Lose Jobs," *USA Today,* July 19, 2011, p. A1.

44. Ronald N. Johnson and Gary D. Liebcap, *The Federal Civil Service System and the Problem of Bureaucracy* (Chicago: University of Chicago Press, 1993).

45. For details on the SES, see www.opm.gov/policy-data-oversight/senior-executive-service/ (accessed 4/7/14).

46. For the details of the Hatch Act, see Daniel Engber, "Can Karl Rove Plot Campaign Strategy on the Government's Dime?," *Slate*, April 21, 2006, www.slate.com/id/2140418 (accessed 7/16/08).

47. Todd Frankel, "Why the CDC Still Isn't Researching Gun Violence, Despite the Ban Being Lifted Two Years Ago," *Washington Post*, January 14, 2015, p. A01.

48. John D. Huber and Charles R. Shipan, *Deliberate Discretion? The Institutional Foundations of Bureaucratic Autonomy* (New York: Cambridge University Press, 2002).

49. David Epstein and Sharyn O'Halloran, *Delegating Powers: A Transaction Cost Politics Approach to Policy Making under Separate Powers* (New York: Cambridge University Press, 1999).

50. Barry R. Weingast, "Caught in the Middle: The President, Congress, and the Political-Bureaucratic System," in *Institutions of American Democracy: The Executive Branch*, ed. Joel D. Aberbach and Mark A. Peterson (New York: Oxford University Press, 2006).

51. Keith Whittington and Daniel P. Carpenter, "Executive Power in American Institutional Development," *Perspectives on Politics* 1 (2003): 495–513.

52. Roger Noll, Mathew McCubbins, and Barry Weingast, "Administrative Procedures as Instruments of Political Control," *Journal of Law, Economics, and Organization* 3 (1987): 243–77.

53. Lisa Rein, "Climate Scientists to Be Grilled by Congressional Investigators, but Their E-mails Are Still Off-Limits," *Washington Post*, November 16, 2015, www.washingtonpost.com/news/federal-eye/wp/2015/11/16/climate-scientists-to-be-grilled-by-congressional-investigators-but-their-emails-are-still-off-limits (accessed 8/29/16).

54. Mathew McCubbins and Thomas Schwartz, "Congressional Oversight Overlooked: Fire Alarms vs. Police Patrols," *American Journal of Political Science* 28 (1984): 165–79.

55. McCubbins and Schwartz, "Congressional Oversight Overlooked."

56. Steven J. Balla and John R. Wright, "Interest Groups, Advisory Committees, and Congressional Control of the Bureaucracy," *American Journal of Political Science* 45 (2001): 799–812.

57. Daniel P. Carpenter, "The Gatekeeper: Organizational Reputation and Pharmaceutical Regulation at the FDA" (unpublished paper, Harvard University, 2006).

58. Terry M. Moe, "Political Control and the Power of the Agent," *Journal of Law, Economics, and Organization* 22 (2006): 1–29.

59. See David Weil, "OSHA: Beyond the Politics," *Frontline*, January 9, 2003, www.pbs.org/wgbh/pages/frontline/shows/workplace/osha/weil.html (accessed 7/17/08).

Chapter 13

1. Burgess Everett and Glenn Thrush, "McConnell Throws Down the Gauntlet: No Scalia Replacement under Obama," Politico.com, February 13, 2016, www.politico.com/story/2016/02/mitch-mcconnell-antonin-scalia-supreme-court-nomination-219248#ixzz49VnIxZGz (accessed 5/23/16).

2. The union case was *Friedrichs v. California Teachers Association* and the immigration case was *United States v. Texas*.

3. www.whitehouse.gov/scotus (accessed 5/23/16).

4. *United States v. Texas*, 579 U.S. ____ (2016).

5. *Fisher v. University of Texas*, 579 U.S. ____ (2016),

6. Ralph Ketcham, *The Antifederalist Papers and the Constitutional Convention Debates* (New York: Penguin Putnam, 2003), p. 304.

7. Lester S. Jayson, ed., *The Constitution of the United States of America: Analysis and Interpretation* (Washington, DC: U.S. Government Printing Office, 1973), p. 585.

8. David G. Savage, *Guide to the U.S. Supreme Court,* 4th ed. (Washington, DC: CQ Press, 2004), pp. 5–7.

9. Winfield H. Rose, "*Marbury v. Madison*: How John Marshall Changed History by Misquoting the Constitution," *Political Science and Politics* 36:2 (April 2003): 209–14. Rose argues that in a key quotation in the case Marshall intentionally left out a clause of the Constitution that suggests that Congress *did* have the power to expand the original jurisdiction of the Court. Other constitutional scholars reject this argument.

10. *Marbury v. Madison*, 5 U.S. 1 Cranch 137 (1803).

11. Revisionist historians, legal scholars, and political scientists have challenged the landmark status of *Marbury v. Madison*. For example, Michael Stokes Paulsen's *Michigan Law Review* article points out that *Marbury* was not cited in subsequent Supreme Court cases as a precedent for judicial review until the late nineteenth century. Legal scholars in the early twentieth century were the first to promote the idea that *Marbury* was a landmark decision. Paulsen also notes that when the opinion was delivered in 1803 it was not controversial. Even the Jeffersonian Democrats, who were at odds with Marshall's Federalists, thought that it was a reasonable decision and not the institutional power grab that modern accounts describe. Finally, Marshall made a very narrow case for judicial review, arguing that the Supreme Court could declare legislation that was contrary to the Court's interpretation of the Constitution null and void only if it concerned judicial powers. Revisionists argue that what appear to be broad claims of judicial power in *Marbury* (e.g., the Court has the power "to say what the law is") are taken out of the context of a much more narrow claim of power. Michael Stokes Paulsen, "Judging Judicial Review: *Marbury* in the Modern Era: The Irrepressible Myth of *Marbury*," *Michigan Law Review* 101 (August 2003): 2706–43.

12. *Ware v. Hylton*, 3 U.S. 199 (1796).

13. *Wal-Mart v. Dukes*, 564 U.S. (2011). However, in 2011 the Court struck down any class-action claim unless there was "convincing proof of a companywide discriminatory pay and promotion policy"—statistical evidence of pay disparities would not suffice. David Savage, "Supreme Court Blocks Huge Class-Action Suit against Wal-Mart," *Los Angeles Times*, June 21, 2011, http://articles.latimes.com/2011/jun/21/nation/la-na-court-walmart-20110621 (accessed 7/13/16).

14. *Lujan v. Defenders of Wildlife*, 504 U.S. 555 (1992).

15. United States Courts, Judges & Judgeships, Federal Judgeships, www.uscourts.gov/judges-judgeships/authorized-judgeships (accessed 7/1/16).

16. *Ledbetter v. Goodyear Tire & Rubber Co.*, 550 U.S. 618 (2007).

17. "Judicial Selection in the States," Ballotpedia.org, https://ballotpedia.org/Judicial_selection_in_the_states (accessed 5/24/16).

18. See, for example, a case involving the West Virginia state supreme court and $3 million in campaign spending by a coal company that had a case pending before the court, *Caperton v. A. T. Massey Coal Co.*, 556 U.S. 868 (2009). The Court ruled that the losing party's due process rights under the Fourteenth Amendment had been violated when the justice who benefited from the campaign spending did not recuse himself from the case. Given the disproportionate and significant spending by Massey and the timing of the spending, the majority ruled:

"On these extreme facts the probability of actual bias rises to an unconstitutional level."

19. Paul Brace and Brent D. Boyea, "State Public Opinion, the Death Penalty, and the Practice of Electing Judges," *American Journal of Political Science* 52:2 (April 2008): 360–72.

20. Richard P. Caldarone, Brandice Canes-Wrone, and Tom S. Clark, "Partisan Labels and Democratic Accountability: An Analysis of State Supreme Court Abortion Decisions," *Journal of Politics* 71 (2009): 560–73.

21. Stephen Ware, "The Missouri Plan in National Perspective," *Missouri Law Review* 74 (2009): 751–75.

22. "President Bush Discusses Judicial Accomplishments and Philosophy," Cincinnati, Ohio, October 6, 2008, georgewbush-whitehouse.archives.gov/news/releases/2008/10/20081006-5.html (accessed 12/14/11).

23. Paul Kane, "Reid, Democrats Trigger 'Nuclear' Option; Eliminate Most Filibusters on Nominees," *Washington Post*, November 21, 2013, www.washingtonpost.com/politics/senate-poised-to-limit-filibusters-in-party-line-vote-that-would-alter-centuries-of-precedent/2013/11/21/d065cfe8-52b6-11e3-9fe0-fd2ca728e67c_story.html (accessed 5/2/14).

24. John Roberts, U.S. Supreme Court, "2007 Year-End Report on the Federal Judiciary," January 1, 2008, www.supremecourt.gov/publicinfo/year-end/2007year-endreport.pdf (accessed 9/26/16).

25. For a critical account of the Supreme Court's reduced caseload, which dates back to the Rehnquist Court, see Philip Allen Lacovara, "The Incredible Shrinking Court," *American Lawyer*, December 1, 2003, pp. 53–58.

26. *New Jersey v. New York*, No. 120 Orig., 118 S.Ct. 1726 (1998), and *Kansas v. Colorado*, No. 105 Orig., 125 S.Ct. 526 (2004).

27. Henry J. Abraham, *The Judiciary: The Supreme Court in the Governmental Process*, 7th ed. (Boston: Allyn and Bacon, 1987), p. 25, says that original jurisdiction has been invoked "about 150 times." A Lexis search revealed an additional 27 original jurisdiction cases between 1987 and December 2004. See U.S. Department of Justice, Help/Glossary, www.usdoj.gov/osg/briefs/help.html, for a basic discussion of the Supreme Court's original jurisdiction.

28. Amanda L. Tyler, "Setting the Supreme Court's Agenda: Is There a Place for Certification?," *George Washington Law Review Arguendo* 78 (May 2010): 101–18.

29. Savage, *Guide to the U.S. Supreme Court*, p. 848.

30. See Thomas G. Walker and Lee Epstein, *The Supreme Court of the United States: An Introduction* (New York: St. Martin's Press, 1993), pp. 80–85, for a more detailed discussion of these concepts and citations to the relevant Court cases.

31. *Shaw v. Reno*, 509 U.S. 630 (1993).

32. *Elk Grove Unified School District v. Newdow*, 542 U.S. 1 (2004).

33. Gregory A. Caldeira and John R. Wright, "The Discuss List: Agenda Building in the Supreme Court," *Law and Society Review* 24 (1990): 813.

34. Walker and Epstein, *Supreme Court*, p. 89; Ryan C. Black and Ryan J. Owens, *The Solicitor General and the United States Supreme Court: Executive Influence and Judicial Decisions* (New York: Cambridge University Press, 2012).

35. U.S. Supreme Court, "The Court and Its Procedures," www.supremecourt.gov/about/procedures.pdf (accessed 9/26/16).

36. Lee Epstein, Jeffrey A. Segal, Harold J. Spaeth, and Thomas G. Walker, *The Supreme Court Compendium: Data, Decisions, and Developments*, 3rd ed. (Washington, DC: CQ Press, 2003), Table 7-25.

37. Gregory A. Caldeira and John R. Wright, "*Amicus Curiae* before the Supreme Court: Who Participates, When, and How Much?," *Journal of Politics* 52 (August 1990): 803.

38. Garrett Epps, "Clarence Thomas Breaks His Silence," *The Atlantic*, February 29, 2016, www.theatlantic.com/politics/archive/2016/02/clarence-thomas-supreme-court/471582/ (accessed 5/27/16).

39. *Smith v. Allwright*, 321 U.S. 649 (1944).

40. Walker and Epstein, *Supreme Court*, p. 110.

41. Lee Epstein, William M. Landes, and Richard A. Posner, "Are Even Unanimous Decisions in the United States Supreme Court Ideological?," *Northwestern University Law Review* 106:2 (2012): 702.

42. Adam Liptak, "Compromise at the Court Veils Its Rifts: Roberts' Handiwork, Unanimous Rulings," *New York Times*, July 2, 2014, pp. A1, A17. For the recent term see Kedar Bhatia, "Final October Term 2015 Stat Pack," June 29th, 2016, www.scotusblog.com/wp-content/uploads/2016/06/SB_unanimity_OT15.pdf, accessed 7/1/16.

43. Lee Epstein and Thomas G. Walker, *Constitutional Law for a Changing America: Institutional Powers and Constraints*, 5th ed. (Washington, DC: CQ Press, 2004), p. 31.

44. Forrest Maltzman and Paul J. Wahlbeck, "Strategic Policy Considerations and Vote Fluidity on the Burger Court," *American Journal of Political Science* 90 (1996): 581–92; Forest Maltzman, James F. Spriggs II, and Paul J. Wahlbeck, *Crafting Law on the Supreme Court: The Collegial Game* (New York: Cambridge University Press, 2000).

45. Thomas M. Keck, *The Most Activist Supreme Court in History: The Road to Modern Judicial Conservatism* (Chicago: University of Chicago Press, 2004).

46. Robert Dahl, "Decision-Making in a Democracy: The Supreme Court as a National Policy-Maker," *Journal of Public Law* 6 (1957): 279–95, is the classic work on this topic. More recent work challenged Dahl's methods but largely supports the idea that the Court follows the will of the majority.

47. Jeffrey A. Segal, Richard J. Timpone, and Robert M. Howard, "Buyer Beware? Presidential Success through Supreme Court Appointments," *Political Research Quarterly* 53:3 (September 2000): 557–73; Gregory A. Caldeira and Charles E. Smith Jr., "Campaigning for the Supreme Court: The Dynamics of Public Opinion on the Thomas Nomination," *Political Research Quarterly* 58:3 (August 1996): 655–81.

48. William Mishler and Reginald S. Sheehan, "The Supreme Court as a Countermajoritarian Institution? The Impact of Public Opinion on Supreme Court Decisions," *American Political Science Review* 87:1 (March 1993): 87–101.

49. David O'Brien, *Storm Center: The Supreme Court in American Politics*, 4th ed. (New York: W. W. Norton, 1996).

50. We thank Dan Smith for raising this point.

Take a Stand

a. Richard S. Beth, "Cloture Attempts on Nominations: Data and Historical Development," Congressional Research Service Report 7-5700, June 23, 2013, www.senate.gov/CRSReports/crs-publish.cfm?pid=%270E%2C*P%2C%3B%3C%20P%20%20%0A (accessed 5/2/2014); "President Obama's Judicial Nominations," 113th Congress, American Bar Association, www.americanbar.org/content/dam/aba/uncategorized/GAO/2014apr16_obamanomchart.authcheckdam.pdf (accessed 5/2/13).

Chapter 14

1. Robert W. Wood, "Clinton Vows Estate Tax Hikes, While Trump Vows Repeal," *Forbes*, August 9, 2016, www.forbes.com/sites/robertwood/2016/08/09/hillary-vows-estate-tax-hikes-while-trump-vows-repeal/#292b60055c0f (accessed 9/21/16).

2. Steve Eder and Megan Twohey, "Donald Trump Acknowledges Not Paying Federal Income Taxes for Years," *New York Times*, October 10, 2016, www.nytimes.com/2016/10/10/us/politics/donald-trump-taxes.html?_r=0 (accessed 10/23/16).

3. Richard Rubin, "Donald Trump's Tax Plan Would Reduce Taxes by $4.4 Trillion to $5.9 Trillion, Group Says," *Wall Street Journal*, September 19, 2016, www.wsj.com/articles/donald-trumps-tax-plan-would-reduce-taxes-by-4-4-trillion-to-5-9-trillion-group-says-1474297940 (accessed 9/21/16).

4. Neil Irwin, "How Hillary Clinton and Donald Trump Differ on Taxes," *New York Times*, August 12, 2016, www.nytimes.com/2016/08/13/upshot/how-hillary-clinton-and-donald-trump-differ-on-taxes.html?_r=0 (accessed 9/21/16).

5. See William T. Bianco, *Trust: Representatives and Constituents* (Ann Arbor: University of Michigan Press, 1994), Chapter 6, for a discussion of the repeal of the Catastrophic Coverage Act.

6. James Q. Wilson, *Bureaucracy: What Government Agencies Do and Why They Do It* (New York: Basic Books, 1989).

7. The classic work on the appropriations process in the prereform era is Richard Fenno's *The Power of the Purse: Appropriation Politics in Congress* (Boston: Little, Brown, 1966). D. Roderick Kiewiet and Mathew D. McCubbins reexamined the appropriations process in the postreform era and found that the appropriations committees have maintained much of their power; see *The Logic of Delegation: Congressional Parties and the Appropriations Process* (Chicago: University of Chicago Press, 1991).

8. See Charles M. Cameron, *Veto Bargaining: Presidents and the Politics of Negative Power* (New York: Cambridge University Press, 2000), for a general discussion of the strategic elements of issuing veto threats.

9. Joe Soss, *Unwanted Claims: The Politics of Participation in the U.S. Welfare System* (Ann Arbor: University of Michigan Press, 2000).

10. Greg Jaffe and Ed O'Keefe, "Obama Accepts Resignation of VA Secretary Shinseki," *Washington Post*, May 30, 2014, www.washingtonpost.com/politics/shinseki-apologizes-for-va-health-care-scandal/2014/05/30/e605885a-e7f0-11e3-8f90-73e071f3d637_story.html (accessed 7/23/14).

11. Daniel P. Carpenter, *The Forging of Bureaucratic Autonomy: Reputations, Networks, and Policy Innovation in Executive Agencies, 1862–1928* (Princeton, NJ: Princeton University Press, 2001).

12. U.S. Department of the Treasury, "Duties and Functions," www.treasury.gov/education/duties (accessed 8/5/08).

13. U.S. Department of the Treasury, "FAQs: Currency: Production and Circulation," www.treasury.gov/education/faq/currency/production.shtml; United States Mint, "Coin Production Figures," www.usmint.gov/about_the_mint/index.cfm?action=ProductionFigures and www.moneyfactory.gov/uscurrency/annualproductionfigures.html (accessed 6/11/14).

14. The stages model was first presented in James E. Anderson, *Public Policy Making* (New York: Praeger, 1974). Also see Thomas R. Dye, *Understanding Public Policy*, 15th ed. (New York: Pearson, 2017).

15. John Kingdon, *Agendas, Alternatives, and Public Policy* (Boston: Little, Brown, 1984).

16. Frank R. Baumgartner and Bryan D. Jones, *Agendas and Instability in American Politics*, 2nd ed. (Chicago: University of Chicago Press, 2009); Nikolaos Zahariadis, "The Shield of Heracles: Multiple Streams and the Emotional Endowment Effect," *European Journal of Political Research* 54:3 (August 2015): 466–81.

17. Graeme Boushey, *Policy Diffusion Dynamics in America* (New York: Cambridge University Press, 2010).

18. Charles R. Shipan and Craig Volden, "The Mechanisms of Policy Diffusion," *American Journal of Political Science* 52:4 (October 2008): 840–57.

19. The classic article on deflation is Irving Fisher, "The Debt-Deflation Theory of Great Depressions," *Econometrica*, 1933, https://fraser.stlouisfed.org/docs/meltzer/fisdeb33.pdf (accessed 6/2/16).

20. John Maynard Keynes, *The General Theory of Employment, Interest and Money* (1936; repr., New York: Macmillan, 2007).

21. These figures come from the Congressional Budget Office, "Historical Budget Data," www.cbo.gov (accessed 4/18/08). Tax revenue fell from 19.6 percent of GDP in 1981, the last year before the tax cuts went into effect, to 18.1 percent of GDP in 1988, the last year of the Reagan presidency. Individual income tax revenue fell from 9.3 percent to 8 percent of GDP over the same period, so most of the decrease in revenue was due to lower individual income taxes. While overall government spending did increase during the 1982–1983 recession, spending from the beginning of Reagan's term to the end dropped slightly from 22.2 percent to 21.2 percent of GDP.

22. Office of Management and Budget, "Budget of the United States Government, Fiscal Year 2011," www.whitehouse.gov/omb/budget/Overview/ (accessed 2/16/10).

23. The payroll tax figure comes from Congressional Budget Office, "The Distribution of Household Income and Federal Taxes, 2010," December 2013, Table 3, p. 13, http://cbo.gov/sites/default/files/cbofiles/attachments/44604-AverageTaxRates.pdf (accessed 6/30/14), and the income tax figure from Drew DeSilver," High-income Americans pay most income taxes, but enough to be 'fair'?," Pew Research Center, April 13, 2016, www.pewresearch.org/fact-tank/2016/04/13/high-income-americans-pay-most-income-taxes-but-enough-to-be-fair (accessed 10/23/16).

24. Congressional Budget Office, "The Distribution of Household Income and Federal Taxes, 2013," June, 2016, Figure 5, p. 12, www.cbo.gov/publication/51361 (accessed 10/23/16).

25. "The Structure and Functions of the Federal Reserve System," Federal Reserve System.org, www.federalreserveeducation.org/about-the-fed/structure-and-functions (accessed 6/2/16).

26. Milton Friedman, "The Quantity Theory of Money: A Restatement," in *The Optimum Quantity of Money and Other Essays* (Chicago: Aldine, 1969), p. 52.

27. In reality, under the Monetary Control Act (MCA) of 1980, the reserve requirement can range from 8 percent to 14 percent for all demand deposits greater than $25 million. In the original law, banks with demand deposits under $25 million had to have a reserve of only 3 percent. The amount that is subject to the lower reserve requirement is increased every year to reflect overall money supply and currently is about $71 million. See Board of Governors of the Federal Reserve System, "Reserve Requirement," www.federalreserve.gov/monetarypolicy/reservereq.htm#table1 (accessed 2/7/12).

28. In December 2002, the discount rate was effectively discontinued as an active policy tool and was pegged to 1 percent above the targeted FFR (which means that the "discount rate" is oddly named—it really should be called the premium rate). In the economic crisis of 2008–2009 the Fed

temporarily dropped the difference between the FFR and the discount rate to .25 percent and then to .50 percent, where it remains today; see the December 2002 *Federal Reserve Bulletin* (pp. 482–83). See also "Frequently Asked Questions— Discount Window Lending Programs," Federal Reserve, www. frbdiscountwindow.org/en/Frequently_Asked_Questions. aspx (accessed 6/3/16).

29. William Greider, *Secrets of the Temple: How the Federal Reserve Runs the Country* (New York: Simon and Schuster, 1987), pp. 295–98.

30. Board of Governors of the Federal Reserve System, Credit and Liquidity Programs and the Balance Sheet, www. federalreserve.gov/monetarypolicy/bst_recenttrends.htm (accessed 2/16/10).

31. Board of Governors of the Federal Reserve System, Credit and Liquidity Programs and Balance Sheets, Recent Balance Sheet Trends, www.federalreserve.gov/monetarypolicy/ bst_recenttrends.htm (accessed 6/3/16).

32. Alan Greenspan's tenure spanned the presidencies of Reagan, Bush, and Clinton and the second Bush. See Federal Reserve Board, "Membership of the Board of Governors of the Federal Reserve System, 1914," www.federalreserve.gov/bios/ boardmembership.htm, for a list of all Federal Reserve Board members (accessed 8/5/08).

33. Edward R. Tufte, *Political Control of the Economy* (Princeton, NJ: Princeton University Press, 1978); Douglas Hibbs, "The Partisan Model of Macroeconomic Cycles: More Theory and Evidence for the United States," *Economics and Politics* 6 (1994): 1–23.

34. Jim Granato, "The Effect of Policy-Maker Reputation and Credibility on Public Expectations," *Journal of Theoretical Politics* 8 (1996): 449–70; Irwin L. Morris, *Congress, the President, and the Federal Reserve: The Politics of American Monetary Policy-Making* (Ann Arbor: University of Michigan Press, 2000).

35. John B. Taylor, *Economics*, 4th ed. (New York: Houghton Mifflin, 2003), Chapter 10. Some economics textbooks also define regulation of externalities, such as pollution, as economic regulation.

36. Zachary A. Goldfarb, David Cho, and Binyamin Appelbaum, "Treasury to Rescue Fannie and Freddie," *Washington Post*, September 7, 2008, p. A1.

37. Peter Baker, "A Professor and a Banker Bury Old Dogma on Markets," *New York Times*, September 21, 2008, p. A1.

38. U.S. Department of Treasury, "TARP Tracker from September 2008 to Date," www.treasury.gov/initiatives/financial-stability/reports/Pages/TARP-Tracker.aspx#All (accessed 6/11/14).

39. Renae Merle, "U.S. Stock Markets Soar on Financial Rescue Plan," *Washington Post*, September 19, 2008; Howard Schneider, Neil Irwin, and Binyamin Appelbaum, "Treasury to Temporarily Guarantee Money Market Funds," *Washington Post*, September 19, 2008, www.washingtonpost.com/wp-dyn/content/article/2008/09/19/AR2008091901306.html (accessed 7/19/16).

40. Theda Skocpol, *Social Policy in the United States: Future Possibilities in Historical Perspective* (Princeton, NJ: Princeton University Press, 1995), p. 37.

41. Skocpol, *Social Policy in the United States*, pp. 145–60.

42. David M. Kennedy, *Freedom from Fear: The American People in Depression and War, 1929–1945* (New York: Oxford University Press, 2001); Byron W. Daynes, William Pederson, and Michael P. Riccards, eds., *The New Deal and Public Policy* (New York: St. Martin's Press, 1998).

43. Robert Dallek, *Flawed Giant: Lyndon Johnson and His Times, 1961–1973* (New York: Oxford University Press, 1998); Irving Berstein, *Guns or Butter: The Presidency of Lyndon Johnson* (New York: Oxford University Press, 1996).

44. Bernadette D. Proctor, Jessica L. Semega, and Melissa A. Kollar, "Income and Poverty in the United States: 2015," September 2016, U.S. Census, Table B-2, p. 43.

45. Bernadette D. Proctor, Jessica L. Semega, and Melissa A. Kollar, "Income and Poverty in the United States: 2015," September 2016, U.S. Census, Table B-2, p. 51.

46. Emmanuel Saez, "Striking It Richer: The Evolution of Top Incomes in the United States (Updated with 2014 Preliminary Estimates)," University of California, Berkeley, June 25, 2015, https://eml.berkeley.edu/~saez/saez-UStopincomes-2014.pdf (accessed 6/7/16).

47. Eric J. Toder, Benjamin H. Harris, and Katherine Lim, "Distributional Effects of Tax Expenditure," Tax Policy Center, July 21, 2009, www.taxpolicycenter.org/UploadedPDF/411922_expenditures.pdf (accessed 6/17/10).

48. Dean Baker, *The Conservative Nanny State: How the Wealthy Use the Government to Stay Rich and Get Richer*, May 2006, www. conservativenannystate.org (accessed 6/1/14).

49. Chris Edwards and Jeff Patch, "Corporate Welfare," in *Cato Handbook for Policymakers*, 7th ed., Cato Institute, 2009, www. cato.org/pubs/handbook/hb111/hb111-26.pdf (accessed 9/24/12).

50. Paul N. Van de Water and Arloc Sherman, "Social Security Keeps 20 Million Americans out of Poverty: A State-by-State Analysis," Center on Budget and Policy Priorities, August 11, 2010, www. cbpp.org/cms/?fa=view&id=3260 (accessed 9/16/10).

51. Social Security Administration, Office of Retirement and Disability Policy, and Office of Research, Evaluation, and Statistics, "Fast Facts & Figures about Social Security, 2009," SSA Publication No. 13-11785, July 2009, http://retirement.gov/policy/docs/chartbooks/fast_facts/2009/fast_facts09.pdf (accessed 2/19/10).

52. See the *2008 OASDI Trustees Report*, www.ssa.gov/OACT/TR/TR08/II_project.html#wp105643 (accessed 10/3/16).

53. Social Security Administration, *2010 OASDI Trustees Report*, Figure II D4, www.ssa.gov/OACT/TR/2010/trLOF.html (accessed 9/16/10).

54. See Congressional Budget Office, "Menu of Social Security Options," May 25, 2005, www.cbo.gov/publication/16532?, for a detailed account of the fiscal impact of the various proposals (accessed 10/3/16).

55. "Health Insurance Coverage: Early Release of Estimates from the National Health Interview Survey, January–September, 2015," U.S. Department of Health and Human Services, February, 2016, www.cdc.gov/nchs/data/nhis/earlyrelease/insur201602.pdf (accessed 6/9/16).

56. Organization for Economic Cooperation and Development, "OECD Health Statistics, 2015," July 7, 2015, Figure 2, www. oecd.org/unitedstates/Country-Note-UNITED%20STATES-OECD-Health-Statistics-2015.pdf, U.S. data from "National Health Expenditures, 2014, Highlights," Centers for Medicaid and Medicare Services, December 3, 2015, www.cms.gov/Research-Statistics-Data-and-Systems/Statistics-Trends-and-Reports/NationalHealthExpendData/NationalHealthAccountsHistorical.html (accessed 6/9/16).

57. Department of Health and Human Services, Centers for Medicare and Medicaid Services, "Brief Summaries of Medicare and Medicaid," www.cms.hhs.gov/MedicaidGenInfo/03_TechnicalSummary.asp (accessed 8/11/08).

58. Department of Health and Human Services, *2015 Actuarial Report on the Financial Outlook for Medicaid*, Table 3, p. 14, www.medicaid.gov/Medicaid-CHIP-Program-Information/By-Topics/Financing-and-Reimbursement/Downloads/medicaid-actuarial-report-2015.pdf (accessed 9/27/16).

59. U.S. Department of Health and Human Services, Office of the Assistant Secretary for Planning and Evaluation, *ASPE FMAP 2017 Report*, December 29, 2015, Table 1, https://aspe.hhs.gov/basic-report/fy2017-federal-medical-assistance-percentages (accessed 9/27/16).

60. *2016 Medicare Trustees Report*, June 22, 2016, Table V.F2, p. 214, www.cms.gov/Research-Statistics-Data-and-Systems/Statistics-Trends-and-Reports/ReportsTrustFunds/Downloads/TR2016.pdf (accessed 7/18/16).

61. Medicaid.gov, Annual Enrollment Reports, "2015 Number of Children Ever Enrolled Report," www.medicaid.gov/chip/downloads/fy-2015-childrens-enrollment-report.pdf (accessed 7/18/16).

62. Congressional Budget Office, "Cost Estimates for H.R. 4872, Reconciliation Act of 2010 (Final Health Care Legislation)," March 20, 2010, www.cbo.gov/doc.cfm?index=11355 (accessed 9/24/12).

63. David Nather and Susan Levine, "A Brief History of Obamacare Delays," Politico.com, March 25, 2014, www.politico.com/story/2014/03/obamacare-affordable-care-act105036.html#ixzz33QRP8biR (accessed 6/2/14).

64. Namrata Uberoi, Kenneth Finegold, and Emily Gee, "Health Insurance Coverage and the Affordable Care Act, 2010–2016," March 3, 2016, Health and Human Services, ASPE Issue Brief, https://aspe.hhs.gov/sites/default/files/pdf/187551/ACA2010-2016.pdf (accessed 6/10/16).

65. "Medicaid Enrollment Data Collected through MBES, July–September 2015 Medicaid MBES Enrollment Report," posted March 2016, Medicaid.gov, www.medicaid.gov/medicaid-chip-program-information/program-information/medicaid-and-chip-enrollment-data/medicaid-enrollment-data-collected-through-mbes.html (accessed 6/10/16).

66. Eligibility information for food stamps may be found at U.S. Department of Agriculture Department, Food and Nutrition Services, Supplemental Nutrition Assistance Program (SNAP), U.S. Department of Agriculture, "Latest Available Month," www.fns.usda.gov/pd/supplemental-nutrition-assistance-program-snap (accessed 6/10/16).

67. U.S. Department of Labor, "Unemployment Insurance Data Summary," http://workforcesecurity.doleta.gov/unemploy/content/data_stats/datasum16/DataSum_2016_1.pdf (accessed 6/10/16).

68. 2016 EITC Income Limits, Maximum Credit Amounts and Tax Law Updates, Internal Revenue Service, www.irs.gov/credits-deductions/individuals/earned-income-tax-credit/eitc-income-limits-maximum-credit-amounts-next-year (accessed 6/10/16).

69. Internal Revenue Service, "EITC Awareness Day: IRS Kicks-Off Tax Season Alerting Low- and Moderate-Income Workers of Significant Tax Benefit," www.irs.gov/uac/Newsroom/EITC-Awareness-Day-IRS-Kicks-Off-Tax-Season-Alerting-Low-and-Moderate-Income-Workers-of-Significant-Tax-Benefit (accessed 6/1/14).

70. R. Kent Weaver, *Ending Welfare as We Know It* (Washington, DC: Brookings Institution Press, 2000).

71. "Chart Book: TANF at 19," Center on Budget and Politics Priorities, March 29, 2016, www.cbpp.org/research/family-income-support/chart-book-tanf-at-19 (accessed 6/10/16).

72. U.S. Department of Education, Race to the Top Fund, www2.ed.gov/programs/racetothetop/index.html (accessed 2/23/10).

Take a Stand

a. The comment was in response to the takeover of a federal wildlife refuge in Oregon. Rubio called for the occupiers to lay down their arms but showed sympathy for their central demand that the federal government cede control over much of the Bureau of Land Management land. "Marco Rubio on Oregon Federal Land Business," *Des Moines Register* editorial board interview, January 6, 2016, www.desmoinesregister.com/videos/news/elections/presidential/caucus/2016/01/06/78384514/ (accessed 6/4/16).

b. John Tierney, "The Sagebrush Solution," *New York Times*, July 26, 2005, p. A19. Additional information was drawn from www.highcountrynews.org.

c. A very detailed account of this saga may be found in Raymond B. Wrabley Jr., "Managing the Monument: Cows and Conservation in the Grand-Staircase-Escalante National Monument," *Journal of Land, Resources and Environmental Law* 29:2 (2009): 253–80.

Chapter 15

1. Mark Mazzeti and Eric Schmitt, "C.I.A. Missile Strike May Have Killed Pakistan's Taliban Leader," *New York Times*, August 6, 2009, p. A7.

2. For an example of the isolationist approach, see Patrick J. Buchanan, *A Republic, Not an Empire*, updated ed. (Washington, DC: Regnery, 2002).

3. Robert O. Keohane, *After Hegemony: Cooperation and Discord in the International System* (1984; repr., Princeton, NJ: Princeton University Press, 2005).

4. The distinction was first made in E. H. Carr, *The Twenty Years' Crisis, 1919–1939: An Introduction to the Study of International Relations* (London: Macmillan, 1939). Realism was elaborated as a general theory in Hans Morgenthau, *Politics among Nations: The Struggle for Power and Peace* (New York: Knopf, 1948). For a general overview, see Jonathan Haslam, *No Virtue like Necessity: Realist Thought in International Relations since Machiavelli* (New Haven, CT: Yale University Press, 2002).

5. A synoptic account of the United States as a world power, which takes the story up to the 2003 invasion of Iraq, is Niall Ferguson, *Colossus: The Price of America's Empire* (New York: Penguin Press, 2004).

6. Samuel Flagg Bemis, *John Quincy Adams and the Foundations of American Foreign Policy* (New York: Knopf, 1949); Ernest R. May, *The Making of the Monroe Doctrine* (Cambridge, MA: Harvard University Press, 1975). The latter stresses domestic political considerations and argues that the Monroe Doctrine was "actually the by-product of an election campaign."

7. Daniel M. Smith, *The Great Departure: The United States and World War I, 1914–1920* (New York: Wiley, 1965).

8. Thomas J. Knock, *To End All Wars: Woodrow Wilson and the Quest for a New World Order* (New York: Oxford University Press, 1992).

9. Margaret MacMillan, *Paris 1919: Six Months That Changed the World* (New York: Random House, 2001).

10. John M. Cooper, *Breaking the Heart of the World: Woodrow Wilson and the Fight for the League of Nations* (New York: Cambridge University Press, 2001).

11. John Lewis Gaddis, *Strategies of Containment* (New York: Oxford University Press, 2005).

12. Tony Smith, "Making the World Safe for Democracy in the American Century," *Diplomatic History* 23:2 (1999): 173–88.

13. Winston Churchill, "Sinews of Peace (Iron Curtain)," Westminster College, Fulton, Missouri, March 5, 1946,

available from the Churchill Centre at www.winstonchurchill. org/i4a/pages/index.cfm?pageid=429 (accessed 8/2/08). See also Klaus Larres, *Churchill's Cold War: The Politics of Personal Diplomacy* (New Haven, CT: Yale University Press, 2002).

14. George F. Kennan, "The Sources of Soviet Conduct," *Foreign Affairs* 25:4 (July 1947): 566–82.

15. Robert L. Beisner, *Dean Acheson: A Life in the Cold War* (New York: Oxford University Press, 2006); Dean Acheson, *Present at the Creation* (New York: W. W. Norton, 1969).

16. Michael J. Hogan, *The Marshall Plan: America, Britain, and the Reconstruction of Western Europe* (New York: Cambridge University Press, 1987). See also Martin Schain, ed., *The Marshall Plan: Fifty Years Later* (New York: Palgrave, 2001).

17. Marc Trachtenberg, *A Constructed Peace: The Making of the European Settlement, 1945–1963* (Princeton, NJ: Princeton University Press, 1999).

18. The balance of military power between NATO and the Warsaw Pact throughout the Cold War is traced in David Miller, *The Cold War: A Military History* (New York: St. Martin's Press, 1998).

19. Robert A. Packenham, *Liberal America and the Third World* (Princeton, NJ: Princeton University Press, 1973). For an overview, see David P. Forsythe, "Human Rights in U.S. Foreign Policy: Retrospect and Prospect," *Political Science Quarterly* 105:3 (Autumn 1990): 435–54.

20. Lawrence Freedman, *Kennedy's Wars: Berlin, Cuba, Laos, and Vietnam* (Oxford: Oxford University Press, 2002).

21. William J. Duiker, *Sacred War: Nationalism and Revolution in a Divided Vietnam* (New York: McGraw-Hill, 1995).

22. Henry Kissinger, *Years of Upheaval* (Boston: Little, Brown, 1982); Jussi Hanhimäki, *The Flawed Architect: Henry Kissinger and American Foreign Policy* (New York: Oxford University Press, 2004).

23. Raymond Garthoff, *Détente and Confrontation: American-Soviet Relations from Nixon to Reagan* (Washington, DC: Brookings Institution Press, 1994).

24. Francis Fukuyama, *The End of History and the Last Man*, updated ed. (New York: Free Press, 2006).

25. For a summary of American human rights policy, see John W. Dietrich, "U.S. Human Rights Policy in the Post–Cold War Era," *Political Science Quarterly* 121:2 (Summer 2006): 269–94.

26. Joseph Nye, *Soft Power: The Means to Success in World Politics* (New York: Hachette Book Group, 2009).

27. Samuel P. Huntington, *The Clash of Civilizations and the Remaking of World Order* (New York: Free Press, 2002).

28. Louis Fisher, *Presidential War Power* (Lawrence: University Press of Kansas, 2004).

29. John Mueller and Mark G. Stewart, *Chasing Ghosts: The Policing of Terrorism* (New York: Oxford University Press, 2015).

30. David Hoffman and David B. Ottaway, "Panel Drops Covert-Acts Notification; in Compromise, Bush Pledges to Inform Hill in All but Rare Cases," *Washington Post*, October 27, 1989, p. A1.

31. Dahlia Lithwick, "The Enemy Within," *Slate*, June 12, 2008, www.slate.com/id/2193468 (accessed 10/3/16).

32. Somini Sengupta, "As Musharraf's Woes Grow, Enter an Old Rival, Again," *New York Times*, April 6, 2007, p. A3; Leslie Wayne, "Airbus Seeks a Welcome in Alabama," *New York Times*, June 19, 2007, p. C1.

33. Cecila Kang, "Huawei's U.S. Competitors among Those Pushing for Scrutiny of Chinese Tech Firm," *Washington Post*, October 10, 2012, p. D1.

34. See Pew Research Center, "The U.S. Public's Pro-Israel History," July 19, 2006, http://pewresearch.org/pubs/39/the-u.s.-publics-pro-israel-history (accessed 10/3/16).

35. Pew Research Center, "U.S. Public Seldom Has Welcomed Refugees into Country," November 19, 2015, www. pewresearch.org/fact-tank/2015/11/19/u-s-public-seldom-has-welcomed-refugees-into-country/ (accessed 5/13/16).

36. A directory of NGOs can be found at the Department of Public Information site, Nongovernmental Organization Section, www.un.org/dpi/ngosection/asp/form.asp (accessed 8/2/08).

37. See Amnesty International, "The Secretive and Illegal U.S. Programme of Rendition," April 5, 2006, www.amnesty.org/ en/news-and-updates/feature-stories/secretive-and-illegal-us-programme-of-rendition-20060405 (accessed 8/12/08).

38. United States International Trade Commission, "Harmonized Tariff Schedule of the United States (2010), Revision 2," www. usitc.gov/docs/tata/hts/bychapter/1002htsa.pdf (accessed 9/14/10).

39. Colum Lynch, "U.N. Backs Broader Sanctions on Tehran; Security Council Votes to Freeze Some Assets, Ban Arms Exports," *Washington Post*, March 25, 2007, p. A1.

40. William B. Quandt, *Camp David: Peacemaking and Politics* (Washington, DC: Brookings Institution Press, 1986).

41. U.S. Department of State, *Treaties in Force*, January 1, 2007, www.state.gov/s/l/treaty/treaties/2007/index.htm (accessed 8/12/08).

42. Lisa L. Martin, "The President and International Commitments: Treaties as Signaling Devices," *Presidential Studies Quarterly* 35:3 (2005): 440–65.

43. Johanna Neuman and Megan K. Stack, "Americans' Beirut Exodus Underway; Hundreds Are Evacuated by Ship and Helicopter," *Los Angeles Times*, July 20, 2006, p. A10. The Clinton administration resorted to cruise missile attacks five times: three against Iraq (1993, 1996, 1998), one in 1995 against Bosnian Serb forces in the former Yugoslavia, and one against targets in Afghanistan and Sudan in 1998. James Mann, "Foreign Policy of the Cruise Missile," *Los Angeles Times*, December 23, 1998, p. 5.

44. A comprehensive account of the Afghanistan invasion and its aftermath is in Barnett R. Rubin, "Saving Afghanistan," *Foreign Affairs* 86:1 (January/February 2007): 57–78.

45. P. J. Huffstutter, "A Town Gives until It Hurts," *Los Angeles Times*, November 7, 2003, p. A1.

46. Pew Research Center, "Fewer Americans See Solid Evidence of Climate Change," October 22, 2009, http://people-press.org/ report/556/global-warming (accessed 2/17/10).

47. Steven Erlanger, "Syrian Conflict Poses the Risk of Wider Strife," *New York Times*, February 12, 2012, p. A1.

48. For an optimistic review, see Joseph E. Stiglitz, *Making Globalization Work* (New York: W. W. Norton, 2007).

49. Benjamin Applebaum, "Perils of Globalization When Factories Close and Towns Struggle," *New York Times*, May 17, 2015, p. A1.

50. Fred Kaplan, "North Korea's Nuclear Test Isn't as Dangerous as Kim Jong-un Wants Us To Believe," *Slate*, January 6, 2016., http://www.slate.com/articles/news_and_politics/ politics/2016/01/north_korea_s_nuclear_test_isn_t_as_ dangerous_as_kim_jong_un_wants_us_to.html (accessed 6/20/16).

Study Guide Answer Key

Chapter 1

1. C
2. B
3. C
4. D
5. D
6. C
7. A
8. E
9. A
10. E
11. C

Chapter 2

1. B
2. E
3. C
4. C
5. B
6. D
7. B
8. D
9. B
10. D
11. B
12. A
13. A
14. C
15. B

Chapter 3

1. C
2. B
3. B
4. C
5. C
6. B
7. B
8. B
9. A
10. D
11. B
12. D

Chapter 4

1. D
2. B
3. C
4. A
5. D
6. A
7. D
8. C
9. B
10. C
11. C
12. B
13. C

Chapter 5

1. A
2. C
3. B
4. E
5. E
6. B
7. C
8. E
9. A
10. B
11. C
12. C
13. D

Chapter 6

1. D
2. B
3. A
4. B
5. E
6. D
7. B
8. C
9. C
10. A
11. B
12. E
13. B
14. A

Chapter 7

1. A
2. E
3. B
4. E
5. A
6. A
7. E
8. C
9. C
10. A

Chapter 8

1. A
2. D
3. B
4. B
5. B
6. C
7. E
8. A
9. C
10. B
11. A
12. C
13. C

Chapter 9

1. E
2. A
3. C
4. B
5. E
6. C
7. A
8. B
9. D
10. A

Chapter 10

1. D
2. E
3. B
4. A
5. D
6. B
7. D
8. A
9. C
10. E
11. B
12. B

Chapter 11	Chapter 12	Chapter 13	Chapter 14	Chapter 15
1. A	1. C	1. A	1. A	1. C
2. A	2. A	2. D	2. C	2. A
3. C	3. D	3. B	3. D	3. E
4. D	4. E	4. A	4. A	4. C
5. A	5. B	5. E	5. D	5. D
6. B	6. C	6. B	6. A	6. D
7. B	7. A	7. C	7. B	7. B
8. D	8. B	8. A	8. B	8. C
9. B	9. D	9. E	9. C	9. A
10. A	10. C	10. B	10. E	10. B
11. D	11. A	11. B	11. A	11. C
12. C	12. E	12. D	12. E	12. D
	13. A	13. A	13. B	13. D
	14. B	14. B	14. A	14. B
			15. B	15. A

Credits

Line Art

Chapter 1, What Do the Numbers Say?: Map: "2016 Presidential Election, Purple America," by Robert J. Vanderbei, Princeton University. www.princeton.edu/~rvdb/JAVA/election2016/. Reprinted by permission of the author.
Figure 6.4: Graph from "Public's Policy Priorities Reflect Changing Conditions at Home and Abroad," Pew Research Center, Washington, DC (January, 2015) www.people-press.org/2015/01/15/publics-policy-priorities-reflect-changing-conditions-at-home-and-abroad/. Reprinted with permission.
Figure 7.5: Figure from "A Deep Dive Into Party Affiliation," Pew Research Center, Washington, DC (April, 2015) www.people-press.org/2015/04/07/a-deep-dive-into-party-affiliation/. Reprinted with permission.
Chapter 15, What Do the Numbers Say?: Graph: "Terrorism in the United States." Copyright © 2015 Gallup, Inc. All rights reserved. The content is used with permission; however Gallup retains all rights of republication.

Photographs

ii–iii: Zach Gibson/Getty Images

Chapter 1

2–3: John Moore/Getty Images; **4:** Alex Milan Tracy/Sipa USA/Newscom; **7 (left):** U.S. Army Photo by Staff Sgt. Russell Bassett; **7 (right):** AP Photo/*Houston Chronicle*, Brett Coomer; **10:** Allison Shelley/For *The Washington Post* via Getty Images; **11:** Andrew Harrer/Bloomberg via Getty Images; **12:** Rick Wilking/AFP/Getty Images; **13 (left):** Nano Calvo/Alamy Stock Photo; **13 (center):** Gordon Chibroski/*Portland Press Herald* via Getty Images; **13 (right):** AF archive/Alamy Stock Photo; **17 (top):** Essdras M Suarez/*The Boston Globe* via Getty Images; **17 (bottom):** © Flip Schulke/CORBIS/Corbis via Getty Images; **19:** AP Photo/*The Salt Lake Tribune*, Scott Sommerdorf; **22:** Rob Crandall/Alamy Stock Photo

Chapter 2

26–27: Win McNamee/Getty Images; **29:** Bettmann/Getty Images; **32:** © North Wind Picture Archives—All rights reserved; **34:** Bettmann/Getty Images; **40:** © Leonard de Selva/Corbis via Getty Images; **41 (top):** Library of Congress/Getty Images; **41 (bottom):** Francis G. Mayer/Corbis/VCG/via Getty Images; **43:** Pete Marovich/Bloomberg via Getty Images; **45 (top center):** Bob Barket/Stringer/Getty Images; **45 (top right):** Spx Chrome/Getty Images; **45 (center):** Jewel Samad/Getty Images; **45 (center right):** Spx Chrome/Getty Images; **45 (bottom left):** Jewel Samad/Getty Images; **45 (bottom center):** Mark Wilson/Getty Images; **46:** AP Photo/Musadeq Sadeq; **48:** Porter Gifford/Getty Images; **51 (left):** © Everett Collection Inc./Alamy Stock Photo; **51 (right):** © Everett Collection Inc./Alamy Stock Photo; **52:** AP Photo/Gary Gardiner

Chapter 3

56–57: AP Photo/John Bazemore; **58:** Patsy Lynch/FEMA; **62:** AP Photo/Eric Gay; **64:** Image copyright © The Metropolitan Museum of Art. Image source: Art Resource, NY; **67:** Bettmann/Getty Images; **69 (top left):** Dennis Flaherty/Getty Images; **69 (top center):** Ivana Star/Getty Images; **69 (top right):** Space Images/Getty Images; **69 (center left):** Food Collection/Getty Images; **69 (center):** 3alexd/Getty Images; **69 (center right):** Sigrid Gombert/Getty Images; **69 (bottom left above):** Ivana Star/Getty Images; **69 (bottom left below):** Food Collection/Getty Images; **69 (bottom center left):** Joe Raedle/Getty Images; **69 (bottom center right):** Caia Image Closed/Getty Images; **69 (bottom right):** Michael Betts/Getty Images; **70:** Bettmann/Getty Images; **76:** © Will & Deni McIntyre/Corbis via Getty Images; **78:** Karen Bleier/AFP/Getty Images; **80:** Kevin Maloney/Getty Images; **81:** Mario Tama/Getty Images; **82:** Justin Sullivan/Getty Images; **84:** AP Photo/David Zalubowski

Chapter 4

88–89: Ty Wright/Getty Images; **91 (left):** AP Photo; **91 (right):** William Thomas Cain/Getty Images; **93 (top left):** Ty Wright/Stringer/Getty Images; **93 (top center):** Spx Chrome/Getty Images; **93 (top right):** John Parra/Getty Images; **93 (center left):** Spx Chrome/Getty Images; **93 (center):** Bloomberg/Getty Images; **93 (center right):** Image Navi/Getty Images; **93 (bottom):** Stockbyte/Getty Images; **98:** © Eric Reed/ZUMA Press, Inc./Alamy Stock Photo; **99:** Chip Somodevilla/Getty Images; **102:** J. Lawler Duggan/For *The Washington Post* via Getty Images; **104:** William Campbell/Getty Images; **105:** AP Photo/Patrick Semansky; **106:** Stacy Walsh Rosenstock/Alamy Stock Photo; **108 (left):** © Scott Houston/Corbis via Getty Images; **108 (right):** Evelyn Hockstein/For *The Washington Post*/Getty Images; **110:** David McNew/Getty Images; **111:** AP Photo; **113:** Bettmann/Getty Images; **114:** Reuters/Intelwire.com; **116:** AP Photo/Michael Stravato

Chapter 5

122–123: John Moore/Getty Images; **126 (left):** Library of Congress; **126 (right):** HB Lindsey/Underwood Archives/Getty Images; **128:** Michael Salas/Time Life Pictures/Getty Images; **130:** © Steven Ferdman/Everett Collection/Alamy Live News; **131:** Charles Ommanney/*The Washington Post* via Getty Images; **133 (left):** Centralized Bond Hearing Court via AP; **133 (right):** Brian Snyder/Reuters/Newscom; **134:** Feidin Santana via AP Images; **136:** Granger, NYC—All rights reserved; **140:** AP Photo/Bill Hudson; **141:** Radius Images/Alamy Stock Photo; **147 (left):** David Schaffer/Getty Images; **147 (right):** Tetra Images/Getty Images; **149:** © 2012 Marilyn Humphries/Newscom; **151:** Mario Tama/Getty Images; **153:** Jose Luis Magana/Reuters/Newscom; **154:** Kevin Lamarque/Reuters/Newscom **155:** Scott Olson/Getty Images

Chapter 6

160–161: Spencer Platt/Getty Images; 162 (left): Fox/Photofest; 162 (right): Larry Downing/Reuters/Newscom; 163: Mark Ralston/AFP/Getty Images; 164 (left): AP Photo/Rich Pedroncelli; 164 (right): AP Photo/David J. Phillip; 167: Matthew Cavanaugh/EPA/Newscom; 169: Jeff Malet Photography/Newscom; 173 (top left): Tetra Images/Getty Images; 173 (top center): Daniel Grill/Getty Images; 173 (top right): Evirgen/Getty Images; 173 (bottom left): John Lamb/Getty Images; 173 (bottom center): Image Navi/Getty Images; 173 (bottom right): Hero Images/Getty Images; 181: CALVIN AND HOBBES © 1994 Watterson. Dist. By UNIVERSAL UCLICK. Reprinted with permission. All rights reserved; 183: Stacy Walsh Rosenstock/Almay Stock Photo

Chapter 7

190–191: © Bryan Smith via ZUMA Wire; 192 (left): AP Photo/Paul Sancya; 192 (center): Jason Reed/Reuters/Newscom; 192 (right): AP Photo/Chuck Burton; 193: © Corbis via Getty Images; 194: Granger, NYC—All rights reserved; 200: John Leyba/*The Denver Post* via Getty Images; 205: Joe Raedle/Getty Images; 206: AP Photo/M. Spencer Green; 209 (left): Jewel Samad/AFP/Getty Images; 209 (center left): Jewel Samad/AFP/Getty Images; 209 (center right): Daniel Acker/Bloomberg via Getty Images; 209 (right): Gary Coronado/Pool via Bloomberg/Getty Images; 210: AP Photo/Charles Dharapak; 212 (top): Stephen M. Dowell/*Orlando Sentinel* via AP; 212 (bottom): Chris Kleponis/Getty Images

Chapter 8

216–217: Justin Sullivan/Getty Images; 218: AP Photo/Ronda Churchill; 220: Luke Sharrett/Bloomberg via Getty Images; 222: Brian Blanco/Getty Images; 228 (top): Bill Clark/CQ Roll Call/Getty Images; 228 (bottom): Courtesy Alberto Tomas Halpern/Newspaper Tree; 231 (top): CQ Roll Call via AP Images/Tom Williams; 231 (bottom): AP Photo/Paul Vernon; 235: Courtesy Priorities USA; 236: Drew Angerer/Stringer/Getty Images; 239: Brendan Smialowski/AFP/Getty Images; 240: Win McNamee/Getty Images; 242: AP Photo/J. Scott Applewhite; 245: Chip Somodevilla/Getty Images; 246: Brooks Kraft/Getty Images

Chapter 9

250–251: © Richard Levine/Alamy Stock Photo; 254 (left): Business Wire via Getty Images; 254 (right): ZUMA Press, Inc./Alamy Stock Photo; 259: Tom Williams/Roll Call/Getty Images; 263 (top center): Pressmaster/Shutterstock; 263 (top right): Yuri Arcurs/Getty Images; 263 (center left): Image Source/Getty Images; 263 (center): Tetra Images/Getty Images; 263 (center right): Greg Bajor/Getty Images; 263 (bottom left): Mark Wilson/Getty Images; 264: AP Photo/Elaine Thompson; 265: Andrew Burton/Getty Images; 268: Ron Sachs/picture-alliance/dpa/AP Images; 270: Olivier Douliery/Sipa USA/via AP Images; 272 (left): Will & Deni McIntyre/Science Source/Getty Images; 272 (right): AP Photo/Robert F. Bukaty

Chapter 10

276–277: AP Photo/Carolyn Kaster; 279: Granger, NYC—All rights reserved; 282: AP Photo/Jim Urquhart; 284: Al Drago/CQ Roll Call/Getty Images; 287: AP Photo/The Kenosha News, Bill Siel; 292: Kevin Lamarque/Reuters/Corbis via Getty Images; 295: Win McNamee/Getty Images; 298: Ethan Miller/Getty Images; 303 (row 1, left): Mark Wilson/Getty Images; 303 (row 1, right): Mark Wilson/Getty Images; 303 (row 2, left): Chip Somodevilla/Getty Images; 303 (row 2, center): Jewel Samad/Getty Images; 303 (row 2, right): Chip Somodevilla/Getty Images; 303 (row 4, right): Mark Wilson/Getty Images; 303 (row 5, left): Mark Wilson/Getty Images; 303 (row 5, center): Mark Wilson/Getty Images; 303 (row 5, right): Jewel Samad/Getty Images; 305: AP Photo/Senate TV; 307: Pete Marovich/Bloomberg via Getty Images; 309: AP Photo/The Porterville Recorder, Chieko Hara

Chapter 11

312–313: Pete Marovich/Bloomberg via Getty Images 315: Brooklyn Museum/Corbis via Getty Images; 316: World History Archive/Newscom; 319: Jacquelyn Martin/AP; 321 (row 1, left): Jewel Samad/AFP/Getty Images; 321 (row 1, right): Debbi Smirnoff/Getty Images; 321 (row 2, left): Image Source/Getty Images; 321 (row 2, center): Jewel Samad/AFP/Getty Images; 321 (row 2, right): Samuel Corum/Anadolu Agency/Getty Images; 321 (row 3, left): Jewel Samad/AFP/Getty Images; 321 (row 3, right): Lawrence Jackson/The White House via Getty Images; 321 (row 4, left): Jewel Samad/AFP/Getty Images; 321 (row 4, right): Dennis Flaherty/Getty Images; 324: AP Photo/Pablo Martinez Monsivais; 327: AP Photo/Pablo Martinez Monsivais; 328: Al-Mayadeen via AP video; 330 (left): Aude Guerrucci-Pool/Getty Images; 330 (right): Gage Skidmore/Alamy Stock Photo; 334: Deborah Gembara/Reuters/Newscom; 337: AP Photo/Saul Loeb, Pool

Chapter 12

340–341: © Ryan Garza/Detroit Free Press via ZUMA Wire; 343: Photo by U.S. Coast Guard via Getty Images; 345 (top left): Dennis Flaherty/Getty Images; 345 (top center): United States Environmental Protection Agency; 345 (top right): Spx Chrome/Getty Images; 345 (center left): United States Environmental Protection Agency; 345 (center): Jewel Samad/Getty Images; 345 (center right): United States Environmental Protection Agency; 345 (bottom left): Jewel Samad/Getty Images; 345 (bottom center): United States Environmental Protection Agency; 346: Zach Bolinger/Icon Sportswire via AP Images; 347: CARLSON © 2005 Milwaukee Journal Sentinel. Reprinted with permission of UNIVERSAL UCLICK. All rights reserved; 349: Bettmann/Getty Images; 351: Justine Lane/EPA/Newscom; 359: Matthew Eisman/Getty Images for Common Sense Media; 360: Chip Somodevilla/Getty Images; 361: David Paul Morris/Stringer/Getty Images; 362: AP Photo/J. Scott Applewhite; 364: Conor Ralph/*The Flint Journal-MLive.com* via AP; 367: Dmitri Kessel/The LIFE Picture Collection/Getty Images

Chapter 13

370–371: Al Drago/CQ Roll Call/Getty Images; 375: © North Wind Picture Archives—All rights reserved; 377: AP Photo/Vince Bucci, Pool; 379: Chip Somodevilla/Getty Images; 381 (top): Glow Images/Getty Images; 381 (center left): Alexsandar Nakic/Getty Images; 381 (center right): Spx Chrome/Getty Images; 381 (bottom): Mark Ralston/AFP/Getty Images; 382: Kevin Dietsch/UPI/Newscom; 385: © 2005 JD Crowe, The Mobile Register, and PoliticalCartoons.com; 390: © Art Lien; 391: © Christy Bowe/Globe Photos/ZUMAPRESS.com; 394: Larry Downing/Reuters/Newscom; 396: Steve Liss/The LIFE Images Collection/Getty Images; 398: © Bettmann/Corbis via Getty Images

Chapter 14

402–403: © *The New York Times*/Redux; 404: Frederic J. Brown/AFP/Getty Images; 406: Joshua Roberts/Reuters/Newscom; 409 (top left): Drew Angerer/Getty Images; 409 (top center): Alex Wong/Getty Images; 409 (top right): Mark Wilson/Getty Images; 409 (bottom left): Molly Riley/AFP/Getty Images; 409 (bottom center): Dennis Flaherty/Getty Images; 409 (bottom right): Alex

Wong/Getty Images; **412:** ZUMA Press, Inc./Alamy Stock Photo; **423:** J.M. Eddins, Jr./MCT via Getty Images; **424 (left):** David R. Frazier/DanitaDellmont.com "Danita Dellmont Photography"/Newscom; **424 (right):** © Scott J. Ferrell/Congressional Quarterly/Alamy; **425:** © Alex Webb/Magnum Photos; **427 (top):** AP Photo/Lauren Victoria Burke; **427 (bottom):** Andrew Harrer/Bloomberg via Getty Images; **429:** © Everett Collection Inc./Alamy Stock Photo; **435:** Gary Markstein/Copley News Service/Newscom

Chapter 15

444–445: AP Photo/Aleppo Media Center, AMC; **448:** Timothy A. Clary/AFP/Getty Images; **450:** AP Photo; **452:** AP Photo/Al Jazeera; **453:** Mohammed Mohammed Xinhua News Agency/Newscom;

455: Joe Klamar/AFP/Getty Images; **457:** Saul Loeb/AFP/Getty Images; **459 (row 1, left):** Dennis Flaherty/Getty Images; **459 (row 1, center):** Roberto Schmidt/AFP/Getty Images; **459 (row 1, right):** Xinhua/Gamma-Rapho via Getty Images; **459 (row 2, left):** Jewel Samad/AFP/Getty Images; **459 (row 2, center):** Stocktrek Images/Getty Images; **459 (row 2, right):** Jewel Samad/AFP/Getty Images; **459 (row 3, left):** Jewel Samad/AFP/Getty Images; **459 (row 3, center):** Jewel Samad/AFP/Getty Images; **459 (row 3, right):** Molly Riley/AFP/Getty Images; **459 (row 4, left):** Dennis Flaherty/Getty Images; **459 (row 4, right):** Raphye Alexius/Getty Images; **460:** Jim Watson/AFP/Getty Images; **464:** AP Photo; **467:** © Peter Turnley/Corbis via Getty Images; **468 (left):** Imaginechina via AP Images; **468 (right):** Gilles Sabrie/*The New York Times*/Redux; **470:** © Bryan Denton/Corbis via Getty Images; **472:** KCNA/EPA/Newscom

Glossary/Index

AT&T, 112
attorneys, 114
autonomy under federalism, 59
Axelrod, David, 329

baby-boom generation, 432, 432–33
Americans born between 1946 and 1964, who will be retiring in large numbers over the next 20 years.

Baker, James, 330
Bakke, Allan, 154
Bakke, Regents of the University of California v., 154

balanced budget, 416, 417 A spending plan in which the government's expenditures are equal to its revenue.

Baldwin, Tammy, 285, 286
ballots, 219, 220–21
Baltimore, Barron v., 65, 95
banks, 64, 74, 330, 331
Barron v. Baltimore, 65, 95
Baumgartner, Frank R., 413
BCRA (Bipartisan Campaign Reform Act), 102, 233
Bear Stearns, 426
Becerra, Xavier, 327
BellSouth, 112
Benishek, Dan, 228
Benton v. Maryland, 96
Berlin Wall, 467
Bernanke, Ben, 422, 427
Bevin, Matt, 88

bicameralism, 278 The system of having two chambers within one legislative body, like the House and Senate in the U.S. Congress.

Biden, Joe, 243, 327, 330, 331

Bill of Rights, 90, 94, 125 The first 10 amendments to the Constitution; they protect individual rights and liberties.
    campaign spending and, 236
    creation of, 41–42, 91, 94, 119
    privacy rights in, 115
    public awareness of, 162
    selective incorporation and, 95, 96
    see also specific amendments and liberties

bills
    debating, 304–5
    filibuster of, 304
    into laws, process of, 301–7, 311
        conventional, 301, 302, 304–5, 305
        deviations from conventional, 303, 305–6
        differences between House and Senate, 306–7
        resolving discrepancies in, 305
    markups in, 304
    types of, 301

bin Laden, Osama, 322, 451, 452
BIPAC (Business-Industry Political Action Committees), 254
Bipartisan Campaign Reform Act (BCRA), 102, 233
Birmingham, A.L., 137, 139, 140
Bismarck, Otto von, 307
black codes, *see* Jim Crow laws
Black Lives Matter movement, 133, 138

block grants, 72 Federal aid provided to a state government to be spent within a certain policy area, but the state can decide how to spend the money within that area.

"blue states," 15–16, 25
Board of Education I, Brown v., 127, 136, 138, 140, 397, 398
Board of Education II, Brown v., 127, 141
Board of Education of Ewing Township, Everson v., 96
Boehner, John, 276, 409
Boeing, 252
Bollinger, Grutter v., 147
Bond, United States v., 79
Border Patrol, U.S., 455
Boren, Craig v., 147
Bowers v. Hardwick, 144–45
BP oil well explosion in 2010, 343
Brady Bill, 108
Brandeis, Louis, 80
Brandenburg v. Ohio, 101
brand names, political, 196
Brazile, Donna, 192
Brennan Center for Justice, 131
Breyer, Stephen, 383, 394
briefs, 389–90

broadcast media, 184 Communications technologies, such as television and radio, that transmit information over airwaves.
    see also media

Brown, Albert G., 279
Brown, Michael, 102, 133
Brown v. Board of Education I, 127, 136, 138, 140, 397, 398
Brown v. Board of Education II, 127, 141

budget deficits, 416, 417 The amount by which a government's spending in a given fiscal year exceeds its revenue.

budget making, 407, 408, 409, 410 The processes carried out in Congress to determine how government money will be spent and revenue will be raised.

Buffett, Warren, 430
Bunning, David, 88

bureaucracy, 340–69 The system of civil servants and political appointees who implement congressional or presidential decisions; also known as the *administrative state*.

control of, 360, 360–65, 362, 364, 368
definition of, 342, 367
economic policy and role of, 411, 412
expertise and its consequences for, 346–48, 347, 348
history of, 349, 349–51, 350, 351, 367
human face of, 357, 357–59, 359, 368
modern federal, 340, 341, 342, 352–55, 353, 354, 355, 356, 368
political appointees and senior executive service positions, 358–59
political process and, 8, 12–13
problem of control and, 347–48, 348
public opinion on, 347–48
red tape and, 346–47
size of, 353–55, 355, 356
standard operating procedures of, 347
tasks of, 342–43, 344, 345–46
types of workers in, 357

bureaucratic drift, 360–65 Bureaucrats' tendency to implement policies in a way that favors their own political objectives rather than following the original intentions of the legislation.

bus boycott, 136, 138
Bush, George H. W., 167, 316, 323, 326
Bush, George W., 167, 316, 323, 331
    appointments made by, 88, 151, 383
    bureaucracy and, 351, 351
    Cheney's expanded role under, 330–31
    Congress and, 43
    in 2000 election, 212, 226
    financial crisis of 2008–2009 and, 426, 427
    immigration issue and, 124, 156
    judges nominated by, 384
    national supremacy and, 75
    No Child Left Behind Act and, 76, 412
    pardons granted by, 325
    social policies of, 430
    unilateral actions of, 333
    vetoes issued by, 326
    War on Terror and, 45, 451
Bush, Jeb, 167, 237
Bush, Laura, 331

Bush Doctrine, 451 The foreign policy of President George W. Bush, under which the United States would use military force preemptively against threats to its national security.

business cycle, 418 The normal pattern of expansion and contraction of the economy.

Business-Industry Political Action Committees (BIPAC), 254

Cabinet, 331–32 The group of 15 executive department heads who implement the president's agenda in their respective positions.

cabinet departments, 355
    see also specific departments

clear and present danger test, 101
Established in *Schenck v. United States*, this test allows the government to restrict certain types of speech deemed dangerous.

Clear Channel Communications, 184
Clinton, Bill, 316, 323
    appointments made by, 151, 383
    civil rights and, 150, 151
    in 1992 election, 226
    federalism and, 72
    foreign policy of, 316
    Gore's relationship with, 331
    impeachment of, 308
    vetoes issued by, 326
    welfare reforms and, 316, 438
Clinton, Hillary, 18
    addressing AIPAC convention, 457
    2016 election and, 2–4, 190, 192, 216, 220, 241, 246, 246, 312
        advertising in, 233
        economic policy in, 402, 403, 404–5, 428
        electoral college and, 225, 226
        nomination of, 223, 241, 243
        swing states and, 223, 245
        Trump's threats to jail, if elected, 22
    as first spouse, 331
    as secretary of state, 307, 307

closed primary, 206, 208, 219 A primary election in which only registered members of a particular political party can vote.

cloture, 304 A procedure through which the Senate can limit the amount of time spent debating a bill (cutting off a filibuster) if a supermajority of 60 senators agree.

Club for Growth, 196
Clyburn, James, 327
Coast Guard, 342

coattails, 239 The idea that a popular president can generate additional support for candidates affiliated with his or her party. Coattails are weak or nonexistent in most American elections.

coercion, 254 A method of eliminating nonparticipation or free riding by potential group members by requiring participation, as in many labor unions.

coercive federalism, 56, 68, 71, 72, 74–76 A form of federalism in which the federal government pressures the states to change their policies by using regulations, mandates, and conditions (often involving threats to withdraw federal funding).

Cold War, 449–51, 450, 467 The period of tension and arms competition between the United States and the Soviet Union that lasted from 1945 until 1991.

collective action problems, 6–7, 14 Situations in which the members of a group would benefit by working together to produce some outcome, but each individual is better off refusing to cooperate and reaping benefits from those who do the work.

collusion, 388
Colorado
    Columbine High School shooting in, 80
    gay rights in, 145
Colorado, Wolf v., 96
color-blind jurisprudence, 141–43, 152
Columbine High School, 80
commander in chief, 319, 322
commerce
    congressional authority over, 64, 78–80, 79
    state authority over, 64, 64
commerce clause, 78–80, 79, 80

commercial speech, 106, 106 Public expression with the aim of making a profit. It has received greater protection under the First Amendment in recent years but remains less protected than political speech.

committee system, 298–300, 299, 309

common law, 377 Law based on the precedent of previous court rulings rather than on legislation. It is used in all federal courts and 49 of the 50 state courts.

Common Sense (Paine), 31
Commonwealth of Independent States (CIS), 60
Communications Decency Act, 107
communities, 166
Community Development Block Grants, 72
Compassionate Use Act, 82

competitive federalism, 76 A form of federalism in which states compete to attract businesses and jobs through the policies they adopt.

compromise
    at the Constitutional Convention, 34–40, 42
    slavery and, 39–40

concurrent powers, 59 Responsibilities for particular policy areas, such as transportation, that are shared by federal, state, and local governments.

concurrent resolutions, 301
concurring opinions, 392
Confederacy, 65, 126
confederal battle flag, 102

confederal government, 60 A form of government in which states hold power over a limited national government.

confederations, 8, 253 Interest groups made up of several independent, local organizations that provide much of their funding and hold most of the power.

conference, 197, 391 The organization of Republicans within the House and Senate that meets to discuss and debate the party's positions on various issues in order to reach a consensus and to assign leadership positions.

conference committees, 298 Temporary committees created to negotiate differences between the House and Senate versions of a piece of legislation that has passed through both chambers.

conflict, 8–11, 10, 23
    in Constitutional Convention, 29, 29–33, 30–31, 35
    cultural values and, 15–17, 25
    economic interests and, 15, 17
    in foreign policy issues, 466–72, 467, 474
    gender and, 17, 18
    ideology and, 18–19
    public opinion differences as cause of, 11
    racial and ethnic differences and, 17–18, 18
    resolving, 20–22, 25
Congress, 276–311
    allocation of power to, 6, 77–80
    Articles of Confederation and, 29–30, 33
    bicameralism of, 279
    caucuses and conferences in, 197
    civil rights legislation of, 140, 148–50, 151
    commerce clause and, 64, 78–80, 79, 80
    constituency service in, 287, 287–88
    constitutional amendments and, 47, 49, 50, 97, 101
    Constitution and, 33, 279
    creation of laws in, 80, 114, 115
    descriptive representation in, 280, 281
    economic policy and role of, 407, 408, 409, 410
    election to, 279, 288
    electoral connection and, 283–85, 285, 287, 287–91, 290
    enumerated powers of, 50
    exclusive powers of, 42–43
    executive orders and, 318–19, 320
    executive privilege and, 327
    foreign policy and, 454, 456, 458
    fund-raising in, 285, 287
    Guantánamo Bay and, 45, 334, 334
    gun control and, 160, 319
    home style in, 285, 286
    incumbency advantage in, 284–85, 285, 287
    interest groups and lobbying of, 259
    oversight by, 307–8, 311, 362–63
    party unity in, 297, 297–98
    party votes in, 296, 296–97
    polarization of, 297, 297–98
    power of the purse and, 42, 46
    president's relationship with, 279, 280

"consent of the governed," 32 The idea that government gains its legitimacy through regular elections in which the people living under that government participate to elect their leaders.

conservative, 18–19, 81, 163, *163*, 176, 177 One side of the ideological spectrum defined by support for lower taxes, a free market, and a more-limited government; generally associated with Republicans.

considerations, 163, 165, *165* The many pieces of information a person uses to form an opinion.

constitutional authority (presidential), 317, 318 Powers derived from the provisions of the Constitution that outline the president's role in government.

constitutional interpretation, 376 The process of determining whether a piece of legislation or governmental action is supported by the Constitution.

constructivism, 447, 448 The idea that foreign policy is shaped by how a state's leaders define the national interest, ideology, and other factors.

containment, 450 An important feature of American Cold War policy in which the United States used diplomatic, economic, and military strategies in an effort to prevent the Soviet Union from expanding its influence.

cooperative federalism, 67, 68, 70, 70, 71, 77, 83 A form of federalism in which national and state governments work together to provide services efficiently. This form emerged in the late 1930s, representing a profound shift toward less concrete boundaries of responsibility in national-state relations.

Council of Economic Advisors (CEA), 414 A group of economic advisers, created by the Employment Act of 1946, that provides objective data on the state of the economy and makes economic-policy recommendations to the president.

culture wars, 15 Political conflict in the United States between "red-state" Americans, who tend to have strong religious beliefs, and "blue-state" Americans, who tend to be more secular.

due process rights, 95, 109–15, *113*, 120, 145 The idea that laws and legal proceedings must be fair. The Constitution guarantees that the government cannot take away a person's "life, liberty, or property, without due process of law." Other specific due process rights are found in the Fourth, Fifth, Sixth, and Eighth Amendments, such as protection from self-incrimination and freedom from illegal searches.

Dukes, Betty, *149*
Duncan v. Louisiana, *96*

earmarks, 293 Federally funded local projects attached to bills passed through Congress.

Earned Income Tax Credit (EITC), 437–38
Ebola virus, 233

economic depression, 414 A deep, widespread downturn in the economy, like the Great Depression of the 1930s.

economic growth, 315, 316
economic individualism, 15
economic interests
    Constitution and, *32*, 32–33
    political conflict and, 15, *17*
economic policy, 402–28, 441
    bureaucracy and role in, 411, *412*
    congressional role in, 407, *408*, *409*, 410
    in 2016 election, 402, 404
    financial crisis of 2008-2009 and, 426–28, *427*
    fiscal theories and policies in, 416, 418–20, *419*, *420*, *421*
    goals of, 414–16, *415*
    government regulation and impact on, 423–24, 426, *426*
    monetary theories and polices in, 421–23, *423*
    presidential role in, *408*, *409*, 410–11
    trade policies and, *470*, 470–71
    see also public policy

economic sanctions, 463–64 Penalties applied by one country or group of countries on another, usually in the form of tariffs or other trade barriers.

economic stimulus package, 75
education, 7, 77
    desegregation of, 74, 127, 136, *138*, 139–41, *141*, 150
    government and, 77
    No Child Left Behind Act and, *76*, 439
    Race to the Top program and, 412, 439
    social policies on, 412, 438–40
Education Amendments (1972), Title IX of, *137*, 148–49
Edwards, George C., III, 336
EEOC (Equal Employment Opportunity Commission), 142, 144

Eighth Amendment, 50–51, *52*, *94*, *96*, 114–15
Eisenhower, Dwight, *138*, 150, 315, 334
EITC (Earned Income Tax Credit), 437–38
elastic clause, *see* necessary and proper clause
elderly people, civil rights of, 125

election cycle, 227 The two-year period between general elections.

Election Day, 219, 237
electioneering, 266–68, *267*, *268*
elections, 216–49
    of 1828, 193
    of 1860, 126
    of 1916, 315
    of 1932, 315
    of 1952, 228
    of 1968, 228
    of 1976, 228
    of 1980, 228, 351
    of 1992, 226
    of 2000, 212, *212*, 226, 227
    of 2004, *226*
    of 2008, 204, 205, 226, 321
    of 2010, 26, 76, 204
    of 2012, 26, 205, 207, *226*, 226, 241–42, 245
    of 2014, 26, 235, 242, *242*
    of 2016, 12, 16, 171, 173, 183, 190, *191*, 204, 205, 209, 213, 216, *217*, *218*, 220, 222, 223, 225, 226, 228, 232, 233, 234, *234*, *235*, 237, 241–46, 244, 245, 246, 248, *298*, *309*, 402, *403*, 404–5, 419, 428, 440, *445*, 476
    campaigns in, 227–37, 247
        advertising in, 102, 232–33, *233*, 234
        campaign financing in, 233–37
        debates in, 232
        fund-raising for, 285, 287
        permanent, 228, 230, *230*
        promises and platforms in, *231*, 231–32
    Constitution and, 219
    functions of, 218–19
    media and, 8, 13
    minor political parties and, *212*, 212–13
    national conventions in, 222, 222–23
    political process and, 13
    presidential, *221*, 221–27, *222*, *223*, 226, 229
    primary and caucus stage in, 204, 206, 208, 219, 221–22
    recruiting and nominating candidates in, 204–6, *206*
    rules and requirements of, 219, 247
    runoff, 220
    stages of, 219
    states' role in, 59
    voter turnout in, 237–38, *238*, 248
    voting cues in, 239, *239*
    voting methods and ballot counting in, 220–21
    voting requirements in, 219
    wave, 239–40, *240*

electoral college, 38, 61, 223, 223–26 The body that votes to select America's president and vice president based on the popular vote

in each state. Each candidate nominates a slate of electors who are selected to attend the meeting of the college if their candidate wins the most votes in a state or district.

electoral connection, 283–85, *285*, *287*, 287–91, 290 The idea that congressional behavior is centrally motivated by members' desire for reelection.

electoral votes, 223, 223–27, 227
Eleventh Amendment, 49, 56, 62
Emancipation Proclamation, 315
employment
    discrimination in, *136*, 141, 142
    full, as economic policy goal, 414
Endangered Species Act, 69, 113
Engle v. Vitale, 97
English as official language, 154–55

entitlement, 434 Any federal government program that provides benefits to Americans who meet requirements specified by law.

enumerated powers, 50 Powers explicitly granted to Congress, the president, or the Supreme Court in the first three articles of the Constitution. Examples include Congress's power to "raise and support Armies" and the president's power as commander in chief.

Environmental Protection Agency (EPA), 69, 340, *364*, *364*, 366
environmental racism, 133
environment and environmentalism
    contaminated water in Flint, Michigan, 133, 340, *341*, 342, *364*, 366
    federalism and, 69
    grazing rights, 425
EOP (Executive Office of the President), 329–30, 439
EPA (Environmental Protection Agency), 69, 340, *364*, *364*, 366
Equal Employment Opportunity Commission (EEOC), 142, 144

equality, 21 In the context of American politics, "equality" means equality before the law, political equality (one person, one vote), and equality of opportunity (the equal chance for everyone to realize their potential), but not material equality (equal income or wealth).
    civil rights and, 125, *136*
    economic, 15, *17*, 18
    political, 21–22, 23, 25

Equal Pay Act, *136*
equal protection clause, 90, 125, 145
    African Americans and, 126
    women and, 143–44
Equal Rights Amendment, *137*, 149

equal time provision, 184 An FCC regulation requiring broadcast media to provide equal air time on any non-news programming to all candidates running for an office.

Era of Good Feelings, 193

establishment clause, 93, 97, 98 Part of the First Amendment that states "Congress shall make no law respecting an establishment of religion," which has been interpreted to mean that Congress cannot sponsor or favor any religion.

ethnicity, 17
European Union (EU), 60
Everson v. Board of Education of Ewing Township, 96
Every Student Succeeds Act in, 11

exclusionary rule, 111, 111 The principle that illegally or unconstitutionally acquired evidence cannot be used in a criminal trial.

executive agreement, 324 An agreement between the executive branch and a foreign government, which acts as a treaty but does not require Senate approval.

executive branch, 329–32, 330
    allocation of power to, 6, 43
    checks and balances on, 36
    foreign policy and role of, 454–56, 455
    structure of, 353, 353–55, 354
    see also president, U.S.; vice president, U.S.

Executive Office of the President (EOP), 329–30, 439 The group of policy-related offices that serve as support staff to the president.

executive orders, 318–19, 319, 320, 323 Proclamations made by the president that change government policy without congressional approval.

executive privilege, 325, 327–28 The right of the president to keep executive branch conversations and correspondence confidential from the legislative and judicial branches.

Facebook, 103, 183, 252

factions, 6, 32, 34 Groups of like-minded people who try to influence the government. American government is set up to avoid domination by any one of these groups.

Falwell, Jerry, 106
families, 166, 167
Family Leave Act, 79
Family Research Council (FRC), 252
FBI (Federal Bureau of Investigation), 5
FCC (Federal Communications Commission), 184

FDA (Food and Drug Administration), 340, 347, 363, 364
Federal Aviation Administration, 13
federal bureaucracy, see bureaucracy
Federal Bureau of Investigation (FBI), 5
Federal Civil Rights Act, 138

federal civil service, 350 A system created by the 1883 Pendleton Civil Service Act in which bureaucrats are hired on the basis of merit rather than political connections.

Federal Communications Commission (FCC), 184 A government agency created in 1934 to regulate American radio stations and later expanded to regulate television, wireless communications technologies, and other broadcast media.

Federal Election Commission, 102, 233 The government agency that enforces and regulates election laws; made up of six presidential appointees, of whom no more than three can be members of the same party.

Federal Election Commission, Citizens United v., 102, 233
Federal Emergency Management Agency (FEMA), 58, 429
Federal Employees Political Activities Act, 359

federal funds rate (FFR), 422 The interest rate that a bank must pay on an overnight loan from another bank.

federal government, see government, federal
Federal Home Mortgage Corporation, 426

federalism, 6, 56–86 The division of power across the local, state, and national levels of government.
    assessing, 81, 81, 83, 83–84
    balance of power under, 38–39, 60–63, 80
    civil rights and, 83
    coercive, 56, 68, 71, 72, 74–76
    competitive, 76
    constitutional framework for, 60–63
    cooperative, 67, 68, 70, 70, 71, 77, 83
    court structure and, 378–79, 380, 381
    definition of, 58
    dual, 65, 65–67, 67, 70, 71, 74, 77
    early, 63–65, 64
    environmental policy and, 69
    fiscal, 71, 71–72
    ideological complexities of, 81
    "layer cake" model of, 68, 70, 71
    levels of government and autonomy in, 59–60
    "marble cake" model of, 68, 70
    modern, 70, 71–72, 74–81, 83–84, 86
    New Federalism, 71, 72

picket fence, 68, 70, 71
    see also government, federal

Federalist Papers, 31, 32, 41, 374

Federalists, 33, 53, 193, 194, 374 Those at the Constitutional Convention who favored a strong national government and a system of separated powers.
    Constitutional Convention and, 33, 35
    government control by, 64
    separation of powers and, 41–42, 47, 62

federal judges, 370, 371, 382, 382–83, 384, 385
Federal Meat Inspection Act, 350

federal preemptions, 75 Impositions of national priorities on the states through national legislation that is based on the Constitution's supremacy clause.

Federal Reserve System, 26 An independent agency that serves as the central bank of the United States to bring stability to the nation's banking system.
    banking system overseen by, 44, 421–23, 423
    Treasury Department and, 411

Federal Speedy Trial Act, 114
Federal-State Unemployment Compensation Program, 437
FEMA (Federal Emergency Management Agency), 58, 429
feminism, 18
Ferguson, Missouri, 133
Ferguson, Plessy v., 127
FFR (federal funds rate), 422
Fifteenth Amendment, 49, 66, 95, 126
Fifth Amendment, 66, 94, 95, 96, 112–14, 113, 115, 145
fifth party system, 194, 194

fighting words, 105 Forms of expression that "by their very utterance" can incite violence. These can be regulated by the government but are often difficult to define.

filibuster, 304, 384, 385, 385 A tactic used by senators to block a bill by continuing to hold the floor and speak—under the Senate rule of unlimited debate—until the bill's supporters back down.

Fillmore, Millard, 315

filtering, 186 The influence on public opinion that results from journalists' and editors' decisions about which of many potential news stories to report.

financial crisis of 2008–2009, 324, 426–28, 427
Financial Stability Plan, 427

fire alarm oversight, 308, 363 A method of oversight in which members of Congress respond to complaints about the bureaucracy or problems of implementation only as they arise rather than exercising constant vigilance.

First Amendment, *92, 94, 96, 97–107*, 115
    freedom of assembly and, *92, 96, 104, 104*
    freedom of religion and, 88, *92, 93, 96, 97–99, 98, 99, 118, 119*
    freedom of speech and, 51, 66, 88, 91, 92, *100–107, 102, 104, 106, 120*
    freedom of the press and, 66, 67, *92, 96, 104–5, 105*
First Continental Congress, *30*
first party system, *194*
first spouses (presidential spouses), 331
FISA (Foreign Intelligence Surveillance Act), 112

fiscal federalism, 71, 71–72 A form of federalism in which federal funds are allocated to the lower levels of government through transfer payments or grants.

fiscal policy, 407, 416, 418–20, 419, 420, 421 Government decisions about how to influence the economy by taxing and spending.
    see also taxes and tax policies

Fisher v. Univ. of Texas, 147
FiveThirtyEight, 182

527 organization, 196, 266 A tax-exempt group formed primarily to influence elections through voter mobilization efforts and to issue ads that do not directly endorse or oppose a candidate. Unlike PACs, they are not subject to contribution limits and spending caps.

flag desecration, 102, *102*
Flag Protection Act, 102
Flint, Mich.
    public water supply, 133, 340, *341,* 342, *364,* 366
Flores, City of Boerne v., 79
Florida
    2000 election and, 212
    jury duty in, 129
    Orlando shooting in June 2016, 160
    as a swing state, 250
Florida, Seminole Tribe v., 79
Food and Drug Administration (FDA), 340, 347, 363, 364
Ford, Gerald, 228, 316, 451
Ford, Henry, 422
foreign aid, *463, 463,* 464
Foreign Intelligence Surveillance Act (FISA), 112
Foreign Miners Tax, 129

foreign policy, 444–74 Government actions that affect countries, corporations, groups, or individuals outside America's borders.
    Congress and, 454, 456, *458*
    definition of, 446, 473
    federal courts and, 456–57
    history of, 448–52, *450, 452*
    interest groups and, 457, *457,* 460
    media and, 460
    military component of, 465–66
    NGOs and international organizations in, 461
    political conflict in, 466–72, *467,* 474
    president's role in, 322, 324, *324,* 454–56, *458*
    public opinion and, 460
    terrorism and, *see* terrorism
    theories of, 446–48, *448*
    tools of, 462–66, *463, 464, 465,* 474
    weapons of mass destruction and, 469–70, 472, *472*
    see also specific presidents

Founders of the United States, 5–6, 21, 28, 29, *29,* 31–32, 52, 61, 85
Fourteen Points, 449
Fourteenth Amendment, 49, 66, 77–78, *78,* 80, 90, 94–95, 115, 128, 140
    due process clause of, 145
    equal protection clause of, 90, 125, 126, 143–44, 145
Fourth Amendment, *94, 96,* 109–12, *111,* 115
fourth party system, *194*

framing, 186 The influence on public opinion caused by the way a story is presented or covered, including the details, explanations, and context offered in the report.

France, 60, 165, *165*
Francis, Pope, 430
Frankfurter, Felix, 391
Franklin, Benjamin, 40
FRC (Family Research Council), 252
Freedmen's Bureau, 127
freedom, civil liberties and, 88, *89,* 125
freedom of assembly, *92, 96, 104, 104*
freedom of religion, 88, *89, 92, 93, 96, 97–99, 98, 99, 118, 119*
freedom of speech, 51, 66, *92, 96,* 100–107, *102, 104, 106, 120*
freedom of the press, 66, 67, *92, 96,* 104–5, *105*
Freedom Riders, *138*

free exercise clause, 97, 98–99, 99 Part of the First Amendment that states that Congress cannot prohibit or interfere with the practice of religion.

free market, 6, 15, 25, 415, 425 An economic system based on competition among businesses without government interference.

free rider problem, 6–7, 14 The incentive to benefit from others' work without making a contribution, which leads individuals in a collective action situation to refuse to work together.

French and Indian War (1754–1763), 29
French Revolution, 100
Fugitive Slave Act, 126

full employment, 414 The theoretical point at which all citizens who want to be employed have a job.

full faith and credit clause, 62–63 Part of Article IV of the Constitution requiring that each state's laws be honored by the other states. For example, a legal marriage in one state must be recognized across state lines.

Garland, Merrick, 43, 318, 370, *371*
Garner, Tyron, 116, *116,* 145
Garrett, Alabama v., 79
Gates, Bill, 419, 424
gay men and lesbians
    civil rights of, 80, 116, *116,* 118, 125, 129–30, *130,* 134, 136, 137, 144–45, 150
    Constitution and, 48
    discrimination against, 83
    marriage and, *see* same-sex marriage
    military and, 150, *151,* 156
GCT (Grand Canyon Trust), 425
GDP (gross domestic product), 72, 73, 415, 435, *463*
Geithner, Timothy, 427
gender
    federal district judges and, *383*
    juries and, 134
    laws concerning, 78–79, *79*
    political conflict and, 17, 18
    see also women and women's rights
gender discrimination, *136, 137,* 144, *145, 149,* 377

general election, 219 The election in which voters cast ballots for House members, senators, and (every four years) a president and vice president.

general-election campaigns, 230–33, *231, 233*
General Services Administration (GSA), *362*
General Social Survey, *168*
Georgia, 144–45
Georgia, Chisholm v., 62, 65
Gerry, Elbridge, 41, 91, 94, 288

gerrymandering, 288–90 Attempting to use the process of re-drawing district boundaries to benefit a political party, protect incumbents, or change the proportion of minority voters in a district.

"get out the vote" (GOTV), 230
Gibbons v. Ogden, 64, 65
GI Bill of Rights, 414, 438
Gideon, Clarence, 114
Gideon v. Wainwright, 96, 114

Budget Committee of, *299, 408*
constitutional requirements of candidates for, *221*
earmarks in, 293
election to, 279
gun control and, 160
incumbents in, 239-40, *240,* 284, *285,* 287
Intelligence Committee of, *299,* 456
Majority Leader in, *294,* 295
Minority Leader in, *294,* 295
Natural Resources Committee of, 298, *299*
redistricting and, 142-43
rules and procedures in, 13
Rules Committee in, *299, 300, 306*
Senate *vs.,* 279
Speaker of, 293, *294, 295*
typical workdays for, *285, 286*
Veterans' Affairs Committee of, *299,* 308
whip system of, 295
see also Congress
Housing and Urban Development, Department of, 315
Hoyer, Steny, *192, 327*
Huawei, 457
Hudson River, *365*
human nature, Founders' views on, 32
Humphrey, Hubert, 308
Hurricane Katrina, 405
Hustler, 106

IAEA (International Atomic Energy Agency), 470
Idaho, 315

idealism, 447-48 The idea that a country's foreign policy decisions are based on factors beyond self-interest, including upholding important principles or values.

ideological polarization, 176, 177, 197-98, 198, 297, 297-98 The effect on public opinion when many citizens move away from moderate positions and toward either end of the political spectrum, identifying themselves as either liberals or conservatives.

ideology A cohesive set of ideas and beliefs used to organize and evaluate the political world.
definition of, 19
federalism and, 81
polarization of, 176, 177, 197-98, *198,* 297, 297-98
political conflict and, 18-19
public opinion and, 163, *163,* 176, 177

IGOs (intergovernmental organizations), 60, 461
"I Have a Dream" (King), *139*
Illinois, 289
IMF (International Monetary Fund), 60, 137, 461

immigration and immigrants, 18, *18,* 124, 127-29
in Arizona, 122, *123,* 155-56
illegal, 124, *155,* 155-56
public opinion on, 156
Trump and, 124, 155, 169
immigration policy, 4, *4*

impeachment, 6, 46, 308 A negative or checking power over the other branches that allows Congress to remove the president, the vice president, or other "officers of the United States" (including federal judges) for abuses of power.

implied powers, 50 Powers supported by the Constitution that are not expressly stated in it.

income, 132-33, *136,* 430
income inequality, 15, *17,* 18, *136,* 144, *145,* 430

income support, 437-38, 439 Government programs that provide support to low-income Americans, such as welfare, food stamps, unemployment compensation, and the EITC.

income tax, 49

incumbency advantage, 284-85, *285,* 287 The relative infrequency with which members of Congress are defeated in their attempts for reelection.

incumbent A politician running for reelection to the office he or she currently holds.
definition of, 218
high reelection rates of, 239-40, *240*
retrospective evaluations of, 218-19

independent agencies, 352 Government offices or organizations that provide government services and are not part of an executive department.

Indian Removal Act, 128
individualism, economic, 15
industrialization, 70, 315

inflation, 414-15, *415* The increase in the price of consumer goods over time.

In re Oliver 333 U.S. 257, 96

inside strategies, 260-64, *264* The tactics employed within Washington, D.C., by interest groups seeking to achieve their policy goals.

institutional interest groups, 252
intelligence agencies, 455-56
intercontinental railroad, 128

interest group, 10, 13, 15, 250-75 An organization of people who share common

political interests and aim to influence public policy by electioneering and lobbying.
campaign contributions by, 235
definition of, 252-53, 274
electioneering and, 266-68, *267, 268*
financial expenditures of, 256-60, *257, 258*
foreign policy and, 457, *457,* 460
inside strategies of, 260-64, *264*
litigation strategies and, 264, *264*
membership benefits and incentives in, *254,* 254-55
membership size and role in, 253-54
organizational structures of, 253-54
outside strategies of, 260, 262, 263, 264-69, *265, 266, 267, 268*
political influence and power of, 269-72, *270, 272,* 275
regulations imposed on, 259
resources used by, 255
social policy and role of, 412-13
staff and revolving door of, 255-56
types of, 252
see also lobbying and lobbyists

intergovernmental organizations (IGOs), 60, 461 Organizations that seek to coordinate policy across member nations.

intermediate scrutiny, 100 The middle level of scrutiny the courts can use when determining whether a law is constitutional. To meet this standard, the law or policy must be "content neutral," must further an important government interest in a way that is "substantially related" to that interest, and must use means that are a close fit to the government's goal and not substantially broader than is necessary to accomplish that goal.

intermediate scrutiny test, 144, *146, 147*
Internal Revenue Service (IRS), 7
International Atomic Energy Agency (IAEA), 470

internationalism, 447, 449 The idea that a country should be involved in the affairs of other nations, out of both self-interest and moral obligation.

International Monetary Fund (IMF), 60, 137, 461 A nongovernmental organization established in 1944 to help stabilize the international monetary system, improve economic growth, and aid developing nations.

international organizations, 461
Internet, 106-7
cyberbullying, 103
as major source for information about politics, 182-83
interracial marriage, 127
Interstate Commerce Act, 424
Interstate Commerce Commission, 315, 350, 424
interstate highway system, 315

LGBTQ community, 129, *130*
  see also gay men and lesbians
Libby, Lewis "Scooter," 325

libel, 105–6 Written false statements that damage a person's reputation. They can be regulated by the government but are often difficult to distinguish from permissible speech.

liberal, 18–19, 81, 163, 176, 177 One side of the ideological spectrum defined by support for stronger government programs and more market regulation; generally associated with Democrats.

Libertarians, 19, *19*, 176, 177, 212 Those who prefer very limited government and therefore tend to be conservative on issues such as welfare policy, environmental policy, and public support for education but liberal on issues of personal liberty such as free speech, abortion, and the legalization of drugs.

liberty, 20–21, 23, 25, 33 Political freedom, such as the freedom of speech, press, assembly, and religion. These and other legal and due process rights protecting individuals from government control are outlined in the Bill of Rights of the U.S. Constitution.

Libya, *459*
Lilly Ledbetter Fair Pay Act, *137*, 144

limited government, 29, 52 A political system in which the powers of the government are restricted to prevent tyranny by protecting property and individual rights.

Lincoln, Abraham, 65, 126, 162, 280, 315
literacy tests, 127
litigation strategies and interest groups, 264, *264*

living Constitution, 48, 51, 393 A way of interpreting the Constitution that takes into account evolving national attitudes and circumstances rather than the text alone.

lobbying, 250, *251*, 252 Efforts to influence public policy through contact with public officials on behalf of an interest group.
  astroturf, 265
  definition of, 252
  direct, 260–61
  drafting legislation and regulations in, 261
  financial spending on, 256–60, *257*, *258*
  grassroots, 265, *265*
  media used in, 268–69
  mobilizing public opinion, 265–66
  restrictions on, 259
  see also interest groups

Locke, John, 36
Lockett, Clayton, 115
Lockheed Martin Corporation, 256

logrolling, 293 A form of reciprocity in which members of Congress support bills that they otherwise might not vote for in exchange for other members' votes on bills that are very important to them.

Lopez, Alfonso, 78
Lopez, United States v., 78, 79
Louisiana, Duncan v., 96
Louisiana Purchase, 449
Louisville, desegregation in, *141*

Madison, James, 6, 21, 30, 32, 34, *34*, 36, 47, 64, 97, 288
Madison, Marbury v., 46–47, 374–75, *375*

Majority Leader, 242, 294, 295 The elected head of the party holding the majority of seats in the House or Senate.

majority opinions, 392
majority rule, 34–35

majority voting, 220 A voting system in which a candidate must win more than 50 percent of votes to win the election. If no candidate wins enough votes to take office, a runoff election is held between the top two vote-getters.

Malcolm X, *139*
Malloy v. Hogan, 96

mandatory spending, 418, 419 Expenditures that are required by law, such as the funding for Social Security.

Manning, Bradley, *105*
Mapp, Dollree, *111*
"marble cake" model of federalism, *68*, 70
Marbury v. Madison, 46–47, 374–75, *375*
March on Washington, *139*
margin of error, 170
marijuana
  drug-sniffing dogs in searches for, 110, *110*
  medical use of, 81, 82, *82*
marketplace of ideas, 107

markup, 304 One of the steps through which a bill becomes a law, in which the final wording of the bill is determined.

marriage
  interracial, 127
  same-sex, *see* same-sex marriage
Marshall, John, 47, *375*
  Marbury v. Madison and, 46–47, 374–75
  McCulloch v. Maryland and, 48
Marshall, Thurgood, 48, 395
Marshall Plan, 450, *450*
Mars rover, 340, 347
Martin, Trayvon, 133
Maryland, Benton v., 96
Maryland, McCulloch v., 48, 64, *65*, 66

Mason, George, 41, 91, 94
Massachusetts, 81, 104

mass associations, 253–54 Interest groups that have a large number of dues-paying individuals as members.

mass media, 182 Sources that provide information to the average citizen, such as newspapers, television networks, radio stations, and websites.
  see also media

mass survey, 170–71 A way to measure public opinion by interviewing a large sample of the population.

Mayhew, David, 283, 284
McCain, John, 205, 293, 312
McCain-Feingold Act, *see* Bipartisan Campaign Reform Act (BCRA)
McCarthy, Kevin, *309*
McCaskill, Claire, 276
McConnell, Mitch, *242*, 370
McCulloch v. Maryland, 48, 64, *65*, 66
McDonald v. Chicago, 96
McHenry, James, 40
Meadows, Mark, *409*
media, 182–86, 188
  deregulation of, 184
  election coverage and, 8, 13
  foreign policy and, 460
  hostile, 185
  Internet-based news sources in, 182–83
  in lobbying campaigns, 268–69
  news, 182–86, *185*, 188
  regulation of, 184
  sources, 182–83

media conglomerates, 184 Companies that control a large number of media sources across several types of media outlets.

media effects, 184–86 The influence of media coverage on average citizens' opinions and actions.

Medicaid, 56, 75, 76, 80, 315, 429, 434–35, 436 An entitlement program funded by the federal and state governments that provides health care coverage for low-income Americans who would otherwise be unable to afford health care.

medical marijuana, 81, 82, *82*

Medicare, 26, 274, 315, 347, 429, 434–36, 436, 440 The federal health care plan created in 1965 that provides coverage for retired Americans for hospital care (Part A), medical care (Part B), and prescription drugs (Part D).

Merkel, Angela, 112
Merrill Lynch, 426
Mexican Americans, 128, *128*
Mexican-American War, 128, 315, 322

Mexico, 124
Mica, John, 362
Michael M. v. Superior Court, 147
Michigan
    busing in Detroit, 141
    Flint's public water supply, 133, 340, *341*, *342*, *364*, 366
Microsoft, 424, *424*
military
    foreign policy and, 465–66
    gays in, 150, *151*, 156
    sexual assault and, 276, *277*, 278
military funerals, protests at, 101, 118
millennials, political affiliation of, 19

Miller test, 107 Established in *Miller v. California*, this three-part test is used by the Supreme Court to determine whether speech meets the criteria for obscenity. If so, it can be restricted by the government.

Miller v. California, 107
"Millionaires" Amendment, 102
minimum wage, 404, *404*
Minnesota, Near v., 96

Minority Leader, 294, 295 The elected head of the party holding the minority of seats in the House or Senate.

minority rights, 34
minor political parties, 212, 212–13
Miranda, Ernesto, 112

Miranda rights, 112–13, *113* The list of civil liberties described in the Fifth Amendment that must be read to a suspect before anything the suspect says can be used in a trial.

Mischiefs of Faction, 183
Mississippi, 116, *139*
Missouri, *102*, 156
Missouri Compromise, 66, 126

monarchy, 7, 21, 31 A form of government in which power is held by a single person, or monarch, who comes to power through inheritance rather than election.

monetarist theory, 421 The idea that the amount of money in circulation (the money supply) is the primary influence on economic activity and inflation.

monetary policy, 407, 421–23 Government decisions about how to influence the economy using control of the money supply and interest rates.

Moniz, Ernest, 332
Monkey Cage, The, 183
monopolies, 64, *64*, 424, *424*
Monroe, James, 314, 449

Monroe Doctrine, 314, 449 The American policy, initiated under President James Monroe in 1823, stating that the United States would remain neutral in conflicts between European nations and that these nations should stop colonizing or occupying areas of North and South America.

Montana, 76, 108, 315
Montgomery, Ala., civil rights movement in, 136, 137, *138*, 139

mootness, 388 The irrelevance of a case by the time it is received by a federal court, causing the Court to decline to hear the case.

Morrill Act, 438
Morrison, United States v., 79

most-favored-nation status, 462 A standing awarded to countries with which the United States has good trade relations, providing the lowest possible tariff rate. WTO members must give one another this preferred status.

Motor Voter Act, 74
MSNBC, 185

multilateral action, 447 Foreign policy carried out by a nation in coordination with other nations or international organizations.

mutually assured destruction, 450–51 The idea that two nations that possess large stores of nuclear weapons—like the United States and the Soviet Union during the Cold War—would both be annihilated in any nuclear exchange, thus making it unlikely that either country would launch a first attack.

NAACP (National Association for the Advancement of Colored People), 131, 139
Nader, Ralph, 212, *212*
NAFTA (North American Free Trade Agreement), 316, 451, 462
NASA, 340, 347
National Aeronautics and Space Administration (NASA), 7
National Association for the Advancement of Colored People (NAACP), 131, 139
National Beer Wholesalers Association (NBWA), 258

national committee, 195 An American political party's principal organization, comprising party representatives from each state.

National Economic Council (NEC), 410 A group of economic advisers created in 1993 to work with the president to coordinate economic policy.

National Federation of Independent Business v. Sebelius, 79
National Forest Service, 298
National Guard, 5, 150
National Independent Automobile Dealers Association (NIADA), 253
National Institutes of Health (NIH), 346
National Labor Relations Act, 429
National Labor Relations Board v. Jones & Laughlin Steel Corporation, 65, 67
National Organization for Women (NOW), 148
National Organization of Women, 103
National Recovery Administration, 429
National Republican Congressional Committee (NRCC), 197
National Republican Senatorial Committee (NRSC), 197
National Review, 182
National Review Online, 182
National Rifle Association (NRA), 107, 160, 252–53, 270
national security, 90, 118
National Security Agency (NSA), 112, 118, 167, 456

National Security Council (NSC), 330, 454 Within the EOP, an agency that advises the president on matters of foreign policy.

national supremacy, 64, 74–75

national supremacy clause, 39, 61 Part of Article VI, Section 2, of the Constitution stating that the Constitution and the laws and treaties of the United States are the "supreme Law of the Land," meaning national laws take precedence over state laws if the two conflict.

National Turkey Federation, 270, *270*
National Women's Soccer League (NWSL), 149

nation building, 448 The use of a country's resources, including the military, to help create democratic institutions abroad and prevent violence in other countries.

Nation of Islam, 17
Native Americans, 125, 128
NATO (North Atlantic Treaty Organization), 60, 450, 459, 464

natural rights, 32 Also known as "unalienable rights," the Declaration of Independence defines them as "Life, Liberty, and the pursuit of Happiness." The Founders believed that upholding these rights should be the government's central purpose.

NBWA (National Beer Wholesalers Association), 258
Near v. Minnesota, 96
NEC (National Economic Council), 410

outside strategies, 260, 262, 263, 264–69, 265, 266, 267, 268 The tactics employed outside Washington, D.C., by interest groups seeking to achieve their policy goals.

Oval Office, 329–30

oversight, 307, 307–8, 311, 362–63 Congressional efforts to make sure that laws are implemented correctly by the bureaucracy after they have been passed.

ownership society, 430 The term used to describe the social-policy vision of President George W. Bush, in which citizens take responsibility for their own social welfare and the free market plays a greater role in social policy.

PACs (political action committees), 196, 234, 234, 266–68, 267, 268
Paine, Thomas, 31
Pakistan, 453, 469

paradox of voting, 237–38 The question of why citizens vote even though their individual votes stand little chance of changing the election outcome.

pardons, 325
parents and political opinions, 166, 167
Paris, Treaty of, 375
Paris terrorist attacks in 2015, 165, 165
Parks, Rosa, 136, 138
Parliament, British, 28, 38

parliamentary system, 8, 38 A system of government in which legislative and executive power are closely joined. The legislature (parliament) selects the chief executive (prime minister), who forms the cabinet from members of the parliament.

partisan redistricting, 288–90

party coalitions, 201, 202, 203, 203 The groups that identify with a political party, usually described in demographic terms such as African-American Democrats or evangelical Republicans.

Party Decides, The, 190

party identification (party ID), 198, 200, 200–201, 201 A citizen's loyalty to a specific political party.

party in government, 192, 192, 197–98, 198 The group of officeholders who belong to a specific political party and were elected as candidates of that party.

party in the electorate, 192, 192, 198, 200, 200–201, 201, 202, 203, 203 The group of citizens who identify with a specific political party.

party organization, 192, 192, 195–97 A specific political party's leaders and workers at the national, state, and local levels.

party platform, 207, 210 A set of objectives outlining the party's issue positions and priorities. Candidates are not required to support their party's platform.

party principle, 193 The idea that a political party exists as an organization distinct from its elected officials or party leaders.

party system, 193, 194 Periods in which the names of the major political parties, their supporters, and the issues dividing them have remained relatively stable.

party unity, 297, 297–98 The extent to which members of Congress in the same party vote together on party votes.

party vote, 296, 296–97 A vote in which the majority of one party opposes the position of the majority of the other party.

payroll taxes, 419

peak associations, 252, 254 Interest groups whose members are businesses or other organizations rather than individuals.

Pearl Harbor, 449
Pelosi, Nancy, 303, 327
Pence, Mike, 331
Pentagon Papers, 105
per curiam opinions, 392
Pericles, 14
Perkins, Tony, 88
permanent campaign, 228, 230, 230
Perot, Ross, 212, 226
Perry, Rick, 76
Persian Gulf War, 316
Personal Responsibility and Work Opportunity Act, 72
Pew Research Center, 173196
Philippines, 451
Phoenix, 122

picket fence federalism, 68, 70, 71 A more refined and realistic form of cooperative federalism in which policy makers within a particular policy area work together across the levels of government.

Pinckney, Charles, 91

plaintiff, 376 The person or party who brings a case to court.

Planned Parenthood, 115, 409

plea bargain, 376 An agreement between a plaintiff and a defendant to settle a case before it goes to trial or the verdict is decided. In a civil case, this usually involves

an admission of guilt and an agreement on monetary damages; in a criminal case, this often involves an admission of guilt in return for a reduced charge or sentence.

Pledge of Allegiance, 388
Plessy v. Ferguson, 127
Plouffe, David, 329

pluralism, 35 The idea that having a variety of parties and interests within a government will strengthen the system, ensuring that no group possesses total control.

plurality opinions, 392

plurality voting, 220 A voting system in which the candidate who receives the most votes within a geographic area wins the election, regardless of whether that candidate wins a majority (more than half) of the votes.

pocket veto, 305, 325, 326 A president's ability to veto a piece of legislation by taking no action on it (possible only when Congress is not in session).

Pointer v. Texas, 96
polarization
    ideological, 176, 177
    of political parties, 197–99, 198, 297, 297–98
police, 109, 112–13

police patrol oversight, 362–63 A method of oversight in which members of Congress constantly monitor the bureaucracy to make sure that laws are implemented correctly.

police powers, 59 The power to enforce laws and provide for public safety.

policy agenda, 405 The set of desired policies that political leaders view as their top priorities.

policy mood, 179, 179–80 The level of public support for expanding the government's role in society; whether the public wants government action on a specific issue.

political action committee (PACs), 196, 234, 234, 266–68, 267, 268 An interest group or a division of an interest group that can raise money to contribute to campaigns or to spend on ads in support of candidates. The amount a PAC can receive from each of its donors and the amount it can spend on federal electioneering are strictly limited.

political appointees, 342, 358–59 People selected by an elected leader, such as the president, to hold a government position.

political campaigns, media and, 8
political parties, 190–215

progressive, 419–20 Taxes that require upper-income people to pay a higher tax rate than lower-income people, such as income taxes.

proportional allocation, 221 During the presidential primaries, the practice of determining the number of convention delegates allotted to each candidate based on the percentage of the popular vote cast for each candidate. All Democratic primaries and caucuses use this system, as do some states' Republican primaries and caucuses.

protectionism, 129 The idea under which some people have tried to rationalize discriminatory policies by claiming that some groups, like women or African Americans, should be denied certain rights for their own safety or well-being.

public goods, 6 Services or actions (such as protecting the environment) that, once provided to one person, become available to everyone. Government is typically needed to provide public goods because they will be under-provided by the free market.

public opinion, 160–82, 187 Citizens' views on politics and government actions.

public policy, 405–7, *406, 413, 441* A law, rule, statute, or edict that expresses

the government's goals and provides for rewards and punishments to promote their attainment.

see also economic policy; social policy

purposive benefits, 254 Satisfaction derived from the experience of working toward a desired policy goal, even if the goal is not achieved.

rational basis test, 143–44, 146, 147 The use of evidence to suggest that differences in the behavior of two groups can rationalize unequal treatment of these groups.

realignment, 195 A change in the size or composition of the party coalitions or in the nature of the issues that divide the parties. Realignments typically occur within an election cycle or two, but they can also occur gradually over the course of a decade or longer.

realism, 447–48 The idea that a country's foreign policy decisions are motivated by self-interest and the goal of gaining more power.

recess appointment, 318 Selection by the president of a person to be an ambassador or the head of a department while the Senate is not in session, thereby bypassing Senate approval. Unless approved by a subsequent Senate vote, recess appointees serve only to the end of the congressional term.

redistributive tax policies, 15, 25 Politics, generally favored by Democratic politicians, that use taxation to attempt to create social equality (for example, higher taxation of the rich to provide programs for the poor).

redistricting, 142–43, 288–90, 290 Re-drawing the geographic boundaries of legislative districts. This happens every 10 years to ensure that districts remain roughly equal in population.

red tape, 346–47 Excessive or unnecessarily complex regulations imposed by the bureaucracy.

regressive, 419 Taxes that take a larger share of poor people's income than wealthy people's income, such as sales taxes and payroll taxes.

regulation, 342–43, 344, 345–46, 346 A rule that allows the government to exercise control over individuals and corporations by restricting certain behaviors.

remedial legislation, 78 National laws that address discriminatory state laws. Authority for such legislation comes from Section 5 of the Fourteenth Amendment.

republicanism, 31 As understood by James Madison and the framers, the belief that a form of government in which the interests of the people are represented through elected leaders is the best form of government. Our form of government is known as a republican democracy.

Republican National Committee (RNC), 192–93, 207
Republican Party, 192, *194*
  as brand name, 196
  campaign fund-raising and support provided by, 207, *207*
  Civil War amendments passed by, 126
  congressional conference of, 197
  economic policy and, 15
  formation of, 315
  founding and history of, 193–95, *194*
  identification with, 167–68, 177
  ideology and, 18, 197–98, *198*
  party coalitions in, 201, *202*, 203, *203*
  party identification in electorate of, 198, *200*, 200–201, *201*
  presidential platforms of, 207, 210
  race and, 17, *17*, 203, *203*, 244
  see also elections
research and development, 346

reserved powers, 39 As defined in the Tenth Amendment, powers that are not given to the national government by the Constitution, or not prohibited to the states, are reserved by the states or the people.

reserve requirement, 422 The minimum amount of money that a bank is required to have on hand to back up its assets.

resolutions, types of, 301
resources used by interest groups, 255
retrospective evaluations, 218–19
reverse discrimination, 152, 154
revisionary power, 374
Revolutionary War, 30, *30*, 34

revolving door, 256 The movement of individuals from government positions to jobs with interest groups or lobbying firms, and vice versa.

RFRA (Religious Freedom Restoration Act), 99
Rhode Island, 37
Rice, Condoleezza, 451
rights of criminal defendants, 109–15, *113*, 120
"rights revolution," 74
right to bear arms, 107–8, *108*, 120
right to legal counsel, 114
RNC (Republican National Committee), 192–93, 207
Roberts, John G., Jr., 58, 372, 383, *391*, 394
Robinson, Jackie, 127
Robinson v. California, 96
Roe v. Wade, 115–16, 137

Rogers, Will, 196

roll call vote, 296, 296–97 A recorded vote on legislation; members may vote yes, no, abstain, or present.

Romney, Mitt
  in 2012 election, 242, 245, 312
  as governor of Massachusetts, 81
Roof, Dylann, 133, *134*
Roosevelt, Eleanor, *429*
Roosevelt, Franklin Delano, *70*, *194*, 315, *316*, 382, 411, 428–29
Roosevelt, Theodore, 26, 315
Rosen, Jeffrey, 103
Rubio, Marco, 209, 237
rules, influence on political process, 13
Rumsfeld, Hamdan v., 45

runoff election, 220 Under a majority voting system, a second election held only if no candidate wins a majority of the votes in the first general election. Only the top two vote-getters in the first election compete in the runoff.

Ryan, Paul, 190, 192–93, *287*, 409

Sallie Mae, 250, 252
SALT I (Strategic Arms Limitation Treaty), 451
same-sex marriage, *10*, 62, 145, 151, *151*, 381
  Defense of Marriage Act and, 62–63, 81, 145
  marriage licenses for, 88, *89*
  public opinion on, 129, 156

sample, 170, 171, 172, 173 Within a population, the group of people surveyed in order to gauge the whole population's opinion. Researchers use samples because it would be impossible to interview the entire population.

sample size, 170, 172, 173

sampling error, 170, 172, 173 The predicted difference between the average opinion expressed by survey respondents and the average opinion in the population, sometimes called the *margin of error*. Increasing the number of respondents lowers the sampling error.

Sanders, Bernie, 220, 241, 243, 428, 440
Sandford, Dred Scott v., 65, *65*, 66, 94, 126, 375
Sandoval, Alexander v., 155
Sandy Hook Elementary School shootings, 108, 318–19
Scalia, Antonin, 111, 370, 383, *391*, 394, 395
Schattschneider, E. E., 10
Schenk, Charles, 101
Schilb v. Kuebel, 96
school desegregation, 74, *138*, 139–41, *141*, 150

school prayer, 97–98
Schumer, Charles, 219–20
Scott, Dred, 66
Scott, Walter, 133, *134*
SCOTUSblog (Supreme Court blog), 182
scrutiny, strict, 100
searches and seizures, 109–12, *111*, 115
search warrants, 109, 110, 111
Sears, David O., 168
Seattle, desegregation in, *141*
Sebelius, Kathleen, 308
Sebelius, National Federation of Independent Business v., 79
secession, 64–65, 126
Second Amendment, *94*, 95, *96*, 107–8, *108*, 120
Second Continental Congress, 29, *30*
second party system, *194*
Sedition Act, 100
segregation, 67, *67*, 127, 136
  de jure *vs.* de facto, 141
  "separate but equal" doctrine and, 127, 136, *138*, 139–40
Select Committee on Energy Independence and Global Warming, 298

select committees, 298 Committees in the House or Senate created to address a specific issue for one or two terms.

selective incentives, 254, 254–55 Benefits that can motivate participation in a group effort because they are available only to those who participate, such as member services offered by interest groups.

selective incorporation, 95, 96 The process through which the civil liberties granted in the Bill of Rights were applied to the states on a case-by-case basis through the Fourteenth Amendment.

self-incrimination, 74, 112–13

semi-closed primary, 206, 219 A primary where anyone who is a registered member of the party or registered as an Independent can vote.

Seminole Tribe v. Florida, 79
Senate, U.S.
  "advice and consent" of, 43, *43*, 50, 308
  Agriculture Committee of, 298, *299*
  appointments confirmed by, 317, 318, *382*, 382–83, 385
  Appropriations Committee of, *299*
  bills in, 306–7
  Budget Committee of, *299*, 408
  constitutional requirements of candidates for, 221
  earmarks in, 293
  federal court appointments and, 384, 385, *385*
  Foreign Relations Committee in, *299*
  gun control and, 160
  House *vs.*, 279

Senate structure, holding more importance and authority than other committees.

Stanton, Elizabeth Cady, 136
State, Department of, 454

state capacity, 346 The knowledge, personnel, and institutions that the government requires to effectively implement policies.

state-level judges, 379, 382

State of the Union, 324 An annual speech in which the president addresses Congress to report on the condition of the country and to recommend policies.

states
    Constitutional Convention and, 35–36
    economic differences among, 83, *83*
    see also government, state

states' rights, 64–65, 75–80, *78, 80* The idea that states are entitled to a certain amount of self-government, free of federal government intervention. This became a central issue in the period leading up to the Civil War.

states' sovereign immunity, 87–88, *88*

statutory authority (presidential), 317, 318 Powers derived from laws enacted by Congress that add to the powers given to the president in the Constitution.

statutory interpretation, 376 The various methods and tests used by the courts for determining the meaning of a law and applying it to specific situations. Congress may overturn the courts' interpretation by writing a new law; thus, it also engages in statutory interpretation.

stealth democracy, 11
Stevens, John Paul, 394
Stewart, Potter, 107
stock markets, 315
Stone, Harlan Fiske, 391
Stonewall Rebellion, 129, *130*

straight tickets, 239 A ballot on which a voter selects candidates from only one political party.

Strategic Arms Limitation Treaty (SALT I), 451

strict construction, 393 A way of interpreting the Constitution based on its language alone.

strict scrutiny, 100 The highest level of scrutiny the courts can use when determining whether a law is constitutional. To meet this standard, the law or policy must be shown to serve a "compelling state interest"

or goal, it must be narrowly tailored to achieve that goal, and it must be the least restrictive means of achieving that goal.

strict scrutiny test, 143–44, *146, 147*
student loans, 250, *251, 252*, 273
Student Nonviolent Coordinating Committee (SNCC), 137

substantive representation, 280 When a member of Congress represents constituents' interests and policy concerns.

suicide, assisted, 82
Superior Court, Michael M. v., 147
Super PACs, 266–67, *268*
Supplemental Nutrition Assistance Program (SNAP), 437

supply-side economics, 418 The theory that lower tax rates will stimulate the economy by encouraging people to save, invest, and produce more goods and services.

Supreme Court, 378–79
    ACA and, 56, 75, 80, 88
    access to, 386–89, *387,* 400
    affirmative action and, 152–54
    appointments to, 43, 317–18, 370, *371, 382,* 382–83, *384, 385*
    briefs for, 389–90
    campaign finance reforms and, 102
    case criteria of, 387–89
    chief justices of, 374
    civil liberties and, 88, 90
    civil rights issues and, 66, *67,* 74, 83, 126, 136, *138,* 139–45, *141, 147,* 148, 152–54, 155, 486
    color-blind jurisprudence of, 141–43, 152
    conferences of justices, 391
    constitutional interpretation by, 6, 51, 61, 64, 77, 95–118, 376, 378–79
    deadlock in, after Scalia's death, 370
    death penalty and, 51, 115
    decision making of, 393–97, *394, 395, 396,* 396–97, 400
    executive privilege ruling of, 327
    FDR's court-packing plan for, 382
    federalism and, 64, *64,* 65, 65–66, 74, 77–80, *79,* 82, 83
    foreign policy and, 456–57
    freedom of speech and, 66, 100, 101, 102, 104, 105, 106, 107
    hearing cases before, 389–92, *390, 391,* 400
    judicial activism of, 141–43, 396
    judicial restraint of, 372, 396
    judicial review by, 46–47, 374–76, *375*
    jurisdiction of, 373
    Lemon test and, 98
    opinion writing in, *391,* 391–92
    oral arguments in, *390,* 390–91
    public knowledge of, *162*
    public opinion and, 396–97
    religion and, 88, 97–99, *98, 99*
    rules of access for, 386–87

same-sex marriage and, 10, 62, 62–63, 81, 145, 151, *381*
states' rights and, 77–80, *78, 80*
statutory interpretation by, 376
strategic approach to, 394, 396
Voting Rights Act and, 77, 78, 131
workload of, 386, *387*
writ of *certiorari* and, 386–87
see also specific cases
surveillance, 109, 110, 112, 118, 167
surveys
    large-scale, 171
    mass, 170–71
    problems with, 171–75, *174*
    wording of, 171, 174, *174*
Sweden, 60
swing states, 223, *223,* 250

symbolic speech, 101–2, *102,* 103 Nonverbal expression, such as the use of signs or symbols. It benefits from many of the same constitutional protections as verbal speech.

Syria, 43, 46, 322, 444, 446, 457, 469

Taliban, 469
Tammany Hall, *193*
Taney, Roger, 65
TANF (Temporary Assistance to Needy Families), 72, 438
Tanzania, 451

tariff, 462 A tax levied on imported and exported goods.

TARP (Troubled Asset Relief Program), 426
taxes and tax policies
    Articles of Confederation problems with, 30–31, 39
    cuts in, 419–20
    in 2016 election, 402, 404, 419–20
    federal authority over, 42, 64
    local authority over, 60
    payroll, 419
    redistributive, 15, 25
    regressive *vs.* progressive, 419–20
    state authority over, 64
    top marginal tax rates and, 420, *421*
    Trump and, 232
Tea Act (1773), 29
Tea Party, *19,* 26, 27, 38, 52, 76, 138, 196, 242, 412

Temporary Assistance to Needy Families (TANF), 72, 438 The welfare program that replaced AFDC in 1996, eliminating the entitlement status of welfare, shifting implementation of the policy to the states, and introducing several new restrictions on receiving aid. These changes led to a significant decrease in the number of welfare recipients.

Tenth Amendment, 38, 56, 61, 77, 94
terrorism, 451–52, *452,* 469
    drone attacks against, 328, 452, 453, *453*

Voter Registration Information

State	Registration Deadline before Election*	Early Voting Permitted?**	Identification Required to Vote?**	More Information
Alabama	14 days	No	Photo ID requested	alabamavotes.gov
Alaska	30 days	Yes	ID requested; photo not required	elections.alaska.gov
Arizona	29 days	Yes	ID required; photo not required	azsos.gov/election
Arkansas	30 days	Yes	ID requested; photo not required	sos.arkansas.gov
California	15 days	Yes	No	sos.ca.gov
Colorado	8 days by mail or online; no in-person deadline	Yes (all voting by mail)	ID requested; photo not required	sos.state.co.us
Connecticut	14 days by mail; 7 days in person; election-day registration permitted	No	ID requested; photo not required	ct.gov/sots
Delaware	24 days	No	ID requested; photo not required	elections.delaware.gov
District of Columbia	30 days by mail or online; no in-person deadline	Yes	No	dcboee.org
Florida	29 days	Yes	Photo ID requested	dos.myflorida.com/elections
Georgia	28 days	Yes	Photo ID required	sos.ga.gov
Hawaii	30 days	Yes	Photo ID requested	hawaii.gov/elections
Idaho	25 days	Yes	Photo ID requested	idahovotes.gov
Illinois	27 days	Yes	No	elections.il.gov
Indiana	29 days	Yes	Photo ID required	in.gov/sos/elections
Iowa	10 days	Yes	No	sos.iowa.gov
Kansas	21 days	Yes	Photo ID required	kssos.org
Kentucky	29 days	No	ID requested; photo not required	elect.ky.gov
Louisiana	30 days	Yes	Photo ID requested	sos.la.gov
Maine	21 days by mail; no in-person deadline	Yes	No	maine.gov/sos
Maryland	21 days	Yes	No	elections.state.md.us
Massachusetts	20 days	No	No	www.sec.state.ma.us
Michigan	30 days	No	Photo ID requested	michigan.gov/sos
Minnesota	21 days	Yes	No	mnvotes.org
Mississippi	30 days	No	Photo ID required	sos.ms.gov
Missouri	Fourth Wednesday prior to election	No	ID requested; photo not required	sos.mo.gov
Montana	30 days by mail; no in-person deadline	Yes	ID requested; photo not required	sos.mt.gov

State	Registration Deadline before Election*	Early Voting Permitted?**	Identification Required to Vote?**	More Information
Nebraska	Third Friday prior to election by mail; second Friday prior to election in person	Yes	No	www.sos.ne.gov
Nevada	31 days by mail; 21 days in person	Yes	No	nvsos.gov
New Hampshire	10 days; election-day registration permitted	No	ID requested; photo not required	sos.nh.gov
New Jersey	21 days	Yes	No	njelections.org
New Mexico	28 days	Yes	No	sos.state.nm.us
New York	25 days	No	No	www.elections.ny.gov
North Carolina	25 days	Yes	No	ncsbe.gov
North Dakota	No voter registration required	Yes	Photo ID required	vote.nd.gov
Ohio	30 days	Yes	ID required; photo not required	sos.state.oh.us
Oklahoma	24 days	Yes	ID requested; photo not required	ok.gov/elections
Oregon	21 days	Yes (all voting by mail)	No	sos.oregon.gov
Pennsylvania	30 days	No	No	votespa.com
Rhode Island	30 days; election-day registration permitted	No	Photo ID requested	www.elections.state.ri.us
South Carolina	30 days	No	ID requested; photo not required	scvotes.org
South Dakota	15 days	Yes	Photo ID requested	sdsos.gov
Tennessee	30 days	Yes	Photo ID required	tn.gov/sos/election
Texas	30 days	Yes	Photo ID requested	votetexas.gov
Utah	30 days by mail; 7 days in person	Yes	ID requested; photo not required	elections.utah.gov
Vermont	Wednesday before the election	Yes	No	www.sec.state.vt.us/elections
Virginia	22 days	No	Photo ID required	sbe.virginia.gov
Washington	30 days by mail and online; 8 days in person	Yes (all voting by mail)	ID requested; photo not required	sos.wa.gov/elections/
West Virginia	21 days	Yes	No	sos.wv.gov
Wisconsin	20 days by mail; election-day registration permitted	Yes	Photo ID required	www.sos.state.wi.us
Wyoming	14 days; election-day registration permitted	Yes	No	soswy.state.wy.us

* Information collected from Project Vote Smart, votesmart.org/elections/voter-registration (accessed 9/1/16).

** Information collected from National Conference of State Legislatures, www.ncsl.org (accessed 9/1/16). In states where an ID is "requested," voters who do not bring ID to the polls may be required to sign an affidavit of identity, vote on a provisional ballot, have a poll worker vouch for their identity, or take additional steps after Election Day to make sure their vote is counted.